【青岛市图书馆馆藏旧版西文文献总书目】

——英、德、法语专辑

主　编　于　婧　马云超

编　者　（按姓氏笔画为序）

于　婧　马云超　王　璇　王丹妮　尹立丽

刘　华　刘　佳　曲　玲　李晨曦　张晶辉

中国海洋大学出版社

·青岛·

图书在版编目(CIP)数据

青岛市图书馆馆藏旧版西文文献总书目:英、德、法语专辑 / 于婧,马云超主编. —青岛:中国海洋大学出版社,2014.5

ISBN 978-7-5670-0602-7

Ⅰ.①青… Ⅱ.①于…②马… Ⅲ.①西文图书—图书馆目录—青岛市 Ⅳ.①Z822.1

中国版本图书馆 CIP 数据核字(2014)第 088477 号

出版发行 中国海洋大学出版社
社　　址 青岛市香港东路 23 号　　**邮政编码** 266071
出 版 人 杨立敏
网　　址 http://www.ouc-press.com
电子信箱 pankeju@126.com
订购电话 0532—82032573(传真)
责任编辑 潘克菊　　**电　　话** 0532—85902533
印　　制 青岛海蓝印刷有限责任公司
版　　次 2014 年 6 月第 1 版
印　　次 2014 年 6 月第 1 次印刷
成品尺寸 210 mm×285 mm
印　　张 42
字　　数 1080 千
定　　价 128.00 元

TSINANFU
TSINGTAU UNDER THREE FLAGS
WILSON LEON GODSHALL
SHANTUNG
ON THE SHANTUNG FRONT
TSINGTAO
A HISTORICAL, POLITICAL AND ECONOMIC SURVEY

BRITTLE BEHAVIOR OF ENGINEERING STRUCTURES
Earl R. Parker
Life in Early America
THE PRINCE AND THE PAUPER
SAMUEL L. CLEMENS
A. HALL & CO
Joseph C. Lincoln
THE STONE ARITHMETIC
PRIMARY
DEATH COMES FOR THE ARCHBISHOP
WILLA CATHER
I CAPTURE THE CASTLE
DODIE SMITH
A FREE and RESPONSIBLE PRESS

旧版英语文献

凡 例

一、本书文献是按《中国图书分类法》22 大类分类，著录按《中国文献编目规则》和《西文文献著录条例》规定格式。

二、本书著录项目主要包括题名项、责任者项、版本项、出版者项、出版年项、中文提要。

具体格式为：

正题名：副题名/责任者．—版本．—出版地：出版者，出版日期

页数；尺寸

三、本书为了尊重历史文献的本来面目，尽量在著录文字中采用原始文献中所用文字和词语。

四、本书文献均收藏于青岛市图书馆。

五、本书正文按《中国图书馆分类法》排列，后附按以英、德、法语字母顺序排序的书名索引，读者可通过书名索引的检索途径查找和检索本书。

目　录

《中国图书馆分类法》类目

英语专辑

A 马克思主义、列宁主义……

A122/E57
The Peasant War in Germany/Frederick Engels; introduction by D. Riazanov; translated from the German by Moissaye J. Olgin. —New York: International Publishers, c1926.
191 p. ;18 cm.

A21/L563
Imperialism, The Highest Stage of Capitalism/V. I. Lenin. —Moscow: Foreign Languages Publishing House, c1947
154 p. ;19 cm.

A22/L563
Materialism and Empirio-Criticism: Critical Comments on a Reactionary Philosophy/V. I. Lenin. —Moscow: Foreign Languages Publishing House, c1947
391 p. ;20 cm.

A221/L563
Two Tactics of Social-Democracy in the Democratic Revolution/V. I. Lenin. —Moscow: Foreign Languages Publishing House, c1947
155 p. ;20 cm.

A221. 2/L563O58
One Step Forward, Two Steps Back/V. I. Lenin. —Moscow: Foreign Languages Publishing House, c1947
115 p. ;20 cm.

A226/L563
The Proletarian Revolution and the Renegade Kautsky/V. I. Lenin. —Moscow: Foreign Languages Publishing House, c1947
127 p. ;20 cm.

A324/S775(O)
Problems of Leninism/J. Stalin. —Moscow: Foreign Languages Publishing House, c1947
642 p. ;22 cm.

A732/K95(2)
Memories of Lenin. Vol. II/Nadezbda K. Krupskaya. —New York: International Publishers, [?]
ix, 243 p. ;19 cm.

A74/A374
Joseph Stalin: a Short Biography/G. F. Alexandrov... [et al.]. . —Moscow: Foreign Languages Pub. House, 1949.
206 p. ;20 cm.

A74/F714
Stalin on Lenin/Foreign Languages Publishing House. —Moscow: Foreign Languages Publishing House, c1946
95 p. ;21 cm.

A742/L655
Stalin/Isaac Don Levine. —New York: Blue Eibbon Books, Inc. , c1931
421 p. ;21 cm.

A81/J83
The Labour Theory of Value in Karl Marx/H. W. B. Joseph. —London: Oxford University Press, c1923
176 p. ;19 cm.

B 哲学

B/R468

Philosophy and Theology/Ernest Rhys. —London: J. M. Dent & Sons Ltd. , c[?]

xviii, 320, 4 p. ;18 cm.

B-49/F145

I Believe: The Personal Philosophies of Certain Eminent Men and Women of Our Time/Clifton Fadiman. —[S. l. : s. n.], c1939

xiv, 429 p. ;22 cm.

B-53/C682

Readings in political philosophy/Francis William Coker. —Rev. and enl. ed. . —New York: The Macmillan Company, c1938, 1948.

xvi, 717 p. ;22 cm.

B0/P332

Introduction to Philosophy/Paulsen. —[S. l]: Henry Holt and Company, [?]

xxii, 437 p. ;22 cm.

B0/R888

The Spirit of Modern Philosophy/Josiah Royce. —Boston: Houghton Mifflin Company, c1920

xv, 519 p. ;21 cm.

B0/R961

An Outline of Philosophy/Bertrand Russell. —London: G. Allen & Unwin, ltd. , c1927.

vi, 317, [1] p. ;23 cm.

B016. 8/M168

Interpreting the Universe/John Macmurray. —London: Faber and Faber, [?]

164 p. ;19 cm.

B023/RR651-3

Courses of Study/J. M. Robertson. —3rd ed. —Rewritten to Date. —London: Watts & Co. , 1908.

xii, 526 p. ;21 cm.

B08/M156-2

An Introduction to Social Philosophy/John S. Mackenzie. —2nd ed. . —Glasgow: James Maclehose & Sons, c1895

xv, 454 p. ;20 cm.

B08/R186

Modern Classical Philosophers: Selections Illustrating Modern Philosophy From Bruno to Spencer/Comp. by Benjamin Rand. —Boston: Houghton, Mifflin and Company, c1908.

xiii, 740 p. ;23 cm.

B081. 1/L885-2(1)

Metaphysic: In Three Books Ontology, Cosmology and Psychology. Vol. I/Hermann Lotze. —2nd ed. . —Oxford: The Clarendon Press, c1887

xx, 390 p. ;20 cm.

B081. 1/L885-2(2)

Metaphysic: In Three Books Ontology, Cosmology and Psychology. Vol. II/Hermann Lotze. —2nd ed. . —Oxford: The Clarendon Press, c1887

xx, 324 p. ;20 cm.

B1/B964

The Seas of God: Great Stories of the Human Spirit/Whit Burnett. —New York: J. B. Lippincott Company, c1944

585 p. ;21 cm.

B1/E66(3)

A History of Philosophy/Johann Eduard Erdmann. —London: George Allen & Unwin Ltd., c1921

356 p. ;22 cm.

B1/H521

History of Philosophy Thilly/Henry Holt and Company. —[S. l.]: Henry Holt and Company, [?]

xv, 612 p. ;21 cm.

B1/H698(1)

A History of Modern Philosophy. Vol. 1: A Sketch of the History of Renaissance to Our Own Day/Harald Hoeffding. —London: Macmillan and Co., Ltd., c1924

xvii, 532 p. ;20 cm.

B1/H698(2)

A History of Modern Philosopy: A Sketch of the History of Philosophy from the Close of the Renaissance to Our Own Day. Vol. II/Harald Hoeffding. —London: Macmillan and Co., Ltd., c1924

ix, 600 p. ;22 cm.

B1/L258

Classical (Imaginary) Conversations: Greek, Roman, Modern/Walter Savage Landor. —New York: M. Walter Dunne, Publisher, c1901

xv, 418 p. ;23 cm.

B1/S412

Schwegler's History of Philosophy/Schwegler. —New York: D. Appleton and Company, [?]

469 p. ;20 cm.

B1/W373

History of Philosophy/Alfeed Weber. —New York: Charles Scribner's Sons, c1896

xiii, 604 p. ;20 cm.

B1/W763

A History of Philosophy: With Especial Reference to The Formation and Development of Its Problems and Conceptions/W. Windelband. —New York: The Macmillan Company, c1914

xv, 726, 6 p. ;23 cm.

B2/D733

Confucianism and Taoism/Robert K. Douglas. —New York: Pott, Young, & Co., c1879

287 p. ;17 cm.

B22/D733

Oracles of Nostradamus/Robert K. Douglas. —London: Wyman and Sons, c1879

287 p. ;17 cm.

B222.25/F115-2

A Systematical Digest of the Doctrines of Confucius/Ernst Faber. —2nd ed.. —Germany: The General Evangelical Protestant Missionary Society, 1873

137 p. ;24 cm.

B222.5/H975-2

The Mind of Mencius, or, Political Economy Founded Upon Moral Philosophy: A Systematic Digest of the Doctrines of the Chinese Philosopher Mencius, B. C. 325. /Hutchinson. —2nd ed. —Tokyo: Nippon Seikokwai Shuppan Kwaisha, c1897

xvi, 316 p. ;22 cm.

B5/M523

The Dawn of Modern Thought: Descartes Spinoza Leibniz/S. H. Mellone. —London: Oxford University Press, c1930

124 p. ;19 cm.

B502/W763-3

History of Ancient Philosophy/W. Windelband. —3th ed.. —New York: Charles Scribner's Sons, c1910

xv, 393 p. ;21 cm.

B502.1/L848

Discourses of Epictetus/George Long. —New York: D. Appleton and Company, c1912

1 v. ;21 cm.

B502.232/F756

The Political Philosophies of Plato and Hegel/M. B. Foster. —Oxford: The Clarendon Press, c1935

xiii, 205 p. ;19 cm.

B502.232/J87

Plato: Apology, Crito, Phaedo, Symposium, Republic/B. Jowett. —New York: Walter J. Black, c1942

viii, 511 p. ;19 cm.

B502.232/N475

Lectures on the Republic of Plato/Richard Lewis Nettleship. —London: Macmillan and Co., Ltd., c1897

364 p. ;21 cm.

B502.232/P718R425

The Republic of Plato/Plato. —London: J. M. Dent & Sons Ltd., c1935

xlii, 325, 15 p. ;17 cm.

B502.233/L863

Aristotle: On Man in the Univers/Louise Ropes Loomis. —New York: Walter J. Black, c1943

xliii, 443 p. ;19 cm.

B502.233/P478

The Nicomachean Ethics of Aristotle/F. H. Peters. —4th ed.. —London: Kegan Paul, Trench, Trubner & Co., Ltd., c1893

359 p. ;18 cm.

B502.233/R827

Aristotle/W. D. Ross. —London: Methuen & Co., Ltd., c1923

vii, 300 p. ;22 cm.

B516/K95

The Philosophy of the Present in Germany/by Oswald Kuelpe... [et al.]; tr. from the 5th German ed. by Maud Lyall Patrick and G. T. W. Patrick. Authorized translation. —London: G. Allen & Company, ltd., c1913.

ix, 256 p. ;19 cm.

B516.22/L525

The Monadology and Other Philosophical Writings/Leibniz. —London: Oxford University Press, c1898

x, 437 p. ;20 cm.

B516.22/M577

Leibniz/John Theodore Merz. —Edinburgh: William Blackwood and Sons, [?]

vii, 216 p. ;17 cm.

B516.31/K16

Perpetual Peace: A Philosophical Essay/Immanuel Kant; edited, with an introduction, by Lewis White Beck. —London: George Allen & Unwin Ltd., c1903.

xi, 203 p. ;19 cm.

B516.31/K16-10

Fundamental Principles of the Metaphysic of Ethics/Immanuel Kant. —10th. ed. —London: Longmans, Green and Co., c1932

102 p. ;19 cm.

B516.31/L748

The Philosophy of Immanuel Kant/A. D. Lindsay. —London: T. C. & E. C. Jack, Ltd.,

[?]
89 p. ;17 cm.

B516. 31/W339
The Philosophy of Kant Explained/by John Watson. —Glasgow: James Maclehose and sons, c1908.
xi, 515 p. ;22 cm.

B516. 35/C587
Hegel's Ethical Teaching: Its Development, Significance, and Limitations/W. S. Chang. —Shanghai: The Commercial Press, c1925
x, 137 p. ;23 cm.

B516. 35/L886
Hegel Selections/J. Loewwenberg. —London: Charles Scribner's Sons, c1929
xliii, 468 p. ;17 cm.

B516. 41/S373
The Wisdom of Life and other Essays/Arthur Schopenhauer. —New York: M. Walter Dunne, Publisher, c1901
xii, 332 p. ;23 cm.

B516. 41/S373
Essays of Schpenhauer: the Scott Library/Schopenhauer. —[S. l. : s. n.], [?]
xxxiv, 220 p. ;17 cm.

B516. 47/N592
Thus Spake Zarathustra/Friedrich Nietzsche. —New York: The Modern Library, [?]
325 p. ;18 cm.

B520. 232/J87
Dialogues of Plato/Benjamin Jowett. —New York: D. Appleton and Company, c1912
xix, 476 p. ;21 cm.

B561/H424
The Belief in Personal Immortality/E. S. P. Haynes. —London: Watts & Co. , c1918
viii, 156 p. ;17 cm.

B561/M875
Locke Berkeley Hume/C. R. Morris. —Oxford: the Clarendon Press, c1931
1v;21 cm.

B561/M953
Contemporary British Philosophy: Personal Statements (first series)/J. B. Baillie. [et al.]; edited by J. H. Muirhead. . —London: George Allen & Unwin Ltd. , 1924.
432 p. ;22 cm.

B561. 22/H682
Leviathan/Thomas Hobbes. —London: J. M. Dent Sons, Ltd. , [?]
392 p. ;18 cm.

B561. 22/S663
Hobbes's Leviathan: Reprinted from the Edition of 1651/W. G. Pogson Smith. —Oxford: The Clarendon Press, c1929
xxxi, 557 p. ;23 cm.

B561. 24/L239
Locke Selections/Sterling P. Lamprecht. —London: Charles Scribner's Sons, c1928
lv, 348, 6 p. ;17 cm.

B561. 24/L813
An Essay Concerning Human Understanding/John Locke. —Oxford: The Clarendon Press, c1924
xlviii, 380 p. ;19 cm.

B561. 24/L814
An Essay Concerning Human Understanding/John Locke. —London: George Routledge And Sons, [?]
xvi, 645 p. ;19 cm.

B561.291/H921(1)

A Treatise of Human Nature. Volume I/David Hume. —London: J. M. Dent & Sons, c1911

xxx, 258 p. ;18 cm.

B561.291/H921

Hume Selections/David Hume. —London: Charles Scribner's Sons, c1927

xxv, 401 p. ;17 cm.

B561.4/R598

The Principles of State Interference: Four Essays on the Political Philosophy of Mr. Herbert Spencer, J. S. Mill and T. H. Green/David G. Ritchie. —London: Swan Sonnenschein & Co., Ltd., c1902

xi, 172 p. ;18 cm.

B561.45/S745

First Principles/Herbert Spencer. —New York: A. L. Burt. Publisher, [?]

xv, 483, 6 p. ;19 cm.

B561.45/S745-6

First Principles/Herbert Spencer. —New York: A. L. Burt. Publisher, [?]

xviii, 550 p. ;20 cm.

B561.49/C286

Sartor Resartus: The Life and Opinions of Herr Teufelsdroeckh/Thomas Carlyle. —Tokyo: Kenkyusha, c1928

xii, 380 p. ;19 cm.

B561.59/F841

Locke/Alexander Campbell Fraser. —Edinburgh: William Blackwood and Sons, [?]

x, 299 p. ;17 cm.

B561.59/W668

Spinoza Selections/John Wild. —London: Charles Scribner's Sons, c1930

lxi, 479 p. ;17 cm.

B563.1/E52(2)

The Chief Works of Benedict De Spinoza. vol. II/R. H. M. Elwes. —Revised ed.. —Revised ed.: George Bell and Sons, c1903

xxii, 420, 26 p. ;18 cm.

B563.1/S758(1)

The Chief Works of Benedict de Spinoza. vil. I/Benedict de Spinoza. —London: George Bell and Sons, c1900

xxxiii, 387, 29 p. ;19 cm.

B563.1/S758

Ethic/Benedict de Spinoza. —London: Oxford University Press, c1930

xcix, 297 p. ;22 cm.

B563.1/S758I

Improvement of the Understanding, Ethics and Correspondence/Benedict De Spinoza. —New York: M. Walter Dunne, Publisher, c1901

xxxiii, 427 p. ;23 cm.

B565.21/D445D611

A Discourse on Method/Rene Descartes. —London: J. M. Dent & Sons Ltd., c1912

xxiv, 254 p. ;18 cm.

B565.21/R259

The Discourse on Method and Metaphysical Meditations of Rene Descartes/Gertrude Burford Rawlings. —London: Walter Scott, [?]

xxxi, 227 p. ;18 cm.

B565.24/M779(1)

The Spirit of the Laws. Volume I/Baron de Montesquieu. —New York: D. Appleton and Company, c1912

xliii, 447 p. ;21 cm.

B565.24/M779(O)

Montesquieu: Persian Letters/Montesquieu. —

London: George Routledge & Sons Ltd. , [?]
359 p. ;19 cm.

B565. 24/M779

Persian and Chinese Letters: Being the Lettres Persanes/Charles Louis Baron de Montesquieu. —New York: M. Walter Dunne, Publisher, c1901
xiii, 427 p. ;23 cm.

B565. 26/R864

Ideal Empires and Republics: Rousseau's Social Contract More's Utopia Bacon's New Atlantis Campanella's City of the Sun/Jean Jacques Rousseau. —New York: M. Wal Terdunne, Publisher, c1901
xx, 317 p. ;23 cm.

B565. 49/B493

Creative Evolution/Herni Bergson. —London: Macmillan and Co, Ltd. , c1920
xv, 425, 6 p. ;22 cm.

B656. 2/M214

Descartes/J. P. Mahaffy. —Edinburgh: William Balckwood and Sons, [?]
vi, 211 p. ;18 cm.

B712/P174(1)

Contemporary American Philosophy: Personal Statements. Vol. I/. —London: George Allen & Unwin Ltd. , c1930
450 p. ;22 cm.

B712/P174(2)

Contemporary American Philosophy: Personal Statements. Vol. II/[?]. —London: George Allen & Unwin Ltd. , c1930
447 p. ;22 cm.

B712. 41/R961

Emerson: The Wisest American/Phillips Russell. —New York: Blue Ribbon Books, c1929
320 p. ;21 cm.

B712. 44/J27

Pragmatism: A New Name for Some Old ways of Thinking/William James. —London: Longmans, Green, and Co. , c1908
xii, 307 p. ;22 cm.

B712. 49/F297

The Destiny of Man Viewed in the Light of His Origin/John Fiske. —Boston: Houghton, Mifflin and Company, c1884
vii, 121 p. ;18 cm.

B712. 51/D519

Reconstruction in Philosophy/John Dewey. —New York: Henry Holt and Company, c1920
vii, 224 p. ;18 cm.

B712. 59/C155

The Persistent Problems of Philosophy/Calkins. —New York: The Macmillan Company, c1912
xxvi, 577 p. ;20 cm.

B81/D519

How We Think/John Dewey. —Boston: D. C. Heath & Co. , c1910
vi, 224 p. ;19 cm.

B81/J89-3

Principles of Logic/George Hayward Joyce. —3rd ed. . —New York: Longmans, Green & Co. , c1929
431 p. ;22 cm.

B81-06/K21-4

Ethics and the Materialist Conception of History/Karl Kautsky. —4th ed. . —Chicago: Charles H. Kerr & Company, [?]
206 p. ;17 cm.

B812/J43

Elementary Lessons in Logic: Deductive and Inductive with Questions and Examples and a Vocabulary of Logical Terms/W. Stanley Jevons.—New York: The Macmillan Company, c1916

viii, 340, 8 p.;18 cm.

B812.4/G795-16(1)

A Treatise on the Law of Evidence. Vol. I/Simon Greenleaf..—16th ed..—Boston: Little, Brown, 1899

cxxxiv, 991 p.;24 cm.

B812.4/G795-16(2)

A Treatise on the Law of Evidence. Vol. II/Simon Greenleaf.—16th ed..—Boston: Little, Brown, 1899

xcvi, 638 p.;24 cm.

B812.4/G795-16(3)

A Treatise on the Law of Evidence. Vol. III/Simon Greenleaf..—16th ed..—Boston: Little, Brown, 1899

xiii, 542;24 cm.

B82/B811-2

Ethical Studies/F. H. Bradley.—2nd ed..—Oxford: The Clarendon Press, c1927

xii, 344 p.;23 cm.

B82/B863

Five Types of Ethical Theory/C. D. Broad.—London: Kegan Paul, Trench, Trubner & Co., Ltd., c1930

xxv, 288 p.;22 cm.

B82/C316

The Theory of Morals: An Introduction to Ethical Philosophy/E. F. Carritt.—London: Oxford University Press, c1928

xii, 143 p.;19 cm.

B82/C865

Constructive Ethics: A Review of Modern Moral Philosophy/W. L. Courtney.—London: Chapman and Hall, Ltd., c1895

xii, 318 p.;23 cm.

B82/D519

Ethics/John Dewey, James H. Tufts.—London: G. Bell & Sons, Ltd., c1910

xiii, 618 p.;21 cm.

B82/E94

The Morality of Punishment: With some Suggestions for a General Theory of Ethics/A. C. Ewing.—London: Kegan Paul, Trench, Trubner& Co., Ltd., c1929

xiv, 233 p.;22 cm.

B82/F453-2

Moral Theory: An Introduction to Ethics/G. C. Field.—2nd ed..—London: Methuen & Co., Ltd., c1932

x, 214 p.;19 cm.

B82/G795-5

Prolegomena to ethics/the late Thomas Hill Green; edited by A. C. Bradley.—5th ed..—Oxford: Clarendon Press, 1906.

xxxix, 470 p.;20 cm.

B82/J63

A Study of the Ethics of Spinoza/Harold H. Joachim.—Oxford: The Clarendon Press, c1901

xiv, 316 p.;22 cm.

B82/J83

Some Problems in Ethics/H. W. B. Joseph.—Oxford: Clarendon, c1931

135 p.;19 cm.

B82/L528

The Individual and the Social Order: An Introduction to Ethics and Social Philosophy/Joseph

A. Leighton. —London: D. Appleton and Company, c1926
xix, 578 p. ;21 cm.

B82/M156-5
A Manual of Ethics/John S. Mackenzie. —London: University Tutorial Press, c1915
xxii, 500, 4 p. ;18 cm.

B82/M156-6
A Manual of Ethics/John S. Mackenzie. —6th ed.. —London: University Tutorial Press, c1929
xii, 426 p. ;19 cm.

B82/M821
Principia Ethica/George Edward Moore. —Cambridge: The University Press, c1929
xxvii, 232 p. ;23 cm.

B82/M953
The Elements of Ethics/John H. Muirhead. —London: John Murray Albemarle Street, W. , [?]
xiv, 292 p. ;19 cm.

B82/R186
The Classical Moralists/B. Rand.. —Boston: Houghton Mifflin Co. , c1909.
xviii, 797 p. ;22 cm.

B82/R222-2(1)
The Theory of Good and Evil: A Treatise on Moral Philosophy. Volume I/Hastings Rashdall. —2nd ed.. —London: Oxford University Press, c1924
xx, 312 p. ;23 cm.

B82/R222-2
The Theory of Good and Evil: A Treatise on Moral Philosophy/Hastings Rashdall. —2nd ed.. —London: Oxford University Press, c1924
xv, 464 p. ;23 cm.

B82/R658
Essays Toward Truth: Studies in Orientation/Kenneth Allan Robinson, William Benfield Pressey, James Dow Mccallum. —New York: Henry Holt and Company, c1924
vii, 395 p. ;19 cm.

B82/S163
Ethics/C. W. Saleeby, M. D.. —New York: Frederick A. Stokes Company, [?]
117 p. ;18 cm.

B82/S713
On the Ethics of Naturalism/W. R. Sorley. —London: Willian Blackwood and Sons, 1885
xii, 292 p. ;20 cm.

B82/S745
The Data of Ethics/H. Spencer. —London: Williams & Norgate, c1907.
viii, 264 p. ;21 cm.

B82-051/C311
Morals and Politics: Theories of Their Relation from Hobbes and Spinoza to Marx and Bosanquet/E. F. Carritt. —Oxford: The Clarendon Press, c1935
216 p. ;19 cm.

B82-051/C316
Ethical and Political Thinking/E. F. Carritt. —Oxford: The Clarendon Press, c1947
xx, 186 p. ;19 cm.

B82-051/M953
Rule and End in Morals/John H. Muirhead. —London: Oxford University Press, c1932
vi, 120 p. ;20 cm.

B82-052/P351
The Approach to the Social Question: An Introduction to the Study of Social Ethics/Francis Greenwood Peabody. —New York: The Macmil-

lan Company, c1912
vii, 210 p. ;19 cm.

B82-057/S828-2
The Science of Ethics/Leslie Stephen. —2nd ed.. —London: Smith, Elder, & Co., c1907
xxvi, 444 p. ;20 cm.

B82-061/B985
Three Sermons on Human Nature and Dissertation on Virtue/Joseph Butler. —London: G. Bell and Sons Ltd., c1931
xxvii, 81 p. ;18 cm.

B82-064/M645
Utilitarianism/John Stuart Mill. —13th ed.. —London: Longmans, Green And Co., c1897
96, 32 p. ;23 cm.

B82-067/S568
The Methods of Ethics/Henry Sidgwick. —London: Macmillan and Co., Ltd., c1913
xxxvi, 528 p. ;23 cm.

B82-09/R724
A Short History of Ethics, Greek and Modern/R. A. P. Rogers. —London: Macmillan and Co., Ltd., c1911
xxii, 302 p. ;19 cm.

B82-09(5)/L433(1)
History of European Morals From Augustus to Charlemagne vol. 1/William Edward Hartpole Lecky. —London: Longmans, Green, and Co., c1911
xxiv, 407 p. ;18 cm.

B82-095/S568
Outlines of the History fo Ethics for English Readers/Henry Sidgwick. —London: Macmillan and Co., Ltd., c1931
xxvi, 337 p. ;18 cm.

B821/B128-4
The Essaysor Counsels, Civil and Moral and the Wisdom fo the Ancients/Francis Bacon. —4th ed.. —Boston: Little, Brown and Company, c1864
xxvi, 360 p. ;17 cm.

B821/C286
Heroes and Hero-Worship/Thomas Carlyle. —London: Collins Clear-Type Press, [?]
312 p. ;16 cm.

B821/F979
A Comparative Study of Life Ideals: the Way of Decrease and Increase with Interpretations and Illustrations from the Philosophies of the East and the West/by Yu-lan Fung.. —Shanghai: The Commercial Press, Ltd., c1927.
xii, 264 p. ;19 cm.

B824/D773-3
Social Credit/C. H. Douglas. —3rd ed., rev. and enl.. —London: Eyre & Spottiswoode, c1934
xi, 212 p. ;19 cm.

B825/B964
The Seas of God: Great Stories of the Human Sprit/Whit Burnett. —Philadelphia: J. B. Lippincott Company, c1944
585 p. ;21 cm.

B825/G318
The Mirrors of Wall Street/Anonymous. —New York: G. P. Putnam's Sons, c1933
268 p. ;23 cm.

B825/G884
Understanding Yourself: The Mental Hygiene of Personality/Ernest R. Groves. —New York: Emerson Books, Inc., c1944
279 p. ;21 cm.

B825/K63

How to Develop Self-confidence in Speech & Manner/Grenville Kleiser. —New York: Funk & Wagnalls Company, c1910

vii, 288 p. ;19 cm.

B825/L735(O)

The Importance of Living/Yutang Lin. —[S. l. : s. n.], c1939

xvi, 459 p. ;21 cm.

B825/M298

Little Visits with Creat Americans or Success Ideals and How to Attain Them/Orison Swett Marden. —New York: The Success Company, c1905

352 p. ;20 cm.

B825/M621

Famous Boys: A Book of Brave Endeavour/Charles D. Michael. —London: S. W. Partridge & Co. , Ltd. , [?]

1 v. ;19 cm.

B825-49/S641

Character/Smiles, Samuel. —London: John Murray, Albemarle Street, W. , c1910

xiv, 428, 7 p. ;20 cm.

B829/HSI

Studies in Chinese Diplomatic History/Ching-Lin Hsia. —Shanghai: The Commercial Press, c1926

xii, 226 p. ;23 cm.

B83/B741

Three Lectures on Aesthetic/Bernard Bosanquet. —London: Macmillan and Co. , Ltd. , 1923.

ix, 118 p. ;20 cm.

B834. 3/W873

Care of Clothing: Woman's Institute Library of Dressmaking/The Woman's Institute of Domestic Arts and Sciences. —Scranton: The Woman's Institute of Domestic Arts and Sciences, c1925

1 v. ;23 cm.

B837. 128. 5/H681

Oil for the Lamps of China/(1882-1967) Alice Tisdale Hobart. —New York: The Bobbs-Merrill Company, c1933.

403 p. ;21 cm.

B84/F841-4

Selections from Berkeley/Alexander Campbell Fraser. —4th ed. . —Oxford: The Clarendon Press, c1891

liii, 402, 8 p. ;20 cm.

B84/H698

Outlines of Psychology/Harald Hoeffding. —London: Macmillan and Co. , Ltd. , c1901

xi, 365 p. ;18 cm.

B84/S365

Human Nature: A First Book in Psychology/Max Schoen. —New York: Harper & Brothers Publishers, c1930

xviii, 504 p. ;22 cm.

B84/T319

The Measurement of Intelligence: An Explanation of and a Complete Guide for the Use of the Stanford Revision and Extension of the Binet-Simon Intelligence Scale/Lewis M. Terman. —Boston: Houghton Mifflin Company, c1916

xviii, 362 p. ;19 cm.

B84/W965

An Introduction to Psychology/Wilhelm Wundt. —New York: The Macmillan Company, c1912

xi, 196 p. ;19 cm.

B84-09/B111(1)

History of Psychology: A Sketh and an Interpretation. vol. I. from the Earliest Time to John Locke. /James Mark Baldwin. —London: Watts & Co. , c1913

xv, 136 p. ;18 cm.

B841/C853

My Method: Including American Impressions/ Emile Coue. —New York: Doubleday, Page & Company, c1923

xx, 201 p. ;19 cm.

B841. 7/F855

Mental Tests: Their History, Principles and Applications/Frank N. Freeman. —Boston: Houghton Mifflin Company, c1926

ix, 503 p. ;19 cm.

B842/G539

The Story of Our Minds: The Science of Psychology Our Mental States and Processes-What, They Are-What They Mean/Robert Chenault Givler. —New York: P. F. Collier & Son Corporation Publishers, c1940

407 p. ;20 cm.

B844. 1/A547

Happy Childhood: The Development and Guidance of Children and Youth/John E. Anderson. —New York: D. Appleton-century Company, c1933

xix, 321 p. ;21 cm.

B844. 1/H741

The Psychology of Subnormal Children/Leta S. Hollingworth. —New York: The Macmillan Company, c1930

xix, 288 p. ;19 cm.

B844. 2/H741

The Psychology of the Adolescent/Leta S. Hollingworth. —New York: D. Appleton and Company, c1930

xii, 227 p. ;21 cm.

B844. 6/S326

The Promises Men Live by a New Approach to Economics/Harry Scherman. —New York: Random House, c1938

xxvi, 492 p. ;23 cm.

B845/B287-2

Relation of Psychology to Music/E. F. Bartholomew. —2nd ed. . —Rock Island: The New Era Publishing Company, c1899

286 p. ;19 cm.

B845. 9/E47(6)

Studies in the Psychology of Sex: Sex in Relation to Society. Vol. VI/Havelock Ellis. —Philadelphia: F. A. Dabis Company, Publishers, c1917

xvi, 656 p. ;22 cm.

B848/L323-3

Increasing Personal Efficiency: The Psychology of Personal Progress/Donald A. Laird. —New York: Harper & Brothers, Publishers, c1936

xii, 294 p. ;21 cm.

B848. 4/M298

Little Visits with Great Americans, or, Success Ideals and How To Attain Them/Orison Swett Marden. —New York: The Success Company, c1905

742 p. ;20 cm.

B848. 4/M298

Heading for Victory, or, Getting the Most Out of Life/Orison Swett Marden. —New York: Success Magazine Corporation, c1922

vi, 535 p. ;19 cm.

B848.4/M298B365

How to Be Great/Orison Swett Marden.—Shanghai: The Commercial Press, Ltd., c1927

150 p.;16 cm.

B848.4/M839

On Compromise/John Viscount Morley.—London: Macmillan and Co., Ltd., c1923

x, 248 p.;20 cm.

B848.4-49/K62

How to Use Your Mind: A Psychology of Study/Harry D. Kitson.—Philadelphia: J. B. Lippincott Company, c1921

245 p.;18 cm.

B849/H529(2)

Psychology Applied to Life and Work. vol. 2/Harry Walker Hepner.—Washington: Prentice-Hall Inc., c1941

iv, 369-770 p.;21 cm.

B871.22/G721

Papers Relating to the Foreign Relations of the United States/Government Printing Office.—Washington: Government Printing Office, c1920

cii, 1444 p.;22 cm.

B9/B214

Practical Problems in Religion/Rev. Rudolph G. Bandas.—Chicago: The Bruce Publishing Company, c1934

192 p.;19 cm.

B9/B293

The Religions of the World/George A. Barton.—Chicago: The University of Chicago Press, c1917, 1919

xiii, 406 p.;20 cm.

B9/H329

Into the Way of Peace/Communicants of the English Church.—London: The Religious Book Club, c1941

192 p.;20 cm.

B9/L735

The Return to Religion/Henry C. Link.—New York: The Macmillan Company, c1941

181 p.;20 cm.

B91/M861

Who Moved the Stone/Frank Morison.—New York: The Century Co., c1930

vii, 294 p.;20 cm.

B91/P316

The Social Basis of Religion/Simon N. Patten.—New York: the Macmillan Company, c1912

xviii, 247 p.;19 cm.

B91/S539(2)

Justice and Charity. Part II, The Individual Problem and the Cross/Fulton J. Sheen.—Washington: National Council of Catholic Men, [?]

78 p.;19 cm.

B911/C155

Religion and Life/Raymond Calkins.—New York: Harper & Brothers Publishers, c1935

115 p.;18 cm.

B92/H975

The Ordeal of Western Religion/Paul Hutchinson.—Boston: Houghton Mifflin Company, c1933

xiv, 139 p.;19 cm.

B920/B985

The Analogy of Religion, Natural and Revealed, to the Constitution and Course of nature: to which are added two brief dissertations. I. of personal identity. II. of the nature of virtue/Joseph Butler.—London: George Bell & Sons,

1898
546 p. , 48 p. ;19 cm.

B920/D795
Natural Law in the Spiritual World/Henry Drummond. —New York: John W. Lovell Company, [?]
xxiv, 414 p. ;19 cm.

B920/H254
Religious Living/Georgia Harkness. —New York: Association Press, c1940
iii, 65 p. ;19 cm.

B920/P913
The Religious Consciousness: a Psychological Study/James Bissett Pratt. —New York: Macmillan, 1921.
viii, 488 p. ;22 cm.

B920/S917
Psychology of Religious Experience: Studies in the Psychological Interpretation of Religious Faith/Francis L. Strickland. —New York: The Abingdon Press, c1924
320 p. ;21 cm.

B921/C652
The Red Theology in the Far East/Charles Coates. —London: Chas. J. Thynne & Jarvis. Ltd. , c1926
202 p. ;19 cm.

B921/S811-3
After Dogmatic Theology, What?: Materialism or A spiritual Philosophy and Natural Religion/Giles B. Stebbins. —3rd ed. . —Detroit: Thorndike Nourse, c1884
144 p. ;20 cm.

B922/S296
First Religious Instructions for Little Ones/Albert Schaffler. —New York: Joseph F. Wagner, c1901
iv, 208, xxxiv p. ;20 cm.

B928. 2/D691(1)
Social Life of the Chinese: With some Account of their Religious, Governmental, Educational, and Business Customs and Opinions. Vol. I/Justus Doolittle. —New York: Harper & Vrothers, Publishers, c1876
xxxii, 490 p. ;21 cm.

B929/C443(1)
Foundations of the Nineteenth Century. vol. 1/Houston Stewart Chamberlain. —London: John Lane the Bodley Head Ltd. , c1910
580 p. ;19 cm.

B929/C443(2)
Foundations of the Nineteenth Century. vol. II/Houston Stewart Chamberlain. —London: John Lane the Bodley Head Ltd. , c1910
580 p. ;19 cm.

B929/H793
The History of Religions/E. Washburn Hopkins. —New York: The Macmillan Company, c1926
624 p. ;20 cm.

B929. 382/S756-5
Lucius Flavus: An Historical Tale of the Time Immediately Preceding the Destruction of Jerusalem/Reverend Joseph Spillmann. —5th ed. . —London: B. Herder Book Co. , c1919
619 p. ;20 cm.

B932-61/E25
A Dictionary of Nonclassical Mythology/Marian Edwardes, Lewis Spence. —London: J. M. Dent & Sons Ltd. , [?]
xii, 214 p. ;17 cm.

B948/R349

Truth and Tradition in Chinese Buddhism: A Study of Chinese Mahayana Buddhism/Karl Ludvig Reichelt, Kathrina Van Wagenen Bugge. —Shanghai: The Commercial Press, Ltd., c1928

x, 330 p.; 21 cm.

B96/W556

Islam and Missions: Being Papers Read at the Second Missionary Conference on Behalf of the Mohammedan World at Lucknow, January 23-28, 1911/E. M. Wherry, S. M. Zwemer, C. G. Mylrea. —New York: Fleming H. Revell Company, c1911

298 p.; 21 cm.

B96/Z97

The Mohammedan World of To-Day: Being Papers Read at the First Missionary Conference on Behalf of the Mohammedan World Held at Cairo April 4th-9th, 1906/S. M. Zwemer, E. M. Wherry, James L. Barton. —New York: Fleming H. Revell Company, c1906

302 p.; 21 cm.

B97/518

The Pastoral Epistles/J. H. Bernard. —London: Fetter Lane, E. C., c1906

lxxvii, 192 p.; 17 cm.

B97/B471

Christianity and our World/John C. Bennett. —New York: Association Press, c1936

ix, 70 p.; 19 cm.

B97/B627

Edinburgh Sermons/Hugh Black. —London: Hodder and Stoughton, c1906

xi, 300 p.; 20 cm.

B97/B985(3)

The Lives of the Saints. vol. III/Rev. Alban Butler. —New York: P. J. Kenedy & Sons, c1933

xii, 405 p.; 23 cm.

B97/B985(4)

The Lives of the Saints. vol. VI/Rev. Alban Butler. —New York: P. J. Kenedy & Sons, c1937

xv, 407 p.; 23 cm.

B97/B985(5)

The Lives of the Saints. vol. V/Rev. Alban Butler. —New York: P. J. Kenedy & Sons, c1936

xvi, 383 p.; 23 cm.

B97/C156-3

The Four Gospelsa/Charles J. Callan, Charles J. Callan. —3rd ed.. —New York: Joseph F. Wagner(Inc)., c1918

xxx, 561 p.; 23 cm.

B97/C797

The Master-Christian/Marie Correlli. —London: Metuen & Co., c1900

634 p.; 18 cm.

B97/G874-4

The History of the Passion of our Lord Jesus Christ/James Groenings. —4th Revised ed.. —London: B. Herder Book Company, c1919

xiv, 461 p.; 19 cm.

B97/H357

The Greater Men and Women of the Bible: Moses-Samson/James Hastings. —Edinburgh: T. & T. Clark, c1914

x, 520 p.; 23 cm.

B97/H835-2

Man's Triumph: With God in Christ/Frederick A. Houck. —2nd Revised ed.. —London: B. Herder Book Co., c1940

xiii, 244 p. ;19 cm.

B97/K92

Christianity's Problem in the Far East/Andrew J. Krzesinski. —South Bend: Fides Publishers, c1945

125 p. ;20 cm.

B97/L468

In the Likeness of Christ/Rev. Edward Leen. —New York: Sheed & Ward, c1940

xxiv, 361 p. ;20 cm.

B97/M848

The Crises of the Christ/G. Campbell Morgan. —New York: Fleming H. Revell Company, c1903

477 p. ;21 cm.

B97/P111

Days of Our Years/Pierre Van Paassen. —New York: New York Publishing Co. , Inc. , c1949

577 p. ;24 cm.

B97/P238

Sadhu Sundar Singh Called of God/Arthur Parker. —New York: Fleming H. Revell Company, c1920

xvi, 171 p. ;19 cm.

B97/P949-R

The Rule of ST. Francis: the Religious Vows and the Rule/A Priest of the English Province, O. F. M. . —London: The Salesian Press, c1933

98 p. ;19 cm.

B97/R994

The Book of Genesis: In the Revised Version with Introduction and Notes/Herbert E. Ryle. —Cambridge: Cambridge University Press, c1914

lxviii, 477 p. ;17 cm.

B97/S

The God of Our Fathers/H. P. S. . —New York: Fleming H. Revell Company, c1923

156 p. ;19 cm.

B97/S613

The Fact of Christ: A series of Lectures/P. Carnegie Simpson. —New York: Pleming H. Revell Company, [?]

1v;21 cm.

B97/S849

The Stronghold of Prophecy: Irrefutable Evidence from Fulfilled Prophecy that the Scriptures are the Infallible Word of God/Herbert Stewart. —London: Marshall, Morgan & Scott, Ltd. , [?]

127 p. ;19 cm.

B97/S919

So Great Salvation/J. F. Strombeck. —Moline: Strombeck Agency, Inc. , c1940

152 p. ;19 cm.

B97/S919-4

So Great Salvation/J. F. Strombeck. —Moline: Strombeck Agency, Inc. , c1943

152 p. ;19 cm.

B97-54/R261

The China Christian Year Book 1934-1935/F. Rawlinson. —Shanghai: Christian Literature Society, 1937.

xxxii, 458 p. ;19 cm.

B971/A457-2

The Life and Teachings of Jesus Christ: In the Words of the King James Version/Charles A. McAlpine. —2 ed. . —New York: The Coverdale Bible Press, c1937

191 p. ;21 cm.

B971/E36

The Abingdon Bible Commentary/Frederick Carl Eiselen, Edwin Lewis, David G. Downey. —New York: The Avingdon Press, c1929

xvi, 1452 p. ; 24 cm.

B971/H811

The Twentieth Century New Testament: A Translation into Modern English made form the Original Greek/Horace Marshall & Son.. —London: Horace Marshall & Son., c1902

xiv, 513 p. ; 19 cm.

B971/I61(1)

Studies in the Scriptures. Series 1, "the Plan of the Ages"/International Bible Students Association. —London: International Bible Students Association, c1913

356, 14 p. ; 19 cm.

B971/I61(3)

Studies in the Scriptures. Series III, Thy Kingdom Come/International Bible Students Association. —London: International Bible Students Association, c1913

384 p. ; 19 cm.

B971/I64

The Time is at Hand/International Bible Students Association. —London: International Bible Students Association, c1913

371 p. ; 19 cm.

B971/M161

Expositions of Holy Scripture: Isaiah(Chaps. I to XLVIII)/Alexander Maclaren. —New York: Hodder & Stoughton, [?]

viii, 403 p. ; 22 cm.

B971/M323

Stories from the Bible/Walter de La Mare. —New York: Cosmopolitan Book Corporation, c1929

xvii, 393 p. ; 24 cm.

B971/M374

The Bible is True: The Lessons of the 1925-1934 Excavations in Bible Lands Summarized and Explained/Sir Charles Marston. —London: Eyre and Spottiswoode, c1934

xiv, 284 p. ; 21 cm.

B971/P735

The Gospel According to St John/A. Plummer. —Cambridge: Cambridge University Press, c1913

lxiv, 382 p. ; 17 cm.

B971/S451-2

The Teaching of Bible Classes: Principles and Methods with Special Reference to Classes of Young Men and Boys/Edwin F. See. —New York: Young Men's Christian Association Press, c1907

viii, 181 p. ; 19 cm.

B971/S667

The Bible in the Making in the Light of Modern Research/J. Paterson Smyth. —New York: James Pott & Company, c1914

219 p. ; 19 cm.

B971/T486

Land and the Book; or, Biblical Illustrations Drawn From Manners and Customs, the Scenes and Scenery of the Holy Land/W. M. Thomson. —London: T. Nelson and Sons, Paternoster Row, c1881

xvii, 716 p. ; 18 cm.

B971/V561

The Holy Bible/King James Version. —Chicago: John C. Winston Company, [?]

255 p. ; 19 cm.

B971. 1/G779

A Critical Introduction to the Old Testament/George Buchanan Gray. —New York: Charles Scribner's Sons, c1924

xi, 253 p. ;19 cm.

B971. 1/K67

The Religious Teaching of the Old Testament/Albeert C. Kundson. —New York: The Abingdon Press, c1918

416 p. ;21 cm.

B971. 2/O12

The New Testament of Our Lord and Saviour Jesus Christ: A New Translation/Nihil Obstat. —New York: Sheed & Ward, c1945

573 p. ;22 cm.

B971-62/U78(4)

The New Biblical Guide: Popular Edition. Vol. IV/John Urquhart. —London: Marshall Brothers, [?]

xx, 428 p. ;19 cm.

B975/B167

Christian Missions and A New World Culture/Archibald G. Baker. —Chicago: Willett, Clark & Company, c1934

xiii, 322 p. ;20 cm.

B975/B286

One Hundred Revival Sermons and Outlines/Frederick Barton. —New York: Doubleday, Doran & Company, Inc. , c1929

xiii, 455 p. ;21 cm.

B975/B873

The Candle of the Lord and Other Sermons/Phillips Brooks. —London: Macmillan and Co. , c1884

vii, 370 p. ;19 cm.

B975/B942

The Pilgrim's Progress From This World to That Which Is to Come/John Bunyan. —London: J. M. Dent & Sons ltd. , c1907.

xvii, 383 p. ;18 cm.

B975/D795

The New Evangelism/Henry Drummond. —London: Hodder and Stoughton, [?]

vii, 210 p. ;19 cm.

B975/F748

Living Under Tension Sermons on Christianity Today/Harry Emerson Fosdick. —New York: Harper & Brothers, c1941

ix, 253 p. ;19 cm.

B975/G367

Christian Politeness: for the Use of Schools, Academies, Colleges, and Seminaries, as Well as for Private Study /M. M. Gerend. —Milwaukee: J. H. Yewdale and Sons Co. , c1904

298 p. ;20 cm.

B975/G975

Raths to Power: Central Church Sermons/Frank W. Gunsanulus. —New York: Fleming H. Revell Company, c1905

362 p. ;cm. 20 cm.

B975/H146(1)

Along the Mission Trail. I, In the Philippines/Bruno Hagspiel. —Illinois: Mission Press, c1925

267 p. ;22 cm.

B975/H146(3)

Along the Mission Trail. III, In New Guinea/Bruno Hagspiel. —Illinois: Mission Press, c1926

270 p. ;22 cm.

B975/H749

Patriotism is not Enough/John Haynes Holmes. —London: George Allen & Unwin

Ltd. , c1925
viii, 209 p. ;19 cm.

B975/J72
Letters to Missionary/R. F. Johnston. —London: Watts & Co. , c1918
xxvi, 158 p. ;19 cm.

B975/M367
The Missionary/Edison Marshall. —New York: Triangle Books, c1942
288 p. ;19 cm.

B975/M612
One Hundred Prayer Meeting Talks and Plans/F. B. Meyer. —New York: Richard R. Smith, Inc. , c1930
544 p. ;21 cm.

B975/P217
Life of Christ/Giovanni Papini. —New York: Harcourt, Brace and Company, c1923
416 p. ;22 cm.

B975/R975
Riches/J. F. Rutherford. —New York: Watch Tower, c1936
379 p. ;18 cm.

B975/S539(2)
Freedom. Part II, Personal Freedom/Fulton J. Sheen. —Washington: National Catholic Welfare Conference, [?]
90 p. ;19 cm.

B975/T865
Alternative to Futility/Elton Trueblood. —New York: Harper & Brothers Publishers, c1948
124 p. ;19 cm.

B975/W664(1930)
Lesson Commentary for Sunday Schools 1930/Charles P. Wiles, D. Burt Smith. —Philadelphia: The United Lutheran Publication House, [?]
316 p. ;23 cm.

B975/W664(1939)
Lesson Commentary for Sunday Schools 1930/Charles P. Wiles, D. Burt Smith. —Philadelphia: The United Lutheran Publication House, [?]
319 p. ;23 cm.

B975/W664(1940)
Lesson Commentary for Sunday Schools 1940/Charles P. Wiles, D. Burt Smith. —Philadelphia: The United Lutheran Publication House, [?]
319 p. ;23 cm.

B975/W664
Lesson Commentary for Sunday Schools 1935/Charles P. Wiles, D. Burt Smith. —Philadelphia: The United Lutheran Publication House, [?]
316 p. ;23 cm.

B975/W689
A Textual Concordance of the Holy Scriptures: Arranged Especially for Use in Preaching/Rev. Theomas David Williams. —New York: Benziger Brothers, c1908
848 p. ;22 cm.

B975/Y68-2
The Enthusiasm of God/Dinsdale T. Young. —2nd ed.. —Cincinnati: Jennings and Graham, [?]
255 p. ;19 cm.

B976. 1/DE65
The Last Plague of Egypt/Baron Harry D'Erlanger. —London: Lovat Dickson & Thompson Limited Publishers, c1936
304 p. ;22 cm.

B976. 1/E97
Holy Communion/Blessed Peter Julian Ey-

mard. —New York: The Sentinel Press, c1940
xi, 330 p. ;17 cm.

B976. 1/J58
The Way of Perfection/St. Theresa of Jesus. —Westminster: The Newman Bookshop, c1948
xxx, 274 p. ;20 cm.

B976. 1/M265
Maryknoll Mission Letters: China: Extracts from the Letters and Diaries of the Pioneer Missioners of the Catholic Foreign Misson Society of America/The Macmillan Company. —New York: The Macmillan Company, c1923
xvi, 364 p. ;24 cm.

B976. 1/P733
Baptism & Confirmation/Raoul Plus. —New York: Benziger Brothers, c1930
156 p. ;15 cm.

B976. 1/R936
Radio Replies: In Defence of Religion Given from the Catholic Broadcasting Station 2sm Sydney, Australia/Rev. Dr. Rumble. —Minnesota: The Cathedral Press, c1938
xvii, 347 p. ;22 cm.

B976. 1/S348
Catholic Mission History/Schmidlin, Joseph. —Techny: Mission Press, V. D. , c1933
xiv, 861 p. ;24 cm.

B976. 1/S392(2)
I Teach Catechism. vol. II, Grades III, Iv and v/M. A. Schumacher. —New York: Benziger Brothers, Inc. , c1946
xxi459, xxxviii p. ;20 cm.

B976. 1/W698
Imperial Government and Catholic Missions in China During the years 1784-1785/Bernward H. Willeke. —New York: The Franciscan Institute, c1948
xiv, 227 p. ;23 cm.

B976. 1-09/W389
A Short History of the Catholic Church/Hermann Wedewer, Joseph McSorley. —London: B. Herder, c1916
357 p. ;19 cm.

B976. 1-61/H535(15. 10)
The Catholic Encyclopedia: An International Work of Reference on the Constitution, Doctrine, Discipline, and History of the Catholic Church. Fifteen Volumes and Index Volume X/Charles G. Herbermann, Edward A. Pace. —New York: The Encyclopedia Press, Inc. , c1911
xv, 800 p. ;26 cm.

B976. 1-61/H535(15. 4)
The Catholic Encyclopedia: An International Work of Reference on the Constitution, Doctrine, Discipline, and History of the Catholic Church. Fifteen Volumes and Index Volume Iv/Charles G. Herbermann, Edward A. Pace. —New York: The Encyclopedia Press, Inc. , c1908
xv, 799 p. ;26 cm.

B976. 1-61/H535(16)
The Catholic Encyclopedia: An International Work of Reference on the Constitution, Doctrine, Discipline, and History of the Catholic Church. Vol. 16/Charles G. Herbermann. —61th ed. . —New York: The Encyclopedia Press, Inc. , c1914
ix, 959 p. ;26 cm.

B976. 1-62/O32
The Official Catholic Directory: For the Year of Our Lord 1928/P. J. Kenedy & Sons. —New York: P. J. Kenedy & Sons, c1928
1 v. ;27 cm.

B976. 3/M612

The Epistle to the Philippians: A Devotional Commentary/Rev. F. B. Meyer. —London: The Religious Tract Society, 1905

261 p. ;20 cm.

B976. 3/S651

The Book of Mormon: An Account Written by the Hand of Mormon Upon Plates Taken from the Plates of Nephi/Translated by Joseph Smith. —Salt Lake City: The Church of Jesus Christ of Latter-Day Saints, c1948.

568 p. ;19 cm.

B977/C454

The Religion of Youth: Being Addresses Given at Alpin College/Melville Chaning-Pearce. —London: Hodder and Stoughton, Ltd. , c1934

xxv, 309 p. ;18 cm.

B977/C652

The New Archeological Discoveries and Their Bearing Upon the New Testament and Upon the Life and Times of the Primitive Church/Camden M. Cobern. —New York: Funk & Wagnalls Company, c1917

xxxiv, 697 p. ;23 cm.

B977/F597

Heritage of Beauty: Pictorial Studies of Modern Christian Architecture in Asia and Africa/Daniel Johnson Fleming. —New York: Friendship Press, c1937

95 p. ;26 cm.

B977/H174

Women in the Y. M. C. A. Record/Mary Ross Hall, Helen Firman Sweet. —New York: Association Press, c1947

ix, 149 p. ;21 cm.

B977/H893

Loyola and The Educational System of The Jesuits/Thomas Hughes. —New York: Charles Scribner's Sons, c1902

ix, 302 p. ;18 cm.

B977/I61

Women and Girls in the Young Men's Christian Association: A Study of Current Practices/The International Committee of the Young Men's Christian Associations. —New York: The International Committee of the Young Men's Christian Associations, c1946

89 p. ;23 cm.

B977/J65

The Chants of the Vatican Gradual/Dom Dominic Johner. —Collegeville: St. John's Abbey Press, c1940

xiii, 500 p. ;20 cm.

B977/M332-4

The Official Handbook of the Legion of Mary/Concilium Legionis Mariae. —4th American ed. . —[S. l.]: Concilium Legionis Mariae, c1941

296 p. ;19 cm.

B977/P882

The Groth of Christian Personality: A Study of the Pupil for Teacher of Religion in Home and School/Wilfred Evans Powell. —St. Louis: The Bethany Press, c1929

255 p. ;19 cm.

B977/S959

Training a Staff: A Manual for Young Men's Christian Association Executives/Paul Super. —New York: Association Press, c1920

xx, 300 p. ;22 cm.

B977. 2/G448

Mission Problems and Mission Methods in South China/J. Campbell Gibson. —New York: Fleming H. Revell Company, c1901

332 p. ;20 cm.

B977. 561/S549

The Impatience of a Parson: A Plea for the Recovery of Vital Christianity/H. R. L. Sheppard. —New York: Doubleday, Doran & Company, Inc. , c1928

xviii, 227 p. ;19 cm.

B977. 712/H893

Witnesses in Criminal Trials of Clerics: An historical synopsis and Commentary/Rev. James Austin Hughes. —Washington: The Caatholic University of America, c1937

ix, 140 p. ;22 cm.

B977. 712/K63

Diocesan Consultors/Peter J. Klekotka. —[S. l: s. n.], c1920

179 p. ;23 cm.

B978/B741

Main Issues Confronting Christendom/Harold A. Bosley. —New York: Harper & Brothers Publishers, c1948

xi, 204 p. ;21 cm.

B978/F818

Vicars and Prefects Apostolic: A Dissertation/ Rev. Francis Joseph Winslow. —New York: Rev. Francis Joseph Winslow, c1924

141 p. ;23 cm.

B978/J76

Christ at the Round Table/E. Stanley Jones. —London: Hodder and Stoughton, c1928

320 p. ;20 cm.

B978/O44

Christianity and the Race Problem/J. H. Oldham. —London: Student Christian Movement, c1925

xx, 280 p. ;22 cm.

B978/R956

Mornings in Florence Being Simple Studies of Christian Art for English Travellers/John Ruskin. —New York: John W. Lovell Company, [?]

1 v. ;19 cm.

B978/S

Ignorance in Relation to the Imputability of Delicts: An Historical Synopsis and Commentary/Innocent Robert Swoboda. —Washington, D. C. : The Catholic University of America Press, c1941

xii, 271 p. ;23 cm.

B978/S691

The Tabernacle, The Priesthood, and the Offerings/Henry W. Soltau. —London: Paternoster Square, [?]

viii, 474 p. ;19 cm.

B978/S877

The Gospel of the Kingdom: Studies in Social Reform and What to Do: A Course of Study on Living Social Problems in the Light of the Gospel of Jesus Christ/Josiah Strong. —New York: The American Institute of Social Service, c1912

197 p. ;24 cm.

B978/V867

Christian Faith and Democracy/Gregory Vlastos. —New York: Association Press, c1939

80 p;19 cm.

B979/G566

The Jesus of History/by T. R. Glover; with a foreword by the Archbishop of Canterbury. . —New York: Association Press, 1928.

xiv, 225 p. ;20 cm.

B979/G646

The Jesuits/Alban Goodier. —New York: The Macmillan Company, c1930

ix, 83 p. ;17 cm.

B979/L366

Church History: A Complete History of the Catholic Church to the Present Day/Rev. John Laux. —New York: Benziger Brothers, c1930

xix, 620 p. ;20 cm.

B979/S395-22

Illustrated Bible History of the Old and New Testaments for the Use of Catholic Schools/Ignatius Schuster. —22nd ed.. —London: B. Herder Book Co. , c1935

x, 388 p. ;19 cm.

B979/W177

A History of the Christian Church/Williston Walker. —New York: Charles Scribner's Sons, c1918

xiii, 624 p. ;21 cm.

B979. 2/N521-7

Demon Possession and Allied Themes/John L. Nevius. —7th ed.. —Chicago: Fleming H. Revell Company, [?]

518 p. ;19 cm.

B979. 712/R691

Forty Years in the Philippines: A History of The Philippine Mission of The Presbyterian Church in the United States of America 1899-1939/James B. Rodgers. —New York: The Board of Foreign Missions of The Presbyterian Church in the United States of America, c1940

viii, 205 p. ;23 cm.

B979. 9/A131

Silhouettes of My Contemporaries/Lyman Abbott. —New York: Doubleday, Page & Company, c1922

x, 361 p. ;21 cm.

B979. 9/F494

A Portrait of Peter/J. Alexander Findlay. —London: Hodder and Stoughton, c1935

ix, 232 p. ;18 cm.

B979. 9/G464

Forty Years a Country Preacher/George B. Gilbert. —New York: Grosset & Dunlap Publishers, c1939

xiii, 319 p. ;21 cm.

B979. 9/H624

Henry Ward Beecher: An American Portrait/Paxton Hibben. —New York: George H. Doran Company, c1927

xiv, 361 p. ;23 cm.

B979. 9/J82

Saint Francis of Assisi/Johannes Joergensen. —New York: Longmans, Green and Co. , c1944

xv, 428 p. ;21 cm.

B979. 9/M647

Charles G. Finney: He Prayed Down Revivals/Basil Miller. —2nd ed.. —Michigan: Zondervan Publishing House, [?]

137 p. ;20 cm.

B979. 92/M257

Adveniat Regnum Tuum: The Story of China's First Cardinal/Louis J. Maloof. —Tsingtao: Mission Press, c1946

52 p. ;17 cm.

B979. 954. 6/B712

St. John Bosco's Early Apostolate/G. Bonetti. —London: Burns Oates & Washbourne Ltd. , c1934

xv, 511 p. ;21 cm.

B979. 956. 1/B871

Hudson Taylor: The Man Who Believed God/Marshall Broomhall. —London: The China Inland Mission, c1931

xii, 244, 4 p. ;19 cm.

B979. 956. 1/W261-2

Life of Saint Madeleine Sophie: Foundress of the Society of the Sacred Heart of Jesus 1779-1865/Margaret Ward. —2nd ed.. —Roehampton: Convent os the Sacred Heart, c1925

xii, 662 p. ;23 cm.

B979. 971. 2/B329

Mary Baker Eddy: The Truth and the Tradition/Ernest Sutherland Bates, John V. Dittemore. —New York: Alefed A. Knopf, c1932

v, 476 p. xxxiv p. ;24 cm.

B979. 971. 2/M425

Character-Building in China: The Life-Story of Julia Brown Mateer/Robert Mccheyne Mateer. —New York: Fleming H. Revell Company, c1912

1 v. ;19 cm.

B979. 971. 2/W783

This Circle of Earth: The Story of John H. Dietrich/Carleton Winston. —New York: G. P. Putnam's Sons, c1942

ix, 271 p. ;22 cm.

B991/A211

Astrology: Your Place in the Sun/Evangeline Adams. —New York: Dodd, Mead & Company, c1928

xx, 343 p. ;21 cm.

B997. 12/C514

Cheiro's Book of Numbers/Cheiro. —New York: New York Publishing Company, Inc., c1926

x, 304 p. ;21 cm.

C 社会科学总论

C52/C754

Notes on Life and Letters/Joseph Conrad. —London: J. M. Dent and Sons Ltd., c1921

xii, 354 p. ;20 cm.

C52/L735

Between Tears and Laughter/Lin Yutang. —New York: Blue Ribbon Books, c1943

vii, 216 p. ;20 cm.

C623. 5/B889(6)

The New Triangle Arithmetics. Grade Six/Leo J. Brueckner, C. J. Anderson. —Chicago: The John C. Winston Company, c1935

vii, 279, 21 p. ;19 cm.

C831-54/E63(1931)

The Statesman's Year-Book: Statistical and Historical Annual of the States of the World for the Year 1931/M. Epstein. —London: Macmillan and Co., Ltd., c1931

xxxiv, 1642 p. ;19 cm.

C831-54/E63(1934)

The Statesman's Year-Book: Statistical and Historical Annual of the States of the World for the Year 1934/M. Epstein. —London: Macmillan and Co., Ltd., c1934

xxxiv, 1478 p. ;19 cm.

C831-54/E63(1935)

The Statesman's Year-Book: Statistical and Historical Annual of the States of the World for

the Year 1935/M. Epstein. —London: Macmillan and Co. , Ltd. , c1937
xxxvi, 1502 p. ;19 cm.

C831-54/E63(1936)
The Statesman's Year-Book: Statistical and Historical Annual of the States of the World for the Year 1936/M. Epstein. —London: Macmillan and Co. , Ltd. , c1936
xxxiii, 1493 p. ;20 cm.

C831-54/E63(1937)
The Statesman's Year-Book: Statistical and Historical Annual of the States of the World for the Year 1937/M. Epstein. —London: Macmillan and Co. , Ltd. , c1937
xxxvi, 1502 p. ;19 cm.

C831-54/E63(1940)
The Statesman's Year-Book: Statistical and Historical Annual of the States of the World for the Year 1940/M. Epstein. —London: Macmillan and Co. , Ltd. , c1940
xxxviii, 1488 p. ;19 cm.

C831-54/E63(1941)
The Statesman's Year-Book: Statistical and Historical Annual of the States of the World for the Year 1941/M. Epstein. —London: Macmillan and Co. , Ltd. , c1941
xxxvi, 1486 p. ;19 cm.

C831-54/E63(1947)
The Statesman's Year-Book: Statistical and Historical Annual of the States of the World for the Year 1947/M. Epstein. —London: Macmillan and Co. , Ltd. , c1947
xxv, 1441 p. ;19 cm.

C837. 12/S397(1936)
The American Year Book: A Ricord of Events and Progress Year 1936/William M. Schuyler. —New York: Thomas Nelson & Sons, c1937
xxii, 958 p. ;20 cm.

C837. 12/S397
The American Year Book: A Ricord of Events and Progress Year 1938/William M. Schuyler. —New York: Thomas Nelson & Sons, c1939
xxiii, 977 p. ;20 cm.

C837. 12/U58(1946. 67)
Statistical Abstract of the United States: 1946, Sixty-Seventh Number/U. S. Department of Commerce, Buearu of Foreign and Domestic Commerce. —Washington: Government Printing Office, c1946
xii, 1039 p. ;23 cm.

C837. 12/U58-68(1947)
Statistical Abstract of the United States: 1947, Sixty-Eighth Edition/U. S. Department of Commerce, Buearu of Foreign and Domestic Commerce. —68th ed. . —Washington: Government Printing Office, c1946
xiii, 1038 p. ;23 cm.

C91/C167
The Making of Society: An Outline of Sociology/edited by Robert Bierstedt. —New York: Modern Library, c1937
xx, 557 p. ;19 cm.

C91/C689-4
Social Theory/G. D. H. Cole. —4th. ed. . —London: Methuen & Co. , Ltd. , 1930
219 p. ;20 cm.

C91/D744
Society and its Problems: An Introduction to the Principles of Sociology/Grove Samuel Dow. —New York: Thomas Y. Crowell Company, c1920
xiv, 594 p. ;21 cm.

C91/G442

More That Must Be Told/Philip Gibbs. —New York: Harper & Brothers Publishers, c1817

407 p. ;21 cm.

C91/G453

The Principles of Sociology: An Analysis of the Phenomena of Association and of Social Organization/by Franklin Henry Giddings. —New York: The Macmillan Company, c1916.

xxvi, 476 p. ;23 cm.

C91/K59

Fundamentals of Sociology: With Special Emphasis upon Community and Educational Problems/Edwin A. Kirkpatrick. —Boston: Houghton Mifflin Company, c1916

x, 291 p. ;19 cm.

C91/K69

Tragedies of Eastern Life: An Introduction to the Problems of Social Psychology/Lim Boon Keng. —Shanghai: The Commercial Press, Ltd. , c1927

264 p. ;19 cm.

C91/L15

Social and Philosophical Studies/Lafargue, Paul. —Chicago: Charles H. Kerr & Company, c1906

165 p. ;16 cm.

C91/R823

The Social Trend/Edward Alsworth Ross. —New York: The Century Co. , c1922

235 p. ;19 cm.

C91/S635

An Introduction to the Study of Society/Albion W. Small and George E. Vincent. —New York: American Book Company, c1894.

384 p. ;19 cm.

C91-09/H436

The Scocial and Political Ideas of Some English Thinkers of the Augustan Age/F. J. C. Hearnshaw. —London: George G. Harrap and Company Ltd. , c1928

246 p. ;23 cm.

C912/A211

A Book of Earnest Lives/W. H. Davenport Adams. —8th ed.. —London: Swan Sonnenschein & Co. , c1902

vii, 403 p. ;20 cm.

C912/G464

Wisdom of the Ages: A Treasury of the World's Most Inspired Thought/M. Gilbert. —New York: New York Pub. Co. , c1936.

382 p. ;20 cm.

C912. 1/C289

How to Win Friends and Influence People/Dale Carnegie. —New York: Simon and Schuster, c1937

x, 340 p. ;21 cm.

C912. 1/D578

The Habits of Good Society: A Handbook for Ladies and Gentlemen/G. W. Dillingham Co. , Publishers. —New York: G. W. Dilling ham Co. , Publishers, [?]

x, 312 p. ;19 cm.

C912. 1/M429

Men, Places, and Things/William Mathews. —Chicago: S. C. Griggs and Company, c1888

viii, 386 p. ;19 cm.

C912. 1/U55

The Life of the Spirit and the Life of To-day/Evelyn Underhill. —New York: E. P. Dutton & Company, c1922

xi, 311 p. ;21 cm.

C912. 3/V292

The Temple of Costly Experience/Daniele Vare. . —[S. l. : s. n.], 1939.

xix, 252 p. ;18 cm.

C912. 6/C289

Little Known Facts About Well Known People/by Dale Carnegie. —[S. l. : s. n.], [?]

246 p. ;19 cm.

C912. 6/D718

Why We Behave Like Human Beings/George A. Dorsey. —New York: Blue Ribbon Books, c1925

xiv, 512 p. ;22 cm.

C912. 6/McD731-20

An Introduction to Social Psychology/William McDougall. —20th ed. . —London: Methuen & Co. , Ltd. , c1926

440 p. ;20 cm.

C912. 6/R823

Social Psychology and Outing and Source Book/Edward Alsworth Ross. —New York: The Macmillan Company, c1921

xvi, 372 p. ;19 cm.

C912. 6/U72

The Social Good/Edward J. Urwick. —London: Methuen & Co. , Ltd. , c1927.

vii, 246 p. , 1 l. ;23 cm.

C912. 6/W337

Behaviorism/John B. Watson. —Revised ed. . —New York: W. W. Norton & Company, INC. , c1924

xi, 308 p. ;22 cm.

C912. 68/H654

The Investment of Influence: A Study of Social Sympathy and Service/Newell Dwight Hillis. —Chicago: Fleming H. Revell Company, c1897

295 p. ;18 cm.

C912. 68/L528

The Governing of Men: General Principles and Recommendations Based on Experience at a Japanese Relocation Camp/Alexander H. Leighton. —Princeton: Princeton University Press, c1945

xvi, 404 p. ;22 cm.

C912. 8/J12

A Community Center: What It Is and How to Organize It/Henry E. Jackson. —New York: The Macmillan Company, c1918

xiii, 159 p. ;20 cm.

C912. 81/P235

The City/Robert E. Park, Ernest W. Burgess, Roberick D. McKenzie. —Chicago: The University of Chicago Press, c1925

xi, 239 p. ;20 cm.

C913/R323

The Modern Family/Ruth Reed. —New York: Alfred A. Knopf, c1929

x, 182 p, xix;22 cm.

C913. 11/A561

The Healthy Home and Community/J. Mace Andress. —Boston: Ginn and Company, c1945

viii, 338 p. ;21 cm.

C913. 11/M396

Family Disor-Ganization/Ernest R. Mowrer. —Chicago: The University of Chicago Press, c1927

xvii, 317 p. ;20 cm.

C913. 14/F785

Creative and Sexual Science: or Manhood, Womanhood and Their Mutual Inter-Relations/O. S. Fowler. —Washington D. C. : [s. n.], [?]

1052 p. ;23 cm.

C913. 14/H174

Youth and Its Problems: The Sex Life of a Man/Winfield Scott Hall. —Philadelphia: The John C. Winston Company Publishers, c1919

xiii, 266 p. ;19 cm.

C913. 14/P267

The Gay Illiterate/Louella O. Parsons. —New York: Doubleday, Doran and Co. , Inc. , c1944

194 p. ;20 cm.

C913. 2/S883-16

Married Love: A New Contribution to the Solution of Sex Difficulties/Marie Carmichael Stopes. —16th ed.. —New York: G. P. Putnam's Sons, c1924

xxi, 169 p. ;19 cm.

C913. 3/K94

The Fight for Life/Paul De Kruif. —New York: Harcourt, Brace and Company, c1938

342 p. ;22 cm.

C913. 3/W132

The Simple Life/Charles Wagner. —London: Sir Isaac Pitman & Sons, Ltd. , c1911

188 p. ;16 cm.

C913. 5/C754

Out to Win/Rev. Joseph P. Conroy. —New York: Benziger Brothers, c1919

181, 13 p. ;19 cm.

C913. 5/F785

Starting in Life: What each calling offers ambitious boys and young men/Nathaniel C. Fowler. —Boston: Little, Brown, and Company, c1910

xxiii, 411 p. ;22 cm.

C913. 5/M888

Youth: Its Care and Culture. /J. Mortimer-Granville. —London: The Walter Scott Publishing Co. , Ltd. , [?]

129 p. ;15 cm.

C913. 68/J11

Japanese Women/The Japanese Woman's Commission. —Chicago: World's Columbian Exposition, c1893

159 p. ;22 cm.

C913. 68/S225

Woman and the New Race/Marcaret Sanger. —New York: Eugenics Publishing Company, c1920

xi, 234 p. ;19 cm.

C913. 68/W598

Women Who Have Ennobled Life/Lilian Whiting. —Philadelphia: The Union Press, c1915

260 p. ;21 cm.

C913. 8/Q3

Social Pathology/Stuart Alfred Qqeen, Delbert Martin Mann. —New York: Thomas Y. Crowell Company, c1925

xxi, 690 p. ;20 cm.

C916/R823

Social Control: A Survey of the Foundations of Order/Edward Alsworth Ross Ross. —New York: The Macmillan Company, c1912

xii, 461 p. ;19 cm.

C92/C311

The Population Problem: A Stupt in Human Evolution/A. M. Carr-Saunders. —Oxford: The Clarendon Press, c1922

516 p. ;21 cm.

C92/C877

The Problem of Population/Harold Cox. —New York: G. P. Putnam's Sons, c1923

ix, 244 p. ;21 cm.

C92/M261(1)

An Essay on Population. Vol. 1/T. R. Malthus. —London: J. M. Dent & Sons Ltd. , [?]

xviii, 315 p. ;17 cm.

C92/M261(2)

An Essay on Population. Vol. 2/T. R. Malthus. —London: J. M. Dent & Sons Ltd. , [?]

xviii, 285 p. ;18 cm.

C924.24/R447

Population Problems/Edward Byron Reuter. —Philadelphia: J. B. Lippincott Company, c1923

xvii, 338 P. ;20 cm.

C93/B293

The Man Nobody Knows/Bruce Barton. —New York: Grosset & Dunlap Publishers, c1924

219 p. ;21 cm.

C93/L681

Education for Leadership/Ley Fall Tsang. —Tsingtao: [s. n.], 1935

ii, 102 p. ;21 cm.

C931.2/D911

The Principles of Industrial Management/John C. Duncan. —New York: D. Appleton and Company, c1911

xviii, 323 p. ;19 cm.

C931.4/L477

Office Management/Baen E. Lee. —Shanghai: The Commercial Press, Ltd. , c1928

xiii, 202 p. ;21 cm.

C955.2/K95

The Spirit of the Chinese People/Ku Hung-Ming. —Peking: The Peking Daily News, c1915

168 p. ;20 cm.

政治、法律

D0/B144

Physics and Politics: or, Thoughts on the Application of the Principles of "Natural Selection" and "Inheritance" to Political Society/Walter Bagehot. —New York: D. Appleton and Company, c1912

228 p. ;19 cm.

D0/B967

Political Ideals/C. Delisle Burns. —London: Oxford University Press, c1931

358 p. ;15 cm.

D0/G234

Political Science and Government/James Wilford Garner. —[S. l. : s. n.], [?]

x, 821 p. ;21 cm.

D0/G394

Introduction to Political Science/Raymond Garfield Gettell. —Boston: Ginn and Company, c1910

xx, 421 p. ;21 cm.

D0/L434

Elements of Political Science/Stephen Leacock. —Boston and New York: Houghton, Mifflin and Company, c1906

ix, 417 p. ;20 cm.

D0/M645

Considerations on Representative Government/John Stuart Mill.—people's ed..—London: Longman, Green, Longman, Roberts, and Green, [?]
viii, 141 p. ;20 cm.

D01/B917

The Economic Theory of the Leisure Class/Nikolai Bukharin.—New York: International Publishers, c1927
220 p. ;22 cm.

D03/R347

Success among Nations/Emil Reich.—New York: Happer & Brothers Publishers, c1904
x, 293 p. ;21 cm.

D03/W913

The Modern State/Leonard Woolf... [et al.]; edited by Mary Adams..—London: George Allen & Unwin Ltd., c1933
320 p. ;19 cm.

D033/S534

The Intelligent Woman's Guide to Socialism, Capitalism, Sovietism and Fascism/Bernard Shaw.—New York: Brentano's Publishers, c1928
xlvi, 495 p. ;24 cm.

D033.3/A856

The Fascist: His State and His Mind/E. B. Ashton.—New York: Putnam, c1937
xiv, 303 p. ;22 cm.

D033.3/R347

Imperialism: Its Prices; Its Vocation/Emil Reich.—London: Hutchinson & Co., c1905
xii, 177 p. ;19 cm.

D066/H669

Armaments: The Race and the Crisis/Francis W. Hirst.—London: Cobden-Sanderson, c1937
171 p. ;22 cm.

D068/L351

Manchuria Cradle of Conflict/Owen Lattimore.—New York: The Macmillan Company, c1932
xvi, 311 p. ;22 cm.

D068/L488

The Riddle of the Rhine: Chemical Strategy in Peace and War/Victor Lefebure.—London: W. Collins Sons & Co., Ltd., c1921
279 p. ;22 cm.

D068/S274

Sabotage!: The Secret war Against America/Michael Sayers, Albert E. Kahn.—New York: Happer & Brothers Publishers, c1942
266 p. ;21 cm.

D08/D392

Democracy Today and Tomorrow/by Eduard Benes.—[S. l. : s. n.], 1940.
xiv p., 1 l., 244 p. ;21 cm.

D081/B433

Equality/Edward Bellamy.—New York and London: D. Appleton and Company, c1912
xii, 480 p. ;18 cm.

D082/M645U89

Utilitarianism Liberty & Representative Government/John Stuart Mill.—London: J. M. Dent & Sons Ltd., c1910
xxv, 393 p. ;18 cm.

D082/S634

The Powers and Aims of Western Democracy/William Milligan Sloane.—New York: Charles Scribner's Sons, c1919
xiii, 489 p. ;21 cm.

D091/H436

The Social and Political Ideas of some Great Thinkers of the Sixteenth and Seventeenth Centuries: A Series of Lectures Delivered at King's College University of London During the Session 1925-26/F. J. C. Hearnshaw. —London: George G. Harrap & Company Ltd. , c1926

219 p. ;22 cm.

D091/P776

An Introduction to the History of the Science of Politics/Frederick Pollock. —London: Macmillan and Co. , Ltd. , c1923

xii, 138 p. ;18 cm.

D091.6/P361

The History of the Fabian Society/Edward R. Pease. —New and Revised ed. . —New York: International Publishers, c1926

306 p. ;20 cm.

D091.6/S534-1931

Fabian Essays in Socialism/G. Bernard Shaw. —1931 ed. . —London: The Fabian Society, c1931

xlix, 220 p. ;22 cm.

D095.124/K93

The Conquest of Bread/Peter Kropotkin. —New York: Vanguard Press, c1906

xiv, 214 p. ;18 cm.

D095.654/R864S678

The Social Contract and Discourse/Jean-Jacques Rousseau. —New York: J. M. Dent & Sons Ltd. , c1932

xlvii, 287 p. ;18 cm.

D178.53/N619

Fishes and Shells of the Pacific World/John T. Nichols. —New York: The Macmillan Company, c1945

201 p. ;21 cm.

D5/B877

Partisan Politics: The Evil and the Remedy/Brown, James Sayles. —Philadelphia: J. B. Lippincott Company, c1897

221 p. ;21 cm.

D5/C689

A Guide to Modern Politics/G. D. H. and Margaret Cole. —London: Victor Gollancz, 1934.

559 p. ;19 cm.

D5/G978

The Future of Bolshevism/Waldemar Gurian. —London: Sheed & Ward, c1936

125 p. ;19 cm.

D5/J12

Europe Since the War: A Sketch of Political Development 1918-1932/J. Hampden Jackson. —London: Victor Gollancz Ltd. , c1933

144 p. ;19 cm.

D5/L779

First Principles in Politics/William Samuel Lilly. —New York: G. P. Putnam's Sons, c1899

ix, 322 p. ;22 cm.

D5/P866

This World of Nations: Foundations, Institutions, Practices/Pitman B. Potter. —New York: The Macmillan Company, c1929

xix, 366 p. ;22 cm.

D5/R374

World Politics: At the End of the Nineteenth Century/Paul S. Reinsch. —New York: The Macmillan Company, c1908

xviii, 366 p. ;19 cm.

D5/S464

The Truth Behind the News 1918-1928/George

Seldes. —London: Faber & Gwyer, [?]
355 p. ;22 cm.

D5/S464
You Can't Print That!: The Truth Behind the News, 1918-1928/George Seldes. —New York: Payson & Clarke, Ltd. , 1929.
465 p. ;23 cm.

D5/W689
One World/Wendell L. Willkie. —New York: Simon and Schuster, c1943
ix, 206 p. ;21 cm.

D50/A935
The Governments of Europe/Frederic Austin. —New York: The Macillan Company, c1913
xiv, 668 p. ;22 cm.

D50/C912(O)
The Fifteen Decisive Battle of the World from Marathon to Waterloo. /Creasy, E. S. —London: George Routledge & Sons, [?]
440 p. ;16 cm.

D50/C912
The Fifteen Decisive Battle of the World from Marathon to Waterloo. /Creasy, E. S. —New York: Hurst & Company Publishers, [?]
543 p. ;15 cm.

D50/G441
An Introduction to World Politics/Herbert Adams Gibbons. —New York: The Century Co. , c1922
xiii, 595 p. ;23 cm.

D50/H885
The Far East in World Politics: A Study in Recent History/G. F. Hudson. —London: Oxford University Press, H. Milford, c1937
vii, 276 p. ;20 cm.

D50/L617
The Awakening of the East: Siberia-Japan-China/Fierre Leroy-Beaulieu. —New York: Mcclure, Phillips & Co. , c1900
xxvii, 298 p. ;19 cm.

D50/R374
Intellectual and Political Currents in the Far East/Paul S. Reinsch. —Boston: Houghton Mifflin Company, c1912
viii p. , 1 l. , 395 p. , 1 l. ;21 cm.

D50/R374C
Colonial Administration/Paul S. Reinsch. —New York: The Macmillan Company, c1905
viii, 422 p. ;19 cm.

D50/W913
International Government/L. S. Woolf. —London: George Allen & Unwin Ltd. , c1916
xxiii, 388 p. ;21 cm.

D502/A132
Japanese Expansion and American Policies/James Francis Abbott. —New York: The Macmillan Company, c1916
vii, 268 p. ;19 cm.

D502/P132
Dollars and World Peace/Kirby Page. —New York: George H. Doran Company, c1927
214 p. ;20 cm.

D502/S243
How Belgium Saved Europe/Charles Sarolea. —London: William Heinemann, c1915
vii, 226 p. ;18 cm.

D51/A583
Must It Be War/Norman Angell. —London: Labour Book Service, [?]
256 p. ;20 cm.

D51/H325

The War in Outline 1914-1918/Liddell Hart. —New York: The Modern Library, c1936

xx, 285 p. ;17 cm.

D51/P832

Fascism/Odon Por. —London: The Labour Publishing Company Ltd. , c1923

270, xli, p. ;19 cm.

D51/T182

The Truth About the Treaty/Andre Tardieu. —Indianapolis: The Bobbs-Merrill Company Publishers, c1921

473 p. ;23 cm.

D513/B825

Fascism Make or Break?: German Experience since the 'June Days'/R. Braun. —London: Martin Lawrence Ltd. , c1935

133 p. ;19 cm.

D521/C751

The Future of Freedom in the Orient/Ralph Coniston. —New York: W. W. Norton & Company, Inc. , c1947

233 p. ;21 cm.

D526/B517

Espionage/H. R. Berndorff. —London: Eveleigh Nash & Grayson Ltd. , c1930

254 p. ;22 cm.

D56/H567

Good Neighbors: Argentina Brazil Chile Seventeen other Countries/Hubert Herring. —London & New Haven: Yale University Press, c1941

ix, 381 p. ;24 cm.

D56/K46

Social Evolution/Benjamin Kidd. —New York: Grosset & Dunlap Publishers, c1894

ix, 404 p. ;19 cm.

D562/J82

The Blood of the Nation: A Study of the Decay of Races Through the Survival of the Unfit/David Starr Jordan. —Boston: American Unitarian Association, c1910

82 p. ;17 cm.

D57/G481

Poverty and Dependency: Their Relief and Prevention/John Lewis Gillin. —Rev. ed. . —New York: Century, c1925

x, 836 p. ;23 cm.

D58/C283

Better Living in the Postwar World/Norman V. Carlisle. —New York: The Macmillan Company, c1944

xi, 288 p. ;21 cm.

D58/R285

The Reader's Digest. V. 26, No. 154/Rumford Press. —[S. l.]: Rumford Press, c1935

128 p. ;20 cm.

D58/S674

People on Our Side/Edgar Snow. —New York: Random House, c1944

xii, 322 p. ;21 cm.

D59/M864

Politics and History/John Viscount Morley. —London: Macmillan and Co. , Ltd. , c1923

v, 317 p. ;20 cm.

D59/W754

The State Elements of Historical and Practical Politics: A Sketch of Institution History and Administration/Woodrow Wilson. —Boston: D. C. Heath & Co. , Publishers, c1890

xxxvi, 686 p. ;19 cm.

D6/G472

China and The Chinese/Herbert Allen Ciles. —New York: The Columbia University Press, c1902

ix, 229 p. ;19 cm.

D6/N521

China and the Chinese: A General Description of the Country and its Inhabitants; Its Civilization and from of Government; Its Religious and Social Institutions; Its Intercourse with other Nations and Its Present Condition and Prospects/John L. Nevius. —New York: Harper & Brothers, Publishers, 1869

456 p. ;20 cm.

D6/R222

What's Right with China: An Answer to Foreign Criticisms/O. D. Rasmussen. —Shanghai: The Commercial Press, Ltd. , c1928

xx, 249 p. , 1 leaf, [251]-255 p. ;22 cm.

D6/W959

Chinese Government and Politics/Chin-Fang Wu. —Shanghai: The Commercial Press, Ltd. , c1934

xv, 473 p. ;23 cm.

D6-53/N158

China's New Nationalism and Other Essays/Harley Farnsworth MacNair. —Shanghai: The Commercial Press, c1928

xi, 423 p. ;19 cm.

D60/L437

Reconstruction in China: A Record of Progress And Achievement in Facts and Figures /Tang Leang-Li. —Shanghai: China United Press, c1935

xiv, 401 p. ;25 cm.

D609. 9/L359

The Development of China/by Kenneth Scott Latourette. —Boston: Houghton Mifflin, 1917.

xi, 273 p. ;21 cm.

D609. 9/L735

The Vigil of a Nation/Lin Yutang. —New York: The John Day Company, c1944

vii, 262 p. ;21 cm.

D609. 9/S667

The Crisis in China/George B. Smyth, Rev. Gilbert Reid, Charles Johnston. —New York: Happer & Brothers Publishers, c1900

v, 271 p. ;19 cm.

D62/B337

Modern Democracy in China/Mingchien Joshua Bau. —Shanghai: The Commercial Press, Ltd. , c1927

x, 467 p. ;21 cm.

D62/T289

Vital Factors in China's Problems: Readings in Current Literature/Lee Teng-Hwee. —Shanghai: The Commercial Press, Ltd. , c1928

xi, 458 p. d19 cm. ;

D668/N864(1)

Report of the Hon. Richard Feetha, C. M. C. : Judge of the Supreme Court of the Union of South Africa to the Shanghai Municipal Council. Volume 1. —Containing Parts I, II and III/North Daliy News and Herald, Ltd. —Shanghai: North Daliy News and Herald, c1931

372 p. ;24 p.

D669/L989

Social Life of the Chinese(in Peking)/Jermyn Chi-Hung Lynn. —Peking: China Booksellers Ltd. , c1928

182 p. ;17 cm.

D669/T972

The Chinese at Home/H. Twitchell. —Lon-

don: George Newnes, Ltd. , [?]
xii, 305 p. ;22 cm.

D673. 73/P238-2
John Chinaman and A Few Others/E. H. Farker. —2nd ed.. —London: John Murray, Albemarle Street, c1902
xx, 380 p. ;20 cm.

D73/A142
Chaos in Asia/Hallett Abend. —New York: Ives Washburn, Inc. , c1939
313 p. ;22 cm.

D730. 2/G977I59
Inside Asia/John Gunther. —London: Hamish Hamilton, 1939.
x p. , 1 ?, 599 p. ;22 cm.

D731/D594
The New Far East/Arthur Diosy. —London: Cassell and Company, Ltd. , c1898
xii, 374 p. ;22 cm.

D731/McK33
The Unveiled East/F. A. McKenzie. —New York: E. P. Dutton And Company, c1907
viii, 347 p. ;22 cm.

D731. 1/T161
Political Status of Mongolia/Tennyson Tan. —Shanghai: The Mercury Press, c1932
144 p. ;24 cm.

D731. 263. 8/D761
Korea of the Japanese/Drake, H. B. —London: John Lane the Bodley Head Ltd. , c1930
225 p. ;22 cm.

D731. 268/U58
Fifteen Years Among the Top-Knots or Life in Korea/L. H. Underwood. —Boston: American Tract Society, c1904
xvii, 354 p. ;20 cm.

D731. 3/B993
Government by Assassination/Hugh Byas. —New York: Alfred A Knopf, c1942
ix, 369, viii p. ;22 cm.

D731. 3/H899(1)
Fifty Years of New Japan (Kaikoku Gojunen Shi). Volume 1/Marcus B. Huish. —New York: E. P. Dutton & Company, c1909
xi, 646 p. ;23 cm.

D731. 3/H899(2)
Fifty Years of New Japan (Kaikoku Gojunen Shi). Volume II/Marcus B. Huish. —New York: E. P. Dutton & Company, c1909
xi, 616 p. ;23 cm.

D731. 369/E53
The Japanese Nation: A Social Survey/John F. Embree. —New York: Farrar & Rinehart, Inc. , c1945
xi, 308 p. ;21 cm.

D733. 8/S291
The Effect of Western Influence on Native Civilisations in the Malay Archipelago/B. Schrieke. —Batavia: G. Kolff & Co. , c1929
vii, 247 p. ;27 cm.

D733. 88/C689
The Peoples of Malaysia/Fay-Cooper Cole. —New York: D. Van Nostrand Company, inc. , c1945
xiv, 354 p. ;21 cm.

D735. 1/K35
The Ageless Indies/Raymond Kennedy. —New York: The John Day Company, c1942
xvi, 208 p. ;20 cm.

D735. 1/K45

The Indian Federation: An Exposition and Critical Review/Ahmad Khan. —London: Macmillan and Co. , Ltd. , c1937

xii, 450 p. ;22 cm.

D735. 1/T467

The Reconstruction of India/Edward Thompson. —London: Faber & Faber Ltd. , [?]

vii, 320 p. ;21 cm.

D735. 181/D618

Ships of Youth: A Study of Marriage in Modern India/Maud Diver. —London: William Blackwood & Sons Ltd. , [?]

558 p. ;19 cm.

D737. 4/C877

Diversions of A Diplomat in Turkey/Samuel S. Cox. —New York: Charles L. Webster & Co. , c1887

xix, 685 p. ;23 cm.

D737. 46/D991

Constantinople and Its Problems: Its Peoples, Customs, Religions and Progress/Henry Otis Dwight. —New York: Fleming H. Revell Company, c1901

298 p. ;20 cm.

D738. 2/A283

The Women of Israel, or, Characters and Sketches from the Holy Scriptures and Jewish History/Grace Aguilar. —London: George Routledge and Sons, Ltd. , [?]

576 p. ;19 cm.

D738. 281/M647-6

The Secret of the Jew: His life-His family/Rabbi David Miller. —6th ed. . —Oakland: [s. n.], c1930

iv, 507 p. ;20 cm.

D747/B916

Impressions of South Africa/James Bryce. —New York: The Century Co, c1900

lx, 517 p. ill. ;21 cm.

D75/G977-1940

Inside Europe: Again Completely Revised/John Gunther. —1940 war ed. —New York: Harper & Brothers Publishers, c1940.

xxii, 602 p. ;21 cm.

D75/T282

The Whispering Gallery of Europe/Major-General A. C. Temperley. —London: Collins Clear-Type Press, c1938

359 p. ;23 cm.

D75/W453

What is Coming?: A European Forecast/H. G. Wells. —New York: The Macmillan Company, c1916

294 p. ;20 cm.

D750. 64/F533

The Republican Tradition in Europe/H. A. L. Fisher. —New York: G. P. Putnam's Sons, c1911

xii, 361 p. ;22 cm.

D751. 12/K69

The New Russia/Eight Talks Broadcast. —London: Faber and Faber Ltd. , [?]

126 p. ;19 cm.

D751. 2/D759

Russian Affairs/Geoffrey Drage. —New York: E. P. Dutton & Co. , c1904

xvi, 738 p. ;23 cm.

D751. 2/M637

Russia and Its Crisis/Paul Milyoukov. —Chicago: The University of Chicago Press, c1906

xiii, 589 p. ;20 cm.

D751.2/M863

Rousseau and His Era. Vol. II/Morley, John Viscount.—London: Macillan and Co., Ltd., c1923

xii, 340 o.;20 cm.

D751.2/M863(1)

Rousseau and his Era. Vol. I/John Viscount Morley.—London: Macillan and Co., Ltd., c1873

xii, 329 p.;20 cm.

D751.2/R212

Russia in 1919/Arthur Ransome.—New York: B. W. Huebsch Mcm. xix, c1919

x, 232 p.;18 cm.

D751.2/T472

Russian Politics/Herbert M. Thompson.—New York: Henry Holt and Company, c1896

xi, 289 p.;20 cm.

D751.20/H662

Humanity Uprooted/Maurice Hindus.—New York: Blue Ribbon Books, Inc., c1934

xix, 369 p.;21 cm.

D751.236/K89

In Stalin's Secret Service: An Expose of Russia's Secret Policies by the Former Chief of the Soviet Intelligence in Western Europe/W. G. Krivitsky.—Shanghai: The Far Eastern Book Co., c1940

xv, 273 p.;20 cm.

D751.28/K89

I Chose Freedom: The Personal and Political Life of a Soviet Official/Victor Kravchenko.—New York: Charles Scribner's Sons, c1946

496 p.;21 cm.

D751.3/B928-3

Poland: Key to Europe/Raymond Leslie Buell.—3rd ed..—New York: Alered A. Knope, c1938

xi, 406, xv p.;21 cm.

D751.3/P558

Poland/W. Alison • Phillips.—London: Williams and Norgate, [?]

vi, 256, 7 p.;17 cm.

D751.6/G356

My Four Years in Germany/James W. Gerard.—London: Hodder and Stoughton, c1917

xiv, 320 p.;22 cm.

D751.6/G356M995

My Four Years in Germany/James W. Gerard.—New York: Grosset & Dunlap Publishers, c1917

xvi, 328 p.;19 cm.

D751.60/H143

Germany after Hitler/Paul Hagen.—New York: Farrar & Rinehart, Inc., [?]

240 p.;19 cm.

D751.60/L429

Germany: The Last Four Years/Walter Layton.—[S. l.]: Eyre & Spolttiswoode, c1934

vii, 116 p.;22 cm.

D751.664/B798

The Spirit and Structure of German Fascism/Robert A. Brady.—London: Victor Gollancz Ltd., c1937

383 p.;22 cm.

D752.2/C537

Sweden: The Middle Way/Marquis W. Childs.—New York: Yale University Press, c1936

xvi, 171 p.;24 cm.

D752. 2/L793

A Sovereign People: A Study of Swiss Democracy/Henry Demarest Lloyd. —New York: Doubleday, Page & Company, c1907

xvi, 273 p. ;21 cm.

D754. 6/L848

Land-Reclamation in Italy: Rural Revival in the Building of a Nation/Cesare Longobardi. —London: P. S. King & Son, Ltd. , c1936

xii, 243 p. ;22 cm.

D754. 6/M376

Italy Against the World/George Martelli. —London: Chatto and Windus, c1937

xii, 316 p. ;23 cm.

D755. 1/W784

The Spanish in the Southwest/Rosa V. Winterburn. —New York: American Book Company, c1903

224 p. ;19 cm.

D756. 064/L345

The Rise of European liberalism: An Essay in Interpretation/Harold J. Laski. —London: George Allen & Unwin Ltd. , c1936.

xl, 287 p. ;23 cm.

D756. 1/C133

England Today: Some Information for Peoples of other Countries/G. Caiger. —Tokyo: Kaitakusha, [?]

154 p. ;19 cm.

D756. 1/C286

Past and Present/Thomas Carlyle. —London: J. M. Dent & Sons Ltd. , c1915

xvi, 304 p. ;17 cm.

D756. 1/C689

The People's Front/G. D. H. Cole. —London: Victor Goliancz Ltd. , c1937

366 p. ;19 cm.

D756. 1/L294

My England/George Lansbbury. —London: Selwyn & Blount, Ltd. , [?]

254, [32] p. ;22 cm.

D756. 1/L674-2

Government of Dependencies/an essay by Sir Geoger Cornewall Lewis; with an introduction by Jacob Gould Schurman. —Rev. ed. —Washington [D. C.] & London: M. Walter Dunne, [1901]

xx, 216, 99 p. ;24 cm.

D756. 1/R649

Evolution of States/J. M. Robertson. —New York: G. P. Putnam's Sons, c1913

ix, 487 p. ;22 cm.

D756. 1/S495

Britain and The Dictators: A Survey of Post-War British Policy/R. W. Seton-Wartson. —London: Bentley House, c1938

xviii, 459 p. ;22 cm.

D756. 12/K35

Why England Sleept/John F. Kennedy. —New York: Wilfred Funk, Inc. , c1940

xxx, 252 p. ;21 cm.

D756. 14/P799

Falsehood in War-Time: Containing An Assortment of Lies Circulated throughout the Nations during the Great War/Arthur Ponsonby. —London: George Allen & Unwin Ltd. , c1940

192 p. ;18 cm.

D756. 164/A883

The Labour Party in Perspective/C. R. Attlee. —London: Victor Gollancz Ltd. , c1937

287 p. ;19 cm.

D756.19/M875

A History of Political Ideas/by C. R. Morris and Mary Morris..—New York: G. P. Putnam, 1930.

xii, 194 p. ;19 cm.

D756.38/P111

Earth Could be Fair/Pierre Van Paassen.—New York: The Dial Press, c1946

509 p. ;21 cm.

D756.5/M379

French Liberal Thought in the Eighteenth Century: A Study of Political Ideas From Bayle to Condorcet/Kingsley Martin.—London: E. Benn Ltd., c1929.

xviii, 313 p., 1 l. ;23 cm.

D756.5/P967

The Pleasant Land of France/Rowland E. Prothero.—London: Thomas Nelson And Sons, [?]

379 p. ;16 cm.

D756.569/B822

French Traits: An Essay in Comparative Criticism/W. C. Brownell.—New York: harles Scribner's Sons, c1918

411 p. ;21 cm.

D759/H417(1)

A Political and Social History of Modern Europe. Vol. I/Carlton J. H. Hayes.—New York: The Macillan Company, c1918

597 p. ;21 cm.

D759/H417(2)

A Political and Social History of Modern Europe. Vol. II/Carlton J. H. Hayes.—New York: The Macillan Company, c1918

757 p. ;21 cm.

D771.18/H975

The Unknown Country: Canada and Her People/Bruce Hutchison.—Toronto: Longmans, Green & Company, c1943

x, 386 p. ;21 cm.

D771.2/A425

Washington Merry-Go-Round./Rovert S. Allen.—New York: Blue Ribbon Books, Inc., c1933.

5 p. l., 9-366 p. ;22 cm.

D771.2/A425W314

Washington Merry-Go-Round/Horace Liveright, Inc.,—New York: Horace Liveright inc., c1931

366 p. ;21 cm.

D771.2/A512(1920)

Circular Instructions. Nos. 701-1000(January 29, 1920 to February 2, 1926)/American Consultant Service.—[S. l. : s. n.], [?]

1 v. ;23 cm.

D771.2/A512

Circular Instructions. Nos. 1-400(January 3, 1911 to April 21, 1915)/American Consultant Service.—[S. l. : s. n.], [?]

1 v. ;23 cm.

D771.2/A583

The Public Mind: Its Disorders: Its Exploitation/Norman Angell.—New York: E. P. Dutton & Company, c1927

ix, 232 p. ;22 cm.

D771.2/A583L645

Let the People Know/Norman Angell.—New York: The Viking Press, c1943

viii, 245 p. ;21 cm.

D771.2/B786

The Tragic Era: The Revolution after Lin-

coln/Claude G. Bowers. —Boston: Houghton Mifflin Company, c1929
xxii, 567 p. ;23 cm.

D771.2/B928
Isolated America/Raymond Buell. —New York: Alfred A. Knopf, Inc., c1940
xiii, 457, xiii p. ;22 cm.

D771.2/C311
America Challenged: A Preface to A Point of View/Lewis F. Carr. —New York: The Macmillan Company, c1929
322 p. ;22 cm.

D771.2/E24
Civics Through Problems: A Social and Governmental Civics/James B. Edmonson, Arthur Dondineau. —New York: The Macmillan Company, c1935
xiv, 621 p. ;20 cm.

D771.2/F174
Our Civic Life: Civics and Citizenship/Emil F. Faith, A. H. Edgerton. —New York: Mentzer, Bush & Company, c1941
xxii, 426 p. ;21 cm.

D771.2/F352
A Little Democracy Is a Dangerous Thing/ Charles W. Ferguson. —New York: Association Press, c1948
126 p. ;19 cm.

D771.2/G721
United States Government Manual 1947: Revised to December 1, 1946/Government Information Service. —Washington: Office of Government Reports, c1947
713 p. ;21 cm.

D771.2/G721-2
United States Government Manual 1947: Revised Through June 1, 1947/Government Information Service. —2nd ed.. —Washington: Office of Government Reports, c1947
713 p. ;21 cm.

D771.2/H217
The Strange Career of Mr. Hoover Under Two Flags/John Hamill. —New York: William Faro, Inc., c1931
381 p. ;22 cm.

D771.2/H325
Actual Government as Applied under American Conditions/Albert Bushnell Hart. —New ed.. —London and Bombay: Longmans, Green and Co., c1906
xliv, 559 p. ;20 cm.

D771.2/H325L471
Lected Addresses and Public Papers of Woodrow Wilson/Lbert Bushnell Hart. —New York: the Modern Library, c1918
v, 316 p. ;17 cm.

D771.2/H685
Freedom of the Press: A Framework of Principle: A Report from the Commission on Freedom of the Press/William Ernest Hocking. —Chicago: The University of Chicago Press, c1947
xi, 243 p. ;20 cm.

D771.2/J66
Addresses and Papers of Theodore Roosevelt/ Willis Fletcher Johnson. —New York: The Unit Book Publishing Co., c1909
510, vi p. ;18 cm.

D771.2/J82
Imperial Democracy: A Study of the Relation of Government by the People, Equality before the Law, and Other Tenets of Democracy, to the Demands of A Vigorous Foreign Policy and Other Demands of Imperial Dominion/David Starr Jor-

dan. —New York: D. Appleton and Company, c1899
viii, 293 p. ;19 cm.

D771. 2/K24
Government in Action: 1944 Edition/Robert E. Keohane, Mary Pieters Keohane, Joseph D. McGoldrick. —New York: Harcourt, Brace and Company, c1944
xviii, 875 p. ;20 cm.

D771. 2/K29
Life in Modern America/Mary G. Kelty. —Boston: Ginn and Company, c1946
vii, 527, xvi p. ;21 cm.

D771. 2/L746
The Roosevelt Revolution: First Phase/Ernest K. Lindley. —London: Victor Gollance Ltd. , c1934
287 p. ;19 cm.

D771. 2/L914
Political Essays/James Russell Lowell. —Boston: Houghton, Mifflin and Company, c1888.
326 p. ;20 cm.

D771. 2/O23
Pressure Politics: The Story of the Anti-Saloon League/Peter H. Odegard. —New York: Columbia University Press, c1928
x, 299 p. ;23 cm.

D771. 2/P349
America's Place in the World/Nathaniel Peffer. —New York: The Viking Press, c1945
236 p. ;20 cm.

D771. 2/P478(1)
The Public States of America. Volume I/Richard Peters. —Boston: Little, Brown, and Company, c1861
cxxii, 755 p. ;26 cm.

D771. 2/P481
The Public Statutes at Large United States of America/Richard Peters. —Boston: Little, Brown and Company, c1867
xii, 644, 176 p. ;26 cm.

D771. 2/R323
Municipal Government in the United States/by Thomas Harrison Reed.... —New York: The Century Co. , [c1926]
vii p. , 2 l. , 3-378 p. ;23 cm.

D771. 2/S817
Lincoln Steffens Speaking/Lincoln Steffens. —New York: Harcourt, Brace and Company, c1936
xii, 315 p. ;21 cm.

D771. 2/S914
Union Now With Britain/Clarence K. Streit. —New York: Harper & Brothers Publishers, c1941
xv, 240 p. ;21 cm.

D771. 2/U58(1)
Register of the Department of State. April 1, 1948/United States Government Printing Office. —Washington: United States Government Printing Office, c1948
507 p. ;24 cm.

D771. 2/U58(2)
Register of the Department of State. December 1, 1946/United States Government Printing Office. —Washington: United States Government Printing Office, c1947
513 p. ;24 cm.

D771. 2/U58(1938)
Register of the Department of State. October 1, 1938/United States Government Printing Office. —Washington: United States Government

Printing Office, c1938
vii, 232 p. ;25 cm.

D771. 2/U58P273
Participation of the United States Government in International Conferences/United States Government Printing Office. —Washington: United States Government Printing Office, 1947
xi, 292 p. ;24 cm.

D771. 2/V984
The New Politics/Frank Buffington Vrooman. —London: Oxford University Press (American Branch), c1911
300 p. ;22 cm.

D771. 2/W168
The Expansion of Western Ideals and The World's Peace/Charles Waldstein. —New York: John Wilson and Son, c1899
ix, 194 p. ;18 cm.

D771. 2/W449
An Intelligent American's Guide to the Peace/under the general editorship of and with an introduction by Sumner Welles. —New York: Dryden Press, c1945.
vi, 370 p. ;29 cm.

D771. 2/W747
Middle America/by Charles Morrow Wilson.. —New York: W. W. Norton & Company, Inc., [1944]
317 p. ;22cm.

D771. 2/W873
American Politics: Political Parties and Party Problems in the United States/James Albert Woodburn. —New York: G. P. Putnam's Sons, c1903
ix, 314 p. ;22 cm.

D771. 2/W947
Civil Government in the United States/A. O. Wright. —Madison: Midland Publishing Co., c1897
7, 350 p. ;19 cm.

D771. 2-53/D519(1)
Characters and Events: Popular Essays in Social and Political Philosophy. Volume I/John Dewey. —New York: Henry Holt and Company, c1929
x, 431 p. ;21 cm.

D771. 2-53/D519(2)
Characters and Events: Popular Essays in Social and Political Philosophy. Volume II/John Dewey. —New York: Henry Holt and Company, c1929
vi, 435-861 p. ;21 cm.

D771. 2-62/D618
United States Government Manual. 1948/Division of The Federal Register, The National Archives. —Washington: Division of the Federal Register, c1948
722 p. ;23 cm.

D771. 20/B368
Readings in American Government and Politics/Charles A. Beard. —New York: The Macmillan Company, c1911
xxiii, 624 p. ;21 cm.

D771. 20/B868
A Few Brass Tacks/Louis Bromfield. —New York: Harper & Brother Publishers, c1946
303 p. ;21 cm.

D771. 20/M463
An Outline of Municipal Government/Chester C. Maxey. —New York: Doubleday, Page & Company, c1925
xvii, 388 p. ;21 cm.

D771.20/R878

Problems of City Government/L. S. Rowe.—New York: D. Appleton and Company, c1908

358 p.;20 cm.

D771.22/B368

American Government and Politics/Charles A. Beard.—New York: The Macmillan Company, c1911

viii, 772 p.;20 cm.

D771.22/B368-5

American Government and Politics/Charles A. Beard.—5th ed..—New York: The Macmillan Company, c1929

viii, 820 p.;22 cm.

D771.22/B917(1)

The American Commonwealth.. v. 1, The National Government-The State Governments/by James Bryce.—New York: The Commonwealth Publishing Company, c1908

xvii, 724, 24 p.;20cm.

D771.22/B917-2(1)

The American Commonwealth.. v. 1, The National Government-The State Governments/by James Bryce..—2nd ed., rev..—New York: The Commonwealth Publishing Company, c1908

xiii, 808 p.;21cm.

D771.22/B917-2(2)

The American Commonwealth.. v. 2, The party system-public opinion-illustrations and reflections-social institutions /by James Bryce.—2nd ed., rev..—New York: The Commonwealth Publishing Company, c1908

v, 843 p.;20cm.

D771.22/J76

Readings on Parties and Elections in the United States/Chester Lloyd Jones.—New York: The Macmillan Company, c1912

xv, 354 p.;20 cm.

D771.22/L808(2)

Forms of federal practice. Vol. II/Comp., arranged and annotated by Frank O. Loveland..—Cincinnati, O.: The W. H. Anderson Company, c1903.

1205-2277 p.;24 cm.

D771.22/M212(1947)

American Government: A Consideration of the Problems of Democracy/Frank Abbott Magruder.—Boston: Allyn and Bacon, c1947

x, 710, 44 p.;19 cm.

D771.22/M212(1948)

American Government: A Consideration of the Problems of Democracy/Frank Abbott Magruder.—Boston: Allyn and Bacon, c1948

x, 710, 44 p.;19 cm.

D771.22/M212

American Government: A Consideration of the Problems of Democracy/Frank Abbott Magruder.—Boston: Allyn and Bacon, c1948

720, 43 p.;19 cm.

D771.22/M463-3

The American Problem of Govern/Chester C. Maxey.—3rd. ed..—New York: F. S. Crofts & Co., c1939

ix, 596 p.;23 cm.

D771.22/R374

Readings on American Federal Government/Paul S. Reinsch.—Boston: Ginn and Company, c1909

xii, 850 p.;21 cm.

D771.22/W548

The New Democracy/Walter E. Weyl.—New York: The Macmillan Company, c1914 x, 370, 13 p. ;19 cm.

D771.222/E37

The New Citizenship: A Study of American Politics/Seba Eldridge. —New York: Thomas Y. Crowell Company Publishers, c1929

vii, 357 p. ;20 cm.

D771.223/U58-2

Official Congressional Directory/United States Government Printing Office. —2nd ed.. —Washington: United States Government Printing Office, c1946

xx, 916 p. ;23 cm.

D771.223-66/D419

Twenty-Third Report to Congress on Lend-Lease Operations: For the Period Ended September 30, 1946/Department of State. —Washington: U. S. Government Printing Office, c1941

76 p. ;23 cm.

D771.224/C334

The Story of American Democracy/Mabel B. Casner, Ralph H. Gabriel. —New York: Harcourt, Brace and Company, c1942

xvi, 632 p. ;24 cm.

D771.224/E37

Major Problems of Democracy: A Study of Social Conditions in the United States/Seba Eldridge, Carroll D. Clark. —New York: The Century Co., c1928

xv, 585 p. ;20 cm.

D771.224/G676

American Democracy Today and Tomorrow/Ryllis Alexander Goslin, Omar Pancoast Goslin, Helen Frances Storen. —New York: Harcourt, Brace and Company, c1942

xviii, 589 p. ;24 cm.

D771.224/M394

Progressive Democracy: Addresses and State Papers of Alfred E. Smith/with an introduction by Henry Moskowitz. —New York: Harcourt, Brace and Company, c1928

xiii, 392 p. ;23 cm.

D771.224/McC743

Presidential Campaigns/George Murray Mcconnel. —Chicago: Rand, McNally & Co., c1908

243 p. ;20 cm.

D771.224/T632(1)

Democracy in America. Volume 1/Alexis De Tocqueville. —New York: D. Appleton and Company, c1912

xlviii, 418 p. ;21 cm.

D771.224/T632(2)

Democracy in America. volume 2/Alexis De Tocqueville. —New York: D. Appleton and Company, c1912

iv, 419-868 p. ;21 cm.

D771.224/W739

The Rights and Duties of American Citizenship/Westel Woodbury Willoughby. —New York: American Book Company, c1898

336 p. ;19 cm.

D771.225/K41

The Flag of the United States: Your Flag and Mine/Harrison Summers Kerrick. —Columbus: The Champlin Printing Co., c1925

142 p. ;26 cm.

D771.231/U58

Register of the Department of State: October 1, 1940/United States Government Printing Office. —Washington: United States Government Printing Office, c1940

251 p. ;24 cm.

D771.235/R956
Forward with Science/Rogers D. Rusk. —New York: Alfred A Knopf, c1944
xiv, 307, v p. ;22 cm.

D771.238/C774
Chinese Immigration/Mary Roberts Coolidge. —New York: Henry Holt, 1909.
x, 531 p. ;19 cm.

D771.238/H841
Immigration and Labor: The Economic Aspects of European Immigration to the United States/Isaac A. Hourwich. —New York: G. P. Putnam's Sons, c1912
xvii, 544 p. ;22 cm.

D771.238/S438
These Foreigners/William Seabrook. —New York: Harcourt, Brace and Company, c1938
ix, 358 p. ;21 cm.

D771.25/M718
Politics and Criminal Prosecution/Raymond Moley. —New York: Minton, Balch & Company, c1929
xii, 241 p. ;20 cm.

D771.26/B866
The American Character/D. W. Brogan. —New York: Alfreda. Knopf, c1944
xxi, 168 p. ;22 cm.

D771.26/D663
The Citizen and Commonwealth: A Part of the New American Citizen/Charles F. Dole. —[S. l. : s. n.], [?]
154 p. ;18 cm.

D771.26/D994
Citizenship of the United States/Frederick Van Dyne. —New York: The Lawyer's Co-operative Publishing Co., c1904
xxvii, 385 p. ;23 cm.

D771.262/W747
Things as They Are: Mission Work in Southern India/Amy Wilson-Carmichael. —London: Morgan and Scott, c1904
xvi, 303 p. ;20 cm.

D771.264/P349
The White Man's Dilemma: Climax of the Age of Imperialism/Nathaniel Peffer. —New York: The John Day Company, c1927
ix, 312 p. ;21 cm.

D771.264/R263
An Introduction to Political Parties and Practical Politics/P. Orman Ray. —New York: Charles Scribner's Sons, c1913
xiii, 493 p. ;19 cm.

D771.269/Z89
Gold Coast and Slum: A Sociological Study of Chicago's Near North Side/Harvey Warren Zorbaugh. —Chicago: The University of Chicago Press, c1929
xv, 287 p. ;20 cm.

D771.27/S644
Working with the People/Charles Sprague Smith. —New York: A. Wessels Company, c1904
xvi, 161 p. ;18 cm.

D771.27/W279
American Charities/Amos Griswold Warner. —Revised ed.. —New York: T. Y. Crowell & Company, c1894, 1908
xvii, 510 p. ;19 cm.

D771.28/F174
Our Civic Life: Civics and Citizenship/Emil F. Paith, A. H. Edgerton. —New York: Mentzer, Bush & Company, c1941

xxii, 426 p. ;21 cm.

D771. 28/F563

The American Way of Life: A History/Harold Underwood Faulkner, Tyler Kepner, Hall Bartlett. —Revised ed. . —New York: Happer & Brothers Publishers, c1941, 1945

xviii, 739 p. ;24 cm.

D771. 28/G778

Wonder and Workers/William S. Gray. —Chicago: Scott, Fresman and Company, c1946

544 p. ;20 cm.

D771. 28/K29

Life in Early American/Mary G. Kelty. —Boston: Ginn and Company, c1941

viii, 413 p. ;20 cm.

D771. 28/W899

The Way our People Lived: An Intimate American History/W. E. Woodward. —New York: E. P. Dutton & Company, Inc. , c1945

413 p. ;22 cm.

D771. 281/R787

The Record of A Happy Marriage/Isabel Scott Rorick. —Boston: Houghton Mifflin Company, c1942

211 p. ;21 cm.

D771. 283/H325

Community Organization/Joseph Kinmont Hart. —New York: The Macmillan Company, c1927

230 p. ;19 cm.

D771. 283/MacG238

The Rural Community/Llewellyn MacGarr. —New York: The Macmillan Company, c1923

xv, 239 p. ;19 cm.

D771. 286. 8/J66

Brave Women and Their Deeds of Heroism/Joseph Johnson. —London: Gall and Inglis, [?]

240 p. ;19 cm.

D771. 288/S654

Counterfeiting: Crime against the People/Laurence Dwight Smith. —New York: W. W. Norton & Company Inc. , c1944

254 p. ;21 cm.

D771. 288/W916(1)

Prostitution in The United States. Volume I, Prior to the Entrance of the United States into the World War/Howard B. Woolston. —New York: The Century Co. , c1921

xiii, 360 p. ;20 cm.

D771. 289/W721

Our Rural Heritage: The Social Psychology of Rural Development/James Mickel Williams. —New York: Alfred A Knopf Mcm. xxv, c1925

xvii, 246 p. ;24 cm.

D771. 29/F413

The History of Political Theory and Party Organization in the United States/Simeon D. Fess. —Boston: Ginn and Company, c1910

vi, 451 p. ;20 cm.

D771. 29/J72

History of American Politics/Alexander Johnston. —New York: Henry Holt and Company, c1881

x, 274 p. ;16 cm.

D7712. 85/L752

The Revolt of Modern Youth/Judge Ben B. Lindsey, Wainwright Evans. —New York: New York, c1925

xii, 364 p. ;21 cm.

D80/B928-2

International Relations/Raymond Leslie Buell. —revised ed. —London: Sir Isaac Pitman & Sons, Ltd. , c1929

xvii, 838 p. ;21 cm.

D80/F754

The Practice of Diplomacy: As Illustrated in the Foreign Relations of the United States/John W. Foster. —Boston: Houghton, Mifflin and Company, c1906

401 p. ;22 cm.

D80/L345

Problems of Peace: Lectures Delivered at the Geneva Institute of International Relations/H. J. Laski, A. E. Zimmern. —London: George Allen & Unwin Ltd. , c1932

xv, 301 p. ;19 cm.

D81/B916

International Relations/James Bryce. —New York: The Macmillan Company, c1922

xii, 275p. ;20cm.

D81/C686

Geographic Aspects of International Relations (Lectures on the Harris Foundation 1937)/Charles C. Colby. —Chicago: The University of Chicago Press, c1938

xi, 295 p. ;19 cm.

D81/E26

Heading for War: What You Ought to Know & Fear/W. H. Edwards. —New York: Payson & Clarke Ltd. , c1928

162 p. ;19 cm.

D81/F533

League or War? /Fisher, Irving. —New York: Harper & Brother Publishers, c1923

xi, 268 p. ;22 cm.

D81/W235

War Is Not Inevitable: Problems of Peace/Frank Walters, Edgar Ansel Mowrer, Douglas Reed. —London: Peace Book Co. , c1938

299 p. ;19 cm.

D81-53/M391-2

The Evolution of World-Peace/F. S. Marvin. —2nd ed.. —London: Oxford University Press, c1933

209 p. ;19 cm.

D813/H913

The Two Hague Conferences and their Contributions to international law/William I. Hull. —Boston: Ginn & Company, c1908

xiv, 516 p. ;20 cm.

D813/N946

Versailles/Karl Friedrich Nowak. —New York: Payson and Clarke Ltd. , c1929

287 p. ;23 cm.

D813. 1/A374

From Paris to Locarno and After: The League of Nations and the Search for Security, 1919-1928/F. Alexander. —London: J. M. Dent & Sons Ltd. , [?]

246 p. ;19 cm.

D813. 1/P776

The League of Nations/Frederick Pollock. —London: Stevens and Sons, Ltd. , c1920

xv, 251 p. ;22 cm.

D813. 4/F754

Arbitration and the Hague Court/John W. Foster. —Boston: Houghton, Mifflin and Company, c1904

147 p. ;20 cm.

D813. 7-532/G721

First Session of the General Conference of the

United Nations Educational, Scientific and Cultural Organization: Paris, November 19-December 10, 1946/Report of the United States Delegation With Selected Documents. —Washington: United States Government Printing, c1947
vii, 157 p. ;24 cm.

D814.21/T756
The World After the Peace Conference: Being An Epilogue to the 'History of the Peace Conference of Paris' and A Prologue to the 'Survey of International Affairs, 1920-1923'/Arnold J. Toynbee. —London: Humphrey Milford, c1926
91 p. ;25 cm.

D815/A583
Geneva and the Drift to War/Norman Angell, J. B. Condliffe. —London: George Allen & Unwin Ltd., c1938
xiii, 234 p. ;19 cm.

D815/B658
Peace and Disarmament/Leon Blum. —London: Jonathan Cape Thirty Bedford Square, c1932
202 p. ;20 cm.

D815/C142
What Makes a War End? /H. A. Calahan. —New York: The Vanguard Press, c1944
260 p. ;21 cm.

D815/C311
International Relations Since the Peace Treaties/E. H. Carr. —London: Macmillan and Co., Ltd., c1937
viii, 284 p. ;19 cm.

D815/G463
The Unequal Treaties: China and the Foreigner/by Rodney Gilbert; with a foreword by H. E. Morriss. —London: J. Murray, c1929.
xi, 248 p. ;23 cm.

D815/I16
The Washington Conference and After: A Historical Survey/Yamato Ichihashi. —California: Stanford University Press, c1928
xii, 443 p. ;20 cm.

D815/J76
Hitler's Drive to the East/F. Elwyn Jones. —London: Victor Gollancz Ltd., c1937
126 p. ;19 cm.

D815/M645
Democracy and the Eastern Question: The problem of the far east as demonstrated by the great war, and its relation to the United States of America/Thomas F. Millard. —New York: The Century Co., c1919
ix, 446 p. ;21 cm.

D815/M818
Imperialism and World Politics/Parker Thomas Moon. —New York: Macmillan, c1936
xiv p., 583 p. ;23 cm.

D815/T744
Asia Answers/Ralph Townsend. —New York: G. P. Putnam's Sons, 1936.
xiv, 272 p. ;22 cm.

D815.1/B167-2
Disarmament/P. J. Noel Baker. —2nd ed.. —Washington D. C: The Hogarth Press, c1927
xiv, 352 p. ;22 cm.

D815.7/L668(2)
The Personal Rights Series. No. II, Socialism and Individualism/J. H. Levy. —[S. l. : s. n.], [?]
155 p. ;18 cm.

D816/A142
Treaty Ports/Hallett Abend. —New York:

Doubleday, Doran & Company, Inc., c1944
vii, 271 p.;21 cm.

D816/O11
The Great European Treaties of the Nineteenth Century/Augustus Oakes, R. B. Mowat. —London: Oxford University Press, c1921
xii, 403 p.;19 cm.

D82/B637
China and the Far East: Clark University Lectures/George H. Blakeslee. —New York: Thomas Y. Crowell & Co., c1910
xxii, 455 p.;21 cm.

D82/J83
Foreign Diplomacy in China 1894-1900: A Study in Political and Economic Relations with China/Philip Joseph. —London: George Allen & Unwin Ltd., c1928
458 p.;22 cm.

D822/B347
Shanghai'37/Vicki Baum. —New York: Doubleday, Doran & Company, Inc., c1939
619 p.;18 cm.

D822/B623
Japan in China/T. A. Bisson. —New York: The Macmillan Company, c1938
417 p.;22 cm.

D822/K11
Japan in China: Her Motives and Aims/K. K. Kawakami. —London: John Murray, Albemarle Street, W., c1938
xviii, 188 p.;19 cm.

D826/C736
Treaties and Agreements With and Concerning China, 1894-1919/Compiled and edited by John V. A. Macmurray. —London: Oxford University Press, c1921.
xlvi, 928 p.;26 cm.

D826/E56
Shangtung: Treaties and Agreements/The Endowment. —Washington: The Endowment, c1921
x, 120 p.;24 cm.

D829/G347
The Tinder Box of Asia/George E. Sokolsky. —London: George Allen & Unwin Ltd., c1932
ix, 376 p.;21 cm.

D829.12/P865
The Outbreak in China: Its Causes/Rev. F. L. Hawks Pott. —New York: James Pott & Company, c1900.
vi, 124 p.;20 cm.

D829.15/M468
Treaties Between the Empire of Chian and Foreign Powers: Together with Regulation for the Conduct of Foreign Trade, Conventions, Agreements, Regulations, Etc., the Peace Protocol of 1901, and the Commercial Treaty of 1902/William Frederick • Mayers. —Shanghai: The "North-China Herald" Office, c1902
xiv, 332 p.;24 cm.

D829.313/W362
The Truth about China and Japan/B. L. P. Weale. —New York: Dodd, Mead & Co., 1919.
248 p.;21 cm.

D83/K46
Changing Asia/Egon Erwin Kisch. —New York: Alfred. A. Knopf, c1934
267, viii p.;22 cm.

D831.131/H632
Manchoukuo-soviet Border Issues/Noboru Hidaka. —[S. l.]: The Manchuria Daily News,

c1938
261 p. ;22 cm.

D831. 3/L389
Danger from the East/Richard E. Lauterbach. —New York: Harper & Brothers Publishers, c1947
xi, 430 p. ;21 cm.

D831. 3/T136
War and Diplomacy in the Japanese Empire/Tatsuji Takeuchi. —London: George Allen & Unwin, Ltd. , c1935
xix, 505 p. ;23 cm.

D831. 32/I79
Japan Must Fight Britain/by Lt. Comdr. ; translated by Instructor-Capt. G. V. Rayment. —London: Paternoster House, [1937]
288 p. ;23 cm.

D837. 12/D419
Occupation of Germany Policy and Progress 1945-46/The Department of State United States of America. —Washinton D. C. : United States Government Printing Office, c1947
viii, 241 p. ;24 cm.

D837. 12/P928
European Recovery and American Aid/The President's Committee on Foreign Aid. —Washington: [s. n.], c1947
x, 286 p. ;24 cm.

D837. 12/S841
Lend-lease: Weapon for Victory/Edward R. Stettinius. —New York: The Macmillan Company, c1944
xiv, 358 p. ;22 cm.

D837. 12/W449
The Time for Decision/Sumner Welles. —New York: Harper & Brothers Publishers, [1944]
vii, 431 p. ;22 cm.

D851. 2/D883
The Road to Teheran: The Story of Russia and America, 1781-1943/Foster Rhea Dulles. —New York: Overseas Editions, Inc. , c1944
244 p. ;17 cm.

D851. 22/D883
The Road to Teheran: the Story of Russia And America, 1781-1943/Foster Rhea Dulles. —Princeton: Princeton University Press, c1944
vi, 279 p. ;21 cm.

D851. 6/V292
Laughing Diplomat/Daniele Vare. —[S. l. : s. n.], [?]
448 p. ;22 cm.

D851. 62/H432
Germany and World Peace/Sven Hedin. —London: Hutchison & Co. , c1937
viii, 358 p. ;22 cm.

D852/M936
A History of European Diplomacy, 1815-1914/by R. B. Mowat. —London: E. Arnold, 1923.
viii, 308 p. ;23 cm.

D854. 60/M115
Italy's Foreign and Colonial Policy 1914-1937/Maxwell H. H. Macartney, Paul Cremona. —London: Oxford University Press, c1938
vii, 353 p. ;22 cm.

D855. 1/H417
Wartime Mission in Spain: 1942-1945/Carlton J. H. Hayes. —New York: The Macmillan Company, c1945
viii, 313 p. ;21 cm.

D856. 1/B862
British Historical & Political Orations from

the XIIth to the XXth Century/J. M. Dent & Sons Ltd. —London: J. M. Dent & Sons Ltd. , [?]
351 p. ;18 cm.

D856. 1/K35
Britain Faces Germany/A. L. Kennedy. —London: J ohn Dickinson & Co. , Ltd. , c1937
194 p. ;19 cm.

D856. 12/H496
Failure of A Mission: Berlin 1937-1939/Nevile Henderson. —London: Hodder and Stoughton Ltd. , c1940
x, 318 p. ;19 cm.

D871. 2/(1916)
Papers Relating to the Foreign Relations of the United States with Annual Message of the President Transmitted to Congress December 5, 1916/Government Printing Office. —Washinton: Government Printing Office, c1925
lxxvi, 1008 p. ;23 cm.

D871. 2/C743
Uncle Sam Abroad: Our Foreign Serice Consular and Diplomatic/J. E. Conner. —Chicago: Rand, McNally & Company, c1900
201 p. ;19 cm.

D871. 2/F754
The Practice of Diplomacy: As Illustrated in the Foreign Relations of the United States/John W. Foster. —Boston: Houghton, Mifflin and Company, c1906
401 p. ;23 cm.

D871. 2/G721(2)
Papers Relating to the Foreign Relations of the United States with the Annual Message of the President Transmitted to Congress December 3, 1907. Part 2/Government Printing Office. —Washington: Government Printing Office, c1910
xl, 550-1313 p. ;23 cm.

D871. 2/G721(1887)
Papers Relating to the Foreign Relations of the United States for the Year 1887/Government Printing Office. —Washington: Government Printing Office, c1887
lxvii, 1149 p. ;23 cm.

D871. 2/G721(1899)
Papers Relating to the Foreign Relations of the United States with the Annual Message of the President Transmitted to Congress December 5, 1899/Government Printing Office. —Washington: Government Printing Office, c1901
xcii, 823 p. ;23 cm.

D871. 2/G721(1906. 1)
Papers Relating to the Foreign Relations of the United States with the Annual Massage of the President Transmitted to Congress/Government Printing Office. —Washington: Government Printing Office, c1909
ciii, 868 p. ;23 cm.

D871. 2/G721(1906. 2)
Papers Relating to the Foreign Relations of the United States with the Annual Massage of the President Transmitted to Congress. Part 2/Government Printing Office. —Washington: Government Printing Office, c1909
xlix, 869-1666 p. ;23 cm.

D871. 2/G721(1907. 1)
Papers Relating to the Foreign Relations of the United States with the Annual Massage of the President Transmitted to Congress. part 1/Government Printing Office. —Washington: Government Printing Office, c1910
cxii, 587 p. ;23 cm.

D871. 2/G721(1908)
Papers Relating to the Foreign Relations of the

United States with Annual Message of the President Transmitted to Congress December 8, 1908/Government Printing Office. —Washington: Government Printing Office, c1912

ci, 848 p. ;23 cm.

D871.2/G721(1910.6)

Papers Relating to the Foreign Relations of the United States with Annual Message of the President Transmitted to Congress December 6, 1910/Government Printing Office. —Washington: Government Printing Office, c1912

cxii, 884 p. ;23 cm.

D871.2/G721

Papers Relating to the Foreign Relations of the United States/Government Printing Office. —Washington: Government Printing Office, c1902

lxxx, 574 p. ;23 cm.

D871.2/G721G

Papers Relating to the Foreign Relations of the United States/Government Printing Office. —Washington: Government Printing Office, c1884

lxx, 619 p. ;24 cm.

D871.2/G721GP

Papers Relating to the Foreign Relations of the United States/Government Printing Office. —Washington: Government Printing Office, c1905

lxxxvii, 894;23 cm.

D871.2/G721P214(1898)

Papers Relating to the Foreign Relations of the United States with the Annual Massage of the President Transmitted to Congress/Government Printing Office. —Washington: Government Printing Office, c1901

xcv, 1191 p. ;23 cm.

D871.2/G721P214(1930)

Papers Relating to the Foreign Relations of the United States 1918/United States Government Printing Office. —Washington: United States Government Printing Office, c1930

cxi, 877 p. ;24 cm.

D871.2/G721P214

Papers Relating to the Foreign Relations of the United States/Government Printing Office. —Washington: Government Printing Office, c1904

lxxxiii, 823 p. ;23 cm.

D871.2/G721P214R382F714

Papers Relating to the Foreign Relations of the United States/Government Printing Office. —Washington: Government Printing Office, c1906

xciii, 953 p. ;23

D871.2/H659

American Consular Jurisdiction in the Orient/Frank E. Hinckley. —Washington: W. H. Lowdermilk and Company, c1906

xx, 283 p. ;23 cm.

D871.2/K69

The Americans in Santo Domingo/Melvin M. Knight. . —New York: Vanguard Press, c1928

xix, 189 p. ;20 cm.

D871.2/M255(1)

Treaties, Conventions, International Acts, Protocols and Agreements between the United States of America and Other Powers 1776-1909. Volume I/William M. Malloy. —Washington: Government Printing Office, c1910

xxvi, 1230 p. ;23 cm.

D871.2/M255(2)

Treaties, Conventions, International Acts, Protocols and Agreements between the United States of America and Other Powers 1776-1909. Volume II/William M. Malloy. —Washinton: Government Printing Office, c1910

xxvi, 1231-2491 p. ;23 cm.

D871.2/S551

Have We A Far Eastern Policy? /Charles H. Sherrill. —New York: Charles Scribner's Sons, c1920

xvi, 307 p. ;19 cm.

D871.2/U58

Regulations Prescribed for the Use of The Consular Service of the United States/The United States Government Printing Office. —Washington: The United States Government Printing Office, c1896

xix, 871 p. ;22 cm.

D871.2/U58

Foreign Service List July 1, 1947/(?). —Washington: United States Government Printing Office, c1947

iii, 191 p. ;24 cm.

D871.2/U85

The Challenge of the Future: A Study in American Foreign Policy/Roland G. Usher. —Boston: Houghton Mifflin Company, c1916

xx, 350 p. ;21 cm.

D871.2/W314

Papers Relating to the Foreign Relations of the United States/Washington Government Printing Office. —Washington: Washington Government Printing Office, c1926

clxvi, 1242 p. ;24 cm.

D871.2-53/G721

Papers Relating to the Foreign Relations of the United States/Government Printing Office. —Washington: Government Printing Office, c1883

liii, 557 p. ;23 cm.

D871.2-53/G721P214

Papers Relating to the Foreign Relations of the United States/Government Printing Office. —Washington: Government Printing Office, c1873

lxi, 732 p. ;23 cm.

D871.2-62/U67(1937)

The Department of State Register of the Department of State/United States Government Printing Office. —Washington: United States Government Printing Office, c1937

viii, 396 p. ;25 cm.

D871.20/C592

Memorandum on the Monroe Doctrine/J. Reuben Clark. —Washington: US Government Printing Office, c1930

xxv, 238 p. ;23 cm.

D871.22/D419

Report to Congress on Foreign Surplus Disposal: October 1947/Department of State. —Washington: Department of State, c1947

32 p. ;23 cm.

D871.22/K22

American-Japanese Relations An Inside View of Japan's Policies and Purposes/Kiyoshi K. Kawakami. —New York: Fleming H. Revell Company, c1912

370 p. ;21 cm.

D871.22/W916

America's Foreign Policy: Essays and Addresses/Theodore Salisbury Woolsey. —New York: The Century Co., c1898

x, 293 p. ;18 cm.

D871.232/M169

The Chinese Abroad: Their Position and Protection, a Study in International Law and Relations/by Harley Farnsworth MacNair; with an introduction by the Hon. V. K. Wellington Koo; and a foreword by Fong F. Sec. —3rd ed. —Shanghai: The Commercial Press, Ltd., c1926.

xxii, 340 p. ;21 cm.

D871.26/M647(2)

Treaties and Other International Acts of the United States of America. Volume 2/United States Government Printing Office. —Washington: United States Government Printing Office, c1931

xxix, 662 p. ;26 cm.

D871.26/M647(3)

Treaties and Other International Acts of the United States of America. Volume 3/United States Government Printing Office. —Washington: United States Government Printing Office, c1933

xxiv, 833 p. ;26 cm.

D871.26/M647(4)

Treaties and Other International Acts of the United States of America. Volume 4/United States Government Printing Office. —Washington: United States Government Printing Office, c1934

xxvi, 855 p. ;26 cm.

D871.26/M647(5)

Treaties and Other International Acts of the United States of America. Volume 5/United States Government Pringting Office. —Washington: United States Government Pringting Office, c1937

xxvi, 1103 p. ;26 cm.

D871.26/U58

National Documents: State Papers So Arranged as to Illustrate the Growth of Our Country from 1606 to the Present Day/Unit Book Publishing Co. , —New York: Unit Book Publishing Co. , c1904

494, iv p. ;18 cm.

D873.02/B721

The American Mediterranean/Stephen Bonsal. —New York: Moffat, Yard and Company, c1912

xiv, 488 p. ;21 cm.

D9/C734

Report of the Commission on Extraterritoriality in China, Peking, September 16, 1926: being the report to the governments of the Commission appointed in pursuance to Resolution v of the Conference on the Limitation of Armaments/Commission on Extraterritorial Jurisdiction in China. —Washington: Govt. Print. Off. , 1926.

xiv, 156 p. ;23 cm.

D90/V788

Common-Sense in Law/Paul Vinogradoff. —New York: Henry Holt and Company, [?]

256 p. ;17 cm.

D901/B476

An Introduction to the Principles of Morals and Legislation/Jeremy Bentham. —Oxford: The Clarendon Press, c1789

xxv, 378, 8 p. ;19 cm.

D908/G646(1)

Comparative Administrative Law: An Analysis of the Administrative Systems National and Local, of the United States, England, France and Germany. vol. I/Frank J. Goodnow. —Student's ed. —New York: G. P. Putnam's Sons, c1893

xxxv, 327 p. ;22 cm.

D91/H875(1910)

Synopses of the Laws of the United States of America, with Instructions for Taking Depositions, the Execution and Acknowledgment of Deeds, Wills, etc. 1910/The Hubbell Publishing Company. —Cambridge: H. O. Houghton & Co. , c1910

1191 p. ;22 cm.

D91/H875(1911)

Synopses of the Laws of the United States of America, with Instructions for Taking Depositions, the Execution and Acknowledgment of Deeds, Wills, etc. 1911/The Hubbell Publishing Company.—Cambridge: H. O. Houghton & Co., c1911

1202 p.;22 cm.

D91/H875(1912)

Synopses of the Laws of the United States of America, with Instructions for Taking Depositions, the Execution and Acknowledgment of Deeds, Wills, etc./The Hubbell Publishing Company.—Cambridge: H. O. Houghton & Co., c1912

25-1170 p.;22 cm.

D91/H875(1914)

Synopses of the Laws of the United States of America, with Instructions for Taking Depositions, the Execution and Acknowledgment of Deeds, Wills, etc./The Hubbell Publishing Company.—Cambridge: H. O. Houghton & Co., c1914

1334 p.;22 cm.

D91/H875(1914)

Synopses of the Laws of the United States of America, with Instructions for Taking Depositions, the Execution and Acknowledgment of Deeds, Wills, etc./The Hubbell Publishing Company.—Cambridge: H. O. Houghton & Co., c1914

1198 p.;22 cm.

D91/H875(1918)

Synopses of the Laws of the United States of America, with Instructions for Taking Depositions, the Execution and Acknowledgment of Deeds, Wills, etc./The Hubbell Publishing Company.—Cambridge: H. O. Houghton & Co., c1917

1315 p.;22 cm.

D91/H875(1919)

Synopses of the Laws of the United States of America, with Instructions for Taking Depositions, the Execution and Acknowledgment of Deeds, Wills, etc./The Hubbell Publishing Company.—Cambridge: H. O. Houghton & Co., c1919

1334 p.;22 cm.

D91/H875(1920)

Synopses of the Laws of the United States of America, with Instructions for Taking Depositions, the Execution and Acknowledgment of Deeds, Wills, etc./The Hubbell Publishing Company.—Cambridge: H. O. Houghton & Co., c1920

1350 p.;22 cm.

D91/H875(1922)

Synopses of the Laws of the United States of America, with Instructions for Taking Depositions, the Execution and Acknowledgment of Deeds, Wills, etc. 1922/The Hubbell Publishing Company.—Cambridge: The Hubbell Publishing Company, c1922

1378 p.;22 cm.

D91/H875(1923)

Synopses of the Laws of the United States of America, with Instructions for Taking Depositions, the Execution and Acknowledgment of Deeds, Wills, etc./The Hubbell Publishing Company.—Cambridge: H. O. Houghton & Co., c1923

1411 p.;22 cm.

D91/H875(1924)

Synopses of the Laws of the United States of America, with Instructions for Taking Depositions, the Execution and Acknowledgment of Deeds, Wills, etc. 1924/The Hubbell Publishing

Company. —[S. l.]: The Hubbell Publishing Company, c1924
1427 p. ;22 cm.

D91/H875(1925)
Synopses of the Laws of the United States of America, with Instructions for Taking Depositions, the Execution and Acknowledgment of Deeds, Wills, etc. 1925/The Hubbell Publishing Company. —[S. l.]: The Hubbell Publishing Company, c1925
1458 p. ;22 cm.

D91/H875(1927)
Synopses of the Laws of the United States of America, with Instructions for Taking Depositions, the Execution and Acknowledgment of Deeds, Wills, etc. /The Hubbell Publishing Company. —Cambridge: H. O. Houghton & Co. , c1927
1458 p. ;22 cm.

D91/H875
Synopses of the Laws of the States, Provinces of Canada, Mexico, and Porto Rico, with Instructions for Taking Depositions, the Execution and Acknowledgment of Deeds, Wills, etc. /The Hubbell Publishing Company. —[S. l.]: H. O. Houghton & Co. , c1912
1206 p. ;23 cm.

D91/H875P976
Synopses of the Laws of the United States of America, with Instructions for Taking Depositions, the Execution and Acknowledgment of Deeds, Wills, etc. /The Hubbell Publishing Company. —Cambridge: H. O. Houghton & Co. , c1918
1334 p. ;22 cm.

D91/H875S992
Synopses of the Laws of the United States of America, with Instructions for Taking Depositions, the Execution and Acknowledgment of Deeds, Wills, etc. /The Hubbell Publishing Company. —Concord: The Rumford Press, c1921
1379 p. ;22 cm.

D910/B644(1-44)
Cyc. Annotations to Cyclopedia or Law and Procedure. 1-40 Cyc. /De Witt C. Blashfield. —New York: The American Book Company, c1913
xiv, 2335-3811 p. ;26 cm.

D910/W659-2(1)
A Treatise on the Anglo-American System of Evidence in Trials at Common Law including the statutes and judicial decisions of all jurisdictions of the United States and Canada. volumes 1/John Henry Wigmore. —2nd ed. —Boston: Little, Brown, and Company, c1923
lxxxvi, 720 p. ;26 cm.

D911/C438
Outlines of Constitutional Law With Notes on Legal History/Dalzell Chalmers, Cyril Asquith. —London: Sweet & Maxwell, Ltd. , c1922
xi, 326, 31 p. ;22 cm.

D911. 05/S651
Cases on Selected Topics in the Law of Municipal Corporations/Jeremiah Smith. —Cambridge: The Harvard Law Review Publishing Association, c1898
xi, 260 p. ;23 cm.

D913/B949-3
The Law of Torts: A Concise Treatise on the Civil Liability at Common Law and Under Modern Statutes Actionable Wrongs to Person and Property/Francis M. Burdick. —3rd ed. —Albany, New York: Banks & Company, c1915
xcix, 612 p. ;22 cm.

D913/P132-2(2)

The Law of Contracts. Vol. II/William Herbert Page. —2nd ed. —Cincinnati: The W. H. Anderson Company, c1920

xxv, 658-1428 p. ;26 cm.

D913/P132-2(4)

The Law of Contracts. Vol. VI/William Herbert Page. —2nd ed. —Cincinnati: The W. H. Anderson Company, c1920

xxv, 3170-6546 p. ;26 cm.

D913/P132-2(5)

The Law of Contracts. Vol. V/William Herbert Page. —2nd ed.. —Cincinnati: The W. H. Anderson Company, c1921

xx, 2574-3169 p. ;26 cm.

D913.99/H936

Commercial Law of China/William S. Hung. —[S. l. : s. n.], c1932

xix, 307 p. ;20 cm.

D914.04/A316

Notes and Commentaries on Chinese Criminal Law/Ernest Alabaster. —London: Luzac & Company, c1899

lxxii, 675 p. 22 cm. ;22 cm.

D915.13/A131-2

Modes of Proving the Facts/Austin Abbott. —2nd ed. —Rochester: The Lawyers' Co-operative Publishing Company, c1901

xxi, 653 p. ;23 cm.

D915.18-62/C596-2

Handbook of Criminal Procedure/WM. L. Clark. —2nd ed. St. Paul: West Publishing Co. , c1895

xi, 748 p. ;23 cm.

D916.5/S531(1932)

Fiftieth Year the Lawyers Directory 1932/ Sharp & Alleman Co. , Publishers. —Philadelphia: Sharp & Alleman Co. , Publishers, c1932

2398 p. ;23 cm.

D917/E47

The Criminal/Havelock Ellis. —London: The Walter Scott, 1910

xxx, 440 p. ;19 cm.

D917/H724

Murder out Yonder: An Informal Study of Certain Classic Crimes in Back-Country America/ Stewart H. Holbrook. —New York: The Macmillan Company, c1944

255 p. ;22 cm.

D918/S679-2

Modern Criminal Investigation/Harry Soderman, John J. O'Connell. —Revised ed.. —New York: Funk & Wagnalls Company, c1935, 1940 and 1945

xiii, 478 p. ;20 cm.

D92/C518

The Chinese Supreme Court Decisions: Relating to General principles of Civil Law, Obligations, and Commercial Law/translated by F. T. Cheng. —Peking: The Commission on Extra-territoriality, 1923.

229 p. ;25 cm.

D922.221.1/W947

Code of Customs Regulations and Procedure/ Stanley F. Wright, A. C. E Braud. —Shanghai: Statistical Department of the Inspectorate General of Customs, c1933

xi, 306 p. ;25 cm.

D923.4-62/A445

Handbook on the Protection of Trade-Marks Patents, Copyrights and Trade-Names in China/ Norwood F. Allman. —Shanghai: Kelly & Walsh, Ltd. , c1924

iii, 207 p. ;22 cm.

D924/C454

The Criminal Code of the Republic of China: Embodying the Law Governing the Application of the Criminal Code and The Penal Code of Army, Navy and Air Forces of The Republic of China/Chao-Yuen C. Chang. —Shanghai: Kelly & Walsh, Ltd. , c1935

183 p. ;26 cm.

D925.2=6/C734

The Regulations Relating to Criminal Procedure of the Republic of China/The Commission on Extraterritoriality. —Peking: The Commission on Extraterritoriality, c1923

131 p. ;25 cm.

D927.658/N852

The Ordinances of Hongkong for 1909/Noronha & Co. ,—Hongkong: Noronha & Co. , c1909

1 v. ;24 cm.

D935.11/I27

The New Constitution of India/Courtenay Ilbert, Hon. Lord Meston. —London: University of London Press, Ltd. , c1923

212 p. ;19 cm.

D954.59/G795

A Handbook of Greek Constitutional History/A. H. J. Greenidge. —London: Macmillan and Co. , Ltd. , c1902

xvii, 276 p. ;19.5 cm.

D956.11/B144

The English Constitution/Walter Bagehot. —London: Kegan Paul, c1925

lxxiv, 300 p. ;19 cm.

D956.11/M113

The English Constitution/Jesse Macy. —New York: The Macmillan Company, c1906

xxiii, 534 p. ;21 cm.

D970.9/H875

Synopses of the Laws/The Hubbell Publishing Co. ,—Washington: The Hubbell Publishing Co. , c1911

1202 p. ;22 cm.

D971.2/A131-3

Clerks' and Conveyancers' Assistant: A Collection of Forms of Conveyancing, Contracts, and Legal Proceedings/Benj. V. Abbott, Austin Abbott. —3rd ed. . —New York: Baker, Voorhis and Company, c1911

xi, 1686 p. ;23 cm.

D971.2/A567(14)

American Law and Procedure. Volume XIV, Statutory Construction/James DeWitt Andrews. —Chicago: La Salle Extension University, c1910

417 p. ;24 cm.

D971.2/B621-8

The Principles of Equity: A Treatise on the System of Justice Administered in Courts of Chancery/Geo. Tucker Bispham, Sharswood Brinton. —8th ed. . —New York: The Banks Law Publishing Co. , c1911

826 p. ;23 cm.

D971.2/B622-8(2)

New Commentaries on The Criminal Law upon A New System of Legal Exposition. Volume II, The Specific Offences/Joel Prentiss Bishop. —8th ed. —Chicago: T. H. Flood and Company, c1892

xi, 927 p. ;24 cm.

D971.2/B691(5)

Everybody's Legal Adviser. Volume V/Albert S. Bolles. —New York: Funk & Wagnalls Com-

pany, c1922
899-1113 p. ;17 cm.

D971. 2/C938
Principles of Procedure in Deliberative Bodies/ George Glover Crocker. —New York: G. P. Putnam's Sons, c1889
vi, 167 p. ;15 cm.

D971. 2/D921-7(1)
A Book of Forms for Practice in the Courts, and for Conveyancing; also, for the Use of Public Officers and Men of Business Generally. Vol. I/ James D. Dunlap. —7th and Revised ed. —Philadelphia: The George T. Biset Company, c1913
1232 p. ;24 cm.

D971. 2/F754-4(2)
A Treatise on Federal Practice Civil and Criminal. Vol. II/Roger Foster. —4th ed.. —Chicago: Callaghan and Company, c1909
xi, 954-1965 p. ;24 cm.

D971. 2/G721-2
Digest of the Published Opinions of the Attorneys-General, and of the Leading Decisions of the Federal Courts, with Reference to International Law, Treaties, and Kindred Subjects/ Government Printing Office. —Washington: Government Printing Office, c1877
vii, 290 p. ;23 cm.

D971. 2/H172(2)
American Law and Procedure. vol. II/James Parker Hall, James DeWitt Andrews. —Chicago: La Salle Extension University, c1910, 1911
xxii, 435 p. ;24 cm.

D971. 2/H174(1)
American Law and Procedure. vol. I/James Parker Hall, James DeWitt Andrews. —Chicago: La Salle Extension University, c1910
liv, 378 p. ;24 cm.

D971. 2/H174(3)
American Law and Procedure. vol. III/James Parker Hall, James DeWitt Andrews. —Chicago: La Salle Extension University, c1910, 1911
xv, 429 p. ;24 cm.

D971. 2/H174(5)
American Law and Procedure. Vol. V/James Parker Hall. —Chicago: La Salle Extension University, c1911
xvi, 442 p. ;24 cm.

D971. 2/H174(6)
American Law and Procedure. Vol. VI/James Parker Hall. —Chicago: La Salle Extension University, c1911
xx, 492 p. ;24 cm.

D971. 2/H174(7)
American Law and Procedure. Vol. VII/James Parker Hall. —Chicago: La Salle Extension University, c1911
xvii, 451 p. ;24 cm.

D971. 2/H174(8)
American Law and Procedure. Vol. VIII/ James Parker Hall. —Chicago: La Salle Extension University, c1911
xvi, 410 p. ;24 cm.

D971. 2/H174(10)
American Law and Procedure. Vol. X/James Parker Hall. —Chicago: La Salle Extension University, c1910, 1911
xx, 458 p. ;24 cm.

D971. 2/H174(11)
American Law and Procedure. Vol. XI/James Parker Hall. —Chicago: La Salle Extension University, c1910, 1911
xvii, 417 p. ;24 cm.

D971. 2/H174(12)

American Law and Procedure. Vol. XII/James Parker Hall. —Chicago: La Salle Extension University, c1910, 1911

xx, 408 p. ;24 cm.

D971. 2/H174

American Law and Procedure/James Parker Hall, James DeWitt Andrews. —Chicago: La Salle Extension University, c1910

xiv, 425 p. ;24 cm.

D971. 2/H177

Constitution Law/James Parker Hall. —Chicago: Lasalle Extension University, c1910, 1911

xiv, 457 p. ;24 cm.

D971. 2/H749-12(2)

Commentaries on American Law. Vol. II/O. W. Holmes. —12th ed. —Boston: Little, Brown and Company, c1896

x, 647 p. ;24 cm.

D971. 2/H749-12(3)

Commentaries on American Law. Vol. III/O. W. Holmes, John M. Gould. —12th ed. —Boston: Little, Brown and Company, c1896

viii, 514 p. ;24 cm.

D971. 2/H749-14(4)

Commentaries on American Law. Vol. Iv/O. W. Holmes, John M. Gould. —14th ed. —Boston: Little, Brown and Company, c1896

vii, 742 p. ;24 cm.

D971. 2/K37-12(1)

Commentaries on American Law. Vol. I/James Kent. —12th ed. —Boston: Little, Brown and Company, c1896

ccxci, 548 p. ;24 cm.

D971. 2/M153(3)

Corpus Juris: Being a Complete and Systematic Statement of the Whole Body of the Law as Embodied in and Developed by All Reported Decisions. V. III/edited by William Mack and William Benjamin Hale. —New York: The American Law Book Co. , c1915

xxi, 1449 p. ;26 cm.

D971. 2/M153(4)

Corpus Juris: Being a Complete and Systematic Statement of the Whole Body of the Law as Embodied in and Developed by All Reported Decisions. V. IV/edited by William Mack and William Benjamin Hale. —New York: The American Law Book Co. , c1916.

xxi, 1476 p. ;26 cm.

D971. 2/M153(7)

Corpus Juris: Being a Complete and Systematic Statement of the Whole Body of the Law as Embodied in and Developed by All Reported Decisions. V. VII/edited by William Mack and William Benjamin Hale. —New York: The American Law Book Co. , c1916

xxi, 1181 p. ;26 cm.

D971. 2/M153(8)

Corpus Juris: Being a Complete and Systematic Statement of the Whole Body of the Law as Embodied in and Developed by All Reported Decisions. V. VIII/edited by William Mack and William Benjamin Hale. —New York: The American Law Book Co. , c1916.

xxiv, 1151 p. ;26 cm.

D971. 2/M153(9)

Corpus Juris: Being a Complete and Systematic Statement of the Whole Body of the Law as Embodied in and Developed by All Reported Decisions. V. IX/edited by William Mack and William Benjamin Hale. —New York: The American Law Book Co. , c1916

xxvi, 1295 p. ;26 cm.

D971. 2/M153(10)

Corpus Juris: Being a Complete and Systematic Statement of the Whole Body of the Law as Embodied in and Developed by All Reported Decisions. V. X/edited by William Mack and William Benjamin Hale. —New York: The American Law Book Co. , c1917

xviii, 1247 p. ;26 cm.

D971. 2/M153(11)

Corpus Juris: Being a Complete and Systematic Statement of the Whole Body of the Law as Embodied in and Developed by All Reported Decisions. V. 11/edited by William Mack and William Benjamin Hale. —New York: The American Law Book Co. , c1917

xxx, 1238 p. ;26 cm.

D971. 2/M153(12)

Corpus Juris: Being a Complete and Systematic Statement of the Whole Body of the Law as Embodied in and Developed by All Reported Decisions. V. XII/edited by William Mack and William Benjamin Hale. —New York: The American Law Book Co. , c1917

xxxi, 1315 p. ;26 cm.

D971. 2/M153(13)

Corpus Juris: Being a Complete and Systematic Statement of the Whole Body of the Law as Embodied in and Developed by All Reported Decisions. V. 13/edited by William Mack and William Benjamin Hale. —New York: The American Law Book Co. , c1917

xxv, 1263 p. ;26 cm.

D971. 2/M153(14)

Corpus Juris: Being a Complete and Systematic Statement of the Whole Body of the Law as Embodied in and Developed by All Reported Decisions. V. 14/edited by William Mack and William Benjamin Hale. —New York: The American Law Book Co. , c1919.

xviii, 11388 p. ;26 cm.

D971. 2/M153(15)

Corpus Juris: Being a Complete and Systematic Statement of the Whole Body of the Law as Embodied in and Developed by All Reported Decisions. V. XV/edited by William Mack and William Benjamin Hale. —New York: The American Law Book Co. , c1918

xxiX, 1455 p. ;26 cm.

D971. 2/M153(16)

Corpus Juris: Being a Complete and Systematic Statement of the Whole Body of the Law as Embodied in and Developed by All Reported Decisions. V. XVI/edited by William Mack and William Benjamin Hale. —New York: The American Law Book Co. , c1918

xvi, 1381 p. ;26 cm.

D971. 2/M153(17)

Corpus Juris: Being a Complete and Systematic Statement of the Whole Body of the Law as Embodied in and Developed by All Reported Decisions. V. 17/edited by William Mack and William Benjamin Hale. —New York: The American Law Book Co. , c1919.

ix, 1379 p. ;26 cm.

D971. 2/M153(18)

Corpus Juris: Being a Complete and Systematic Statement of the Whole Body of the Law as Embodied in and Developed by All Reported Decisions. V. XVIII/edited by William Mack and William Benjamin Hale. —New York: The American Law Book Co. , c1919

xxiv, 1408 p. ;26 cm.

D971. 2/M153(21)

Corpus Juris: Being a Complete and Systematic Statement of the Whole Body of the Law as Embodied in and Developed by All Reported Decisions. V. XXI/edited by William Mack and Wil-

liam Benjamin Hale. —New York: The American Law Book Co. , c1920
xvi, 1263 p. ;26 cm.

D971. 2/M153(22)
Corpus Juris Being A Complete and Systematic Statement of the Whole Body of The Law As Embodied in And Developed By All Reported Decisions. Volume XXII/William Mack, William Benjamin Hale. —New York: The American Law Book Co. , c1920
1294 p. ;27 cm.

D971. 2/M153(25)
Corpus Juris: Being a Complete and Systematic Statement of the Whole Body of the Law as Embodied in and Developed by All Reported Decisions. V. XXV/edited by William Mack and William Benjamin Hale. —New York: The American Law Book Co. , c1921
xix, 1217 p. ;26 cm.

D971. 2/M153(26)
Corpus Juris: Being a Complete and Systematic Statement of the Whole Body of the Law as Embodied in and Developed by All Reported Decisions. V. 23/edited by William Mack and William Benjamin Hale. —New York: The American Law Book Co. , c1926.
xxii, 1206 p. ;26 cm.

D971. 2/M153(27)
Corpus Juris: Being a Complete and Systematic Statement of the Whole Body of the Law as Embodied in and Developed by All Reported Decisions. V. XXVII/edited by William Mack and William Benjamin Hale. —New York: The American Law Book Co. , c1922
xvi, 1108 p. ;26 cm.

D971. 2/M153(28)
Corpus Juris: Being a Complete and Systematic Statement of the Whole Body of the Law as Embodied in and Developed by All Reported Decisions. V. 28/edited by William Mack and William Benjamin Hale. —New York: The American Law Book Co. , c1922
xvii, 1322 p. ;26 cm.

D971. 2/M153(29)
Corpus Juris: Being a Complete and Systematic Statement of the Whole Body of the Law as Embodied in and Developed by All Reported Decisions. V. XXIX/edited by William Mack and William Benjamin Hale. —New York: The American Law Book Co. , c1922
xvii, 1165 p. ;26 cm.

D971. 2/M153(30)
Corpus Juris: Being a Complete and Systematic Statement of the Whole Body of the Law as Embodied in and Developed by All Reported Decisions. V. XXX/edited by William Mack and William Benjamin Hale. —New York: The American Law Book Co. , c1923.
xii, 1167 p. ;26 cm.

D971. 2/M153(31)
Corpus Juris: Being a Complete and Systematic Statement of the Whole Body of the Law as Embodied in and Developed by All Reported Decisions. V. 31/edited by William Mack and William Benjamin Hale. —New York: The American Law Book Co. , c1923
x, 1200 p. ;26 cm.

D971. 2/M153(32)
Corpus Juris: Being a Complete and Systematic Statement of the Whole Body of the Law as Embodied in and Developed by All Reported Decisions. V. 32/edited by William Mack and William Benjamin Hale. —New York: The American Law Book Co. , c1923.
xviii, 1358 p. ;26 cm.

D971. 2/M153(33)

Corpus Juris: Being a Complete and Systematic Statement of the Whole Body of the Law as Embodied in and Developed by All Reported Decisions. V. 33/edited by William Mack and William Benjamin Hale. —New York: The American Law Book Co., c1930.

xx, 1215 p. ;26 cm.

D971. 2/M153(35)

Corpus Juris: Being a Complete and Systematic Statement of the Whole Body of the Law as Embodied in and Developed by All Reported Decisions. V. 35/edited by William Mack and William Benjamin Hale. —New York: The American Law Book Co., c1924.

xix, 1255 p. ;26 cm.

D971. 2/M153(36)

Corpus Juris: Being a Complete and Systematic Statement of the Whole Body of the Law as Embodied in and Developed by All Reported Decisions. V. 36/edited by William Mack and William Benjamin Hale. —New York: The American Law Book Co., c1924

xxii, 1289 p. ;26 cm.

D971. 2/M153(38)

Corpus Juris: Being a Complete and Systematic Statement of the Whole Body of the Law as Embodied in and Developed by All Reported Decisions. V. 38/edited by William Mack and William Benjamin Hale. —New York: The American Law Book Co., c1925

xxiii, 1385 p. ;26 cm.

D971. 2/M153(39)

Corpus Juris: Being a Complete and Systematic Statement of the Whole Body of the Law as Embodied in and Developed by All Reported Decisions. V. 39/edited by William Mack and William Benjamin Hale. —New York: The American Law Book Co., c1925

xii, 1397 p. ;26 cm.

D971. 2/M153(40)

Corpus Juris: Being a Complete and Systematic Statement of the Whole Body of the Law as Embodied in and Developed by All Reported Decisions. V. XL/edited by William Mack and William Benjamin Hale. —New York: The American Law Book Co., c1926

xx, 1497 p. ;26 cm.

D971. 2/M153(42)

Corpus Juris: Being a Complete and Systematic Statement of the Whole Body of the Law as Embodied in and Developed by All Reported Decisions. Vol. XLII/William Mack, Donald J. Kiser. —New York: The American Law Book Co., c1927

xviii, 1416 p. ;26 cm.

D971. 2/M153(43)

Corpus Juris: Being a Complete and Systematic Statement of the Whole Body of the Law as Embodied in and Developed by All Reported Decisions. V. 43/edited by William Mack and William Benjamin Hale. —New York: The American Law Book Co., c1927

1352 p. ;26 cm.

D971. 2/M153(46)

Corpus Juris: Being a Complete and Systematic Statement of the Whole Body of the Law as Embodied in and Developed by All Reported Decisions. Vol. XLVI/William Mack, Donald J. Kiser. —New York: The American Law Book Co., c1928

xxix, 1388 p. ;26 cm.

D971. 2/M153(47)

Corpus Juris: Being a Complete and Systematic Statement of the Whole Body of the Law as Embodied in and Developed by All Reported Decisions. V. 47/edited by William Mack and William

Benjamin Hale. —New York：The American Law Book Co.，c1929.

vi，1376 p.；26 cm.

D971.2/M153(48)

Corpus Juris：Being a Complete and Systematic Statement of the Whole Body of the Law as Embodied in and Developed by All Reported Decisions. V. 48/edited by William Mack and William Benjamin Hale. —New York：The American Law Book Co.，c1929

ix，1229 p.；26 cm.

D971.2/M153(49)

Corpus Juris：Being a Complete and Systematic Statement of the Whole Body of the Law as Embodied in and Developed by All Reported Decisions. Vol. XLIX/William Mack，Donald J. Kiser. —New York：The American Law Book Co.，c1930

x，1350 p.；26 cm.

D971.2/M153(51)

Corpus Juris：Being a Complete and Systematic Statement of the Whole Body of the Law as Embodied in and Developed by All Reported Decisions. V. 51/edited by William Mack and William Benjamin Hale. —New York：The American Law Book Co.，c1930.

xii，1255 p.；26 cm.

D971.2/M153(52)

Corpus Juris：Being a Complete and Systematic Statement of the Whole Body of the Law as Embodied in and Developed by All Reported Decisions. V. 52/edited by William Mack and William Benjamin Hale. —New York：The American Law Book Co.，c1931.

lxxxii，1193 p.；26 cm.

D971.2/M153(53)

Corpus Juris：Being a Complete and Systematic Statement of the Whole Body of the Law as Embodied in and Developed by All Reported Decisions. V. 53/edited by William Mack and William Benjamin Hale. —New York：The American Law Book Co.，c1933.

xxxii，1294 p.；26 cm.

D971.2/M153(54)

Corpus Juris：Being a Complete and Systematic Statement of the Whole Body of the Law as Embodied in and Developed by All Reported Decisions. V. 54/edited by William Mack and William Benjamin Hale. —New York：The American Law Book Co.，c1931.

xxxii，1125 p.；26 cm.

D971.2/M153(55)

Corpus Juris：Being a Complete and Systematic Statement of the Whole Body of the Law as Embodied in and Developed by All Reported Decisions. V. LV/edited by William Mack and William Benjamin Hale. —New York：The American Law Book Co.，c1931

xxviii，1347 p.；26 cm.

D971.2/M153(56)

Corpus Juris：Being a Complete and Systematic Statement of the Whole Body of the Law as Embodied in and Developed by All Reported Decisions. V. 56/edited by William Mack and William Benjamin Hale. —New York：The American Law Book Co.，c1932.

xxxii，1287 p.；26 cm.

D971.2/M153(57)

Corpus Juris：Being a Complete and Systematic Statement of the Whole Body of the Law as Embodied in and Developed by All Reported Decisions. V. 57/edited by William Mack and William Benjamin Hale. —New York：The American Law Book Co.，c1932.

xxxii，1157 p.；26 cm.

D971.2/M153(60)

Corpus Juris: Being a Complete and Systematic Statement of the Whole Body of the Law as Embodied in and Developed by All Reported Decisions. Vol. LX/William Mack, Donald J. Kiser. —New York: The American Law Book Co., c1932

xxxi, 1216 p.; 26 cm.

D971.2/M153(61)

Corpus Juris: Being a Complete and Systematic Statement of the Whole Body of the Law as Embodied in and Developed by All Reported Decisions. V. 61/edited by William Mack and William Benjamin Hale. —New York: The American Law Book Co., c1933.

xxx, 1753 p.; 26 cm.

D971.2/M153(62)

Corpus Juris: Being a Complete and Systematic Statement of the Whole Body of the Law as Embodied in and Developed by All Reported Decisions. V. LXII/edited by William Mack and William Benjamin Hale. —New York: The American Law Book Co., c1933

xxxii, 1164 p.; 26 cm.

D971.2/M153(63)

Corpus Juris: Being a Complete and Systematic Statement of the Whole Body of the Law as Embodied in and Developed by All Reported Decisions. V. 63/edited by William Mack and William Benjamin Hale. —New York: The American Law Book Co., c1933.

xxx, 1211 p.; 26 cm.

D971.2/M153(64)

Corpus Juris: Being a Complete and Systematic Statement of the Whole Body of the Law as Embodied in and Developed by All Reported Decisions. V. 64/edited by William Mack and William Benjamin Hale. —New York: The American Law Book Co., c1933.

xxxii, 1315 p.; 26 cm.

D971.2/M153(66)

Corpus Juris: Being a Complete and Systematic Statement of the Whole Body of the Law as Embodied in and Developed by All Reported Decisions. V. 66/edited by William Mack and William Benjamin Hale. —New York: The American Law Book Co., c1934.

xxxii, 1603 p.; 26 cm.

D971.2/M153(67)

Corpus Juris: Being a Complete and Systematic Statement of the Whole Body of the Law as Embodied in and Developed by All Reported Decisions. V. 67/edited by William Mack and William Benjamin Hale. —New York: The American Law Book Co., c1934.

xxxii, 1466 p.; 26 cm.

D971.2/M153(68)

Corpus Juris: Being a Complete and Systematic Statement of the Whole Body of the Law as Embodied in and Developed by All Reported Decisions. V. 68/edited by William Mack and William Benjamin Hale. —New York: The American Law Book Co., c1934.

xxxii, 1349 p.; 26 cm.

D971.2/M153(69)

Corpus Juris: Being a Complete and Systematic Statement of the Whole Body of the Law as Embodied in and Developed by All Reported Decisions. Volume LXIX/William Mack, William Benjamin Hale. —New York: The American Law Book Co., c1934

xxxi, 1322 p.; 27 cm.

D971.2/M153(70)

Corpus Juris: Being a Complete and Systematic Statement of the Whole Body of the Law as Embodied in and Developed by All Reported Decisions. V. 70/edited by William Mack and William

Benjamin Hale. —New York: The American Law Book Co. , c1935.
xxvi, 1194 p. ;26 cm.

D971. 2/M153(71)
Corpus Juris: Being a Complete and Systematic Statement of the Whole Body of the Law as Embodied in and Developed by All Reported Decisions. V. 71/edited by William Mack and William Benjamin Hale. —New York: The American Law Book Co. , c1937.
xxii, 1654 p. ;26 cm.

D971. 2/M153(72)
Corpus Juris: Being a Complete and Systematic Statement of the Whole Body of the Law as Embodied in and Developed by All Reported Decisions. V. 72/edited by William Mack and William Benjamin Hale. —New York: The American Law Book Co. , c1937.
xxxii, 3639 p. ;26 cm.

D971. 2/M153(1938)
Corpus Juris: 1938 Annotations Internal Revenue-Workmen's Compensation/William Mack. —New York: The American Law Book Company, c1938
1633 p. ;26 cm.

D971. 2/M153(14A)
Corpus Juris: Being a Complete and Systematic Statement of the Whole Body of the Law as Embodied in and Developed by All Reported Decisions. V. 14A/edited by William Mack and William Benjamin Hale. —New York: The American Law Book Co. , c1921
xxv, 1434 p. ;26 cm.

D971. 2/U58(5)
United States Code: 1946 Edition. Volume Five/United States Government Printing Office. —Washington: United States Government Printing Office, c1948
xix, 6294-8043 p. ;27 cm.

D971. 2/U58(1929. 4)
The Code of the District of Columbia (To March 4, 1929)/United States Government Printing Office. — Washington: United States Government Printing Office, c1930
xvi, 807 p. ;28 cm.

D971. 2/U58(1946. 1)
United States Code: 1946 Edition: Containing the General and Permanent Laws of the United States, in force on January 2, 1947. volume one/ United States Government Printing Office. — Washington: United States Government Printing Office, c1947
xlvii, 1127 p. ;27 cm.

D971. 2/U58(1946. 5)
United States Code: 1946 Edition. Supplement V/United States Government Printing Office. — Washington: United States Government Printing Office, c1948
1 v p. ;27 cm.

D971. 2/U58
United States Code: 1946 Edition. Supplement I/United States Government Printing Office. — Washington: United States Government Printing Office, c1948
198-1919 p. ;27 cm.

D971. 2/W317
Navigation Laws of the United States/Washington Government Printing Office. —Washington: Washington Government Printing Office, c1915
585 p. ;23 cm.

D971. 2/W553(3)
A Digest of the International Law of the United States.. Vol. 3/edited by F. Wharton. — Washington: Government Printing Office, 1886.

837 p. ;23 cm.

D971. 2-61/M153(19)

Cyclopedia of Law and Procedure. Vol. XIX/ William Mack, LL. D..—New York.—Popular ed. : The American Law Book Company, [etc.], c1912.

1464 p. ;26 cm.

D971. 2-61/M153(20)

Cyclopedia of Law and Procedure. Vol. XX/ William Mack, LL. D..—Popular ed.—New York: The American Law Book Company, [etc.], c1906

1494 p. ;25 cm.

D971. 2-61/M153(21)

Cyclopedia of Law and Procedure. Vol. XXI/ William Mack.—New York: The American Law Book Company, c1906

1743 p. ;27 cm.

D971. 2-61/M153(23)

Cyclopedia of Law and Procedure. Vol. XXIII/ William Mack, LL. D..—Popular ed.—New York: The American Law Book Company, [etc.], c1906

1623 p. ;25 cm.

D971. 2-61/M153(26)

Cyclopedia of Law and Procedure. Vol. XXVI/ William Mack, LL. D..—Popular ed.—New York: The American Law Book Company, [etc.], c1907

1611 p. ;25 cm.

D971. 2-61/M153(29)

Cyclopedia of Law and Procedure. Vol. XXIX/ William Mack, LL. D..—Popular ed.—New York: The American Law Book Company, [etc.], c1908

1696 p. ;25 cm.

D971. 2-61/M153(30)

Cyclopedia of Law and Procedure. Vol. XXX/ William Mack, LL. D..—Popular ed..—New York: The American Law Book Company, [etc.], 1908

1644 p. ;25 cm.

D971. 2-61/M153(34)

Cyclopedia of Law and Procedure. Vol. XXXIV/William Mack, LL. D..—Popular ed..—New York: The American Law Book Company, [etc.], 1910.

1829 p. ;25 cm.

D971. 2-61/M153(36)

Cyclopedia of Law and Procedure. Vol. XXXVI/William Mack, LL. D..—Popular ed..—Popular ed. : The American Law Book Company, [etc.], c1910

1651 p. ;25 cm.

D971. 2-61/M153(37)

Cyclopedia of Law and Procedure. Vol. XXXVII/William Mack, LL. D..—Popular ed..—New York: The American Law Book Company, [etc.], 1911.

336-1799 p. ;26 cm.

D971. 2-61/M153(38)

Cyclopedia of Law and Procedure. Vol. XXXVIII/William Mack, LL. D..—Popular ed..—New York: The American Law Book Company, [etc.], 1911.

2117 p. ;26 cm.

D971. 2-61/M153(39)

Cyclopedia of Law and Procedure. Vol. XXXIX/William Mack, LL. D..—Popular ed..—New York: The American Law Book Company, [etc.], c1912.

2123 p. ;26 cm.

D971.2-62/L415

The Lawyers Directory. 1936: Summary of Contents/The Lawyers Directory, Inc. ,—Cincinnati: The Lawyers Directory, Inc. , c1936

736 p. ;25 cm.

D971.2-62/S531

The Lawyers Directory. 1932/Sharp & Alleman Co. ,—Philadelphia: Sharp & Alleman Co. , c1932

2398 p. ;23 cm.

D971.205/B366(1)

A Selection of Cases on The Conflict of Laws. Vol. 1, Jurisdiction: Remedies/Joseph Henry Beale. —Cambridge: The Harvard Law Review Publishing Association, c1900

xviii, 496 p. ;25 cm.

D971.205/B366(3)

A Selection of Cases on The Conflict of Laws. Vol. III, The Recognition and Enforcement of Rights with a Summary of the Conflict of Laws/Joseph Henry Beale. —Cambridge: The Harvard Law Review Publishing Association, c1902

xviii, 548 p. ;25 cm.

D971.209/L869

Cases of the Conflict of Laws: Selected From Decisions of English and American Courts: American Casebook Series/Ernest G. Lorenzen. —St. Paul: West Publishing Company, c1909

xxi, 784 p. ;26 cm.

D971.21/B393

The Constitution of The United States 1787-1927/James M. Beck. —New York: George H. Doran, c1927

ix, 207 p. ;19 cm.

D971.21/T747

Our Constitution: Why and How It Was Made-Who Made It, and What It Is/Edward Waterman Townsend. —New York: Moffat, Yard & Company, c1906

322 p. ;21 cm.

D971.21/W842-2(1)

A Treatise on the American Law of Administration. Vol. I. /J. G. Woerner. —2nd ed. —Boston: Little, Brown, and Company, c1899

clxxii, 643 p. ;24 cm.

D971.21-53/H217(2)

The Federalist: A Commentary on the Constitution of the United States. Vol. II, English Constitution Bagehot/Alexander Hamilton, James Madison, John Jay. —New York, London: M. Walter Dunne, c1901

xii, 225 p. ;23 cm.

D971.21-53/H271(1)

The Federalist: A Commentary on the Constitution of the United States. Vol. I, Being a Collection of Essays/Alexander Hamilton, James Madison, John Jay. —New York, London: M. Walter Dunne, c1901

xxiv, 427 p. ;23 cm.

D971.215/E37(1920)

Federal Statutes Annotated. Supplement, 1920: Containing all the Laws of the United States of a General, Permanent and General Nature Enacted by the Sixty-sixth and Sixty-seventh Congresses between January 1, 1920 and Dec. 21, 1921 with Supplemental Notes Continuing the Annotation in the Prior Volumes/Harold N. Eldridge. —New York: Edward Thompson Company, c1921

xxiii, 1000 p. ;25 cm.

D971.215/E37(1923)

Federal Statutes Annotated. Supplement, 1923: Containing all the Laws of the United States of a General, Permanent and General Nature Enacted by the Sixty-sixth and Sixty-seventh Congresses between Dec. 31, 1922 and Dec. 31, 1923 with Supplemental Notes Continuing the Annotation in the Prior Volumes/Harold N. Eldridge. —New York: Edward Thompson Company, c1924

xxiii, 1040 p. ;25 cm.

D971.215/E37-2(1921)

Federal Statutes Annotated. Supplement, 1921: Containing all the Laws of the United States of a General, Permanent and General Nature Enacted by the Sixty-sixth and Sixty-seventh Congresses between Dec. 19, 1920 and Dec. 31, 1921 with Supplemental Notes Continuing the Annotation in the Prior Volumes/Harold N. Eldridge. —2nd ed.. —New York: Edward Thompson Company, c1922

xxi, 990 p. ;25 cm.

D971.215/K51-2(3)

Federal Statutes Annotated: Containing all the Laws of the United States of a General, Permanent and Public Nature in Force on the First Day of January, 1916. Vol. III, Dairy Products to Internal Revenue/William M. Mckinney. —2nd ed.. —New York: Edward Thompson Company, c1917

1090 p. ;25 cm.

D971.215/K51-2(4)

Federal Statutes Annotated: Containing all the Laws of the United States of a General, Permanent and Public Nature in Force on the First Day of January, 1916. Vol. IV, Internal Revenue (Continued) to Judiciary/William M. Mckinney. —2nd ed.. —New York: Edward Thompson Company, c1917

1081 p. ;25 cm.

D971.215/K51-2(6)

Federal Statutes Annotated: Containing all the Laws of the United States of a General, Permanent and Public Nature in Force on the First Day of January, 1916. Vol. VI, Judiciary(Concluded) to Passports/William M. Mckinney. —2nd ed. —New York: Edward Thompson Company, c1918

1286 p. ;25 cm.

D971.215/McK51-2(1)

Federal Statutes Annotated: Containing all the Laws of the United States of a General, Permanent and Public Nature in Force on the First Day of January, 1916. Vol. I, Dairy Products to Internal Revenue/William M. Mckinney. —2nd ed.. —New York: Edward Thompson Company, c1916

1240 p. ;25 cm.

D971.215/McK51-2(2)

Federal Statutes Annotated: Containing all the Laws of the United States of a General, Permanent and Public Nature in Force on the First Day of January, 1916. Vol. II, Dairy Products to Internal Revenue/William M. Mckinney. —2nd ed.. —New York: Edward Thompson Company, c1917

1217 p. ;25 cm.

D971.215/McK51-2(5)

Federal Statutes Annotated: Containing all the Laws of the United States of a General, Permanent and Public Nature in Force on the First Day of January, 1916. Vol. V, Dairy Products to Internal Revenue/William M. Mckinney. —2nd ed.. —New York: Edward Thompson Company, c1917

1245 p. ;25 cm.

D971.225/C734

Principles of Labor Legislation/John R. Commons and John B. Andrews; prepared in Co-operation with the American bureau of industrial research. —New York: Harper & Brothers, [1916]

524 p. ;21 cm.

D971. 23/W843

A Treatise on the American Law of Guardianship of Minors and Persons of Unsound Mind/J. C. Woerner. —Boston: Little, Brown, and Company, c1897

lvi, 581 p. ;24 cm.

D971. 239. 9/B167

Business Law/A. E. Baker. —Chicago: Metropolitan Text Book Co. , c1919

249 p. ;22 cm.

D971. 239. 9-62/G487-2

Manual of Commercial Law/Stephen W. Gilman, J. B. Geijsbeek. —2nd ed.. —[Tokyo]: The Bobbs-Merrill Company, c1913

xiv, 736 p. ;23 cm.

D971. 239. 9-62/S745

A Manual of Commercial Law/Edward W. Spencer. —Indianapolis: Press of Charles E. Hollenbeck, c1898

xiii, 639, 47 p. ;21 cm.

D971. 24/B857

Cyclopedia of Criminal Law/Hascal R. Brill. —Chicago: Callaghan and Company, c1922

xxiv, 1003 p. ;26 cm.

D971. 24/W553-9(1)

A Treatise on Criminal Law. Volume I/Francis Wharton. —9th ed. —Philadelphia: Kay & Brother, c1885

xi, 860 p. ;24 cm.

D971. 26/G568

The Promoter of Justice: His Rights and Duties/John Carroll Glynn. —Washington D. C. : The Catholic University of America, c1936

xx, 337 p. ;24 cm.

D971. 263/L766

American Inquisitors: A Commentary on Dayton and Chicago/Walter Lippmann. —New York: The Macmillan Company, c1928

viii, 120 p. ;20 cm.

D971. 265/L415

The Lawyers Directory 1948/The Lawyers Directory, Inc. ,—Cicinnati: The Lawyers Directory, Inc. , c1948

682 p. ;25 cm.

D971. 265-62/M384(1)

Martindale-Hubbell Law Directory. Volume II/Martindale-Hubbell, Inc. ,—Summit: Martindale-Hubbell, Inc. , c1947

1 v. ;25 cm.

D971. 265-62/M384(2)

Martindale-Hubbell Law Directory. Volume II/Martindale-Hubbell, Inc. ,—Summit: Martindale-Hubbell, Inc. , c1947

1 v. ;25 cm.

D971. 265-62/M384(3)

Martindale-Hubbell Law Directory. Volume III/Martindale-Hubbell, Inc. ,—Summit: Martindale-Hubbell, Inc. , c1947

1 v. ;25 cm.

D971. 27/P785

Pomeroy's Equity Jurisprudence and Equitable Remedies(Six Volumes); Pomeroy's Equity Jurisprudence(In Four Volumes); A Treatise on Equitable Remedies (In Two Volumes)/John Norton Pomeroy. —San Francisco: Bancroft-Whitney Company, c1905

lviii, 519 p. ;23 cm.

D971. 27/P785-3(3)

Pomeroy's Equity Jurisprudence and Equitable Remedies(Six Volumes)Pomeroy's Equity Jurisprudence(In Four Volumes)A Treatise on Equitable Remedies (In Two Volumes)/John Norton Pomeroy. —3rd ed. San Francisco: Bancroft-Whitney Company, c1905

xv, 975-1314 p. ;23 cm.

D9712.1/C647

Our Constitution: Its Story, Its Meaning, Its Use/A. J. Cloud. —Chicago: Scott, Foresman and Company, c1923

224 p. ;19 cm.

D975.614/F855

The Famous Cases of Dr. Thorndyke/R. Austin Freeman. —London: Hodder & Stoughton, [?]

viii, 1080 p. ;19 cm.

D99/B853

The Law of Nations: An Introduction to the International Law of Peace/J. L. Brierly. —Oxford: The Clarendon Press, c1928

viii, 228 p. ;19 cm.

D99/H181-5

A Treatise on International Law/by William Edward Hall; edited by A. Pearce Higgins. —5th ed.. —Oxford: The Clarendon Press, c1904

xxiv, 764, 8 p. ;22 cm.

D99/L419-8

A Handbook of Public International Law/by T. J. Lawrence. —8th ed.. —London: Macmillan and Co., Ltd., 1912.

xiv, 189 p. ;18 cm.

D99/M645

The End of Exterritoriality in China/Thomas F. Millard. —Shanghai: The A. B. C. Press, c1931

278 p. ;20 cm.

D99/M821(1)

A Digest of International Law. Vol. I/John Bassett Moore. —Washington: Government Printing Office, c1906

lxxix, 939 p. ;24 cm.

D99/M821(2)

A Digest of International Law: As Embodied in Diplomatic Discussions, Treaties and Other International Agreements, International Awards, the Decisions of Municipal Courts, and the Writings of Jurists... Vol. 2/by John Bassett Moore. —Washington: Government Printing Office, c1906

viii, 1123 p. ;24 cm.

D99/M821(3)

A Digest of International Law. Vol. III/by John Bassett Moore. —Washington: Government Printing Office, c1906.

vii, 1022 p. ;24 cm.

D99/M821(4)

A Digest of International Law. Vol. IV/John Bassett Moore. —Washington: Government Printing Office, c1906

vii, 806 p. ;21 cm.

D99/M821(5)

A Digest of International Law: As Embodied in Diplomatic Discussions, Treaties and Other International Agreements, International Awards, the Decisions of Municipal Courts, and the Writings of Jurists... Vol. 5/by John Bassett Moore.. —Washington: Government Printing Office, c1906

870 p. ;24 cm.

D99/M821(7)

A Digest of International Law. Vol. VII/John Bassett Moore. —Washington: Government Printing Office, c1906

x, 1109 p. ;24 cm.

D99/M821(8)

A Digest of International Law. Vol. VIII/John Bassett Moore. —Washington: Government Printing Office, c1906

iv, 458 p. ;24 cm.

D99/W916

Introduction to the Study of International Law: An Aid in Teaching, and in Historical Studies/Theodore D. Woolsey. —5th ed. —New York: Charles Scribner's Sons, c1879

xvii, 526 p. ;21 cm.

D99-62/W746

Handbook of International Law/George Grafton Wilson. —St. Paul, Minn. : West Publishing Company, c1910

xxi, 623 p. ;23 cm.

D990/L419

The Principles of International Law/T. J. Lawrence. —Boston: D. C. Heath & Co. , Publishers, c1895

xxi, 745 p. ;21 cm.

D993. 7/S893

Consular Cases and Opinions/Ellery C. Stowell. —Washington, D. C. : John Byrne & Co. , c1909

xxxvi, 811 p. ;24 cm.

D993. 8/P688(4)

Treaties, Conventions, International Acts, Protocols, and Agreements Between the United States of America and Other Powers. Vol. 4/Government Printings Office. —Washington: Government Printings Office, c1938

B-15, 3919-5755 P. ;24 cm.

D994/W577(1)

Damages in International Law. Vol. I/Marjorie M. Whiteman. —Washington: United States Government Printing Office, c1937

viii, 826 p. ;25 cm.

D994/W577(2)

Damages in International Law. Vol. II/Marjorie M. Whiteman. —Washington: United States Government Printing Office, c1937

iv, 829-1549 p. ;25 cm.

D995/O69

The Rights of War and Peace: Including the Law of Nature and of Nations/translated from the original Latin of Grotius, with notes and ill. from political and legal writers, by A. C. Campbell; with an Introd. by David J. Hill. . —Hyperion reprint ed. . —Washington: M. Walter Dunne, c1901.

x, 423 p. ;24 cm.

D995/S647

International Law: As Interpreted During the Russo-Japanese War/F. E. Smith, N. W. Sibley. —Boston: The Boston Book Co. , c1905

xi, 494 p. ;26 cm.

D995/T136

Cases on International Law During the Chino-Japanese War/Sakuye Takahashi. —Cambridge: The University Press, c1899

xxviii, 219 p. ;23 cm.

D997. 5/L796(1)

Extraterritorial Cases. Volume 1/Charles Sumner Lobingier. —Manila: Bureau of Printing, c1920

lxi, 1049 p. ;23 cm.

D997. 5/L796(2)

Extraterritorial Cases. Volume II/Charles Sumner Lobingier. —Shanghai: Chinese American Publishing Co. , c1928

lxixvi, 862 p. ;23 cm.

D998/F628

A Collection of Nationality Laws of Various Countries as Contained in Constitutions, Statutes and Treaties/Richard W. Flournoy, Manley O. Hudson. —London: Oxford University Press, c1929

xxiii, 776 p. ;25 cm.

D998. 871. 2/H119(2)

Digest of International Law. Vol. II/Green Haywood Hackworth. —Washington, D. C. : U. S. Government Printing Office, c1941

v, 829 p. ;25 cm.

军事

E-61/C923

A Dictionary of Military Terms: English-Japanese, Japanese-English/H. T. Creswell. —American ed. . —American ed. —Chicago: The University of Chicago Press, c1942

1226, 175 p. ;16 cm.

E0/W132-5

Organization and Tactics/Arthur L. Wagner. —5th ed. . —Kansas City: Hudson-Kimberly Republishing Co. , c1894

xxi, 551 p. ;22 cm.

E073/H241

A Student in Arms/Donald Hankey. —London: Andrew Melrose, Ltd. , c1917

302 p. ;19 cm.

E112. 44/McC988R763

Romeo in Moon Village/George Barr Mccutcheon. —New York: Dodd, Mead and Company, c1924

344 p. ;20 cm.

E153/S844(O)

A History of Sea Power/William Oliver Stevens, Allan Westcott. —New York: Doubleday, Doran & Company, Inc. , c1941

434 p. ;22 cm.

E153/S844

A History of Sea Power/William Oliver Stevens, Allan Westcott. —New York: Doubleday, Doran & Company, Inc. , c1942

467 p. ;22 cm.

E19/J65

From the Land of Silent People/Robert St. John. —New York: Halcyon House, c1942

353 p. ;22 cm.

E19/T161

When Japan Comes to War/O. Tanin, E. Yohan. —London: Lawrence & Wishart, [?]

271 p. ;21 cm.

E195. 2/G878

The Years of War (1942-1945)/V. Grossman. —Moscow: Foreign Languages Publ. House, c1946.

451 p. ;22 cm.

E291/L439

The Arrow War with China/Charles S. Leavenworth. —London: Sampson Low, Marston & Company Ltd. , c1901

xiv, 232 p. ;19 cm.

E516/S314

Germany's High Sea Fleet in the World War/Admiral Scheer. —New York: Peter Smith, c1934

xiv, 375 p. ;22 cm.

E516. 51/B527

Cavalry: A Popular Edition of "Cavalry in War and Peace"/Bernhardi. —New York: George H. Doran, c1914

238 p. ;19 cm.

E561. 45/L933V489

Verena in the Midst: A Kind of a Story/E. V. Lucas. —London: Methued & Co. , Ltd. , c1920

x, 251, 8 p. ;19 cm.

E561. 5/V858

The British Army from Within/E. Charles Vivian. —New York: George H. Doran Company, c1914

176 p. ;19 cm.

E712/W238

The Airman's Almanac/Francis Walton. —New York: Farrar & Rinehart, Inc. , c1945

511 p. ;21 cm.

E712. 3/U58(1911)

Infantry Drill Regulations. 1911/United States Army. —Washington: Government Printing Office, c1911

221 p. ;15 cm.

E712. 44/K41-2

Organization, Powers, and Duties of Health Authorities: An Analysis of the Laws and Regulations Relating Thereto in Force in the United States/J. W. Kerr, A. A. Moll. —2nd ed. —Washington: Government Printing Office, c1912

452 p. ;23 cm.

E712. 5/U58

Unarmed Defense for the American soldier/United States Government Printing Office. —Washington: United States Government Printing Office, c1942

315 p. ;18 cm.

E712. 53/A358

Makers of Naval Tradition/Carroll Storrs Alden. —San Francisco: Ginn and Company, c1942

xiv, 378 p. ;20 cm.

E712. 53-62/U58-13

The Bluejackets' Manual/United States Naval Institute. —13th ed. —Annapolis: United States Naval Institute, c1946

vii, 622 p. ;19 cm.

E712. 54/DeS498

Victory Through Air Power/Alexander P. De Seversky. —New York: Simon and Schuster, c1942

xiv, 354 p. ;21 cm.

E8/H867

40 O. B. or How the War was Won/Hugh Cleland Hoy. —London: Hutchinson & Co. , (Publishers) Ltd. , c1932

287 p. ;22 cm.

E8/S582

The Invisible Weapons/J. C. Silber. —London: Hutchinson & Co. , c1932

288 p. ;22 mc

E914-64/U58(D)

Astronomical Navigation Tables: Latitudes 15°-19° North and South. Volume. D/United States Navy Department. —Washington: United States Government, c1941

231 p. ;25 cm.

E914-64/U58(K)

Astronomical Navigation Tables: Latitudes 45°-49° North and South. Volume. K/United States Navy Department. —Washington: United States Government, c1941

231 p. ;25 cm.

E914-64/U58(L)

Astronomical Navigation Tables: Latitudes 50°-54° North and South. Volume. L/United States Navy Department. —Washington: United States Government, c1941

231 p. ;25 cm.

E925. 64/D618

Firedrake: The Destroyer That Wouldn't Give up/A. D. Divine. —New York: E. P. Dutton & o. , Inc. , c1943

250 p. ;21 cm.

E925-43/H564

Range and Ballistic Tables, 1935/Ernest E. Herrmann. —[S. l. : s. n.], [?]

v, 124 p. ;28 cm.

E95/F452-2

A Text-Book Field Fortification/G. J. Fiebeger. —2nd ed. Revised. —New York: John Wiley & Sons, c1909

xiii, 174 p. ;21 cm.

E965/C843

Pigeon Heroes: Birds of War and Messengers of Peace/Marion B. Cothren. —New York: Coward-Mccann Inc. , c1944

47 p. ;23 cm.

E965/D389

Animal Reveille/Richard Dempewolff. —New York: Doubleday, Doran & Company, Inc. , c1943

xiii, 272 p. ;22 cm.

F 经济

F-29/T877

The Tsingtao Hong List: 1935/青岛泰晤士报. —Tsingtao: The Tsingtao Times Publishing Co. , c1935

1 v. ;21 cm.

F-61/S619

Business Terms, Phrases and Abbreviations With Equivalents in Franch, German, Spanish, and Italian and Facsimile Documents/Sir Isaac Pitman & Sons, Ltd. ,—London: Sir Isaac Pitman & Sons, Ltd. , [?]

vi, 231, 32 p. ;19 cm.

F-61/S619-4

Business Terms, Phrases and Abbreviations With Equivalents in Franch, German, Spanish, and Italian and Facsimile Documents/Sir Isaac Pitman & Sons, Ltd. ,—4th ed. . —London: Sir Isaac Pitman & Sons, Ltd. , [?]

vi, 273, 14 p. ;18 cm.

F0/B752(1)

Principles of Economics. vol. I/O. Fred Boucke. —New York: The Macmillan Company, c1925

xii, 560 p. ;22 cm.

F0/B752(2)

Principles of Economics. vol. II/O. Fred Boucke. —New York: The Macmillan Company, c1925

x, 520 p. ;22 cm.

F0/B877

The Economics of the Recovery Program/ Douglass V. Brown, Edward Chamberlin, Seymour E. Harris. —New York: Whittlesey House, c1934

xii, 188 p. ;19 cm.

F0/B938

Introduction to the Study of Economics/ Charles Jesse Bullock. —New York: Silver, Burdett and Company, c1897

581 p. ;19 cm.

F0/B993

Applied Economics/Raymond T. Bye, William W. Hewett. —New York: Alfred A. Knopf, c1928

vi, 655 p. ;24 cm.

F0/C466

Outlines of Political Economy: New Edition/ Sydney Chapman. —London: Longmans, Green and Co. , c1925

xvi, 463 p. ;19 cm.

F0/C592

Readings in the Economics of War/J. Maurice Clark, Walton H. Hamilton, Harold G. Moulton. —Chicago: The University of Chicago Press, c1918

xxxi, 676 p. ;23 cm.

F0/C782

The Trend of Economics/by Morris Albert Copeland, Sumner Hubert Slichter [etc.]. . . ed, with an introduction, by Rexford Guy Tugwell. —New York: A. A. Knopf, 1924.

xi, 556 p. ;25 cm.

F0/E37

An Introduction to Political Economy/Rechard T. Ely. —New York: Hunt & Eaton, c1892

358 p. ;20 cm.

F0/E37

Elementary Principles of Economics: Together with a Short Sketch of Economic History/Richard T. Ely and George Ray Wicker. —4th. Rev. ed. . —New York: Macmillan, c1911.

388 p. ;19 cm.

F0/G348

Progress and Poverty: an Inquiry Into the Cause of Industrial Depressions, and of Increase of Want With Increase of Wealth: the Remedy/ Henry George. —New York: Doubleday, Page & Company, c1879

xviii, 568 p. ;20 cm.

F0/H185

Why the Capitalist?: A Refutation of the Doctrines Prevailing in Conventional Political Economy/Frederick Haller. —Chicago: John F. Higgins, c1914

277, xvii p. ;19 cm.

F0/J66

Economics and the Good Life/by F. Ernest Johnson. —New York: Association Press, c1934.

xii, 186 p. ;19 cm.

F0/M367-8

Principles of Economics: An Introductory Volume/Alfred Marshall. —8th ed. . —London: Macmillan and Co. , Ltd. , c1938

xxxiv, 871 p. ;22 cm.

F0/M481

An Introduction to Economic Analysis and Pol-

icy/by J. E. Meade. —London: Oxford University Press, c1936
xv, 396 p. ;20 cm.

F0/M681
A Preface to Economics/Broadus Mitchell. —New York: Henry Holt and Company, c1932
xi, 574 p. ;22 cm.

F0/S392(46)
Harvard Economic Studies: An Inquiry into Profits, Capital, Credit, Interest, and the Business Cycle. Vol. 46/Joseph A. Schumpeter. —Cambridge: Harvard University Press, c1936
1 v. ;20 cm.

F0/S438-2
Principles of Economics/Henry Rogers Seager. —2nd ed. , Revised and Enlarged. —New York: Henry Holt Company, c1913, 1917
xx, 662 p. ;21 cm.

F0/S464
Principles of Economics/Edwin R. A. Seligman. —New York: Longmans, Green and Co. , c1921
liv, 711 p. ;20 cm.

F0/S464-5
Principles of Economics/Edwin R. A. Seligman. —5th ed. —New York: Longmans, Green and Co. , c1912
liv, 711 p. ;20 cm.

F0/S587
The Ground Work of Economics: For Matriculation and Higher School Certificate Candidates/H. A. Silverman. —London: Sir Isaac Pitman & Sons, Ltd. , c1929
ix, 370, 35 p. ;19 cm.

F01/E21
Economics: Principles and Problems/Lionel D. Edie. —New York: Thomas Y. Crowell Company, c1926
xx, 799 p. ;23 cm.

F012/S783
Some Economic Factors in Modern Life/Josiah Stamp. —London: P. S. King & Son, Ltd. , c1929
vii, 279 p. ;22 cm.

F014. 5/S836-2
Principles of Business Economics/James Stephenson. —2nd ed. —London: Sir Isaac Pitman & Sons, Ltd. , c1934
xv, 853 p. ;23 cm.

F032. 2/B971
Profit Sharing, Its Principles and Practice: a Collaboration/by Arthur W. Burritt, Henry S. Dennison, Edwin F. Gay, Ralph E. Heilman, Henry P. Kendall. —New York and London: Harper & Brothers, c1918
x, 328 p. ;23 cm.

F09/H257
History of Economic Thought: A Critical Account of the Origin and Development of the Economic Theories of the Leading Thinkers in the Leading Nations/Lewis H. Haney. —New York: The Macillan Company, c1917
xvii, 567 p. ;20 cm.

F091. 3/P371
The Invariable Standard and Measure of Value/by J. Taylor Peddie. —2nd ed. —London: P. S. King & Son, 1928.
xix, 241 p. ;22 cm.

F091. 33/R488
The Principles of Political Economy & Tacation/David Ricardo. —London: J. M. Dent & Sons, Ltd. , [?]
300 p. ;18 cm.

F091. 33/S642(1)

An Inquiry Into the Nature and Causes of the Wealth of Nations/Adam Smith. —London: J. M. Dent and Sons Ltd. , c1929

xvi, 441, 4 p. ;18 cm.

F091. 33/S645(2)

An Inquiry into the Nature and Causes of the Wealth of Nations. vol. 2/Adam Smith. —London: Oxford University Press, c1904

viii, 687, 8 p. ;16 cm.

F091. 33/S645

Select Chapters and Passages from the Wealth of Nations of Adam Smith/Adam Smith. —[S. l. : s. n.], c1776

xii, 285 p. ;18 cm.

F091. 349/V394

The Theory of the Leisure Class/Thorstein Vehlen. —[S. l. : s. n.], [?]

viii, 404 p. ;19 cm.

F091. 352. 1/H417

Prices and Production/Friedrich A. Hayek. —London: George Routledge & Sons, Ltd. , 1941

xiv, 162 p. ;19 cm.

F1/C331

This Economic World and How It May Be Improved/Thomas Nixon Carver, Hugh W. Lester. —Chicago: A. W. Shaw Company, c1928

432 p. ;23 cm.

F11/C967

International Economic Policies: A Survey of the Economics of Diplomacy/William Smith Culbertson. —New York: D. Appleton-Century Company Incorporated, c1925

xviii, 575 p. ;21 cm.

F110/082(2)

Modern Business Routine: Explained and Illustrated. . Vol. 2/R. S. Osborne. —London: Effingham Wilson, c1914

x, 317, 31 p. ;22 cm.

F110/O81(1)

Modern Business Routine: Explained and Illustrated. v. 1, home trade/by R. S. Osborne. —London: Effingham Wilson, c1916

ix, 237, 31 p. ;22 cm.

F112/H734

Economic Essays/Jacob H. Hollander. —New York: The Macmillan Company, c1927

viii, 368 p. ;22 cm.

F114. 45/C743

The United States in the Orient: The Nature of the Economic Problem/Charles A. Conant. —Boston: Houghton, Mifflin and Company, c1901

x, 237 p. ;18 cm.

F115/F529

Oil Imperialism: the International Struggle for Petroleum/Louis Fischer. —New York: International, c1926

256 p. ;20 cm.

F119. 44/K44

The Economic Consequences of the Peace/John Maynard Keynes. —New York: Harcourt, Brace and Howe, c1920.

vii, 298 p. ;21 cm.

F119. 9/A425

The New Europe/Nellie B. Allen. —Boston: Ginn and Company, c1913, 1920

xii, 435 p. ;19 cm.

F119. 9/H893

The Advanced Class-book of Modern Geography: Physical-Political-Commercial/William

Hughes. —London: George Philio & Son, Ltd. , c1904

xvii, 866 p. ;19 cm.

F119. 9/S651

Industrial and Commercial Geography/J. Russell Smith. —New York: Henry Holt and Company, c1913

xi, 914 p. ;22 cm.

F119. 9/S651

Our Industrial world/J. Russell Smith. —Chicago: The John C. Winston Company, [?]

viii, 406 p. ;25 cm.

F119. 9/S785-3(1)

An Intermediate Commercial Geography. Part I, Commodities and World Trade/L. Dudley Stamp. —3rd ed. —London: Longmans, Green and Co. , c1931

xiv, 262 p. ;22 cm.

F12/C978

The Capital Question of China/Lionel Curtis. —London: Macmillan and Co. , c1932

xix, 322 p. ;22 cm.

F12. 45/R939F275

Favorites/Damon Runyon. —Tower books ed. . —Cleveland: The World Publishing Company, c1935

192 p. ;21 cm.

F127. 51/O32-2

The Shanghai Directory. 1938/The Office of the North-China Daily News & Herald, Ltd. ,—rev. ed. . —Shanghai: The Office of the North-China Daily News & Herald, Ltd. , c1938

559 p. ;26 cm.

F129/S957

The International Development of China/by Sun Yat-sen, with 16 maps in the text and a folding map at end. . —New York: G. P. Putnam's sons, c1922

xvi, 265 p. ;21 cm.

F129. 951/H376

Shanghai: City for Sale/Ernest O. Hauser. —New York: [s. n.], c1940

323 p. ;20 cm.

F15/C689

The Intelligent Man's Review of Europe Today/G. D. H. Cole, Margaret Cole. —London: Victor Gollancz Ltd. , c1933

864 p. ;18 cm.

F151. 29/M461-2(2)

An Economic: History of Russia. volume two/James Mavor. —2nd ed. —London: J. M. Dent & Sons Ltd. , c1925

xxii, 630 p. ;23 cm.

F156. 1/E46

The English Cooperatives/Sydney R. Elliott. —New Haven: Yale University Press, c1937

212 p. ;24 cm.

F156. 14/K73

The Economic Development of the British Overseas Empire/L. C. A. Knowles. —2nd ed. rev. . —London: G. Routledge and Sons, Ltd. , c1928.

xv, 555 p. ;23 cm.

F156. 19/M559-2

Outlines of the Economic History of England: A Study in Social Development/H. O. Meredith. —2nd ed. . —London: Sir Isaac Pitman & Sons, Ltd. , c1930

x, 421, 24 cm. ;22 cm.

F156. 193. 32/W329

An Economic History of England/Charlotte

M. Waters. —London: Humphrey Milford, c1925
xviii, 610 p. ;19 cm.

F171. 2/D412
America Conquers Britain: A Record of Economic War/Ludwell Denny. —New York: Alfred A. Knopf, Inc. , c1930
429, xvi p. ;25 cm.

F171. 24/G721(1912)
Reports of the Department of Commerce and Labor 1912: Report of the Secretary of Commerce and Labor and Reports of Bureaus. /Govt. Print. Off.. —Washington: Govt. Print. Off. , c1913
881 p. ;23 cm.

F224/G795
Complete Mercantile Arithmetic/H. P. Green. —[S. l. : s. n.], [?]
ix, 553 p. ;18 cm.

F23/M143
A First Year in Bookkeeping and Accounting/George A. Macfarland, Irving D. Rossheim. —New York: D. Appleton and Company, c1913
viii, 227 p. ;22 cm.

F230/H968
Principles of Accounting/by George R. Husband and Olin E. Thomas.. —[S. l. : s. n.], 1935.
X, 801 p. ;22 cm.

F230/R878-1924(1-2)
Accountancy and Business Management. Parts one and Two/Harry M. Rowe. —1924 ed. —Chicago: The H. M. Rowe Company, c1922, 1923
268 p. ;23 cm.

F231/C278
Bookkeeping and Accounting: Advenced Principles Illustrated Through a Retall Store System/P. A. Carlson[etc.]. —Washington: South-Western Publishing Company, c1943
vi, 144 p. ;21 cm.

F231. 4/C454
Modern Bookkeeping for Chinese Students/Yo-Liang Chang. —Shanghai: The Commercial Press, 1927.
201 p. ;23 cm.

F231. 4/E52
Bookkeeping for Today: Elementary Course/Fayette H. Elwell. —[S. l. : s. n.], [?]
x, 436 p. ;23 cm.

F234/R878(1927)
Rowe's Bookkeeping and Accountancy: Complete Text Presenting the Art of Bookkeeping in Accordance with the Principles of Modern Accountancy/Harry M. Rowe. —1927 ed.. —Baltmore: The H. M. Company, c1927
vi, 264 p. ;23 cm.

F240/B658
Labor Economics/Solomon Blum. —New York: Henry Holt and Company, c1925
ix, 579 p. ;22 cm.

F244/D632
Wages/Maurice Dobb; With an Introduction by J. M. Keynes.. —London: Nisbet, c1928
ix, 169 p. ;19 cm.

F249. 712/L657
Labor: Today and Tomorrow/Aaron Levenstein. —New York: Alfred A. Knopf, c1945
253, xiv p. ;21 cm.

F27/B595
The Cause of Business Depressions/Hugo Bilgram. —Philadelphia: J. B. Lippincott Company, c1914

xvii, 531 p. ;21 cm.

F27/C289

The Empire of Business/Andrew Carnegie. —London: Harper & Brothers, Publishers, c1906

345 p. ;21 cm.

F27/C487

A New Deal/Stuart Chase. —New York: The Macmillan Company, c1933

257 p. ;20 cm.

F27/R628

Organizing a Business/Maurice H. Robinson. —Chicago: La Salle Extension University, c1936.

269 p. ;22 cm.

F27/R936

Tomorrow's Business/Beardsley Ruml. —New York: Farrar & Rinehart, Inc. , c1945

238 p. ;21 cm.

F27/V394

The Theory of Business Enterprise/Thorstein Veblen. —New York: Charles Scribner's Sons, c1936

vi, 400 p. ;20 cm.

F27-62/H769(1912)

The Directory & Chronicle for China, Japan, Corea, Malay States, Siam, Netherlands India, Borneo, The Philippines, &C. for the year 1912/The Hongkong Daily Press, Ltd. —London: The Hongkong Daily Press, Ltd. , c1920

1818 p. ;23 cm.

F27-62/H769(1920)

The Directory & Chronicle for China, Japan, Corea, Malay States, Siam, Netherlands India, Borneo, The Philippines, &C. for the year 1920/The Hongkong Daily Press, Ltd. —London: The Hongkong Daily Press, Ltd. , c1920

xliii, 1596, lxxxvi p. ;23 cm.

F270/G174

Organization and Management/Lee Galloway. —New York: Alexander Hamilton Institute, c1909

xvii, 503 p. ;22 cm.

F270/H498

A Decade of Group Work/Charles E. Hendy. —New York: Association Press, c1948

xiii, 189 p. ;21 cm.

F275/L736-3

Problems in Business Finance/Edmond Earle Lincoln. —3rd ed. —Chicago: A. W. Shaw Company, c1921

li, 547 p. ;23 cm.

F276. 6/S554

Corporation Finance/Edward Sherwood Mead. —revised ed. —New York: D. Appleton and Company, c1915

xiv, 478 p. ;19 cm.

F279. 1-61/H769

The Directory & Chronicle for China, Japan, Corea, Indo-China, Straits Settlements, Malay States, Siam, Netherlands India, Borneo, The Philippines, etc. /The Hongkong Daily Press, Ltd. ,—Hongkong: The Hongkong Daily Press, Ltd. , c1921

xl, 468-1640, lxxii p. ;23 cm.

F279. 2-61/U58

The United Corporation of China Tientsin Branch/United Publishing Co. ,—Tientsin: United Publishing Co. , c[19--?]

1 v. ;28 cm.

F279. 313/M679

An Outline of the Missubishi Enterprises/the Mitsubishi Goshi Kaisha. —[S. l. : s. n.], c1926

77 p. ;23 cm.

F279. 712/C734

Reorganization of Federal Business Enterprises: A Report to Congress by the Commission on Organization of the Executive Branch of the Government, March 1949/The Commission on Organization of the Executive Branch of the Government. —Washington: U. S. Government Printing Office, c1949

129 p. ;23 cm.

F279. 712/D659

The Dollar Directory January 1948. /The Dollar Directory Co. ,—Shanghai: The Dollar Directory Co. , [19-?].

1 v. (various papings). ;26 cm.

F279. 712/O14

The New Dealers/Unofficial Observer. —New York: The Literary Guid, c1934

ix, 414 p. ;23 cm.

F279. 712. 1/S556(1)

The Small Business. Course 1, Orgnization: Based on Business Principles and Management/ Bernard A. Shilt, W. Harmon Wilson. —Washington, D. C. : South-Western Publishing Company, c1944

vii, 312 p. ;21 cm.

F3/K94

Hunger Fighters/by Paul de Kruif; illustrated by Zadig. —New York: Blue Ribbon Books, c1928.

376 p. ;23 cm.

F316/U69

Botts in War, Botts in Peace: Eathworms can Take Anything/William Hazlett Upson. —New York: Farrar & Rinchart, Inc. , c1933

327 p. ;19 cm.

F32/O32

Report of the China-United States Agricultural Mission/Office Foreign Agricultural Relations. —Washington: Office Foreign Agricultural Relations, c1947

xiv, 265 p. ;27 cm.

F321. 1/T111

Land and labour in China/R. H. Tawney. —London: George Allen & Unwin Ltd. , 1932

207 p. ;21 cm.

F371. 2/B448(2)

The Book of Rural Life: Knowledge and Inspiration: Board of Trade to Compass. II/The Bellows-Durham Company. —Chicago: The Bellows-Durham Company, c1925

609-1238 p. ;25 cm.

F371. 2/B448(4)

The Book of Rural Life: Knowledge and Inspiration: Board of Trade to Compass. IV/The Bellows-Durham Company. —Chicago: The Bellows-Durham Company, c1925

1897-2556 p. ;25 cm.

F371. 2/B448(5)

The Book of Rural Life: Knowledge and Inspiration: Board of Trade to Compass. V/The Bellows-Durham Company. —Chicago: The Bellows-Durham Company, c1925

2557-3191 p. ;25 cm.

F371. 2/B448(9)

The Book of Rural Life: Knowledge and Inspiration: A Guide to the Best in Modern Living. IX/The Bellows-Durham Company. —Chicago: The Bellows-Durham Company, c1925

5029-5624 p. ;25 cm.

F371. 2/B448(10)

The Book of Rural Life: Knowledge and Inspiration. Vol. X/The Bellows-Dutham Company. —

Chicago: The Bellows-Durham Company, c1925
5625-6210 p. ;25 cm.

F371. 2-54/K67
Yearbook of the United States Department of Agriculture/Seaman Asahel Knapp. —Washington: Government Printing Office, c1912
732 p. ;23 cm.

F4/D565
The Industrial Revolution/Frederick C. Dietz. —London: G. Bell And Sons Ltd. , c1930
xi, 115 p. ;19 cm.

F41/H875
Eastern Industrialization and Its Effect on the West: With Special Reference to Great Britain and Japan/by G. E. Hubbard, assisted by Denzil Baring; with a Conclusion by Professor T. E. Gregory. —London: Oxford University Press, H. Milford, c1935.
xxii, 418 p. ;22 cm.

F416. 471/C678
Combustion on Wheels: An Informal History of the Automobile Age/David L. Cohn. —Boston: Houghton Mifflin Company, c1944
272 p. ;20 cm.

F471. 29/V394
Absentee Ownership and Business Enterprise in Recent Times: the Case of America/Thorstein Veblen. —New York: B. W. Huebsch, inc. , c1923.
445 p. ;20 cm.

F506. 72/H785
Railroad Accounting/by William E. Hooper. —New York: D. Appleton and Company, 1915.
xi, 461 p. ;22 cm.

F517. 12-62/U58
Merchant Vessels of the United States. 1939/United States Department of Commerce. —[S. l. : s. n.], c[1939]
774 p. ;23×29 cm.

F53/J66(1)
Railroad Traffic and Rates. Vol. I/Emory R. Johnson and Grover G. Huebner. —New York: D. Appleton and Co. , 1921.
xv, 523 p. ;22 cm.

F532. 9/K37
Railway Enterprise in China: An Account of Its Origin and Development/Percy Horace Kent. —London: Edward Arnold, c1908
ix, 304 p. ;23 cm.

F537. 12/H887
The Railroad Freight Service/Grover G. Huebner, Emory R. Johnson. —New York: D. Appleton and Company, c1926
xiv, 589 p. ;22 cm.

F550. 7-65/P187
Rules and Regulations: Governing Navigation of the Panama Canal and Adjacent Waters/The Panama Canal Press. —Mount Hope: The Panama Canal Press, c1947
152 p. ;23 cm.

F550. 72/A615
Ocean Shipping: Elements of Practical Steamship Operation/Robert Edwards Annin. —New York: The Century Co. , c1920
xiv, 427 p. ;20 cm.

F550. 72/J66
Principles of ocean transportation/by Emory R. Johnson. . —New York: D. Appleton and Company, c1918.
xxi, 513 p. , 7 plates;22 cm.

F626. 22/C649-5

The ABC Universal Commercial Electric Telegraphic Code/W. Clausen-Thue. —5th ed.. —New York: American Code Company, c1901

1400 p. ;24 cm.

F637. 12/U58(1)

United States Official Postal Guide. Part I, Domestic Postal Service Including International Money Order Business/United States Government Printing Office. —Washington: United States Government Printing Office, c1945

792 p. ;23 cm.

F637. 12/U58(2)

United States Official Postal Guide. Part II/United States Government Printing Office. —Washington: United States Government Printing Office, c1945

792 p. ;23 cm.

F637. 12/U58(1934)

United States Official Postal Guide: July 1934/United States Government Printing Office. —Washington: United States Government Printing Office, c1934

1336 p. ;23 cm.

F7/C734-5

Commercial Knowledge: Adapted for Chinese Students/Commercial knowledge. —5th ed. —Tokyo: The Nakanishiya, c1908.

244 p. ;19 cm.

F7-09/H174

The Elements of Commercial History/by Fred Hall. —London: Sir Isaac Pitman & Sons, Ltd., [19-?]

vii, 156 p. ;19 cm.

F71/B877

Principles of Commerce: A Study of the Mechanism, the Advantages, and the Transportation Costs of Foreign and Domestic Trade/Harry Gunnison Brown. —New York: The Macmillan Company, c1920.

xxiii p., 1 l., 154, 188, 207 p. ;21 cm.

F71/H678

The Science of Wealth/Hobson, J. A.. —London: Williams & Norgate, c1911

vii, 256 p. ;18 cm.

F71-09/C454

Commercial history and organization＝商業史及組織/by Yuan-Chieh Chang and Feng Chun Yang. —Shanghai: The Commercial Press, c1926.

xxii, 386 p. ;19 cm.

F710/K16

Essentials of Business Arithmetic: A Self-teaching Course/Edward M. Kanzer, William L. Schaaf. —Washington: D. C. Heath and Company, c1943

viii, 476, 37 p. ;19 cm.

F713. 32/S678

The Retail Text: A Course in Retail Sales Development/Socony-Vacuum Oil Company, Inc.,—[S. l.]: Socony-Vacuum Oil Company, Inc., c1946

193 p. ;28 cm.

F713. 359/B298

Royal Spades Auction Bridge/Bascule. —London: Longmans, Green And Co., c1913

xii, 180 p. ;16 cm.

F713. 5/W873

Marketing/Tonzoo C. Woo. —Shanghai: The Commercial Press, Ltd., c1924

xviii, 253 p. ;19 cm.

F713. 50/C766-2

Marketing: Methods and Policies/Paul D. Con-

verse. —New York: Prentice-Hall, Inc. , c1924
xv, 619 p. ;21 cm.

F713. 55/H868
The Consumption of Wealth/by Elizabeth Ellis Hoyt. —New York: The Macmillan Company, c1928.
xiv, 344 p. ;21 cm.

F713. 8/F242
The Typography of Advertisements That Pay: How to Choose and Combine Type Faces, Engravings and All the Other Mechanical Elements of Modern Advertisement Construction/Gilbert P. Farrar. —New York: D. Appleton and Company, c1918
xvi, 282 p. ;19 cm.

F713. 8/K63-2
Advertising Procedure/Otto Kleppner. —rev. ed. —New York: Prentice-Hall, Inc. , c1939
xvii, 582 p. ;23 cm.

F713. 8/N248
Developing Marketable Products and Their Packagings/Ben Nash. —New York: McGraw-Hill, 1945.
xii, 404 p. ;23cm.

F713. 8/S213-2
Advertising: Theory and Practice/C. H. Sandage. —revised ed. —Chicago: Richard D. Irwin, Inc. , c1945
xiii, 747 p. ;23 cm.

F715. 5/K16
Essentials of Business Arithmetic: A Self-teaching Course/Edward M. Kanzer, William L. Schaaf. —Washington: D. C. Heath and Company, c1943
viii, 476 p. ;19 cm.

F726/A583
The Theory of International Prices: History, Criticism and Restatement/by James W. Angell Awarded the David A. Wells prize for the year 1924-25 and published from the income of the David A. Wells Fund. —Cambridge: Harvard University Press, c1926
xiv, 571 p. ;23 cm.

F737. 12-62/B927(1933)
Custom House Guide: An Importer's Encyclopedia United States Customs Tariff-Customs Ports-Customs Regulations/John F. Budd. —ed. 1933. —New York: Custom House Guide, c1933
xx, 1600 p. ;23 cm.

F737. 12-62/B927(1947)
Custom House Guide: United States Customs Tariff, Customs Ports, Internal Revenue Code Customs, Shipping and Commerce Regulations Reciprocal Trade Agreements. 1947 Edition/ed. by John F. Budd. —New York: American Import & Export Bulletin, c1947.
1 v. ;24 cm.

F737. 12-62/B927-1946
Custom House Guide: United States Customs Tariff, Customs Ports, Internal Revenue Code Customs, Shipping and Commerce Regulations Reciprocal Trade Agreements/ed. by John F. Budd. —1946 ed. —New York: American Import & Export Bulletin, c1946.
1 v. ;24 cm.

F737. 129/C289(2)
The American Business Manual. Volume II, The Plant/Edward M. Carney, George M. O'Neil, Maurice V. Genez. —New York: P. F. Collier & Son, c1911
384 p. ;20 cm.

F737. 129/C289(3)
The American Business Manual. Volume III,

The Plant/Edward M. Carney, George M. O'Neil, Maurice V. Genez. —New York: P. F. Collier & Son, c1911
384 p. ;20 cm.

F74/C669
Universal Trade Code. /Code Compiling Company, Inc. ,—New York: Code Compiling Company, Inc. , c1921
iv, 634 p. ;17 cm.

F74/H684
International Trade: An Application of Economic Theory/John A. Hobson. —London: Methuen & Co. , c1904
xii, 202 p. ;19 cm.

F740/B324-4
The Theory of International Trade With Some of Its Applications to Economic Policy/C. F. Bastable. —4th ed. . —London: Macmillan and Co. , Ltd. , c1903
xvi, 197 p. ;19 cm.

F741/F538
International Commercial Polices with Special Reference to the United States/George Mygatt Fisk, Paul Skeels Peirce. —New York: The Macmillan Company, c1925
xii, 322 p. ;20 cm.

F744/C945
The Tariff: An Interpretation of a Bewildering Problem/by George Crompton. . —New York: The Macmillan Company, c1927.
ix, 226 p. ;23 cm.

F752/I59(1)
Foreign Trade of China, 1927. Part I, Report and Abstract of Statistics/The Inspectorate General of Customs. —Shanghai: The Inspectorate General of Customs. , c1928
635 p. ;28 cm.

F752/K29
Returns of Trade and Trade Reports for the Year 1903. Part II, Reports and Statistics for Each Port/Kelly & Walsh, Ltd. ,—Shanghai: Kelly & Walsh, Ltd. , c1904
xviii, 943 p. ;28 cm.

F752/R386
The Foreign Trade of China/C. F. Remer. —Shanghai: The Commercial Press, Ltd. , c1928
xii, 269 p. ;21 cm.

F752/S797-2
Code of Customs Regulations and Procedure/Statistical Department of the Inspectorate General of Customs. —2nd ed. . —Shanghai: Statistical Department of the Inspectorate General of Customs, c1935
xii, 461 p. ;25 cm.

F752/S797-3
Code of Customs Regulations and Procedure/Statistical Department of the Inspectorate General of Customs. —3rd ed. (Revised and Enlarged). —Shanghai: Statistical Department of the Inspectorate General of Customs, c1937
xiii, 562 p. ;25 cm.

F752/W953-2
Gode of Customs Regulations and Procedure/Stanley F. Writht. —2nd ed. , Revised and Enlarged. —Shanghai: Statistical Department of Inspectorate General of Customs, c1935
xii, 463 p. ;25 cm.

F752. 5/W337-2
The Principal Articles of Chinese Commerce (import and export)/Ernest Watson. . —2nd ed. —Shanghai: Published by Order of the General of Customs, c1941.
537 p. ;26 cm.

F753. 13/A798

The Secret of Japan's Trade Expansion/Isoshi Asahi. —Tokyo：The International Association of Japan，c1934

xiii，130，64 p. ;19 cm.

F753. 13/K75

Foreign Trade Business Methods on Japaness Principles and Practices/Denzo K. Koyama. —Tokyo：Maruzen Company，Ltd.，c1934

xix，293 p. ;22 cm.

F755. 165. 9/A826-3

Modern Tariff History：Germany-United States-France/Percy Ashley. —New 3rd ed.. —New York：E. P. Dutton & Company，c1926

x，365 p. ;22 cm.

F757. 12/S923

Expansion：Under New World-Conditions/Josiah Strong. —New York：The Baker and Taylor Company，c1900

310 p. ;19 cm.

F757. 12/U28(1931)

Merchant Vessels of the United States：Year Ended June 30，1931/United States Government Printing Office. —Washington：United States Government Printing Office，c1931

1068 p. ;26 cm.

F757. 12/U58

Merchant Vessels of the United States：Year Ended June 30，1932/United States Government Printing Office. —Washington：United States Government Printing Office，c1932

1121 p. ;26 cm.

F757. 12. 2/U58(1923)

Customs Regulations of the United States：Prescribed for the Instruction and Guidance of Customs Officers/U. S. Treasury Department Bureau of Customs. —Washington：United States Government Printing Office，c1924

x，792 p. ;24 cm.

F757. 125. 2/U58(1931)

Customs Regulations of the United States：Prescribed for the Instruction and Guidance of Customs Officers/U. S. Treasury Department Bureau of Customs. —ed. of 1931. —Washington：United States Government Printing Office，c1932

x，975 p. ;21 cm.

F757. 125. 2/U58(1937)

Customs Regulations of the United States：Prescribed for the Instruction and Guidance of Customs officers/U. S. Treasury Department Bureau of Customs. —ed. of 1937. —Washington：United States Government Printing Office，c1937

xi，921 p. ;21 cm.

F757. 128. 2/P187

The trade of the United States with China/by Shu-lun Pan. —New York：China Trade Bureau，c1924.

xix，365 p. ;23 cm.

F760. 2/U54(1)

Standard Commodity Classification. Volume I/United States Government Printing Office. —Washington：United States Government Printing Office，c1943

xxxiv，652 p. ;23 cm.

F768. 4/F219

Manual for the Leather Trade/I. G. Farbenindustrie Aktiengesellschaft. —Frankfurt：I. G. Farbenindustrie Aktiengesellschaft，[?]

184 p. ;18 cm.

F81/S679

Wealth，Virtual Wealth and Debt：The Solution of the Economic Paradox/Frederick Soddy. —London：George Allen & Unwin Ltd.，

c1926
320 p. ;22 cm.

F811/H697
Metallurgy of Copper/H. O. Hofman. —New York: McGraw-Hill Book Company, Inc. , c1914
xiv, 556 p. ;23 cm.

F815. 616/R356
Britain and the War Debts/Leonard J. Reid. —London: Herbert Jenkins, c1933
108 p. ;19 cm.

F815. 659/F538
French Public Finance: In the Great War and Today/Harvey E. Fisk. —New York: Bankers Trust Company, c1922
363 p. ;17 cm.

F817. 12/D419
Wealth, Debt, and Taxation/Department of Commerce and Labor Special Reports of the Census Office. Washington: Government Printing Office, c1907
xi, 1234 p. ;30 cm.

F817. 12/S464-7
Essays in Taxation/by Edwin R. A. Seligman. —7th ed. —New York: Printed for the Columbia University Press by The Macmillan Company, c1905.
x, 434 p. ;23 cm.

F817. 12/W853
Co-operative Credit for the United States/Henry W. Wolff. —New York: Sturgis & Walton Company, c1917
vi, 349 p. ;19 cm.

F817. 123/G721(2)
Reports of the Department of the Interior for the Fiscal Year Ended June 30, 1907. Vol. 2/Washington: Government Printing Office, c1908
vii, 523-1214 p. ;24 cm.

F817. 126/G441
The Public Debt of the United States/J. S. Gibbons. —New York: Charles Scribner & Co. , c1867
xii, 276 p. ;20 cm.

F82/K51
Money: A Study of the Theory of the Medium of Exchange/David Kinley. —special China ed. . —Shanghai, China: Macmillan, [c1904]
xviii, 415 p. ;19 cm.

F820/E46
This Money Business: A Simple Account of the Institutions and Working of the Banking and Financial World/Barnard Ellinger. —London: P. S. King & Son Ltd. , c1933
141 p. ;22 cm.

F822/W129
Chinese Currency and Banking/Srinvas R. Wagel. —Shanghai: North-China Daily News & Herald Ltd. , c1915
455 p. ;25 cm.

F822. 0/C532
Silver and Prices in China: Report of the Committee for the Study of Silver Values and Commodity Prices, Ministry of Industries. /[?]. —Shanghai: Commercial Press, c1935
xxi, 245 p. , [8] folded leaves;23 cm.

F83/F841
Great Britain and The Gold Standard: A Study of the Present World Depression/H. F. Frader. —London: Macmillan and Co. , Ltd. , c1933
xi, 205 p. ;22 cm.

F83/S177
Recovery: The Second Effort/Sir Arthur Salter. —London: G. Bell and Sons Ltd. , c1933

xxxv, 306 p. ;21 cm.

F830/T161

China's New Currency System/Tang Leang-li. —Shanghai: China United Press, c1936

ix, 138 p. ;25 cm.

F830. 4/M165

The Elements of Banking/Henry Dunning Macleod. —New York: Longmans, Green, and Co. , c1902

xvi, 308, 40 p. ;19 cm.

F830. 59-62/M734(1931)

Tate's Money Manual/William F. Spalding. —London: Effingham Wilson, c1931

xii, 116, 28 p. ;22 cm.

F830. 59-62/S734(2)

Tate's Money Manual. Vol. II/William F. Spalding. —London: Sir Isaac Pitman & Sons, Ltd. , c1933

ix, 178, 28 p. ;22 cm.

F830. 73/C591

The A B C of the Foreign Exchanges: A Practical Guide/George Clare. —London: Macmillan and Co. , Ltd. , c1911

xiv, 160 p. ;19 cm.

F830. 9/S734-28

Tate's Modern Cambist: a manual of the world's monetary systems, the foreign exchanges, the stamp duties on bills of exchange in foreign Countries, the principal rules governing bills of exchange and promissory notes, foreign weights and measures and bullion and exchange operations/by William F. Spalding. —28th ed.. —London: Sir Isaac Pitman & Sons, Ltd. , c1929

xiv, 734 p. ;22 cm.

F830. 91/C883

Understanding the Stock Market: A Handbook for the Investor/by Alliston Cragg. —New York: New York Publishing Company, 1929.

xvi, 276 p;21 cm.

F830. 91/F533

The Stock Market Crash and After/Irving Fisher. —New York: The Macmillan Company, c1930

xxvi, 286 p. ;20 cm.

F835. 2/P763

The History, Law, and Practice of the Stock Exchange/A. P. Poley. —London: Sir Isaac Pitman and Sons, Ltd. , c1907

338 p. ;21 cm.

F835. 619/F538

English Public Finance from the Revolution of 1688: with Chapters on the Bank of England/Harvey E. Fisk. —New York: Bankers Trust Company, 1920.

241 p. ;18 cm.

F835. 619/H847

The Banks in the Clearing House/William Howarth. —London: Effingham Wilson, c1905

227 p. ;18 cm.

F835. 65/P314

The Bank of France in Its Relation to National and International Credit/Maurice Patron. —Washington: Govt. Print. Off. , 1910.

181 p. ;23 cm.

F837. 12/F538

Our Public Debt: An Historical Sketch with a Description of United States Securities/Harvey E. Fisk. —New York: Bankers Trust Company, 1919.

126 p. ;18 cm.

F837.129/H529

A History of in the United States: With a Brief Description of the Currency Systems of all Commercial Nations/A. Barton Hepburn. —New York: The Macmillan Company, c1915

xv, 552 p. ;22 cm.

G 文化、科学、教育、体育

G05/V235

Business and Education/Frank A. Vanderlip. —New York: Duffield and Company, c1907

562 p. ;19 cm.

G131.3/N731

Lectures on Japan: An Outline of the Development of the Japanese People and Their Culture/Inazo Nitobe. —Tokyo: Kenkyusha, c1936

xii, 393 p. ;20 cm.

G131.32/F949-3

Tea Cult of Japan: An Aesthetic Pastime/Yasunosuke Fukukita. —3rd. ed.. —Japan: Board of Tourist Industry, c1937

77 p. ;19 cm.

G137.122/B972

Studies in Nature and Literature/John Burroughs. —Boston: Houghton Mifflin Company, c1875

112 p. ;18 cm.

G171.2/M643

Literature and Life in America/Dufley Miles, Robert C. Pooley. —Chicago: Scott, Foresman and Company, c1943

xviii, 726 p. ;23 cm.

G171.2/P316

The New Basis of Civilization/Simon N. Patten. —New York: The Macmillan Company, c1908

vii, 220 p. ;19 cm.

G206/C734

A Free and Responsible Press: A General Report on Mass Communication: Newspapers, Radio, Motion Pictures, Magazines, and Books/The Commission on Freedom of the Press. —Chicago: The University of Chicago Press, c1947

xii, 138 p. ;20 cm.

G210/W946

Elements of Journalism/Mary J. J. Wrinn. —Revised ed.. —New York: Harper & Brothers Publishers, c1929, 1939

xvii, 376 p. ;24 cm.

G212/B646

Newspaper Writing and Editing/Willard Grosvenor Bleyer. —Boston: Houghton Mifflin Company, c1913

ix, 365 p. ;20 cm.

G212/MacD731

Interpretative Reporting/Curtis D. MacDougall. —Revised ed.. —New York: The Macmillan Company, c1948

x, 751 p. ;21 cm.

G212.2/H993-3

Newspaper Handbook: Treating Grammar, Punctuation, Rhetoric, Diction, Journalistic Structure, Typographical Style, Accuracy, Headlines, Proofreading, Copyreading, Type,

Cuts, Libel, Applied Ethics, Story Paterns, and News Values/Grant Milnor Hyde. —3rd ed.. —New York: D. Appleton-Century Company, c1941

xix, 337 p. ;20 cm.

G213-44/G212

Headlines and Deadlines: a Manual for Copyeditors/Robert E. Garst and Theodore M. Bernstein. —New York: Columbia University Press, c1940

217 p. ;21 cm.

G219. 712/B475

Ballyhoo/Silas Bent. —New York: Boni and Liveright, c1927

xviii, 398 p. ;21 cm.

G219. 712/J76

Journalism in the United States/Robert W. Jones. —New York: E. P. Dutton & Company, Inc. , c1947

728 p. ;22 cm.

G239. 13/L433

Publications Issued by the League of Nations/the league of nations. — [S. l. : s. n.], c1935

312 p. ;20 cm.

G239. 561. 2-53/M875

The Spectator. Essays 1-L/John Morrison. —London: Macmillan and Co. , [?]

xxviii, 311 p. ;18 cm.

G259. 712/F755

High School Administration/Herbert H. Foster. —New York: The Century Co. , c1928

xvii, 665 p. ;20 cm.

G40/B274

Common Sense in Education and Teaching/P. A. Barnett. —New York: Longmans, Green, and Co. , c1901

327 p. ;19 cm.

G40/T974

Science and Education in China/George Ranson Twiss. —Shanghai: The Commercial Press, Ltd. , c1925

ix, 361 p. ;19 cm.

G40-05/D272

Teaching the Social Studies/Edgar Dawson. —New York: The Macmillan Company, c1927

xvi, 405 p. ;20 cm.

G40-052. 2/R961

Education and the Good Life/Bertrand Russell. —New York: Horace Liveright, c1926

vi, 319 p. ;21 cm.

G40-09/B988

A Cultural History of Education: Reassessing Our Educational Traditions/R. Freeman Butts. —New York: McGraw-Hill Book Company, Inc. , c1947

ix, 726 p. ;23 cm.

G42/A545

English Teaching Efficiency in China/Elam Jonathan Anderson. —Shanghai: The Commercial Press, Ltd. , c1925

xviii, 182 p. ;22 cm.

G42/B974

Supervision and the Improvement to Teaching/William H. Burton. —New York: D. Appleton and Company, c1924

xx, 510 p. ;19 cm.

G423/B663

How to Make a Curriculum/Franklin Bobbitt. —Boston: Houghton Mifflin Company, c1924

292 p. ;19 cm.

G423/C877
Curriculum-Adjustment in the Secondary School/Philip W. L. Cox. —Philadelphia: J. B. Lippincott Company, c1925
vi, 311 p. ;19 cm.

G423/D261
Our Evolving High School Curriculum/Calvin Olin Davis. —New York: World Book Company, c1905
ix, 301 p. ;20 cm.

G423/Mcm. 979
How to Organize the Curriculum/Charles A. Mcmurry. —New York: The Macmillan Company, c1924
vii, 358 p. ;19 cm.

G423. 04/S671
Foundations of Curricula Sociological Analyses/David Snedden. —New York: Bureau of Publications, c1927
196 p. ;24 cm.

G424. 1/P238
General Methods of Teaching in Elementary Schools/Samuel Chester Parker. —Revised ed. —Boston: Ginn and Company, c1919
xx, 336 p. ;20 cm.

G424. 1/T456
Principles and Technique of Teaching: An Introduction to the Study of the Teaching Art/Frank W. Thomas. —Boston: Houghton Mifflin Company, c1924
xxiv, 410 p. ;19 cm.

G424. 2/B146
Classroom Management: Its Principles and Technique/William Chandler Bagley. —New York: The Macmillan Company, c1926
xvii, 306 p. ;19 cm.

G44/B694
Everyday Psychology for Teachers/Frederick Elmer Bolton. —New York: Charles Scribner's Sons, c1923
x, 443 p. ;20 cm.

G44/B966
The Normal Mind: An Introduction to Mental Hygiene and the Hygieni of School Instruction/William H. Burnham. —New York: D. Appleton-Century Company, c1936
xviii, 702 p. ;21 cm.

G44/C351
A Humane Psychology of Education/Jaime Castiello. —New York: Fordham University, c1938
xxiii, 254 p. ;18 cm.

G44/J27
Talks to Teachers on Psychology: and to Students on Some of Life's Ideals/William James. —New York: Henry Holt and Company, c1899
ix, 301 p. ;21 cm.

G44/S795
Psychology in Education/Daniel Starch, Hazel M. Stanton, Wilhelmine Koerth. —New York: D. Appleton-Century Company, c1941
x, 722 p. ;22 cm.

G44/S897
An Introduction to Child Study/Ruth Strang. —New York: The Macmillan Company, c1930
xiii, 550 p. ;20 cm.

G449. 4/S633
The Second Giant Quiz Book/Rosejeanne Slifer, Louise Crittenden. —New York: Crown Publishers, c1939
282 p. ;21 cm.

G45/L922

Everyday Problems of the Country Teacher: A Textbook and Handbook of Country-School Practice/Frank J. Lowth. —New York: The Macillan Company, c1927

xii, 563 p. ;20 cm.

G451/H738

The Teacher's Technique/Charles Elmer Holley. —New York: The Century Co. , c1922.

x, 378 p. ;21 cm.

G451.2/C486

The Commonwealth Teacher-Training Study/W. W. Charters, Douglas Waples. —Chicago: The University of Chicago Press, c1929

xx, 666 p. ;23 cm.

G472/B468

Principles of School Administration/Benjamin, Harold. —New York: McGraw-Hill Book Company, Inc. , c1946

388 p. ;23 cm.

G472.3/L673

Personnel Problems of the Teaching Staff: A Study of Some of the Outstanding Personnel Management Problems That Arise in the Administration and Supervision of a Public School System/Ervin Eugenen Lewis. —New York: The Century Co. , c1925

xvii, 460 p. ;21 cm.

G479/B491

Theories and Facts for Students of Longevity and Health/Thomas Bersford. —San Francisco: Thomas Bersord, c1908

128 p. ;19 cm.

G479/G233

The Road to Adolescence/Joseph Garland. —Cambridge: Harvard University Press, c1934

viii, 293 p. ;21 cm.

G479/S751

Confidential Talks with Young Men/Lyman B. Sperry. —New York: Fleming H. Revell Company, [?]

179 p. ;19 cm.

G512.71/W373

Problems in Public School Administration: A Plan and Work Book for Public School Administrators/Oscar F. Weber. —New York: The Century Co. , c1930

xxxviii, 726 p. ;20 cm.

G52/H874(1.2)

Vocational Education in China. Bulletin I, 1923 Vol II/Huang Yen-pei. —2nd. ed. . —Shanghai: The Commercial Press, c1925

54 p. ;19 cm.

G521/C535

Reconstruction of Modern Educational Organizations in China/Chiling Yin. —Shanghai: Commercial Press, Ltd. , c1924

xviiii, 171 p. ;19 cm.

G529/D623

A History of Democratic Education in Modern China/Lu-dzai Djung. —Taipei: Cheng Wen Pub. Co. , c1934.

xxxiii, 258 p. ;20 cm.

G556.128-54/D281(1938)

The Public and Preparatory Schools Year Book/C. H. Deane[etc.]. —London: H. F. Deane and Sons the Year Book Press Ltd. , c1938

xxx, 1064 p. ;18 cm.

G556.18/R691

The Old Public School of England/John Rodgers. —London: B. T. Batsgord, Ltd. , c1938

xvi, 112 p. ;22 cm.

G571.2/C486

Curriculum Construction/W. W. Charters.—New York: The Macmillan Company, c1929

xii, 352 p. ;20 cm.

G571.2/C616

The Goose-Step: A Study of American Education/Upton Sinclair.—Revised ed.—[S. l.]: The Cornwall Press, Inc., c1922

x, 488 p. ;21 cm.

G571.2/C853

School and Society in Chicago/George S. Counts.—New York: Harcourt, Brace & Company, c1928

viii, 367 p. ;21 cm.

G571.2/C962

Public School Administration: A Statement of the Fundamental Principles Underlying the Organization and Administration of Public Education/Ellwood P. Cubberley.—Boston: Houghton Mifflin, c1922.

xviii, 479 p. ;20 cm.

G571.2/G721

Bibliography of Education for 1908-9/Government Printing Office.—Washington: Government Printing Office, c1909

134 p. ;23 cm.

G571.2/K69

Education in the United States/Edgar W. Knight.—Boston: Ginn and Company, c1929

xi, 588 p. ;21 cm.

G571.2/L693

Some Phases of Popular Control of Education in the United States: An Analytical study of Legal Status Relating to State Control of Education/Chien-Hsun Li.—Shanghai: The Commercial Press, Ltd., c1928

xvi, 256 p. ;23 cm.

G571.2/McD.L791

Student Personnel Work at Northwestern University/Esther McD. LLoud-Hones.—New York: Harper & Brother Publisher, c1929

xx, 253 p. ;21 cm.

G571.2-49/F737(1)

The American Educator: A New and Thoroughly Modern Reference Work Designed to Meet the Needs of Every Age. vol. 1/Ellsworth D. Foster, James Laughlin Hughes.—Chicago: Bellows-Durham Company, c1929

527 p. ;24 cm.

G571.2-49/F737(2)

The American Educator: A New and Thoroughly Modern Reference Work Designed to Meet the Needs of Every Age. vol. 2/Ellsworth D. Foster, James Laughlin Hughes.—Chicago: Bellows-Durham Company, c1929

529-1024 p. ;24 cm.

G571.2-49/F737(6)

The American Educator: A New and Thoroughly Modern Reference Work Designed to Meet the Needs of Every Age. vol. 6/Ellsworth D. Foster, James Laughlin Hughes.—Chicago: Bellows-Durham Company, c1929

2577-3072 p. ;24 cm.

G571.2-49/F737(7)

The American Educator: A New and Thoroughly Modern Reference Work Designed to Meet the Needs of Every Age. vol. 7/Ellsworth D. Foster, James Laughlin Hughes.—Chicago: Bellows-Durham Company, c1929

3073-3568 p. ;24 cm.

G571.2-49/F737(8)

The American Educator: A New and Thoroughly Modern Reference Work Designed to

Meet the Needs of Every Age. vol. 8/Ellsworth D. Foster, James Laughlin Hughes. —Chicago: Bellows-Durham Company, c1929

3569-4053 p. ;24 cm.

G571. 2-49/F737(8. 3)

The American Educator: A New and Thoroughly Modern Reference Work Designed to Meet the Needs of Every Age. vol. 8. 3/Ellsworth D. Foster, James Laughlin Hughes. —Chicago: Bellows-Durham Company, c1929

1025-1536 p. ;24 cm.

G571. 2-49/F737(8. 5)

The American Educator: A New and Thoroughly Modern Reference Work Designed to Meet the Needs of Every Age. vol. 8(5)/Ellsworth D. Foster, James Laughlin Hughes. —Chicago: Bellows-Durham Company, c1929

2065-2567 p. ;24 cm.

G571. 25/S243-30

A Handbook of Private Schools for American Boys and Girls an Annual Survey/Porter Sargent. —30th ed.. —Boston: [s. n.], c1947

1071 p. ;18 cm.

G571. 26/R156

Public School Finance/Homer P. Rainey. —New York: The Century Co. , c1929

xix, 385 p. ;20 cm.

G571. 28/C962(2)

State and County School Administration. Vol II, Source book/Ellwood P. Cubberley, Edward C. Elliott. —New York: The Macmillan Company, c1927

xxi, 729 p. ;19 cm.

G571. 28/C962

The Principal and His School: The Organization, Administration, and Supervision of Instruction in an Elementary School/Ellwood P. Cubberley. —Boston: Houghton Mifflin Company, c1923

xviii, 571 p. ;19 cm.

G571. 28/W873(28)

The Badger: Being A Year Book of the University of Wisconsin Compiled by the Junior Class. Volume Twenty-Eight/Koksan J. Woo. —[S. l. : s. n.], [?]

696 p. ;27 cm.

G610/M781-7

The Montessori Method/Maria Motessori. —7th ed.. —New York: Frederick A. Stokes Company, c1912

xlii, 377 p. ;20 cm.

G613. 2/N338

The Open Door: For Children Learning English/Elma A. Neal. —New York: The Macmillan Company, c1927

98 p. ;20 cm.

G62/G939-3

A Laboratory Guide in Elementary Bacteriology/William Dodge Frost. —3rd revised ed. —New York: The Macmillan Company, c1909

395 p. ;22 cm.

G622/K61

The Catholic Teacher's Companion: A Book of Self-Help and Guidance/Felix M. Kirsch. —New York: Beniger Brothers, c1924

xxx, 747 p. ;17 cm.

G622/S732

The Platoon School: A Study of the Adaptation of the Elementary School Organization to the Curriculum/Charles L. Spain. —New York: The Macmillan Company, c1924

xviii, 255 p. ;19 cm.

G622. 4/F854

Modern Elementary School Practice/George E. Freeland. —New York: The Macmillan Company, c1920

xiv, 408 p. ;19 cm.

G623. 3/S213(3)

Junior High School English. Book 3/Richard L. Sandwick. —Boston: D. C. Heath & Co. , c1920

vii, 188 p. ;19 cm.

G623. 31/L784(2)

Living English: For Junior Middle Schools. Book II/Chan Wen Hu. —Shanghai: The World Book Co. , Ltd. , c1946

ii, 102 p. ;19 cm.

G623. 31/L784(3)

Living English: For Junior Middle Schools. Book III/Chan Wen Hu. —Shanghai: The World Book Co. , Ltd. , c1946

ii, 108 p. ;19 cm.

G623. 31/L784(5)

Living English: For Junior Middle Schools. Book V/Chan Wen Hu. —Shanghai: The World Book Co. , Ltd. , c1946

ii, 146 p. ;19 cm.

G623. 4/S651(6)

Geography of Europe, Asia, Africa: For Elementary Schools. Grade 6/J. Russell Smith. —Chicago: The John C. Winston Company, c1945

384 p. ;25 cm.

G623. 41/McG965

Adventuring in Young America/Edna McGuire, Claude Anderson Phillips. —New York: The Macmillan Company, c1931

370 p. ;19 cm.

G623. 45/S651(5)

Geography of the Americas for Elementary Schools. Grade 5/J. Russell Smith. —Chicago: The John C. Winston Company, c1946

viii, 394 p. ;25 cm.

G623. 45/S651(6)

Geography of Europe, Asia, Africa for Elementary Schools. Grade 6/J. Russell Smith. —Chicago: The John C. Winston Comapany, c1945

viii, 384, 66 p. ;25 cm.

G623. 5/H174-4

Elementary Trigonometry/H. S. Hall, S. R. Knight. —4th ed. . —[S. l. : s. n.], c1936

xv, 415 p. ;18 cm.

G623. 5/Y73

Elementary Mathematical Analysis/John Wesley Young. —New York: The Macmillan Company, c1924

xii, 548 p. ;19 cm.

G623. 5-44/Y1

Pratical Problems in Arithmetic: Book IV for Sixth Grade/Wilbur M. Yeincst. —Washington: Webster Publishing Company, c1930

60 p. ;19 cm.

G623. 56/S878

The Stone Arithmetic/John C. Stone. —Chicago: Benj. H Sanborn & Co. , c1925, 1931

xiv, 306 p. ;19 cm.

G623. 6/Y67

First Book of Botany: Designed to Cultivate The Observing Powers of Children/Eliza A. Youmans. —New York: D. Appleton ans Company, c1878

Lv;19 cm.

G623. 71/G453

Elementary Music/Thaddeus P. Giddings, Will

Earhart, Ralph L. Baldwin. —Boston: Ginn and Company, c1923
192 p. ;21 cm.

G623. 71/McC743(2)
The Music Hour. Second Book/Osbourne Mcconathy[etc.]. —New York: Silver, Burdett and Company, c1928
124 p. ;21 cm.

G623. 71/T914(1)
The New Nomal Music Course. Book One/John W. Tufts and H. E. Holt. —New York: Silver, Burdett and Company, c1910
144 p. ;20 cm.

G623. 75/C294(2)
Stories Pictures Tell. Book Two/Flora L. Carpenter. —Chicago: Rand McNally & Company, c1918
vii, 57 p. ;19 cm.

G623. 75/C294(3)
Stories Pictures Tell. Book Three/Flora L. Carpenter. —Chicago: Rand McNally & Company, c1918
vii, 67 p. ;19 cm.

G623. 75/N532
Integrated Handwork for Elementary Schools: Teachers' Guide in Use and Techniques/Louis V. Newkirk. —New York: Silver Burdett Company, c1940
viii, 342 p. ;25 cm.

G624/F837
Textbook Selection/R. H. Franzen, F. B. Knight. —Baltimore: Warwick & York, Inc. , c1922
94 p. ;18 cm.

G624. 56/B889(3)
Arithmetic We Use. Grade 3/Leo J. Brueckner, Foster E. Grossnickle, Elda L. Merton. —Philadelphia: The John C. Winston Company, c1942
278 p. ;20 cm.

G624. 56/B889(4)
Arithmetic We Use. Grade 4/Leo J. Brueckner, Foster E. Grossnickle, Elda L. Merton. —Philadelphia: The John C. Winston Company, c1942
278 p. ;20 cm.

G624. 56/B889(5)
Arithmetic We Use. Grade 5/Leo J. Brueckner, Foster E. Grossnickle, Elda L. Merton. —Philadelphia: The John C. Winston Company, c1942
311 p. ;20 cm.

G624. 56/B889(6)
Arithmetic We Use. Grade 6/Leo J. Brueckner, Foster E. Grossnickle, Elda L. Merton. —Philadelphia: The John C. Winston Company, c1942
312 p. ;20 cm.

G624. 56/B889(7)
Arithmetic We Use. Grade 7/Leo J. Brueckner, Foster E. Grossnickle, Elda L. Merton. —Philadelphia: The John C. Winston Company, c1943
308 p. ;20 cm.

G624. 56/B889(8)
Arithmetic We Use. Grade 8/Leo J. Brueckner, Foster E. Grossnickle, Elda L. Merton. —Philadelphia: The John C. Winston Company, c1943
311 p. ;20 cm.

G624. 6/H631
Elementary Dynamics of Particles and Solids/W. M. Hicks. —Reprinted from the 3rd ed. . —Reprinted from the 3rd ed. —Tokyo: [s. n.], c1898
viii, 401 p. ;19 cm.

G630/S655

Junior High School Education: Its Principles and Procedures/Maurice M. Smith. —New York and London: McGraw-Hill Book Company, Inc. , c1942

470 p. ;23 cm.

G632. 3/U28

The Supervision of Secondary Subjects/Willis L. Uhl. —New York: D. Appleton and Company, c1929

xvi, 673 p. ;19 cm.

G632. 3/U31

Secondary School Curricula/Willis L. Uhl. —New York: The Macmillan Company, c1927

xx, 582 p. ;20 cm.

G632. 479/S836

Stephenson's Eighth Grade Examination Question and Answer Books: 1923 Supplement/Compiled by Sam C. Stephenson. —Nebraska: Sam C. Stephenson, c1923

73 p. ;23 cm.

G633. 2/A526

American Government: A Text-book for Secondary Schools/Roscoe Lewis Ashley. —New York: The Macmillan Company, c1904

xx, 356 p. ;19 cm.

G633. 34/W257-2

Theme-Building: The Essentials of High-School Composition/C. H. Ward. —Revised ed. —Chicago: Scott, Foresman and Company, c1924

xviii, 540 p. ;19 cm.

G633. 41/C734

New Manual of English Grammar with Chinese Translations (for Middle Schools)/Commercial Press, Ltd. ,—Shanghai: Commercial Press, Ltd. , c1924

245 p. ;19 cm.

G633. 51/R419-2

Outlines of Ceneral History for Eastern Students/V. A. Renouf. —2nd ed. —London: Macmillan and Co. , Ltd. , c1907

xxii, 501 p. ;22 cm.

G633. 54/K29

The Old-World Beginning of America/Mary G. Kelty. —Boston: Ginn and Company, c1932

ix, 379 p. ;20 cm.

G633. 56/L848(3)

The World for Senior Students. Book III/Longmans, Green, and Co. ,—Revised ed. —London: Longmans, Green, and Co. , c1907

viii, 562 p. ;19 cm.

G633. 57/F933

The New Geography of China: A Senior Middle School Textbook/Chester G. Fuson. —Shanghai: The Commercial Press, Ltd. , c1933

xii, 260 p. ;23 cm.

G633. 58/S528

The Story of Our Continent: A Reader in the Geography and Geology of North America for the Use of Schools/N. S. Shaler. —Boston: Ginn & Company, c1899

v, 290 p. ;19 cm.

G633. 6/C976

A Course in General Mathematics/Clinton Harvey Currier, Emery Ernest Watson. —[S. l. : s. n.], [?]

viii, 413 p. ;19 cm.

G633. 6/S645(2)

General High School Mathematics. Book II/David Eugene Smith, John Albert Foberg, William David Reeve. —[S. l: s. n.], [?]

viii, 472 p. ;19 cm.

G633.62/D955

Practical School Algebra/Clement V. Dutell. —London: G. Bell and Sons, Ltd. , c1928

xii, 320, lx p. ;18 cm.

G633.63/S642

Modern-School Solid Geometry/Eolland R. Smith, John R. Clark. —New York: World Book Company, c1939

258 p. ;20 cm.

G633.7/R333

Physics: A Simplified Text for Review in Questions and Answers/Regents Publishing Co. , Inc. —New York: Regents Publishing Co. , c1947

84 p. ;17 cm.

G633.7/S849

Physics for Secondary Schools/Oscar M. Stewart, Burton L. Cushing. —Revised ed. . —Boston: Ginn and Company, c1946

vi, 768 p. ;19 cm.

G633.8/K33

Smith's Elementary Chemistry/rev. and rewritten by James Kendall. —London: G. Bell and Sons. Ltd. , c1925

xvi, 442 p. ;18 cm.

G633.951/G453

Intermediate Music/Thaddeus P. Giddings, Will Earhart, Ralph L. Baldwin, Elbridge W. Newton. —Boston: Ginn and Company, c1924

224 p. ;21 cm.

G633.951/T914(1)

The New Normal Music Course. Book One/John W. Tufts, H. E. Holt. —Boston: Silver, Burdett and Company, c1910

144 p. ;20 cm.

G633.951/T914(2)

The New Normal Music Course. Book Two/John W. Tufts, H. E. Holt. —Boston: Silver, Burdett and Company, c1911

224 p. ;20 cm.

G634/E49(1)

Junior High School Literature. Book One/William H. Elson, Christine M. Keck. —Chicago: Scott, Foresman and Company, c1920

xiv, 624 p. ;19 cm.

G634/E49(2)

Junior High School Literature. Book Two/William H. Elson, Christine M. Keck. —Chicago: Scott, Foresman and Company, c1920

660 p. ;19 cm.

G634.34/H566

New Composition and Rhetoric for Schools/Robert Herrick, Lindsay Todd Damon. —Chicago: Scott, Foresman and Company, c1911

508 p. ;19 cm.

G634.41/L735

Selected English Writings of Chinese Middle School Students/H. D. Ling. —Shanghai: The World Book Co. , Ltd. , c1928

iii, 161 p. ;19 cm.

G634.41/T799(1)

Junior English in Action. Book One/J. C. Tressler. —Revised ed. . —Boston: D. C. Teath and Company, c1937

xiv, 402 p. ;19 cm.

G634.41/W256

Sentence and Theme (Abridged-with Drills): a Foundation for High-school Composition/C. H. Ward. . —Chicago: Scott, Foresman, c1929.

xx, 304 p. ;19 cm.

G634. 55/R845

Living in the Peoples' World/Lawrence V. Roth, Stillman M. Hobbs. —Chicago: Laidlaw Brothers Publishers, c1947

704 p. ;22 cm.

G634. 6/D955(2)

The New Day Junior Mathematics. Book Two/ Fletcher Durell, J. A. Foberg, Ralph S. Newcomb. —New York: Charles E. Merrill Company, c1932

xii, 338, xxviii p. ;19 cm.

G634. 653/P977-5

An Elementary Treatise on Conic Sections and Algebraic Geometry/G. Hale Puckle. —5th ed. . —Tokyo: Rairaido, c1896

vi, 379 p. ;19 cm.

G639. 712/I52

Principles of Secondary Education/Alexander Inglis. —Boston: Houghton Mifflin Company, c1918

xvi, 741 p. ;19 cm.

G639. 712/K75

The American Secondary School/Leonard V. Koos. —Boston: Ginn and Company, c1927

xii, 755 p. ;19 cm.

G640/N551

The Aim of a University Education/John Henry Newman. —[S. l. : s. n.], [?]

251 p. ;18 cm.

G642. 3/B512

A College Course in Writing from Models/ Frances Campbell Berkeley. —New York: Henry Holt and Company, c1910

xiii, 478 p. ;19 cm.

G649. 712/B223

Teacher in America/Jacques Barzun. —Boston: Little, Brown and Company, c1945.

321 p. ;21 cm.

G649. 712/B639

American Universities and Colleges/David Allan Robertson. —New York: Charles Scribner's Sons, c1928

xii, 884 p. ;22 cm.

G649. 712/F264

Facing Life/W. H. P. Faunce. —Tokyo: The Kobunsha Co. , Ltd. , c1940

103, 20 p. ;19 cm.

G649. 712/N911

Terms of Admission to the Colleges of the College Entrance Examination Board/College Entrance Examination Board. —New York: College Entrance Examination Board, c1948

iv, 223 p. ;23 cm.

G649. 712/O77

The Approbation of Religious Institutes: A Dissertation/Clement Raymond Orth. —Washington: Catholic University of America, c1931

170 p. ;23 cm.

G649. 712/W314-2

Fifty Years in Constantinople and Recollections of Robert College/George Washburn. —2nd ed. —Boston: Houghton Mifflin Company, c1911

xxx, 319 p. ;22 cm.

G649. 712/W837

Educational Guide to the United States for use of Chinese and Other Oriental Students/J. Wong-Quincey. —Shanghai: Commerical Press, Ltd. , c1921

iii, 634 p. ;23 cm.

G649. 712. 8/U58(3)

University of Michigan Official Publication:

Register of Staff and Graduates July 1, 1946, Through June 30, 1947. Section III/The University. —Ann Arbor: The University, c1947
642 p. ;23 cm.

G723/D955
A First Book in Algebra/Fletcher Durell. —New York: Charles E. Merrill Company, c1919
iv, 339, xli p. ;19 cm.

G771. 223/J73-3
Principles of Guidance/Arthur J. Jones. —3rd ed.. —New York: McGraw-Hill Book Company, Inc. , c1945
xx, 502 p. ;21 cm.

G78/B293
Safed and Keturah: The Third Series of the Parables of Safed the Sage/William E. Barton. —Boston: The Pilgrim Press, c1921
180 p. ;19 cm.

G78/C525(1)
Letters to His Son: On the Fine Art of becoming o Man of the World and a Gentlman. Vol. 1/Earl of Chesterfield. —New York: M. Walter Dunne, Publisher, c1901
xi, 408 p. ;23 cm.

G78/C525(2)
Letters to His Son: On the Fine Art of becoming o Man of the World and a Gentlman. Vol. II/Earl of Chesterfield. —New York: M. Walter Dunne, Publisher, c1901
xi, 435 p. ;23 cm.

G78/K15
The Pre-school Age: A Mother's Guide to a Child's Occupation/Minnie Watson Kamm. —Boston: Little, Brown, and Company, c1926
viii, 216 p. ;19 cm.

G78/W419
The Training of Children in the Christian Family/Luther Allan Weigle. —Boston: The Pilgrim Press, c1922
ix, 224 p. ;19 cm.

G79/D578
The Art of Conversation: With Directions for Self Education/G. W. Dillingham Co. , Pubilshers. —New York: G. W. Dillingham Co. , Pubilshers, [?]
vi, 207 p. ;19 cm.

G792/L986
The Mind at Work in Studying, Thinking and Reading: A Source Book and Discussion Manual/R. L. Lyman. —Chicago: Scott, Foresman and Company, c1924
349 p. ;20 cm.

G8-49/G736
Esquire's First Sports Reader/Herbert Graffis. —New York: A. S. Barnes & Company, c1945
292 p. ;24 cm.

G80/F597(2)
Physical Culture Classics. vol. 2/Wm. F. Fleming. —New York: E. R. Dumont, c1909
256 p. ;20

G80/M143(8. 1)
Physical Culture. Vol. 8. No. 1/Bernarr Macfadden. —New York: Physical Culture Publishing Company, c1902
196 p. ;24 cm.

G80-05/F597
Physical Culture Classics. Vol. 1/WM. F. Fleming. —New York: The United School of Physical Culture, c1909
248 p. ;21 cm.

G811/D225

Sport in the Highland of Kashmir: Being a Narrative of an Eight Months' Trip in Baltistan and Ladak, and a Lady's Experiences in the Latter Country; Together with Hints for the Guidance of Sportsmen/Henry Zouch Darrah. —London: Rowland Ward, Ltd. , c1898

xviii, 506 p. ;23 cm.

G811. 9/S861

Torch-Bearers of History/Amelia H. Stirling. —London: T. Nelson and Sons, c1894

174 p. ;19 cm.

G812/H717

Physical Education in China/GunSun Hoh. —Shanghai: The Commerical Press, Ltd. , c1926

xvii, 314 p. ;21 cm.

G845/H645

Forty Years of First-Class Lawn Tennis/G. W. Hillyard. —London: Williams & Norgate, Ltd. , c1925

xi, 267 p. ;22 cm.

G849. 3/B877

How to Play Golf: Golf Lessons and Comment: How I Play Golf/Innis Brown. —New York: American Sports Publishing Company, c1935

158 p. ;17 cm.

G849. 319/B425

Golf Faults Illustrated/G. W. Beldam, J. H. Taylor. —London: William Clowes and Sons, [?]

174 p. ;22 cm.

G875. 3/C712

The Boy's Book of Model Aeroplanes/Francis A. Collins. —New York: D. Appleton-Century Company, c1943

vii, 262 p. ;19 cm.

G89/F888

Good Games/Jean Hosford Fretwell. —New York: Rand McNally & Company, c1930

160 p. ;23 cm.

G894/S787-34(1)

Stanley Gibbons Limited Priced Catalogue of Stamps of the Whole World 1928. Part I, British Empire/Stanley Gibbons, Ltd. , —34th ed. . —London: Stanley Gibbons, Ltd. , c[1928]

xvi, 1248, 72 p. ;18 cm.

G894. 1/P213-3

Standard Postage Stamp Catalogue of China and Treaty Ports/S. A. Pappadopulo. —Shanghai: Stephens Stamo Co. , c1935

1 v. ;21 cm.

G895/R896

The Book of Camping: Camping Essentials for the Leader/Robert Rubin. —New York: Association Press, c1949

viii, 152 p. ;21 cm.

G897/M234

Sure You Can Fish!: Tackle Shortages Need not Stop You/Harlan Major. —New York: Funk & Wagnalls Company, c1942

xiv, 124 p. ;23 cm.

G898/H255

The Fun Encyclopedia: An All-Purpose Plan Book for Those Interested in Recreation for Clubs, Schools, Churches, and the Home/E. O. Harbin. —[S. l.]: Abingdon Cokesbur, [?]

1008 p. ;24 cm.

G898/H255

Phunology: A Collection of Tried and Provel Plans for Play, Fellowship, and Profit/E. O. Harbin. —Nashville: Cokesbury Press, c1930

ix, 454 p. ;20 cm.

G898/H945

James Hunter's Book of Indoor Entertainments/James Hunter.—London: Hodder & Stoughton Ltd. , c1935

659 p. ;19 cm.

G898/R421

Betcha Can't Do It !: A Hundred and Two Stunts and Practical Jokes/Alexander Van Rensselaer.—[S. l. : s. n.], c1941

xvi, 168 p. ;19 cm.

G898. 2/S779

Judge's Cross Word Puzzle Omnibus/The Staff of Judge.—New York: Blue Ribbon Books, c1929, 1930, 1931

1 v. ;20 cm.

H 语言、文字

H0/B666

The Loom of Language/Frederick Bodmer.—New York: W. W. Norton & Company, Inc. , c1944

512 p. ;12×17 cm.

H019/B181

Our Inheritance Speeches and Addresses/Stanley Balawin.—New York: Doubleday, Doran & Company, Inc. , c1928

xvi, 349 p. ;20 cm.

H019/B433

Bell's Standard Elocutionist: Principles and Exercises/David Charles Bell, Alexander Melville Bell.—London: Hodder and Stoughton, [?]

xvi, 528 p. ;17 cm.

H019/B877

Poems of Pep and Point for Public Speakers/Will H. Brown.—Cincinnati: The Standard Publishing Company, c1918

327 p. ;19 cm.

H019/C583

Two Patriotic Pageants/Classes in the English and History Departments of the New Jersy State Normal School.—Boston: Walter H. Baker & Co. , c1921

132 p. ;19 cm.

H019/D125

The Principles of Public Speaking: A Practical Text Book for Colleges/Maynard Lee Daggy.—Madison: Democrat Printing Company, c1909

x, 436 p. ;20 cm.

H019/H429(1)

Orations: From Homer to William McKinley. Vol. I /Mayo W. Hazeltine.—New York: P. F. Collier and Son, [?]

438 p. ;19 cm.

H019/H429(2)

Orations: From Homer to William McKinley. Vol. II/Mayo W. Hazeltine.—New York: P. F. Collier and Son, [?]

ii, 1763-2192 p. ;19 cm.

H019/H429(3)

Orations: From Homer to William McKinley. Vol. III/Mayo W. Hazeltine. —New York: P. F. Collier and Son, [?]

iii, 875-1318 p. ;19 cm.

H019/H429(4)

Orations: From Homer to William McKinley. Vol. V/Mayo W. Hazeltine. —New York: P. F. Collier and Son, [?]

iii, 1319-1762 p. ;19 cm.

H019/H429(5)

Orations: From Homer to William McKinley. Vol. V/Mayo W. Hazeltine. —New York: P. F. Collier and Son, [?]

ii, 1763-2192 p. ;19 cm.

H019/H429(6)

Orations: From Homer to William McKinley. Vol. VI/Mayo W. Hazeltine. —New York: P. F. Collier and Son, [?]

2193-2625 p. ;19 cm.

H019/H429(7)

Orations: From Homer to William McKinley. Vol. VII/Mayo W. Hazeltine. —New York: P. F. Collier and Son, [?]

iii, 2627-3068 p. ;19 cm.

H019/H429(8)

Orations: From Homer to William McKinley. Vol. VIII/Mayo W. Hazeltine. —New York: P. F. Collier and Son, [?]

iii, 3070-3508 p. ;19 cm.

H019/H429(9)

Orations: From Homer to William McKinley. Vol. IX/Mayo W. Hazeltine. —New York: P. F. Collier and Son, [?]

3511-3953 p. ;19 cm.

H019/H429(10)

Orations: From Homer to William McKinley. Vol. X/Mayo W. Hazeltine. —New York: P. F. Collier and Son, [?]

ii, 3955-4417 p. ;19 cm.

H019/H429(11)

Orations: From Homer to William Mckinley. vol. 11/Mayo W. Hazeltine. —New York: P. F. Collier and Son, [?]

4420-4819 p. ;20 cm.

H019/H429(13)

Orations: From Homer to William McKinley. Vol. XIII/Mayo W. Hazeltine. —New York: P. F. Collier and Son, [?]

5259-5680 p. ;20 cm.

H019/H429(14)

Orations: From Homer to William McKinley. Vol. XIV/Mayo W. Hazeltine. —New York: P. F. Collier and Son, [?]

5681-6120 p. ;20 cm.

H019/H429(15)

Orations: From Homer to William Mckinley. vol. 15/Mayo W. Hazeltine. —New York: P. F. Collier and Son, [?]

ii, 6122-6560 p. ;20 cm.

H019/H429(16)

Orations: From Homer to William McKinley. Vol. XVI/Mayo W. Hazeltine. —New York: P. F. Collier and Son, [?]

ii, 6561-6993 p. ;19 cm.

H019/H429(17)

Orations: From Homer to William McKinley. Vol. XVII/Mayo W. Hazeltine. —New York: P. F. Collier and Son, c1902

ii, 6995-7734 p. ;19 cm.

H019/H429(18)

Orations：From Homer to William McKinley. Vol. XVIII/Mayo W. Hazeltine. —New York：P. F. Collier and Son，c1902

ii，7435-7878 p. ;19 cm.

H019/H429(20)

Orations：From Homer to William McKinley. Vol. XX/Mayo W. Hazeltine. —New York：P. F. Collier and Son，[?]

ii，8321-8766 p. ;20 cm.

H019/H429(22)

Orations：From Homer to William McKinley. Vol. XXII/Mayo W. Hazeltine. —New York：P. F. Collier and Son，[?]

ii，9207-9650 p. ;19 cm.

H019/H429(23)

Orations：From Homer to William Mckinley. vol. XXIII/Mayo W. Hazeltine. —New York：P. F. Collier and Son，[?]

9651-10090 p. ;20 cm.

H019/H429(25)

Orations：From Homer to William Mckinley. vol. 25/Mayo W. Hazeltine. —New York：P. F. Collier and Son，[?]

4819-5257 p. ;20 cm.

H019/H429(25)

Orations：From Homer to William McKinley. Vol. XXV/Mayo W. Hazeltine. —New York：P. F. Collier and Son，[?]

ii，10545-11114 p. ;19 cm.

H019/H479(24)

Orations：From Homer to William McKinley. Vol. XXIV/Mayo W. Hazeltine. —New York：P. F. Collier and Son，[?]

ii，10091-10544 p. ;20 cm.

H019/M753

Principles and Types of Speech/Alan H. Monroe. —Washington：Scott，Foresman and Company，c1944

xii，543 p. ;21 cm.

H02/L673

Specimens of the forms of Discourse/E. H. Lewis. —New York：Henry Holt and Company，c1900

viii，367 p. ;17 cm.

H026. 1/I86

Pitman's Shorthand Instructor：A Complete Exposition of Sir Isaac Pitman's System of Shorthand/Isaac Pitman. —London：Sir Isaac Pitman & Sons，Ltd. ，[?]

xiii，301 p. ;17 cm.

H026. 1/P685

Course in Isaac Pitman Shorthand/Isaac Pitamn. —Toronto：The Commercial Text Book Company，c1913

240，23 p. ;16 cm.

H026. 3/T531(5)

Language in Action. Grade Five/A. L. Threlkeld，Frances M. Noar，Dale Zeller. —Chicago：J. B. Lippincott Company，c1934

xxxi，513 p. ;19 cm.

H05/S562

The Rhetoric of Oratory/Edwin Du Bois Shruter. —New York：The Macmillan Company，c1912

x，309 p. ;19 cm.

H126. 1/G819

Advanced Shorthand：A Self-teaching Course，Based on Gregg Speed Building/John Robert Gregg. —New York：The Gregg Publishing Company，[1943]

316 p. ;22 cm.

H126. 1/W516

Lesson Plans in Gregg Shorthand/Lula May Westenhaver. —New York: The Gregg Publishing Company, c1925

xix, 185 p. ;19 cm.

H152. 3/C436-9

A Digest of the Law of Bills of Exchange, Promissory Notes, Cheques, and Negotiable Securities/Sir M. D. Chalmers; assisted by Kenneth Chalmers. . —9th ed. . —London: Stevens & Sons, Ltd. , 1927

2 p. l. , iii-li, 500 p. ;22 cm.

H19/H654-3(2)

The Chinese Language: How To Learn It. Vloeme II/Walter Hillier. —3rd ed. , Revised. —Wisconsin: C. N. Caspar Co. , c1923

i, 250, 109 p. ;21 cm.

H19/H654-7

The Chinese Language And How To Learn It: A Manual for Beginners/Walter Hillier. —7th. ed. . —Wisconsin: C. N. Caspar Co. , c1924

297 p. ;21 cm.

H31/B187

Constructive English: Derivation, Spelling, Pronunciation, Grammar, Usage, Capitalization, Functuation, and Letter Writing, with Exercises/Francis Kingsley Ball. —Boston: Ginn, c1923.

xxii, 458 p. ;18 cm.

H31/B571(3)

English for Use. Book Three/John H. Beveridge, Belle M. Ryan, William D. Lewis. —Chicago: The John C. Winston Company, c1935

xiv, 450 p. ;19 cm.

H31/C734-2(2)

New Textbook of English Grammar. Volume II: For Middle Schools/Commercial Press, Ltd. ,—2nd ed. . —Shanghai: Commercial Press, Ltd. , 1920

ix, 178-397 p. ;20 cm.

H31/C877

The Arts of Writing, Reading, and Speaking/Edward W. Cox. —New York: G. W. Dillingham Co. , [?]

264 p. ;19 cm.

H31/D313

Actual Business English/P. H. Deffendall. —New York: The Macmillan Company, c1924

x, 224 p. ;19 cm.

H31/H279

Origins and Meanings of Popular Phrases & Names: Including Those Which Came Into Use During the Great War. /Basil Hargrave. —London: T. Werner Laurie, c1932.

376 p. ;21 cm.

H31/H429

The Second Book of Observation, Thought and Expression or Seeing, Thinking, Knowing, Talking and Writing/M. W. Hazen. —New York: Silver Rurdett and Company, c1899

288 p. ;19 cm.

H31/I18

Business English/Smimasa Idichi. —Kojimachi: Kenkyu Sha, c1924

vi, 273 p. ;20 cm.

H31/L523(30)

The Penguin New Writing. 30/John Lehmann. —London: Penguin Books, c1947

192 p. ;19 cm.

H31/M488

My Adventure in England/A. W. Medley. —Tokyo: Taibundo, [?]

195 p. ;18 cm.

H31/N118

Business English and Correspondence/Thomas G. Nacayama. —Tokyo: Sugiyama Book Company, c1927

viii, 490 p. ;22 cm.

H31/P866(2)

Oral and Written English Complete Book. Book two/Milton C. Potter, H. Jeschke. —Boston: Ginn and Company, c1917

iv, 418, xxxiv p. ;19 cm.

H31/P866

Oral and Written English Complete Book/Milton C. Potter, H. Jeschke. —Boston: Ginn and Company, c1921

iv, 418, xxxiv p. ;19 cm.

H31/R643

English for Social Living: A Program Including 25 Statements of Practic by Teachers in the Field/Holland D. Roberts, Walter V. Kaulfers, Grayson N. Kefauver. —New York: McGraw-Hill Book Company, Inc., c1943

xiii, 266 p. ;23 cm.

H31/S132

Saito's Advance English Lessons/H. Saito. —[S. l.]: The S. E. G. Press, c1901

1051 p. ;19 cm.

H31/T166(1)

Correct English: First Course. /William M. Tanner. —Boston: Ginn and Co., c1931

xii, 452, xvi p. ;19 cm.

H31/T166(2)

My English. Book Two/William M. Tanner, Frank J. Platt. —Boston: Ginn and Company, c1941

xv, 399 p. ;19 cm.

H31/T799(2)

English in Action. Course Two/J. C. Tressler. —Boston: D. C. Heath and Company, c1929, 1930

ix, 243 p. ;20 cm.

H31/T799(3)

English in Action. Course Three/J. C. Tressler. —Boston: D. C. Heath and Company, c1929

x, 307 p. ;21 cm.

H31/T799-4(1)

English in Action. Course One/J. C. Tressler. —4th ed.. —Boston: D. C. Heath and Company, [?]

xii, 468 p. ;21cm.

H31/T799-4(2)

English in Action. Course Two/J. C. Tressler. —4th ed.. —Boston: D. C. Heath and Company, c1945

xiv, 466 p. ;21cm.

H31/T799-4(3)

English in Action. Course Three/J. C. Tressler. —4th ed.. —Boston: D. C. Heath and Company, [?]

xii, 467 p. ;21cm.

H31/T799-4(4)

English in Action. Course Four/J. C. Tressler. —4th ed.. —Boston: D. C. Heath and Company, c1945

xiv, 466 p. ;21 cm.

H31/T799-4

English in Action/J. C. Tressler. —4th ed.. —Boston: D. C. Heath and Company, c1945

xiv, 464 p. ;21cm.

H31/W913

College Handbook of Composition/Edwin C. Woolley, Franklin W. Scott. —Boston: D. C. Heath and Company, c1928

xix, 396 p. ;17 cm.

H311.9/C568

Select Orations of Cicero/Cicero. —Boston: Ginn and Company, c1896

lxv, 495 p. , 194 p. ;19 cm.

H312/G819

Gregg Shorthand: A Light-Line Phonography for the Million/John Robert Gregg. —New York: The Gregg Publishing Company, c1929

xiv, 173 p. ;17 cm.

H313/B792

The Saurus of English Words and Phrases. 1/ A. Boyle. —London: J. M. Dent. & Co. , c1912

305 p. ;18 cm.

H313/D548(1)

Household Words. Vol. I/Charles Dickens. —Leipzig: Bernhard Tauchnitz, c1851

vi, 380 p. ;16 cm.

H313/D548(3)

Household Words. Vol. III/Charles Dickens. —Leipzig: Bernhard Tauchnitz, c1851

vi, 416 p. ;16 cm.

H313/D548(4)

Household Words. Vol. IV/Charles Dickens. —Leipzig: Bernhard Tauchnitz, c1851

vi, 422 p. ;16 cm.

H313/D548(6)

Household Words. Vol. VI/Charles Dickens. —Leipzig: Bernhard Tauchnitz, c1851

vi, 419 p. ;16 cm.

H313/D548(9)

Household Words. Vol. IX/Charles Dickens. —Leipzig: Bernhard Tauchnitz, c1851

vi, 424 p. ;16 cm.

H313/D548(11)

Household Words. Vol. XI/Charles Dickens. —Leipzig: Bernhard Tauchnitz, c1852

vi, 433 p. ;16 cm.

H313/D548(13)

Household Words. Vol. XIII/Charles Dickens. —Leipzig: Bernhard Tauchnitz, c1853

vi, 434 p. ;16 cm.

H313/D548(15)

Household Words. Vol. XV/Charles Dickens. —Leipzig: Bernhard Tauchnitz, c1852

350 p. ;16 cm.

H313/D548(16)

Household Words. Vol. XVI/Charles Dickens. —Leipzig: Bernhard Tauchnitz, c1852

vi, 364 p. ;16 cm.

H313/D548(18)

Household Words. Vol. XVIII/Charles Dickens. —Leipzig: Bernhard Tauchnitz, c1853

vi, 394 p. ;16 cm.

H313/D548(21)

Household Words. Vol. XXI/Charles Dickens. —Leipzig: Bernhard Tauchnitz, c1853

vi, 374 p. ;16 cm.

H313/D548(29)

Household Words. Vol. XXIX/Charles Dickens. —Leipzig: Bernhard Tauchnitz, c1851

lxx, 340 p. ;16 cm.

H313/D548(30)

Household Words. Vol. XXX/Charles Dickens. —Leipzig: Bernhard Tauchnitz, c1855

vi, 366 p. ;16 cm.

H313/D548(34)

Household Words. Vol. XXXIV/Charles Dickens. —Leipzig: Bernhard Tauchnitz, c1856

vi, 378 p. ;16 cm.

H313/D548(35)

Household Words. Vol. XXXV/Charles Dickens. —Leipzig: Bernhard Tauchnitz, c1856

vi, 378 p. ;16 cm.

H313/D548(36)

Household Words. Vol. XXXVI/Charles Dickens. —Leipzig: Bernhard Tauchnitz, c1856

lxxiv, 302 p. ;16 cm.

H313/D548(XXVIII)

Household Words. Vol. XXVIII/Charles Dickens. —Leipzig: Bernhard Tauchnitz, c1851

vi, 422 p. ;16 cm.

H313/F982

30 Days to A More Powerful Vocabulary/Wilfred Funk. —New York: Wilfred Funk, Inc., c1943

vii, 248 p. ;19 cm.

H313/Z94

Science Terms Made Easy/A. E. Zucker, Charles Packard. —Shanghai: Commercial Press, Ltd., c1920

ix, 164 p. ;19 cm.

H313.2/C883

English Synonyms Explained/George Crabb. —Shanghai: Commercial Press, Ltd., c1913

597 p. ;19 cm.

H313.3/W256

The Chairman's Guide and Secretary's Companion/Ward Lock & Co., Ltd., —London: Ward Lock & Co., Ltd., c1914

176 p. ;19 cm.

H313.3-61/F813

Dictionary of Slang and Colloquial English/John S. Framer, W. E. Henley. —Tokyo: Maruzen Co., Ltd., [?]

viii, 533 p. ;22 cm.

H314/F245

The Grammar School: Speller and Definer/E. D. Farrell. —New York: The Catholic Publication Society Co., c1889

225 p. ;19 cm.

H314/F912

American English Grammar: The Grammatical Structure of Present-Day American English with Especial Reference to Social Differences or Class Dialects/Charles Carpenter Fries. —New York: Appleton-Century-Crofts, Inc., [?]

313 p. ;21 cm.

H314/K16

Higher English Grammar/Naibu Kanda. —Shanghai: The Commercial Press, Ltd., c1927

169 p. ;19 cm.

H314/K16-2

English Grammar for Beginners/Naibu Kanda. —Revised ed.. —Tokyo: Sanseido, c1904

80 p. ;19 cm.

H314/K62(2)

The Mother Tongue. Book II, An Elementary English Grammar/George Lyman Kittredge. —Revised ed.. —Boston: Ginn and Company, c1908

xxii, 454 p. ;19 cm.

H314/L351

A Complete English Grammar for Chinese

Students/David Lattimore. —Shanghai: Commercial Press, c1923.

x, 518 p. ;18 cm.

H314/L525(O)

A New English Grammar/M. A. Leiper. —Shanghai: The Macmillan Company Publisher, c1923

x, 362 p. ;19 cm.

H314/N457

Idiom, Grammar, and Synthesis: A Manual of Practical and Theoretical English for High School and University Students/J. C. Nesfield. —London: Macmillan and Co., Ltd., c1922

vii, 471 p. ;19 cm.

H314/S132

Practical English Grammar. Vol. II/Saito. —東京: 興文社工場, c1898

307 p. ;19 cm.

H314/S642

English Grammar: Correct and Effective use/Kate Smith, Ethel B. Magee. —Boston: Ginn and Company, c1928

x, 357 p. ;19 cm.

H314/S648

Longmans' Briefer Grammar/George J. Smith. —New York: Longmans, Green and Co., c1903

226 p. ;20 cm.

H314/S961

An Advanced English Grammar/N. Suruda. —Kokyo: Kokyo Taibunsha, c1936

80 p. ;19 cm.

H314/Y45

English Grammar/Julin Khedau Yen-Fuh. —Shanghai: Commercial Press, c1913

x, 239 p. ;19 cm.

H314/Y9

English Grammar/Julin Khedau Yen-Fuh. —Shanghai: The Commercial Press, Ltd., c1927

x, 239 p. ;19 cm.

H314.1/T758

Trabue-Stevens Speller/M. R. Trabue, B. A. Stevens. —New York: Row, Peterson and Company, c1929

xv, 57, xxv p. ;19 cm.

H314.2/S132(2)

Higher English Lessons: Higher Second Year. No. 2, Verbs/H. Saito. —Tokyo: Kobunsha, c1902

326 p. ;20 cm.

H315/A939

The Automatic Letter Writer/A. W. Shaw Company. —Chicago: A. W. Shaw Company, c1914

192 p. ;26 cm.

H315/B827-15

Commercial Composition and Correspondence/Henry Freer Bray. —15th ed.. —Tokyo: Maruzen Company, Ltd., c1922.

364 p. ;22 cm.

H315/B873

Essay and Letter Writing With Models and Outlines/F. H. Brooksbank. —London: Macmillan and Co., Ltd., c1908

xii, 263 p. ;17 cm.

H315/D313

Actual Business Correspondence/P. H. Deffendall. —New York: The Macmillan Company, c1923

ix, 267 p. ;19 cm.

H315/F342(2)

English Commercial Correspondence. Book II/S. W. Fenton. —Shanghai: The Commercial Press, Ltd., c1927

281-665 p.; 19 cm.

H315/F974

Writing Craftsmanship: Models and Readings/Maurice Garland Fulton. —New York: The Macmillan Company, c1926

xiii, 498 p.; 20 cm.

H315/F974C697

College life: Its Conditions and Problems/Maurice Garland Fulton. —New York: The Macmillan Company, c1922

xxii, 524 p.; 19 cm.

H315/G219

Manual of Composition and Rhetoric/John Hays Gardiner, George Lyman Kittredge and Sarah Louise Arnold. —Boston: Ginn & Company, c1907

xi, 500 p.; 18 cm.

H315/G341

Outlines of Composition and Rhetoric/John Franklin Genung, Charles Lane Hanson. —Boston: Ginn and Company, c1915

vii, 406 p.; 19 cm.

H315/H243

Style Manual of the Department of State: For Use in the Preparation of Correspondence and State Papers/Margaret M. Hanna, Alice M. Ball. —Washington D. C.: United States Government Printing Office, c1937

xvi, 375 p.; 25 cm.

H315/H341

Practice Handbook in English Composition for College Students/P. Caspar Harvey. —New York: The Macmillan Company, c1930

xix, 350 p.; 19 cm.

H315/L353

Freshman Composition/Henry Burrowes Lathrop. —New York: The Century Co., c1921

xxii, 369 p.; 19 cm.

H315/L693

A Manual of Commercial Correspondence and Commercial Forms/Li Ung Bing. —Shanghai: The Commercial Press, c1927

xix, 173 p.; 20 cm.

H315/L845

The Study and Practice of Writing English/Gerhard R. Lomer, Margaaret Shmun. —Boston: Houghton Mifflin Company, c1946

v, 342 p.; 19 cm.

H315/P252

English Ways and By-ways/Leighton Parks. —New York: Charles Scribner's Sons, c1922

x, 232 p.; 20 cm.

H315/P361

The Principles of Composition/Henry G. Pearson. —Boston: D. C. Heath & Co., Publishers, c1897, 1898

xiv, 151 p.; 19 cm.

H315/S444-2(1)

Elementary Composition for Chinese Students. Volume I/Fong F. Sec. —Rev. ed.. —Shanghai: Commercial Press, Ltd., c1916

182 p.; 19 cm.

H315/T166

Composition and Rhetoric/William M. Tanner. —Boston: Ginn and Co., c1922.

xiii, 500 p., xxxix; 20 cm.

H315/T559

English Composition and Rhetoric/Lin Tien-Lan. —Shanghai: Chung Hwa Book Company, [?]

ii, 293 p. ;19 cm.

H315/W256

The Complete Letter-writer for Ladies and Gentlemen/Ward, Lock & Co. , Ltd. ,—London: Ward, Lock & Co. , Ltd. , [?]

1 v. ;19 cm.

H315/Y11

English Correspondence in Foreign Trade/T. Yasunda, M. Nishiyama. —Tokyo: Sekibundo, c1936

3, 266 p. ;23 cm.

H315. 9/L693(1)

Translation Exercises. Book 1, From Chinese to English/Li Ung Bing. —Shanghai: Commercial Press, Ltd. , c1913

65 p. ;19 cm.

H316/A512W377

Webster's Elementary-School Dictionary: Abridge from Webster's New International Dictionary/American Book Company. —New York: American Book Company, c1914

xvi, 702 p. ;20 cm.

H316/C734

Practical Synonyms/The Commercial Press, Ltd. ,—Shanghai: The Commercial Press, Ltd. , c1926

208 p. ;19 cm.

H316/C734

A Chinese-English Dictionary/The Commercial Press. —Shanghai: The Commercial Press, Limmited, c1930

282, 10 p. ;19 cm.

H316/C993

Apleton's New English-Spanish and Spanish-English Dictionary/Arturo Cuyas, Antonio Llano. —New York: D. Appleton-Century Company, c1942

xxvii, 539 p. ;21 cm.

H316/C993-3

Appleton's New English-Spanish and Spanish-English Dictionary/Arturo Cuyas, Antonio Liano. —3th ed. . —New York: D. Appleton-Century Company, c1903

xxvii, 539 p. ;21 cm.

H316/D354

Chambers's Twentieth Century Dictionary of the English Language/Rev. Theomas Davidson. —London: W. & R. Chambers, Ltd. , c1908

viii, 1207 p. ;21 cm.

H316/F362

A Standard Dictionary of the English Language/James C. Ferald, Francis A. March. —New York: Funk & Wagnalls Company, c1897, 1905, 1906, 1914, 1915

921 p. ;24 cm.

H316/F785-3

The Pocket Oxford Dictionary of Current English/Compiled by F. G. Fowler and H. W. Fowler. —3th ed. . —Oxford: Clarendon P. , c1936

xvi, 1034 p. ;17 cm.

H316/f786

Modern English Usage/Francis George Fowler. —London: [s. n.], [?]

viii, 742 p. ;19 cm.

H316/L673

The Winston Dictionary/William Dodge Lewis, Henry Seidel Canby. —College ed. . —New York: P. F. Coller & Son Corporation Publish-

ers, c1943
xx, 1260 p. ;22 cm.

H316/L677
The Winston Simplified Dictionary/William D. Lewis, Edgar A. Siinger. —Chicago: The John C. Winston Company, c1924
xxii, 824 p. ;19 cm.

H316/L677-IN
The Winston Simplified Dictionary/William D. Lewis, Edgar A. Siinger. —Intermediate ed.. —Chicago: The John C. Winston Company, c1929
xxii, 940 p. ;20 cm.

H316/L743
A Pocket-Dictionary of the English and German Languages: Giving the Pronunciation According to the Phonetic System of Toussaint Langenscheidt/Hermann Lindemann. —9th Revised ed.. —New York: the Internation News Company, c1911
xliv, 563, 16 p. ;16 cm.

H316/M568-5
Webster's Collegiate Dictionary/G. & C. Merriam Co. ,—5th ed.. —Springfield: G. & C. Merriam Co. , c1947
xxxiv, 1274 p. ;22 cm.

H316/M568-5
Thin Paper Webster's Collegiate Dictionary / G. & C. Merriam Co. , Publishers. —5th ed.. —Springfield: G. & C. Merriam Co. , Publishers, c1947
xxxiv, 1275 p. ;22 cm.

H316/O81(1)
The World Book. Volume One/M. V. O'shea, George H. Locke. —Chicago: W. F. Quarrie & Company, c1922
656 p. ;24 cm.

H316/O81(2)
The World Book. Volume Two/M. V. O'shea, George H. Locke. —Chicago: W. F. Quarrie & Company, c1922
657-1328 p. ;24 cm.

H316/O81(3)
The World Book. Volume Three/M. V. O'shea, George H. Locke. —Chicago: W. F. Quarrie & Company, c1923
1329-2000 p. ;24 cm.

H316/O81(4)
The World Book. Volume Four/M. V. O'shea, George H. Locke. —Chicago: W. F. Quarrie & Company, c1922
2001-2640 p. ;24 cm.

H316/O81(6)
The World Book. Volume Six/M. V. O'shea, George H. Locke. —Chicago: W. F. Quarrie & Company, c1922
3281-3952 p. ;24 cm.

H316/O81(7)
The World Book. Volume Seven/M. V. O'shea, George H. Locke. —Chicago: W. F. Quarrie & Company, c1922
3953-4608 p. ;24 cm.

H316/O81(8)
The World Book. Volume 8/M. V. O'shea, George H. Locke. —Chicago: W. F. Quarrie & Company, c1922
4609-5248 p. ;24 cm.

H316/O81(9)
The World Book. Volume Nine/M. V. O'shea, George H. Locke. —Chicago: W. F. Quarrie & Company, c1922
5249-5888 p. ;24 cm.

H316/O81(10)

The World Book. Volume Ten/M. V. O'shea, George H. Locke. —Chicago: W. F. Quarrie & Company, c1922

5889-6528 p. ;24 cm.

H316/P361-41

Pears' Cyclopaedia/A. & F. Pears Ltd. ,—41st ed. . —London: A. & F. Pears Ltd. , c1932

960 p. ;20 cm.

H316/R732

Thesaurus of English Words and Phrases: Classified and Arranged So as to Facilitate the Expression of Ideas and Assist in Literary Composition/Peter Mark Roget. —New York: Thomas Y. Crowell Company, [?]

xlv, 270 p. ;20 cm.

H316/W377-3

Webster's Collegiate Dictionary/G. &C. Merriam Co. ,—3rd ed. —Springfield: G. & C. Merriam Co. , c1930

xxxii, 1222 p. ;22 cm.

H316/W377-5

Webster's Collegiate Dictionary/Meviam Webster. —5th ed. . —Springfield: G. & C. Merriam Co. , Publishers, c1940

xxvi, 1274 p. ;23 cm.

H316/W384

Improved Pronouncing Dictionary of the English Language/Noah Webster. —London: Ward, Lock & Co. , Ltd. , [?]

viii, 416, 24 p. ;17 cm.

H316/W718

Collins' Graphic English Dictionary/A. M. Williams. —London: Collin's Clear-Type Press, [?]

1411 p. ;22 cm.

H316/W777

The Winston Dictionary for School/The Winston Dictionary Staff. —Chicago: The John C. Winston Company, c1945

x, 950, 24 p. ;22 cm.

H316/W783

The Winston Dictionary for Schools/The Winston Dictionary Staff. —Chicago: The John C. Winston Company, c1945

x, 950, 24 p. ;22 cm.

H319. 4/B167(6)

Everyday Classics: Sixth Reader/Franklin T. Banker and Ashiey H. Thorndike. —New York: The Macmillan Company, c1924

416 p. ;19 cm.

H319. 4/C559

Stories from China/T. K. CHU. —London: Kenganpaul, Trench, Trubner & Co. , Ltd. , c1937

84 p. ;15 cm.

H319. 4/C887(1)

English Prose. Vol. I/H. Craik. —New York: The Macmillan Company, [?]

604 p. ;20 cm.

H319. 4/C887(2)

English Prose. Vol. II/H. Craik. —New York: The Macmillan Company, [?]

599 p. ;20 cm.

H319. 4/C887(4)

English Prose. Vol. IV/H. Craik. —New York: The Macmillan Company, [?]

636 p. ;20 cm.

H319. 4/D194(4)

The Background Series of English Readers. Book IV, Stories from Classical Mythology/Annina Periam Danton. —Shanghai: The Commer-

cial Press, c1926
xvi, 190 p. ;19 cm.

H319.4/D194(5)
The Background Series of English Readers. Book V, Stories from the Hebrew and Greek/ Annina Periam Danton. —Shanghai: The Commercial Press, c1927
xiii, 357 p. ;19 cm.

H319.4/D548(4)
Novels and Tales: Reprinted from Household Words. Vol. IV/Charles Dickens. —Leipzig: Bernhard Tauchnitz, c1857
354 p. ;16 cm.

H319.4/D548(5)
Novels and Tales: Reprinted from Household Words. Vol. V/Charles Dickens. —Leipzig: Bernhard Tauchnitz, c1857
358 p. ;16 cm.

H319.4/D548(9)
Novels and Tales: Reprinted from Household Words. Vol. IX/Charles Dickens. —Leipzig: Bernhard Tauchnitz, c1858
322 p. ;16 cm.

H319.4/D548(11)
Novels and Tales: Reprinted from Household Words. Vol. XI/Charles Dickens. —Leipzig: Bernhard Tauchnitz, c1859
362 p. ;16 cm.

H319.4/E49(6)
Elson-Gray Basic Readers. Book Six/William H. Elson[etc.]. —Chicago: Scott, Foresman and Company, c1931, 1936
465 p. ;19 cm.

H319.4/G297(2)
Commercial Press Science Readers. Volume I/ N. Gist Gee. —Shanghai: The Commercial Press, Ltd., c1929
183 p. ;19 cm.

H319.4/G297(5)
Commercial Press Science Readers. Volume V/ N. Gist Gee. —Shanghai: The Commercial Press, Ltd., c1928
192 p. ;19 cm.

H319.4/G783
Guidebook for More Friend and Neighbors/ William S. Gray. —Chicago: Scott, Foresman and Company, c1946
176 p. ;21 cm.

H319.4/G783-1946
Guidebook for More Friend and Neighbors/ William S. Gray. —the 1946-47 ed. —Chicago: Scott, Foresman and Company, c1946
239 p. ;21 cm.

H319.4/G929
The Story of the English/H. A. Guerber. —New York: American Book Company, c1898
356 p. ;19 cm.

H319.4/H217
Sunshine Stories/Annie I. Hamilton. —Shanghai: The Commercial Press, Ltd., c1926
185 p. ;20 cm.

H319.4/H462(1)
Reading and Literature. Book One/Melvin E. Haggerty. —New York: World Book Company, c1905
viii, 567 p. ;20 cm.

H319.4/H462(2)
Reading and Literature. Book Two/Melvin E. Haggerty. —New York: World Book Company, c1905
ix, 566 p. ;20 cm.

H319.4/M494

Living Upstairs: Reading for Profit and Pleasure/Francis Meehan. —New York: E. P. Dutton & Co., Inc., c1943

256 p.;21 cm.

H319.4/N786

Merry Hearts and Bold/Witty Fenner Nolen. —Boston: D. C. Heath and Company, c1942

viii, 437 p.;20 cm.

H319.4/N786

Merry Hearts and Bold/Barbara Nolen. —Boston: D. C. Heath and Company, c1942

viii, 437 p.;20 cm.

H319.4/O93

From a Friend to a Friend/Our Sunday Visitor Press. —Indiana: Our Sunday Visitor Press, [?]

155 p.;18 cm.

H319.4/S167

From Panama to Cape Horn: A South American Reader/Ethel Imogene Salisbury. —Chicago: World Book Company, c1927

vii, 294 p.;20 cm.

H319.4/W177

The Study Readers/Alberta Walker, Mary R. Parkman. —New York: Charles E. Merrill Company, c1924

ix, 320 p.;19 cm.

H319.4/W246

Fifty Popular Chinese Folk-stories: With Chinese Notes/I-Ting Wang. —Shanghai: The World Book Co., Ltd., c1929

85 p.;19 cm.

H319.4/W676

Practice Exercises in Silent Reading and Study/J. A. Wiley. —Iowa: Professor J. A. Wiley Iowa State Teachers College Cedar Falls, c1928

368 p.;19 cm.

H319.4/Y94

Sophomore English Readings/C. C. Yu. —Shanghai: Chung Hwa Book Co., Ltd., c1934

ii, 466 p.;18 cm.

H319.4/Y94-3

Representative Masterpieces/Yu Nanqiu. —3th. ed.. —Shanghai: Southeastern Book Company, c1930

517 p.;19 cm.

H319.4: I16/B855

Selected Speeches on Public Questions/John Bright. —London: J. M. Dent & Sons Ltd., c1907

xiii, 271 p.;17 cm.

H319.4: I561/S192

Romeo and Juliet/Cambridge University. —Cambridge: Cambridge University, 1936

238 p.;17 cm.

H319.4: I561.44/R285

The Cloister and the Hearth/Charles Reade. —Shanghai: Chung Hwa Book Co., Ltd., [?]

iv, 174 p.;19 cm.

H319.4: N/M427

Enough and to Spare: Mother Earth Can Nourish Every Man in Freedom/Kirtley F. Mather. —New York and London: Harper & Brothers, c1944

186 p.;19 cm.

H319.9/C337

District School Dialogues for All Occasions: Choice Selections That Assure Pleasant and Pleasurable Entertainments in School, Church or Parlor/Carleton B. Case. —Chicago: Shrewesbury Publishing Co., c1928

155 p.;18 cm.

H319. 9/S253

Anglo-Japanese Conversation Lessons/Henry Satoh. —Tokyo: H Hayashi. , c1896

457 p. ;15 cm.

H319. 9/Y94

Students' English Conversation/Wang Yuan-Chang. —Shanghai: The Commercial Press, Ltd. , c1924

viii, 131 p. ;19 cm.

H32/A211

French/John Adams. —London: Hodder and Stoughton, Ltd. , [?]

xv, 206 p. ;19 cm.

H32/D671(1)

Modern French Course. Book One/Mathurin Dondo. —Boston: D. C. Heath and Company, c1945

ix, 367 p. ;21 cm.

H32/F765(1)

The Mastery of French: Direct Method. Book One/G. P. Fougeray. —New York: Iroquois Publishing Company, Inc. , c1922, 1923

xxxvii, 429 p. ;21 cm.

H324/F841

A French Grammar for Schools and Colleges Together With a Brief Reader and English Exercises /W. H. Fraser. —Boston: Heath, c1901

551 p. ;18 cm.

H326/W511-2

Junior Classic French Dictionary: French-English and English-French/J. E. Wessely. —Revised ed. . —Chicago: Follett Publishing Company, c1946

272 p. ;17 cm.

H329. 9/C471

Practical Exercises on French Conversation/C. A. Chardenal. —New ed. . —London: Librairie Hachette, c1928

viii, 192 p. ;17 cm.

H33/A425(1)

German. Book One/Philip Schuyler Allen, Dorothea Von Harjes Davis. —Chicago: Scott, Foresman and Company, c1938

432 p. ;23 cm.

H33/H536

German and English Languages/F. C. Herbert, L. Hirsch. —Philadelphia: David McKay Company, [?]

1 v. ;18 cm.

H33/O89-9

First German Book/Emil Otto, Franz Lange. —9th ed. . —London: Sampson Low, Marston & Co. , c1906

vii, 103 p. ;20 cm.

H33/V959-3

Essentials of German/B. J. Vos. —3rd ed. . —New York: Henry Holt and Company, c1913

287 p. ;20 cm.

H334/A425

A First German Grammar/Philip Schuyler Allen, Paul Hermann Phllipson. —Boston: Ginn and Company, c1916

xiv, 436 p. ;19 cm.

H334/A917

Chambers's Advanced German Grammar/Carl Eduard Aue. —London: W. & R. Chambers, Ltd. , c1905

418 p. ;18 cm.

H334/J54

A German Grammar for Schools and Colleges/

Edward S. Joynes. —Boston: D. C. Heath & Co. , Publishers, c1887, 1898, 1904
ix, 436 p. ;18 cm.

H334/M927
Spoken German: Basic Course Units 1-12/William Gamwell Moulton, Fenni Karding Moulton. —Washington, D. C. : Linguistic Society of America, c1944
ix, 269 p. ;14 cm.

H34/I11(2)
Elcamino Real: Understanding our Spanish-Speaking Neighbors. Book Two/Edith Moore Iarrett. —Boston: Houghton Mifflin Company, c1943
xvi, 622 p. ;22 cm.

H34/J37(1)
El Camino Real. Book One: Understanding our Spanish-Speaking Neighbors/Edith Moore Jarrett, Beryl J. M. Mcm. anus. —New ed. . —Boston: Houghton Mifflin Company, c1946
xxii, 494 p. ;22 cm.

H34/W684
New First Spanish Book/Lawrence A. Wilkins. —New York: Henry Holt and Company, c1925
xxiv, 388, lxx p. ;19 cm.

H34/W684
New Second Spanish Book/Lawrence A. Wilkins. —New York: Henry Holt and Company, c1926
xxi, 442, cxxiii p. ;19 cm.

H34/W691
First Spanish Course/Howard Willard. —Boston: D. C. Heath and Company, c1941
310 p. ;21 cm.

H346/K59
Handy Dictionary of the English and Spanish Languages/F. A. Kirkpatrick. —Philadelphia: David McKay Company, c1946
450 p. ;17 cm.

H346/W515
Junior Classic Spanish Dictionary: Spanish-English and English-Spanish/Wessely. —Revised ed. . —Chicago: Follett Publishing Company, c1946
vi, 215 p. ;17 cm.

H35/B711-6
Bondar's Simplified Russian Method: Conversational and Commercial/D. Bondar. —6th ed. —New York: Pitman Publishing Corporation, [?]
xxvi, 323 p. ;22 cm.

H35/M821(2)
Practical Russian. Book II/E. A. Moore, Gleb Struve. —London: Edward Arnold & Co. , c1946
138 p. ;19 cm.

H351. 2/P859
Russian: Textbook of the Russian Language for english-Speaking People. Part I/Nina Potapova. —Moscow: Foreign Languages Publishing House, c1945
310 p. ;22 cm.

H353. 1/F692-2
Second Russian Book: A Practical Manual of Russian Verbs/Nevill Forbes. —2nd ed. . —Oxford: The Clarendon Press, c1917
x, 336 p. ;19 cm.

H77/G781(2)
Latin for Today. Second-year Course/Mason D. Gray, Thornton Jenkins. —Boston: Ginn and Company, c1928
xxiv, 154 p. ;19 cm.

H77/J52(1)

Latin and the Romans. Book One/Thornton Jenkins, Anthony Pelzer Wagener. —Boston: Ginn and Company, c1942

xv, 466 p. ;23 cm.

H77/J52(2)

Latin and the Romans. Book two/Thornton Jenkins, Anthony Pelzer Wagener. —Boston: Ginn and Company, c1942

xiv, 584 p. ;23 cm.

H77/P359

Essentials of Latin for Beginners/Henry Carr Peason. —New York: American Book Company, c1905

342 p. ;18 cm.

H771/C697

First Year Latin/Collar, William C. ;Daniell, M. Grant. —Boston: Ginn and Company, c1901

xiv, 313 p. ;19 cm.

H771.6/M298

Cassell's Latin Dictionary: Latin-English, English-Latin/J. R. V. Marchant, Joseph F. Charles. —London: Cassell and Company, Ltd. , [?]

xiv, 927 p. ;22 cm.

H771-61/P969

Junior Classic Latin Dictionary: Latin-English and English-Latin/Antonio J. Provost. —Chicago: Wilcox & Follett Company, c1944

212 p. ;18 cm.

文学

I0/B144(1)

Literary Studies. Vol. I/Walter Bagehot. —London: J. M. Dent & Sons, [?]

xviii, 387 p. ;18 cm.

I0/B144(2)

Literary Studies. Vol. II/Walter Bagehot. —London: J. M. Dent & Sons, [?]

381 p. ;18 cm.

I0/Z27

Some Writers and Some Books/Tseu Yih Zan. —Shanghai: The Commercial Press, c1926

229 p. ;20 cm.

I06/B471

Arnold Bennett: How to Form It With Detailed Instructions for Collecting a Complete library of English Literature/Arnold Bennett. —London: Hodder and Stoughton, [?]

vii, 143 p. ;19 cm.

I06/F453

Readings from English and American Literature/Warter Taylor Field. —Boston: Ginn and Company, c1919

x, 512 p. ;20 cm.

I06/Q6

Studies in Literature/Arthur Quiller-Couch. —New York: G. P. Putnam's Son, c1918

iv, 324 p. ;24 cm.

I106/H887

Horizons: A Book of Criticism/Francis Hackett. —New York: B. W. Huebsch, 1919

368 p. ;21 cm.

I106/T737(1)

Prose and Poetry Adventures. Part I/Donald Maclean Tower, Cora J. Russell, Christine W. West. —New York: The L. W. Singer Company, c1945

x, 598 p. ;21 cm.

I106/T737(2)

Prose and Poetry Adventures. Part II/Donald Maclean Tower, Cora J. Russell, Christine W. West. —New York: The L. W. Singer Company, c1945

viii, 184 p. ;21 cm.

I106/T737

Prose and Poetry Journeys/Donald Maclean Tower, Cora J. Russell, Christine W. West. —New York: The L. W. Singer Company, c1945

x, 566 p. ;21 cm.

I106/W279(11)

Library of the World's Best Literature, Ancient and Modern. Vol. XI/Charles Dudley Warner. —New York: J. A. Hill & Company, c1896-1902.

ix, 4285-4688 p. ;23 cm.

I106/W279(25)

Library of the World's Best Literature, Ancient and Modern. Vol. XXV/Charles Dudley Warner. —New York: J. A. Hill & Company, c1896-1902.

ix, 9777-10152 p. ;23 cm.

I106/W959

Introductory Lessons to English Literature/ Compiled by Wu Hsien-Shu; edited by Joseph Whiteside.. —Shanghai: The Commercial Press, 1929.

193 p. ;19 cm.

I106. 3/D923

Eight Famous Elizabethan Plays/Esther Cloudman Dunn. —New York: The Modern Library, c1932

xvi, 721 p. ;18 cm.

I106. 4/C593

A Manual of the Short Story Art/Glenn Clark. —New York: The Macmillan Company, c1922

xix, 252 p. ;19 cm.

I106. 6/K95

Essays in Exposition/Benjamin P. Kurtz, Herbert E. Cory. —Boston: Ginn and Company, c1914

lvii, 521 p. ;19 cm.

I106. 9/H313

Hebraic Literature: Translations from The Talmud Midrashim and Kabbala/Maurice H. Harris. —New York: M. Walter Dunne, Publisher, c1901

xvi, 395 p. ;23 cm.

I109/H436(1)

A History of English Literature. Vol. 1/Lafcadio Hearn. —Canada: The Hokuseido Press, c1927

iii, 478, 60, xii p. ;26 cm.

I109. 2/S539

Oriental Literature: The Dabistan or School of Manners, The Original Persian. The Religious Beliefs, Observances, Philosophic Opinions and Social Customs of the Nations of the East/David Shea, Anthony Troyer. —New York: M. Walterdunne, Publisher, c1901

xv, 411 p. ;23 cm.

I11/B181

Thirty More Famous Stories Retold/James Baldwin. —New York: American Book Compa-

ny, c1905
235 p. ;19 cm.

I11/B455
The Fabric of Fiction/Douglas Bement. —New York: Harcourt, Bract and Company, c1943
xii, 644 p. ;24 cm.

I11/C946(2)
A Library of Universal Literature: Comprising Science, Biography, Fiction and the Great Orations. Part Two, Biography/Oliver Cromwell. —New York: P. F. Collier and Son, [?]
ix, 600 p. ;20 cm.

I11/R511
Essays. vol. xiv/James A. Richards. —New York: J. A. Richards, Inc. , c1924
iv, 508 p. ;20 cm.

I11/S525(2)
From Beowulf to Thomas Hardy. Volume II, From Goldsmith to Thomas Hardy/Robert Shafer. —New York: Doubleday, Page and Company, c1927
xxv, 779 p. ;23 cm.

I11/S992
Five Great Modern Irish Plays/John M. Synge. —New York: The Modern Library, c1941
xiii, 332 p. ;18 cm.

I11/Z94(2)
Western Literature. Volume II, The Bible and the Middle Ages/A. E. Zucker. —Shanghai: The Commercial Press, Ltd. , c1924
xvii, 534 p. ;21 cm.

I11/Z94-2(1)
Western Literature. Volume I, Greece and Rome/A. E. Zucker. —2nd ed. . —Shanghai: The Commercial Press, Ltd. , c1924
xvii, 534 p. ;21 cm.

I11/Z94-2(3)
Western Literature. Volume III, The Renaissance/A. E. Zucker. —2nd ed. . —Shanghai: The Commercial Press, Ltd. , c1924
xiii, 526 p. ;21 cm.

I12/A932
The Winged Horse: The Story of the Poets and their Poetry/Joseph Auslander, Frank Ernest Hill. —New York: Doubleday, Doran & Company, Inc. , c1944
xiv, 451 p. ;23 cm.

I12/B784
Library of the World's Best Poetry/M. M. Browning. —[S. l. : s. n.], [?]
548 p. ;24 cm.

I12/B798
The Standard Book of the British and American Verse/Nella Braddy. —New York: The New York Publishing Company, c1932
xviii, 778 p. ;21 cm.

I12/B847
Under the Tent of the Sky: A Collection of Poems about Animals Large and Small/John E. Brewton. —New York: The Macmillan Company, c1946
xvi, 205 p. ;23 cm.

I12/R542
By the Light of the Lone Star/Grace Dupree Ridings. —Dallas: The Kaleidograph Press, c1936
140 p. ;24 cm.

I12/R588
Barrack-Room Ballads and Other Verses/Rudpard Ripling. —Boston, London: The Edinburgh Society, c1899

180 p. ;21 cm.

I12/W894

Poetry of the Victorian Period/George Benjamin Woods. —Chicago: Scott, Foresman and Company, c1930

xviii, 11112 p. ;24 cm.

I13/H874

The Best One-Act Plays/Henry Huizinga. —Shanghai: The Commercial Press, Ltd. , c1930

341 p. ;20 cm.

I13/H899

The Best Long Plays: With Introductions and Notes/Henry Huizinga. —Shanghai: The Commmercial Press, Ltd. , c1933

551 p. ;23 cm.

I13/P523(26)

Continental Drama: Calderon Corneille Racine Moliere Lessing Schiller. Volume 26/P. F. Collier & Son Company. New York: P. F. Collier & Son Company, c1910

489 p. ;20 cm.

I13/S224

New Plays for Christmas/A. P. Sanford. —New York: Dodd, Mead & Company, c1934

vii, 269 p. ;19 cm.

I14/B562

Humorous Tales from 'Blackwood'/Lt. —Col. L. A. Bethell. —London: WM. Blackwood & Sons Ltd. , c1935

554 p. ;19 cm.

I14/C525

A Century of Detective Stories/G. K. Chesterton. —London: Hutchinson & Co. , [?]

1019 p. ;22 cm.

I14/F873

Great Detective Stories of the World/Joseph Lews French. —[S. l.]: Albert & Charles Boni, c1924, 1929

396 p. ;19 cm.

I14/F873G786(1)

Great Pirate Stories. Vol. I/Joseph Lews French. —New York: Tudor Publishing Co. , c1936

1 v. ;21 cm.

I14/F932

A Red and A White Rose/H. A. Frommelt. —Techny: Mission Press, S. V. D. , c1930

126 p. ;17 cm.

I14/H313

The World's Wit and Humor: An Encyclopedia of the Classic Wit and Humor of All Ages and Nations/Joel Chandler Harris. —New York: The Review of Reviews Company, c1906

xi, 290 p. ;19 cm.

I14/H313(3)

My Life and Loves. Vol. Three/Frank Harris. —[S. l. : s. n.], [?]

268 p. ;18 cm.

I14/H536

Jolly Annual for Girls/Jessie Leckie Herbertson. —[S. l.]: Wm. Collins, [?]

194 p. ;27 cm.

I14/J58

The Book of the Short Story/Alexander Jessup, Henry Seidel Canby. —New York: D. Appleton and Company, c1903

507 p. ;19 cm.

I14/L848-6

Love Your Enemies/Helena Long. —Techny: Mission Press, S. V. D. , c1926

117 p. ;17 cm.

I14/M447

The Pocket Book of Western Stories/Harry E. Maule. —New York: Pocket Books, Inc. , c1945

xiv, 320 p. ;16 cm.

I14/O36

Three Types of Story-Tellers/E. Ohashi. —Tokyo: Keibundo, c1926

177, 15 p. ;19 cm.

I14/S113

A Century of Historical Stories/Rafael Sabatini. —London: Hutchinson & Co. , [?]

xiii, 1022 p. ;22 cm.

I14/S113

A Century of Sea Stories/Rafael Sabatini. —London: Hutuchinson & Co. , [?]

1024 p. ;22 cm.

I14/S271

Modern English Novelists: Thomas Hardy and Henry James/Torajiro Sawamura. —Tokyo: Kenkyusha, c1926

vii, 258 p. ;18 cm.

I14/S274

The World's Great Crime Stories/Dorothy L. Sayers. —New York: Blue Ribbon Books, Inc. , c1932

vi, 855 p. ;22 cm.

I14/S644

Short Stories Old and New/C. Alphonso Smith. —Boston: Ginn and Company, c1916

iv, 292 p. ;17 cm.

I14/T454(4)

The Royal Readers. No. IV/Thomas Nelson and Sons. —London: Thomas Nelson and Sons, c1914

viii, 288 p. ;17 cm.

I14/T459

Atlantic Narratives Moder Short Stories/ Charles Swain Thomas. —Boston: The Atlantic Monthle Press, c1918

ix, 390 p. ;19 cm.

I16/B882

Victorian Prose Masters: Thackeray-Carlyle-George Eliot-Matthew Arnold-Ruskin-George Meredith/W. C. Brownell. —New York: Charles Scribners Sons, c1926

viii, 289 p. ;21 cm.

I16/F687

Life Began Yesterday/Stephen Foot. —London: William Heinemann Ltd. , c1938.

213 p. ;

I16/P989(O)

Representative Essays/George Haven Putnam. —New York: G. P. Putnam's Sons, c1908

vi, 395 p. ;19 cm.

I16/S395

A Treasury of the World's Great Letters from Ancient days to Our Own Time/M. Lincoln Schuster. —New York: Simon and Schuster Inc. , c1940

xlviii, 563 p. ;22 cm.

I17/McF295

World's Great: Tales of the Sea/William McFee. —Cleveland and New York: The World Publishing Company, c1944

446 p. ;20 cm.

I18/E49(1)

Elson Junior Literature. Book One/William H. Elson, Christine M. Keck, Mary H. Burris. —Chicago: Scott, Foresman and Company, c1932

512 p. ;20 cm.

I18/E49(2)

Elson Junior Literature. Book Two/William H. Elson, Christine M. Keck, Mary H. Burris.—Chicago: Scott, Foresman and Company, c1932

542 p. ;20 cm.

I18/E49(7)

Child-Library Readers. Book Seven/William H. Elson, Mary H. Burris.—Chicago: Scott, Foresman and Company, c1930

512 p. ;19 cm.

I18/E49(8)

Child-Library Readers. Book Eight/William H. Elson, Mary H. Burris.—Chicago: Scott, Foresman and Company, c1929

560 p. ;19 cm.

I18/O97

East of the Sun and West of the Moon Also Dick Whittington and His Cat and Rumpelstiltzkin/F. A. Owen Publishing Company.—New York: F. A. Owen Publishing Company, [?]

80 p. ;18 cm.

I206/W746

Chinese Literature/with Critical and Biographical Sketches by Epiphanius Wilson... [et al.].—revised ed..—New York: P. F. Collier, c1900.

vii, 302, 149 p. ;24 cm.

I210.6/L926

The True Story of Ah Q/Lu Hsuen.—Shanghai: The Commercial Press, c1927

vii, 100 p. ;19 cm.

I222/L693

Wang Kuei and Li Hsiang-Hsiang/Li Chi.—Peking: Foreign Languages Press, c1954

33 p. ;26 cm.

I222.3/C559

The Li Sao: An Elegy on Encountering Sorrows/translated into English verse with introduction notes, Commentaries, and vocabulary, by Lim Boon Keng, with an introduction note by H. E. Sir Hugh Clifford and prefaces by H. A. Giles, and others..—Shanghai: The Commercial Press, c1929

xi, 200 p. ;19 cm.

I231.3/L133

Japan Talks/Amar Lahiri.—Canada: The Hokuseido Press, c1940

xii, 227 p. ;19 cm.

I242/G472-3

Strange Stories from A Chinese Studio/Herbert A. • Giles.—3rd ed..—Shanghai: Kelly & Walsh Ltd., c1916

xxiii, 488 p. ;19 cm.

I246.57/L735

Moment in Peking: A Novel of Contemporary Chinese Life/Lin Yutang.—New York: The John Day Company, c1939

815 p. ;22 cm.

I246.8/S562

Hsi Shih: Beauty of Beauties: A Romance of Ancient China about 495-472 B. C./Shu Chiung.—Shanghai: Kelly and Walsh Ltd., c1931

xvi, 116 p. ;21 cm.

I247.45/Y1

The Mountain Village/Chun-Chan Yeh.—London: Sylvan Press, c1947

230 p. ;19 cm.

I266/MacN158

China's New Nationalism and Other Essays/Harley Farnsworth MacNair.—Shanghai, China: The Commercial Press, Ltd., c1925.

3 p. leaves, [v]-xi, 398 p. ;20 cm.

I266.1/L735

The Little Critic: Essays, Satires and Sketches on China (First Series: 1930-1932)/Lin Yutang. —Shanghai: The Commercial Press, Ltd., c1935

x, 299 p.;19 cm.

I266.1/L735

With Love and Irony/Lin Yutang. —[S. l.: s. n.], [?]

291 p.;20 cm.

I267/L693

My Country and My People/Lin Yutang. — New York: Halcyon House, c1935.

xviii, 382 p.;21 cm.

I267/L693C853

My Country and My People/Lin Yutang. — London: William Heinemann Ltd., c1936

xviii, 362 p.;22 cm.

I267/L735

Confucius Saw Nancy and Essays about Nothing/Lin Yutang. —Shanghai: The Commercial Press, Ltd., c1936

viii, 301 p.;19 cm.

I271.2/A512(5)

The Encyclopedia Americana. Volume 5/Americana Corporation. —1944 ed. —New York: Americana Corporation, c1944

720 p.;

I271.2/A512(11)

The Encyclopedia Americana. Volume 11/Americana Corporation. —1944 ed. —New York: Americana Corporation, c1944

762 p.;

I271.2/A512(29)

The Encyclopedia Americana. Volume 29/Americana Corporation. —1944 ed. —New York: Americana Corporation, c1944

743 p.;

I276/G849

China's Story: In Myth, Legend, Art, and Annals/William Elliot Griffis. —Boston: Houghton Mifflin Company, c1911

xii, 302 p.;19 cm.

I276.3/B471

Plum Blossoms and Blue Incense and Other Stories of the East/James W. Benntt, Soong Kwen-Ling. —Shanghai: The Commercial Press, Ltd., c1926

330 p.;19 cm.

I287.2/R974

Chinese Children's Rhymes/Ruth Hsue. — Shanghai: The Commercial Press, Ltd., c1935

xxiv, 98 p.;19 cm.

I313.11/W116

Gleanings from Japanese Literature/K. Wadagaki. —Tokyo: Nampokusha, c1919

387, 30 p.;16 cm.

I313.44/K75

The Gold Demon/Koyo Ozaki. —Tokyo: Selbundo, [?]

xiii, 561 p.;19 cm.

I313.45/H436

Shadowings/Lafcadio Hearn. —London: Sampson Low, Marston, & Company, c1900

268 p.;19 cm.

I313.45/H659

Flower and Soldiers/Ashihei Hino. —Tokyo: Kenkyusha, c1939

ii, 213 p.;19 cm.

I313.45/L848-6

The Queen's Nephew: A Narration from the Early Japanese Mission/Helena Long.—6th. ed..—[S.l]: Mission Press, c1919, 1930

149 p.;17 cm.

I313.45/S756-4

The Wonderful Flower of Woxindon: An Historical Romance of Time of Queen Elizabeth/Rev. Joseph Spillmann.—4th ed.—London: B. Herder, c1896

vii, 494 p.;19 cm.

I313.55/I16

Japanese Lady in Europe/Haruko Ichikawa.—Tokyo: Kenkyusha Co., c1937

380 p.;20 cm.

I313.7/S756

Cross and Chrysanthemum: An Historical Tale/Rev. Joseph Spillmann.—London: R. & T. Washbourne, Ltd., [?]

viii, 398 p.;19 cm.

I313.73/H436

Kotto: Being Japanese Curios, with Sundry Cobwebs/Lofcadio Hearn.—New York: The Macmillan Company, c1910

vii, 251 p.;19 cm.

I319.4/E49(5)

The Elson Readers. Book 5/William H. Elson, Christine M. Keck.—Chicago: Scott, Foresman and Company, c1928.

418 p.;19 cm.

I319.4/E49(6)

The Elson Readers. Book 6/William H. Elson, Christine M. Keck.—Chicago: Scott, Foresman and Company, c1929.

448 p.;19 cm.

I326/C639

Nouveau Dictionnaire Anglais-Francais Et Francais-Anglais/E. Clifton.—Pairs: Librairie Garnier Freres, [?]

xii, 658, xx, 673 p.;19 cm.

I336.45/S524

The Upheaval in far Cathay/Hing Shang.—Shanghai: The Shanghai Mercury, Ltd., c1904

188 p.;20 cm.

I337.44/S111

Selected Stories/Saki.—London: Penguin Books Ltd., c1939

xiv, 216 p.;18 cm.

I341.45/S775

The Heart of a Woman and Other Themes/Samuel W. Stagg.—Manila: M. P. H., c1927

1 v.;21 cm.

I351.25/T125

Gitanjali/Rabindranath Tagore.—London: Macmillan and Co., Ltd., c1919

xxii, 101 p.;18 cm.

I351.44/C319

Many Shall Come/Patrick J. Carroll.—Indiana: The Ave Maria Press, c1937

380 p.;19 cm.

I351.45/B545

The Sky is Red/Giuseppe Berto.—New York: James Laughlin, c1948

397 p.;21 cm.

I351.45/B669

The King Tree/Baroness Van Boecop.—New York: Doubleday, Doran & Company, Inc., c1944

242 p.;20 cm.

I351. 45/G195

The Three R's/Ganpat. —London: Hodder and Stoughton Ltd. , [?]

viii, 316 p. ;19 cm.

I371. 73/B974A158

The Arabian Nights' Entertainments or the Book of a Thousand Nights and a Night/Richard F. Burton. —New York: The Modern Library, c1932

xiv, 823 p. ;18 cm.

I371. 73/G649

The Arabian Nights/Earle • Goodenow. —New York: Grosset & Dunlap Publishers, c1946

337 p. ;20 cm.

I371. 73/L265

The Arabian Nights' Entertainments, Stories from the Thousand and One Nights told for young people/M. A. L. Lane. —Boston: Ginn and Company, 1915.

x, 364 p. ;18 cm.

I372/K45

The Sufistic Quatrains of Omar Khayyam/Edward Fitzgrald. —London: M. Walter Dunne, Publisher, c1901

xxv, 395 p. ;24 cm.

I374. 072/G437

Ottoman Literature: The Poets and Poetry of Turkey/E. J. W. Gibb. —New York: M. Walter Dunne, Publisher, c1901

xvi, 351 p. ;23 cm.

I38. 245/S617

East of Eden/I. J. Singer. —New York: Alered A. Knope, c1939

402 p. ;21 cm.

I382. 45/A274

The Bridal Canopy/S. J. Agnon. —New York: Doubleday, Doran & Company, Inc. , c1937

xix, 373 p. ;21 cm.

I470. 45/C643

The Turning Wheels/Stuart Cloete. —Boston: [Houghton Mifflin Company], c[1937]

21 cm.

I478. 55/M889

In the Steps of St. Paul/H. V. Morton. —New York: Dodd, Mead & Company, c1942

xi, 499 p. ;21 cm.

I5/M379

Statesman's Year-Book: Statistical and Historical Annual of the States of the Civilised World for the Year 1877/Frederick Martin. —London: Macmillan and Co. , c1877

xlvi, 784 p. ;19 cm.

I500. 3/M438

The Chief European Dramatists: Twenty-One Plays from the Drama of Greece, Rome, Spain, France, Italy, Germany, Denmark, and Norway, from 500 B. C. to 1879 A. D. /Brander Matthews. —Boston: Houghton Mifflin Company, c1916

xi, 786 p. ;21 cm.

I500. 4/W927(2)

The Best Continental Short Stories of the Day. Vol. II/The World Book, Co. , Ltd. —Shanghai: The World Book, Co. , Ltd. , c1929

253, 17 p. ;18 cm.

I511. 345/G878

The Years of War(1941-1945)/Vassili Grossman. —Moscow: Foreign Languages Publishing House, c1946

450 p. ;22 cm.

I512. 3/T251

The Plays of Anton Techekov/Anton Tchek-

ov. —New York: Modern Library, [?]

xi, 300 p. ;18 cm.

I512. 44/D722B863(O)

The Brothers Karamazov/Fyodor Dostoyecsky. —New York: The Modern Library, [?]

939 p. ;18 cm.

I512. 44/D928P984(O)

Crime and Punishment/Fyodor Dostoevsky. —[New York]: The Macmillan Company, c1927

xi, 554 p. ;21 cm.

I512. 44/G635

Oblomov/Ivan Goncharov. —London: George Allen & Unwin, Ltd. , c1915

317 p. ;19 cm.

I512. 44/P637

The Volga Falls to the Caspian Sea/Boris Pilnyak. —New York: Mcm. xxxi, c1931

353 p. ;20 cm.

I512. 44/T654L897

Where Love Is There God Is Also and What Men Live by/Count Lyof Nikolayevitch Tolstoi. —New York: Thomas Y. Crowell Company, c1925

62 p. ;18 cm.

I512. 44/T654S497

Tales of Sevastopol /Lev Tolstoy; translated by J. Fineberg; illustrated and designed by Pyotr Pavlinov. —Moscow: Foreign Languages Pub. , c1946.

165 p. ;26 cm.

I512. 44/T936

Virgin Soil/Ivan Turgenieff. —New York: Thomas Y. Crowell & Co. , c1877

315 p. ;19 cm.

I512. 45/A357

The Fifth Seal/Mark Aldanov. —New York: Chariles Scribner's Sons, c1943

482 p. ;20 cm.

I512. 45/E33

The Storm/Ilya Ehrenburg. —Moscow: Foreign Languages Publishing House, c1948

735 p. ;22 cm.

I512. 45/F294

The Family/Nina Fedorova. —Boston: Little, Brown and Company, c1943

346 p. ;21 cm.

I512. 45/F495

Port Arthur: A Historical Narrative/J. Fineberg. —Moscow: Foreign Languages Publishing House, c1947

784 p. ;22 cm.

I512. 45/G156

Donbas Sketches/Boris Galin. —Moscow: Foreign Languages Publishing House, 1948

281 p. ;20 cm.

I512. 45/G244

Crime & Punishment/Constance Garnett. —New York: The Macillan Company, c1923

493 p. ;19 cm.

I512. 45/G661

Decadence/Maxim Gorki. —London: Cassell and Company, Ltd. , c1927

323 p. ;19 cm.

I512. 45/H662

Mother Russia/Maurice Hindus. —New York: Halcyon House, c1942, 1943

xii, 395 p. ;21 cm.

I512. 45/H662B855

The Bright Passage/Maurice Hindus. —New

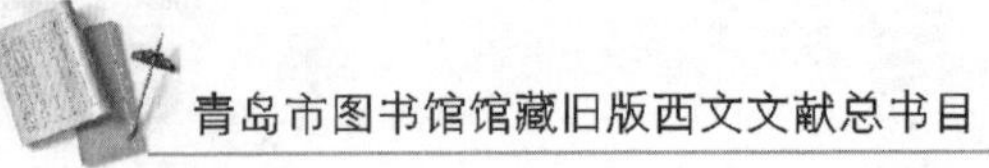

York: Doubleday & Company, Inc., c1947
xiv, 370 p.;22 cm.

I512.45/H662M918
Mother Russia/Maurice Hindus. —New York: Doubleday, Doran and Company, Inc., c1942, 1943
xii, 395 p.;23 cm.

I512.45/L955
Nisso/P. Luknitky. —Moscow: Foreign Languages Publishing House, c1949
482 p.;20 cm.

I512.45/O44
The World is not Enough/Zoe Oldenbourg. —New York: Pantheon Books, c1948
499 p.;22 cm.

I512.45/P273
Big Family/Bellamy Partridge. —New York: Whittlesey House, c1941
xiv, 323 p.;22 cm.

I512.45/S559
And Quiet Flows the Don/Mikhail Sholokhov. —London: Putnam, c1929
ix, 755 p.;20 cm.

I512.45/S565
Such as we/Pierre Sichel. —New York: Reynal & Hitchcock, c1948
629 p.;21 cm.

I512.45/SYO
Alitet Goes to the Hills/Tikhon Syomushkin. —Moscow: Foreign Languages Publishing House, c1948
301 p.;19 cm.

I512.45/V561
Men With a Clear Conscience/P. Vershigora. —Moscow: Foreign Languages Publishing House, c1949
441 p.;20 cm.

I512.49/B431
Selected Philosophical Works/V. G. Belinsky. —Mosow: Foreign Languages Publishing House, c1948
li, 552 p.;22 cm.

I512.55/G873
Across The North Pole to America/M. Gromov. —Moscow: Foreign Languages Publishing House, c1939
37 p.;15 cm.

I513.44/S572
Quo Vadis: A Narrative of the Time of Nero/by Henryk Sienkiewicz; translated from the Polish by Jeremiah Curtin. —New York: Book League of America, c1925.
422 p;21 cm.

I513.44/S572
Quo Vadis/Henryk Sienkiewicz. —Boston: Little, Brown, and Company, c1897
541 p.;20 cm.

I513.44/S572Q9
Quo Vadis/Henryk Sienkiewicz. —[S. l.: s. n.], [?]
447 p.;18 cm.

I513.45/C754(O)
Lord Jim/Joseph Conrad. —New York: The Modern Library, c1921
417 p.;18 cm.

I513.45/C754
Lord Jim/Joseph Conrad. —Educational Ed.. —New York: Doubleday, Doran & Co., Inc., c1928
417 p.;19 cm.

I513. 45/R458(1)

The Peasants. Spring/Ladislas Reymont. —New York: Alfred A. Knopf, Inc., c1925

329 p.;19 cm.

I513. 45/R458(2)

The Peasants. Summer/Ladislas Reymont. —New York: Alfred A. Knopf, Inc., c1925

287 p.;19 cm.

I513. 45/R458

The Peasants. Autumn/Ladislas Reymont. —New York: Alfred A. Knopf, c1924

261 p.;19 cm.

I515. 45/F663

Imperial Tokay/Yolanda Foldes. —London: Robert Hale Ltd., [?]

272 p.;19 cm.

I515. 45/F663I

The Street of the Fishing Cat/Jolán Földes. —London: Ivor Nicholson and Watson Ltd., c1937

317 p.;20 cm.

I515. 45/K77

Arrival and Departure/Arthur Koestler. —New York: The Macmillan Company, c1944

180 p.;22 cm.

I515. 45/K77T429

Thieves in the Night: Chronicle of An Experiment/Arthur Koestler. —New York: The Macmillan Company, c1946

357 p.;22 cm.

I515. 45/K86

Nero/Desider Kostolanyi. —London: The Camelot Press Ltd., c1928

288 p.;19 cm.

I516/C699

Selections from Early German Literature/Klara Hechtenberg Collitz. —New York: American Book Company, c1910

284 p.;19 cm.

I516. 07/G599

Library of World's Classics: Conversations With Eckermann/Johann Wolfgang Von Goethe. —New York: M. Walterdunne, Publisher, c1901

xii, 397 p.;24 cm.

I516. 34/G599F267

Faust/Johann Wolfgang Goethe. —New York: Modern Library, c1912

xx, 258 p.;18 cm.

I516. 34/G599F267(O)

Faust: A Dramatic Poem/Goethe. —Boston: Ticknor and Fields, c1838

320 p.;18 cm.

I516. 35/B915

Hegel's Educational Ideas/William M. Bryant. —New York: Werner School Book Company, c1896

214 p.;16 cm.

I516. 45/B619

Augustus/Guenther Brikenfeld. —London: Constable & Co Ltd., c1935

viii, 396 p.;19 cm.

I516. 45/C411

Great German Short Novels ans Stories/Bennett A. Cerf. —New York: The Modern Library Inc., c1933

ix, 475 p.;18 cm.

I516. 45/C545

Christine/Alice Choimondeley. —London: Macmillan and Co., Ltd., c1917 vi, 256, 8 p. ;19 cm.

I516. 45/F194

Old Hert Goes on a Journey/Hans Fallada. —New York: Putnam, c1936

291 p. ;19 cm.

I516. 45/F299

Cat Across the Path/Ruth Feiner. —London: George G. Harrap & Co. , Ltd. , c1935

382 p. ;18 cm.

I516. 45/F422

The Oppermanns/Lion Feuchtwanger. —London: Martin Secker, c1933

460 p. ;19 cm.

I516. 45/F828P466

The Persians are Coming/Bruno Frank. —New York: Alfred A. Knopf, Inc. , c1929

139 p. ;21 cm.

I516. 45/G727

Zero Hour/Georg Grabenhorst. —New York: Brentano's Ltd. , c1928

320 p. ;19 cm.

I516. 45/G776

Count Belisarius/Robert Graves. —London: Cassell, c1938

ix, 526 p. , iv;21 cm.

I516. 45/G947S524

Shannon's Way/A. J. Cronin. —Boston: Little, Brown and Company, c1948

313 p. ;20 cm.

I516. 45/G985

Ambition/Bernhard Guttmann. —New York: Harper & Brothers Publishers, c1930

323 p. ;20 cm.

I516. 45/H618

Hostages/Stefan Heym. —New York: The Sun Dial Press, c1943

362 p. ;21 cm.

I516. 45/H791-6

Simon Dale/Anthony Hope. —6th ed. . —London: Methuen & Co. , c1902

357 p. ;19 cm.

I516. 45/L882

The Angel with Trumpet/Ernst Lothar. —New York: Doubleday, Daran & Co, Inc. , c1944

ix, 457 p. ;20 cm.

I516. 45/L955

Rubber: A Romance of the Dutch East Indies/Madelon H. Lulofes. —London: Caddell and Company, Ltd. , c1933

314 p. ;19 cm.

I516. 45/M281

Joseph the Provider/Thomas Mann. —New York: Alfred A. Knopf, c1944

608 p. ;20 cm.

I516. 45/S454

The Seventh Cross/Anna Seghers. —Boston: Little, Brown and Company, c1942

338 p. ;20 cm.

I516. 45/T439

Farewell to Paradise/Frank Thiess. —New York: Alfred A. Knopf, c1929

183 p. ;20 cm.

I516. 45/W425

The Scorpion/Anna Elisabet Weirauch. —New York: Greenberg Publisher, c1932

396 p. ;19 cm.

I516. 45/W488

Embezzled Heaven/Franz Werfel. —New York: The Viking Press, c1940

427 p. ;21 cm.

I516. 55/L931

The Nile: The Life-Story of a River/Emil Ludwig. —New York: The Viking Press, c1937

xvi, 619 p. ;24 cm.

I516. 88/G864F163

Fairy Tales/Brother Grimm. —Chicago: Rand McNally & Company, c1913

275 p. ;23 cm.

I516. 88/G864G864

Grimm's Fairy Tales: For Children And The Household/The Brothers Grimm. —London: Ward, Lock & Co. , Ltd. , [?]

347 p. ;19 cm.

I516. 99/J35

Priestly Zeal for Souls: Reflections for Priests/John J. Janssen, L. M. Dooley. —New York: Frederick Pustet Co. , c1946

138 p. ;18 cm.

I521. 45/B347

A Tale From Bali/Vicki Baum. —London: Geoffrey Bles, c1937

512 p. ;20 cm.

I521. 45/B347R

Results of An Accident/Vicki Baum. —London: Geoffrey Bles, c1931

315 p. ;19 cm.

I521. 45/B347G751

Grand Hotel/Vicki Baum. —London: Geoffrey Bles, c1931

315 p. ;19 cm.

I521. 45/B347W394

The Weeping Wood/Vicki Baum. —New York: Doubleday, Doran & Company, Inc. , c1944

x, 531 p. ;21 cm.

I521. 45/W488

Twilight of a World/Franz Werfel. —New York: The Viking Press, c1937

692 p. ;21 cm.

I522. 84/J65H465(O)

Heidi/Johanna Spyri. —[S. l. : s. n.], c1938

302, 6 p. ;20 cm.

I533/I12

Pillars of Society and an Enemy of the People/H. Ibsen. —Shanghai: The World Book Co. , Ltd. , c1929

336, 20 p. ;17 cm.

I533. 34/I12

Ghosts; An Enemy of the People; A Doll's House; John Gabriel Borkman/Henrik Ibsen. —New York: The Modern Library, [?]

330 p. ;18 cm.

I533. 34/I12

Four Plays by Ibsen/Clarence Stratton. —Boston: Ginn and Company, c1931

xxv, 566 p. ;19 cm.

I533. 34/I12G411

Ghosts; An Enemy of the People; A Doll's House; John Gabriel Borkman/Henrik Ibsen. —New York: The Modern Library, [?]

252 p. ;17 cm.

I533. 45/G971

The Wind from the Mountains/Trygve Gulbranssen. —New York: G. P. Putnam's Sons, c1937

412 p. ;21 cm.

I533. 45/H198

Growth of the Soil/translated from the Norwegian of Knut Hamsun by W. W. Worster. —New York：A. A. Knopf，c1921.

276 p. ;23 cm.

I533. 45/K47

Shaper of Danger/Axel Kielland. —Boston：Little，Brown and Company，c1945

324 p. ;20 cm.

I533. 45/R744

Giants in the Earth：A Saga of the Prairie/O. E. Rolvaag. —New York：Harper & Brothers Publishers，[?]

xxii. 465p. ;18cm.

I533. 45/U54

The Wild Orchid/Sigrid Undset. —New York：Alfred A. Knopf，c1931

410 p. ;19 cm.

I533. 45/U54

Kristin Lavransdatter/Sigrid Undset. —London：Alfred A. Knopf，1930

945 p. ;21 cm.

I534. 45/J51

The Long Journey/Johannes V. Jensen. —New York：Alfred A. Knopf，c1945

xxi，677 p. ;19 cm.

I534. 88/A544

Hans Andersen's Fairy Tales/Hans Chrislian Andersen. —Chicago：Rand McNally & Company，c1916

286 p. ;23 cm.

I534. 88/A544O

Andersen's Fairy Tales/Hans Andersen. —London：John F. Ahaw & Co.，Ltd.，[?]

1 v. ;28 cm.

I534. 88/A544Z62

Andersen's Fairy Tales/Hans Andersen. —Shanghai：The Commercial Press，Ltd.，c1927

113 p. ;19 cm.

I535. 45/L111

Independent People：An Epic/Halldor Laxness. —New York：Alfred A. Knopf，c1946

vi，470 p. ;22 cm.

I545/L269

The Iliad Homer/Andrew Lang，Walter Leaf，Ernest Myers. —[S. l.]：The Macmillan Company，[?]

xviii，471 p. ;17 cm.

I545. 072/B983

The Odyssey of Homer：Done into English Prose/S. H. Butcher，Andrew Lang. —[S. l：s. n.]，[?]

xviii，435 p. ;17 cm.

I545. 072/B983O22

The Odyssey of Homer/S. H. Butcher，A. Lang. —New York：Random House，[?]

xxiv，383 p. ;18 cm.

I545. 22/L269

The Iliad of Homer/Andrew Lang，Walter Leaf，Ernest Myers. —America：The Macmillan Company，c1905

xviii，471 p. ;17 cm.

I545. 22/L269I28

The Iliad of Homer/Andrew Lang，Walter Leaf，Ernest Myers. —London：J. M. Dent & Sons Ltd.，c1910

xix，440 p. ;17 cm.

I545. 3/L257

Four Famous Greek Plays/Paul Landis. —New

York: The Modern Library, c1929
xviii, 285 p. ;18 cm.

I545. 74/C734
Aesop's Fables/The Commercial Press. —Shanghai: The Commercial Press, Ltd. , c1930
163 p. ;19 cm.

I546. 22/C739(3)
Virgil's Aeneid: Boos I-VI, VIII, IX and Selections from the other books. Vol. III/David Y. Comstock. —Boston: Allyn and Bacon, c1896
vii, 129 431, 129 p. ;19 cm.

I546. 23/A41(O)
The Divine Comedy of Dante Alighieri/Dante Alighieri. —[S. l.]: The Modern Library, c1932
xix, 625 p. ;18 cm.

I546. 4/V292
The Maker of Heavenly Trousers/Daniele Vare. —Shanghai: Popular Book Company, [?]
273 p. ;18 cm.

I546. 4/V292G258
The Gate of Happy Sparrows/Daniele Vare. —[S. l. : s. n.], [?]
xv, 257 p. ;17 cm.

I546. 44/V493
The House by the Medlar-Tree/Giovanni Verga. —New York: Harper & Brothers Publishers, c1890
vii, 300 p. ;18 cm.

I546. 45/J15
Every Other Gift/Naomi Jacob. —London: Hutchinson & Co. , (Publishers)Ltd. , [?]
320 p. ;19 cm.

I546. 45/M236
Kaputt/Curzio Malaparte. —New York: E. P. Dutton & Co. , Inc. , c1946
407 p. ;22 cm.

I551. 4/A283
The Vale of Cedars, or, the Martyr: A Story of Spain in the Fifteenth Century/Grace Aguilar. —London: George Routledge and Sons, Ltd. , [?]
293 p. ;18 cm.

I551. 43/S111O
Don Quixote/Miguel de Cervantes Saavedra. —New York: The Macmillan Company, c1930
xxv, 479 p. ;19 cm.

I551. 45/I12
Mare Nostrum (Our Sea)/Vicente Blasco Ibnaez. —New York: E. P. Dutton & Company, c1919
518 p. ;19 cm.

I561/B561
The Twenty-Fifth Hour/Herbert Best. —London: Jonathan Cape, Inc. , c1940
285 p. ;20 cm.

I561/B815
Kai Lung's Golden Hours/Ernest Bramah. —London: Penguin Books Ltd. , c1938
280 p. ;18 cm.

I561/B996(2)
The Poems & Plays of Lord Byron. Volume Two/Lord Byron. —Lodnon: J. M. Dent & Sons, Ltd. , [?]
vii, 551 p. ;18 cm.

I561/C477
Obiter Dicta/Charles Scribner's Sons. —New York: Charles Scribner's Sons, c1885
232 p. ;18 cm.

I561/C899(1)
Collection of British Authors: Tauchnitz Edi-

tion. Vol I/F. Marion Crawford. —Leipzig: Bernhard Tauchnitz, c1900
247 p. ;16 cm.

I561/E58
An Englishwoman's Love-Letters/[?]. —[London]: [s. n.], c1901
322 p. ;19 cm.

I561/G662-3(3)
The Young Man's Problems. Volume III/James L. Gordon. —3rd ed.. —Shanghai: The Commercial Press, Ltd. , c1924
68 p. ;16 cm.

I561/G738
Redeemed and Other Sketches/R. B. Cunninghame Graham. —London: William Heinemann, Ltd. , c1927
188 p. ;19 cm.

I561/H145(3775. 1)
Collection of British Authors: the Brethren. Vol. I/H. Rider Haggard. —Leipzig: Bernhard Tauchnitz, c1904
279 p. ;16 cm.

I561/H172
Collection of British Authors: The Woman's Kingdom/John Halifax. —Leipzig: Bernhard Tauchnitz, c1868
296 p. ;16 cm.

I561/J65(2)
Recollections. Vol. II/Viscount Morley John. —New York: The Macmillan Company, c1917
vi, 431 p. ;23 cm.

I561/K55
Hypatia, or, New Foes with An Old Face/Charles Kingsley. —London: Cassell and Company, Ltd. , [?]
442 p. ;18 cm.

I561/K55
Collection of British Authors: Hereward the Wake, "Last of the English". Vol. 2/Charles Kingsley. —Leipzig: Bernhard Tauchnitz, c1866
333 p. ;16 cm.

I561/R495
A Voyage to Purilia/Elmer Rice. —London: Victor Gollancz Ltd. , c1930
288 p. ;19 cm.

I561/S431
The Lady of the Lake: In Six Cantos/Walter Scott. —Boston: Educational Publishing Company, [?]
204 p. ;17 cm.

I561/T358
Henry Esmond/W. M. Thackeray. —London: Collins' Clear-Type Press, [?]
456 p. ;16 cm.

I561/W812
Great Tales of Terror and the Supernatural/Herbert A. Wise, Phyllis Fraser. —New York: Random House, c1944
xix, 1080 p. ;21 cm.

I561/Y68
Portrait of A Village/Francis Brett Young. —London: William Heinemann Ltd. , c1937
180 p. ;23 cm.

I561. 06/B415
Seven Men/Max Beerbohm. —New York: Alfred A. Knopf, c1920
237 p. ;23 cm.

I561. 06/B622
Social Backgrounds of English Literature/Ralph Philip Boas, Barbara M. Hahn. —Boston:

Little, Brown, and Company, c1929
xii, 337 p. ;19 cm.

I561.06/B882
English Belles-Lettres: From A. D. 901 to 1834/Thomas Browne, Roger Ascham, John Arbuthnot. —New York: M. Walter Dunne, c1901
ix, 403 p. ;23 cm.

I561.06/M643(4)
Literature and Life. Book Four, English Literature/Dudley Miles, Robert C. Pooley, Edwin Greenlaw. —Chicago: Scott, Foresman and Company, c1935
xviii, 814 p. ;23 cm.

I561.06/R454(8)
The Library of Wit and Humor: British. Volume VIII, Dickens to Kipling/The Review of Reviews Corporation. —New York: The Review of Reviews Corporation, c1930
xi, 292 p. ;18 cm.

I561.06/R454(9)
The Library of Wit and Humor: British. Volume IX, Dickens to Kipling/The Review of Reviews Corporation. —New York: The Review of Reviews Corporation, c1930
xiv, 288 p. ;18 cm.

I561.064/S464(1)
British Moralists.. V. 1/edited by L. A. Selby-Bigge. —Oxford: Clarendon Press, c1897.
lxx, 425 p. ;20 cm.

I561.064/S464(2)
British Moralists.. V. 2/edited by L. A. Selby-Bigge. —Oxford: Clarendon Press, c1897.
451 p. ;20 cm.

I561.07/W894
English Poetry and Prose of the Romantic Movement: Selected and Edited with Notes, Bibliographies, and A Glossary of Proper Names/George Benjamin Woods. —Chicago: Scott, Foresman and Company, c1916
xviii, 1454 p. ;23 cm.

I561.072/O75
A Handbook of the Works of Robert Browning/Sutherland Orr. —London: George Bell and Sons, c1899
viii, 420 p. ;18 cm.

I561.072/S425
Scott Lady of the Lake/Sir Walter Scott. —[S. l: s. n.], [?]
xv, 261 p. ;18 cm.

I561.072/S649
Macaulay's Essay on Milton/Herbert Augustine Smith. —Boston: Ginn and Company, c1898
xxii, 82 p. ;17 cm.

I561.073/D328
Elizabethan drama. 2/Thomas Dekker. —New York: P. F. Collier, c1910.
469-943 p. ;20 cm.

I561.073/H436
Lectures on Shakespeare/Lafcadio Hearn. —Kanda: The Houkuseido Press, c1928
120 p. ;19 cm.

I561.073/L841
The Students' Shakespeare King Lear/Frank Alanson Lombard. —Shanghai: The Commercial Press, Ltd., c1925
viii, 385, xvii p. ;19 cm.

I561.073/R746
Shakespeare's Comedy of The Merchant of Venice: Complete and Unabridged with Notes/William J. Rolfe. —Washington: National Home Library, c1932
134 p. ;17 cm.

I561. 073/S527

Julius Caesar/William Shakespeare. —Boston: Ginn and Company, c1908

lxi, 174 p. ;17 cm.

I561. 073/S766

Shakespeare's Tragedy of Julius Caesar/Homer P. Sprague. —Boston: Silver, Burdett and Co. , c1912

212 p. ;18 cm.

I561. 073/W947

King Lear/William Aldis Wright. —Oxford: The Clarendon Press, [?]

xx, 200 p. ;17 cm.

I561. 076/A757

Essays Literary Critical/Matthew Arnold. —London: J. M. Dent & Sons Ltd. , c1906

xv 380 p. ;18 cm.

I561. 1/D545

Houshold Words/Charles Dickens. —Leipzig: Dernhard Tauchnitz, c1853

lxxviii, 290 p. ;16 cm.

I561. 1/H847

Heroiness of Fiction/W. D. Howells. —New York: Harper & Brothers, Publishers, [?]

274 p. ;21 cm.

I561. 1/I53

The Ingoldsby Legends or, Mirth and Marvels/Thomas Ingoldsby. —London: Ward, Lock & Co. , Ltd. , [?]

xxii, 426 p. ;19 cm.

I561. 1/O75

Life and Letters of Robert Browning. vol. 1/Mrs. Sutherland Orr. —Boston: Houghton, Mifflin and Company, c1892

xii, 324 p. ;20 cm.

I561. 1/S527(2)

Shakespear's Historical Plays, Poems & Sonnets. Vol. II/Shakespeares. —London: J. M. Dent & Sons Ltd. , c1906

887 p. ;18 cm.

I561. 1/S545

Plays, Translations, and Longer Poems/Percy Bysshe Shelley. —London: J. M. Dent & Sons Ltd. , c1936

viii, 439 p. ;17 cm.

I561. 1/T312

The Poems and Plays of Alfred Lord Tennyson/Alfred Lord Tennyson. —New York: The Modern Library, c1938

xviii, 1133 p. ;21 cm.

I561. 1/T358(2)

The Works of William Makepeace Thackeray. Vol. II/William Makepeace Thackeray. —New York: Peter Fenelon Collier, Publisher, [?]

618 p. ;26 cm.

I561. 1/T358(3)

The Works of William Makepeace Thackeray. Vol. III/William Makepeace Thackeray. —New York: Peter Fenelon Collier, Publisher, [?]

661 p. ;26 cm.

I561. 1/T358(6)

The Works of William Makepeace Thackeray. Vol. VI/William Makepeace Thackeray. —New York: Peter Fenelon Collier, Publisher, [?]

601 p. ;26 cm.

I561. 1/T358(8)

The Works of William Makepeace Thackeray. Vol. VIII/William Makepeace Thackeray. —New York: Peter Fenelon Collier, Publisher, [?]

591 p. ;26 cm.

I561. 11/A622

Prose and Poetay of England/Elizabeth Frances Ansorge. —New York: The L. W. Sixger Company, c1943

xiii, 882 p. ;21 cm.

I561. 11/B996

The Poems and Dramas of Lord Byron/Lord Byron. —Chicago: Belford-Clarke Co. , Publishers, c1891

xi, 800 p. ;22 cm.

I561. 11/C592

The Complete Works of William Shakespeare/William George Clark, William Aldis Wright. —New York: Grosset & Dunlap Publishers, [?]

1419 p. ;21 cm.

I561. 11/F115

My Naughtiest Story: An Anthology of Stories chosen by their own Authors/Faber & Faber Ltd. ,—London: Faber & Faber Ltd. , [?]

456 p. ;19 cm.

I561. 11/S527(8)

The Complete Works of William Shakespeare. Vol. VIII/William Shakespeare. —London: Oxford University Press, c1911

487 p. ;15 cm.

I561. 14/G814(1)

Literature and Life. Book One/Edwin Greenlaw, Dudley Miles, Clarence Stratton. —Chicago: Scott, Foresman and Company, c1929

ix, 582 p. ;22 cm.

I561. 14/G814(1)

Literature and Life. Book One/Edwin Greenlaw, William H. Elson, Dudley Miles, Clarence Stratton. —Revised ed. . —Chicago: Scott, Foresman and Company, c1927, 1933

viii, 632 p. ;23 cm.

I561. 14/G814(2)

Literature and Life. Book Two/Edwin Greenlaw, Dudley Miles, Clarence Stratton. —Chicago: Scott, Foresman and Company, c1929

ix, 630 p. ;22 cm.

I561. 14/G814(3)

Literature and Life. Book Three/Edwin Greenlaw, Dudley Miles. —Chicago: Scott, Foresman and Company, c1929

xii, 692 p. ;23 cm.

I561. 14/G814L775(1)

Literature and Life. Book One/Edwin Greenlaw, Dudley Miles, Clarence Stratton. —Chicago: Scott, Foresman and Company, c1927

viii, 582 p. ;24 cm.

I561. 14/M643(4)

Literature and Life. Book Four/Edwin Greenlaw, Dudley Miles, Clarence Stratton. —Chicago: Scott, Foresman and Company, c1929

xviii, 814 p. ;22 cm.

I561. 14/W671

The Best Known Works of Oscar Wilde: including the poems, novels, plays, essays and fairy tales and dialogues. Vol. 6/Oscar Wilde. —New York: Blue Ribbon Books, c1927

620 P. ;22 cm.

I561. 2/A392(1)

The Poems of Alfres, Lord Tennyson. volume: 1 (1830-1856)/Lord Tennyson Alfred. —London: J. M. Dent & Sons Ltd. , c1906

xx, 467 p. ;18 cm.

I561. 2/F949

Modern English Poems/R. Fukuhara. —Tokyo: Kenkyusha, c1929

lvii, 415 p. ;19 cm.

I561. 2/G624
The Poems and Plays of Oliver Goldsmith/Oliver Goldsmith. —London: J. M. Dent & Sons Ltd. , c1914
xxiv, 317 p. ;18 cm.

I561. 2/K57(1)
The Years Between. vol. 1/Rudyard Kipling. —[S. l.]: Methuen and Co. , Ltd. , c1919
x, 99 p. ;17 cm.

I561. 2/M235
Paradise Lost/John Milton. —New York: The Mershon Company, [?]
1 v. ;15 cm.

I561. 2/M396
The Collected Poems of John Masefield/John Masefield. —London: William Heinemann Ltd. , c1931
ix, 784 p. ;19 cm.

I561. 2/O47
The Ways of Life: Two Stories/Mrs. Oliphant. —London: Smith, Elder & Co. , c1897
330 p. ;20 cm.

I561. 2/P161
The Golden Treasury of Songs and Poems/Francis T. Palgrave. —New York: Thomas Y. Crowell Company, c1924
xviii, 554 p. ;18 cm.

I561. 2/P161
The Golden Treasury/Francis T. Palgrave. —London: Macmillan and Co. , Ltd. , c1932
524 p. ;16 cm.

I561. 2/P161G618
The Golden Treasury of Songs and Poems/Francis T. Palgrave. —Tokyo: Kenkyusha, c1929
lv, 668 p. ;18 cm.

I561. 2/P825
The Select Poetical Works of Alexander Pope/Alexander Pope. —Leipzig: Bernhard Tauchnitz, c1848
305 p. ;16 cm.

I561. 2/Q6
The Oxford Book of English Verse 1250-1900/Arthur Quiller-Couch. —Oxford: The Clarendon Press, [?]
xix, 1083 p. ;17 cm.

I561. 2/S431
The Lady of the Lake/Walter Scott. —Chicago: A Flanagan Company, c1924
185 p. ;18 cm.

I561. 2/S431L153
The Lady of the Lake: In Six Cantos/Walter Scott. —Boston: Educational Publishing Company, [?]
204 p. ;17 cm.

I561. 2/S545(2)
The Poetical work of Percy Bysshe Shelley. vol. II, Plays, Translations & Longer Poems/Percy Bysshe Shelley. —London: J. M. Dent & Sons Ltd. , c1907
viii, 439 p. ;18 cm.

I561. 2/S741
The Pocket Book of Verse: Great English and American Poems/M. E. Speare. —New York: Pocket Books, Inc. , c1940
xx, 355 p. ;16 cm.

I561. 2/U61(2)
Modern American and British Poetry. Volume 2, British/Louise Untermeyer. —Washington: Harcourt, Brace and Company, c1942
xxiii, 506 p. ;22 cm.

I561.2/W925

Wordsworth's Shorter Poems/William Wordsworth. —London: Collins' Clear-Type Press, [?]

383 p. ;16 cm.

I561.23/C496(2)

The Complete Works of Geoffrey Chaucer. vol. II/Thomas R. Lounsbury. —New York: Thomas Y. Corowell & Co., Publishers, c1900

465-877 p. ;23 cm.

I561.23/S748(2)

The Faerie Queene. Vol. 2/Edmund Spenser. —London: J. M. Dent & Sons Ltd., [?]

480 p. ;17 cm.

I561.24/B827

Poems of Shelley/Stoford A. Brooke. —London: Macmillan and Co., Ltd., c1922

lx, 340 p. ;16 cm.

I561.24/B827C697

The Collected Poems of Rupert Brooke/Rupert Brooke. —New York: Dodd, Mead and Company, c1915

192 p. ;19 cm.

I561.24/B885(1)

Pauline, Paracelsus, Sordello stc. Volume 1/Robert Browning. —Boston: Houghton, Mifflin and Company, c1890

412, 25 p. ;20 cm.

I561.24/B885

The Complete Poetical Works of Robert Browning/Robert Browning. —New York: The Macmillan Company, c1921

xv, 1359 p. ;19 cm.

I561.24/B885

Red Cotton Night-Cap Country: Aristophanes' Apology: the Inn: Album: Pacchiarotto and How He Worked in Distemper and Other Poems/Robert Browning. —Boston: Houghton, Mifflin and Company, c1890

394 p. ;20 cm.

I561.24/B885C554

Christmas-Eve and Easter Day; Men and Women: In a Balcony/Robert Browning. —Boston and New York: Houghton, Miflin and Company, c1890

444 p. ;20 cm.

I561.24/B996

The Poems & Plays of Lore Byron. Volume Three/Lore Byron. —London: J. M. Den & Sons. Ltd., [?]

537 p. ;18 cm.

I561.24/D414

The Poems of Matthew Arnold: 1840-1866/J. M. Dent & Sons Ltd. —London: J. M. Dent & Sons Ltd., c1908

367 p. ;17 cm.

I561.24/D414P161

Palgrave's Golden Treasury/J. M. Dent & Sons Ltd. —London: J. M. Dent & Sons Ltd., c1906

334 p. ;17 cm.

I561.24/H387

The Poetical Works of Frances Ridley Havergal/Frances Ridley Havergal. —New York: E. P. Dutton & Company, c1893

352 p. ;22 cm.

I561.24/H487

The Poetical Works of Felicia Hemans/Felicia Hemans. —London: Ward, Lock & Co., Ltd., c1912

xxiv, 540 p. ;19 cm.

I561. 24/L853

The Courtship of Miles Standish, Elizabeth and Other Poems/Henry Wadsworth Longfellow. —Boston: Houghton Mifflin Company, c1920

viii, 122 p. ;18 cm.

I561. 24/P964

Legends and Lyrics and Others Poems/Adelaide Anne Procter. —London: J. M. Dent & Sons Ltd. , c1906

xii, 332 p. ;18 cm.

I561. 24/W365

Cowper's Shorter Poems/W. T. Webb. —[S. L: s. n.], [?]

xxxv, 147 p. ;17 cm.

I561. 24/W925

The Poetical Works of Wordsworth/William Wordsworth. —[S. l. : s. n.], [?]

xxxii, 986 p. ;19 cm.

I561. 25/M323

Peacock Pie: A Book of Rhymes/Walter De La Mare. —London: Constable and Company Ltd. , c1913

vii, 112 p. ;23 cm.

I561. 25/M396

Reynard the Fox or the Ghost Heath Run/John Masefield. —New York: The Macmillan Company, c1921

166 p. ;19 cm.

I561. 3/D136

Little Plays/Lena Dalkeith. —London: T. C. & E. C. Jack, Ltd. , [?]

111 p. ;15 cm.

I561. 3/H437

Characters of Shakespear's Play/William Hazlitt. —London: J. M. Dent & Sons, c1906

xxiii, 273 p. ;18 cm.

I561. 3/S527O

The Student's Shakespeare: Romeo and Juliet/Shakespeare. —Shanghai: The Commercial Press, Ltd. , c1925

xii, 251 p. ;19 cm.

I561. 3/S527O

The Tragedy of King Richard the Third/Hudson Shakpespeare. —Boston: Ginn and Company, c1880

lxii, 178 p. ;17 cm.

I561. 33/D414

Shakespeare's Comedies/J. M. Dent & Sons Ltd. —London: J. M. Dent & Sons Ltd. , c1906

847 p. ;17 cm.

I561. 33/G663

Six Plays of Shakespeare: Midsummer Night's Dream, Merchant of Venice: As You Like It, Julius Caesar: Hamlet, Macbeth/Six Plays of Shakespeare. —Stockholm: The Continental Book Company AB, c1946

xxxv, 441 p. ;19 cm.

I561. 33/J81(1)

The Complete Plays of Ben Jonson. vol. 1/Ben Jonson. —London: J. M. Dent & Sons, Ltd. , [?]

xxix, 642 p. ;18 cm.

I561. 33/L218-2

The Oxford and Cambridge edition of tales from Shakespeare/Mary Lamb. —2nd ed. —London: George Gill & Sons, Ltd. , [?]

xi, 204 p. ;18 cm.

I561. 33/S527(O)

A Midsummer-Night's Dream/William Shakespeare. —Philadelphia: Henry Altemus Company, [?]

192, 16 p. ;14 cm.

I561.33/S527G878

Twelfth Night/William Shakespeare. —New York: Grosset and Dunlap, c1909

xliii, 198 p. ;21 cm.

I561.33/S527J94(O)

Julius Caesar/William Shakespeare. —Shanghai: The Commercial Press, c1933

xii, 237 p. ;19 cm.

I561.33/S527J94C128(O)

Julius Caesar/Shakespeare. —Oxford: Oxford University Press, c1923

xlvi, 203 p. ;17 cm.

I561.33/S527J94W(O)

Julius Caesar/William Shakespeare. —Chicago: Wilcox & Follett Company, c1921

83 p. ;20 cm.

I561.33/S527K33

Hamlet, Prince of Denmark/William Shakespeare. —Tokyo: Kenkyusha, c1922

xvi, 268 p. ;20 cm.

I561.33/S527K52

King John/William Shakespeare. —Oxford: The Clarendon Press, [?]

160, 8 p. ;17 cm.

I561.33/S527M113

Shakespeare Select Plays Macbeth/M. G. Clark, William Aldis Wright. —Oxford: Clarendon Press, [?]

xliii, 180 p. ;17 cm.

I561.33/S527M118(O)

Macbeth/William Shakespeare. —Chicago: Wilcox & Follett Company, c1921

x, 136 p. ;17 cm.

I561.33/S527M553G492

The Merchant of Venice/Shakespeare. —Boston: Ginn and Company, c1906

xlvii, 144 p. ;17 cm.

I561.33/S527M553V459N277

The Merchant of Venice: Complete and Unabridged/Shakespeare. —Washington: National Home Library Foundation, c1932

134 p. ;17 cm.

I561.33/S527M942

Much Ado about Nothing/William Shakespeare. —New York: The University Society, c1901

151 p. ;18 cm.

I561.33/S527S527

Shakespeare's Tragedy of King Lear/William J. Rolfe. —New York: American Book Company, c1922

267 p. ;18 cm.

I561.33/S527S527(O)

Shakespeare's Tragedies/William Shakespeare. —London: J. M. Dent & Sons Ltd., c1913

981 p. ;18 cm.

I561.33/S527T158(O)

The Taming of the Shrew/William Shakespeare. —New York: Grosset & Dunlap, [?]

xxxii, 133 p. ;21 cm.

I561.33/S527T282(O)

The Tempest/William Shakespeare. —Oxford: The Clarendon Press, [?]

xx, 156, 8 p. ;17 cm.

I561.33/S527T765(O)

The Tragedy of King Richard the Third/Shakespeare. —Oxford: The Clarendon Press, [?]

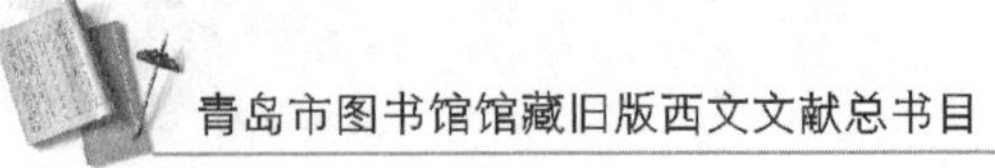

lxiv, 236 p. ;17 cm.

I561.33/S527T765

Coriolanus/William Shadespeare. —New York: The University Society, c1901

196 p. ;18 cm.

I561.33/S527T866

The Ture Annals of Fairyland in the Reign of King Oberon/Shakespeare. —London: J. M. Dent and Sons Ltd. , c1913

xiv, 338 p. ;18 cm.

I561.33/S527Y67(3)

As You Like It. Vol. III/William Shakespeare. —Chicago: Scott, Foresman and Company, c1919

223 p. ;17 cm.

I561.33/S527Y67(16)

As You Like It. Vol. XVI/William Shakespeare. —Chicago: Scott, Foresman and Company, [?]

143 p. ;17 cm.

I561.33/V516

As You Like It/A. W. Verity. —London: Cambridge, c1925

lii, 256 p. ;18 cm.

I561.33/W954

Shakespeare Select Plays: First Part of King Henry IV/William Aldis Wright. —Oxford: The Clarendon Press, [?]

xxiv, 178, 8 p. ;17 cm.

I561.34/M349

The Plays of Christopher Marlowe/Christopher Marlowe. —London: J. M. Dent & Sons Ltd. , c1909

xvii, 488 p. ;18 cm.

I561.34/S527M666

The Minor Elizabeth-an Drama (1) Pre-Shakespearean Tragedies/William Shakespeare. —London: J. M. Dent. & Co. , c1910

311 p. ;18 cm.

I561.34/W668-6

Lady Windermere's Fan: A Play About a Good Woman/Oscar Wilde. —6th ed. —London: Methuen & Co. , Ltd. , c1911

157 p. ;17 cm.

I561.34/W671

Salome: A Tragedy in One Act/Oscar Wilde. —Copyright ed. —Leipzig: Bernhard Tauchnitz, c1909

124 p. ;16 cm.

I561.35/B275

Quality Street, the Admirable Crichton & Mary Rose/James Matthew Barrie. —Tokyo: Kenkyusha, c1928

xxvi, 458 p. ;19 cm.

I561.35/H217

Hangover Square, or the Man with Two Minds: a Story of Darkest Earl's Court in the Year 1939/Patrick Hamilton. —Cleveland: The World Publishing Company, c1944

307 p. ;21 cm.

I561.35/S552

The Plays of Richard Brinsley Sheridan/R. B. Sheridan. . —London: J. M. Dent, c1919.

411 p. ;18 cm.

I561.4/A434

The Knight's Move/Mark Allerton. —London: Odhams Ltd. , [?]

189 p. ;16 cm.

I561.4/A798

Chaytor's/Adrian Alington. —London: Chatto

& Windus, [?]
343 p. ;19 cm.

I561. 4/B798(1)
Eleanor's Victory. Vol. 1/M. E. Braddon. —Leipzig: Bernhard Tauchnitz, c1863
342 p. ;16 cm.

I561. 4/B918
The House of the Four Winds/John Buchan. —London: Hodder and Stoughton, c1935
318 p. ;20 cm.

I561. 4/C525
The Club of Queer Trades/G. K. Chesterton. —London: W. Collins Sons & Co Ltd. , [?]
249 p. ;16 cm.

I561. 4/C712
London Belongs to Me/Norman Collins. —London: Collins Clear-Type Press, c1945
639 p. ;21 cm.

I561. 4/C743
Fishermen of the Banks/James B. Connolly. —London: Faber & Gwyer, [?]
275 p. ;22 cm.

I561. 4/D173
Ariel Dances/Ethel Cook Eliot. —London: Sampson Low, Marston & Co. , Ltd. , [?]
314 p. ;19 cm.

I561. 4/E11
The Golden Fleece, or, Who Wins the Prize/A. L. O. E. —London: T. Nelson and Sons, c1887
131 p. ;17 cm.

I561. 4/F115
Best Mystery Stories of the Year 1932/Faber & Faber Ltd. ,—London: Faber & Faber Ltd. , c1932
485 p. ;19 cm.

I561. 4/H224
Mr. Punch in the Hunting Field/J. A. Hammerton. —London: The Amalgamated Press. Ltd. , [?]
191 p. ;18 cm.

I561. 4/H886
The Purple Land/W. H. Hudson. —New York: Grosset & Dunlap, [?]
260 p. ;21 cm.

I561. 4/J12
The Girls of Cromer Hall/Raymond Jacberns. —London: Thomas Nelson and Sons, Ltd. , [?]
256 p. ;16 cm.

I561. 4/L671
On Actors and the Art of Acting/George Henry Lewes. —Leipzig: Bernhard Tauchnitz, 1875
279 p. ;17 cm.

I561. 4/M283
Linda Shawn/Ethel Mannin. —London: Jarrolds Publishers, [?]
285 p. ;19 cm.

I561. 4/M363
Modern Short Stories/F. ST. Mars, Stanley J. Weyman. —Warick Lane: University of London Press, Ltd. , c1931
158 p. ;17 cm.

I561. 4/M396
Victorious Troy, or, the Hurrring Angel/John Masefield. —London: William Heinemann Ltd. , c1935
309 p. ;19 cm.

I561. 4/M427
Comin' Thro' the Rye/Helen Mathers. —[S.

l. : s. n.], [?]
510 p. ;16 cm.

I561. 4/M449
Creatures of Circumstance/W. Somerset Maugham. —London: William Heinemann Ltd. , c1947
310 p. ;19 cm.

I561. 4/M913
Thursby/Geoffrey Moss. —London: Hutchinson & Co. , [?]
429 p. ;19 cm.

I561. 4/O113
The Return of Silver Chief/Jack O'Brien. —Philadelphia: The John C. Winston Company, c1943
211 p. ;22 cm.

I561. 4/O63
The Laughing Cavalier: A Story of the Ancestor of the Scarlet Pimpernel/Baroness Orczy. —London: Hodder and Stoughton, [?]
284 p. ;18 cm.

I561. 4/R282
Disgrace Abounding/Douglas Reed. —London: Jonathan Cape Thirty Redford Square, c1939
447 p. ;20 cm.

I561. 4/R643
Penguin Parade: New Stories, Poems, Etc. , by Contemporary Writers/Denys Kilham Roberts. —London: Penguin Books Ltd. , c1938
248 p. ;18 cm.

I561. 4/S241
John Walters From the Lieutenant and Others, The Human Touch and No Man's Land/Sapper. —London: Hodder and Staoughton Publishers, [?]
316 p. ;19 cm.

I561. 4/S255
Answer That Bell! /Margaret Baillie Saunders. —London: Hutchinson & Co. , [?]
288 p. ;19 cm.

I561. 4/S495
Woodstock or The Cravalie: : A Tale of the Year Sixteen Hundred and Fifty-one/Walter Scott. —[S. l.]: T. Nelson & Sons, Ltd. , [?]
586 p. ;16 cm.

I561. 4/S646
Tzigane/Eleanor Smith. —London: Hutchinson & Co. , [?]
318 p. ;19 cm.

I561. 4/S775
High Speed/Clinton H. Stagg. —London: John Hamilton Ltd. , [?]
247 p. ;19 cm.

I561. 4/S842
The Minister of State/J. A. Steuart. —London: J. M. Dent & Sons, Ltd. , [?]
392 p. ;18 cm.

I561. 4/S889
The Enchanted Country/Joan Sutherland. —London: Hodder and Stoughton Ltd. , [?]
319 p. ;17 cm.

I561. 4/S897
Jack Brown in China: A Story of the Russo-Japanese War/Herbert Strang. —London: Humphrey Milford Oxford University Press, c1933
viii, 370 p. ;20 cm.

I561. 4/T363(3)
The Virginians: A Tale of the Last Century. Vol. III/W. M. • Thackeray. —Leipzig: Bernhard Tauchnitz, c1854
328 p. ;16 cm.

I561.4/T363

The Newcomers: Memoirs of a Most Respectable Family. Vol. II/W. M. Thackeray. —Leipzig: Bernhard Tauchnitz, c1854

328 p. ;16 cm.

I561.4/W187

The Strange Countess/Edgar Wallace. —London: Hodder and Stoughton, [?]

320 p. ;19 cm.

I561.4/W187K26

The Keepers of the King's Peace/Edgar Wallace. —London: Ward, Look & Co., Ltd., [?]

251 p. ;19 cm.

I561.4/W218

The Green Mirror: A Quiet Story/Hugh Walpole. —London: Macmillan and Co., c1922

473 p. ;20 cm.

I561.4/W256

Nellie of Truro: A Tale From Life/Ward, Lock and Co.,—London: Ward, Lock and Co., [?]

292 p. ;18 cm.

I561.4/W453

The Secret Places of the Heart/H. G. Wells. —London: Cassell and Company, Ltd., c1922

311 p. ;19 cm.

I561.4/W453

The Bulpington of Blup/H. G. Wells. —London: Hutchinson & Co., Ltd., [?]

408 p. ;20 cm.

I561.4/W453

In the Days of the Comet/H. G. Wells. —London: Collins' Clear-Type Press, [?]

281 p. ;17 cm.

I561.4/W594(1)

The Man on the Dover Road. Book 1, 1792/David Whitelaw. —London, New York, Toronto: Hodder and Stoughton, [?]

318 p. ;19 cm.

I561.4/W838

The Man Upstairs and Other Stories/P. G. Wodehouse. —London: Methuen & Co., Ltd., c1922

279, 8 p. ;19 cm.

I561.43/C496C229

Canterbury Tales/Geoffrey Chaucer. —New York: New YorkPublishing Company, Inc., c1934

xvi, 626 p. ;23 cm.

I561.44/A283

Home Influence: A Tale for Mothers and Daughters/Grace Aguilar. —London: George Routledge & Sons, Ltd., [?]

xviii, 421 p. ;18 cm.

I561.44/A283D273

The Days of Bruce: A Story From Scotting History/Grace Aguilar. —London: George Routledge and Sons, Ltd., [?]

506 p. ;19 cm.

I561.44/A552

Boy Trappers in the Rockies/W. B. Anderson. —London: George G. Harrap & Co., Ltd., c1913

285 p. ;21 cm.

I561.44/A625

The Black Poodle and Other Tales/F. Anstey. —London: Longmans, Green, and Co., c1899

269 p. ;19 cm.

I561.44/A933(O)

Pride and Prejudice/Jane Austen. —Tokyo: Kenkyusha, c1929

xxxiii, 503 p. ;19 cm.

I561.44/A933D414

Sense and Sensibility/Jane Austen. —London: J. M. Dent & Sons, Ltd. , c1906

308 p. ;18 cm.

I561.44/A933P945(O)

Pride and Prejudice/Jane Austen. —Stockholm: The Continental Book Company, c1946

345 p. ;19 cm.

I561.44/B121

Keeping up with Lizzie/Irving Bacheller. —New York: Grosset & Dunlap, c1911

158 p. ;18 cm.

I561.44/B527(2)

Not Woode, But Won. : A Novel. Vol. II/Bernhard. —Tauchnitz. —Leipzig: Bernhard Tauchnitz, c1871

vi, 294 p. ;16 cm.

I561.44/B629L865

Lorna Doone/R. D. Blackmore. —New York: Grosset & Dunlap, c1920

646 p. ;21 cm.

I561.44/B647

Adventures in Mashonaland/Rose Blennerhassett, Lucy Sleeman. —London: Macmillan and Co. , c1894

xii, 340 p. ;21 cm.

I561.44/B687

Colonial Reformer/Rolf Boldrewood. —London: Macmillan and Co. , c1895

471 p. ;18 cm.

I561.44/B687C948

The Crooked Stick, or, Pollie's Probation/Rolf Boldrewood. —London: Macmillan and Co. , Ltd. , c1896

339 p. ;18 cm.

I561.44/B696W959(O)

Wuthering Heights/Emily Bronte. —New York: Dodd, Mead & Company, c1947

355 p. ;22 cm.

I561.44/B737

Lavengro and the romany rye/George Borrow. —George Borrow: E. M. Hale and Company, [?]

374 p. ;20 cm.

I561.44/B869(O)

Jane Eyre/Charlotte Bronte. —London: The Continental Book Company, [?]

517 p. ;19 cm.

I561.44/B869

Jane Eyre/Charlotte Bronte. —New York: The Macmillan, c1947

xix, 543 p. ;19 cm.

I561.44/B869J33(O)

Jane Eyre/Charlotte Bronte. —Tokyo: Kenkyusha, c1928

xxvi, 806 p. ;19 cm.

I561.44/B869O

Jane Eyre/Charlotte Bronte. —New York: The Modern Library, [?]

543 p. ;18 cm.

I561.44/B918

Hunting-Tower/Buchan, John. —London: Hodder and Stoughton Ltd. , c1922

318 p. ;19 cm.

I561.44/B918

Annan Water/Robert Buchanan. —London: Chatto and Windus, Piccadilly, c1891

viii, 306 p. ;17 cm.

I561.44/B918G111

Gap in the Curtain/John Buchan. —London: Hodder and Stoughton, c1932

315 p. ;19 cm.

I561.44/B918M435

Matt: A Story of a Caravan/Robert Buchanan. —A New ed.. —London: Chatto & Windus, Piccadilly, c1889

239 p. ;18 cm.

I561.44/B918S524

The Shadow of the Sword/Robert Buchanan. —London: Chatto & Windus, Piccadilly, c1894

xi, 468 p. ;17 cm.

I561.44/B941-2

The Last Days of Pompell/Edward Bulwer. —Leipzig: Bernhard Tauchnitz, c1879

xii, 444 p. ;16 cm.

I561.44/B942(O)

The Pilgrim's Progress/John Bunyan. —Stockholm: The Continental Book Company, c1946

332 p. ;18 cm.

I561.44/B942

The Pilgrim's Progress/John Bunyan. —Stockholm: The Continental Book Company, c1946

319 p. ;18 cm.

I561.44/B968

Carbineer and Scout: A Story of the Great Boer War/E. Harcourt Burrage. —London: Blackie & Son Ltd., [?]

240 p. ;18 cm.

I561.44/C643

Watch for the Dawn/Stuart Cloete. —London: Collins Clear-Type Press, c1939

438 p. ;21 cm.

I561.44/C747

Tales from Shakespeare/Charles, Mary Lamb. —Shanghai: The Commercial Press, Ltd., c1929

339, 39 p. ;19 cm.

I561.44/C747C

Tales from Shakespeare/Charles, Mary Lamb. —Shanghai: Chung Hwa Book Company, Ltd., [?]

iii, 316 p., 54 p. ;19 cm.

I561.44/C754D

Nostromo/Joseph Conrad. —New York: Doubleday, Doran & Company, Inc., [?]

xv, 566 p. ;20 cm.

I561.44/C754N

The Nigger of the Narcissus/Joseph Conrad. —New York, N. Y.: Doubleday, [1914].

190 p. ;21 cm.

I561.44/C754(O)

The Nigger of the "Narcissus"/Joseph Conrad. —London: William Heinemann, c1910

259 p. ;18 cm.

I561.44/C754R

The Rover/Joseph Conrad. —London: T. Fisher Unwin Ltd., c1923

317 p. ;20 cm.

I561.44/C754V

Victory/Joseph Conrad. —New York: The Modern Library, c1921

xvi, 385 p. ;18 cm.

I561.44/C754W526

Under Western Eyes/Joseph Conrad.—10th ed..—London: Methuen & Co., Ltd., c1917

320 p.;19 cm.

I561.44/C754W526-10

Under Western Eyes/Joseph Conrad.—10th ed..—London: Methuen & Co., Ltd., 1925

320 p.;19 cm.

I561.44/C797

Ziska: the Problem of a Wicked Soul/Marie Core.—Bristol: J. W. Arrowsmith Ltd., [?]

1 v;21 cm.

I561.44/C943

Babes in the Wood: A Romance of the Jungles/B. M. Croker.—London: Methuen & Co., Ltd., c1916

295 p.;17 cm.

I561.44/C943B851

Bridget/B. M. Croker.—London: Hutchinson & Co., c1918

288 p.;20 cm.

I561.44/D311S713

Sorrell and Son/Warwick Deeping.—New York: Grosset and Dunlap, c1926

400 p.;21 cm.

I561.44/D314(2)

Robinson Crusoe/Daniel Defoe.—Middlesex: Penguin Books Ltd., c1938

233-436 p.;18 cm.

I561.44/D314A(O)

The Adventures of Robinson Crusoe/Daniel Defoe.—Chicago: The Goldsmith Publishing Company, [?]

252 p.;20 cm.

I561.44/D314(O)

Robinson Crusoe/Daniel Defoe.—Chicago: The John C. Winston Company, c1925

xi, 301 p.;22 cm.

I561.44/D548(1)

Our Mutual Friend. Vol. I./Charles Dickens.—New York: Pollard & Moss, c1887

431 p.;21 cm.

I561.44/D548(2)

The Works of Charles Dickens. Vol. II/Charles Dickens.—Collier's Unanridged ed.—New York: P. F. Collier Publisher, [?]

589-1183 p.;26 cm.

I561.44/D548(O)

A Tale of Two Cities/Charles Dickens.—London: Collins Clear Type Press, c1859, c1929

456 p.;16 cm.

I561.44/D548C(O)

Christmas Books/Charles Dickens..—London: Collins Clear-Type Press, [?]

486 p.;16 cm.

I561.44/D548A191

The Adventures of Oliver Twist/Charles Dickens.—New York: Illustrated Editions Company, [?]

481 p.;21 cm.

I561.44/D548B259

Barnaby Rudge/Charles Dickens.—London: J. M. Dent & Sons Ltd., [?]

xiv, 633 p.;17 cm.

I561.44/D548B259C

Barnaby Rudge/Charles Dickens.—London: Collins' Clear-Type Press, [?]

xiv, 680 p.;17 cm.

I561.44/D548C462
Barnaby Rudge: A Tale of the Riots of'Eighty/Charles Dickens. —London: Champan & Hall Ld., [?]
vii, 391 p.;19 cm.

I561.44/D548C475
The Christmas Carol/Charles Dickens. —New York: The Macmillan Company, c1946
166 p.;19 cm.

I561.44/D548C554
Christmas Books/Charles Dickens.. —Lond.: Jmdent & Sons Ltd., [?]
416 p.;17 cm.

I561.44/D548C554S884
Christmas Stories/Charles Dickens. —London: J. M. Dent & Sons Ltd., c1917
xiii, 708 p.;18 cm.

I561.44/D548C554S884(O)
Christmas Stories/Charles Dickens. —[S. l.]: T. Nelson & Sons, Ltd., [?]
610 p.;16 cm.

I561.44/D548D249
David Copperfield/Charles Dickens. —New York: Random House, c[1850?]
923 p.;18 cm.

I561.44/D548G786(O)
Great Expectations/Charles Dickens. —London: J. M. Dent & Sons, Ltd., c1917
xiii, 453 p.;17 cm.

I561.44/D548G786E25
Great Expectations/Charles Dickens. —London: Edward LLoyd, Ltd., [?]
225 p.;23 cm.

I561.44/D548H258
Hard Times/Charles Dickens. —London: J. M. Dent & Sons Ltd., c1908
xvi, 363 p.;18 cm.

I561.44/D548H838
A Tale of Two Cities/Charles Dickens. —Boston: Houghton Mifflin Company, c1905
xxxix, 389 p.;18 cm.

I561.44/D548L693(2)
The Life and Adventures of Martin Chuzzlewit: His Relatives, Friends, and Enemies. Vol. II/Charles Dickens. —Leipzig: Bernhard Tauchnitz, c1844
470 p.;16 cm.

I561.44/D548L693
The Life and Adventures of Nicholas Nickleby/Charles Dickens. —London: J. M. Dent & Sons Lid, [190-?]
843 p.;18 cm.

I561.44/D548L778(O)
Little Dorrit/Charles Dickens. —London: J. M. Dent & Sons Ltd., c1917
xiv, 784 p.;18 cm.

I561.44/D548M167
A Tale of Two Cities/Charles Dickens. —London: Macmillan and Co., Ltd., c1931
xii, 153 p.;17 cm.

I561.44/D548O48
Oliver Twist, or the Parish Boy's Progress/Charles Dickens. —London: J. M. Dent and Sons Ltd., 1918
xix, 410 p.;18 cm.

I561.44/D548P414
The Posthumous Paper of the Pickwick Club/Charles Dickens. —London: J. M. Dent and Sons, [?]
xxxii, 804 p.;18 cm.

I561.44/D548P467

The Personal History and Experience of David Copperfield the Younger/Charles Dickens.—New York: The Macmillan Company, c1925

xv, 511 p. ;19 cm.

I561.44/D548P594(O)

The Pickwick Papers/Charles Dickens.—London: J. M. Dent & Sons Ltd., c1934

xxxi, 804, 15 p. ;17 cm.

I561.44/D548P862

The Posthumous Paper of the Pickwick Club/Charles Dickens.—London: Thomas Nelson and Sons, [?]

845 p. ;16 cm.

I561.44/D548S627O

Sketches by Boz/Charles Dickens.—London: Chapman & Hall. Ltd, c1867

viii, p. ;20 cm.

I561.44/D548T143(O)

A Tale of Two Cities/Charles Dickens.—Shanghai: The Commercial Press, Ltd., c1928

ii, 520, 72 p. ;19 cm.

I561.44/D548T143T454

Tale of Two Cities and Sketches by Boz/Charles Dickens.—New York: Thomas Y. Crowell & Company, [?]

v, 821 p. ;20 cm.

I561.44/D613

Tancred; The New Crusade/Benjamin Disraeli.—New York: P. F. Collier & Son, [?]

433 p. ;20 cm.

I561.44/D613

Alroy. Ixion in Heaven. The Inferanl Marriage. Popanilla/Right Honorable B. Disraeli.—New ed..—London: Longmans, Green, and Co., c1878

vii, 462 p. ;18 cm.

I561.44/D754

Tales of Terror and Mystery/Arthur Conan Doyle.—New York, N. Y.: Doubleday, c1922

310 p. ;18 cm.

I561.44/D754E96

The Exploits of Brigadier Gerard/A. Conan Doyle.—London: John Murray, c1917

334 p. ;18 cm.

I561.44/D754U54

Uncle Bernac/Aconan Doyle.—London: Hodder & Stoughton, [?]

253 p. ;18 cm.

I561.44/D754W582

The White Company/Doyle.—[S. l.: s. n.], c1891

435 p. ;19 cm.

I561.44/E11

Harold's Bride: A Tale/A. L. O. E..—London: Thomas Nelson and Sons, 1890

228 p. ;19 cm.

I561.44/E42

The Weaver of Raveloe/George Eliot.—London: J. M. Dent & Sons Ltd., c1928

x, 262 p. ;18 cm.

I561.44/E42A193O

Adam Bede/George Eliot.—New York: Dodd, Mead & Company, c1947

507 p. ;22 cm.

I561.44/E42F316(1)

Felix Holt: The Radical. Vol. I/George Eliot.—Leipzig: Bernhard Tauchnitz, c1867

340 p. ;16 cm.

I561. 44/E42F316(2)
Felix Holt: The Radical. Vol. II/George Eliot. —Leipzig: Bernhard Tauchnitz, c1867
320 p. ;16 cm.

I561. 44/E42M645(O)
The Mill on the Floss/George Eliot. —New York: P F Collier & Son Company, c1917
xxiii, 565 p. ;20 cm.

I561. 44/E42S581
Silas Marner/George Eliot. —London: The Continental Book Company AB, c1946
285 p. ;18 cm.

I561. 44/E94
A Great Emergency and Other Tales/Juliana Horatia Ewing. —London: Society for Promoting Christian Knowledge, [?]
310 p. ;18 cm.

I561. 44/E95
Six to Sixteen: A Story for Girls/Juliana Horatia Ewing. —London: George Bell & Sons, c1896
vii, 296 p. ;17 cm.

I561. 44/E95-6
Jan of the Windmill: A Story of the Plains/Juliana Horatia Ewing. —London: George Bell and Sons, c1895
x, 310 p. ;18 cm.

I561. 44/F459H673
The History of Tom Jones: A Foundling/Henry Fielding. —New York: The Modern Library, [?]
xxiii, 861 p. ;18 cm.

I561. 44/F459J83
The History of the Adventures of Joseph Andrews and his friend Mr. Abraham Adams/Henry Fielding. —New York: The Modern Library, c1939
xxxviii, 422 p. ;18 cm.

I561. 44/F852
In the Valley/Harold Frederic. —New York: Charles Scribner's Sons, c1893
xii, 427, 4 p. ;19 cm.

I561. 44/G248
Cranford: A Tals/Elizabeth Cleghorn Gaskell. —London: J. M. Dent. & Co. , c1906
255 p. ;18 cm.

I561. 44/G248G748
Cranford/Gaskell. —Stockholm: The Continental Book Company, c1946
246 p. ;19 cm.

I561. 44/G248G748H518
Cranford/Mrs. Gaskell. —Philadelphia: Henry Altemus, [?]
294 p. ;16 cm.

I561. 44/G619
Five Silver Daughters/Louis Golding. —London: Victor Gollanca Ltd. , c1934
608 p. ;20 cm.

I561. 44/G624(O)
The Vicar of Wakefield/Oliver Goldsmith. —Tokyo: Kenkyusha, c1929
xviii, 282 p. ;19 cm.

I561. 44/G624O48
The Vicar of Wakefield/Oliver Goldsmith. —London: J. M. Dent & Co, c1908
xvi, 222 p. ;18 cm.

I561. 44/G624V628
The Vicar of Wakefield/Oliver Goldsmith. —Stockholm: The Continental Book Company AB, c1946
xxxvi, 283 p. ;18 cm.

I561.44/G784

The Friendly Road：New Adventures in Contentment/David Grayson.—London：Andrew Melrose，Ltd.，c1921

255 p.；17 cm.

I561.44/G973

Travels into Several Remote Nations of the World/Lemuel Gulliver.—London：Penguin Books Ltd.，c1726

xi，280 p.；18 cm.

I561.44/H145

The Witch's Head/H. Rider Haggard.—London：Longmans，Green，and Co.，c1903

344 p.；19 cm.

I561.44/H145B

Black Heart and White Heart and the Wizard/H. Rider Haggard.—London：Hodder and Stoughton，c1924

318 p.；18 cm.

I561.44/H145C719

Colonel Quaritch，V. C.：A Tale of Country Life/H. Rider Haggard.—London：Longmans，Green，and C.，c1901

341 p.；18 cm.

I561.44/H145E68

Eric Brighteyes/H. Rider Haggard.—London：Longmans，Green，and Co.，c1902

xiv，317 p.；18 cm.

I561.44/H243

Spin a Silver Coin：The Story of a Desert Trading Post/Alberta Hannum.—London：Michael Joseph Ltd.，c1947

183 p.；22 cm.

I561.44/H268G795(O)

Under the Greenwood Tree/Thomas Hardy.—London：J. M. Dent & Sons Ltd.，[?]

221 p.；18 cm.

I561.44/H272R437(O)

The Return of the Native/Thomas Hardy.—New York：Grosset & Dunlap，[?]

vii，469 p.；21 cm.

I561.44/H272R437C474

The Return of the Native/Thomas Hardy.—New York：Charles Scribner's Sons，c1917

xvi，412 p.；17 cm.

I561.44/H272R437R186

The Return of the Native/Thomas Hardy.—Chicago：Rand，McNally &Company，Publishiers，[?]

vii，384 p.；21 cm.

I561.44/H436

Kwaidan：Stories and Studies of Strange Things/Hearn，Lafcadio.—Boston：Houghtion Mifflin Company，c1930

240 p.；21 cm.

I561.44/H758

South Riding：An English Landscape/Winifred Holtby.—London：Collins，c1936

xvii，588 p.；20 cm.

I561.44/H791

Half A Hero/Anthony Hope.—London：Ward Lock & Co.，Ltd.，c1901

vi，304 p.；18 cm.

I561.44/H791(O)

The Intrusions of Peggy/Anthony Hope.—London：Smith，Elder，& Co.，c1903

vi，342 p.；18 cm.

I561.44/H791-4

Quisante/Anthony Hope.—4th ed..—London：Methuen & Co.，c1903

375 p. ;18 cm.

I561. 44/H791-6

A Man of Mark/Anthony Hope. —6th ed.. —London: Methuen & Co. , c1902

viii, 264 p. ;18 cm.

I561. 44/H791C732(O)

Comedies of Courtship/Anthony Hope. —London: Ward, Lock & Co. , Ltd. , c1901

346 p. ;18 cm.

I561. 44/H791D665

Dolly Dialogues/Anthony Hope. —London: Victoria House, c1899

144 p. ;18 cm.

I561. 44/H791H435

The Heart of Princess Osra/Anthony Hope. —London: Longmans, Green, and Co. , c1900

336 p. ;18 cm.

I561. 44/H791W827

Mr. Witt's Widow: A Frivolous Tale/Anthony Hope. —London: Ward, Lock & Co. , Ltd. , [?]

243 p. ;18 cm.

I561. 44/I21

Idols in the Heart: A Tale/A. L. O. E.. —London: T. Nelson and Sons, c1891

iv, 270 p. ;19 cm.

I561. 44/I46

Mopsa the Fairy/Jean Ingelow. —London: J. M. Dent Sons Ltd. , [?]

208 p. ;18 cm.

I561. 44/J27(O)

The Ambassadors/Henry James. —New York: Happer & Brothers Publishers. , c1903

432 p. ;21 cm.

I561. 44/J55(O)

Three Men in A Boat: To Say Nothing of the Dog/Jerome K. Jerome. —London: J. W. Arrowsmith Ltd. , c1889

248 p. ;20 cm.

I561. 44/K52

Westward Ho! /Charles Kingsley. —London: T. Nelson and Sons, [?]

694 p. ;16 cm.

I561. 44/K57

Kim/Rudyard Kipling. —New York: Doubleday, Page & Company, c1925

284 p. ;20 cm.

I561. 44/K57S684

Soldiers Three: A Collection of Stories/Rudyard Kipling. —London: Sampson Low. Marston, Searle & Rivington, c1890

1 v. ;22 cm.

I561. 44/K57S775

Stalky & Co. , /Rudyard Kipling. —Leipzig: Bernhard Tauchnitz, c1899

288 p. ;15 cm.

I561. 44/L218T143

Tales From Shakespeare/Charles Lamb, Mary Lamb. —London: Cassell and Company, Ltd. , [?]

318 p. ;18 cm.

I561. 44/L419(O)

Women in love/D. H. Lawrence. —[S. l. : s. n.], 1920, 1922

x, 548 p. ;19 cm.

I561. 44/L419L879

The Lost Girl/D. H. Lawrence. —[S. l.]: World Book Service, c1930

378 p. ;18 cm.

I561.44/L419S698

Sons and Lovers/D. H. Lawrence. —[S. l. : s. n.], [?]

491 p. ;17 cm.

I561.44/L477

Annis Warleigh's Fortunes/Holme Lee. —London: Smith, Elder & Co., 15, Waterloo Place, c1873

436 p. ;18 cm.

I561.44/L667(7)

Scott's Ivanhoe. vol. vii/William D. Lewis. —Boston: Ginn and Company, c1906, 1916

xviii, 597 p. ;19 cm.

I561.44/L998

Ernest Maltravers or the Eleusinia/Edward Bulwer Lytton. —Philadelphia: J. B. Lippincott Company, [?]

xvi, 317 p. ;19 cm.

I561.44/M153

The Fortunes of Hugo/Denis Mackail. —London: William Heinemann Ltd., c1926

287 p. ;19 cm.

I561.44/M362

Masterman Ready/Captain Marryat. —New York: A. L. Burt Company, c1898

xi, 446 p. ;19 cm.

I561.44/M362M627

Mr Midshipman Easy/Captain Marryat. —New York: Grosset & Dunlap Publishers, c1928

vii, 376 p. ;20 cm.

I561.44/M373

Konigsmark/A. E. W. Mason. —London: Hodder & Stoughton Ltd., c1938

413 p. ;20 cm.

I561.44/M719

Blanche: A Story for Girls/Molesworth. —London: W. & R. Chambers, 1894

372 p. ;19 cm.

I561.44/M822

The Brook Kerith: A Syrian Story/George Moore. —Edinburgh: Printed for T. Werner Laurie Ltd., c1916

471 p. ;22 cm.

I561.44/N734

Mine Inheritance/Frederick Niven. —London: Collins, c1940

432 p. ;20 cm.

I561.44/O62

The Mystery of Mr. Bernard Brown/E. Phillips Oppenheim. —[S. l. : s. n.], [?]

253 p. ;18 cm.

I561.44/O63U54

Unravelled Knots/Baroness Orczy. —New York: George H. Doran Company, c1923, 1924, 1925, 1926

399 p. ;19 cm.

I561.44/O97

The Running Footman, or, The Sentimental Servant/John Owen. —London: Victor Gollancz Ltd., c1931

352 p. ;19 cm.

I561.44/P949

The Good Companions/J. B. Priestley. —New York: Harper & Brothers Publishers, c1929

640 p. ;21 cm.

I561.44/R155

Neither Storehouse Nor Barn/Allen Raine. —London: Hutchinson & Co., c1908

316 p. ;19 cm.

I561.44/R285

The Cloister and the Hearth/Charles Reade. —London: J. M. Dent & Sons Ltd. , c1906

iv, 174 p. ;19 cm.

I561.44/R524

Pointed Roofs/Dorothy M. Richardson. —London: Duckworth & Co. , c1915

viii, 312 p. ;19 cm.

I561.44/R956

John Ruskin's "Unto this Last" and Poems/John Ruskin. —[S. l.]: The Hokuseido Press, c1900

173 p. ;19 cm.

I561.44/S431(B)

Ivanhoe: A Romance/Walter Scott. —Tauchnitz ed.. —Tauchnitz edition. Leipzig: Bernhard Tauchnitz, c1845

567 p. ;16 cm.

I561.44/S431(O)

Ivanhoe: A Romance/Walter Scott. —Boston: DeWolfe, Fiske & Co. , Publishers, [?]

xxv, 447 p. ;19 cm.

I561.44/S431(O)

The Fortunes of Nigel/Sir Walter Scott. —London: Adam & Charles Black, c1897

xxix, 478 p. ;20 cm.

I561.44/S431

Kenilworth/Sir Walter Scott. —New York: Dodd, Mead & Company, [?]

450 p. ;19 cm.

I561.44/S431G

Guy Mannering: or, the Astrologer/Sir Walter Scott. —Copyright ed.. —Leipzig: Dernhard Tauchnitz, c1846

467 p. ;16 cm.

I561.44/S431F736

The Fortunes of Nigel/Sir Walter Scott. —London: Collins' Clear-Type Press, [?]

624 p. ;16 cm.

I561.44/S431I93(2)

Ivanhoe: a Romance. vol. II/Sir Walter Scott. —London: Ginn and Company, c1906

xviii, 597 p. ;19 cm.

I561.44/S431I93

Ivanhoe: A Romance/Walter Scott. —New York: Grosset & Dunlap Publishers, [?]

xxvii, 458 p. ;19 cm.

I561.44/S431K33

Kenilworth/Sir Walter Scott. —Copyright ed.. —Leipzig: Bernhard Tauchnitz, c1845

xiv, 497 p. ;16 cm.

I561.44/S431Q926

Quentin Durward; Ivanhoe; Kenilworth/Sir Walter Scott. —New York: The Modern Library, [?]

1138 p. ;21 cm.

I561.44/S431W111

Waverley/Sir Walter Scatt. —[S. l: s. n.], [?]

464 P. ;16 cm.

I561.44/S516

Black Beauty/Anna Sewell. —New York: Rand, McNally & Company, [?]

235 p. ;18 cm.

I561.44/S844

The Short Stories of Robert Louis Stevenson/Robert Louis Stevenson. —New York: Charles Scribner's Sons, c1930

519 p. ;20 cm.

I561.44/S844(2)

New Arabian Nights. Second Series/Robert

Louis Stevenson. —Tokyo: Kenkyusha, c1937
vi, 229 p. ;18 cm.

I561. 44/S844(O)
Dr. Jekyll and Mr. Hyde: The Merry men & Other Tales/Robert Louis Stevenson. —London: J. M. Dent & Sons Ltd. , c1945
243 p. ;17 cm.

I561. 44/S847
Dr, Jekyll and Mr. Hyde and Merry Men/Stevenson, Robert Louis. —London: J. M. Dent & Sons Ltd. , [?]
xii, 244 p. ;17 cm.

I561. 44/S847K46(O)
Kidnapped/R. Louis Stevenson. —[S. l. : s. n.], [?]
327, 8 p. ;19 cm.

I561. 44/S847K46W927
Kidnapped/Robert Louis Stevenson. —Cleveland: The World Publishing Company, c1947
313 p. ;22 cm.

I561. 44/S977G973(O)
Gulliver's Travels into Several Remote Regions of the World: In Four Parts: New Edition/Jonathan Swift. —London: Blackie & Son, Ltd. , [?]
xxiv, 390 p. ;19 cm.

I561. 44/S977G973G(O)
Gulliver's Travels/Jonathan Swift. —London: J. M. Dent & Sons, c1912
xiv, 279 p. ;18 cm.

I561. 44/S977G973T(O)
Gulliver's Travels/Dean Swift. —[S. l.]: T. Nelson & Sons, Ltd. , [?]
xxxii, 320 p. ;16 cm.

I561. 44/S977G973(O)
Gulliver's Travels/Jonathan Swift. —Chicago: The Goldsmith Publishing Company, [?]
253 p. ;20 cm.

I561. 44/S977G973M834
Gulliver's Travels: A Tale of a Tub. The Battle of the Books/Jonathan Swift. —New York: The Modern Library, c1931
xiii, 550 p. ;18 cm.

I561. 44/T358(1)
Vanity Fair. 1/W. M. Thackeray. —Stockholm: The Continental Book Company, [?]
xxii, 437 p. ;18 cm.

I561. 44/T358(2)
Vanity Fair. 2/W. M. Thackeray. —Stockholm: The Continental Book Company, [?]
449(438-878) p. ;18 cm.

I561. 44/T358V258(O)
Vanity Fair: A Novel Without a Hero/W. M. Thackeray. —London: George G. Harrap & Co. Ltd. , c1924
753 p. ;22 cm.

I561. 44/T358V258H293
Vanity Fair/William Makepeace Thackeray. —New York: Harpers, [?]
xiv, 676 p. ;21 cm.

I561. 44/T363
The History of Henry Esmond Esquire/William Makepeace Thackeray. —New York: The Modern Library, [?]
ix, 615 p. ;18 cm.

I561. 44/T363-2
The History of Henry Esmond Esquire/William Makepeace Thackeray. —2nd ed. . —London: The Clarendon Press, c1915
xxxii, 600 p. ;18 cm.

I561. 44/T363C363

Catherine: A Story/W. M. Thackeray. —Leipzig: Bernhard Tauchnitz, c1870

viii, 294 p. ;16 cm.

I561. 44/T363N541

The New Comes: Memirs of a Most Respectable Family/W. M. Thackeray. —Leipzig: Bernhard Tauchnitz, c1855

329 p. ;16 cm.

I561. 44/T468

Griffith John: The Story of Fifty Years in China/R. Wardlaw Thompson. —London: The Religious Tract Society, c1907

xvi, 544 p. ;22 cm.

I561. 44/U65

Secrets of the Courts of Europe: The Confidences of an Ex-Ambassador/Allen Upward. —London: Methuen & Co. , c1897

382 p. ;18 cm.

I561. 44/V118

Children of the Soil: A West Country Romance/Horace Annesley Vachell. —London: Hutchinson & Co. , [?]

224 p. ;19 cm.

I561. 44/W218

Mr. Perrin and Mr. Traill: A Tragi-Comedy/Hugh Walpole. —London: Penguin Books Ltd. , c1938

246 p. ;19 cm.

I561. 44/W218J55

Jeremy and Hamlet/Hugn Walpole. —London: Macmillan and Co. , Ltd. , c1937

311 p. ;19 p.

I561. 44/W453

Her Ladyship's Elephant/David Dwight Wells. —London: William Heinemann, c1905

viii, 258 p. ;19 cm.

I561. 44/W453

The Sleeper Awakes/H. G. Wells. —London: W. Collins Sons & Co. , Ltd. , [?]

258 p. ;18 cm.

I561. 44/W453N

New Worlds for Old/H. G. Wells. —New York: The Macmillan Company, c1907

vii, 333 p. ;20 cm.

I561. 44/W453B862

Mr. Britling Sees it Through/H. G. Wells. —New York: The Macmillan Company, c1917

443 p. ;19 cm.

I561. 44/W453R432

The Research Magnificent/H. G. Wells. —London: Macmillan and Co. , Ltd. , c1915

406 p. ;20 cm.

I561. 44/W454F522

The First Men in the Moon/H. G. Wells. —London: W. Collins Sons and Co. , Ltd. , [?]

254 p. ;19 cm.

I561. 44/W539

Queechy/Elizabeth Wetherell. —London: Ward, Lock and Co. , c[18--]

iv, 448 p. ;18 cm.

I561. 44/W549

The Lively Peggy/Stanley J. Weyman. —New York: Longmans, Green and Co. , c1928

339 p. ;21 cm.

I561. 44/W582

No. 5 John Street/Richard Whiteing. —London: Thomas Nelson and Sons, c[1902]

viii, 284 p. ;16 cm.

I561.44/Y55

The Little Duke/Charlotte M. Yonge. —Akron: The Saalfield Publishing Company, [?]

250 p. ;20 cm.

I561.44/Z29

The Mantle of Elijah/I. Zangwill. —London: William Heinemann, c1900

viii, 424 p. ;19 cm.

I561.45/1

The Dark Wood/Christine Weston. —London: Collins, c1947

256 p. ;20 cm.

I561.45/A159

The Surgeon's Log: Impressions of the Far East/Johnston Abraham. —London: Chapman and Hall, Ltd. , c1911

xiii, 302 p. ;19 cm.

I561.45/A222

Billicks/A. St. John Adcock. —London: Stanley Paul & Co. , c1909

155 p. ;19 cm.

I561.45/A437

The Fashion in Shrouds/Margery Allingham. —London: William Heinemann Ltd. , c1938

437 p. ;20 cm.

I561.45/A437

More work for the Undertaker/Margery Allingham. —London: William Heimenann Ltd. , c1948

320 p. ;19 cm.

I561.45/A437K52

Kingdom of Death/Margery Allingham. —[S. l.]: Lawrence E. Spivak Publisher, c1933

125 p. ;20 cm.

I561.45/A625

A Fallen Idol/F. Anstey. —London: Smith, Elder, & Co. , c1902

334 p. ;18 cm.

I561.45/A625

The Giant's Robe/F. Anstey. —London: Smith, Elder, & Co. , c1900

384 p. ;19 cm.

I561.45/A723

Men Dislike Women/Micael Arlen. —London: William Heinemann Ltd. , c1931

309 p. ;19 cm.

I561.45/A723

The Short Stories of Michael Arlen/Michael Arlen. —London: W. Collins Sons & Co Ltd. , [?]

1 v. ;19 cm.

I561.45/A735

The Case of the Weird Sisters/Charlotte Armstrong. —New York: Coward-Mccann, Inc. , c1943

279 p. ;19 cm.

I561.45/A735

King Cotton/Thomas Armstrong. —London: Collins, c1947

928 p. ;21 cm.

I561.45/A742

The Jasmine Farm/Arnim, Mary Annette (wave) Countess von. —London: William Heinemann Ltd. , c1934

375 p. ;20 cm.

I561.45/A742B464

The Benefactress/Arnim, Mary Annette (wave) Countess von. —London: Macmillan and Co. , Ltd. , [?]

418 p. ;19 cm.

I561.45/A835

The Tempting of Paul Chester/Alice and Claude Askew.—London: Collins' Clear Type Press, [?]

346 p. ;16 cm.

I561.45/A883

The Rich young Man: A Comedy with Digression/G. M. Attenborough.—London: Cassell and Company, Ltd., c1929

317 p. ;19 cm.

I561.45/A926

Silver Wedding/Ruby M. Ayres.—London: Hodder and Stoughton, c1937

300 p. ;18 cm.

I561.45/B181

Oasis/Oliver Baldwin.—London: Grayson & Grayson, c1936

320 p. ;22 cm.

I561.45/B268

A Prince of Good Fellows/Robert Barr.—New York: Mcclure, Phillips & Co., c1902

x, 340 p. ;19 cm.

I561.45/B275(2)

The Little Minister. Vol II/J. M. Barrie.—The Kirriemuir ed..—New York: H. M. Caldwell Company, c1898

326 p. ;18 cm.

I561.45/B329

The Jacaranda Tree/H. E. Bates.—London: M. Joseph, 1949.

223 p. ;21 cm.

I561.45/B446

The Hedge and the Horse/Hilaire Belloc.—London: Cassell and Company Ltd., c1936

300 p. ;19 cm.

I561.45/B471

The Old Wives' Tale/Arnold Bennett.—New York: The Modern Library, [?]

xii, 640 p. ;19 cm.

I561.45/B471L863

The Loot of Cities: Being the Adventures of a Millionaire in Search of Joy (A Fantasia); and other Stories/Arnold Bennett.—London: Thomas Nelson and Sons, Ltd., [?]

254 p. ;19 cm.

I561.45/B471T316

Teresa of Watling Street: A Fantasia on Modern Themes/Arnold Bennett.—London: Ward, Lock & Co., Ltd., c1931

255 p. ;17 cm.

I561.45/B474

The Oakleyites/E. F. Benson.—London: Hodder and Stoughton, [?]

318 p. ;18 cm.

I561.45/B474

From A College Window/Arthur Christopher Benson.—London: Thomas Nelson and Sons, Ltd., [?]

250 p. ;19 cm.

I561.45/B474L866

Lord Raingo/Arnold Bennett.—New York: George H. Doran Company, c1926

393 p. ;20 cm.

I561.45/B474S446

Secret Lives/E. F. Benson.—London: Hodder and Stoughton, c1932

316 p. ;19 cm.

I561.45/B474T779

Travail of Gold/E. F. Benson.—London: Hodder and Stoughton, [?]

320 p. ;19 cm.

I561. 45/B477

Life Story/Phyllis Bentley. —London: Victor Gollancz Ltd. , c1948

297 p. ;19 cm.

I561. 45/B477

Trio/Phyllis Bentley. —London: Victor Gollancz Ltd. , c1930

317 p. ;19 cm.

I561. 45/B47B945

Buried Alive: A Tale of These Days/Arnold Bennett. —New York: Doubleday, Doran & Co. , Inc. , c1944

253 p. ;21 cm.

I561. 45/B512

Jumping Jenny/Anthony Berkeley. —London: Hodder and Stoughton, c1933

316 p. ;19 cm.

I561. 45/B512P949

Mr. Priestley's Problem/Anthony Berkeley. —London: W. Collins Sons & Co Ltd. , [?]

vii, 307 p. ;16 cm.

I561. 45/B554

Pennine/Eardley Beswick. —London: William Heinemann Ltd. , c1936

372 p. ;19 cm.

I561. 45/B632

The Devil's Beacon/Clifton Robbins. —London: Ernest Benn Ltd. , c1933

319 p. ;19 cm.

I561. 45/B636

The Paying Guest/George Blake. —London: Collins Clear-type Press, c1949

256 p. ;21 cm.

I561. 45/B636W526

The Westering Sun/George Blake. —London: Collins, c1947

351 p. ;20 cm.

I561. 45/B694

Diana of the Islands/Ben Bolt. —London: Ward, Lock & Co. , Ltd. , c1931

vi, 256 p. ;17 cm.

I561. 45/B722

Old Mrs. Camelot/Emery Bonett. —Philadelphia: The Blakiston Company, c1944

274 p. ;20 cm.

I561. 45/B725A581

Mr. Angel Comes Aboard/Charles G. Booth. —New York: Doubleday, Daran and Co. , Inc. , c1944

207 p. ;20 cm.

I561. 45/B751

Under the Skin/Phyllis Bottome. —London: Faber and Faber Ltd. , [?]

336 p. ;19 cm.

I561. 45/B751D494

Devil's Due/Phyllis Bottome. —London: Faber and Faber, c1931

336 p. ;19 cm.

I561. 45/B786

The Leopard and Lily/Marjorie Bowen. —London: Methuen & Co. , Ltd. , c1920

288 p. ;19 cm.

I561. 45/B798W982

Wyllard's Weird/M. E. Braddon. —Leipzig: Bernhard Tauchnitz, c1885

279 p. ;16 cm.

I561. 45/B798W982(1)

Wyllard's Weird: A Novel. Vol. 1/M. E. Brad-

don. —Copyright ed. —Leipzig: Bernhard Tauchnitz, c1885
295 p. ;16 cm.

I561.45/B798(2)
Henry Dunbar: The Story of an Outcast. vol. II/M. E. Braddon. —Leipzig: Bernhard Tauchnitz, c1864
314 p. ;16 cm.

I561.45/B798W982(3)
Wyllard's Weird: A Novel. Vol. 3/M. E. Braddon. —Copyright ed.. —Leipzig: Bernhard Tauchnitz, c1885
287 p. ;16 cm.

I561.45/B815
Max Carrados Mysteries/Ernest Bramah. —London: Hodder and Stoughton Ltd., [?]
318 p. ;19 cm.

I561.45/B844
Mrs. May: Some Chapters From the Life of a Char-Lady/Thomas Le Breton. —London: Herbert Jenkins Ltd., [?]
1 v. ;21 cm.

I561.45/B851
Illyrian Spring/Ann Bridge. —London: Chatto & Windus, c1935, 1937
353 p. ;20 cm.

I561.45/B851G
The Ginger Griffin/Ann Bridge. —London: Chatto & Windus, c1934
378 p. ;19 cm.

I561.45/B851P
Peking Picnic/Ann Bridge. —London: Chatto & Windus, c1932
328 p. ;19 cm.

I561.45/B851A543
And Then You Came/Ann Bridge. —London: Chatto and Windus, c1948
319 p. ;20 cm.

I561.45/B851B658
Blue Silver/Victor Bridges. —London: Honner and Stoughton, c1936
316 p. ;19 cm.

I561.45/B862
Born 1925: A Novel of Youth/Vera Brittain. —London: Macmillan & Co., Ltd., c1948
379 p. ;20 cm.

I561.45/B863
Sarah/John Brophy. —London: Collins, c1948
320 p. ;20 cm.

I561.45/B886
The Peregrinations of Penelope/Victor A. Bruce. —London: Heath Cranton Ltd., c1930
173 p. ;19 cm.

I561.45/B918
Adventures of Richard Hannay/John Buchan. —Boston: Houghton Mifflin Company, c1915
374 p. ;19 cm.

I561.45/B918M
The Martyrdom of Madeline/Robert Buchanan. —London: Chatto & Windus' Piccadilly, c1891
viii, 294 p. ;17 cm.

I561.45/B918C353
Castle Gay/John Buchan. —London: Hodder and Stoughton, c1930
320 p. ;19 cm.

I561.45/B918M834
Modern Short Stories/John Buchan. —Lon-

don: Thomas Nelson & Sons, Ltd. , c1926
xii, 239 p. ;16 cm.

I561. 45/B918P294
The Path of the King/John Buchan. —London: Hodder and Stoughton Ltd. , c1928
viii, 310 p. ;19 cm.

I561. 45/B918P954P
A Prince of the Captivity/John Buchan. —London: Hodder and Stoughton, c1933
383 p. ;19 cm.

I561. 45/B918T445(o)
The Thirty-Nine Steps/John Buchan. —New York: Pochet Books, c1915
208 p. ;17 cm.

I561. 45/B922
Aesop Dancing or the Heart of Oliver Goldsmith/J. E. Buckrose. —London: Eveleigh Nash and Grayson Ltd. , c1930
253 p. ;19 cm.

I561. 45/B945B414
Beggar's Horses/Percival Christopher Wren. —London: John Murray, Albemarle Street, W. , c1934
444 p. ;19 cm.

I561. 45/B947
Huntingtower/John Buchan. —London: Hodder and Stoughton Ltd. , c1922
318 p. ;19 cm.

I561. 45/B967
The Fifth of November and Other Tales/Burns and Otes. —London: Burns and Otes, [?]
247 p. ;18 cm.

I561. 45/B974
Heir to Lucifer/Miles Burton. —London: The Crime Club, c1947
192 p. ;19 cm.

I561. 45/B985(O)
The Way of All Flesh/Samuel Butler. —London: Jonathan Cape Ltd. , 1936
356 p. ;18 cm.

I561. 45/C452
Ella Keeps House/Jessie Champion. —London: John Lane, The Bodley Head, [?]
304 p. ;20 cm.

I561. 45/C486
Saint's Getaway/Leslie Charteris. —New York: The Sun Dial Press, c1943
x, 305 p. ;19 cm.

I561. 45/C525
The Innocence of Father Brown/G. K. Chesterton. —Copyright ed. —Leipzig: Bernhard Tauchnitz, c1911
295 p. ;17 cm.

I561. 45/C55
The Sittaford Mystery/Agatha Christie. —London: W. Collins Sons & Co. Ltd. , c1931
250 p. ;19 cm.

I561. 45/C555
The Murder at the Vicarage/Agatha Christie. —Harmondworth: Penguin Books, c1929
255 p. ;18 cm.

I561. 45/C555A
Appointment with Death: A Poirot Mystery/Agatha Christie. —New York: Grosset & Dunlap Publiers, c1937, 1938
301 p. ;19 cm.

I561. 45/C555L
Lord Edgware Dies/Agatha Christie. . —London: W. Collins Sons and Co. , Ltd. , c1933
252 p. ;19 cm.

I561.45/C555H539
Hercule Poirot's Christmas/Agatha Christie. —London: The Crime Club, c1939
251 p. ;20 cm.

I561.45/C555M974
Murder in Mesopotamia/Agatha Christie. —London: The Crime Club, c1936
284 p. ;19 cm.

I561.45/C555M995
The Mysterious Affair at Styles: A Detective Story/Agatha Christie. —New York: Grosset & Dunlap Publishers, c1920
296 p. ;19 cm.

I561.45/C555M995J
The Mysterious Affair at Styles, The Murder on the Links, Poirot Investigates/Agatha Christie. —London: John Lane the Bodley Head Ltd., [?]
1 v. ;19 cm.

I561.45/C555P397
Lord Edgware Dies/Agatha Christie. —London: Penguin Books, c1933
252 p. ;18 cm.

I561.45/C561
The Stronghold/Richard Church. —London: J. M. Dent & Sons Ltd., c1939
420 p. ;20 cm.

I561.45/C689A398
The Affair at Aliquid/G. D. H. and M. Cole. —London: W. Collins Sons & Co. Ltd., c1933
285 p. ;18 cm.

I561.45/C712
The Brownies At No. 9/Freda Collins. —London: George G. Harrap & Co., Ltd., c1936
254 p. ;21 cm.

I561.45/C712B627
Black Ivory/Norman Collins. —London: Collins, c1948
255 p. ;20 cm.

I561.45/C712P397
Penang Appointment/Norman Collins. —London: Victor Gollancz Ltd., c1934
286 p. ;19 cm.

I561.45/C738
Darkness and Day/I. Compton-Burnett. —London: Victor Gollancz Ltd., c1951
235 p. ;19 cm.

I561.45/C743S438
Sea-Borne: Thirty Years Avoyaging/James B. Connolly. —New York: Doubleday, Daran and Company, Inc., c1944
246 p. ;22 cm.

I561.45/C743T874
Truth Comes Limping/J. J. Connington. —Boston: Little Brown and Company, 1938
295 p. ;20 cm.

I561.45/C754
The Nigger of the "Narcissus": A Tale of the Sea/Joseph Conrad. —London: William Heinemann Ltd., c1897
259 p. ;19 cm.

I561.45/C754N898
Nostromo: A Tale of the Seaboard/Joseph Conrad. —New York: Doubleday, Doran & Company, Inc., [?]
xxv, 566 p. ;20 cm.

I561.45/C774
What Katy Did Next/Susan Coolidge. —London: Blackie & Son Ltd., [?]

191 p. ;18 cm.

I561.45/C785A193

Adam and Eve and Pinch Me: Tales/A. E. Coppard. —London: Penguin Books, c1946

168 p. ;18 cm.

I561.45/C789

Devil-Man from Mars/James Corbett. —London: Herbert Jenkins Ltd., c1935

312 p. ;19 cm.

I561.45/C874

Suwarrow Gold and Other Stories of the Great South Sea/James Cowan. —London: Jonathan Cape Ltd., c1936

253 p. ;1 cm.

I561.45/C881

The Magical Realm/Kathleen Coyle. —New York: E. P. Dutton & Co., Inc., c1943

314 p. ;22 cm.

I561.45/C945

The House of Horror/Michael Crombie. —London: Arthur Gray(Books) Ltd., [?]

255 p. ;19 cm.

I561.45/C947

The Citadel/A. J. Crownin. —Boston: Little, Brown and Company, c1938

401 p. ;21 cm.

I561.45/C947G795

The Green Years/A. J. Cronin. —Boston: Little, Brown and Company, c1944

347 p. ;19 cm.

I561.45/D179

Island of the East Indies/Hawthorne Daniel. —New York: G. P. Putnam's Sons, c1944

xiii, 266 p. ;19 cm.

I561.45/D179A778

The Arrogant History of White Ben/Clemence Dane. —New York: The Literary Guide of America, Inc., c1939

viii, 363 p. ;21 cm.

I561.45/D252

The Steeper Cliff/David Davidson. —New York: Random House, c1947

340 p. ;21 cm.

I561.45/D283

The Fifth Tulip/Donald Deane. —London: John Hamilton Ltd. Publishers, [?]

247 p. ;19 cm.

I561.45/D311

Sackcloth Into Silk/Warwick Deeping. —Toronto: Mcclelland and Stewart, Limited Publishers, c1935

423 p. ;19 cm.

I561.45/D311(O)

The Impudence of Youth/Warwick Deeping. —London: Cassell and Company Ltd., c1946

282 p. ;19 cm.

I561.45/D311O44

Old Pybus/Warwick Deeping. —New York: Alfred A Knope, c1928

376 p. ;20 cm.

I561.45/D311R784

Roper's Row/Warwick Deeping. —London: Cassell & Company Ltd., c1929

423 p. ;19 cm.

I561.45/D311S713

Sorrell and Son/Warwick Deeping. —New York: Grosset & Dunlap, c1926

400 p. ;19 cm.

I561. 45/D311T531

Three Rooms/Warwick Deeping. —London: Cassell and Company Ltd. , c1930

316 p. ;18 cm.

I561. 45/D311V198

Valour/Warwick Deeping. —London: Cassell and Company, Ltd. , c1918

339 p. ;19 cm.

I561. 45/D314

Roxana: the Fortunate Mistress/Daniel Defoe. —[S. l.]: The Bibliophilist Society, c1931

xi, 322 p. ;24 cm.

I561. 45/D333

Humbug/E. M. Delafield. —London: Hutchinson & Co. , [?]

288 p. ;19 cm.

I561. 45/D422

Somebody Must/Peter de Polnay. —London: Hutchinson & Co. , [?]

224 p. ;19 cm.

I561. 45/D546C536

Child's History of England with an Introduction/Charles Dickens. —London: J. M. Dent & Sons Ltd. , c1907

xx, 396 p. ;18 cm.

I561. 45/D548J88

Joy and Josephine/Monica Dickens. —London: Michael Joseph, c1948

320 p. ;20 cm.

I561. 45/D687

Jim the Penman/Dick Donovan. —London: George Newnws, Ltd. , [?]

ii, 254 p. ;17 cm.

I561. 45/D754

The Refugees, a Tale of Two Continents /A. Conan Doyle. —London: Eveleigh Nash & Grayson Ltd. , c1922

383 p. ;19 cm.

I561. 45/D754(O)

The Sign of Four/A. Conan Doyle. —London: Hasell, Watson & Viney, Ltd. , c1922

285 p. ;18 cm.

I561. 45/D754S

A Study in Scarlet/A. Conan Doyle. —London: Ward, Lock & Co. , Ltd. , [?]

255 p. ;16 cm.

I561. 45/D754L349

His Last Bow: Some Reminiscences of Sherlock Holmes/Arthur Conan Doyle. —London: John Murray, Albemarle Street, W. , c1917

vii, 305 p. ;19 cm.

I561. 45/D754L796

Lobster Salad/Lynn Doyle. —London: Duckworth, c1922, 1925

320 p. ;19 cm.

I561. 45/D754L879O

The Lost World/Arthur Conan Doyle. —London: Hodder and Stoughton, [?]

252 p. ;18 cm.

I561. 45/D754M533

The Memoirs of Sherlock Holmes/A. Conan Doyle. —London: Wyman & Sons Ltd. , c1923

248 p. ;18 cm.

I561. 45/D754R768

Rodney Stone/A. Conan Doyle. —London: Eveleigh Nash & Grayson Ltd. , c1921

366 p. ;19 cm.

I561. 45/D754S464(O)

Selections from Adventures of Sherlock Holmes/A. Conan Doyle. —Shanghai: The

Commercial Press, Ltd., c1926
224 p. ;16 cm.

I561.45/D797
No Through Road/Clifford J. Druce. —London: Victor Gollancz Ltd., c1935
288 p. ;19 cm.

I561.45/D847
The Masterful Monk/Owen Francis Dudley. —London: Longmans, Green and Co., c1933
314 p. ;19 cm.

I561.45/D885R289
Rebecca/Daphne Du Maurier. —[S. l. : s. n.], [?]
457 p. ;19 cm.

I561.45/D885R289(O)
Rebecca/Daphne Du Maurier. —[S. l. : s. n.], [?]
446 p. ;18 cm.

I561.45/E11
Beyond the Black Waters/A. L. O. E.. —London: Thomas Nelson and Sons, c1890
248 p. ;19 cm.

I561.45/E14
Desire-Spanish Version/Evelyn Eaton. —London: Chapman and Hall Ltd., c1932
285 p. ;19 cm.

I561.45/E22
The Semi-Attached Couple/Emily Eden. —Boston: Houghton Mifflin Company, c1947
xvi, 249 p. ;21 cm.

I561.45/E23
Woman of the Family: A Romantic Novel/May Edginton. —London: Collins Clear-Type Press, c1935
286 p. ;19 cm.

I561.45/E65
Two Names upon the Shore/Susan Ertz. —London: Hodder & Stoughton Ltd., c1947
315 p. ;19 cm.

I561.45/E65S887
The Story of Julian/Susan Ertz. —New York, London: D. Appleton and Company, c1931
311 p. ;19 cm.

I561.45/E92
Ghosts of the Scarlet Fleet/E. R. G. R. Evans. —London: Jarrolds Publishers, c1932
320 p. ;19 cm.

I561.45/E92
Montana Rides Again/Evan Evans. —London: Cassell and Company, 1935
256 p. ;19 cm.

I561.45/E92M764
Montana Rides! /Evan Evans. —New York: Grosset & Dunlap, c1933
300 p. ;19 cm.

I561.45/F118
Unforbidden Fruit/Warner Fabian. —London: Stanley Paul & Co., c1928
288, 11 p. ;19 cm.

I561.45/F172B618
Birds of Prey/Gerar Fairlie. —London: Hodder and Stoughton Ltd., c1932
317 p. ;19 cm.

I561.45/F235
Martin Conisby's Vengeance/Jeffery Farnol. —Boston: Little, Brown, and Company, c1942
vi, 331 p. ;20 cm.

I561.45/F613
The Markenmore Mystery/J. S. Fletcher. —

London: Herbert Jenkins Ltd., [?]
311 p.;19 cm.

I561.45/F613M974
The Murder in the Pallant /J. S. Fletcher.—London: Herbert Jenkins Ltd., [?]
312 p.;19 cm.

I561.45/F623
The Old Ashburn Place/Margaret Flint.—New York: Dodd, Mead & Company, c1936
301 p.;21 cm.

I561.45/F655
The Saint/Antonio Fogazzaro.—London: J. M. Dent & Sons, Ltd., [?]
296 p.;18 cm.

I561.45/F717
Commodore Hornblower/by C. S. Forester.—Boston: Little, Brown and Company, c1945.
3 p., l., [3]-384 p.;20 cm.

I561.45/F717C734
Commodore Hornblower/C. S. Forester.—Boston: Little, Brown and Company, c1945
384 p.;20 cm.

I561.45/F717E11
The Earthly Paradise/C. S. Forester.—[Harmondsworth]: Penguin Books, [c1940]
319 p.;19 cm.

I561.45/F733
Passage to India/E. M. Forster.—New York: Iarcourt, Brace and Company, c1924
322 p.;20 cm.

I561.45/F785
Beauty and Bands/Ellen Thorneycroft Fowler.—London: Constable and Company Ltd., c1920
357 p.;18 cm.

I561.45/F828
Everywoman/Gilbert Frankau.—London: Hutchinson & Co., (Publishers), Ltd., [?]
ix, 448, 32 p.;19 cm.

I561.45/F828M379
Martin Make-Believe: A Romance/Gilbert Frankau.—London: Hutchinson& Co., Ltd., [?]
448 p.;20 cm.

I561.45/F852
The Little Fortune/Arnold Fredericks.—London: Simpkin, Marshall, Hamilton Kent & Co., Ltd., c1917
317 p.;19 cm.

I561.45/F855T498
Dr. Thorndyke Intervenes/R. Austin Freeman.—London: Hodder and Stoughton, Ltd., c1933
317 p.;19 cm.

I561.45/F974
The Plough/Mary Fulton.—London: Duckworth & Co., c1919
302 p.;19 cm.

I561.45/G145
Over the River/John Galsworthy.—London: William Heinemann Ltd., c1933
322 p.;19 cm.

I561.45/G145F
Fraternity/John Galsworthy.—London: William Heinemann, c1909
viii, 344 p.;19 cm.

I561.45/G146
The Forsyte Saga/John Galsworthy.—New York: Charles Scribner's Sons, c1947

xx, 921 p. ;21 cm.

I561.45/G437R859

The Road to Bagdad/George Gibbs. —New York: D. Appleton-Century Company, c1938

233 p. ;20 cm.

I561.45/G441

My American: A Romance/Stella Gibbons. —London: Longmans, Green and Co. , c1939

444 p. ;20 cm.

I561.45/G442

The Cross of Peace/Philip Gibbs. —London: Hutchinson & Co. , (Publishers). Ltd. , [?]

288, 56 p. ;18 cm.

I561.45/G442D219

Darkened Rooms/Philip Gibbs. —New York: Doubleday, Doran & Company, Inc. , c1929

298 p. ;19 cm.

I561.45/G442G786

Great Argument/Philip Gibbs. —London: Hutchinson & Co. , [?]

288, 28 p. ;19 cm.

I561.45/G442N532

The New Crusade/Anthony Gibbs. —London: Hutchinson & Co. , (Publishers), Ltd. , [?]

287, 32 p. ;19 cm.

I561.45/G457B627

Black Narcissus/Rumer Godden. —Boston: Little, Brown and Company, c1939

294 p. ;21 cm.

I561.45/G464

More Than Conquerors/Ariadne Gilbert. —[S. l. : s. n.], c1914

423 p. ;20 cm.

I561.45/G531

The Nether World/George Gissing. —New York: E. P. Dutton & Company, [?]

x, 392 p. ;20 cm.

I561.45/G568

Love Itself/Elinor Glyn. —New York: The Macaulay Company, c1912

301 p. ;19 cm.

I561.45/G578

Gypsy Gypsy/Rumer Godden. —London: Peter Davies, c1940

289 p. ;19 cm.

I561.45/G578

Thc House by the Sea/Jon Godden. —London: Michael Joseph Ltd. & The Book Society Ltd. , c1947

280 p. ;19 cm.

I561.45/G578C218

A Candle for ST. Jude/Rumer Godden. —London: Michael Joseph, c1948

192 p. ;19 cm.

I561.45/G646

Colorado Jim/George Goodchild. —London: W. Collins Sons & Co Ltd. , [?]

247 p. ;18 cm.

I561.45/G646M

The Monster of Grammont/George Goodchild. —New York: The Mystery League, Inc. , c1930

287 p. ;20 cm.

I561.45/G656H615

The Heyday in the Blood/Geraint Goodwin. —London: Jonathan Cape, c1936

287 p. ;20 cm.

I561.45/G678

Sir John Hawkins/Philip Gosse.—London: John Lane the Bodley Head Ltd., c1930

xii, 289 p.;22 cm.

I561.45/G688

The Herb of Grace/Elizabeth Goudge.—London: Hodder and Stoughton, c1948

356 p.;21 cm.

I561.45/G688G

Green Dolphin Street/Elizabeth Goudge.—New York: Coward-Mccann, Inc., c1944

345 p.;20 cm.

I561.45/G778

Killer Conquest/Berkeley Gray.—London: Collins, c1947

192 p.;19 cm.

I561.45/G788A398

Alias Norman Conquest/Berkeley Gray.—London: Collins, c1945

160 p.;19 cm.

I561.45/G799(O)

The Heart of the Matter/Graham Greene.—London: William Heinemann Ltd & The Book Society Ltd., c1948

297 p.;19 cm.

I561.45/G799H435

The Heart of the Matter/Graham Greene.—London: The Reprint Society, c1948

297 p.;19 cm.

I561.45/G799J91

Jubilee Hall; or, "There's no Place Like Home"/The Honble Mrs. Greene.—London: T. Nelson and Sons, Paternoster Row., c1892

220 p.;19 cm.

I561.45/G822

Lords of the Coast/Jackson Gregory.—London: Hodder & Stoughton, c1935

315 p.;19 cm.

I561.45/G822R312

Red Rivals/Jackson Gregory.—London: Hodder & Stoughton Ltd., [?]

318 p.;19 cm.

I561.45/G853

St. Paul's Life of Christ/Gwilym O. Griffith.—London: Hodder and Stoughton, c1928

288 p.;17 cm.

I561.45/G947

The Stars Look Down/A. J. Cronin.—Shanghai: Asia Book Co., Ltd., [?]

701 p.;20 cm.

I561.45/G971

Beyond Sing the Woods/Trygve Gulbranssen.—New York: G. P. Putnam's Sons, c1936

313 p.;21 cm.

I561.45/G976L879

The Lost Glen/Neil M. Gunn.—Edinburgh: The Porpoise Press, c1932

351 p.;19 cm.

I561.45/G976S587

The Silver Darlings/Nell M. Gunn.—New York: George W. Stewart, Publisher, Inc., c1945

384 p.;20 cm.

I561.45/G977

The Shadow of a Vendetta/Archibald C. Gunter.—London: Bulter & Tanner, [?]

320, 16 p.;20 cm.

I561.45/H113

The School of Paris/Robert A. Hamblin.—

London: George Allen & Unwin Ltd., c1924
285 p.;19 cm.

I561.45/H233
Drift/James Hanley.—London: Joiner & Steele, c1932
270 p.;19 cm.

I561.45/H268
Fickle Fortune/Robina F. Hardy.—London: Oliphant Anderson & Ferrier, [?]
192 p.;18 cm.

I561.45/H412
The Lucky Number/Ian Hay.—London: Hodder and Stoughton Ltd., [?]
320 p.;18 cm.

I561.45/H429
Cocktail Alley/Eric Hazelton.—London: Cassell and Company Ltd., c1933
311 p.;19 cm.

I561.45/H487
Three Gentlemen from New Caledonia/R. D. Henmingway, Henry de Halsalle.—London: Stanley Paul & Co, c1915
vii, 358 p.;19 cm.

I561.45/H599
The Little Iliad/Maurice Hewlett.—Philadelphia: J. B. Lippincott Company, c1915
327 p.;20 cm.

I561.45/H615
Arabella/Georgette Heyer.—London: William Heinemann Ltd., c1949
315 p.;19 cm.

I561.45/H615G
The Grand Sophy/Georgette Heyer.—London: William Heinemann Ltd., c1950
348 p.;21 cm.

I561.45/H626
In the Wilderness/Robert Hichens.—London: Methuen & Co., Ltd., c1917
583, 31 p.;18 cm.

I561.45/H626A784
Dr. Artz/Robert Hichens.—New York: Comsmopolitan Book Corporation, c1928, 1929
378 p.;19 cm.

I561.45/H626P222
The Paradine Case/Robert Hichens.—London: Ernest Benn Ltd., c1933
527 p.;19 cm.

I561.45/H626P962
The Prophet of Berkeley Square/Robert Hichens.—New York: Dodd, Mead and Company, c1918
iv, 333 p.;19 cm.

I561.45/H656
Good-bye, Mr. Chips/James Hilton.—London: Hazell, Watson & Viney, Ltd., c1934
127 p.;19 cm.

I561.45/H656(O)
Good-bye Mr. Chips/James Hilton.—Boston: Little, Brown and Company, c1945
125 p.;19 cm.

I561.45/H656S
So Well Remembered/James Hilton.—Boston: Little, Brown and Company, c1945
309 p.;19 cm.

I561.45/H656K69
Knight Without Armour/James Hilton.—London: Ernest Benn Ltd., c1933
287 p.;19 cm.

I561.45/H656L879
Lost Horizon/James Hilton. —New York: Grosset & Dunlap Publishers, c1933
277 p. ;19 cm.

I561.45/H656N912
Nothing So Strange/James Hilton. —Boston: Little, Brown and Company, c1947
308 p. ;20 cm.

I561.45/H656S887
The Story of Dr. Wassell/James Hilton. —Boston: Little, Brown and Company, c1943
xi, 158 p. ;18 cm.

I561.45/H692
God's in His Heaven/James Lansdale Hodson. —London: Victor Gollancz Ltd., c1935
352 p. ;19 cm.

I561.45/H747
In Danger's Hour/Gordon Holman. —London: Hodder and Stoughton Ltd., c1948
217 p. ;23 cm.

I561.45/H765
No Snow in Latching/Michael Home. —London: Methuen & Co., Ltd., c1949
x, 225 p. ;19 cm.

I561.45/H791
A Young Man's Year/Anthony Hope. —London: Methunen & Co., Ltd., c1915
vi, 343, 31 p. ;20 cm.

I561.45/H791-4
The King's Mirror/Anthony Hope. —London: Methuen and Co., c1903
viii, 311 p. ;18 cm.

I561.45/H791C454-6
A Change of Air/Anthony Hope. —London: Methuen & Co., c1901
304 p. ;18 cm.

I561.45/H791T838
Tristram of Blent: An Episode in the story of an Ancient House/Anthony Hope. —London: John Maurray, Albemarle Striit, W, c1901
408 p. ;19 cm.

I561.45/H812
Princess After Dark/Sydney Horler. —London: Hodder and Stoughton, c1934
320 p. ;18 cm.

I561.45/H812L
Lord of Terror: A Paul Vivanti Story/Sydney Horler. —London: Collins 48 Pall Mall, c1935
252 p. ;19 cm.

I561.45/H848
The Solitary Summer/Elizabeth Jane Howard. —New York: Grosset & Dunlap, c1900
190 p. ;20 cm.

I561.45/H893
In Hazard: A Sea Story/Richard Hughes. —London: Chatto & Windus, c1938
1 v. ;21 cm.

I561.45/H921
Bullets Bite Deep/David Hume. —London: Collins, c1935
249 p. ;18 cm.

I561.45/H921G
The Gaol Gates Are Open/David Hume. —London: Collins, c1935
256 p. ;19 cm.

I561.45/H926
The Road to Anywhere/ "Rita" (Mrs. Desmond Humphreys). —London: Hutchinson & Co., (Publishers) Ltd., [?]
288 p. ;19 cm.

I561.45/H973

Interim/R. C. Hutchinson. —New York: Farrar & Rinebart, Inc., c1945

186 p.;19 cm.

I561.45/H975

The Clean Heart/Arthur StuartMen Hutchinson. —Boston: Little, Brown and Company, c1922

403 p.;c19 cm.

I561.45/H975B

Big Business/A. S. M. Hutchinson. —London: Hodder & Stoughton, Ltd., c1932

317 p.;19 cm.

I561.45/H975F853

This Freedom/A. S. M. Hutchinson. —London: Hodder and Stoughton, Ltd., c1922

318 p.;19 cm.

I561.45/H975T342

Testament: A Novel/R. C. Hutchinson. —London: Cassell and Company Ltd., c1938

732 p.;22 cm.

I561.45/H975W784

If Winter Comes/A. S. M. Hutchinson. —New York: Grosset & Dunlap Publishers, c1921

415 p.;21 cm.

I561.45/H986

After Many a Summer Dies the Swan/Aldous Huxley. —[S. l: s. n.], c1939

356 p.;18 cm.

I561.45/I154

The Bishop's Crime/H. C. Bailey. —[S. l.]: Crosset & Dunlap, Publishers, c1940, 1941

viii, 309 p.;19 cm.

I561.45/I27

Before the Fact: A Murder Story Ladies/Francis Iles. —London: Victor Gollance Ltd., c1932

352 p.;19 cm.

I561.45/I54J92

Judy Bovenden/H. C. Bailey. —London: Methuen & Co., Ltd., c1928

v, 250, 8 p.;19 cm.

I561.45/I58

Attack Alarm/Hammond Innes. —London: The Macmillan Company, c1942

284 p.;21 cm.

I561.45/I65

Young Bess/Margaret Irwin. —New York: Harcourt, Brace and Company, c1945

274 p.;21 cm.

I561.45/I65B851

The Bride: The Story of Louise and Montrose/Margaret Irwin. —London: The Reprint Society, c1939

431 p.;20 cm.

I561.45/J12

Twenty-Six Sea Yarns/G. Gibbard Jackson. —London: "the Boys Own Paper" Office, [?]

255 p.;22 cm.

I561.45/J15

Gollantz/Naomi Jacob. —London: Hutchinson & Co., c1948

288 p.;19 cm.

I561.45/J15S

Short Cruises/W. W. Jacobs. —Copyright ed.. —Leipzig: Bernhard Tauchnitz, c1907

288 p.;17 cm.

I561.45/J17

Light Freights/W. W. Jacobs. —London:

Methuen & Co, Ltd. , c1928
vii, 193 p. ;19 cm.

I561. 45/J27B627
The Black Laurel/Storm Jameson. —London: Macmillan, 1948 [c1947]
349 p. ;

I561. 45/J52
Adventures of Bindle/Herbert Jenkins. —London: Herbert Jenkins Ltd. , [?]
312 p. ;19 cm.

I561. 45/J58
The Saga of San Demetrio/F. Tennyson Jesse. —New York: Alfred A. Knopf, c1943
84 p. ;20 cm.

I561. 45/J77
Two Survived: The Story of Tapscott and Widdicombe, who were torpedoed in mid-atlantic and survived seventy days in an open boat/Guy Pearce Jones. —London: Hamish Hamilton, c1941
198 p. ;19 cm.

I561. 45/J78E86
I Spy ! or, Europe Without Tears/Maurice Bethel Jones. —London: George Allen and Unwin Ltd. , c1939
304 p. ;20 cm.

I561. 45/K23
Shepherds in Sackcloth/Sheila Kaye-Smith. —New York: Harper & Brothers Publishers, c1930
379 p. ;19 cm.

I561. 45/K23P731
The Ploughman's Progress/Sheila Kaye-Smith. —London: Cassell and Company, Ltd. , [?]
344 p. ;20 cm.

I561. 45/K23S743
Spell Land: the Story of a Sussex Farm/Sheila Kaye-Smith. —New York: E. P. Dutton and Company, c1926
vii, 319 p. ;20 cm.

I561. 45/K23V172
The Valiant Woman/Sheila Kaye-smith. —London: Cassell and Company Ltd. , c1939
400 p. ;21 cm.

I561. 45/K23V813
Virtue's Tragedy/Efe Kaye. —London: John Macqueen, c1899
317 p. ;19 cm.

I561. 45/K25
The Mimic/E. M. Keate. —London: Sampson Low, Marston & Co. , Ltd. , [?]
310 p. ;19 cm.

I561. 45/K35(O)
Red Sky at Morning/Margaret Kennedy. —New York: Doubeday, Page & Co. , c1927
331 p. ;19 cm.

I561. 45/K35M627
The Midas touch/Margaret Kennedy. —New York: Random House, c1939
viii, 530 p. ;20 cm.

I561. 45/K35W556
Where Stands a Winged Sentry/Margaret Kennedy. —New Haven: Yale University Press, c1941
xv, 251 p. ;21 cm.

I561. 45/K52
The Sun Climbs Slow/Lou King-Hall. —London: Peter Davies, c1946
255 p. ;19 cm.

I561. 45/K57(O)
The light that failed/Rudyard Kipling. —New York: Doubleday & Company, Inc. , c1899
258 p. ;20 cm.

I561. 45/K57(O)
Captains Courageous/Rudyard Kipling. —London: Macmillan and Co. , c1939
vi, 282 p. ;17 cm.

I561. 45/K57D273
The Day's Work: The Works of Rudyard Kipling/Rudyard Kipling. —New York: Doubleday & Mcclure Company, c1899
431 p. ;19 cm.

I561. 45/K57S775
Stalky & Co. , /Rudyard Kipling. —London: Macmillan and Co. , Ltd. , c1929
272 p. ;20 cm.

I561. 45/K62
Olive E. /C. H. B. Kitchin. —London: Constable & Co Ltd. , c1937
324 p. ;19 cm.

I561. 45/L433
Perpetual Fires/Eric Leadbitter. —London: George Allen & Unwin Ltd. , c1918
324 p. ;19 cm.

I561. 45/L528
Pattie Thorne/Netta Leigh. —London: Geoge Stoneman, [?]
177 p. ;19 cm.

I561. 45/L528
The Opal Heart/Marie Connor Leighton. —London: Ward, Lock & Co. , Ltd. , c1920
308 p. ;19 cm.

I561. 45/L673A639
The Apes of God/Wyndham Lewis. —London: Crayson & Grayson, c1931
625 p. ;22 cm.

I561. 45/L735
Magnus Merriman/Eric Linklater. —London: Jonathan Cape, c1934
362 p. ;20 cm.

I561. 45/L814
Ancestor Jorico/William J. Locke. —New York: Dodd, Mead & Company, c1929
339 p. ;19 cm.

I561. 45/L814S479
Septimus/William J. Locke. —New York: John Lane Company, c1909
315 p. ;19 cm.

I561. 45/L817
Slave Market/Vere Lockwood. —London: Herbert Jenkins Ltd. , c1935
312 p. ;19 cm.

I561. 45/L829
A Calf for Venus/Norah Lofts. —London: Michael Joseph Ltd. , c1949
221 p. ;19 cm.

I561. 45/L829H588
Hester Roon/Norah Lofts. —London: Peter Davies, c1940
396 p. ;19 cm.

I561. 45/L865
Relative to Poison/E. C. R. Lorac. —London: The Crime Club, c1947
192 p. ;19 cm.

I561. 45/L872
The Green Brigade/James Lorimer. —London: William Blackwood & Sons Ltd. , c1935
vii, 307 p. ;19 cm.

I561.45/L919

Why They Married/Belloc Lowndes. —London: William Heinemann, c1923

263 p. ;19 cm.

I561.45/L933

Variety Lane/E. V. Lucas. —London: Methuen & Co., Ltd., c1916

vi, 189 p. ;17 cm.

I561.45/M111

Cold Feet/Mahon, Terence. —London: Chapman and Hall, Ltd., c1929

249 p. ;20 cm.

I561.45/M113

The Fortune of Christina M'nab/(S.) Macnaughtan. —London: Thomas Nelson and Sons, [?]

275 p. ;16 cm.

I561.45/M117

Dangerous Ages/Rose Macaulay. —London: Collin's Clear-Type Press, c1922

370 p. ;19 cm.

I561.45/M128

The Clue of The Dead Goldfish/Macclure, Victor. —London: George G. Harrad & Co., Ltd., c1933

254 p. ;19 cm.

I561.45/M135

The Crime Conductor/Philip Macdonald. —London: The Crime Club, c1939

252 p. ;18 cm.

I561.45/M135(O)

Patrol/Philip Macdonald. —London: Penguin Books Ltd., c1937

246 p. ;18 cm.

I561.45/M135

England, Their England/A. G. Macdonell. —London: Macmillan and Co., Ltd., c1933

299 p. ;19 cm.

I561.45/M145

The Red Horizon/Patrick Macgill. —London: Herbert Jenkins Ltd., [?]

306 p. ;19 cm.

I561.45/M152

Assignment in Brittany/Helen Macinnes. —New York: The Sun Dial Press, c1943

1 v. ;21 cm.

I561.45/M152F899

Friends and Lovers/Helen Macinnes. —Boston: Little, Brown and Company, c1947

367 p. ;20 cm.

I561.45/M153

Morning, Noon and Night/Denis Mackail. —London: Hodder & Stoughton, Ltd., c1938

331 p. ;19 cm.

I561.45/M155S726

The South Wind of Love/Compton Mackenzie. —London: Rich & Cowan Ltd., c1937

835 p. ;20 cm.

I561.45/M156

Water on the Brain/Compton Mackenzie. —London: Cassell and Company Ltd., c1933

335 p. ;19 cm.

I561.45/M156H948

Hunting the Fairies/Compton Mackenzie. —London: Chatto and Windus, c1949

281 p. ;19 cm.

I561.45/M156O44

The Old Men of the Sea/Compton Mackenzie. —London: Cassell and Company, Ltd.,

c1924
vii, 343 p. ;18 cm.

I561.45/M156O93
Our Street/Compton Mackenzie. —New York: Doubleday, Doran & Company, Inc., c1934
309 p. ;20 cm.

I561.45/M156R736
Rogues and Vagabonds/Compton • Mackenzie. —London: Cassell and Company, Ltd., c1927
319 p. ;20 cm.

I561.45/M167
The Pastor's Wife/Macmillan and Co., Ltd.,—London: Macmillan and Co., Ltd., c1925
484 p. ;19 cm.

I561.45/M323
The Connoisseur and Other Stories/Malter de la Mare. —New York: Alfred A Knopf, c1926
309 p. ;19 cm.

I561.45/M357
Wickford Point/John P. Marquand. —London: Robert Hale Ltd., c1939
510 p. ;20 cm.

I561.45/M367
The Uncertain Glory/Bruce Marshall. —London: Victor Gollance Ltd., c1935
445 p. ;20 cm.

I561.45/M387
Attic and Area or the Maidservant's Year/Francesca Marton. —London: Hamish Hamilton, c1948
422 p. ;19 cm.

I561.45/M388
The Return of Anthony Trent/Wyndham Martyn. —London: Herbert Jenkins Ltd., [?]
320 p. ;19 cm.

I561.45/M396
Captain Margaret/John Masefield. —[S. l.]: Thomas Nelson and Sons, [?]
384 p. ;16 cm.

I561.45/M396E29
Eggs And Baker or the Days of Trial/John Masefield. —London: William Heinemann Ltd., c1936
298 p. ;19 cm.

I561.45/M396J61
Jim Davis/John Masefield. —New York: Grosset & Dunlat Pulisher, [?]
vii, 244 p. ;21 cm.

I561.45/M396M645
In the Mill/John Masefield. —New York: The Macmillan Company, c1941
158 p. ;21 cm.

I561.45/M398(O)
Running Water/A. E. W. Mason. —New York: The Century Co., 1907
vii, 352 p. ;20 cm.

I561.45/M398D(O)
Dilemmas/A. E. W. Mason. —London: Hodder & Stoughton Ltd., c1934
315 p. ;19 cm.

I561.45/M398O87
No Other Tiger/A. E. W. Mason. —New York: George H. Doran Company, c1927
310 p. ;19 cm.

I561.45/M398P
The Philanderers/A. E. W. Mason. —London: Hodder and Stoughton Ltd., c1926
285 p. ;17 cm.

I561.45/M398S955

The Summons/A. E. W. Mason.—London: Hodder and Stoughton Ltd., [?]

320 p.;19 cm.

I561.45/M398W

They Wouldn't Be Chessmen/A. E. W. Mason.—London: Hodder & Stoughton Ltd., c1935

343 p.;19 cm.

I561.45/M449

Ashenden, or, The British Agent/W. Somerset Maugham.—New York: Doubleday, Doran and Company, Inc., c1941

xiii, 304 p.;20 cm.

I561.45/M449A773

The Razor's Edge/W. Somerset Maugham.—New York: The Armed Services, Inc., c1944

383 p.;12 cm.

I561.45/M449B636

The Razor's Edge/W. Somerset Maugham.—Philadelphia: The Blakiston Company, c1944

250 p.;20 cm.

I561.45/M449S917

Strictly Personal/W. Somerset Maugham.—New York: New York Publishing Co., Inc., c1943

272 p.;21 cm.

I561.45/M454

Hungry Hill/Daphne du Mauier.—Philadephia: The Blakiston Company, [?]

344 p.;20 cm.

I561.45/M454D962

The Progress of Julius/Daphne du Maurier.—London: William Heinemann Ltd., c1933

304 p.;19 cm.

I561.45/M454J49

Jamaica Inn/Daphne du Maurier.—London: Vitor Gollance Ltd., c1936

351 p.;19 cm.

I561.45/M454P221

The Parasites /Daphne du Maurier.—London: Victor Gollancz Ltd., c1949

350 p.;19 cm.

I561.45/M461

The Fate of Jane McKenzie/Nancy Barr Mavity.—London: W. Collins Sons @ Co Ltd., c1933

252 p.;19 cm.

I561.45/M463

Spinster of This Parish/W. B. Maxwell.—New York: Grosset & Dunlap, c1922

397 p.;19 cm.

I561.45/M465

Tudor Green/W. B. Maxwell.—London: Hutchison & Co., (Publishers), Ltd., c1935

527, 48 p.;19 cm.

I561.45/M657

Don't Touch the Body/Arthur Mills.—London: Collins Clear-Type Press, c1947

191 p.;19 cm.

I561.45/M657

The Road/Dorothy Mills.—London: Duck Worth and Co., c1923

276 p., 15 p;18 cm.

I561.45/M683

The Pursuit of Love/Nancy Mitford.—London: The Reprint Society, c1945

2222 p.;19 cm.

I561.45/M847

The Fountain/by Charles Morgan. —New York: Alfred A Knopf, c1932.

450 p. ;19 cm.

I561.45/M981

Leading Lady/D. L. Murray. —London: Hodder and Stoughton Ltd. , c1947

414 p. ;21 cm.

I561.45/MacI58

Above Suspicion/Helen MacInnes. —Boston: Little, Brown and Company, c1945

333 p. ;19 cm.

I561.45/McF295

Command/William McFee. —New York: Doubleday, Page & Company, c1922

337 p. ;19 cm.

I561.45/McK34

Sonia: Between two Worlds/Stephen McKenna. —Harmondsworth: Penguin Books, c1949

448 p. ;18 cm.

I561.45/McK34-5

Sonia: Between two Worlds/Stephen McKenna. —5th. ed.. —London: Methuen & Co. , Ltd. , c1917

404 p. , 31 p. ;19 cm.

I561.45/N489

The Waters of Babylon/Robert Neumann. —London: J. M. Dent & Sons Ltd. , c1939

356, 7 p. ;19 cm.

I561.45/N561

The North Afire: A Picture of What may be/W. Douglas Newton. —London: Methuen & Co. , Ltd. , c1914

200, 31 p. ;19 cm.

I561.45/N616

Evensong/Beverley Nichols. —London: Jonathan Gape & Bedford Square, c1932

288 p. ;19 cm.

I561.45/N616G218

Down the Garden Path/Beverley Nichols. —London: Lonathan Lape, c1933

290 p. ;21 cm.

I561.45/N616S465

Self/Beverley Nichols. —London: Penguin Books Ltd. , c1938

246 p. ;19 cm.

I561.45/N616T357

A Thatched Roof/Beverley Nichols. —London: Jonathan Cape, c1934

285 p. ;20 cm.

I561.45/N861

Trevalion/W. E. Norris. —London: Hutchinson and Co. , c[?]

288 p. ;20 cm.

I561.45/O48

Sing, Morning Star/Jane Oliver. —London: Collins Clear-Type Press, c1949

320 p. ;20 cm.

I561.45/O63

The Triumph of the Scarlet Pimpernel/Baroness Orczy. —London: Hodder and Stoughton Ltd. , [?]

302 p. ;18 cm.

I561.45/O63

Animal Farm/George Orwell. —New York: Harcourt, Brace and Company, c1946

118 p. ;19 cm.

I561.45/O85

The Flame and the Serpent/Hilda Oster-

hout. —London: Victor Collancz Ltd. , c1949
258 p. ;19 cm.

I561. 45/P119J61
Jimmie Dale and the Missing Hour/Frank L. Packard. —London: Hodder & Stoughton Ltd. , c1935
311 p. ;20 cm.

I561. 45/P156
The White Devil of the Black Sea/Lewis Stanton Palen. —London: John Lane the Bodley Head Ltd. , c1924
xviii, 297 p. ;19 cm.

I561. 45/P197
One Fine Day/Mollie Panter-Downes. —London: Hamish Hamilton, c1948
184 p. ;19 cm.

I561. 45/P232
Sayonara (Good-Bye)/John Paris. —London: W. Collins Sons & Co. , Ltd. , c1924
viii, 370 p. ;19 cm.

I561. 45/P232K49
Kimono/John Paris. —London: W. Collins Sons & Co. , Ltd. , c1924
345 p. ;19 cm.

I561. 45/P249
The Acting Second Mate/Sydney Parkman. —London: Hodder and Stoughton, [?]
320 p. ;18 cm.

I561. 45/P346
The Lion Roads/Robert Payne. —London: William Heinemann Ltd. , c1949
258 p. ;18 cm.

I561. 45/P416
The Familiar Stranger/F. E. Penny. —London: Hutchinson & Co. , (Publishers)Ltd. , [?]
336 p. ;19 cm.

I561. 45/P458
Star of India/Alice Perrin. —London, New York: Cassell and Company, Ltd. , c1920
241 p. ;18 cm.

I561. 45/P494A581W721
Angel Pavement/J. B. Priestley. —London: William Heinemann Ltd. , c1930
xiv, 613 p. ;22 cm.

I561. 45/P556
From the Angle of Seventeen/Eden Phillpotts. —London: John Murray, Albemarle Street, W. , c1916
235 p. ;19 cm.

I561. 45/P844F687
The Foot of the Rainbow/Gene Stratton Porter. —London: Hodder & Stoughton, [?]
254 p. ;18 cm.

I561. 45/P949
They Walk in the city: The Lovers in the stone forest/J. B. Priestley. —London: William Heinemann Ltd. , c1936
515 p. ;20 cm.

I561. 45/P949
Three Men in New Suits/J. B. Priestley. —London: William Heinemann Ltd. , c1945
170 cm. ;19 cm.

I561. 45/P949F219
Faraway/J. B. Priestley. —London: William Heinemann Ltd. , c1932
568 p. ;23 cm.

I561. 45/P949F773
Four-In-Hand/J. B. Priestley. —London: William Heinemann Ltd. , c1934
652 p. ;20 cm.

I561.45/P949G646

The Good Companions/J. B. Priestley. —London: William Heinemann Ltd., c1929

vii, 460 p. ;22 cm.

I561.45/P949L645

Let the People Sing: A Novel/John Boynton Priestley. —New York: Harper, 1939.

351 p. ;21 cm.

I561.45/Q3

The Heart of a Princess: A Romance of Today/William Le Queux. —London: Ward, Lock & Co., Ltd., c1920

320 p. ;19 cm.

I561.45/Q3D636

The Doctor of Pimlico: Being the Disclosure of a Great Crime/William Le Queux. —London: Cassell and Company, c1919

309 p. ;19 cm.

I561.45/Q3S578

The Sign of The Stranger/William Le Queux. —London: Ward, Lock & Co., Ltd., [?]

248 p. ;16 cm.

I561.45/R155

The Black Tolts/William MacLeod Raine. —London: Hodder & Stoughton Ltd., c1932

319 p. ;19 cm.

I561.45/R155

The Trail of Danger/Wukkuan Nackeod Raine. —London: Hodder and Stoughton Ltd., c1934

314 p. ;19 cm.

I561.45/R268

Don John's Mountain Home/Ernest Raymond. —London: Cassell & Co., Ltd., c1936

345 p. ;19 cm.

I561.45/R268

The Fulfilment of Daphne Bruno/Ernest Raymond. —London: Cassell and Company, Ltd., c1926

324 p. ;19 cm.

I561.45/R323

Galanty Show/Douglas Reed. —London: Jonathan Cape Thirty Bedford Square, c1947

256 p. ;20 cm.

I561.45/R323

Reasons of Health/Douglas Reed. —London: A. W. Bain & Co., Ltd., c1949

207 p. ;20 cm.

I561.45/R323P962

A Prophet at Home/Douglas Reed. —[S. l.: s. n.], [?]

414 p. ;19 cm.

I561.45/R475

Bricklayer's Arms/John Rhode. —London: The Crime Club, c1945

192 p. ;19 cm.

I561.45/R542-2

Thanks to Sanderson/W. Pett Ridge. —2nd ed.. —London: Methuen & Co., Ltd., c1911

vii, 308, 30 p. ;19 cm.

I561.45/R618

An Honest Living/George Robey. —London: Cassell and Company, Ltd., c1924

302 p. ;18 cm.

I561.45/R639

Eyes of the Wilderness/Charles G. D. Roberts. —London: J. M. Dent & Sons Ltd., c1933

xvi, 267 p. ;21 cm.

I561.45/R639P637

Pilgrim Cottage/Cecil Roberts. —London: Hodder & Stoghtion Ltd., c1933

393 p.;20 cm.

I561.45/R643

Still Glides the Stream/B. Dew Roberts. —London: Chatto & Windus, c1940

vii, 325 p.;19 cm.

I561.45/R649

Ordinary Families/E. Arnot Robertson. —London: The Alden Press, c1933

331 p.;19 cm.

I561.45/R737

The Emperor of America/Sax Rohmer. —London: Cassell and Company, Ltd., c1929

294 p.;19 cm.

I561.45/R795

Golden Glory/F. Hoace Rose. —London: Hodder & Stoughton, c1915

356 p.;18 cm.

I561.45/R851E56

Enchanter's Nightshade/Ann Bridge. —London: Chatto & Windus, c1937

397 p.;19 cm.

I561.45/R961

A New Heaven/G. Warren Russell. —London: Methuen & Co., Ltd., c1919

viii, 247, 31 p.;19 cm.

I561.45/R975

Clara Hopgood/Mark Rutherford. —London: Oxford University Press, 1936

188 p.;19 cm.

I561.45/S113

The Black Swan/Rafael Sabatini. —Boston: Hougton Mifflin Company, c1931

311 p.;19 cm.

I561.45/S119

The Dark Island/V. Sackville-West. —London: The Hogarth Press, c1934

317 p.;19 cm.

I561.45/S241

Ask for Ronald Standish/Sapper. —London: Hodder and Stoughton, c1936

310 p.;19 cm.

I561.45/S241-11

Out of the Blue/Sapper. —11th ed. —London: Hodder and Stoughton Ltd., c1927

320 p.;19 cm.

I561.45/S241B935

Bull-Dog Drummond: The Adventures of a Demobilised Officer Who Found Peace Dull/Sapper. —London: Hoddre and Stoughton Ltd., [?]

320 p.;18 cm.

I561.45/S241K72

Knock-out/Sapper. —London: Hodder and Stoughton, c1933

317 p.;19 cm.

I561.45/S249-10

Jim Brent/Sapper. —10th ed.. —London: Hodder and Stoughton, c1926, 1935

316 p.;18 cm.

I561.45/S274

Murder Must Advertise: A Detective Story/Dorothy L. Sayers. —New York: Harcourt, Brace and Company, c1933

282 p.;20 cm.

I561.45/S274G

Great Short Stories of Detection, Mystery and Horror/Dorothy L. Sayers. —London: Victor Gollancz Ltd., c1948

1147 p. ;19 cm.

I561. 45/S274O54

The Omnibus of Crime/Dorothy L. Sayers. —New York: Harcourt, Brace and Company, c1929

1177 p. ;22 cm.

I561. 45/S431

The Talisman/Walter Scott. —New York: Dodd, Mead & Company, c1946

358 p. ;22 cm.

I561. 45/S431(O)

The Talisman/Walter Scott. —London: Ward, Lock & Bowden, c1895

xi, 365 p. ;26 cm.

I561. 45/S524(1)

Queer Street. Volume I/Edward Shanks. —London: Penguin Books Ltd. , c1938

1-250 p. ;18 cm.

I561. 45/S524(2)

Queer Street. Volume II/Edward Shanks. —London: Penguin Books Ltd. , c1938

251-522 p. ;18 cm.

I561. 45/S528

From all the Seas/Shalimar. —London: William Blackwood & Sons Ltd. , c1933

313 p. ;19 cm.

I561. 45/S528P355

The Peaceful Wanderer/Shalimar (F. C. Hendry). —London: William Blackwood & Sons Ltd. , c1938

313 p. ;19 cm.

I561. 45/S531

The Foolish Gentlewoman/Margery Sharp. —London: Collins Clear-Type Press, c1948

256 p. ;20 cm.

I561. 45/S531B862

Britannia Mews/Margery Sharp. —Boston: Little, Brown and Company, c1946

377 p. ;20 cm.

I561. 45/S531S879

The Stone of Chastity/Marger Sharp. —Cleveland: The World Publishing Company, c1945

280 p. ;20 cm.

I561. 45/S539

We are French/Perley Poore Sheehan, Robert H. Davis. —London: Simpkin, Marshall, Hamilton, Kent & Co. , Ltd. , c1915

viii, 190 p. ;19 cm.

I561. 45/S539M

Mignonette/Joseph Shearing. —London: William Heinemann Ltd. , c1949

286 p. ;19 cm.

I561. 45/S562

No Highway/Nevil Shute. —London: William Heinemann Ltd. , c1948

315 p. ;19 cm.

I561. 45/S562O

Ordeal: A Novel/Nevil Shute. —New York: William Morrow and Company, c1939

280 p. ;21 cm.

I561. 45/S613

Capricorn/Helen Simpson. —London: William Heinemann Ltd. , c1937

305 p. ;19 cm.

I561. 45/S616

The Young Woodcarver of Geneva. /Grace Sinclair. —London: The Book Society, [?]

175 p. ;19 cm.

I561. 45/S627

Below The Watchowers/Margaret Skelton. —London: Leonard Parsons, c1926

445 p. ;19 cm.

I561. 45/S631

Led by Lawrence/Gurney Slade. —London: Frederick Warne and Co. , Ltd. , c1934

288 p. ;20 cm.

I561. 45/S631C755

Conspirator/Humphrey Slater. —New York: Harcourt, Brace and Company, c1948

184 p. ;21 cm.

I561. 45/S634

Angels Weep/Desmond Leslie. —London: T. Werner Laurie Ltd. , c1948

268 p. ;19 cm.

I561. 45/S642

Jake: A Novel/Naomi Royde Smith. —London: Macmillan & Co. , Ltd. , c1935

446 p. ;19 cm.

I561. 45/S644P959

Prisoners of Hope/Constance Smith. —London: A. D. Innes & Company, Ltd. , c1898

327 p. ;20 cm.

I561. 45/S645

Out of Step/Derek Walker Smith. —London: Victor Gollancz Ltd. , c1930

287 p. ;19 cm.

I561. 45/S728

Immortal Dyer/Stephen Southwold. —London: Robert Hale Ltd. , c1935

251 p. ;19 cm.

I561. 45/S741

The Unbroken Heart/Robert Speaight. —London: Cassel and Company Ltd. , c1939

282 p. ;19 cm.

I561. 45/S769

Fame Is the Spur/Howard Spring. —London: Collins Clear-Type Press, c1947

667 p. ;20 cm.

I561. 45/S769H258

Hard Facts/Howard Spring. —New York: The Viking Press, c1944

283 p. ;21 cm.

I561. 45/S775

Mandarin Gardens/H. de Vere Stacpoole. —London: Hutchinson & Co. , (Publishers)Ltd. , [?]

288, 56 p. ;19 cm.

I561. 45/S775

The Gates of Morning/H. De Vere Stacpoole. —London: Hutchinson & Co. , [?]

x, 286 p. ;19 cm.

I561. 45/S775

The Sunstone/H. de Vere Stacpoole. —London: Hutchinson & Co. , (Publishers)Ltd. , [?]

287, 48 p. ;19 cm.

I561. 45/S775G492

Ginger Adams/H. de Vere Stacpoole. —London: Hutchinson & Co. , (Publishers), Ltd. , [?]

288 p. ;19 cm.

I561. 45/S813

They That Go Down in Ships/Marguerite Steen. —New York: Cosmopolitan Book Corporation, c1931

396 p. ;20 cm.

I561. 45/S839

Thunderstorm/G. B. Stern. —London: [s. n.], [?]

224 p. ;19 cm.

I561. 45/S839N739

No Son of Mine/G. B. Stern. —London: Cassell and Company Ltd. , 1948

327 p. ;19 cm.

I561. 45/S839O45

Oleander River/G. B. Stern. —London: Cassell and Company Ltd. , c1937

381 p. ;19 cm.

I561. 45/S839S555

Shining and Free: A Dayin the Life of the Matriarch/G. B. Stern. —London: William Heinemann Ltd. , c1935

291 p. ;19 cm.

I561. 45/S847

The Master of Ballantrae: A Winter's Tale/ Robert Louis Stevenson. —London: W. Foulsham & Co. , Ltd. , [?]

221 p. ;19 cm.

I561. 45/S847

Listening Valley/D. E. Stevenson. —New York: Farrar & Rinehart, c1944

312 p. ;19 cm.

I561. 45/S847T582

Mrs. Tim Gets A Job/D. E. Stevenson. —London: Collins, c1947

256 p. ;20 cm.

I561. 45/S861

Lovers Aren't Company/Monica Stirling. —London: Victor Gollancz Ltd. , c1949

192 p. ;19 cm.

I561. 45/S865

Pink Gods and Blue Demons/Cynthia Stockley. —London: Cassell and Company, Ltd. , [?]

188 p. ;19 cm.

I561. 45/S894S527

Shaken by the Wind: A Story of Fanaticism/ Ray Strachey. —New York: The Macmillan Company, c1928

317 p. ;20 p.

I561. 45/S915

Country Calendar/A. G. Street. —London: Eyre and Spottiswoode, c1935

xiii, 231 p. ;23 cm.

I561. 45/S916

Bright Metal/T. S. Stribling. —London: Nisbet & Co. , Ltd. , c1928

488 p. ;19 cm.

I561. 45/S923

The Bay/L. A. G. Strong. —London: Victor Collancz Ltd. , c1941

280 p. ;20 cm.

I561. 45/S923

The Open Sky/L. A. G. Strong. —London: Victor Gollancz Ltd. , c1939

445 p. ;20 cm.

I561. 45/S923S438

Sea Wall/L. A. G. Strong. —London: Victor Gollancz Ltd. , c1933

360 p. ;19 cm.

I561. 45/S966

The Arches of the Years/Halliday Sutherland. —New York: Wiliam Morrow and Company, c1933

293 p. ;22 cm.

I561. 45/S973

The Boat Race Murder/R. E. Swartwout. —London: Grayson & Grayson, 1933

287 p. ;19 cm.

I561.45/S978-2
Oquette/Frank Swinnerton. —2nd ed. —London: Methuen & Co., Ltd., c1921
304 p.;19 cm.

I561.45/SR995
One of Three/Netta Syrett. —London: Hurst & Blackett, Ltd., [?]
288 p.;19 cm.

I561.45/T114
Uneasy Giant/Paul Tabori. —London: Sampson Low, Marston & Co., Ltd., c1949
ix, 419 p.;19 cm.

I561.45/T124
Seventy North/Taffrail. —London: Hodder and Stoughton, c1930
320 p.;19 cm.

I561.45/T124M627
Mid-Atlantic/Taffrail. —London: Hodder and Stoughton, c1936
318 p.;20 cm.

I561.45/T445
Peace Breaks Out/Angela Thirkell. —New York: Alfred A. Knopf, c1947
370 p.;19 cm.

I561.45/T445
The Old Bank House/Angela Thirkell. —New York: Alfred A. Knopf, c1949
345 p.;22 cm.

I561.45/T445L897
Love Among the Ruins/Angela Thirkell. —London: Hamish Hamilton, c1948
382 p.;19 cm.

I561.45/T445P786
Pomfret Towers/Angela Thirkell. —London: Hamish Hamilton, c1938
316 p.;19 cm.

I561.45/T445P945
Private Enterprise/Angela Thirkell. —London: Hamish Hamilton, c1947
381 p.;19 cm.

I561.45/T498
The Vandekkers/Russell Thorndiks. —London: Thornton Butterworth Ltd., c1929
318 p.;19 cm.

I561.45/T544
The Miracle/E. Temple Thurston. —London: Hutchinson & Co., [?]
288 p.;19 cm.

I561.45/T552
The Devil's Plaything/Annie O. Tibbits. —London: Federation Press Ltd., [?]
190 p.;18 cm.

I561.45/T556
See How They Run/Tickell, Jerrard. —London: William Heinemann Ltd., 1936
320 p.;21 cm.

I561.45/T581
Icedrome/Frank Tilsley. —London: Eyre & Spottiswoode, c1949
360 p.;19 cm.

I561.45/T654W763
The Wind is Rising/H. M. Tomlinson. —Boston: Little, Brown and Company, c1942
271 p.;20 cm.

I561.45/T659
The Sea and the Jungle/H. M. Tomlinson. —New York: the Modern Library, c1928
x, 332 p.;19 cm.

I561.45/T766

Here Lies Love/Peter Traill. —London: Grayson & Grayson, c1933

285 p. ;19 cm.

I561.45/T859

All's Well, Billy/Lady Troubridge. —London: Methuen & Co., Ltd., c1918

283, 31 p. ;19 cm.

I561.45/T948

Homicide Haven/J. V. Turner. —London: The Crime Club, c1935

284 p. ;19 cm.

I561.45/V128

More About Peggy/Mrs. De Horne Vaizey. —London: Lutterworth Press, [?]

287 p. ;19 cm.

I561.45/W119

Mist on the Saltings/Henry Wade. —London: Constable and Company Ltd., c1933

340 p. ;19 cm.

I561.45/W187

The Black Abbot/Edgar Wallace. —London: Hodder and Stoughton Ltd., [?]

319 p. ;19 cm.

I561.45/W187B627

The Black Abbot/Edgar Wallsce. —New York: A. L. Burt Company Publishers, c1926, 1927

319 p. ;19 cm.

I561.45/W187C

The Crimson Circle/Edgar Wallace. —Toronto: Hodder and Stoughton Ltd., [?]

320 p. ;19 cm.

I561.45/W196

The Joker/Edgar Wallace. —London: Hodder and Stoghton Ltd., [?]

320 p. ;19 cm.

I561.45/W216

Master Mariner: A Novel/Leo Walmsley. —London: Collins Clear-Type Press, c1948

288 p. ;20 cm.

I561.45/W218

Roman Fountain/Hugh Walpole. —[S. l.: s. n.], c1940

301 p. ;19 cm.

I561.45/W218A157

Above the Dark Circus: An adventure/Hugh Walpole. —London: Macmillan and Co., Ltd., c1931

xi, 272 p. ;20 cm.

I561.45/W218C236

Captain Nicholas: A Modern Comedy/Hugh Walpole. —London: Macmillan and Co., Ltd., c1934

ix, 469 p. ;19 cm.

I561.45/W218D

The Dark Forest/Hugh Walpole. —London: Macmillan and Co., Ltd., c1936

1 v;21 cm.

I561.45/W218J65

John Cornelius: His Life and Adventures/Hugh Walpole. —New York: Doubleday, Doran & Company, Inc., c1937

xiv, 425 p. ;20 cm.

I561.45/W218J65M167

John Cornelius: His Life and Adventures/Hugh Walpole. —London: Macmillan and Co., Ltd., c1937

xiv, 532 p. ;19 cm.

I561.45/W218M167

The Old Ladies/Hugh Walpole. —London: Macmillan and Co., c1924

x, 304 p. ;20 cm.

I561.45/W218O44

The Old Ladies/Hugh Walpole. —New York: George H. Doran Company, c1924

305 p. ;20 cm.

I561.45/W218P921

A Prayer for My Son/Hugh Walpole. —New York: Doubeday, Doran & Company, c1936

355 p. ;20 cm.

I561.45/W238(O)

The Compleat Angler/Izaak Walton. —London: The Continental Book Company, c1946

xliv, 215 p. ;18 cm.

I561.45/W256C867

Cousin Philip/Mrs Humphry Ward. —London: W. Collins Sons & Co., Ltd., c1919

274 p. ;19 cm.

I561.45/W279

A Secret of the Marsh/Oliver Warner. —London: Chatto & Windus, c1927

221 p. ;19 cm.

I561.45/W284

The Corner that Held Them/Sylvia Townsend Warner. —London: Chatto & Windus, c1948

vii, 310 p. ;21 cm.

I561.45/W337

Odd Shoes/Winifred Watson. —London: Methuen & Co., Ltd., c1936

422 p. ;19 cm.

I561.45/W354

Wheels Within Wheels: A Story of the Crisis/Alec Waugh. —London: Cassell and Company, Ltd., c1933

314 p. ;19 cm.

I561.45/W365

Precious Bane/Mary Webb. —New York: E. P. Dutton & Company, Inc., c1926

xvi, 356 p. ;19 cm.

I561.45/W453(O)

The Passionate Friends: A Novel/H. G. Wells. —London: W. Collins Sons & Co., Ltd., [?]

252 p. ;19 cm.

I561.45/W453

Mr. Britling Sees it Through/H. G. Wells. —Chicago: M. A. Donohue & ompany, c1916

443 p. ;19 cm.

I561.45/W453D273

In the Days of the Comet/H. G. Wells. —London: W. Collins Sons & Co., Ltd., [?]

281 p. ;19 cm.

I561.45/W453S

The Soul of a Bishop/H. G. Wells. —New York: The Macillan Company, c1917

341 p. ;20 cm.

I561.45/W453T

Tono-Bungay/H. G. Wells. —New York: The Modern Library, c1908

460 p. ;18 cm.

I561.45/W455(O)

Kipps: The Story of a Simple Soul/H. G. Wells. —London: W. Collins Sons & Co., Ltd., c1924

330 p. ;18 cm.

I561.45/W477

Pilgrim's Rest/Patricia Wentworth. —London: Hodder & Stoughton Ltd., c1948

283 p. ;19 cm.

I561. 45/W516

The Meaning of Treason. /Rebecca West. —New York: The Viking Press, c1945, 1946, 1947

305 p. ;21 cm.

I561. 45/W541

The Rose and the Yew Tree/Mary Westmacott. —London: William Heinemann Ltd. , c1948

221 p. ;19 cm.

I561. 45/W557

The Launching of Roger Brook/Dennis Wheatley. —London: Hutghinson & Co. , (Publishers) Ltd. , [?]

381 p. ;23 cm.

I561. 45/W573

Because of the Lockwoods/Dorothy Whipple. —London: Butler & Tanner Ltd. , c1949

358 p. ;19 cm.

I561. 45/W573P958

The Priory/Dorothy Whipple. —London: John Murray, c1939

528 p. ;20 cm.

I561. 45/W582

She Faded into Air/Ethel Lina White. —London: Collins Clear-Type Press, c1941

252 p. ;19 cm.

I561. 45/W684

Being Met Together/Vaughan Wilkins. —New York: The Macmillan Company, c1944

x, 510 p. ;22 cm.

I561. 45/W721

All Hallows' Eve/Charles Williams. —New York: Pelleginin & Cudahy, c1948

xviii, 273 p. ;21 cm.

I561. 45/W729

The Cowboy Countess/C. N. & A. M. Williamson. —London: Methuen & Co. , Ltd. , c1917

249, 31 p. ;18 cm.

I561. 45/W838B642

Blandings Castle and Elsewhere/P. G. Wodehouse. —London: Herbert Jenkins Ltd. , c1935

311 p. ;19 cm.

I561. 45/W838H

The Luck of the Bookins/P. G. Wodehouse. —London: Herbert Jenkins, c1935

311 p. ;19 cm.

I561. 45/W838H832

Hot Water/P. G. Wodehouse. —London: Herbert Jenkins Ltd. , [?]

312 p. ;19 cm.

I561. 45/W838J

Jill the Reckless/P. G. odehouse. —2nd ed. . —London: Herbert Jenkins Ltd. , [?]

313 p. ;19 cm.

I561. 45/W838L

Laughing Gas/P. G. Wodehouse. —London: Herbert Jenkins Ltd. , London, c1936

311 p. ;19 cm.

I561. 45/W838M

Money for Nothing/P. G. Wodehouse. —London: Herbert Jenkins Ltd. , c1928

312 p. ;19 cm.

I561. 45/W838S955

Summer Moonshine/P. G. Wodehouse. —London: Herbert Jenkins Ltd. , c1938

312 p. ;19 cm.

I561. 45/W838U34

Ukridge/P. G. Wodehouse. —London: Herbert

Jenkins Ltd. , [?]
256 p. ;19 cm.

I561. 45/W913C734
The Common Reader/Virginia Woolf. —London: The Hogarth Press, c1929
305 p. ;18 cm.

I561. 45/W913L723
To the Lighthouse/Virginia Woolf. —New York: The Modern Library, c1937
xiii, 310 p. ;18 cm.

I561. 45/W931
Public Affaires/Barbara Worsley-Gough. —London: Victor Gollancz Ltd. , c1932
302 p. ;19 cm.

I561. 45/W945
Good Gestes/Percival Christopher Wren. —London: John Murray, Albemarle Street, W. , c1929
332 p. ;19 cm.

I561. 45/W945
Father Gregory: A Tale of Hindostan/Percival Christopher Wren. —London: John Murray, Albemarle Street, W. , c1913
320 p. ;19 cm.

I561. 45/W945A188
Action and Passion/Percival Christopher Wren. —London: John Murray, c1933
507 p. ;20 cm.

I561. 45/W945B371
Beau Sabreur/Percival Christopher Wren. —New York: Frederick A. Stokes Company, c1926
x, 370 p. ;19 cm.

I561. 45/W945S615
Sinbad the Soldier/Percival Christopher Wren. —London: John Murray, Albemarle Street, W. , c1935
362, 15 p. ;20 cm.

I561. 45/W945U176
Valiant Dust/Percival Christopher Wren. —London: John Murray, Albemarle Street, W. , c1932
359 p. ;19 cm.

I561. 45/W953
Beyond the Rim/S. Fowler Wright. —London: Jarrolds Publishers, c1932
318 p. ;18 cm.

I561. 45/W988
A Mediterranean Mystery/Fred. E. Wynne. —London: Herbert Jenkins Ltd. , [?]
312 p. ;20 cm.

I561. 45/Y31P976
This Publican/Dornford Yates. —London: Ward, Lock & Co. , Ltd. , c1938
320 p. ;19 cm.

I561. 45/Y68
They Seek a Country/Francis Brett Young. —New York: Grosset & Dunlap Publishers, c1937
602 p. ;21 cm.

I561. 45/Y68
Dr. Bradley Remembers/Francis Brett Youny. —London: William Heinemann Ltd. , c1938
745 p. ;20 cm.

I561. 45/Y68B627
Black Roses/Francis Brett Young. —New York: Harper & Brothers, c1929
325 p. ;19 cm.

I561. 45/Y68C495
Chatterton Square/E. H. Young. —London: Jonathan Cape Thirty Bedford Square, c1947
367 p. ;20 cm.

I561.45/Y68C581

The City of Gold/Francis Brett Young. —London: The Book Club, c1940

548 p. ;20 cm.

I561.45/Y68W582

White Ladies/Francis Brett Young. —New York: Harper & Brothers Publishers, c1935

492 p. ;21 cm.

I561.453/S894

Elizabeth and Essex: A Tragic History/Lytton Strachey. —New York: Harcourt, Brace and Company, c1928

296 p. ;21 cm.

I561.455/M396

Sard Harker: A Novel/John Masefield. —New York: The Macmillan Company, c1938

412 p. ;19 cm.

I561.456/C555

The Hollow: A Hercule Poirot Mystery/Agatha Christie. —New York: Dodd, Mead & Company, c1946

279 p. ;20 cm.

I561.456/C555D278

Death on the Nile/Agatha Christie. —London: The Crime Club, c1937

284 p. ;19 cm.

I561.456/D754

The Captain of The Pole-Star/A. Conan Doyle. —London: Hodder and Stoughton, [?]

258 p. ;17 cm.

I561.456/D754M995

The Mystery of Cloomber/A. Conan Doyle. —London: Hodder and Stoughton, [?]

259 p. ;18 cm.

I561.456/M135

Eath on My Left/Philip Macdonald. —London: The Crime Club Ltd., c1935

254 p. ;18 cm.

I561.456/W187

MR. Justice Maxell/Edgar Wallace. —London: Ward, Lock & Co., Ltd., c1923

251 p. ;17 cm.

I561.456/W187P766

The Edgar Wallace Police Van: Four Complete Police Novels in One Volume/Edgar Wallace. —London: Hodder and Stoughton, [?]

1166 p. ;19 cm.

I561.457/W218

The Young Enchanted: A Romantic Story/Hugh Walpole. —London: Macmillan and Co., Ltd., c1938

xii, 427 p. ;18 cm.

I561.5/C833

The Marriage of Josephine/Coryn, Marhorie. —New York: D. Appleton-Century Company, c1945

312 p. ;20 cm.

I561.5/D333

Straw Without Bticks: I Visit Soviet Russia/E. M. Delafield. —London: Macmillan and Co., Ltd., c1937

ix, 262 p. ;19 cm.

I561.5/D333P969

The Provincial Lady in America/E. M. Delafield. —London: Macmillan and Co., Ltd., c1934

viii, 251 p. ;19 cm.

I561.5/H875

Elephant & Seladang Hunting in the Federated Malay States/Theodore R. Hubback. —London:

Rowland Ward, Ltd. , c1905
xiii, 288 p. ;22 cm.

I561. 5/J52
Mrs Bindle: Some Incidents from the Domestic Life of the Bindles/Herbert Jenkins. —London: Herbert Jenkins Ltd. , [?]
312 p. ;20 cm.

I561. 54/B936
The Log of A Sea-Waif: Being Recollections of the First Four Years of My Sea Life/Frank T. Bullen. —London: Macmillan and Co. , Ltd. , c1899
xii, 349 p. ;18 cm.

I561. 55/B668
A Japanese Omelette: A British Writer's Impressions on the Japanese Empire/Major R. V. C. Bodley. —[S. l. : s. n.], [?]
xiv, 242 p. ;19 cm.

I561. 55/C366(O)
Guilty Men/Cato. —[S. l. : s. n.], [?]
144 p. ;18 cm.

I561. 55/C789
Man-eaters of Kumaon/with an introduction by Sir Maurice Hallet... and a preface by Lord Linlithgow..—New York: Oxford University Press, 1946.
235 p. ;21cm.

I561. 55/G929
The Story of the Thirteen Colonies/H. A. Guerber. —New York: American Book Company, c1898
342 p. ;19 cm.

I561. 55/M889-13
The Heart of London/H. V. Morton. —13th ed. . —London: Methuen & Co. , Ltd. , c1931
x, 208 p. ;17 cm.

I561. 55/S795
A Winter in Arabia/Freya Stark. —London: John Murray, c1940
327 p. ;23 cm.

I561. 6/C286
Scottish & other Miscellanies/Thomas Carlyle. —London: J. M. Dent & Sons Ltd. , [?]
339 p. ;18 cm.

I561. 6/D681
"... And Nothing Long"/Ranald MacDonell. —London: Constable & Co Ltd. , c1938
328 p. ;20 cm.

I561. 6/D883
Mungo Park's Travels/L. F. Dullam. —London: Henry Frowde and Hodder & Stoughton, [?]
256 p. ;20 cm.

I561. 6/E26
An Anthology of English Prose from Bede to R. L. S/S. L. Edwards. —London: J. M. Dent & Sons. Ltd. , [?]
xvi, 400 p. ;18 cm.

I561. 6/G218
The Garden of Friendship/T. N. Foulis. —London: T. N. Foulis, Ltd. , [?]
172 p. ;19 cm.

I561. 64/C233(3)
Critical and Miscellaneous Essays Kings of Norway Etc. . volume III/Thomas Carlyle. —London: Chapman and Hall, Ltd. , c1869
1 v. ;18 cm.

I561. 64/D548
American Notes/Charles Dickens. —London: Thomas Nelson and Sons, c1904
416 p. ;16 cm.

I561.64/D548P544(O)
Pictures from Italy and American Notes for General Circulation/Charles Dickens. —New York: Pollard & Moss, c1888
459, 477 p. ;19 cm.

I561.64/E53
English Traits Representative Men and Others Essays/Ralgh Waido Emerson. —London: J. M. Dent, c1908
375 p. ;

I561.64/F942
Essays in Literature and History/J. A. Froude. —London: J. M. Dent & Sons Ltd. , c1906
xxiii, 326 p. ;17 cm.

I561.64/H431
Table Talk or Original Essays/William Hazlitt. —London: J. M. Dent, c1908
337 p. ;17 cm.

I561.64/M117
Miscellaneous Essays and the Lays of Ancient Rome/Thomas Babington Macaulay. —London: J. M. Dent & Sons Ltd. , c1915
xvi, 528 p. ;18 cm.

I561.65/B233
Enjoying Life and Other Literary Remains/W. N. P. Barbellion. —London: Chatto & Windus, c1919
xvi, 246 p. ;19 cm.

I561.65/B471
How to Live on 24 Hours a Day/Arnold Bennett. —Tokyo: The Hekeseido Press, [?]
xviii, 99 p. ;19 cm.

I561.65/B918
Pilgrim's Way: An Essay in Recollection/John Buchan. —Boston: Houghton Mifflin Company, c1940
336 p. ;21 cm.

I561.65/K57
Limits and Renewals/Rudyard Kipling. —London: Macmillan and Co. , Ltd. , c1932
viii, 400 p. ;19 cm.

I561.65/K57(1)
From Sea to Sea and Others Sketches: Letters of Travel. Volume I/Rudyard Kipling. —London: Macmillan and Co. , c1900
xiv, 497 p. ;18 cm.

I561.65/K57(2)
From Sea to Sea and Others Sketches: Letters of Travel. Volume II/Rudyard Kipling. —London: Macmillan and Co. , c1900
ix, 437 p. ;18 cm.

I561.65/K57F
From Sea to Sea: Letters of Marque/Rudyard Kipling. —New York: Doubleday, Page & Company, c1924
187 p. ;19 cm.

I561.65/L415
Seven Pillars of Wisdom: a Triumph/T. E. Lawrence. —New York: Doubleday, Doran & Company, Inc. , c1926.
669 p. ;26 cm.

I561.65/M979(2)
The Letters of Katherine Mansfield. vol. II/J. Middleton Murry. —London: Constable & Co Ltd. , c1928
271 p. ;19 cm.

I561.65/R196
Up and Down The China Coast/Ranger. —London: Denis Archer, c1936
286, 28 p. ;23 cm.

I561.65/Y5

Golden Horn/Francis Yeats-Brown. —London: Victor Gollancz Ltd., c1932

287 p.;22 cm.

I561.7/G212

Miss Smith's Fortune & Other Stories/Charles Garvice. —London: Skeffington & Son, Ltd., [?]

288 p.;19 cm.

I561.73/B617

Love or Money: and Other Stories/George A. Birmingham. —London: Methuen & Co., Ltd., c1935

249 p.;19 cm.

I561.73/B632

Humorous Tales/WM. Blackwood & Sons Ltd.,—Edinburgh and London: WM. Blackwood & Sons Ltd., c1935

554 p.;19 cm.

I561.73/E95

The Brownies: And Other Tales/Juliana Horatia Ewing. —8th ed..—London: George Bell and Sons, York St., Covent Garden, c1892

229 p.;17 cm.

I561.73/G464

Robin Hood and the Men of the Greenwood/Henry Gilbert. —Chicago: The Goldsmith Publishing Company, [?]

252 p.;20 cm.

I561.73/S838

Robin Hood and His Merry Men/Sara Hawks Sterling. —New York: Grosset & Sunlap Publishers, c1921

360 p.;21 cm.

I561.74/H974

Thou Hast A Devil: A Fable/Ray Coryton Hutchinson. —London: Purnell and Sons, c1928

320 p.;18 cm.

I561.8/E95

Melchior's Dream and Other Tales/Juliana Horatia Ewing. —London: George Bell and Sons, c1886

xiii, 293 p.;18 cm.

I561.8/K57

The Second Jungle Book/Rudyard Kipling; with decorations by John Lockwood Kipling, C. I. E. —New York: Doubleday, Pace & Company, c1927.

299 p.;20 cm.

I561.8/K57C

The Second Jungle Book/Rudyard, Kipling. —Leipzig: Bernhard Tauchnitz, c1897.

286, 31 p.;16 cm.

I561.84/A389

When the North wind Blows/Charles E. Alford. —London: George G. Harrap& Co., Ltd., c1936

95 p.;19 cm.

I561.84/B147

National Velvet/Enid Bagnold. —New York: William Morrow and Company, c1935

303 p.;21 cm.

I561.84/B147N277

National Velvet/Enid Bagnold. —London: William Heinemann Ltd., c1935

268 p.;19 cm.

I561.84/B433

Wee Macgregor/J. J. Bell. —Edinburgh: The moray Press, c1933

xx, 206 p.;19 cm.

I561. 84/K55

Yeast: A Problem/Charles Kingsley. —London: Macmillan and Co. , c1893

xvii, 272 p. ;19 cm.

I561. 84/O149

Dwarf's Blood/Edith Olivier. —New York: The Viking Press, c1931

278 p. ;19 cm.

I561. 84/S224

The Happy Harfords/Mary Bourchier Sanford. —London: Collins' Clear-Type Press, [?]

128 p. ;19 cm.

I561. 84/S616

Holiday House: A Book for the Young/Catherine Sinclair. —London: Blackie and Son Ltd. , [?]

224 p. ;18 cm.

I561. 84/S844G877

Treasure Island/Robert Louis Steveson. —New York: Grosset & Dunlap Publishers, c1947

341 p. ;21 cm.

I561. 84/S844T784

Treasure Island/Robert Louis Stevenson. —Chicago: Donohue, Henneberry & Co. , [?]

235 p. ;15 cm.

I561. 84/S844T784O

Treasure Island/Robert Louis Stevenson. —Chicago: The Goldsmith Publishing Company, [?]

248 p. ;19 cm.

I561. 85/B886

The Book of Tales for Little folks/Marjory Bruce. —London: George G. Harrap & Co. , Ltd. , c1932

284 p. ;23 cm.

I561. 85/B936

Helen's Lovers and other Tales/Gerald Bullett. —London: William Heinemann Ltd. , c1932

283 p. ;20 cm.

I561. 85/H645

The Exciting Family/M. D. Hillyard. —London: Blackie & Son Ltd. , [?]

94 p. ;20 cm.

I561. 85/R888

Royal Readers/T. Nelson and Sons. —London: T. Nelson and Sons, c1917

192 p. ;17 cm.

I561. 85/R888N424

Royal Readers/T. Nelson and Sons. —London: T. Nelson and Sons, c1906

vi, 192 p. ;17 cm.

I561. 85/S452

Bears, Boars, and Bulls, and Other Animals: True Stories for Children/Seeley, Jackson, & Halliday. —London: Seeley, Jackson, & Halliday, [?]

172 p. ;17 cm.

I561. 85/S622

In Far Japan: A Story of English Children/Mrs. Isla Sitwell. —London: T. Nelson and Sons, c1896

188 p. ;19 cm.

I561. 88/C319A398(O)

Alice's Adventures in Wonderland; Through the Looking-Glass; The Hunting of the Snark/Lewis Carroll. —New York: The Modern Library, [?]

xxi, 351 p. ;19 cm.

I561. 88/C319A398G878

Alice in Wonderland and Through the Looking

Glass/Lewis Carroll. —[S. l.]: Grosset & Dunlap, Publishers, c1946
295 p. ;21 cm.

I561. 88/G738H546
The Wind in the Willows/Kenneth Grahame. —New York: The Heritage Press, c1940
xiv, 190 p. ;24 cm.

I561. 88/M135
The Princess and Curdie/George Macdonald. —New York: Grosset & Dunlap, c1908
305 p. ;21 cm.

I561. 88/M659
Winnie the Pooh/A. A. Milne. —New York: E. P. Dutton & Co. , Inc. , c1926
ix, 158 p. ;20 cm.

I561. 99/B737
The Bible in Spain: The Jorneys, Adventures, and Imprisonments of An Englishman/George Borrow. —London: T. Nelson and Sons, c1894
xvi, 555 p. ;20 cm.

I561. 99/C536-34
Golden Bells, or, Hymns for Our Children/Children's Special Service Mission. —34th ed. . —London: Children's Special Service Mission, [?]
163 p. ;14 cm.

I561. 99/M878-2
The Return of the Angels: Sunday Evening in a Glasgow Pulpit/Rev. G. H. Morrison. —2nd ed. . —London: Hodder and Stoughton, c1909
xii, 335 p. ;20 cm.

I561. 99/S425
The Gospel and Its Tributaries/Ernest Findlay Scott. —Edinburgh: T. & T. Clark, c1928
x, 295 p. ;23 cm.

I562. 11/G624
The Select Works of Oliver Goldsmith/Oliver Goldsmith. —Leipzig: Bernhard Tauchnitz, c1842
vi, 399 p. ;16 cm.

I562. 3/S534T531
Three Plays for Puritans/Bernard Shaw. —New York: Dodd, Mead & Company, c1900
xli, 301 p. ;19 cm.

I562. 45/B617
Send for Dr. O'Grady/George A. Birmingham. —London: Hodder and Stoughton, [?]
285 p. ;19 cm.

I562. 45/B995
Destiny Bay/Donn Byrne. —New York: The Sun Dial Press, c1942
350 p. ;19 cm.

I562. 45/D322
The Just Steward/Richard Dehan. —London: William Heinemann, [?]
587 p. ;18 cm.

I562. 45/D926
Guerrilla: A Novel/Lord Dunsany. —New York: The Bobbs-Merrill Company, c1944
252 p. ;21 cm.

I562. 45/G437
Lovely is the Lee/Robert Gibbings. —New York: E. P. Dutton & Company, Inc. , c1945
256 p. ;22 cm.

I562. 45/G624
The Vicar of Wakefield/Oliver Goldsmith. —London: Blackie & Son, Ltd. , [?]
224 p. ;18 cm.

I562. 45/H835
Farewell Happy Fields/Norah Hoult. —Lon-

don: William Heinemann Ltd., c1948
324 p.;19 cm.

I562.45/S874(O)
Dracula/Bram Stoker.—New York: Modern Library, c1897
ix, 418 p.;18 cm.

I562.7/Y41
Irish Fairy and Folk Tales/W. B. Yeats.—New York: The Modern Library, [?]
xviii, 351 p.;17 cm.

I563.45/A518
Jenny Heysten's Career/Jo van Ammers-Kueller.—New York: E. P. Dutton & Co., Inc., c1930
260 p.;19 cm.

I563.45/F224
The Son of Marietta/Johan Fabricius.—London: Victor Gollancz Ltd., c1936
1053 p.;23 cm.

I565/H895
Dramatic Works of Victor Hugo/Victor Hugo.—London: George Bell and Sons, c1904
xvii, 430, 25 p.;19 cm.

I565.072/W985
Francois Villon/D. B. Wyndham-Lewis.—New York: Coward-Mccann, Inc., c1928
xix, 407 p.;23 cm.

I565.34/R839C994
Cyrano De Bergerac: A Play in Five Acts/Edmond Rostand.—London: F. Tennyson Neely, c1898
x, 307 cm.;20 cm.

I565.4/K24
My Adventures in Bolshevik Russia/Odette Keun.—[S. l.: s. n.], [?]
320 p.;19 cm.

I565.43/R114
Gargantua and Pantagruel/Rabelais.—New York: Modern Library, c1928
xii, 543 p.;18 cm.

I565.44/B171C853
The Country Doctor/Honore De Balzac.—London: J. M. Dent and Sons Ltd., c1911
xv, 287 p.;18 cm.

I565.44/B171C867
Cousin Pons/Honore de Balzac.—New York: Mckinlay, Stone & Mackenzie, [?]
v, 306, 27 p.;19 cm.

I565.44/D886(1)
The Count of Monte Cristo. Vol. one/Alexandre Dumas.—New York: P. F. Collier & Son Company Publishers, [?]
iv, 644 p.;20 cm.

I565.44/D886(2)
The Romances of Alexandre Dumas. Vol. 2/La Dame De Monsoreau.—Boston: Little Brown and Company, c1893
vii, 512 p.;19 cm.

I565.44/D886(3)
The Count of Monte Cristo. Vol. 3/Alexandre Dumas.—Boston: Little Brown and Company, c1889
vi, 532 p.;19 cm.

I565.44/D886(O)
The Romances of Alexandre Dumas/La Dame De Monsoreau.—Boston: Little Brown and Company, c1893
xvi, 361 p.;19 cm.

I565.44/D886T(O)
The Three Musketeers/Alexandre Dumas.—

New York: The Modern Library, [?]
596 p. ;18 cm.

I565.44/D886(O)
The Three Musketeers/Alexandre Dumas.—[S. l.]: T. Nelson & Sons, Ltd., [?]
602 p. ;17 cm.

I565.44/D886C527
Chevalier De Maison-Rouge/Alexandre Dumas.—Boston: Little Brown and Company, c1890
xiv, 512 p. ;19 cm.

I565.44/D886D538(1)
The Two Dianas. Volume One/Alexandre Dumas.—Boston: Little Brown and Company, c1891, 1892
xv, 526 p. ;19 cm.

I565.44/D886D538(2)
The Two Dianas. Volume Two/Alexandre Dumas.—Boston: Little Brown and Company, c1891, 1892
xv, 565 p. ;19 cm.

I565.44/D886R333
The Regent's Daughter/Alexandre Dumas.—Boston: Little Brown and Company, c1891, 1893
xviii, 386 p. ;18 cm.

I565.44/D886W253
The War of Women/Alexandre dumas.—Boston: Little Brown and Company, c1895
xii, 315 p. ;19 cm.

I565.44/H895
The Hunchback of Notre-Dame/Victor Hugo.—Oxford: Wordsworth Editions Ltd., c1993
429p. ;19cm.

I565.44/H895H932B724
The Hunchback of Notre Dame/Victor Hugo.—New York: The Book League America, [?]
350 p. ;20 cm.

I565.44/H895L622
Les Miserables/Victor Hugo.—New York: Thomas Y. Crowell & Co., c1887
224 p. ;20 cm.

I565.44/H895T454
Les Miserables. In Five Volumes/Victor Hugo.—Illustrated ed..—New York: Thomas Y. Crowell & Co., c1887
viii, 284 p. ;20 cm.

I565.44/M149
The Heptameron: Tales and Novels of Marguerite Queen of Navarre/Arthur Machen.—New York: Alfred A Knopf, c1925
xxvi, 385 p. ;21 cm.

I565.44/M257
The Herb of Grace/Hector Malot.—New York: Rand McNally & Company, c1925
x, 492 p. ;23 cm.

I565.44/P944
The History of Manon Lescaut and the Chevalier des Crieux/L'abbe Prevost.—London: George Routledge & Sons Ltd., [?]
266 p. ;19 cm.

I565.44/S925
The Charterhouse of Parma/Stendhal.—New York: Modern Library, c1925
lxxxi, 343 p. ;18 cm.

I565.44/S944
The Mysteries of Paris/Eugene Sue.—Chicago, New York: M. A. Donohue & Company, [?]
1312 p. ;19 cm.

I565. 44/V454M995

The Mysterious Island/Jules Verne. —New York: A. L. Burt Company, [?]

564 p. ;20 cm.

I565. 44/V935

Candide/Voltaire. —New York: The Modern Library, [?]

xiii, 236 p. ;18 cm.

I565. 44/Z86N175

Nana/Emile Zola. —New York: The Modern Library Publishers, c1928

xii, 517 p. ;17 cm.

I565. 45/C211

The Plague/Albert Camus. —New York: Alfred A. Knopf, c1948

278 p. ;22 cm.

I565. 45/C395

Sutter's Gold/Blaise Cendrars. —New York: Blue Ribbon Books, c1926

179 p. ;21 cm.

I565. 45/D328

Friends and Lovers/Maurice Dekobra. —London: T. Werner Laurie Ltd. , c1934

251 p. ;19 cm.

I565. 45/D693

The Twelve Best Short Stories of the French Language/Auguste Dorchanin. —London: Gowans & Gray, Ltd. , c1920

306 p. ;cm.

I565. 45/D886(1)

The Three Musketeers. V. 1/Alexander Dumas. —New York: Pocket Books, Inc. , c1940

xii, 400 p. ;17 cm.

I565. 45/F917

First on the Rope/R. Frison-Roche. —London: Methuen & Co. , Ltd. , c1949

267 p. ;19 cm.

I565. 45/H487

Maria Chapdelaine: A Tale of the Lake St. John Country/Louis Hemon. —New York: The Macmillan Company, c1944

288 p. ;19 cm.

I565. 45/H487M332

Maria Chapdelaine: A Tale of the Lake St. John Country/Louis Hemon. —New York: The Modern Library, c1934

xvii, 288 p. ;18 cm.

I565. 45/H891

Ninety-Three. Vol. 1/Victor Hugo. —New York: Thomas Y. Crowell & Co. , c1888

v. 1;20 cm.

I565. 45/M331

The Disaster/Paul and Victor Marguerite. —London: Grening & Co. , Ltd. , c1911

xv, 415 p. ;18 cm.

I565. 45/M452

The Great Short Stories of Guy de Maupassant/Guy de Maupassant. —New York: Pocket Books, Inc. , c1939

367 p. ;16 cm.

I565. 45/M452B561

The Best Stories of Guy De Maupassant/Guy De Maupassant. —New York: Modern Library, c1925

xi, 251 p. ;18 cm.

I565. 45/M454

The Unknown Sea/Francois Mauriac. —London: Eyre & Spottiswoode, c1948

207 p. ;20 cm.

I565. 45/M645
Maquis/George Millar. —London: William Heinemann Ltd., 1945
364 p.; 19 cm.

I565. 45/P792
Home Is the Hunter/Gontran de Poncins. —New York: Reynal & Hitchcock, c1943
271 p.; 21 cm.

I565. 45/P993
The Portable Rabelais/Samuel Putnam. —New York: The Viking Press, c1946
623 p.; 17 cm.

I565. 45/R184
When the Mountain Fell/C. F. Ramuz. —New York: Pantheon Books, Inc., c1947
221 p.; 19 cm.

I565. 45/R239
The Honorable Picnic/Thomas Raucat. —New York: The Viking Press, c1927
319 p.; 19 cm.

I565. 45/R673
Finch's Fortune/Mazo De La Roche. —Boston: Little, Brown, and Company, c1943
443 p.; 20 cm.

I565. 45/R757
Verdun/Jules Romains. —New York: Alfred A. Knopf, c1939
xii, 500 p.; 20 cm.

I565. 45/S346
The Seventh Age or Saint Saturnin/Jean Schlumberger. —London: Victor Gollanca Lts., c1933
320 p.; 19 cm.

I565. 45/V131
Playing with Fire/Roger Vailland. —London: Chatto & Windus, c1948
244 p.; 19 cm.

I565. 45/V481
Lena/Roger Vercel. —New York: Random House, c1937
276 p.; 20 cm.

I565. 45/V486
Troubled Waters/Roger Vercel. —New York: Random House, c1940
245 p.; 21 cm.

I565. 45/V688
The Spider and the Fly/Alfred de Vigny. —London: Stanley Paul & Co., Ltd., c1925
382 p.; 18 cm.

I561. 45/W453
The Wheels of Chance: A Bicycling Idyll/H. G. Wells. —New York: The Macmillan Company, c1913
viii, 320 p.; 19 cm.

I565. 5/L856
Was Hitler's Prisoner Leaves From a Prison Diary/Stefan Lorant. —London: Penguin Books Ltd., c1935
viii, 278 p.; 18 cm.

I565. 53/B478
French Belles-Lettres/Joel Benton. —New York: M. Walter Dunne, Publisher, c1901
xiii, 415 p.; 23 cm.

I565. 54/H891
History of a Crime (Deposition of A Wintenss)/Victor Hugo. —New York: Thomas Y. Crowell & Co., c1888
245, 238 p.; 20 cm.

I565. 6/V531
The Tour of the World in Eighty Days/Jules

Verne. —New York: A. L. Burt Company, Publishers, [?]
316 p. ;19 cm.

I565. 65/M219
Turkestan Solo: On Woman's Expedition From the Tien Shan to the Kizil Kum/Ella K. Maillart. —New York: G. P. Putnam's Sons, c1934
307 p. ;22 cm.

I565. 73/L338
The Fifteen Joys of Marriage/Antoine De La Sale. —London: George Routledge & Sons Ltd. , c[1926]
241 p. ;19 cm.

I611. 44/B687
Plain Living: A Bush Idrll/Rolf Boldrewood. —London: Macmillan and Co. , Ltd. , c1899
316 p. ;18 cm.

I611. 44/B687B132
In Bad Company and Other Stories/Rolf Boldrewood. —London: Macmillan and Co. , Ltd. , c1901
514 p. ;20 cm.

I611. 44/B687C643
Sealskin Cloak/Rolf Boldrewood. —London: Macmillan and Co. , Ltd. , 1899
505 p. ;18 cm.

I611. 44/B687M
The Miner's Right: A Tale of the Australian Goldfields/Rolf Boldrewood. —London: Macmillan and Co. , Ltd. , c1903
389 p. ;18 cm.

I611. 44/B687S773
The Squatter's Dream: A Story of Australlan Life/Rolf Boldrewood. —London: Macmillan and Co. , Ltd. , c1899
312 p. ;18 cm.

I611. 44/B687S982
A Sydney-Side Saxon/Rolf Boldrewood. —London: Macmillan and Co. , 1893
237 p. ;19 cm.

I611. 44/B725
A Maker of Nations/Guy Boothby. —London: Ward, Lock & Co. , Ltd. , c1900
342 p. ;18 cm.

I611. 45/B789
Lucinda Brayford/Martin Boyd. —New York: E. P. Dutton & Company, Inc. , c1948
439 p. ;21 cm.

I611. 45/C475
Wrong Turning/Joan Charles. —London: W. H. ALLEN, c1948
361 P. ;19 cm.

I611. 45/D219
The Timeless Land/Eleanor Dark. —New York: The Macmillan Company, c1941
ix, 499 p. ;22 cm.

I611. 45/D537D273
The Days of Ofelia/Gertrude Diamant. —Boston: Houghton Mifflin Company, c1942
226 p. ;21 cm.

I611. 45/E37
Plaque with Laurel/M. Barnard Eldershaw. —London: George G. Harrap & Co. , Ltd. , c1937
303 p. ;19 cm.

I611. 45/F594
Ships and Men of Old Van Diemen's Land/Vanished Fleets. —New York: New York Publishing Co. , Inc. , c1931
297 p. ;21 cm.

I611. 45/H534

Capricornia/Xavier Herbert. —New York: D. Appleton-Century Company, c1943

xiv, 648 p. ;21 cm.

I611. 45/L234

Kilgour's Mare/Henry G. Lamond. —New York: William Morrow and Company, c1943

124 p. ;21 cm.

I611. 45/L748

Pan in the Pariour/Norman Lindsay. —New York: Farrar & Rinehart, Incorporated Publishers, c1933

346 p. ;19 cm.

I611. 45/L778

The Black Stocking/Conyth Little. —London: The Crime Club, c1947

192 p. ;19 cm.

I611. 45/M821

The Rage of the Vulture/Alan Moorehead. —London: Hamish Hamilton, c1948

253 p. ;19 cm.

I611. 45/P913

Lift up Your Eyes/Ambrose Pratt. —Melbourne: Robertson & Mullens, c1935

362 p. ;19 cm.

I611. 45/W582

Peter Domanig: Morning in Vienna/Victor White. —New York: The Bobbs-Merrill Company, c1944

704 p. ;21 cm.

I611. 55/M878

Malayan Postscript/Ian Morrison. —London: Faber and Faber Ltd. , [?]

196 p. ;21 cm.

I611. 6/B687

Old Melbourne Memories/Rolf Boldrewood. —London: Macmillan and Co. , c1899

xii, 259 p. ;18 cm.

I611. 73/B796

Selected Austrian Short Stories/Marip Buscu. —London: Humphrey Milford, 1928

290 p. ;16 cm.

I612. 45/M365

Died in the Wool/Ngaio Marsh. —Boston: Little Brown and Company, c1945

270 p. ;19 cm.

I612. 45/M365D278

Death and the Dancing Footman/Ngaio Marsh. —New York: Grosset & Dunlap Publishers, c1941

364 p. ;19 cm.

I712. 45/B461

The Devil and Daniel Webster/Stephen Vincent Bent. —New York: Farrar & Rinehart, c1937

61 p. ;21 cm.

I711. 44/C743

Black Rock: A Tale of the Selkirks/Ralph Connor. —London: Hodder and Stoughton, c1906

vi, 96 p. ;21 cm.

I711. 4/P238

An Adventurer of the North/Gilbert Parker. —London and New York: Thomas Nelson and Sons, [?]

287 p. ;16 cm.

I711. 44/P238P

Pierre and His People/Gilbert Parker. —London: Hodder and Stoughton, [?]

259 p. ;17 cm.

I711. 4/P238T

The Trail of the Sword/Gilbert Parker. —London: George Newnes Ltd. , [?]

320 p. ;18 cm.

I711. 45/B268

The Laughing Queen: A Romance of Cleopatra/Barrington. —London: George G. Harrap & Co. , Ltd. , c1929

317 p. ;19 cm.

I711. 45/B328

African Intrigue/Alfred, Batson. —New York: Publishing Company, Inc. , 1933.

viii, 307 p. ;24 cm.

I711. 45/C743

The Prospector: A Tale of the Crow's Nest Pass/Ralph Connor. —London: Hodder and Storghton Publishers, c1906

viii, 472 p. ;19 cm.

I711. 45/D621W555

What Happened at Midnight/Franklin W. Dixon. —New York: Grosset and Dunlap, c1931

iv, 213 p. ;20 cm.

I711. 45/F853

Mrs. Mike: The Story of Katherine Mary Flannigan/Benedict Freedman, Nancy Freedman. —New York: Coward-Mccann, Inc. , c1947

312 p. ;21 cm.

I711. 45/G739

Earth and High Heaven/Gwethalyn Graham. —Philadelphia and New York: J. B. Lippincott, c1944

288 p. ;21 cm.

I711. 45/L434

Laugh with Leacock/Stephen Leacock. —New York: Dodd, Mead & Company, c1913, 1915

x, 339 p. ;19 cm.

I711. 45/L434M

My Remarkable Uncle and Other Sketches/Stephen Leacock. —New York: Dodd, Mead & Company, c1944

308 p. ;20 cm.

I711. 45/M787A613

Anne's House of Dreams/L. M. Montgomery. —New York: A. L. Burt Company Publishers, c1917

344 p. ;19 cm.

I711. 45/MacL567

Two Solitudes/Hugh MacLennan. —New York: Duell, Sloan and Pearce, c1945

370 p. ;21 cm.

I711. 45/R673

Whiteoak Harvest/Mazo De La Roche. —London: Macmillan and Co. , Ltd. , c1936

vi, 329 p. ;20 cm.

I711. 45/R673B

The Building of Jalna/[by] Mazo De La Roche. . —London: Macmillan & Co. , Ltd. , 1945

312 p. ;19 cm.

I711. 45/R673J26

Jalna/Mazo De La Roche. —Boston: Little, Brown and Company, c1928

347 p. ;20 cm.

I711. 45/R673R437

Return to Jalna/Mazo De La Roche. —London: Macmillan & Co. , Ltd. , c1948

viii, 408 p. ;19 cm.

I711. 45/R673W582

Whiteoak Harvest/Mazo De La Roche. —Boston: Little, Brown and Company, c1936

vii, 378 p. ;20 cm.

I711.45/R673Y

Young Renny/Mazo De La Roche. —Tauchnitz ed.. —Leipzig: Bernhard Tauchnitz, c1935

265 p. ;18 cm.

I711.5/C187

Arctic Patrols: Stories of the Royal Canadian Mouted Police/Captain William Campbell. —Milwaukee: The Bruce Publishing Company, c1936

335 p. ;21 cm.

I711.65/H161

This is Ontario/Katherine Hale. —Toronto: The Ryeron Press, c1937, 1946

xi, 245 p. ;21 cm.

I711.65/L434

Arcadian Adventures with the Idle Rich/Stephen Leacock. —London: The Mayflower Press, [?]

304 p. ;19 cm.

I711.73/C743

The Foreigner: A Tale of Saskatchewan/Ralph Connor. —New York: Grosset and Dunlap, c1909

384 p. ;19 cm.

I711.73/C743H578

The Foreigner/Ralph Connor. —New York: Hodder & Stoughton, c1909

382 p. ;19 cm.

I711.73/H957

The Oath of the Huron Chieftain: A Narrative from the Early Canadian Missions/Anthong Huonder. —[S. l.]: Mission Press, c1930

135 p. ;17 cm.

I712/C653

Exit Laughing/Irvin S. Cobb. —New York: New York Publishing Co., Inc., c1942

572 p. ;21 cm.

I712/D554

The Department of Queer Complaints/Carter Dickson. —New York: William Morrow & Company, Inc., c1940

125 p. ;20 cm.

I712/F354

In Those Days: An Impression of Change/Harvey Fergusson. —New York: Alfred A. Knopf, Inc., c1929

267 p. ;19 cm.

I712/G287

Shakespeare and the Founders of Liberty in America/Charles Mills Gayley. —New York: The Macmillan Company, c1917

270 p. ;19 cm.

I712/H484(1)

Friends in Council: A Series of Readings and Discourse Thereon. Vol. I/Arthur Helps. —New York: John W. Lovell Company, [?]

301 p. ;19 cm.

I712/H484(2)

Friends in Council: A Series of Readings and Discourse Thereon. Vol. II/Arthur Helps. —New York: John W. Lovell Company, [?]

266 p. ;19 cm.

I712/H484(3)

Friends in Council: A Series of Readings and Discourse Thereon. Vol. III/Arthur Helps. —New York: John W. Lovell Company, [?]

261 p. ;19 cm.

I712/H484(4)

Friends in Council: A Series of Readings and Discourse Thereon. Vol. IV/Arthur Helps. —New York: John W. Lovell Company, [?]

303 p. ;19 cm.

I712/J12

Round Corners/H. C. L. Jackson. —Detroit: Arnold-Powers, Inc. , c1945

328 p. ;19 cm.

I712/P397

Essays by Present-Day Writers/Raymond Woodbury Pence. —New York: The Macmillan Company, c1924

xiv, 360 p. ;19 cm.

I712/U61

The Ogden Nash: Pocket Book/Louis Untermeyer. —New York: Readers' League of America, c1944

viii, 147 p. ;16 cm.

I712/W734S132(O)

Saints and Strangers/George F. Willison. —New York: Reynal & Hitchcock, c1945

511 p. ;21 cm.

I712. 06/A622

Prose and Poetry of America/Rlizabetii Frances Ansorge, Harriet Marcelia Lucas. —New York: The L. W. Singer Company, c1942

xii, 820 p. ;22 cm.

I712. 06/H436

Essays on American Literature/Lafcadio Hearn. —Kanda: The Hokuseiod Press, c1929

xxxviii, 250 p. ;25 cm.

I712. 06/R454(4)

The Library of Wit and Humor: American. Volume IV, "M. Quad" to Mary Wilkins/[?]. —New York: The Review of Reviews Corporation, c1930

xiv, 289 p. ;18 cm.

I712. 07/A622

Prose and Poetry for Enjoyment/Elizabeth Frances Ansorge, Harriet Marcelia Lucas, Raymond F. Mccoy. —New York: The L. W. Singer Company, c1942

xi, 755 p. ;21 cm.

I712. 07/M113

The Spirit of American Literature/John Macy. —New York: Boni and Liveright, c1913

347 p. ;17 cm.

I712. 09/B873

The Flowering of New England 1815-1865/Van Wyck Brooks. —New York: E. P. Dutton & Co. , Inc. , c1936

550 p. ;20 cm.

I712. 094/B873

The World of Washington Irving/Van Wyck Brooks. —New York: E. P. Dutton & Company, Inc. , c1944

387 p. ;22 cm.

I712. 1/A622

Prose and Poetry of America/Raymond F. Mecoy. —New York: The L. W. Singer Company, c1942

xii, 820 p. ;21 cm.

I712. 1/B972(15)

The Writings of John Burroughs. xv, The Summit of the Years/John Burroughs. —Boston: Houghton Mifflin Company, c1913

vii, 297 p. ;19 cm.

I712. 1/C669

The Best Tales of Edgar Allan Poe/Sherwin Cody. —New York: The Modern Library Publishers, c1924

xix, 476 p. ;17 cm.

I712.1/F699

A House Party: An Account of the stories told at a gathering of famous American authors/Paul Leicester Ford.—Boston: Small, Maynard & Company, c1901

418 p. 19 cm. ;

I712.1/H327

Stories and Poems and other Uncollected Writings/Bret Harte.—Boston: Houghton Mifflin Company, c1914

xxvii, 432 p. ;18 cm.

I712.1/L914

Among My Books/James Russell Lowell.—London: J. M. Dent Sons Ltd., [?]

296 p. ;18 cm.

I712.1/S972

Frontier Days/Oliver G. Swan.—New York: Grosset & Dunlap Publishers, c1928

350 p. ;25 cm.

I712.11/G783

Paths and Pathfinders/William S. Gray, Robert C. Pooley, Fred G. Walcott.—Chicago: Scott, Foresman and Company, c1946

528 p. ;20 cm.

I712.11/H487

Men at War: The Best War Stories of All Time/Ernest Hemingway.—New York: Crown Publishers, 1942,

xxxi, 1072 p. ;22 cm.

I712.11/J58

The Best American Humorous Short Stores/Alexander Jessup.—New York: A. S. Barnes & Co., Inc., [?]

xxx, 276 p. ;19 cm.

I712.11/J58(2)

The Best American Humorous Short Stories. Vol. II/Alexander Jessup.—New York: The Modern Library Publishers, [?]

xxx, 276 p. ;17 cm.

I712.11/J58(O)

The Best American Humorous Short Stories/Alexander Jessup.—New York: Boni and Liverighte, c1920

276 p. ;16 cm.

I712.11/M114(3)

Critical, Historical and Miscellaneous Essays and Poems. Volume III/Thomas Babington Maculay.—Chicago: The Midland Book Company, [?]

825 p. ;19 cm.

I712.12/OB853

The Best Short Stories of 1917 and the Yearbook of the American Short Story/Edwar J. O'Brien.—Boston: Small, Maynard & Company Publishers, c1918

xxvi, 600 p. ;19 cm.

I712.12/OB853(1925)

The Best Short Stories of 1925 and the Yearbook of the American Short Story/Edwar J. O'Brien.—Boston: Small, Maynard & Company Publishers, c1924

xvii, 449 p. ;19 cm.

I712.125/U61

This Singing World: A Collection of Modern Poetry For Young People/Louis Untermeyer.—New York: Harcourt, Brace and Company, c1935

xii, 375 p. ;20 cm.

I712.15/E53

The Complete Essays and Other Writings of Ralph Waldo Emerson/Ralph Waldo Emerson.—New York: The Modern Library, c1940

xxiii, 930 p. ;18 cm.

I712.2/A211
Innocent Merriment: An Anthology of Light Verse/Franklin P. Adams. —New York: New York Publishing Co., Inc., c1942
xvi, 523 p.; 22 cm.

I712.2/B275
Auld Licht Idylls/J. M. Barrie. —New York: R. F. Fenno & Company, c1894
192 p.; 20 cm.

I712.2/B636
Graded Poetry: Sixth Year/Katherine D. Blake, Georgia Alexander. —New York: Charles E. Merrill Co., c1905
96 p.; 17 cm.

I712.2/C789
Walt: The Good Gray Poet Speaks for Himself/Elizabeth Corbett. —New York: Frederick A. Stokes Company, c1928
331 p.; 19 cm.

I712.2/G313
Very Young Verses/Barbara Peck Geismer, Antoinette Brown Suter. —Boston: Houghton Mifflin Company, c1945
xii, 210 p.; 20 cm.

I712.2/H674
The Collected Poems of Velma Hitchcock/Velma Hitchcock. —New York: G. P. Putnam's Sons, c1939
269 p.; 21 cm.

I712.2/H875
The Golden Flute: An Anthology of Poetry for Young Children/Alice Hubbard, Adeline Babbitt. —New York: The John Day Company, c1932
xi, 320 p.; 21 cm.

I712.2/H889
My Poetry Book: An Anthology of Modern Verse for Boys and Girls/Grace Thompson Huffard. —Chicago: The John C. Winston, c1934
xxii, 504 p.; 22 cm.

I712.2/L853
The Poetical Works of Henry Wadsworth Longfellow/Henry Wadsworth Longfellow. —London: Peacock, Mansfield and Britton, c1911
viii, 630 p.; 19 cm.

I712.2/L914(1)
Poems. I/James Russell Lowell. —Boston: Houghton, Mifflin and Company, c1890
x, 312 p.; 20 cm.

I712.2/L914(2)
Poems. II/James Russell Lowell. —Boston: Houghton, Mifflin and Company, c1894
438 p.; 20 cm.

I712.2/L914(3)
Poems. III/James Russell Lowell. —Boston: Houghton, Mifflin and Company, c1896
vi, 290 p.; 20 cm.

I712.2/R613
The Little Book of Modern Verse: A Selection from the Work of Contemporaneous American Poets/Jessie B. Rittenhouse. —Boston: Houghton, Mifflin Company, c1913
xvi, 211 p.; 17 cm.

I712.2/U61
Rainbow in the Sky/Louis Untermeyer. —New York: Harcourt, Brace and Company, c1935
xxvii, 498 p.; 23 cm.

I712.2/W187
On Such a Night/Zella Wallace. —New York: Henry Harrison, Poetry Publisher, c1940
63 p.; 20 cm.

I712. 24/B877

The Ring and the Book/Robert Browning. —Boston: Houghton, Mifflin and Company, c1898

477 p. ;20 cm.

I712. 24/L914

Poems/James Russell Lowell. —New York: Hurst and Company, [?]

v, 229 p. ;15 cm.

I712. 24/P743

Prose Tales/Edgar Allan Poe. —Tokyo: Kenkyusha, c1922

xviii, 313 p. ;19 cm.

I712. 24/W614

Leaves of Grass/Walt Whitman. —Tokyo: Kenkyusha, c1928

xvii, 345 p. ;19 cm.

I712. 25/D261-23

Davis' Anthology of Newspaper Verse for 1941/Athie Sale • Davis. —23rd ed.. —Henry Harrison: Poetry Publisher, c1941

288 p. ;19 cm.

I712. 25/L748

Collected Poems/Vachel Lindsay. —New York: The Macmillan Company, c1941

lxii, 464 p. ;20 cm.

I712. 25/S529

V-Letter and Other Poems/Karl Shapiro. —New York: Reynal and Hitchcock, [?]

viii, 63 p. ;22 cm.

I712. 3/B393

Imagination and Four Other One Act Plays for Boys and Girls/Warren Beck. —Boston: Walter H. Baker Company, c1925

xi, 158 p. ;19 cm.

I712. 3/C678

One-Act Plays/Helen Louise • Cohen. —New York: Harcourt, Brace and Company, c1921

lxi, 342 p. ;19 cm.

I712. 3/G618

The Story of Gilbert and Sullivan/Isaac Goldberg. —New York: Crown Publishers, c1935

xviii, 588 p. ;24 cm.

I712. 3/H645

The Iron Horse/Edwin C. Hill. —New York: Gorsset & Dunlap Publishers, c1924

xv, 329p. ;19 cm.

I712. 3/W671

Salome the Importance of Being Earnest Lady Windermere's Fan/Oscar Wilde. —New York: The Modern Library Publishers, [?]

216 p. ;17 cm.

I712. 35/K21

Of Thee I Sing/George S. Kaufman, Morrie Ryskind. —New York: Alfred • A • Knopf, c1932

214 p. ;20 cm.

I712. 35/O23

Six Play of Clifford Odets/Clifford Odets. —New York: The Modern Library, c1933, 1935, 1936, 1937, 1939

x, 433 p. ;18 cm.

I712. 35/ON411

The Emperor Jones, Anna Christie, The Hairy Ape/Eugenie O'Neill. —New York: The Modern Library, c1937

xix, 260 p. ;18 cm.

I712. 35/S927

Mrs. Miniver/Jan Struther. —New York: Grosset & Dunlap Publishers, c1940, 1942

x, 287 p. ;19 cm.

I712.4/A228
Out of the Hurly-Burly, or, Life in An Odd Corner/Max Adeler. —London: Ward, Lock & Co., Ltd., [?]
398 p. ;19 cm.

I712.4/A228H111
In Happy Hollow/Max Adeler. —London: Ward, Lock & Co., Ltd., c1903
320 p. ;18 cm.

I712.4/A379
Short Stories and Essays/W. J. Alexander. —Toronto: The Ryerson Press, c1928
xii, 435 p. ;19 cm.

I712.4/A447
Frossia/E. M. Almedingen. —New York: Harcourt, Brace and Company, [?]
358 p. ;21 cm.

I712.4/B728
Three Pilgrims and A Tinker/Mary Borden. —New York: Alfred A. Knopf, Inc., 1925
303 p. ;19 cm.

I712.4/B969
The Bedside Book of Famous American Stories/Angus Burrell, Bennett A. Cerf. —[S. l. : s. n.], [?]
xvii, 1347 p. ;20 cm.

I712.4/C776
The Wept of Wish-Ton-Wish: A Tale/J. Fenimore Cooper. —New York: D. Apleton & Company, [?]
442 p. ;20 cm.

I712.4/C776C434
The Chainbearer, or, The Littlepage Manuscripts/J. Fenimore Cooper. —New York: D. Apleton & Company, [?]
490 p. ;20 cm.

I712.4/C776D312
The Deerslayer, or, The First War-Path/J. Fenimore Cooper. —New York: D. Apleton & Company, [?]
612 p. ;20 cm.

I712.4/C776J12
Jack Tier, or, The Florida Reef/J. Fenimore Cooper. —New York: D. Apleton & Company, [?]
510 p. ;20 cm.

I712.4/C776M553
Mercedes of Castile, or, The Voyage to Cathay/J. Fenimore Cooper. —New York: D. Apleton & Company, [?]
538 p. ;20 cm.

I712.4/C776W357
The Ways of the Hour: A Tale/J. Fenimore Cooper. —New York: D. Appleton & Company, [?]
488 p. ;20 cm.

I712.4/D188
The Flame of Life/Gabriele D'annunzio. —New York: The Modern Library, [?]
403 p. ;17 cm.

I712.4/D536
In the Whirl of Life: Nightmare in Reality/Captain N. A. Diakoff. —Bangkok: The Boon Ruang Press, c1931
114 p. ;18 cm.

I712.4/D621
Footprints Under the Window/Franklin W. Dixon. —New York: Grosset & Dunlap, c1933
iii, 218 p. ;19 cm.

I712.4/F228

Real Stories Form Our History: Romance and Adventure in Authentic Records of the Development of the United States/John T. Faris. —Boston: Ginn and Company, c1916

xi, 308 p. ;19 cm.

I712.4/F699

Trying out Torchy/Sewell Ford. —New York: Grossst & Dunlap, c1911

342 p. ;19 cm.

I712.4/G223

Mom Counted Six/Mac Gardner. —New York: Harper & Brothers Publishers, c1944

267 p. ;21 cm.

I712.4/H893

The Delicate Ape; Six Silver Handles; The Deep Blue Sea/Dorothy B. Hughes. —New York: Detective Book Club, c1944

1 v. ;

I712.4/L981

In the Golden Days/Edna Lyall. —New York: New York Publishing Company, [?]

402 p. ;18 cm.

I712.4/M878

The Red Triangle: Being Some Further Chronicles of Martin Hewitt, Investigator/Arthur Morrison. —Boston: L. C. Page & Company, c1903

304 p. ;19 cm.

I712.4/McC988

Sherry/George Barr Mccutcheon. —New York: Dodd, Mead and Company, c1919

374 p. ;20 cm.

I712.4/O'B853(1918)

The Best Short Stories of 1918 and the Yearbook of the American Short Story/Edward J. O'Brien. —Boston: Small, Maynard & Company, c1919

xvii, 441 p. ;19 cm.

I712.4/O'B853

The Best Short Stories 1935 and the Yearbook of the American Story/Edward J. O, Brien. —Boston: Houghton Mifflin Company, c1935

xvii, 389 p. ;21 cm.

I712.4/R578

The Case of Jennie Brice/Mary Roberts Rinehart. —New York: Dell Publishing Company, [?]

190 p. ;16 cm.

I712.4/R888

American Short Stories/James F. Royster. —Chicago: Scott, Foresman and Company, c1925

xxv, 342 p. ;17 cm.

I712.4/S285

Make-Up: A Romance of the Footlights/Alma Sioux Scarberry. —New York: Grosset & Dunlap, c1931

254 p. ;19 cm.

I712.4/S839

The Pocket Companion/Philip van Doren Stern. —New York: Poket Books. Inc. , c1942

viii, 446 p. ;17 cm.

I712.4/W524

David Harum: A Story of American Life/Edward Noyes Westcott. —Lodnon: C. Arthur Pearson, Ltd. , [?]

1 v;21 cm.

I712.4/W729

Rosemary: A Christmas Story/C. N. , A. M. Williamson. —New York: A. L. Burt Company, c1906

140 p. ;20 cm.

I712. 44/1

The King of Arcadia/Francis Lynde. —New York: Charles Scribner's Sons, [c191-?]

viii, 353 p. ;19 cm.

I712. 44/A355

Little Women and Good Wives: Being Stories for Girls/L. M. Alcott. —London: Wars, Lock and Co. , [?]

vii, 313 p. ;18 cm.

I712. 44/A355A926

Aunt Jo's Scrap-Bag/Louisa M. Alcott. —New York: Grosset & Dunlap Publishers, c1929

ix, 354 p. ;21 cm.

I712. 44/A355L778

Little Men: Life at Plumfield With Fo's Boys/Louisa M. Alcott. —Boston: Little, Brown, and Company, c1907

376 p. ;17 cm.

I712. 44/A355L788G374

Little Women or Meg, Jo, Beth, and Amy/Louisa M. Alcott. —London: George G. Harrap & Co. , Ltd. , c1926

vii, 271 p. ;21 cm.

I712. 44/A355O44

An Old-Fashioned Girl/Louisa M. Alcott. —Boston: Little, Brown, and Company, c1926

328 p. ;22 cm.

I712. 44/A355U55

Under the Lilacs/Louisa M. Alcott. —New York: Grosset & Dunlap Publishers, c1877

302 p. ;21 cm.

I712. 44/A562

Ten Boys Who Lived on the Road From Long Ago to Now/by Jane Andrews. —Boston: Ginn and Company, c1913.

ix, 248 p. ;20 cm.

I712. 44/B261

Schoolgirl/Carman Barnes. —New York: Horace Liveright, c1929

viii, 240 p. ;19 cm.

I712. 44/B877C874

Cow-Country/B. M. Bower. —London: Hodder and Stoughton, c1921

252 p. ;19 cm.

I712. 44/C267

Cardigan/Robert W. Chambers. —New York: The Armed Services, Inc. , c1930

318 p. ;12 cm.

I712. 44/C443

The Phantom Filly: A Novel/George Agnew Chamberlain. —Armed Services Editon. —[S. l. : s. n.], [?]

220 p. ;10 cm.

I712. 44/C625

The Prince and the Pauper: A Tale for Youn People of All Ages/Samuel L. Clemens. —Chicago: The Goldsmith Publishing Co. , [?]

252 p. ;20 cm.

I712. 44/C653

Back Home: Being the Narrative of Judge Priest and His People/Irvin S. Cobb. —New York: Grosset & Dunlap, c1912

xi, 348 p. ;19 cm.

I712. 44/C766S732

The Spy: A Tale of the Neutral round/Cooper, J. Fenimore. —New York: D. Appleton & Company, [?]

455 p. ;20 cm.

I712. 44/C776(O)

The Water-Witch: Or, The Skimmer of the sea/J. Fenimore Cooper. —New York: D. Appleton & Company, [?]

471 p. ;20 cm.

I712. 44/C776L(O)

The Last of the Mohicans: A Tale of 1757/James Fenimore Cooper. —New York: Blue Ribbon Books, [?]

vii, 412 p. ;21 cm.

I712. 44/C776O

The Oak-Openings, or, The Bee-Hunter/J. Fenimore Cooper. —New York: Dappleton & Company, c[18--?]

504 p. ;20 cm.

I712. 44/C776P

The Prairie: A Tale/J. Fenimore Cooper. —Chicago and New York: Rand, McNally & Company, [?]

430 p. ;19 cm.

I712. 44/C776

Precaution: A Novel/J. Fenimore Cooper. —New York: D. Appleton & Company, c[18--]

464 p. ;20 cm.

I712. 44/C776B826

The Bravo: A Tale/J. Fenimore Cooper. —New York: D. Appleton & Company, [?]

435 p. ;20 cm.

I712. 44/C776C895

John Masefield or, Vulcan's Peak: A Tale of the Pacific/J. Fenimore Cooper. —New York: D. Appleton & Company, [?]

504 p. ;20 cm.

I712. 44/C776D312

The Deerslayer or the First War-Path/James Fenimore Cooper. —New York: Charles Scribner's Sons, c1925

x, 462 p. ;23 cm.

I712. 44/C776D312(O)

The Deerslayer/James Fenimore Cooper. —New York: J. H. Sears & Company. Inc. , [?]

246 p. ;17 cm.

I712. 44/C776H765

Home as Found: Sequel to Homeward Bound/J. Fenimore Cooper. —New York: D. Appleton & Company, [?]

473 p. ;20 cm.

I712. 44/C776H765H

Homeward Bound or, The Chase: A Tale of the Sea/J. Fenimore Cooper. —New York: D. Appleton & Company, [?]

522 p. ;20 cm.

I712. 44/C776L349(O)

The Last of the Mohicans/James Fenimore Cooper. —Boston: Allyn and Bacon, c1945

ix, 417 p. ;17 cm.

I712. 44/C776M646

Miles Wallingford/Cooper, J. Fenimore. —New York: D. Appleton & Company, [?]

476 p. ;20 cm.

I712. 44/C776N234

The Last of the Mohicans: A Narrative of 1757/James Fenimore Cooper. —New York: The Spencer Press, [?]

xiii, 475 p. ;21 cm.

I712. 44/C776P643

The Pilot: A Tale of the Sea/J. Fenimore Cooper. —New York: D. Appleton & Company, [?]

473 p. ;20 cm.

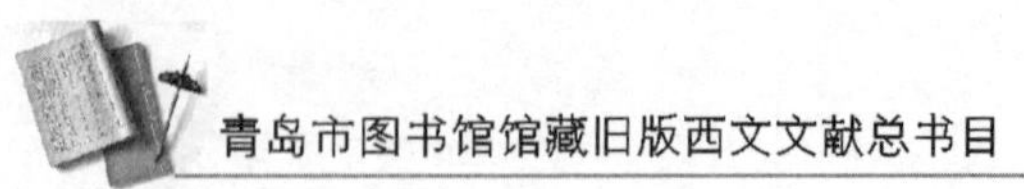

I712.44/C776P662

The Pioneers or, the Sources of the Susquehanna: A Descriptive Tale/J. Fenimore Cooper. —New York: D. Appleton & Company, [?]

506 p. ;20 cm.

I712.44/C776P895

The Prairie/J. Fenimore Cooper. —New York: D. Appleton & Company, [?]

485 p. ;20 cm.

I712.44/C776R312

The Redskins or, Indian and Injin: Being the Conclusion of the Littlepage Mauscripts/J. Fenimore Cooper. —New York: D. Appleton & Company, [?]

538 p. ;20 cm.

I712.44/C776S253

Satanstoe or, the Littlepage Manuscripts/J. Fenimore Cooper. —New York: D. Appleton & Company, [?]

511 p. ;20 cm.

I712.44/C776S438

The Sea-Lion or, the Lost Sealers/J. Fenimore Cooper. —New York: D. Appleton and Company, [?]

482 p. ;21 cm.

I712.44/C891(O)

The Red Badge of Courage/Stephen Crane. —New York: D. Appleton-Century Company, c1895

xxiv, 242 p. ;18 cm.

I712.44/C891A188

Active Service/Stephen Crane. —London: William Heinemann, c1900

315 p. ;18 cm.

I712.44/D261

About Paris/Richard Harding Davis. —New York: Harper & Brothers Publishers, c1895

219 p. ;18 cm.

I712.44/D311

Old Wine and New/Warwick Deeping. —[New York]: [H. Wolff Estate], [?]

387 p. ;19 cm.

I712.44/D911

The Suitable Child/Norman Duncan. —Fleming: H. Reyell Company, c1909

96 p. ;20 cm.

I712.44/D911D636

Doctor Luke of The Labrador/Norman Duncan. —New York: Grosset & Dunlap, c1904

327 p. ;19 cm.

I712.44/E28

The Hoosier Schoolmaster/Edward Eggleston. —New York: Grosset & Dunlaf Publishers, c1892

281 p. ;19 cm.

I712.44/E53

Mine Inheritance/Emily Davant Embree. —Belton: The Cottage Home, c1906

xv, 312 p. ;19 cm.

I712.44/F453

The Love Affairs of a Bibliomaniac/Eugene Field. —New York: Charles Scribner's Sons, c1896

xiii, 253 p. ;18 cm.

I712.44/F514

Claude Lightfoot/Francis J. Finn. —New York: Benziger Brothers, c1893

245 p. ;18 cm.

I712.44/F791

A Mountain Europa; A Cumberland Vendetta; The Last Stetson/John Fox. —New York:

Charles Scribner's Sons, c1909
279 p. ;19 cm.

I712. 44/F791C554
Christmas Eve on Lonesome "Hell-Fer-Sartain" and Other Stories/John Fox. —New York: Charles Scribner's Sons, c1912
v, 245 p. ;20 cm.

I712. 44/F791L778
The Little Shepherd of Kingdom Come/John Fox. —New York: Grosset & Dunlap Publishers, c1931
404 p. ;19 cm.

I712. 44/G151
The Loves of Pelleas and Etarre/Zone Gale. —New York: Grosset and Dunlap, c1907
341 p. ;20 cm.

I712. 44/G677
The Redemption of David Corson/Charles Frederic Goss. —New York: The Bobbs-Merrill Company, c1900
418 p. ;19 cm.

I712. 44/G795H236
Hand and Ring/Anna Katharine Green. —New York: A. L. Burt Company, c1926
vi, 434 p. ;20 cm.

I712. 44/H355L788G878
Little Women or Meg, Jo, Beth, and Amy/Lousia M. Alcott. —New York: Grosset & Dunlap Publishers, c1896, 1910, 1911
440 p. ;19 cm.

I712. 44/H399(O)
The Scarlet Letter/Nathaniel Hawthorne. —New York: The Modern Library, [?]
xvi, 303 p. ;18 cm.

I712. 44/H399H842(O)
The House of the Seven Gables/Nathaniel Hawthorne. —Boston: Houghton Mifflin Company, c1924
422 p. ;18 cm.

I712. 44/H399H842D414
The House of the Seven Gables: A Romance/Nathaniel Hawthorne. —London: J. M. Dent and Sons Ltd. , [?]
xv, 310 p. ;18 cm.

I712. 44/H399M913
Mosses from An Old Manse/Nathaniel Hawthorne. —New York: George Munro, Publisher, [?]
232, 16 p. ;18 cm.

I712. 44/H399S243K33
The Scarlet Letter/Nathaniel Hawthorne. —Tokyo: Kenkyusha, c1928
xxxii, 343 p. ;19 cm.

I712. 44/H399S243L651S698
The Scarlet Letter: A Nomance/Nathaniel Hawthorne. —New York: J. M. Dent Sons Ltd. , c1906
318 p. ;18 cm.

I712. 44/H399S243Z51
The Scarlet Letter/Nathaniel Hawthorne. —London: Zephy Books, c1946
312 p. ;18 cm.

I712. 44/H521
Roads of Destiny/O. Henry. —London: Hodder and Stoughton Ltd. , [?]
307 p. ;18 cm.

I712. 44/H521C112
Cabbages and Kings/O. Henry. —New York: Doubleday, Page & Company, c1914
312 p. ;19 cm.

I712.44/H521F773
The Four Million/O. Henry. —London: Hodder and Stoughton, c1906
256 p.;18 cm.

I712.44/H838
The Neutral Ground/Frank O. Hough. —New York: J. B. Lippincott Company, c1941
526 p.;21 cm.

I712.44/I93
Tales of A Traveller/Irving, Washington. —New York: A. L. Burt Company Publishers, [?]
270, 52 p.;20 cm.

I712.44/J12
Ramona/Helen Jackson. —Boston: Little, Brown and Company, c1907
490 p.;19 cm.

I712.44/J59C853
The Country of the Pointed Firs/Sarah Orne Jewett. —London: Jonathan Cape, c1927
1 v.;21 cm.

I712.44/J724
To Have and to Hold/Mary Johnston. —Boston: Houghton Mifflin Company, c1900
403 p.;19 cm.

I712.44/J73
Sir Mortimer/Mary Jonhston. —London: Archibald Constable and Co., Ltd., c1906
346 p.;17 cm.

I712.44/L736
A Hall & Co., /Joseph c. Lincoln. —New York: D. Appleton-Century Company, c1938
336 p.;20 cm.

I712.44/L766
Martha By-the-Day/Julie M. Lippmann. —New York: Henry Holt and Company, c1913
201 p.;19 cm.

I712.44/L778
The Story of Patrick Henry/Artie Littlefield. —Dansville: F. A. Owen Publishing Company, c1905
1 v.;18 cm.

I712.44/L847W582
White Fang/Jack London. —New York: Grosset & Dunlap Publishers, c1933
276 p.;21 cm.

I712.44/M156
Mr. and Mrs. Pierce: A Story of Youth/Cameron Mackenzie. —New York: Dodd, Mead and Company, c1916
404 p.;19 cm.

I712.44/M531M687(O)
Moby Dick, or The White Whale/Herman Melville. —New York: Grosset & Dunlap Publishers, c1925
viii, 511 p.;19 cm.

I712.44/M531M689
Moby Dick/Herman Melville. —New York: The Modern Library, c1926
xxi, 565 p.;18 cm.

I712.44/M531R192
Moby Dick/Herman Melville. —New York: Random House, c1926
xxi, 565 p.;19 cm.

I712.44/McC988
Mr. Bingle/George Barr Mccutcheon. —New York: Dodd, Mead and Company, c1915
357 p.;19 cm.

I712.44/McC988G744
Graustark: The Story of a Love Behind a

Throne/George Barr Mccutcheon. —New York: Grosset & Dunlap Publishers, c1901
399 p. ;19 cm.

I712. 44/N595
A Hoosier Chronicle/Meredith Nicholson. — Boston: Houghton Migglin Company, c1912
605 p. ;19 cm.

I712. 44/N855
Vandover & the Brute/Frank Norris. —London: William Heinemann, c1914
viii, 311 p. ;19 cm.

I712. 44/P132
Gordon Keith/Thomas Nelson Page. —New York: Charles Scribner's Sons, c1908
ix, 548 p. ;20 cm.

I712. 44/P462
Dan Merrithew/Lawrence Perry. —Chicago: A. C. Mcclurg & Co. , c1910
285 p. ;20 cm.

I712. 44/P558
Plain Mary Smith: A Romance of Red Saunders/Henry Wallace Phillips. —New York: The Century Co. , c1905
318 p. ;20 cm.

I712. 44/P883
An Old Maid's Vengeance/Frances Powell. — New York: Charles Scribner's Sons, c1911
330 p. ;19 cm.

I712. 44/R476
Stepsons of Light/Eugene Manlove Rhodes. — Boston: Houghton Mifflin Company, c1920
317 p. ;19 cm.

I712. 44/R495
Mr. Opp/Alice Hegan Rice. —New York: The Century Co. , c1909
326 p. ;18 cm.

I712. 44/R623
The Ghost Garden: A Novel/Amelie Rives. — New York: Frederick A. Stokes Company, c1918
299 p. ;19 cm.

I712. 44/R939
Damon Runyon Favorites/Damon Runyon. — New York: Pocket Books, Inc. , c1935
ix, 237 p. ;17 cm.

I712. 44/S867
The Wonder-Worker of Padua/Charles Warren Stoddard. —Notre Dame: The Ave Maria, c1896
173 p. ;17 cm.

I712. 44/S892(O)
Uncle Tom's Cabin/Harriet Beecher Stowe. — New York: H. M. Caldwell Company, [?]
419p. ;19cm.

I712. 44/S892
Uncle Tom's Cabin/Harriet Beecher Stowe. — [S. l.]: T. Nelson and Sons, [?]
529 p. ;16 cm.

I712. 44/S911
Michael O'Halloran/Gene Stratton-Porter. — New York: Doubleday, Page & Company, c1915
560 p. ;20 cm.

I712. 44/S911
Laddie: A True Blue Story/Gene Stratton-Porter. —New York: Grosset & Dunlap, c1913
541 p. ;19 cm.

I712. 44/T318
Bruce/Albert Payson Terhune. —New York: Grosset and Dunlap, c1920
204 p. ;20 cm.

I712. 44/T969

The Adventures of Huckleberry Finn/Mark Twain. —New York: The Heritage Reprints, c1912

346 p. ;22 cm.

I712. 44/T969AU

The Adventures of Huckleberry Finn (Tom Sawyer's Comrade)/Mark Twain. —Authorized ed.. —Authorized ed.. —New York: Harper & Brothers Publishers, c1918

404 p. ;21 cm.

I712. 44/T969A111

The Adventures of Huckleberry Finn (Tom Sawyer's Comrade)/Mark Twain. —New York: Harper & Brothers Publishers, c1923

312 p. ;21 cm.

I712. 44/T969A512

The American Claimant and Other Stories and Sketches/Mark Twain. —New York: Harper & Brothers ed.. —New York: P. F. Collier & Son Company, c1896, 1899

397 p. ;20 cm.

I712. 44/T969B218

The £1, 000, 000 Bank-Note and Other New Stories/Mark Twain. —Leipzig: Bernhard Tauchnitz, c1893

280 p. ;16 cm.

I712. 44/T969C742H293

A Connecticut Yankee in King Arthur's Court/Mark Twain. —New York: Harper & Brothers Publishers, [?]

450 p. ;21 cm.

I712. 44/T969C743G878

A Connecticut Yankee in King Arthur's Court/Mark Twain. —New York: Grosset & Dunlap Publishers, c1917

449 p. ;19 cm.

I712. 44/T969L693(O)

Life on the Mississippi/Mark Twain. —New York: Grosset & Dunlap Publishers, c1917

526 p. ;21 cm.

I712. 44/T969S627

Sketches: New and Old/Mark Twain. —New York: Harper & Brothers Publishers, c1875

424 p. ;20 cm.

I712. 44/T969S875

The Stolen White Elephant Etc. /Mark Twain. —A New ed.. —London: Chatto & Windus, c1902

285 p. ;19 cm.

I712. 44/W129B

Billy-Boy/Mary T. Waggaman. —Notre Dame: The Ave Maria Press, c1912

256 p. ;18 cm.

I712. 44/W129J

Josephine Marie/Mary T. Waggaman. —Notre Dame: The Ave Maria, c1921

399 p. ;18 p.

I712. 44/W129T

Tommy Travers/Mary T. Waggaman. —Notre Dame: The Ave Maria, c1912

350 p. ;17 cm.

I712. 44/W324

The Circling Year/Frederic F. Van de Water. —New York: The John Day Company, c1940

222 p. ;21 cm.

I712. 44/W453

Sleeping Dogs/Carolyn Wells. —New York: A. L. Burt Company Publishers, c1929

300 p. ;19 cm.

I712.44/W539

The Wide, Wide World/Elizbeth Wetherell. —Complete ed..—London: Wather Scoott, 24 Warwick Lane, [?]

472 p.;19 cm.

I712.44/W541

Last of the Great Scouts/Helen Cody Wetmore, Zane Grey. —New York: Grosset & Dunlap, c1899

xii, 333 p.;19 cm.

I712.44/W947

The Calling of dan Matthews/Harold Bell Wright. —New York: A. L. Burt Co., c1909

361 p.;19 cm.

I712.44/W947M664

The Mine with the Iron Door/Harold Bell Wright. —New York: D. Appleton and Company, c1923

338 p.;19 cm.

I712.45/1

Strange Negro Stories of The Old Deep South/H. D. "Pop" Howell. —Caligornia: Wetzel Publishing Co., Inc., c1937

295 p.;19 cm.

I712.45/A131

Molly Make-Believe/Eleanor Hallowell Abbott. —New York: The Gentury Co., c1911

211 p.;17 cm.

I712.45/A152

Without Orders/Ablrand. —New York: The Sun Dial Press, c1944

281 p.;19 cm.

I712.45/A211

From Gags to Riches/Joey Adams. —New York: Frederick Fell Inc., c1946

336 p.;21 cm.

I712.45/A211

Revelry/Samuel Hopkins Adams. —New York: Boni & Liveright, c1926

318 p.;18 cm.

I712.45/A217

The Gorgeous Hussy/Samuel Hopkins Adams. —Boston: Houghton Mifflin Company, c1933

549 p.;21 cm.

I712.45/A365

Song of Years/Aldrich, Bess Streeter. —New York: D. Appletion-century Company, c1930

490 p.;21 cm.

I712.45/A365L296

A Lantern in her Hand/Bess Streeter Aldrich. —New York: Grosset & Dunlap Publishers, c1928

306 p.;19 cm.

I712.45/A365S

Spring Came on Forever/Bess Streeter Aldrich. —New York: D. Appleton-Century Company, c1935

332 p.;20 cm.

I712.45/A374R449

Revenge Can Wait/Irene Alexander. —New York: G. P. Putnam's Sons, c1941

268 p.;19 cm.

I712.45/A426

The Forest and the Fort/Hervey Allen. —New York: Farrar & Rinehart, Inc., c1943

344 p.;21 cm.

I712.45/A426A188

Action at Aquila/Hervey Allen. —London: Victor Gollancz Ltd., c1938

448 p.;20 cm.

I712.45/A426A628
Anthony Adverse/Hervey Allen.—New York：Farrar and Rinehart，Inc.，c1933
1244 p.；22 cm.

I712.45/A426B399
Bedford Village/Hervey Allen.—New York：Farrar & Rinehart，Inc.，c1944
305 p.；22 cm.

I712.45/A426T737
Toward the Morning/Hervey Allen.—New York：Rinehart & Company，c1948
458 p.；21 cm.

I712.45/A438A416
All in Good Time/Marguerite Allis.—New York：G. P. Putnam's，c1944
308 p.；22 cm.

I712.45/A438N899
Not Without Peril/Marguerite Allis.—New York：G. P. Putnam's Sons，c1941
405 p.；21 cm.

I712.45/A545
Winesburg，Ohio：A Group of Tales of Ohio Small-Town Life/Sherwood Anderson.—New York：The Modern Library，c1919
xv，303 p.；18 cm.

I712.45/A545(O)
Winesburg，Ohio：A Group of Tales of Ohio Small-Town Life/Sherwood Anderson.—New York：The Modern Library，c1919
xv，303 p.；18 cm.

I712.45/A612
First Come，First Kill/Francis Allan.—New York：Reynal & Hitchcock，c1945
188 p.；19 cm.

I712.45/A649
Tom Swift Circling the Globe/Victor Appleton.—Poughkeepsie：Whitman Publishing Co.，c1927
216 p.；20 cm.

I712.45/A649E37
Tom Swift and his Electric Locomotive or Two Miles a Miles a Minute on the Rails/Victor Appleton.—New York：Grosset & Dunlap Publishers，c1922
212 p.；19 cm.

I712.45/A649T655
Tom Swift and His Sky Racer or The Quickest Flight on Record/Victor Appleton.—New York：Grosset & Dunlap Publishers，c1911
iv，207 p.；19 cm.

I712.45/A723
The Green Hat/Michael Arlen.—New York：Grosset & Dunlap，c1924
303 p.；20 cm.

I712.45/A735
The Innocent Flower：A Macdougal Duff Mystery/Charlotte Armstrong.—New York：Coward-Mccann，Inc.，c1945
185 p.；19 cm.

I712.45/A812
Three Cities/Sholem Asch.—London：Victor Gollancz Ltd.，c1933
862 p.；20 cm.

I712.45/A828
Doctor Serocold：A Page from his Day-book/Helen Ashton.—New York：Doubleday，Doran and Company，Inc.，c1930
305 p.；21 cm.

I712.45/A868
The Avalanche：A Mystery Story/Gertrude

Atherton. —New York: Frederica A. Stokes Company Publishers, c1919
229 p. ;19 cm.

I712. 45/A868B185
Mrs. Balfame/Gertrude Atherton. —London: John Murray, Albemarle Street, W. , c1916
373 p. ;19 cm.

I712. 45/A868C749
The Conqueror: A Dramatized Biography of Alexander Hamilton/Gertrude Atherton. —Philadelphia: J. B. Lippincott Company, c1930, 1943
xii, 536 p. ;21 cm.

I712. 45/A887H241
Hank Winton: Smokechaser/Montgomery M. Atwater. —New York: Random House, Inc. , c1947
210 p. ;21 cm.

I712. 45/A924
The Dases Plan and the New Economics/George P. Auld. —New York: Doubleday, Page & Company, c1927
xvii, 317 p. ;21 cm.

I712. 45/A954
A Yankee Flier With the R. A. F. /Al Avery. —New York: Grosset & Dunlap, c1941
214 p. ;19 cm.

I712. 45/A954Y
A Yankee Flier in the South Pacific/Al Avery. —New York: Grosset & Dunlap, c1943
vii, 208 p. ;19 cm.

I712. 45/A975
Measure of A Man/Dora Aydelotte. —New York: D. Appleton-Century Company, c1942
250 p. ;19 cm.

I712. 45/B121(O)
A Man for the Ages: A Story of the Builders of Democracy/Irving Bacheller. —Indianapolis: The Bobbs-Merrill Company Publishers, c1919
416 p. ;18 cm.

I712. 45/B121W766
The Winds of God: A Tale of the North Country/Irving Bacheller. —New York: Farrar & Rinehart, Inc. , c1941
xiv, 318 p. ;21 cm.

I712. 45/B167
Young Man with a Horn/Docothy Baker. —New York: The Sun Dial Press, c1944
243 p. ;20 cm.

I712. 45/B167S974
Sweet Chariot: A Novel/Frank Baker. —New York: Coward-Mccann, Inc. , c1943
335 p. ;19 cm.

I712. 45/B167Y68
Young Man with a Horn/Dorothy Baker. —London: Readers Union Ltd. , c1939
284 p. ;19 cm.

I712. 45/B181
Skyscraper/Faith Baldwin. —Cleveland: the World Publishing Company, c1944
318 p. ;21 cm.

I712. 45/B181A512
American Family/Faith Baldwin. —New York: Farrar & Rinehart, c1934, 1935
xi, 388 p. ;21 cm.

I712. 45/B181A719
Arizona Star/Faith Baldwin. —New York: Farrar & Rinehart, Inc. , c1944, 1945
vii, 307 p. ;21 cm.

I712.45/B187

The Scarlet Fox: A Novel of Mystery/Eustace Hale Ball. —New York: Grosset & Dunlap Publishiers, c1927

214 p. ;19 cm.

I712.45/B239

Right Half Hollins/Ralph Henry Barbour. —New York: Grosset & Dunlap, c1925

288 p. ;19 cm.

I712.45/B261W821

Within This Present/Margaret Ayer Barnes. —Boston: Houghton Mifflin Company, c1933

611 p. ;21 cm.

I712.45/B274(O)

The Sign of the Cross/Wilson Barrett. —New York: Center Books, c1943

302 p. ;19 cm.

I712.45/B274

Murder at Belle Camille/Monte Barrett. —New York: The Bobbs-Merrill Company, c1943

288 p. ;20 cm.

I712.45/B279F252

Father and His Town/Richard Barry. —Boston: Houghton Mifflin Company, c1941

viii, 299 p. ;22 cm.

I712.45/B329

Fair Stood the Wind for France/H. E. Bates. —Boston: Little, Brown and Company, c1944

270 p. ;20 cm.

I712.45/B329P

The Purple Plain/H. E. Bates. —Boston: Little, Brown and Company, c1947

308 p. ;20 cm.

I712.45/B336D269

Dawn Over the Amazon/Carleton Beals. —New York: Duell, Sloan and Pearce, c1943

vi, 536 p. ;20 cm.

I712.45/B347

Martin's Summer/Vicki Baum. —London: Geoferey Bles, c1933

288 p. ;19 cm.

I712.45/B358

The Bolinvars/Marguerite F. Bayliss. —New York: Henry Holt and Company, c1944

384 p. ;21 cm.

I712.45/B433

Out of This Furnace/Thomas Bell. —Boston: Little, Brown and Company, c1941

413 p. ;21 cm.

I712.45/B433F631

Floods of Spring/Henry Bellamann. —New York: The Sun Dial Press, [?]

374 p. ;20 cm.

I712.45/B433L863

Looking Backward, 2000-1887/Edward Bellamy. —New York: The Modern Library, c1889

x, 276 p. ;19 cm.

I712.45/B433P261

Parris Mitchell of Kings Row/Henry and Katherine Bellamann. —New York: Simon and Schuster, c1948

xi, 333 p. ;21 cm.

I712.45/B433V642

Victoria Grandoler/Henry Bellamann. —New York: Simon and Schuster, c1943

281 p. ;21 cm.

I712.45/B455

Now I Lay Me Down to Sleep/Ludwig Bemelmans. —New York: The Viking Press, c1942

245 p. ;21 cm.

I712. 45/B455W253

My War With the United States/Ludwing Bemelmans. —New York: Viking Press, c1937

151 p. ;18 cm.

I712. 45/B461

A Little Clown Lost/Barry Benefield. —New York: The Century Co. , c1928

317 p. ;19 cm.

I712. 45/B461

Twenty-five Short Stories by Stephen Vincent Benet/Stephen Vincent Benet. —New York: The Sun Dial Press, c1943

xiii, 274 p. ;19 cm.

I712. 45/B461J65-30

John Brown's Body/Stephen Vincent. —30th ed.. —[?]: Property of U. S Navy, c1927

viii, 336 p. ;21 cm.

I712. 45/B477

Inheritance/Phyllis Bentley. —New York: Grosset & Dunlap, c1932

592 p. ;19 cm.

I712. 45/B531

Keep Your Head Down/Walter Bernstein. —New York: The Viking Press, c1945

213 p. ;19 cm.

I712. 45/B531

L'Affaire Jones/Hillel Bernstein. —New York: The Literary Guild of America, c1933

257 p. ;20 cm.

I712. 45/B554

All Sorts and Conditions of Men: An Impossible Story/Walter Besant, James Rice. —New York: Grosset & Dunlap, [?]

448 p. ;19 cm.

I712. 45/B592

The Chinese Parrot: A Charlie Chan Mystery/Earl Derr Biggers. —New York: Pocket Books Inc. , c1944

275 p. ;17 cm.

I712. 45/B592B

Behind that Curtain/Earl Derr Biggers. —New York: Pocket Books, c1942

267 p. ;16 cm.

I712. 45/B592C474

Charlie Chan Carries on/Earl Derr Biggers. —New York: Pocket Books Inc. , c1930

280 p. ;17 cm.

I712. 45/B614

The Land Is Bright/Archie Binns. —New York: Charles Scribner's Sons, c1939

345 p. ;21 cm.

I712. 45/B614M634

Mighty Mountain/Archie Binns. —New York: Charles Scribner's Sons, c1940

440 p. ;21 cm.

I712. 45/B632

Coronado's Children: Tales of Lost Mines and Buried Treasures of the Southwest/J. Frank Dobie. —New York: Grosset & Dunlap Publishers, c1930

xiv, 367 p. ;21 cm.

I712. 45/B632T355

A Texan in England/J. Frank Dobie. —Boston: Little, Brown and Company, c1945

xiii, 285 p. ;20 cm.

I712. 45/B652

Georgie May/Maxwell Bodenheim. —New York: Boni & Liveright, c1928

272 p. ;20 cm.

I712. 45/B694C156

Call for a Chaperon/Sybil Boliho, Cen Fearnley. —New York: William Morrow & Co., c1936

307 p. ;19 cm.

I712. 45/B697F198

Famous Stories of Code and Cipher/Raymond T. Bond. —New York: Rinehart and Company, Incorporated, c1947

xxvi, 342 p. ;21 cm.

I712. 45/B716

Legacy/Charles Bonner. —New York: Alfred A. Knopf, c1940

372 p. ;20 cm.

I712. 45/B751

The Life Line/Phyllis Bottome. —Boston: Little, Brown and Company, c1946

352 p. ;20 cm.

I712. 45/B751S957

Survival/Phyllis Bottome. —New York: The Sun Dial Press, c1944

339 p. ;19 cm.

I712. 45/B751S963

Survival/Phyllis Bottome. —Boston: Little, Brown and Company, c1943

339 p. ;19 cm.

I712. 45/B753

Great American Detective Stories/New York. —Cleveland: the World Publishing Company, c1945

308 p. ;21 cm.

I712. 45/B775

Drums of Destiny/Peter Brourne. —New York: G. P. Putnam's Sons, c1947

570 p. ;22 cm.

I712. 45/B780

The Trail of the White Mule/B. M. Bower. —Boston: Little, Brown and Company, c1922

278 p. ;19 cm.

I712. 45/B784

Dave Dawson at Singapore/R. Sidney Bowen. —New York: The Saalfield Publishing Company, c1942

250 p. ;20 cm.

I712. 45/B786

The Family Failing/B. M. Bower. —New York: Grosset & Dunlap Publishers, c1941

305 p. ;20 cm.

I712. 45/B786S

Shadows Before/Dorothy Bowers. —New York: Doybleday, Doran & Company, Inc., c1940

xvi, 284 p. ;19 cm.

I712. 45/B786

Dave Dawson at Dunkirk/R. Sidney Bowen. —Akron: The Saalfield Publishing Company, c1941

251 p. ;21 cm.

I712. 45/B786A298

Dave Dawson with the air corps/R. Sidney Bowen. —Akron: The Saalfield Publishing Company, c1942

251 p. ;21 cm.

I712. 45/B786D246

Dave Dawson with the Pacific Fleet/R. Sidney Bowen. —Akron: The Saalfield Publishing Company, c1942

249 p. ;20 cm.

I712. 45/B786D246C734

Dave Dawson with the Commandos/R. Sidney

Bowen. —Akron: The Saalfiedld Publishing Company, c1942
248 p. ;20 cm.

I712.45/B786D246D272
Dave Dawson on Convoy Patrol/R. Sieney Bowen. —Akron: the Saalfield Publishing Company, c1941
245 p. ;21 cm.

I712.45/B786D246L694
Dave Dawson in Libya/R. Sidney Bowen. —Akron: The Saalfield Publishing Company, c1941
252 p. ;20 cm.

I712.45/B789
The Perilous Night/Burke Boyce. —New York: The Viking Press, c1942
558 p. ;21 cm.

I712.45/B789B628
Bitter Creek/James Boyd. —New York: Charles Scribner's Sons, c1938, 1939
422 p. ;21 cm.

I712.45/B789D795
Drums/James Boyd. —New York: Charles Scribner's Sons, c1925
492 p. ;18 cm.

I712.45/B789R749
Roll River/James Boyd. —New York: Charles Scribner's Sons, c1935
603 p. ;21 cm.

I712.45/B792
Avalanche/Kay Boyle. —New York: Simon and Schuster, c1944
209 p. ;21 cm.

I712.45/B794
Valley of Vanishing Men/Max Brand. —New York: Dodd, Mead & Company, c1947
199 p. ;19 cm.

I712.45/B799
This Side of Jordan/Roark Bradford. —New York: Harper & Brothers, c1929
255 p. ;19 cm.

I712.45/B815
The Return of Kai Lung/Ernest Bramah. —New York: Sheridan House, c1937
319 p. ;21 cm.

I712.45/B816
This Year's Sin/Florenz Branch. —New York: Phoenix Press, c1945
256 p. ;19 cm.

I712.45/B816F
The Fearful Passage/H. C. Branson. —New York: Simon and Schuster, c1945
249 p. ;20 cm.

I712.45/B817
Dr. Kildare's Search and Dr. Kildare's Hardest Case/Max Brand. —New York: Dodd, Mead & Company, c1943
216 p. ;19 cm.

I712.45/B817H559
The Heroes/Millen Brand. —New York: Simon and Schuster, c1939
336 p. ;21 cm.

I712.45/B817H944
Hunted Riders/Max Brand. —London: Hodder & Stoughton Publishiers, c1936
312 p. ;19 cm.

I712.45/B817K
Dr. Kildare's Crisis/Max Brand. —New York: Grosset & Dunlap Publishers, c1940
206 p. ;19 cm.

I712.45/B817T136
Dr. Kildare Takes Charge/Max Brand. —New York: Grosset & Dunlap, c1940
210 p. ;19 cm.

I712.45/B817T819
Dr. Kildare's Trial/Max Brand. —New York: Grosset & Dunlap Publishers, c1941. 1942
204 p. ;19 cm.

I712.45/B838
Memo to a Firing Squad/Frederick Hazlitt. —New York: Grosset & Dunlap, c1943
275 p. ;19 cm.

I712.45/B838P247
Mrs Parkington/Louis Bromfield. —New York: Harper & Brothers Publishers, c1942, 1943
330 p. ;21 cm.

I712.45/B844
The Rock and the Wind/Viven R. Bretherton. —New York: E. P. Dutton and Company, Inc., c1942
618 p. ;21 cm.

I712.45/B849
O. Henry Memorial Award Prize Stories of 1943/Herschel Brickell. —25th Anniversary ed.. —New York: Doubleday, Doran and Company, Inc., c1943
xxv, 319 p. ;20 cm.

I712.45/B858(O)
Buffalo Coat/Carol Brink. —New York: The Macmillan Company, c1944
421 p. ;21 cm.

I712.45/B859
Deep Summer/Gwen Bristow. —New York: The Blakiston Company, c1937
329 p. ;19 cm.

I712.45/B868
Twenty-Four Hours/Louis Bromfield. —New York: Frederick A. Stokes Company, c1930
463 p. ;19 cm.

I712.45/B868C
Clear the Tracks: The Story of an Old-Time Locomotive Engineer/Joseph Bromley. —New York: Whittlesey House, c1943
288 p. ;21 cm.

I712.45/B868C623
The World We Live in/Louis Bromfield. —Philadelphia: The Blakiston Company, c1940
339 p. ;21 cm.

I712.45/B868G795
The Green Bay Tree/Louis Bromfield. —New York: Frederick A. Stokes Company, c1924
341 p. ;19 cm.

I712.45/B868K34
Kenny/Louis Bromfield. —London: Cassell and Company Ltd., c1949
169 p. ;19 cm.

I712.45/B868M
The Man Who Had Everything/Louis Bromfield. —London: Cassell and Company, c1935
227 p. ;19 cm.

I712.45/B868M236
Malabar Farm/Louis Bromfield. —New York: Harper & Brothers Publishers, c1948
viii, 405 p. ;21 cm.

I712.45/B868P247-9
Mrs. Parkington/Louis Bromfield. —9th ed.. —New York: Harper & Brothers Publishers, c1943
330 p. ;21 cm.

I712.45/B868R154
The Rains Came/Louis Bromfield. —[S. l. : s. n.], c1920
597 p. ;20 cm.

I712.45/B868W668
The Wild Country/Louis Bromfield. —New York: Harper & Brothers, c1948
274 p. ;21 cm.

I712.45/B868WB
The World We Live In/Louis Bromfield. —Philadelphia: The Blakiston Company, c1944
339 p. ;20 cm.

I712.45/B878
A Walk in the Sun/Harry Brown. —New York: Overseas Editions, Inc. , c1944
154 p. ;16 cm.

I712.45/B878A784
Artie Greengroin Ptc. /Harry Brown. —New York: Alfred A. Knopf, c1945
xi, 212 p. ;19 cm.

I712.45/B915S635
Small Town South/Sam Byrd. —Boston: Houghton Mifflin Company, c1942
237 p. ;22 cm.

I712.45/B922
The Good Earth/Pearl S. Buck. —New York: Grosset & Dunlap, c1932.
339 p. ;22 cm.

I712.45/B922
The Promise/Pearl S. Buck. —New York: The Sun Dial Press, c1943
248 p. ;20 cm.

I712.45/B922E13
East Wind: West Wind/Pearl S. Buck. —New York: The John Day Company, c1931
277 p. ;19 cm.

I712.45/B922E13-2
East Wind: West Wind/Pearl S. Buck. —2nd. ed. . —London: Methuen & Co. , Ltd. , c1932
244 p. ;20 cm.

I712.45/B922E96
The Exile/Pearl S. Buck. —New York: Reynal & Hitchcock, c1936
314 p. ;22 cm.

I712.45/B922M918
The Mother/Pearl S. Buck. —London: Methuen & Co. , Ltd. , c1934
244, 8 p. ;19 cm.

I712.45/B922O87
Other Gods: An American Legend/Pearl S. Buck. —[S. l. : s. n.], c1940
381 p. ;19 cm.

I712.45/B922P314
The Patriot/Pearl Buck. —London: Methuen & Co. , Ltd. , c1939
371 p. ;19 cm.

I712.45/B922S698
Sons/Pearl S. Buck. —London: Methuen & Co. , Ltd. , c1932
451, 8 p. ;19 cm.

I712.45/B925
Deep River/Henrietta Buckmaster. —New York: Harcourt, Brace and Company, c1944
512 p. ;12×17 cm.

I712.45/B927
Tarzan: Lord of The Jungle/Edgar Rice Burroughs. —New York: Grosset & Dunlap, c1928
309 cm. ;20 cm.

I712. 45/B927J59

Tarzan and the Jewels of Oper/Edgar Rice Burroughs. —New York: A. L. Burt Company Publishers, c1918

350 p. ; 19 cm.

I712. 45/B954

The Frightened Pigeon/Richard Burke. —New York: G. P. Putnam's Sons, c1944

248 p. ; 21 cm.

I712. 45/B962(O)

Rooster Crows for Day/Ben Lucien Burman. —New York: E. P. Dutton & Company, Inc. , c1945

308 p. ; 21 cm.

I712. 45/B962

Big River to Cross: Mississippi Life Today/Ben Lucien Burman. —New York: Blue Ribbon Books, c1943

294 p. ; 20 cm.

I712. 45/B964

The Quick Brown Fox/W. R. Burnett. —New York: Alfred A. Knopf, c1943

267 p. ; 20 cm.

I712. 45/B964D

Dark Hazard/W. R. Burnett. —New York: Harper & Brothers Publishers, c1933

295 p. ; 21 cm.

I712. 45/B972

Tarzan and the Lost Empire/Edgar Rice Burroughs. —New York: Grosset & Dunlap Publishers, c1929

313 p. ; 19 cm.

I712. 45/B972J95

Jungle Girl/Edgar Rice Burroughs. —New York: Grosset & Dunlap Publishers, c1932

318 p. ; 19 cm.

I712. 45/B972P667

Pirates of Venus/Edgar Rice Burroughs. —London: John Lane The Bodley Head Ltd. , c1935

v, 312 p. ; 19 cm.

I712. 45/B972T176

Tarzan: Lord of the Jungle/Edgar Rice Burroughs. —New York: Grosset and Dunlap, c1928

309 p. ; 20 cm.

I712. 45/B974

Lovejoy/Beatrice Burton. —N. Y. : Doubleday, Doran & Company, Inc. , c1930

309 p. ; 19 cm.

I712. 45/C112

The Cavalier/George W. Cable. —New York: Charles Scribner's Sons, c1901

vii, 311 p. ; 19 cm.

I712. 45/C132L863

Look South to the Polar Star/Holger Cahill. —New York: Harcourt, Brace and Company, c1947

554 p. ; 21 cm.

I712. 45/C135

The Bondman: A New Saga/Hall Caine. —Chicago and New York: Rand, McNally & Company, [?]

357 p. ; 20 cm.

I712. 45/C138E83

The Eternal City/Hall Caine. —London: William Heinemann, c1901

606 p. ; 19 cm.

I712. 45/C147S568

This Side of Innocence/Taylor Caldwell. —New York: Charles Scribner's Sons, c1946

499 p. ;21 cm.

I712. 45/C147T925
The Turnbulls/Taylor Caldwell. —New York: The Sun Dial Press, c1943
517 p. ;20 cm.

I712. 45/C149
The Earth is the Lord's: A Tale of the Rise of Genghis Khan/Taylor Caldwell. —London: Collins, c1941
400 p. ;20 cm.

I712. 45/C149M522
Melissa/Tarlor Caldwell. —New York: Charles Scribner's Sons, c1948
390 p. ;21 cm.

I712. 45/C174T398
There Was a Time/Taylor Caldwell. —New York: Charles Scribner's Sons, c1947
471 p. ;22 cm.

I712. 45/C222D311
The Deepening Stream/Dorothy Canfield. —New York: The Modern Library, c1930
391 p. ;18 cm.

I712. 45/C224
Jam Yesterday/Kathleen Cannell. —New York: William Morrow & Company, c1945
238 p. ;20 cm.

I712. 45/C244T
Trumpet to Arms/Bruce Lancaster. —New York: Grosset & Dunlap Publishers, c1944
379 p. ;19 cm.

I712. 45/C311
As The Earth Turns/Gladys Hasty Carroll. —New York: Grosset & Dunlap, c1933
339 p. ;21 cm.

I712. 45/C311E
The Emperor's Snuff-Box/John Dickson Carr. —4th ed.. —New York: Harper & Brothers Publishers, c1942
298 p. ;20 cm.

I712. 45/C319
The Mastery of Tess/Patrick J. Carroll. —Notre Dame: The Ave Maria Press, c1935
316 p. ;19 cm.

I712. 45/C329
Michaeleen/Patrick J. Carroll. —Notre Dame: The Ave Maria Press, c1931
352 p. ;18 cm.

I712. 45/C337
Such Interesting People/Robert J. Casey. —New York: The Bobbs-Merrill Company, c1943
347 p. ;22 cm.

I712. 45/C337F773
Four Faces of Siva: The Detective Story of A Vanished Race/Robert J. Casey. —New York: Blue Ribbon Books, c1929
xii, 373 p. ;21 cm.

I712. 45/C337W946
Written in Sand/Josephine Young Case. —Boston: Houghton Mifflin Company, c1945
161 p. ;19 cm.

I712. 45/C347P857
C/O Postmaster/Thomas R. St. George. —New York: Thomas Y. Ciowell Co. , c1943
xi, 194 p. ;20 cm.

I712. 45/C363A635(O)
My Antonia/by Willa Sibert Cather... with illustrations by W. T. Benda..—Boston: Houghton Mifflin Co. , c1918.
xiii, [1], 3-418, [2] p. ;19 cm.

I712. 45/C363D278

Death Comes for the Archbishop/Willa Cather. —New York: Alfred A. Knopf, c1926, 1927

299 p. ;19 cm.

I712. 45/C363O58

One of Ours/Willa Cather. —New York: Alfred A. Knopf, Inc. , c1922

459 p. ;19 cm.

I712. 45/C363S524

Shadows on the Rock/Willa Cather. —New York: Alfred A. Knopf, c1931

280 p. ;20 cm.

I712. 45/C411

Modern American Short Stories/Bennett Cerf. —Cleveland: The World Publishing Company, c1945

384 P. ;22 cm.

I712. 45/C411B561

The Best Short Stories of O. Henry/Bennett A. Cerf, Van H. Cartmell. —New York: The Modern Library, c1945

x, 338 p. ;19 cm.

I712. 45/C442

Boomerang/William C. Chambliss. —New York: Harcourt, Brace and Company, c1944

87 p. ;19 cm.

I712. 45/C486S132

The Saint in Miami/Leslie Charteris. —Philadelphia: The Blakiston Company, c1940

299 p. ;19 cm.

I712. 45/C487

Mary Peters/Mary Ellen Chase. —London: Collins, c1935

383 p. ;20 cm.

I712. 45/C487F853

Free Admission/Ilka Chase. —New York: Doubleday & Company, Inc. , c1948

319 p. ;21 cm.

I712. 45/C487W766

Windswept/Mary Ellen Chase. —New York: The Macmillan Company, c1941

440 p. ;22 cm.

I712. 45/C532

Panama Passage/Donald Barr Chidsey. —New York: Doubleday & Company, Inc. , [?]

442 p. ;21 cm.

I712. 45/C555

Easy to Kill/Agatha Christie. —New York: Gulf and Western, c1939.

248 p. ;20 cm.

I712. 45/C561

The Inside of the Cup/Churchill, Winston. —New York: Grosset & Dunlap Publishers, c1912

vi, 513 p. ;20 cm.

I712. 45/C592

Flight into Darkness/Philip Clark. —New York: Simon and Schuster, c1948

212 p. ;19 cm.

I712. 45/C597AB325

Alabam's; Kelly/Donald Henderson Clarke. —Cleveland: The World Publishing Company, c1945

149, 198 p. ;21 cm.

I712. 45/C619

Heaven Below/E. H. Clayton. —New York: Prentice-Hall, Inc. , c1944

282 p. ;23 cm.

I712. 45/C653M785

Mrs. Pomeroy's Reputation/Thomas Cobb. —

London: The Bodley Head, [?]
312 p. ;17 cm.

I712. 45/C672
Neven a Dull Moment/Charles Francis Coe. —New York: Hastings House, c1944
326 p. ;21 cm.

I712. 45/C675L
Lost Paradise: A Boyhood on A Maine Coast Farm/Robert P. Tristram Coffin. —New York: The Macmillan Company, c1934
284 p. ;20 cm.

I712. 45/C678
The Crimson Alibi/Octavus Roy Cohen. —[S. l. : S. n.], [?]
285 p. ;20 cm.

I712. 45/C689T627
A Toast to Tomorrow/Manning Coles. —New York: The Literary Guild of America, Inc. , c1940, 1941
viii, 310 p. ;20 cm.

I712. 45/C692(O)
Escape the Thunder/Lonnie Coleman. —New York: E. P. Dutton & Co. , Inc. , c1944
185 p. ;21 cm.

I712. 45/C699
This Winged World: An Anthology of Aviation Fiction/Thomas Collison. —New York: Coward • Mccann, Inc. , c1943
xxiv, 520 p. ;22 cm.

I712. 45/C743T786
Treading the Winepress/Ralph Connor. —New York: A. L. Burt Company Publishers, c1925
394 p. ;19 cm.

I712. 45/C743T969
The Twenty-one Clues/J. J. Connington. —Boston: Little, Brown and Company, c1941
316 p. ;20 cm.

I712. 45/C774
London After midnight/Marie Coolidge-Rask. —New York: Grosset & Dunlap Publishers, c1928
261 p. ;19 cm.

I712. 45/C776
Preface to A Life/Zona Gale. —New York: D. Appleton and Company, c1926
345 p. ;19 cm.

I712. 45/C776(O)
The Monikins/J. Fenimore Cooper. —New York: Dappleton & Company, [?]
431 p. ;20 cm.

I712. 45/C776R312
The Red Rover: A Tale/J. Fenimore Cooper. —New York: D. Appleton & Company, [?]
494 p. ;20 cm.

I712. 45/C789
The Red-haired Lady/Elizabeth Corbett. —New York: Doubleday, Doran & Company, Inc. , c1945
368 p. ;21 cm.

I712. 45/C833
Out Where the World Begins: A Story of a Far Country/ABE Cory. —New York: George H. Doran Company, c1921
viii, 225 p. ;20 cm.

I712. 45/C837
The Moneyman/Thomas Bertram Costain. . —N. Y. : Doubleday, c1947.
viii, 434 p. ;22 cm.

I712. 45/C837M742
The Moneyman/Thomas B. Costain. —New

York: Staples Press, 1948
428 P. ;19 cm.

I712. 45/C837R544
Ride With Me/Thomas B. Costain. —New York: Doubleday, Doran and Company, Inc. , c1944
x, 595 p. ;21 cm.

I712. 45/C875
Hemingway/Malcalm Cowley. —New York: The Viking Press, c1944
xxiv, 642 p. ;17 cm.

I712. 45/C879M974
Murder in Havana/George Harmon Coxe. —New York: Alfred A. Knopf, c1943
242 p. ;19 cm.

I712. 45/C882
The Just and the Unjust/James Gould Cozzens. —New York: Harcourt, Brace, c1942.
434 p. ;21 cm.

I712. 45/C883
Supper at the Maxwell House: A Novel of Recaptured Nashville/Alfred Leland Crabb. —Indianapolis: The Bobbs-Merrill Company, c1943
372 p. ;21 cm.

I712. 45/C884
A Spectre of Power/Charles Egbert Craddock. —Boston: Houghton, Mifflin and Company, c1903
415 p. ;20 cm.

I712. 45/C891
Yarns From a Windjammer/Mannin Crane. —Boston: Houghton Mifflin Company, c1926
192 p. ;22 cm.

I712. 45/C891A648
The Applegreen Cat: A Mystery Novel/France Crane. —Philadelphia: The Applegreen Cat, c1943
221 p. ;20 cm.

I712. 45/C899M334
Marietta: A Maid of Venice/F. Marion Crawford. —New York: The Macmillan Company, c1902
458 p. ;19 cm.

I712. 45/C899P153
In the Palace of the King: A Love Story of Old Madrid/F. Marion Crawford. —New York: The Macmillan Company, c1901
viii, 867 p. ;20 cm.

I712. 45/C947
Grand Canary: A Novel/A. J. Cronin. —New York: Grosset & Dunlap, c1933
330 p. ;19 cm.

I712. 45/C961
Steps in the Dark/Marten Cumberland. —New York: Doubleday, Doran & Co. , Inc. , c1945
251 p. ;18 cm.

I712. 45/C967
The Twins of Suffering Creek/Ridgwell Cullum. —London: Chapman and Hall, Ltd. , 1912
312 p. ;18 cm.

I712. 45/C975
The Grizzly King: A Romance of the Wild/James Oliver Curwood. —New York: Grosset & Dunlap Publishers, c1915, 1918
ix, 293 p. ;19 cm.

I712. 45/C978C853
The Country Beyond/James Oliver Curwood. —[S. l. : s. n.], [?]
340 p. ;19 cm.

I712. 45/D163

Grandma Called It Carnal/Bertha Damon. —New York: Simon and Schuster, c1938

288 p. ;21 cm.

I712. 45/D163S474

A Sense of Humus/Bertha Damon. —New York: Simon and Schuster, c1943

250 p. ;21 cm.

I712. 45/D188

Defy the tempest/Sylvia G. L. Dannett, Edwin Bennett. —New York: Julian Messner, Inc. , c1944

253 p. ;21 cm.

I712. 45/D246

The Valley of Decision/Marcia Davenport. —New York: Charles Scribner's Sons, c1946

640 p. ;21 cm.

I712. 45/D255M517

The Melting of Molly/Maria Thompson Daviess. —New York: Grosset & Dunlap Publishers, c1912

265 p. ;19 cm.

I712. 45/D261G786

The Great American Novel/Clyde Brion Davis. —New York: Farrar & Rinehart, c1938

309 p. ;21 cm.

I712. 45/D261R291

The Rebellion of Leo McGuire/Clyde Brion Davis. —New York: Farrar & Rinehart, Inc. , c1944

315 p. ;21 cm.

I712. 45/D261R776

The Room Upstairs/Mildred B. Davis. —New York: Simon and Schuster, c1948

245 p. ;19 cm.

I712. 45/D272G238

Garry Grayson's Winning Kick, or, Battling for Honor/Elmer A. Dawson. —New York: Grosset & Dunlap Publishers, c1928

iv, 218 p. ;19 cm.

I712. 45/D272S539

She Came to the Valley/Cleo Dawson. —New York: William Morrow & Company, c1943

388 p. ;20 cm.

I712. 45/D273

Life with Father/Larence Day. —New York: Alfred A. Knopf, c1943

vi, 258 p. ;21 cm.

I712. 45/D273S588

This Simian World/Clarence Day. —New York: Alfred A. Knopf, c1920, 1924.

95 p. ;19 cm.

I712. 45/D311

Stories of Love, Courage and Compassion/Warwick Deeping. —New York: Alfred A. Knopf, Inc. , c1930

821 p. ;21 cm.

I712. 45/D333

"Faster! Faster!"/E. M. Delafield. —New York: Harper & Brothers Publishers, c1936

309 p. ;21 cm.

I712. 45/D336

The Little Apostle on Crutches/Henriette Eugenle Delamare. —New York: Benziger Brothers, c1912

165 p. ;17 cm.

I712. 45/D337A712

Around Old Chester/Margaret Deland. —New York: Harper & Brothers Publishers, c1989

378 p. ;19 cm.

I712. 45/D337H236

The Hands of Esau/Margaret Deland. —New York: Harper & Brothers Publishers, c1914

85 p. ;21 cm.

I712. 45/D337(O)

Partners/Margaret Deland. —New York: Harper & Brothers Publishers, c1891

112 p. ;21 cm.

I712. 45/D337V889

The Voice/Margaret Deland. —New York: Harper & Brothers Publishers, c1902

84 p. ;21 cm.

I712. 45/D357

The Top of the World/Ethel M. Dell. —New York: Grosset & Dunlap Publishers, c1920

ix, 562 p. ;19 cm.

I712. 45/D357J33

Janet March/Flord Dell. —London: John Lane the Bodley Head Ltd. , c1924

457 p. ;19 cm.

I712. 45/D359

Bad Girl/Vina Delmar. —New York: Grosset & Dunlap, c1928

274 p. ;19 cm.

I712. 45/D427

Best Supernatural Stories of H. P. Lovecraft/august Derleth. —Cleveland: The World Publishing Company, c1945

307 p. ;21 cm.

I712. 45/D554

The Curse of the Bronze Lamp/Carter Dickson. —New York: William Morrow & Company, c1945

214 p. ;19 cm.

I712. 45/D579

Comrades/Mary Dillon. —New York: The Century Co. , c1918

396 p. ;20 cm.

I712. 45/D579O44

In Old Bellaire/Mary Dillon. —New York: The Century Co. , c1906

viii, 363 p. ;20 cm.

I712. 45/D583

Winter's Tales/Isak Dinesen. —New York: Random House, c1942

313 p. ;20 cm.

I712. 45/D583B

The Bishop Murder Case/S. S. Van Dine. —London: Cassell and Company, Ltd. , c1929

352 p. ;19 cm.

I712. 45/D583B474

The Benson Murder Case/S. S. Van Dine. —London: Cassell and Company Ltd. , c1931

315 p. ;17 cm.

I712. 45/D583G218

The Garden Murder Case: A Philo Vance Story/S. S. Van Dine. —New York: Grosset & Dunlap Publishers, c1935

332 p. ;19 cm.

I712. 45/D621

The Mystery of Cabin Island/Franklin W. Dixon. —New York: Grosset & Dunlap, c1929

iv, 214 p. ;19 cm.

I712. 45/D645(O)

Hans Brinker, or the Silver Skates a Story of Life in Holland/Mary Mapes Dodge. —Chicago: The Goldsmith Publishing Company, [?]

245 p. ;19 cm.

I712.45/D645H249(O)

Hans Brinker, or the Silver Skates a story of life in Holland/Mary Mapes Dodge. —New York: Rand, McNally & Company Publishers, c1945.

375 p. ;19 cm.

I712.45/D645H249

Hans Brinker or, the Silver Skates/Mary Mapes Dodge. —New York: The John C. Winston Company, c1925

xiv, 325 p. ;22 cm.

I712.45/D674

Christ in Concrete/Pietro Di Donato. —Cleveland: The World Publishing Company, c1937

311 p. ;21 cm.

I712.45/D677

The Lord Is A Man of War/Stanley F. Donath. —New York: Alfred A. Knopf, c1944

338 p. ;20 cm.

I712.45/D695

Dacey Hamilton/Dorothy Van Doren. —New York: Harpee & Brothers Publishers, c1942

303 p. ;21 cm.

I712.45/D733

White Banners/Lloyd C. Douglas. —New York: Grosset & Dunlap, c1936

400 p. ;21 cm.

I712.45/D733L896

White Banners/Lloyd C. Douglas. —London: Lovat Dickson Limited Publishers, c1936

407 p. ;20 cm.

I712.45/D733R

The Robe/Lloyd C. Douglas. —Boston: Houghton Mifflin Company, c1945

508 p. ;20 cm.

I712.45/D733W582

White Banners/Lloyd C. Douglas. —London: Peter Davies, c1936

298 p. ;18 cm.

I712.45/D749

Kansas Irish/Charles B. Driscoll. —New York: The Macmillan Company, c1943

359 p. ;22 cm.

I712.45/D754

Round the Fire Stories/A. Conan Doyle. —Leipzig: Bernhard Tauchnitz, c1908

350 p. ;16 cm.

I712.45/D762

Chrysantha/Margaret Drake. —New York: J. B. Lippincott Company, c1948

252 p. ;21 cm.

I712.45/D765

"God Wills It!": A Tale of the First Grusade/William Stearns Davis. —New York: The Macmillan Company, c1935

x, 552 p. ;19 cm.

I712.45/D771C371

Caius Gracchus/Odin Gregory. —New York: Boni and Liveright Publishers, c1920

172 P. ;22 cm.

I712.45/D828

The Hurricane/Charles Nordhoff, James Norman Hall. —New York: Triangle Books, c1936

257 p. ;19 cm.

I712.45/D911G982

Gus the Great/Thomas W. Duncan. —Philadelphia: J. B. Lippincott Company, c1947

703 p. ;22 cm.

I712.45/D918

Broadway: A Novel/Philip Dunning, George

Abbott. —New York: Grosset &Dunlap, c1927
288 p. ;19 cm.

I712. 45/DD246E13
East Side, West Side/Marcia Davenport. —New York: Charles Scribner's Sons, c1947
376 p. ;23cm.

I712. 45/DeV872
Mountain Time/Bernard DeVoto. —Boston: Little, Brown and Company, c1947
313 p. ;20 cm.

I712. 45/DuB682
Death Comes to Tea/Theodora DuBois. —Boston: Houghton Mifflin Company, c1940
232 p. ;19 cm.

I712. 45/E16
Escape the Night/Eberhart, Mignon G. —New York: Grosset & Dunlap, Publishers, c1944
215 p. ;20 cm.

I712. 45/E24
Chad Hanna/Walter D. Edmonds. —London: Collins, c1940
524 p. ;21 cm.

I712. 45/E24E68
Erie Water/Walter D. Edmonds. —Boston: Little, Brown, and Company, c1944
506 p. ;22 cm.

I712. 45/E24R763
Rome Haul/Walter D. Edmonds. —New York: The Modern Library, c1938
xii, 347 p. ;18 cm.

I712. 45/E36
My Uncle Newt/Frances Eisenberg. —Philadelphia: J. B. Lippincott Company, c1942
320 p. ;21 cm.

I712. 45/E52
Heritage of the River: An Historical Novel of Early Montreal/Muriel Elwood. —New York: Charles Scribener's Sons, c1945
310 p. ;19 cm.

I712. 45/E56
The Werewolf of Paris/Guy Endore. —New York: Grosset & Dunlap Publishers, c1933
325 p. ;20 cm.

I712. 45/E65
Changing Winds/St. John G. Ervine. —New York: The Macmillan Company, c1917
571 p. ;19 cm.

I712. 45/E92
Adventures of the Great Crime-Busters/Clyde Evans. —New York: New Power Publications, c1943
256 p. ;21 cm.

I712. 45/E93
Westward the River/Dale Van Every. —New York: G. P. Putnam's Sons, c1945
275 p. ;21 cm.

I712. 45/F223
The Wilsons/Christopher La Farge. —New York: Coward-Mccann, Inc. , c1940
246 p. ;19 cm.

I712. 45/F223S943
The Sudden Guest/Christopher La Farge. —New York: Coward-Mccann, Inc. , c1946
250 p. ;21 cm.

I712. 45/F235
The Broad Highway/Jeffery Farnol. —Boston: Little, Brown, and Company, c1911
518 p. ;19 cm.

I712.45/F235M995

My Lord of Wrybourne/Jeffery Farnol. —London: Sampson Low, Marston & Co., Ltd., c1948

280 p.;19 cm.

I712.45/F245

Young Lonigan/James T. Farrell. —Cleveland: The World Publishing Company, c1932

201 p.;21 cm.

I712.45/F251

Conceived in Liberty: A Novel of Valley Forge/Howard Fast. —Cleveland: The World Publishing Company, c1939

389 p.;21 cm.

I712.45/F251C

Citizen Tom Paine/Howard Fast. —New York: Bantam Books, c1946.

351 p.;16 cm.

I712.45/F251F853

Freedom Road/Howard Fast. —New York: Book Find Club, c1944

263 p.;21 cm.

I712.45/F251P314

Patrick Henry and the Frigate's Keel: And Other Stories of a Young Nation/Howard Fast. —New York: Duell, Sloan and Pearce, c1936

253 p.;21 cm.

I712.45/F263

Plowman's Folly/Edward H. Faulkner. —New York: Grosset & Dunlap, c1943

155 p.;19 cm.

I712.45/F263I61

Intruder in the Dust/Wiliam Faulkner. —New York: Random House, c1948

247 p.;21 cm.

I712.45/F263L

Light in August/William Faulkner. —London: Chatto & Windus, c1933

480 p.;21 cm.

I712.45/F346

So Big/Edna Ferber. —New York: Grosset and Dunlap, c1924

372 p.;22 cm.

I712.45/F346A512

American Beauty/Edna Ferber. —New York: Doubleday, Doran & Company, Inc., c1931

viii, 313 p.;21 cm.

I712.45/F346C

Cimarron/Edna Ferber. —New York: Grosset and Dunlap, c1930

ix, 388 p.;20 cm.

I712.45/F346S

So Big/Edna Ferber. —Cleveland: The World Publishing Company, c1947

360 p.;21 cm.

I712.45/F354

Chile/Erna Fergusson. —New York: Alfred A. Knopf, Inc., c1943

340, vi p.;22 cm.

I712.45/F453

Gringo Guns/Peter Field. —Cleveland: The World Publishing Company, c1944

307 p.;21 cm.

I712.45/F453S552

Sheriff on the Spot: "A Powder Valley Western"/Peter Field. —New York: William Morrow & Company, c1943

218 p.;19 cm.

I712.45/F514

His First and Last Appearance/Francis J. Finn.—New York: Benziger Brothers, c1900

199 p.;19 cm.

I712.45/F514H296

Harry Dee or Making it out/Francis J. Finn.—New York: Benziger Brothers, c1892

284 p.;19 cm.

I712.45/F529Y3

The Years Between/William J. Fischer.—Techny: Thr Society of The Divine Word, c1911

242 p.;18 cm.

I712.45/F533

Darkness and the Deep/Vardis Fisher.—New York: The Vanguard Press, c1943

296 p.;21 cm.

I712.45/F536

Destination Tokyo/Steve Fisher.—New York: D. Appleton-Century Company, c1944

226 p.;20 cm.

I712.45/F555

Pee-Wee Harris/Percy Keese Fitzhugh.—Racine: Whitman Publishing Co., [?]

191 p.;19 cm.

I712.45/F569F198

Family on the Hill/Ambrose Flack.—New York: Thomas Y. Crowell Company, c1945

247 p.;21 cm.

I712.45/F597

Colonel Effingham's Raid/Berry Fleming.—New York: Duell, Sloan and Pearce, c1943

279 p.;21 cm.

I712.45/F612L968

Lusty Wind for Carolina/Inglis Fletcher.—New York: The Bobbs-Merrill Company, c1944

509 p.;20 cm.

I712.45/F628

The Happy Time/Robert Fontaine.—New York: Simon and Schuster, c1945

269 p.;20 cm.

I712.45/F651L153

A Lady Leaves Home/Eather Forbes.—New York: Grosset & Dunlap, Publishers, c1926

296 p.;20 cm.

I712.45/F651R943

The Running of the Tide/Eather Forbes.—Boston: Houghton Mifflin Company, c1948

632 p.;21 cm.

I712.45/F683

The Secret Shanghai/Jean Fontenoy.—New York: Grey-Hill Press, c1939

188 p.;22 cm.

I712.45/F687H111

The Happy Time/Robert Fontaine.—New York: Simon and Schuster, Inc., c1945

269 p.;20 cm.

I712.45/F692

Mama's Bank Account/Kathryn Forbes.—New York: Harcourt, Brace and Company, c1943

204 p.;21 cm.

I712.45/F692T772

Transfer Point/Karhry Forber.—New York: Harcourt, Brace and Company, c1947

195 p.;21 cm.

I712.45/F693S557

The Ship/C. S. Forester.—Boston: Little, Brown and Company, c1943

x, 281 p.;20 cm.

I712.45/F699D494

The Devil's Stronghold/Leslie Ford.—New York: Charles Scribner's Sons, c1948

209 p.;21 cm.

I712.45/F699F197

False to Any Man/Leslie Ford.—New York: Charles Scribner's sons, c1939

254 p.;19 cm.

I712.45/F717

The Captain from Connecticut/C. S. Forester.—Boston: Little, Brown and Company, c1942

344 p.;20 cm.

I712.45/F829

Claudia: The Story of a Marriage/Rose Franken.—Philadelphia: The Blakiston Company, c1938, 1939

305 p.;19 cm.

I712.45/F853D618

Divided: A Novel/Ralph Freedman.—New York: E. P. Dutton & Co., Inc., c1948

447 p.;21 cm.

I712.45/F917

Amaru: A Romance of the South Seas/Robert Dean Frisbie.—New York: Doubleday, Doran & Co., Inc., c1945

246 p.;19 cm.

I712.45/F965(O)

The Shining Trail/Iola Fuller.—New York: Duell, Sloan and Fearce, c1943

442 p.;22 cm.

I712.45/G137

Double Muscadine/Frances Gaither.—New York: The Macmillan Company, c1949

335 p.;21 cm.

I712.45/G168

Adventures of Hiram Holliday/Paul Gallico.—New York: Ryerson Press, c1943

295 p.;20 cm.

I712.45/G198

Island in the Sky/Ernest K. Gann.—New York: The Viking Press, c1944

181 p.;20 cm.

I712.45/G217

Johnny Chinook: Tall Tales and True from the Canadian West/Robert E. Gard.—London: Longmans, Green & Company, [?]

xix, 360 p.;21 cm.

I712.45/G224

The Case of the Sleepwalker's Miece/Erle Stanley Gardner.—New York: Pocket Books, Inc., c1936

204 p.;17 cm.

I712.45/G226(O)

The Case of the Golddigger's Purse/Erle Stanley Gardner.—New York: The Armed Services, Inc., c1945

352 p.;10×15 cm.

I712.45/G226

The Case of The Lucky Legs/Erle Stanley Gardner.—[S. l.: s. n.], [?]

246 p.;16 cm.

I712.45/G226

The Case of the Lame Canary/Erle Starley Gardner.—New York: Pocket Books, Inc., c1937

189 p.;17 cm.

I712.45/G226C156

The D. A. Calls it Murder/Erle Stanley Gardner.—Philadelphia: The Blakiston Company, c1937

295 p. ;19 cm.

I712. 45/G226C337G618
The Case of the Golddigger's Purse/Erle Stanley Gardner. —New York: Armed Services, Inc. , c1945
1 v;21 cm.

I712. 45/G226D
The D. A. Goes to Trial/Erle Stanley Gardner. —Philadelphia: The Blakiston Company, c1940
283 p. ;19 cm.

I712. 45/G244
Bermuda Calling/David Garth. —New York: G. P. Putnam's Sons, c1944
197 p. ;19 cm.

I712. 45/G259
Aloma of the South Seas/Mac Burney Gates. —New York: Grosset & Dunlap Publishers, c1926
235 p. ;19 cm.

I712. 45/G347
Spin a Yarn Sailor/George G. Harrap & Co. , Ltd. ,—London: George G. Harrap & Co. , Ltd. , c1934
368 p. ;19 cm.

I712. 45/G464
The Case Against Andrew Fane/Anthony Gilbert. —New York: A. L. Burt Company, c1931
290 p. ;19 cm.

I712. 45/G464R758
The Romance of the Last Crusade with Allenby to Jerusalem/Major Vivian Gilbert. —New York: D. Appleton and Company, c1923
235 p. ;19 cm.

I712. 45/G481
The Ringed Horizon/Edmund Gilligan. —New York: Charles Scribner's Sons, c1943
299 p. ;20 cm.

I712. 45/G481G272
The Gaunt Woman/Edmund Gilligan. —New York: The Sun Dial Press, c1944
307 p. ;20 cm.

I712. 45/G481V975
Voyage of the Golden Hind/Edmund Gilligan. —New York: Charles Scribner's Sons, c1945
307 p. ;20 cm.

I712. 45/G489G588
Glencannon Afloat OR Golden Rule and Brass Knuckles on the S. S. Inchcliffe Castle/Guy Gilpatric. —New York: Dodd, Mead & Company, c1944
240 p. ;19 cm.

I712. 45/G489I24
Mr. Glencannon Ignores the War/Guy Gilpatric. —New York: E. P. Dutton & Company, Inc. , c1944
157 p. ;21 cm.

I712. 45/G539
All Cats are Gray/Charles G. Givens. —New York: The Bobbs-Merrill Company Publishers, c1937
358 p. ;21 cm.

I712. 45/G548
The Wheel of Life/Ellen Glasgow. —New York: Doubleday, Page & Company, c1906
747 p. ;21 cm.

I712. 45/G548(O)
In This Our Life/Ellen Glasgow. —New York: Harcourt, Brace and Company, c1941

467 p. ;21 cm.

I712.45/G549

Worrying Won't Win/Montague Glass. —New York: Harper & Brothers Publishers, c1918

229 p. ;19 cm.

I712.45/G571

The Tides of Malvern/Francis Griswold. —New York: Triangle Books, c1941

333 p. ;19 cm.

I712.45/G618

Murder Without Motive/Raymond Leslie Goldman. —New York: Crestwood Publishing Co., Inc., c1938

120 p. ;20 cm.

I712.45/G618F194

Fall Guy for Murder/Lawrence Goldman. —New York: Crestwood Publishing Co., Inc., c1943

128 p. ;19 cm.

I712.45/G619

Magnolia Street/Louis Golding. —New York: Grosset & Dunlap Publishers, c1932

526 p. ;20 cm.

I712.45/G619E54

Mr. Emmanuel/Louis Golding. —New York: The Literary Guild of America, Inc., c1939

444 p. ;21 cm.

I712.45/G619M198

Magnolia Street/Louis Golding. —New York: Grosset & Dunlap Publishers, c1932

607 p. ;20 cm.

I712.45/G621(O)

The Mountain and the Plain/Herbert Gorman. —New York: Farrat & Rinehart, c1936

653 p. ;22 cm.

I712.45/G653

Franklin Street/Philip Goodman. —New York: Alfred A. Knopf, c1942

277 p. ;22 cm.

I712.45/G653

The Fireside Book of Dog Stories/edited by Jack Goodman; with an introduction by James Thurber. —New York: Simon and Schuster, c1943.

xvi, 591 p. ;23 cm.

I712.45/G654

Delilah/Marcus Goodrich. —New York: Farrar & Rinehart, Inc., c1941

496 p. ;20 cm.

I712.45/G671

The Wine of San Lorenzo/Herbert Gorman. —New York: Farrar & Rinehart, Inc., c1945

472 p. ;21 cm.

I712.45/G738W581

Whitey: The Playboy of "Queer People" Runs Riot in Manhattan/Carroll Graham, Garrett Graham. —New York: Grosset & Dunlap, c1931

274 p. ;19 cm.

I712.45/G761L188

The Laird and the Lady/Joan Grant. —London: Methuen & Co., [?]

viii, 281 p. ;19 cm.

I712.45/G778B365

Beppy Marlowe of Charles Town/Elizabeth Janet Gray. —New York: The Viking Press, c1936

281 p. ;21 cm.

I712.45/G778F163

The Fair Adventure/Elizabeth Janet Gray. —New York: The Viking Press, c1948

248 p. ;20 cm.

I712. 45/G778S222

Sandy/Elizabeth Janet Gray. —New York: The Viking Press, c1947

233 p. ;21 cm.

I712. 45/G784F899

Adventures in Friendship/David Grayson. —New York: Grosset & Dunlap Publishers, c1910

232 p. ;19 cm.

I712. 45/G795D451

Desert Episode/George Greenfield. —New York: The Macmillan Company, c1945

130 p. ;21 cm.

I712. 45/G811

Not in Our Stars/Josiah E. Greene. —New York: The Macmillan Company, c1945

588 p. ;21 cm.

I712. 45/G842

The Young Lion Hunter/Zane Grey. —New York: Grosser & Dunlap Publishers, c1911

277 p. ;19 cm.

I712. 45/G842B565

Betty Zane/Zane Grey. —Akron: The Saalfield Publishing Company, [?]

252 p. ;20 cm.

I712. 45/G842D451

Desert Gold: A Romance of the Border/Zane Grey. —New York: Grosset & Dunlap Publishers, c1913

325 p. ;19 cm.

I712. 45/G842H344

The Hash Knife Outfit/Zane Grey. —New York: Grosset & Dunlap, c1933

323 p. ;19 cm.

I712. 45/G842H546

The Heritage of the Desert/Zane Grey. —New York: Grosset & Dunlap Publishers, c1910

297 p. ;19 cm.

I712. 45/G842K33

Ken Ward in the Jungle/Zane Grey. —New York: Grosset & Dunlap Publishers, c1912

308 p. ;19 cm.

I712. 45/G842L349

The Last Trail/Zabe Grey. —New York: Grosset & Dunlap Publishers, [?]

300 p. ;19 cm.

I712. 45/G842L723

The Light of Western Stars/Zane Grey. —New York: Grosset & Dunlap, c1942

376 p. ;19 cm.

I712. 45/G842M233

Majesty's Rancho/Zane Grey. —New York: Grosset & Dunlap Publishers, c1937, 1938

297 p. ;19 cm.

I712. 45/G842T535

Thunder Mountain/Zane Grey. —New York: Harper & Brothers Publishers, c1935

309 p. ;19 cm.

I712. 45/G842T766

The U. P. Trail/Zane Grey. —New York: Grosset & Dunlap Publishers, c1918

409 p. ;19 cm.

I712. 45/G842W

West of the Pecos/Zane Grey. —New York: Grosset & Dunlap, c1937

314 p. ;19 cm.

I712. 45/G976

Ships in the Sky: Compiled from Ussi Greipsson's Notes/Gunnar Gunnarsson. —New

York: The Boss-Merrill Company Publishers, [?]
387 p. ;20 cm.

I712. 45/G986
Air Base/Boone T. Guyton. —New York: Whittlesey House, c1941
xii, 295 p. ;21 cm.

I712. 45/H114
How about Tomorrow Morning? /Helen Haberman. —New York: Prentice-Hall, Inc. , c1945
264 p. ;21 cm.

I712. 45/H174
Salah and His American/Leland Hall. —New York: Alfred A. Knopf, c1935
199 p. ;19 cm.

I712. 45/H176
The Wagnerian Romances/Gertrude Hall. —New York: Alfred A. Knopf, c1925
x, 414 p. ;20 cm.

I712. 45/H177
Lost Island/James Norman Hall. —Boston: Little, Brown and Company, c1944
212 p. ;19 cm.

I712. 45/H196
Tomorrow Fair/Winifred Halsted. —New York: Dodd, Mead & Company, c1943
241 p. ;19 cm.

I712. 45/H224
The Thin Man/Dashiell Hammett. —London: Arthur Barker Ltd. , c1934
284 p. ;19 cm.

I712. 45/H245F899
My Friend Flicka/Mary O Hara. —Philadelphia: J. B. Lippincott Company, c1941
253 p. ;21 cm.

I712. 45/H251
Short Stories of Today/Charles Lane Hanson, William J. Gross. —Boston: Ginn and Company, c1928
xxiv, 392 p. ;17 cm.

I712. 45/H251S884
Stories of the Norsemen/Jean E. Hanson. —Dansville: F. A. Owen Publishing Company, c1905
1 v. ;18 cm.

I712. 45/H263
Lost Waltz: A Story of Exile/Bertita Harding. —New York: The Bobbs-Merrill Company, c1944
312 p. ;22 cm.

I712. 45/H268T216(O)
Tatoosh/Martha Hardy. —New York: The Macmillan Company, c1947
239 p. ;22 cm.

I712. 45/H297
Richard Pryne/Cyril Harri. —New York: Charles Scribner's Sons, c1942
viii, 414 p. ;21 cm.

I712. 45/H313
The Co-Citizens/Corra Harris. —New York: Doubleday, Page & Company, c1915
220 p. ;20 cm.

I712. 45/H313
Trumpets at Dawn/Cyril Harris. —New York: Charles Scribner's Sons, c1944
429 p. ;21 cm.

I712. 45/H318
Queed/Henry Sydor Harrison. —New York: Grosser & Dunlap Publishers, c1911

x, 430 p. ;19 cm.

I712. 45/H318C

Captivating Mary Carstairs/Harrison, Henry Sydonr. —New York: Grosset & Dunlap Publishers, c1911

viii, 346 p. ;20 cm.

I712. 45/H325S626

Mrs. Skaggs's Husbands/Bret Harte. —New York: P. F. Collier & Son, c1900

iv, 352 p. ;19 cm.

I712. 45/H354S559

Short Stories: A Collection of Types if tge Short Story/William Thomson Hastings. —Boston: Hougton Mifflin Company, c1929

402 p. ;21 cm.

I712. 45/H371

Letter from New Guinea/Vern Haugland. —New York: J. J. Little and Ives Company, c1943

148 p. ;19 cm.

I712. 45/H412

The Time is Noon/Hiram Haydn. —New York: Crown Publishers, c1948

561 p. ;21 cm.

I712. 45/H412

Canyon Passage/Ernest Haycox. —Boston: Little, Brown and Company, c1945

264 p. ;19 cm.

I712. 45/H412C212

Canyon Passage/Ernest Haycox. —Boston: Little, Brown and Company, c1945

352 p. ;10 cm.

I712. 45/H418

Who Walk with the Earth/Dorsha Hayes. —New York: Harper & Brothers Publishers, c1945

322 p. ;21 cm.

I712. 45/H432

The Smell to Money/Matthew Head. —Cleveland: The World Publishing Company, c1944

307 p. ;21 cm.

I712. 45/H457

My Ten Years in a Quandary and How They Grew/Brobert Benchley. —New York: Blue Ribbon Books, c1940

viii, 361 p. ;20 cm.

I712. 45/H473

John Payne and the Menace at Hawk's Nest/Kathyn Heisenfelt. —Racine: Whitman Publishing Company, c1943

248 p. ;20 cm.

I712. 45/H487(O)

The Sun Also Rises/Ernest Hemingway. —New York: The Modern Library, 1926

ix, 259 p. ;21 cm.

I712. 45/H487D278

Death in the Afternoon/Ernest Hemingway. —New York: Charles Scribner's Sons, c1932

517 p. ;23 cm.

I712. 45/H487W551

For Whom the Bell Tolls/Ernest Hemingway. —New York: Overseas Editions, Inc. , c1940

470 p. ;16 cm.

I712. 45/H496

The Painted Stallion: A Western Story/George C. Henderson. —New York: Chelsea House, c1930

247 p. ;19 cm.

I712. 45/H498

It Happened on Halfaday Creek/James B. Hendryx. —New York: Doubleday, Doran and

Co, Inc. , c1944
211 p. ;20 cm.

I712. 45/H52(O)
The Gentle Grafter/O. Henry. —New York: A. L. Burt Company, c1908
237 p. ;19 cm.

I712. 45/H521(O)
The Voice of the City: Further Stories of the Four Million/by O. Henry. —London: Hodder and Stoughton, [19-?].
248 p. ;20 cm.

I712. 45/H521
Cabbages and Kings/O. Henry. —London: Hodder and Stoughton Publishers, [?]
288 p. ;19 cm.

I712. 45/H545
Swords & Roses/Joseph Hergesheimer. —New York: Blue Ribbon Books, c1928, 1929
327 p. ;21 cm.

I712. 45/H545B186
Balisand/Joseph Hergesheimer. —New York: Alfred A. Knopf, c1924
371 p. ;19 cm.

I712. 45/H572
Into the Valley: A Skirmish of the Marines/John Hersey. —New York: Pocket Books Inc. , c1943
123 p. ;16 cm.

I712. 45/H572S847
Stevenson's Treasure Island/Frank Willson Cheney Hersey. —Boston: Ginn and Company, c1911
Lxxvi, 249 p. ;18 cm.

I712. 45/H576
The Horse and Buggy Doctor/Arthur E. Hertzler. —New York: Blue Ribbon Books, c1941
x, 322 p. ;20 cm.

I712. 45/H578
School for Eternity/Harry Hervey. —New York: G. P. Putnam's Sons, c1941
340 p. ;21 cm.

I712. 45/H582
The Seekers/Irwin M. Herzig. —New York: J. J. Little & Ives Company, c1925
365 p. ;19 cm.

I712. 45/H611
Those Were the Days: Tales of a long life/Edward Ringwood Hewitt. —New York: Duell, Sloan and Pearce, c1943
xiv, 318 p. ;21 cm.

I712. 45/H615
The Wrath of the Eagles/Frederick Heydenau. —New York: E. P. Dutton & Co. , Inc. , c1943
318 p. ;19 cm.

I712. 45/H616H831
Hostages/Stefan Heym. —New York: G. P. Putnam's Sons, c1942
362 p. ;21 cm.

I712. 45/H681C974
The Cup and the Sword/Alice Tisdale Hobart. —New York: The Bobbs-Merrill Company, c1942
400 p. ;21 cm.

I712. 45/H681P356
The Peacock Sheds His Tall/Alice Tisdale Hobart. —New York: The Bobbs-Merrill Company, c1945
360 p. ;20 cm.

I712. 45/H684G337

Gentleman's Agreement/Laura Z. Hobson. —New York: Simon and Schuster, c1947

275 p. ;21 cm.

I712. 45/H713

The Turning of the Road/Agnes Horsch Hofmaster. —Techny: Mission Press, c1930

180 p. ;19 cm.

I712. 45/H738S187

Samantha in Europe/Marietta Holley. —New York: Funk and Wagnalls Company, c1895

xv, 714 p. ;20 cm.

I712. 45/H747

Sunday Best: The Story of a Philadelphia Family/John Cecil Holm. —New York: Farrar & Rinehart, Inc. , c1943

279 p. ;21 cm.

I712. 45/H747F

The Fleet's in ! /Russell Holman. —New York: Grosset & Dunlap Publishers, c1928

ix, 278 p. ;19 cm.

I712. 45/H749(O)

The Victor/Richard S. Holmes. —New York: Fleming H. Revell Company, c1908

320 p. ;20 cm.

I712. 45/H838C236

Captain Retread/Donald Hough. —New York: W. W. Norton & Company, c1944

218 p. ;21 cm.

I712. 45/H838S674

Snow Above Town/Donald Hough. —New York: W. W. Norton & Company, Inc. , c1943

287 p. ;10×14 cm.

I712. 45/H842

Rogue Male/Geoffrey Household. —Boston: Little, Brown and Company, c1945

280 p. ;20 cm.

I712. 45/H848R142

Ragged Robin/Warren Howard. —New York: Arcadla House Publications, c1937

280 p. ;19 cm.

I712. 45/H868(O)

Bright Intervals/Nancy Hoyt. —New York: Alfred A. Knopf, c1929

246 p. ;20 cm.

I712. 45/H885O61

Open Fire! /Alec Hudson. —New York: The Macmillan Company, c1944

1 v. ;21 cm.

I712. 45/H893

She Goes to War and Other Stories/Rupert Hughes. —New York: Grosset & Dunlap, c1929

303 p. ;19 cm.

I712. 45/H893J65

Johnnie/Dorothy B. Hughes. —New York: Duell, Sloan and Pearce, c1944

219 p. ;19 cm.

I712. 45/H913

Last First/Richard Hull. —London: The Crime Club, c1947

192 p. ;19 cm.

I712. 45/H925

Joshua Moore American/George F. Hummel. —New York: Doubleday, Daran & Company, Inc. , c1943

456 p. ;20 cm.

I712. 45/H939F198

Family Affair/Mary Fassett Hunt. —New York: Harper & Brother Publishers, c1948

280 p. ;21 cm.

I712.45/H959M281
Mannequin/Fannie Hurst. —New York: Grosset & Dunlap Publishers, c1926
297 p. ;19 cm.

I712.45/H965
Men in Sun Helmets/Vic Hurley. —[S. l.]: E. P. Dutton & Co., Inc., [?]
252 p. ;21 cm.

I712.45/H975
The Fire and the Wood: A Love Story/R. C. Hutchinson. —New York: The Litterary Guild of America, Inc., c1940
440 p. ;21 cm.

I712.45/I65
The Making of a Reporter/Will Irwin. —New York: G. P. Putnam's Sons, c1942
440 p. ;23 cm.

I712.45/J12
The Lost Weekend/Charles Jackson. —London: John Land the Bodley Head, c1945
254 p. ;19 cm.

I712.45/J12O93
The Outer Edges/Charles Jackson. —New York: Rinehart and Company, c1948
240 p. ;21 cm.

I712.45/J27
Smoky: The Cow Horse/Will James. —[S. l.: s. n.], [?]
x, 263 p. ;23 cm.

I712.45/J27
Smoky/Will • James. —New York: Charles Scribner's Sons, [?]
x, 263 p. ;24 cm.

I712.45/J27C874
Cowboys North and South/Will James. —New York: Charles Scribner's Sons, c1943
xvii, 217 p. ;21 cm.

I712.45/J27G118
Gabrielle de Bergerac/Henry James. —New York: Boni and Liveright, c1918
153 p. ;19 cm.

I712.45/J27M423
Master Eustace/Henry James. —New York: Thomas Seltzer, c1920
280 p. ;19 cm.

I712.45/J27S693
Smoky: The Cowhorse/Will James. —New York: Charles Scribner's Sons, c1926
x, 308 p. ;19 cm.

I712.45/J28
The Short Stories of Henry James/Henry James. —New York: Random House, c1945
xx, 640 p. ;20 cm.

I712.45/J54
The Salem Frigate/John Jennings. —New York: Doubleday & Company, c1946
ix, 500 p. ;21 cm.

I712.45/J54C156
Call the New World/John Jennings. —New York: The Macmillan Company, c1941
xii, 459 p. ;22 cm.

I712.45/J58
The Best American Humorous Short Stories/Alexander Jessup. —New York: The Modern Library, [?]
xxx, 276 p. ;18 cm.

I712.45/J65
In the Mane of Liberty: A Story of the Ter-

ror/Owen Johnson. —New York: The Century Co. , c1905
viii, 406 p. ;20 cm.

I712. 45/J65G284
The Gay-Dombeys/Harry Johnston. —New York: The Macmillan Company, c1919
xii, 397 p. ;19 cm.

I712. 45/J72
The Little Colonel's Holidays/Annie Fellows Johnston. —Boston: L. C. Page & Company, c1904
232, 7 p. ;20 cm.

I712. 45/J724W819
The Witch/Mary Johnston. —London: Constable and Company Ltd. , c1914
vi, 402 p. ;19 cm.

I712. 45/J76
Still to The West/Nard Jones. —New York: Dodd, Mead & Company, c1946
268 p. ;20 cm.

I712. 45/K11
Eagle at My Eyes/Norman Katkov. —New York: Doubleday & Co. , Inc. , c1948
252 p. ;20 cm.

I712. 45/K16A771
Arouse and Beware /Mackinlay Kantor. —New York: Coward-Mccann, Inc. , c1936
332 p. ;21 cm.

I712. 45/K16V897
The Voice of Bugle Ann/Mackinlay Kantor. —New York: Coward-Mccann, Inc. , c1935
128 p. ;19 cm.

I712. 45/K18
Zotz! /Walter Karig. —New York: Rinehart & Company, Inc. , c1947
xiv, 268 p. ;21 cm.

I712. 45/K18S
Story of A Secret State/Jan Karski. —Boston: Houghton Mifflin Company, c1944
391 p. ;20 cm.

I712. 45/K23
Tambourine Trumpet and Drum/Sheila Kaye-Smith. —New York: Harper & Brothers Publishers, c1943
356 p. ;21 cm.

I712. 45/K26
Nancy Drew Mystery Stories: The Clue of the Broken Locket/Carolyn Keene. —New York: Grosset & Dunlap Publishers, c1934
iv, 219 p. ;19 cm.

I712. 45/K26C649
The Clue in the Diary/Carolyn Keene. —New York: Grosset & Dunlap Pulishers, c1932
iv, 202 p. ;19 cm.

I712. 45/K26M995
The Mystery at the Moss-Covered Mansion/Carolyn Keene. —New York: Crosset & Dunlap Publishers, c1941
v, 215 p. ;19 cm.

I712. 45/K26O44
The Secret of the Old Clock: Nancy Drew Mystery Stories/Carolyn Keene. —New York: Grosset & Dunlap, c1930
iv, 210 p. ;19 cm.

I712. 45/K26R312
The Secret of Red Gate Farm: Nancy Drew Mystery Stories/Carolyn Keene. —New York: Grosset & Dunlap Publishers, c1931
iv, 208 p. ;19 cm.

I712.45/K26S446

The Secret in the Old Attic/Carolyn Keene. —New York: Grosser & Dunlap Publishiers, c1944

216 p. ;19 cm.

I712.45/K26T651

The Mystery of the Tolling Bell/Carolyn Keene. —New York: Grosset & Dunlap Publishers, c1946

213 p. ;19 cm.

I712.45/K28

Three Came Home/Agnes Newton. Keith. —Boston: Little, Brown and Company, c1947

316 p. ;21 cm.

I712.45/K29

Whisper Murder/Vera Kelsey. —New York: Doubleday & Company, Inc., c1946

255 p. ;20 cm.

I712.45/K29-6

Alias Jane Smith/Clarence Budington Kelland. —New York: Harper & Brothers Publishers, c1944

248 p. ;21 cm.

I712.45/K29S277

Scattergood Baines Pulls the Strings/Clarence Budington Kelland. —New York: Harper & Brothers Publishers, c1939

ix, 305 p. ;19 cm.

I712.45/K44

Crescent Carnival/Frances Parkinson Keyes. —New York: Julian Messner, Inc., c1942

xvii, 807 p. ;21 cm.

I712.45/K44C181

Came a Cavalier/Frances Parkinson Keyes. —New York: Julian Messner, Inc., c1947

xxvi, 576 p. ;21 cm.

I712.45/K44R621

The River Road/Frances Parkinson Keyes. —New York: Julian Messner, Inc., c1945

xvi, 747 p. ;21 cm.

I712.45/K49W361

We Followed our Heart to Hollywood/Emily Kimbrough. —New York: Dodd, Mead & Company, c1943

210 p. ;21 cm.

I712.45/K52

Vine of Glory/Mary Jackson King. —New York: The Bobbs-Merrill Company, c1948

357 p. ;21 cm.

I712.45/K57(O)

Puck of Pook's Hill/Rudyard Kipling. —New York, New York: Doubleday & Company, Inc., c1906

253 p. ;21 cm.

I712.45/K59

Winds, Blow Gently/Ronald Kirkbride. —New York: H. Wolff, c1945

313 p. ;21 cm.

I712.45/K63

Men of Marknoll/James Keller, Meyer Berger. —New York: Charles Scrobner's Sons, c1944

191 p. ;21 cm.

I712.45/K65

The Deep/Kaj Klitgaard. —New York: Doubleday, Doran & Co., Inc., c1941

363 p. ;21 cm.

I712.45/K69

Lassie Come-Home/Eric Knight. —Philadellphia: The John C. Winston Company, c1940

248 p. ;22 cm.

I712. 45/K69C

Dr. Christian's Office/Ruth Adames Knight, Jean Hersholt. —New York: Random House, c1944

243 p. ;22 cm.

I712. 45/K69F

Footbridge to Death/Kathleen Moore Knight. —New York: Doubleday & Company, Inc. , c1947

256 p. ;20 cm.

I712. 45/K69T859

The Trouble at Turkey Hill/Kathleen Moore Knight. —New York: Doubleday & Company, Inc. , c1946

219 p. ;20 cm.

I712. 45/K75(2)

Coronet. vol. 2/Manuel Komroff. —New York: Coward-Mccann, Inc. , c1929

349-677 p. ;19 cm.

I712. 45/K91T777

The Thresher/Herbert Krause. —New York: The Bobbs-Merrill Company Publishes, c1946

489 p. ;21 cm.

I712. 45/K92L848

On the Long Tide/Laura Krey. —Boston: Houghton Mifflin Company, c1940

642 p. ;20 cm.

I712. 45/K92T273

And Tell of Time/Laura Krey. —Boston: Houghton Mifflin Company, c1938

712 p. ;21 cm.

I712. 45/K95D219

Darkness of Slumber/Rosemary Kutak. —Philadelphia: J. B. Lippincott Company, c1944

218 p. ;20 cm.

I712. 45/K99

Cappy Ricks Comes Back/Peter B. Kyne. —London: Hodder and Stoughton, c1934

310 p. ;19 cm.

I712. 45/L137S559

If I Should Murder/Patrick Laing. —New York: Phoenix Press, c1945

256 p. ;18 cm.

I712. 45/L187

Before the Wind/Janet Laing. —New York: E. P. Dutton & Company, c1918

viii, 352 p. ;19 cm.

I712. 45/L221

Crag's Foot Farm: A Novel of Leicestershire/Marjory E. Lambe. —[?]: Chapman & Hall Ltd. , c1931

277 p. ;18 cm.

I712. 45/L244

Grand Parade/G. B. Lancaster. —New York: Reynal & Hitchcock, Inc. , c1943

377 p. ;21 cm.

I712. 45/L259

Never Dies the Dream/Margaret Landon. —London: Beinhardt & Evans, c1949

317 p. ;20 cm.

I712. 45/L265

The Fleet in the Forest/Carl D. Lane. —New York: Coward-Mccann, Inc. , c1943

369 p. ;21 cm.

I712. 45/L283

A Lion is in the Streets/Adria Locke Langley. . —Philadelphia: The Blakiston Company, 1945

345 p. ;21 cm.

I712.45/L321

The Collected Short Stories of Ring Lardner/Ring W. Lardner. —New York：The Modern Library，c1929

viii，467 p.；c19 cm.

I712.45/L346

Suds in Your Eye/Mary Lasswell. —Boston：Houghton Mifflin Company，c1945

219 p.；18 cm.

I712.45/L346H

High Time/Mary Lasswell；with frontispiece by George Price. —Boston：Houghton Mifflin，c1944.

174 p.；19 cm.

I712.45/L372

The House in Clewe Street/Mary Lavin. —Boston：Little，Brown and Company，c1944

530 p.；21 cm.

I712.45/L372D

Dark Medallion/Dorothy Langley. —New York：Simon and Schuster，c1945

225 p.；21 cm.

I712.45/L372H842

The House in Clewe Street/Mary Lavin. —London：Penguin Books，c1949

499 p.；18 cm.

I712.45/L389

Heralds of Empire：Being the Story of one Ramsay Stanhope/A. C. Laut. —New York：D. Appleton and Company，c1902

viii，372 p.；19 cm.

I712.45/L419B655

Blood upon the Snow/Hilda Lawrence. —New York：Simon and Schuster，c1944

312 p.；20 cm.

I712.45/L425

Thirty Seconds Over Tokyo/Captain Ted W. Lawson. —New York：Random House，c1943

221 p.；19 cm.

I712.45/L477

The Mysterious Office/Jennette Lee. —New York：Grosset & Dunlap Publishers，c1922

278 p.；19 cm.

I712.45/L477A178

Mr. Achilles /Jennette Lee. —New York：Dodd，Mead and Company，c1912

261 p.；18 cm.

I712.45/L523

The Ballad and the Source/Rosamond Lehmann. —New York：Reynal & Hitchcock，c1945

312 p.；19 cm.

I712.45/L643L983

Lydia Bailey/Kenneth Roberts. —1st ed.. —New York，N. Y.：Doubleday，c1947.

499 p.；22 cm.

I712.45/L673

Breathe upon These/Ludwig Lewisohn. —New York：The Bobbs-Merrill Company，c1944

217 p.；20 cm.

I712.45/L673S425

Scoot's Ivanhoe/W. D. Lews. —Boston：Ginn Company，c1906

xx，536 p.；19 cm.

I712.45/L676

The Man Who Knew Coolidge/Sinclair Lewis. —New York：Harcourt，Brace and Company，c1928

275 p.；20 cm.

I712. 45/L676A613

Ann Vickers/Sinclair Lewis. —London: Jonathan Cape Ltd. , c1933

460 p. ;20 cm.

I712. 45/L676A779

Arrowsmith/Sinclair Lewis. —New York: Grosset & Dunlap Publishers, c1925

448 p. ;21 cm.

I712. 45/L676C

Cass Timberlane: A Novel of Husbands and Wives/Sinclair Lewis. —New York: Random House, c1945

390 p. ;20 cm.

I712. 45/L676E48

Elmer Gantry/Sinclair Lewis. —New York: Harcourt, Brace and Company, c1927

432 p. ;19 cm.

I712. 45/L676G453

Gideon Planish/Sinclair Lewis. —Cleveland: The World Publishing Company, c1943

304 p. ;21 cm.

I712. 45/L676H111

It Can't Happen Here/Sinclair Lewis. —New York: Doubleday, Doran & Company, Inc. , c1935

458 p. ;20 cm.

I712. 45/L676K52

Kingsblood Royal/Sinclair Lewis. —New York: Random House, c1947

348 p. ;21 cm.

I712. 45/L736

The Portygee: A Novel/Joseph C. Lincoln. —New York: D. Appleton and Company, c1920

361 p. ;19 cm.

I712. 45/L736B

The Bradshaws of Harniss/Josephy C. Lincoln. —New York: D. Appleton-Century Company, c1943

379 p. ;20 cm.

I712. 45/L736P273-2

Partners of the Tide/Joseph C. Lincoln. —2nd ed. . —London: Hodder and Stoughton, c1905

400 p. ;19 cm.

I712. 45/L736S

"Shavings": A Novel/Joseph C. Lincoln. —New York: Grosset and Dunlap, c1918

382 p. ;20 cm.

I712. 45/L738

Cap'n Eri: A Story of the Coast/Joseph C. Lincoln. —New York: D. Appleton-Century Company, c1942

viii, 397 p. ;19 cm.

I712. 45/L738B592

The Big Mogul/Joseph C. Lincoln. —New York: A. L. Burt Company Publishers, c1926

386 p. ;19 cm.

I712. 45/L738B635

Blair's Attic/Joseph C. Lincoln, Freeman Lincoln. —New York: Coward-Mccann, Inc. , c1929

369 p. ;19 cm.

I712. 45/L738H174

A. Hall & Co. , /Joseph C. Lincoln. —New York: Grosset & Dunlap Publishers, c1938

326 p. ;20 cm.

I712. 45/L738O93

Out of the Fog/Joseph C. Lincoln. —New York: Grosset & Dunlap Publishers, c1940

360 p. ;19 cm.

I712.45/L775

There Was a Lady/Sarah Litsey. —New York: The Bobbs-Merrill Company Publishers, c1945

253 p. ;21 cm.

I712.45/L813

Hanged for A Sheep: A Mr. and Mrs. North Mystery/Frances Lockridge, Richard Lockridge. —New York: Grosset & Dunlap, c1942

301 p. ;20 cm.

I712.45/L813

I Want to Go Home: A Captain Heimrich Mystery/Richard Lockridge, Frances Lockridge. —Philadelphia: J. B. Lippincott Company, c1948

249 p. ;19 cm.

I712.45/L813R154

Raintree County: ... which had no boundaries in time and space, where lurked musical and strange names and mythical and lost peoples, and which was itself only a name musical and strange/Ross Lockridge. —Boston: Houghton Mifflin Co. , 1948.

xiv, 1066 p. ;22 cm.

I712.45/L814

The Tale of Triona/William J. Locke. —New York: Dodd, Mead and Company, c1922

397 p. ;19 cm.

I712.45/L829

The Golden Fleece/Norah Lofts. —New York: Alfred A. Knopf, Inc. , c1943

249 p. ;20 cm.

I712.45/L829

Jassy/Norah Lofts. —New York: Alfred A. Knopf, c1945

277 p. ;20 cm.

I712.45/L848

Short Shrift/Manning Long. —New York: Duell, Sloan an Pearce, c1945

214p. ;20 cm.

I712.45/L897

No One's Kindness/George Loveridge. —New York: D. Appleton-Cntury Company, c1945

273 p. ;20 cm.

I712.45/L913F252

Father and Glorious Descendant/Pardee Lowe. —Boston: Little, Brown and Company, c1943

322 p. ;21 cm.

I712.45/L913S181

Salute to Freedom/Eric Lowe. —New York: Reynal & Hitchcock, c1938

615 p. ;20 cm.

I712.45/L962

Robbery at Portage Bend/T. Lund. —New York: Claude Kendall, c1933

252 p. ;21 cm.

I712.45/LE57S635

The Small Rain/Madeleine L'Engle. —New York: The Vanguard Press, c1945

371 p. ;19 cm.

I712.45/LW673

Suns Go Down/Flannery Lewis. —New York: The Macmillan Copany, c1937

226 p. ;21 cm.

I712.45/M113(O)

The Voyage/Xharles Morgan. —New York: The Macmillan Company, c1940

508 p. ;22 cm.

I712.45/M114

The Square Circle/Denis Mackall. —Boston:

Houghton Mifflin Companu, c1931
478 p. ;21 cm.

I712. 45/M115
The Uninvited/Dorothy Macardle. —New York: The Sun Dial Press, c1942
viii, 342 p. ;20 cm.

I712. 45/M135(O)
The Egg and I/Betty Macdonald. —New York: J. B. Lippincott Company, c1945
287 p. ;21 cm.

I712. 45/M153
Like Water Flowing/Margaret Mackrang Mackay. —New York: Reynal & Hitchcock, c1938
346 p. ;21 cm.

I712. 45/M252M687
The Mocking Bird is Singing/E. Louise Mally. —New York: Henry Holt and Company, c1944
394 p. ;21 cm.

I712. 45/M281
Stampede/E. B. Mann. —Philadelphia: The Blakiston Company, c1934
299 p. ;19 cm.

I712. 45/M281B658
The Blue-Eyed Kid/E. B. Mann. —Philadelphia: The Blakiston Company, c1932
306 p. ;19 cm.

I712. 45/M283
A Life's Labyrinth/Mary E. Mannix. —Notre Dame: The Ave Maria Press, c1924
252 p. ;19 cm.

I712. 45/M357
So Little Time/John P. Marquand. —Boston: Little, Brown and Company, c1943
594 p. ;21 cm.

I712. 45/M357
The Cruise of the Jasper B. /Don Marquis. —New York: D. Appleton and Company, c1916
319 p. ;19 cm.

I712. 45/M357
The Late George Apley: A Novel in the from of A Memoir/John P. Marquand. —New York: The Modern Library, c1940
vi, 354 p. ;18 cm.

I712. 45/M357
Don't Ask Questions/John P. Marquand. —Sydney: The British Publishers Guild, c1944
186 p. ;18 cm.

I712. 45/M357D235
B. F. 's Daughter/John P. Marquand. —Toronto: Mcclelland and Stewart Ltd. , c1946
439 p. ;20 cm.

I712. 45/M379
The Hills of Home/Curtis Martin. —New York: Literary Classics, Inc. , c1943
185 p. ;19 cm.

I712. 45/M379
Randy Starr After an Air Prize/Eugene Martin. —New York: The Saalfield, c1931
212 p. ;19 cm.

I712. 45/M398
The Hongkong Airbase Murders/Van Wyck Mason. —New York: Grosset & Dunlap, c1937
339 p. ;19 cm.

I712. 45/M398S795
Stars on the Sea/F. van Wyck Mason. —New York: Grosset & Dunlap Publishers, c1940
720 p. ;21 cm.

I712. 45/M447

Up Front/Bill Mauldin. —New York: Henry Holt and Company, c1944

228 p. ;23 cm.

I712. 45/M447B126

Back Home/Bill Mauldin. —New York: William Sloane Associates Publishers, c1947

315 p. ;22 cm.

I712. 45/M454

The Old Fellow/Herrymon Maurer. —New York: The John Day Company, c1943

viii, 296 p. ;21 cm.

I712. 45/M465

The Folded Leaf/William Maxwell. —New York: The Armed Services, Inc. , c1945

383 p. ;10 cm.

I712. 45/M479

Year of the Wild Boar: An American Woman in Japan/Helen Mears. —Philadelphia: J. B. Lippincott Company, c1942

343 p. ;21 cm.

I712. 45/M494

Rusty: A Cocker Spaniel/S. P. Meek. —New York: Alfred A. Knopf, Inc. , c1947

296 p. ;19 cm.

I712. 45/M552D538

Diana of The Crossways/George Meredith. —New York: Boni and Liberght, Inc. , c1917

xiv, 365 p. ;17 cm.

I712. 45/M623

In the Bishop's Carriage/Miriam Michelson. —New York: Crosset & Dunlap Publishers, c1903

280 p. ;20 cm.

I712. 45/M645

Thanks, Angel/Cynthia Millburn. —New York: Gramercy Publishing Co. , c1945

254 p. ;19 cm.

I712. 45/M645F523

Fire Will Freeze/Margaret Millar. —New York: The World Publishing Company, c1944

225 p. ;21 cm.

I712. 45/M645F532R192

Fire Will Freeze/Margaret Millar. —New York: Random House, [?]

225 p. ;19 cm.

I712. 45/M647L441

Lebanon/Caroline Miller. —New York: Doubleday, Doran and Company, Inc. , c1944

234 p. ;20 cm.

I712. 45/M649

First the Blade/May Merrill Miller. —New York: Alfred A. Knopf, c1942

631 p. ;21 cm.

I712. 45/M678

November Night/Miss Tiverton Goes Out. —New York: The Bobbs-Merrill Company Publishers, c1928

325 p. ;19 cm.

I712. 45/M681

Decline and Fall of a British Matron: A Caustic Comedy/Mary Mitchell. —London: William Heinemann Ltd. , c1937

310 p. ;19 cm.

I712. 45/M681

Hugh Wynne: Free Quaker Sometime Brevet Lieutenant-Colonel on the Staff of His Excellency General Washington/S. Weir Mitchell. —New York: D. Appleton-Century Company, c1924

xxxvii, 567 p. ;19 cm.

I712.45/M682V811

Viper's Progress/Mary Mitchell.—London: Methuen & Co., Ltd., c1939

342 p.;19 cm.

I712.45/M717

The Careless Hangman: A Mrs. Pym Story/Nigel Morland.—New York: Farrar & Rinehart, c1941

xi, 294, 5 p.;20 cm.

I712.45/M727

Pride's Way/Robert Molloy.—New York: The Macmillan Company, c1945

355 p.;21 cm.

I712.45/M821S764

Spoonhandle/Ruth Moore.—London: Rich & Cowan, [?]

302 p.;19 cm.

I712.45/M847

Man of Two Worlds: The Novel of a Stranger/Ainsworth Morgan.—New York: Grosset & Dunlap Publishers, c1933

317 p.;19 cm.

I712.45/M872L645

Let the King Beware! /Honore Morrow.—New York: William Morrow and Company, c1936

376 p.;21 cm.

I712.45/M875L695

Liberty Street/I. V. Morris.—New York: Harper & Brothers Publishers, c1944

277 p.;21 cm.

I712.45/M889

The Edged Tool: An Adventure Story/William Morton.—New York: Chelsea House Publishers, c1927.

253 p.;19 cm.

I712.45/M919

Knock on Any Door/Willard Motley.—New York: D. Appleton-Century Company, Inc., c1947

503 p.;21 cm.

I712.45/M955

Black Buttes/Clarence E. Mulford.—New York: Doubleday, Page & Company, c1923

318 p.;19 cm.

I712.45/M955B223

The Bar 20 Rides Again/Clarence E. Mulford.—Philadelphia: The Blakiston Company, c1944

337 p.;19 cm.

I712.45/M955H791

Hopalong Cassidy Takes Cards/Glarence E. Mulford.—New York: Tricngle Books, c1937

269 p.;19 cm.

I712.45/M965(O)

The Winds of the World/Talbot Mundy.—New York: McKinlay, Stone & Mackenzie, c1917

330 p.;18 cm.

I712.45/M965I(O)

The Ivory Trail/Talbot Mundy.—New York: Mckinlay, Stone & Mackenzie, c1919

411 p.;19 cm.

I712.45/M965T398

There Was a Door/Talbot Mundy.—London: Hutchinson & Co., (Publisher)Ltd., [?]

287 p.;19 cm.

I712.45/M978

The Glittering Hill/Clyde F. Murphy.—New York: E. P. Dutton & Co., Inc., c1944

478 p.;20 cm.

I712. 45/M978S

The Scarlet Lily/Edward F. Murphy. —Milwaukee: The Bruce Publishing Company, c1944
239 p. ;20 cm.

I712. 45/MacD675

The Rasp/Philip MacDonald. —New York: Charles Scribner's Sons, c1929
278 p. ;19 cm.

I712. 45/MacD675C

Company Commander/Charles B. MacDonald. —Washington: Infantry Journal Press, c1947
ix, 278 p. ;23 cm.

I712. 45/MacD765S

Sleepy Hores Range/William Colt MacDonald. —Cleveland: The World Publishing Company, c1944
315 p. ;21 cm.

I712. 45/Macm981

Out on A Limbo/Claire Macmurray. —Philadelphia: I. B. Lippincott Company, c1944
191 p. ;21 cm.

I712. 45/MacR134

Dwight Craig/Donals MacRae. —Boston: Houghton Mifflin Company, c1947
398 p. ;21 cm.

I712. 45/McC947

Red Plush: the Story of the Moorhouse Family/Guy Mccrone. —New York: Farrar, Straus and Company, c1947
221 p. ;21 cm.

I712. 45/McC967

The Mark of Zorro/Johnston Mcculley. —New York: Grosset & Dunlap Publishers, c1924
viii, 300 p. ;20 cm.

I712. 45/McC988

The Merivales/George Barr Mccutcheon. —New York: Dodd, Mead & Company, c1929
303 p. ;19 cm.

I712. 45/McF295

Ship to Shore/William McFee. —New York: Random House, c1944
407 p. ;21 cm.

I712. 45/McK34

My Sister Eileen/Ruth Mckenney. —New York: Harcourt, Brace and Company, c1938
xiii, 226 p. ;2 cm.

I712. 45/McM494

Welcome Soldier/Clark Mcmeekin. —New York: D. Appleton-Century Company, c1942
335 p. ;21 cm.

I712. 45/McN399

Bull-dog Drummond's third Round/H. C. McNeile. —New York: Grosset & Dunlap Publishers, c1923
294 p. ;19 cm.

I712. 45/McN411

Heaven is too High/Mildred Masterson McNeilly. —New York: The Hampton Publishing Co. , c1944
432 p. ;21 cm.

I712. 45/MK494

Frog, The Horse That Knew no Master/Colonel S. P. Meek. —New York: Alfred A. Knopf, c1948
302 p. ;19 cm.

I712. 45/N155

Watch out for Willie Carter/Theodore Naidish. —New York: Charils Scribner's Sons, c1944
248 p. ;19 cm.

I712. 45/N274O58

One More Spring/Robert Nathan. —New York: Bantam Books, c1945

128 p. ;17 cm.

I712. 45/N411

Miss Princess/Esther W. Neill. —Notre Dame: The Ave Maria, c1929

268 p. ;19 cm.

I712. 45/N489N946

Now That April's There/Daisy Neumann. —New York: J. B. Lippincott Company, c1944

244 p. ;19 cm.

I712. 45/N684

Step Down, Elder Brother/Josephina Niggli. —New York: Rinehart and Company, Inc. , c1947

viii, 374 p. ;21 cm.

I712. 45/N818L778

The Hurricane/Charles Nordhoff, James Norman Hall. —Boston: Little, Brown, and Company, c1944

257 p. ;21 cm.

I712. 45/N828

Pitcairn's Island/Charles Nordhoff, James Norman Hall. —Boston: Little, Brown, and Company, c1935

viii, 333 p. ;21 cm.

I712. 45/N828

The Hurricane/Charles Nordhoff, James Norman Hall. —New York: The Sun Dial Press, c1941

257 p. ;19 cm.

I712. 45/N853B371

Beauty's Daughter/Kathleen Norris. —Philadelphia: The Bladiston Company, c1934, 1935

354 p. ;19 cm.

I712. 45/N853B371D755

Baker's Dozen/Kathleen Norris. —New York: The Sun Dial Press, c1942

307 p. ;19 cm.

I712. 45/N854

Hands/Charles G. Norris. —New York: Farrar & Rinehart, c1935

546 p. ;21 cm.

I712. 45/N864S

So Dear to My Heart/Sterling North. —New York: Doubleday & Co. , Inc. , c1947

255 p. ;21 cm.

I712. 45/O, H254

Appointment in Samarra/John O'Hara. —London: Faber & Faber Ltd. , [?]

300 p. ;19 cm.

I712. 45/O13

Valiant Dog of the Timberline/Jack O'Brien. —Philadelphia: The John C. Winston Company, c1935

218 p. ;22 cm.

I712. 45/O162

The Olympian: A Story of the City/James Oppenheim. —New York: Harper & Brothers Publishers, c1912

417 p. ;19 cm.

I712. 45/O36

Thunderhead/Mary O'hara. —Philadelphia: J. B. Lippincott Company, c1943

320 p. ;20 cm.

I712. 45/O36G

The Golden Wind/Takashi Ohta, Margaret Sperry. —New York: Charles Boni Paper Books, c1929

269 p. ;18 cm.

I712. 45/O48

Politics and Politicians/F. S. Oliver. —London: Macmillan and Co. , Ltd. , c1934

ix, 93 p. ;19 cm.

I712. 45/O62

Matorni's Vineyard/E. Phillips Oppenheim. —New York: A. L. Burt Company Publishers, c1928

308 p. ;19 cm.

I712. 45/O62A479

The Amazing Quest of Mr. Ernest Bliss/E. Phillips Oppenheim. —London: Hodder and Stoughton Ltd. , c1919

316 p. ;19 cm.

I712. 45/O62B598

Mr. Billingham, The Marquis and Madelon/E. Phillips Oppenheim. —Boston: Little, Brown, and Company, c1929

283 p. ;19 cm.

I712. 45/O62F745

The Fortunate Wayfarer/E. Phillips Oppenheim. —New York: A. L. Burt Company Publishers, c1928

352 p. ;19 cm.

I712. 45/O62G786

The Great Impersonation/E. Phillips Oppenheim. —London: Hodder and Stoughton Publieshers, [?]

318 p. ;18 cm.

I712. 45/O62P954

The Great Prince Shan/E. Phillips Oppenheim. —Boston: Little, Brown, and Company, c1922

303 p. ;19 cm.

I712. 45/O62S732

The Spy Paramount/E. Phillips Oppenheim. —London: Hodder and Stoughton Ltd. , c1935

312 p. ;20 cm.

I712. 45/O62S894

The Strange Boarders of Palace Crescent/E. Phillips Oppenheim. —London: Hodder and Stoughton, c1935

313 p. ;20 cm.

I712. 45/O84

Beasts, Men and Gods/Ferdinand Ossendowski. —New York: E. P. Dutton & Company, c1922

xii, 325 p. ;21 cm.

I712. 45/O85W329

The Waters Under the Earth/Martha Ostern-so. —New York: Dodd, Mead & Company, c1930

319 p. ;19 cm.

I712. 45/OC515

The G-Man's Son/Edward O'Connor. —Chicago: The Goldsmith Publishing Company, c1936

249 p. ;19 cm.

I712. 45/OH254

Green Grass of Wyoming/Mary O'Hara. —New York: J. B. Lippincott Company, c1946

319 p. ;21 cm.

I712. 45/P132

The Tree of Liberty/Elizabeth Page. —New York: Farrar & Rinehart, Inc. , c1939

xii, 985 p. ;22 cm.

I712. 45/P191

We Ride a White Donkey/George Panetta. —New York: Harcourt, Brace and Company, c1944

186 p. ;19 cm.

I712.45/P213

Anything Can Happen/George Papashvily, Helen Waite Papashvily. —New York: Harper and Brothers Publishers, 1945

202 p. ;19 cm.

I712.45/P238

After Such Pleasures/Dorothy Parker. —New York: The Sun Dial Press, 1933.

232 p. ;21 cm.

I712.45/P238C697

The Collected Stories of Dorothy Parker/Dorothy Parker. —New York: The Modern Library, c1930

viii, 362 p. ;19 cm.

I712.45/P261W848

Wolves of the Sea: Being a Tale of the Colonies/Randall Parrish. —London: Jarrolds, [?]

316 p. ;19 cm.

I712.45/P275

Excuse My Dust/Bellamy Partridge. —New York: Whittlesey House, c1943

xiii, 359 p. ;22 cm.

I712.45/P288S438

Sea Level/Anne Parrish. —New York: Harper & Brothers, c1934

373 p. ;21 cm.

I712.45/P289

Manhattan Transfer/John Dos Passos. —London: Constable & Co Ltd., c1927

378 p. ;19 cm.

I712.45/P289

Manhattan Transfer/John Dos Passos. —Boston: Houghton Mifflin Company, c1927

378 p. ;19 cm.

I712.45/P289T727

Tour of Duty/John Dos Passos. —Boston: Houghton Mifflin Company, c1946

336 p. ;21 cm.

I712.45/P363

The Jinx Ship/Howard Pease. —New York: Young Moderns Doubleday & Co., Inc., c1947

324 p. ;20 cm.

I712.45/P373

Swing Low/Edwin A. Peeples. —Boston: Houghton Mifflin Company, c1945

293 p. ;20 cm.

I712.45/P397S559

Short Stories by Present-day Authors/Raymond Woodbury Pence. —New York: The Macmillan Company, c1927

xii, 431 p. ;19 cm.

I712.45/P413H673

The History of Rome Hanks and Kindred Matters/Joseph Stanley Pennell. —New York: Scribner, c1944.

363 p. ;20 cm.

I712.45/P433

Alarum and Excursion/Virginia Perdue. —New York: Doubleday, Doran and Co., Inc., [?]

288 p. ;10×14 cm.

I712.45/P449

The Emperor's Physician/J. R. Perkins. —New York: The Bobbs-Merrill Company, c1944

245 p. ;20 cm.

I712.45/P463

Texas: A World in Itself/George Sessions Perry. —New York: Whittlesey House, c1942

xi, 293 p. ;23 cm.

I712.45/P468

Death in a Domino/Roland Pertwee.—Boston: Houghton Mifflin Company, c1932

268 p.;19 cm.

I712.45/P493

County place/Ann Petry.—London: Michael Joseph, c1948

223 p.;19 cm.

I712.45/P549

Private Purkey's Private Peace/H. I. Phillips.—New York: G. P. Putnam's sons, c1945

ix, 134 p.;20 cm.

I712.45/P558B592

Big Spring: The Casual Biography of a Prairie Town/Shine Philips.—New York: Prentice-Hall, Inc., c1943

231 p.;23 cm.

I712.45/P685

Dragon Lure: Romance of Peking(In the days of Yuan shih-Kai)/Noman Hisdale Pitman.—Shanghai: The Commercial Press, Ltd., c1925

318 p.;19 cm.

I712.45/P743

Murders in the Rue Morgue/Edgar Allen Poe.—New York: J. H. Sears & Company, Inc., Publishers, [?]

246 p.;18 cm.

I712.45/P881V217

The Haunted Hangar/Van Powell.—Akron, Ohio: The Saalfield Publishing Company, [?]

276 p.;21 cm.

I712.45/P882L426

Lay that Pistol Down/Richard Powell.—New York: Simon and Schuster, c1945

210 p.;20 cm.

I712.45/P884P156

Pale Horse, Pale Rider: Three Short Novels/Kathering Anne Porter.—New York: Harcourt, Brace and Company, c1936

264 p.;21 cm.

I712.45/P892

Lost Rapture/Beulah Poynter.—New York: Greenberg Publisher, c1934

249 p.;19 cm.

I712.45/P949A581

Angel Pavement/J. B. Priestley.—New York and London: Harper & Brothers, c1930

494 p.;21 cm.

I712.45/P962

The Boudoir Murder/Milton M. Propper.—New York: Greenberg Publisher, [?]

323 p.;19 cm.

I712.45/P962-4

The Skies of Europe/Frederic Prokosch.—4th ed..—New York: Happer & Brothers Publishers, c1941

500 p.;21 cm.

I712.45/P996

Some Merry Adventures of Robin Hood of Great Renown in Nottinghamshire/Howard Pyle.—New York: Charles Scribner's Sons, c1883, 1902

vii, 176 p.;18 cm.

I712.45/Q3

The Tragedy of X/Ellery Queen.—New York: Grosset & Dunlap Publishers, c1932, 1940

373 p.;19 cm.

I712.45/Q3D

Ten Days' Wonder/Ellery Queen.—Boston: Little, Brown and Company, c1948

265 p. ;19 cm.

I712.45/Q3(O)
The Devil to Pay/Ellery Queen. —New York: Pocket Books, Inc., c1945
200 p. ;16 cm.

I712.45/Q3C141
Calamity Town/Ellery Queen. —New York: Grosset & Dunlap Publishers, c1942
318 p. ;20 cm.

I712.45/Q3H169
Half-Way House: A Novel in Five Parts/Ellery Queen. —[S. l. : s. n.], c1938
319 p. ;19 cm.

I712.45/R155
Bucky Follows A Cold Trail/William MacLeod Raine. —New York: Grosset & Dunlap Publishers, c1937
306 p. ;19 cm.

I712.45/R155B863
The Broad Arrow/William MacLeod Raine. —Philadelphia: The Blakiston Company, c1933
viii, 2922 p. ;19 cm.

I712.45/R186
The Fountainhead/Ayn Rand. —Philadelphia: The Blakiston Company, c1943
753 p. ;20 cm.

I712.45/R234R682
Rocky Mountain Boys or Camping in the Big Game Country/St. George Rathborne. —Chicago: The Goldsmith Publishing Company, [?]
248 p. ;20 cm.

I712.45/R259(O)
The Yearling/Marjorie Kinnan Rawlings. —New York: Chaeles Scribner's Sons, c1940
427 p. ;21 cm.

I712.45/R355
Peter Waring/Forrest Reid. —London: Penguin Books, c1946
253 p. ;18 cm.

I712.45/R384
Arch of Triumph/Erich Maria Remarque; translated from the German by Walter Sorell and Denver Lindley.. —New York: D. Appleton-Century Company, Inc., [1945]
3, 455 p. ;21 cm.

I712.45/R462C978
The Curtain Rises/Quentin Reynolds. —New York: Random House, c1944
353 p. ;22 cm.

I712.45/R495L941
The Lucky Stiff/Craig Rice. —New York: Simon and Schuster, c1945
251 p. ;20 cm.

I712.45/R498(O)
We Took to the Woods/Louise Dickinson Rich. —Philadelphia: J. B. Lippincott Company, c1942
322 p. ;21 cm.

I712.45/R535T784
The Trees/Conrad Richter. —New York: Alfred A. Knopf, c1940
302 p. ;20 cm.

I712.45/R578
Boston Adventure/Mary Roberts Rinehart. —New York: Rinehart & Company, Incorporated, c1947, 1948
348 p. ;21 cm.

I712.45/R578D691
The Door/Mary Roberts Rinehart. —New York: Grosset & Dunlap, c1930

314 p. ;19 cm.

I712. 45/R578L879

Lost Ecstasy/Mary Roberts Rinehart. —London: Hodder and Stoghton Ltd. , c1927

352 p. ;18 cm.

I712. 45/R578W187

The Wall/Mary Roberts Rinehart. —New York: Grosset & Dunlap Publishers, c1938

338 p. ;20 cm.

I712. 45/R632U55

Under the Southern Cross/Elizabeth Robins. —Toronto: The Copp, Clark Co. , Ltd. , c1907

234 p. ;21 cm.

I712. 45/R639N864

Northwest Passage/Kenneth Roberts. —London: Collins Publishers, c1938

709 p. ;21 cm.

I712. 45/R639N864D727

Northwest Passage/Kenneth Roberts. —New York: Doubleday, Doran and Company, Inc. , c1937

709 p. ;21 cm.

I712. 45/R643A793

Arundel: A Chronicle of the Province of Maine and of the Secret Expedition Against Quebec/Kenneth Roberts. —New York: Doubleday, Doran & Company, Inc. , c1930, 1933

632 p. ;20 cm.

I712. 45/R643C236

Captain Caution: A Chronicle of Arundel/Kenneth Roberts. —London: Collins Clear Type Press, c1949

255 p. ;20 cm.

I712. 45/R643O048

Oliver Wiswell/Kenneth Roberts. —New York: Doubleday, Doran & Company, Inc. , c1940

836 p. ;22 cm.

I712. 45/R643T582

The Time of Man/Elizabeth Madox Roberts. —New York: The Viking Press, c1926

382 p. ;19 cm.

I712. 45/R649

Fire Bell in the Night/Constance Robertson. —New York: Henry Holt and Company, c1944

342 p. ;21 cm.

I712. 45/R649O11

Oasis/Willard Robertson. —Philadelphia: J. B. Lippincott Company, c1944

220 p. ;21 cm.

I712. 45/R658P426

The Perfect Round/Henry Morton Robinson. —New York: Harcourt, Brace and Company, c1945

280 p. ;21 cm.

I712. 45/R687

One Angel Less/H. W. Roden. —New York: William Morrow & Company, c1945

216 p. ;19 cm.

I712. 45/R698B275

Barriers Burned Away/E. P. Roe. —New York: Dodd, Mead and Company, c1886

viii, 472, 29 p. ;19 cm.

I712. 45/R722

Dusk at the Grove/Samuel Rogers. —Boston: Little, Brown, and Company, c1934

312 p. ;20 cm.

I712.45/R737

Yu'an Hee See Laughs/Sax Rohmer. —New York: Doubleday, Doran & Company, Inc., c1932

312 p.;19 cm.

I712.45/R788

Unfamiliar Faces/Alice Grant Rosman. —New York: G. P. Putnam's Sons, c1938

312 p.;20 cm.

I712.45/R823L488

The Left Hand Is the Dreamer/Nancy Wilson Ross. —New York: William Sloane Associates, Inc., c1947

300 p.;21 cm.

I712.45/R823T765

The Tragedy of Y: A Drury Lane Mystery/Barnaby Ross. —New York: The Viking Press, c1932

vi, 344 p.;20 cm.

I712.45/R878C975

Curiosity Killed a Cat/Anne Rowe. —New York: William Morrow and Company, c1941

282 p.;20 cm.

I712.45/R939

Hope of Earth/Margaret Lee Runbeck. —Boston: Houghton Mifflin Company, c1947

502 p.;21 cm.

I712.45/R952

Yellowstone Scout/William Marshall Rush. —New York: Longmans, Green and Co., Inc., c1945

184 p.;21 cm.

I712.45/R994

St. George of Weldon/Robert Rylee. —New York: Farrar & Rinehart, Incorporated, c1937

432 p.;21 cm.

I712.45/R994R581

The Ring and the Cross/Robert Rylee. —New York: Alfred A. Knopf, c1947

307 p.;22 cm.

I712.45/S113

The Hounds of God: A Romanc/Rafael Asbatini. —Boston: Houghton Mifflin Company, c1928

327 p.;18 cm.

I712.45/L676C

Cass Timberlane: A Novel of Husbands and Wives/Sinclair Lewis. —New York: Random House, c1945

390 p.;20 cm.

I712.45/L676C

Cass Timberlane: A Novel of Husbands and Wives/Sinclair Lewis. —New York: Random House, c1945

390 p.;20 cm.

I712.45/S324

Lean with the Wind: A Novel of the South Seas/Earl Schenck. —New York and London: Whittlesay House, c1945

338 p.;21 cm.

I712.45/S372

The Burnished Blade/Lawrence Schoonover. —New York: The Macmillan Company, c1948

371 p.;21 cm.

I712.45/S372B

The Burnished Blade/Lawrence Schoonover. —New York: The Macmillan Company, c1948

371 p.;21 cm.

I712.45/S377

Sons of the Morning/Otto Schrag. —New York: Doubleday, Doran and Company, Inc.,

c1945
353 p. ;21 cm.

I712. 45/S425W111
The Wave/Evelyn Scott. —New York: The Literary Guild of America, c1929
625 p. ;21 cm.

I712. 45/S427C719
The Colonel of the Red Huzzars/John Reed Scott. —New York: Grosset & Dunlap, c1905
341 p. ;19 cm.

I712. 45/S438
More than Kind/Caroline Seaford. —London: Victor Gollangz Ltd. , c1935
287 p. ;19 cm.

I712. 45/S448(O)
The Townsman/John Sedges. —New York: The John Day Company, c1945
384 p. ;20 cm.

I712. 45/S452C928
The Crying Sisters/Mabel Seeley. —New York: Grosset & Dunlap Publishers, c1939
292 p. ;19 cm.

I712. 45/S452L773
The Listening House/Mabel Seeley. —New York: Doubleday, Doran & Company, Inc. , c1938
296 p. ;19 cm.

I712. 45/S452W872
Woman of Property/Mabel Seeley. —London: Michael Joseph, c1948
382 p. ;21 cm.

I712. 45/S464
Wings of Lead/Monica Selwin-Tait. —Notre Dame, Indiana: The Avria Press, c1937
302 p. ;19 cm.

I712. 45/S488
The Little French Girl/Anne Douglas Sedgwick. —Boston: Houghton Mifflin Company, c1924
508 p. ;19 cm.

I712. 45/S495
Dragonwyck/Anya Seton. —New York: Lexington Press, c1944
336 p. ;21 cm.

I712. 45/S534
The Young Lions/Jrein Shaw. —New York: Random House, c1948
689 p. ;21 cm.

I712. 45/S544
Captain from Castile/Samuel Shellabarger. —Philadelphia: The Blakiston Company, c1945
503 p. ;21 cm.

I712. 45/S544P954
Prince of Foxes/Samuel Shellabarger. —Boston: Little, Brown and Company, c1947
433 p. ;21 cm.

I712. 45/S553B855
The Bright Promise/Richard Sherman. —Boston: Little, Brown and Company, c1947
373 p. ;20 cm.

I712. 45/S553G573
Goal to Go! /Harold M. Sherman. —New York: Grosset & Dunlap Publisher, c1931
250 p. ;19 cm.

I712. 45/S555P232
Paris-Underground/Etta Shiber. —New York: New York Publishing Co. , Inc. , c1944
vi, 392 p. ;21 cm.

I712.45/S557

Where Nothing Ever Happens/Lee Shippey.—Boston: Houghton Mifflin Company, c1935

256 p. ;19 cm.

I712.45/S562

Pastoral/Nevil Shute.—New York: William Morrow and Company, c1944

246 p. ;21 cm.

I712.45/S562A

Awol: K-9 Commando/Bertrand Shurtleff.—New York: The Bobbs-Merrill Company Publishiers, c1944

283 p. ;21 cm.

I712.45/S616

Priesidential Mission/Sinclair, Ption.—New York: The Viking Press, c1947

x, 645 p. ;21 cm.

I712.45/S616

Years of Illusion/Harold Sinclair.—New York: Doubleday, Doran and Company, Inc., c1941

369 p. ;21 cm.

I712.45/S616R758

Roman Holiday/Upton Sinclair.—London: T. Werner Laurie Ltd., c1931

248 p. ;19 cm.

I712.45/S616T582

In Time of Harvest/John L. Sinclair.—New York: The Mamillan Company, c1943

226 p. ;22 cm.

I712.45/S616W927

World's End/Upton Sinclair.—[S. l. : s. n.], c1940

740 p. ;20 cm.

I712.45/S628

Dithers and Jitters/Cornelia Otis Skinner.—New York: Dodd, Mead & Company, c1944

167 p. ;22 cm.

I712.45/S628E96

Excuse it, Please! /Cornelia Otis Skinner.—New York: Dodd, Mead & Company, c1946

225 p. ;21 cm.

I712.45/S628O93

Our Hearts Were Young and Gay/Cornelia Otls Skinner, Emily Kimbrough.—New York: Dodd, Mead & Company, c1942

247 p. ;19 cm.

I712.45/S628S676

Soap Behind the Ears/Cornelia Otis Skinner.—New York: Dodd, Mead & Company, c1943

231 p. ;22 cm.

I712.45/S631D219

In a Dark Garden/Frank G. Slaughter.—New York: Doubleday & Company, Inc., c1946

433 p. ;21 cm.

I712.45/S642

Rain In the Doorway/Thorne Smith.—[S. l. : s. n.], c1938

365 p. ;17 cm.

I712.45/S643(O)

Tomorrow Will Be Better/Betty Smith.—New York: Harper & Brothers Publishers, c1948

274 p. ;21 cm.

I712.45/S643T784

A Tree Grows in Brooklyn/Betty Smith.—New York: Everybody's Vacation Publishing Co., Inc., c1943

443 p. ;21 cm.

I712.45/S645

I Capture the Castle/Dodle Smith. —London: The Reprint Society, 1949

342 p. ;19 cm.

I712.45/S649L912

Low Man On A Totem Pole/H. Allen Smith. —Philadlphia: The Blakston Commpany, c1941

xv, 205 p. ;19 cm.

I712.45/S662

Turnabout/Thorne Smith. —[S. l. : s. n.], c1933

356 p. ;17 cm.

I712.45/S662S628

Skin and Bones/Thorne Smith. —[S. l. : s. n.], [?]

340 p. ;17 cm.

I712.45/S662S894

The Stray Lamb/Thorne Smith. —New York: The Sun Dial Press, c1942

303 p. ;20 cm.

I712.45/S662T673

Topper takes a trip/by Thorne Smith. —[S. l. : s. n.], c1938.

384 p. ;17 cm.

I712.45/S725

My Family: Right or Wrong/John Philip Sousa. —New York: Doubleday, Doran & Co., Inc., c1943

216 p. ;21 cm.

I712.45/S734

Love at First Flight/Charles Spalding, Otis Carney. —Boston: Houghton Mifflin Company, c1943

160 p. ;20 cm.

I712.45/S741

Doctor Bryson: A Novel/Frank H. Spearman. —New York: Charles Scribner's Sons, c1905

308 p. ;19 cm.

I712.45/S741

Boy: The story of missy's brother/Inez Specking. —New York: Benziger Brothers, c1925

164 p. ;18 cm.

I712.45/S745C539

China Trader/Cornelia Spencer. —[S. l. : s. n.], c1940

362 p. ;20 cm.

I712.45/S779

Boston Adventure/Jean Stafford. —Philaselphia: The Blakiston Company, [?]

390 p. ;20 cm.

I712.45/S779B747

Boston Adventure/Jean Stafford. —New York: Harcourt, Brace and Company, c1944

496 p. ;21 cm.

I712.45/S785S635

The Small General/Robert Standish. —New York: The Macmillan Company, c1945

v, 233 p. ;21 cm.

I712.45/S799B592

The Big Rock Candy Mountain/Wallace Stegner. —New York: Duell, Sloan and Pearce, c1938, 1940, 1942, 1943

515 p. ;20 cm.

I712.45/S799S915

The Street I Know/Harold E. Stearns. —New York: Lee Furman, Inc., c1935

411 p. ;21 cm.

I712. 45/S813S797
States of Grace: A Novel/Francis Steegmuller. —New York: Reynal and Hitchcock, Inc. , c1946
214 p. ;20 cm.

I712. 45/S819
In Dubious Battle/John Steinbeck. —New York: The Modern Library, c1936
343 p. ;18 cm.

I712. 45/S819V598
Elementary Course/John Steinbeck. —New York: The Viking Press, c1947
122 p. ;21 cm.

I712. 45/S819W357
The Wayward Bus/John Steinbeck. —New York: The Viking Press, c1947
312 p. ;21 cm.

I712. 45/S847S897
The Strange Case of Dr. Jekyll and Mr. Hyde and the Master of Ballantrae/Robert Louis Stevenson. —New York: Grosset & Dunlap Publishers, [?]
234 p. ;21 cm.

I712. 45/S866
The Casting Away of Mrs Lecks and Mrs Aleshine/Frank R. Stockton. —New York: D. Appleton-Century Company, c1943
ix, 290 p. ;21 cm.

I712. 45/S866R914
Rudder Grange/Frank R. Stockton. —New York: Charles Scribner's Sons, c1909
292 p. ;19 cm.

I712. 45/S878
An Awakening and What Followed/James Kent Stone. —Notre Dame: The Ave Maria, [?]
345 p. ;20 cm.

I712. 45/S882
The Wind for France/Fair Stood. —Boston: Little, Brown and Company, c1944
270 p. ;19 cm.

I712. 45/S889
The Silent Speaker/Rex Stout. —New York: The Viking Press, c1946
308 p. ;21 cm.

I712. 45/S889T668
Too Many Women/Rex Stout. —London: The Crime Club, c1948
192 p. ;19 cm.

I712. 45/S894
Reap the Wild Wind/Thelma Strabel. —New York: Triangle Books, c1942
viii, 298 p. ;19 cm.

I712. 45/S917P291
The Pastures of Heaven/John Steinbeck. —London: Philip Allan, c1933
302 p. ;19 cm.

I712. 45/S927
Mrs. Miniver/Jan Struther. —New York: Harcourt, Brace and Company, c1940
viii, 272 p. ;21 cm.

I712. 45/S929(O)
Taps for Private Tussie/Jesse Stuart. —New York: E. P. Dutton & Company, Inc. , c1943
303 p. ;22 cm.

I712. 45/S929S897
Stranger in the Earth: The Story of a Search/Thomas Sugrue. —New York: Henry Holt and Company, Publishers, c1948
371 p. ;22 cm.

I712.45/S933

In the Shadow of Gold/Paul Studer. —New York: Greenberg Publisher, c1934

232 p. ;19 cm.

I712.45/S978

Faithful Company: A Winter's Tale/Frank Swinnerton. —New York: Doubleday & Company, Inc., c1948

310 p. ;21 cm.

I712.45/S985

Dayspring/Harry Sylvester. —New York: D. Apleton-Century Company, c1945

294 p. ;20 cm.

I712.45/T176

Mary's Neck/Booth Tarkington. —New York: Doubleday, Doran and Company, Inc., c1932

318 p. ;19 cm.

I712.45/T176C591

Claire Ambler/Booth Tarkington. —New York: Doubleday, Doran & Company, Inc., c1928

253 p. ;18 cm.

I712.45/T176I31

Image of Josephine/Booth Tarkington. —New York: Doubleday, Doran and Company, Inc., c1945

275 p. ;20 cm.

I712.45/T176J39

Penrod Jashber/Booth Tarkington. —New York: Grosset & Dunlap Publishers, c1929

x, 321 p. ;19 cm.

I712.45/T176K11

Kate Fennigate/Booth Tarkington. —London: Hammond, Hammond & Co., Ltd., c1946

398 p. ;19 cm.

I712.45/T176K11D

Kate Fennigate/Booth Tarkington. —New York: Doubleday, Doran & Co., Inc., c1943

359 p. ;21 cm.

I712.45/T176M671

Mirthful Haven/Booth Tarkington. —New York: Doubleday, Doran & Company, Inc., c1930

319 p. ;21 cm.

I712.45/T176(O)

The Magnificent Ambersons/Booth Tarkington. —New York: Doubleday, Page & Company, c1918

516 p. ;19 cm.

I712.45/T176P417(O)

Penrod and Sam/Booth Tarkington. —New York: Grosset & Dunlap, c1916

249 p. ;20 cm.

I712.45/T176P417

Penrod and Sam/Booth Tarkington. —Paris: Louis Conard Publisher, c1918

295 p. ;16 cm.

I712.45/T176P733

The Plutocrat/Booth Tarkington. —New York: Grosset & Dunlap Publishers, c1927

543 p. ;19 cm.

I712.45/T176S497

Seventeen: A Tale of Youth and Summer Time and the Baxter Family Especially William/Booth Tarkington. —New York: Grosset & Dunlap, c1916

329 p. ;19 cm.

I712.45/T176S497(O)

Seventeen/Booth Tarkington. —New York: Grosset & Dunlap Publishers, c1915, 1916

249 p. ;20 cm.

I712.45/T176W927

The World Does Move/Booth Tarkington. —New York: Doubleday, Doran and Company, c1929

294 p.;20 cm.

I712.45/T238C532

Chicken Every Sunday: My life with Mother's Boarders/Rosemay Taylor. —New York: Whittlesey House, c1943

307 p.;21 cm.

I712.45/T245

Out of Order/Phoebe Atwood Taylor. —New York: W · W · Norton & Company, Inc., c1936

280 p.;19 cm.

I712.45/T264

The Double Agent/Hildegarde Tolman Teilhet. —New York: Doubleday, Doran and Company, Inc., c1945

220 p.;20 cm.

I712.45/T318

Wolf/Albert Payson Terhune. —New York: Grosset & Dunlap, c1925

236 p.;20 cm.

I712.45/T318B929

Buff: A Collie and other Dog Stories/Albert Payson Terhune. —New York: Crosset & Sunlap Publishers, c1921

341 p.;20 cm.

I712.45/T318D654

A Dog Named Chips: The Life and Adventures of a Mongrel Scamp/Albert Payson Terhune. —New York: Grosset & Dunlap Publishers, c1931

267 p.;19 cm.

I712.45/T318G846

The Critter and Other Dogs/Albert Payson Terhune. —New York: Grosset & Dunlap, c1936

352 p.;20 cm.

I712.45/T318H

The Heart of a Dog/Albert Payson Terhune. —New York: Doubleday & Company, Inc., c1924

220 p.;20 cm.

I712.45/T318L

Lad: A Dog/Albert Payson Terhune. —New York: E. P. Dutton & Co., Inc., c1919

352 p.;10×14 cm.

I712.45/T318L153

Lad of Sunnybank/Albert Payson Terhune. —New York: Grosset & Dunlap Publishers, c1929

322 p.;21 cm.

I712.45/T318L812

Lochinvar Luck/Albert Payson Terhune. —New York: Grosset & Dunlap Publishers, c1923

vii, 309 p.;20 cm.

I712.45/T318T812

Treve/Albert Payson Terhune. —New York: Grosset & Dunlap Publishers, c1924

312 p.;20 cm.

I712.45/T318W357

The Way of a Dog/Albert Payson Terhune. —New York: Grosset & Dunlap Publishers, c1923

334 p.;19 cm.

I712.45/T369T357

That Stange Sylvester Affair/Lee Thayer. —New York: Dodd, Mead & Company, c1938

264 p.;19 cm.

I712.45/T445

The Brandons/Angela Thirkell. —New York: Grosset & Dunlap, c1939

358 p. ;21 cm.

I712.45/T454

Lone Star Preacher/Lt. Col. John W. Thomason. —New York: Chariles Scribner's Sons, c1944

xii, 296 p. ;21 cm.

I712.45/T476

The Adventure of Christopher Columin/Sylvia Thompson. —Boston: Little, Brown and Company, c1939

318 p. ;21 cm.

I712.45/T569

Dead Ernest: A Leonidas Witherall Mystery/Alice Tilton. —New York: W. W. Norton & Company, c1944

218 p. ;19 cm.

I712.45/T654

All our Yesterdays/H. M. Tomlinson. —New York: Harper & Brothers Publishers, c1930

445 p. ;19 cm.

I712.45/T662

Left in Trust/Juliet Wilbor Tompkins. —Indianapolis: The Bobbs-Merrill Company Publishers, c1929

318 p. ;19 cm.

I712.45/T759

Rough Mesa/John Trace. —New York: Doubleday, Doran and Company, Inc. , c1940

277 p. ;19 cm.

I712.45/T768

Tassels on Her Boots/Arthur Train. —New York: The World Publishing Company, c1944

xii, 301 p. ;21 cm.

I712.45/T779

Trouble-Shooter: The Story of A Northwoods Prosecutor/Robert Traver. —New York: The Viking Press, c1943

294 p. ;22 cm.

I712.45/T868O

The Raft/Robert Trumbull. —New York: Henry Holt and Company, c1942

vii, 204 p. ;20 cm.

I712.45/T877

Adversary in the House/Irving Stone. —New York: Doubleday & Co. , Inc. , c1947

432 p. ;22 cm.

I712.45/T895

The Dove/Wilson Tucker. —New York: Rinehart & Company, Inc. , c1948

218 p. ;19 cm.

I712.45/T967

Hidden Blood/W. C. Tuttle. —Boston: Houghton Mifflin Company, c1943

244 p. ;20 cm.

I712.45/T969T655

Tom Sawyer Detective and Other Stories/Mark Twain. —New York: Groddet & Dunlap Publishers, c1878

216 p. ;19 cm.

I712.45/U69

Keep 'Em Grawling: Earthworms at War/William Hazlett Upson. —New York: Farrar & Rinehart, Inc. , c1940, 1941, 1942

339 p. ;19 cm.

I712.45/V222

The Destroying Angel/Louis Joseph Vance. —Toronto: The Copp, Clark Co. , Ltd. , c1912

vii, 325 p. ;19 cm.

I712. 45/V222

Escape/Ethel Vance. —London: Collins Clear-Type Press, c1939

381 p. ;20 cm.

I712. 45/V222R425

Reprisal/Ethel Vance. —Boston: Little, Brown and Company, c1942

334 p. ;21 cm.

I712. 45/V390

The Tattooed Countess: A Romantic Novel with A Happy Ending/Carl Van Vechten. —New York: Alfred A. Knopf, c1924

286 p. ;19 cm.

I712. 45/V665

Salome: The Wandering Jewess/George Sylvester Viereck, Paul Eldridge. —[S. l. : s. n.], 1938.

464 p. ;20 cm.

I712. 45/W119

My Mother is a Violent Woman/Tommy Wadelton. —New York: Cpward-Mccann, Inc. , c1940

121 p. ;19 cm.

I712. 45/W125B259

Barney's Fortune/Mary T. Waggaman. —Notre Dame: The Ave Maria, c1923

315 p. ;17 cm.

I712. 45/W129

Jerr's Job/Mary T. Waggaman. —Notre Dame: The Ave Maria, c1920

340 p. ;18 cm.

I712. 45/W129

Lorimer Light/Mary T. Waggaman. —Notre Dame: The Ave Mara, c1924

320 p. ;17 cm.

I712. 45/W129

Lady Bird/Mary T. Waggaman. —Notre Dame: The Ave Maria, c1929

336 p. ;17 cm.

I712. 45/W129S848

Sergeant Tim/Mary T. Waggaman. —Notre Dame: The Ave Maria, [?]

335 p. ;17 cm.

I712. 45/W146

The Hucksters/Frederic Wakeman. —New York: Grosset & Dunlap Publishers, c1946

307 p. ;21 cm.

I712. 45/W146H882

The Hucksters/Frederic Wakeman. —New York: Rinehart and Company, c1946

307 p. ;21 cm.

I712. 45/W158L968

Lustre in the Sky/R. G. Waldeck. —New York: Doubledya & Company, Inc. , c1946

434 p. ;22 cm.

I712. 45/W182B847

The Brewers' Big Horses/Mildred Walker. —New York: Harcourt, Brace and Company, c1940

441 p. ;21 cm.

I712. 45/W182Q1

The Quarry/Mildred Walker. —New York: Harcourt, Brace and Company, c1947

339 p. ;21 cm.

I712. 45/W187

New Frontiers/Henry A. Wallace. —New York: Reynal & Hitchcock, c1934

vi, 314 p. ;21 cm.

I712.45/W217

Reaching for the Stars/Nora Waln. —[S. l. : s. n.], [?]

380 p. ;21 cm.

I712.45/W218

The Inquisitor/Hugh Walpole. —London: Macmillan and Co., Ltd., c1935

xii, 618 p. ;19 cm.

I712.45/W256O63

Oracles of Nostradamus/Charles A. Ward. —New York: The Modern Library, c1940

xxiv, 366 p. ;19 cm.

I712.45/W256T342

The Testing of Diana Mallory/Humphry Ward. —New York: Harper & Brothers Publishers, c1908

548 p. ;19 cm.

I712.45/W279

New Song in a Strange Land/Esther Warner. —Boston: Houghton Mifflin Company, c1948

302 p. ;21 cm.

I712.45/W363

Shorter Novels of Herman Melville/Raymond Weaver. —Ameria: Liveright Publishing Corp., c1928

li, 328 p. ;22 cm.

I712.45/W371C728

Comrades of the Saddle or the Young Riders of the Plains/Frank V. Webster. —New York: The Saalfield Publishing Company, [?]

206 p. ;20 cm.

I712.45/W381D121

Daddy-Long-Legs/Jean Webster. —New York: Grosset & Dunlap Publishers, c1912

304 p. ;19 cm.

I712.45/W381D285

Dear Enemy/Jean Webster. —New York: Grosset & Dunlap Publishers, c1915

350 p. ;19 cm.

I712.45/W418

What's In It for Me? /Jerome Weidman. —London: William Heinemann Ltd., c1939

386 p. ;20 cm.

I712.45/W425

The Story of Mrs. Murphy/Natalie Anderson Scott. —New York: E. P. Dutton & Company, Inc., c1947

445 p. ;21 cm.

I712.45/W453

Patty Fairfield/Carolyn Wells. —New York: Dodd, Mead & Company, c1929

247 p. ;19 cm.

I712.45/W511

Apartment in Athens/Glenway Wescott. —New York: Harper & Brothers Publishers, c1945

268 p. ;21 cm.

I712.45/W516A598

Animal Fair/Evelyn West. —New York: J. B. Lippincott Company, c1945

277 p. ;20 cm.

I712.45/W539

Fiddler' Green or the Strange Adventure of Tommy Lawn/Albert Richard Wetjen. —London: Chapman & Hall Ltd., c1931

xix, 251 p. ;19 cm.

I712.45/W553

The Children/Edith Wharton. —New York: D. Appleton and Company, c1928

347 p. ;20 cm.

I712.45/W553H542

Here and Beyond/Edith Wharton.—New York: D. Appleton & Company, c1926

324 p. ;20 cm.

I712.45/W573

The Giant Joshua/Maurine Whipple.—Boston: Houghton Mifflin Company, c1941

ix, 637 p. ;20 cm.

I712.45/W577(O)

The Secret of the Storm Country/Grace Miller White.—New York: Grosset & Dunlap Publishers, c1916

352 p. ;19 cm.

I712.45/W577

Wild Geese Calling/Stewart Edward White.—New York: Doubleday, Doran, 1940.

viii, 577 p. ;22 cm.

I712.45/W577P763

Pole Star/Stewart Edward White, Harry Devighne.—New York: Doubleday, Doran & Company, Inc., c1935

viii, 452 p. ;20 cm.

I712.45/W577T374

They Were Expendable/W. L. White.—New York: Harcourt, Brace and Company, c1942

vii, 209 p. ;21 cm.

I712.45/W582

A Certain Rich Man/William Allen White.—New York: The Macmillan Company, 1909.

434 p. ;20 cm.

I712.45/W582W819

The Witch in the Wood/T. H. White.—New York: G. P. Putnam's Sons, c1939

270 p. ;21 cm.

I712.45/W588

Northwest Raiders/Samuel Alexander White.—New York: Phoenix Press, c1945

256 p. ;19 cm.

I712.45/W588

The Silent Places/Stewart Edward White.—New York: Grosset & Dunlap Publishers, c1904

304 p. ;19 cm.

I712.45/W588D

Wild Geese Calling/Stewart Edward White.—New York: Doubleday, Doran & Company, Inc., c1941

viii, 577 p. ;21 cm.

I712.45/W636

The Wayfarers/Dan Wickenden.—New York: William Morrow and Company, c1945

309 p. ;20 cm.

I712.45/W636D182

Dangerous Ground/Francis Sill Wickware.—New York: Doubleday & Company, Inc., c1946

220 p. ;20 cm.

I712.45/W636R943

The Running of the Deer/Dan Wickenden.—London: J. M. Dent & Sons Ltd., c1938

384 p. ;20 cm.

I712.45/W638

All the King's Horses/Margaret Widdemer.—New York: Farrar & Rinehart, c1930

300 p. ;19 cm.

I712.45/W647

Morning in America/Willard Wiener.—New York: Farrar & Rinehart, Inc., c1942

303 p. ;21 cm.

I712.45/W668P611

The Picture of Dorian Grlay/Oscar Wilde.—

New York: Boni and Liveright Inc. , [?]
255 p. ;17 cm.

I712. 45/W671
The Ides of March/Thornton Wilder. —New York: Harper & Brothers Publishers, c1948
viii, 246 p. ;21 cm.

I712. 45/W671B851
The Bridge of San Luis Rey/Thornton Wilder. —US: Albert & Charles Boni, Inc. , c1927
235 p. ;21 cm.

I712. 45/W671B851L848
The Bridge of San Luis Rey/Thornton Wilder. —London: Longmans, Green and Co. , c1928
vii, 139 p. ;20 cm.

I712. 45/W673
The Woman of Andors/Thornton Wilder. —London: Longmans, Green and Co. , c1930
104 p. ;20 cm.

I712. 45/W673B855
Bright Feather/Robert Wilder. —New York: G. P. Putnam's Sons, c1948
408 p. ;21 cm.

I712. 45/W673H
Heaven's My Destination/Thornton Niven Wilder. —London: Longmans Green and Co. , c1934
244 p. ;19 cm.

I712. 45/W678
Never Let Me Go/Gale Wilhelm. —New York: William Morrow and Company, c1945
215 p. ;20 cm.

I712. 45/W716
Salar the Salmon/Henry Williamson. —Boston: Little, Brown, and Company, c1942
300 p. ;21 cm.

I712. 45/W721
O. Henry Memorial Award Prize Stories of 1931/Blanche Colton Williams. —New York: Doubleday, Doran & Company, Inc. , c1931
xxix, 392 p. ;20 cm.

I712. 45/W721F853
It's a Free Country/Ben Ames Williams. —Boston: Houghton Mifflin Company, c1945
130 p. ;20 cm.

I712. 45/W721L439
Leave Her to Heaven/Ben Ames Williams. —Boston: Houghton Mifflin Company, c1944
429 p. ;20 cm.

I712. 45/W721R312
The Red Mass/Valentine Williams. —Boston: Houghton Mifflin Company, c1925
x, 310 p. ;19 cm.

I712. 45/W721S897
The Strange Woman/Ben Ames Williams. —New York: The Sun Dial Press, c1941
507 p. ;21 cm.

I712. 45/W746
Professor How Could You! /Harry Leon Wilson. —New York: Cosmopolitan Book Corporation, c1924
340 p. ;19 cm.

I712. 45/W746A919
At the Mercy of Ciberius/Augusta Evans Wilson. —New York: A. L. Burt Company, c1887
537 p. ;19 cm.

I712. 45/W795
Gallows Hill/Frances Winwar. —New York: Henry Holt and Company, c1937
292 p. ;18 cm.

I712.45/W819
The Classics in Slang/H. C. Witwer. —New York: Grosset & Dunlap, c1927
vi, 331 p. ;19 cm.

I712.45/W819
The Leather Pushers/H. C. Witwer. —New York: Grosset & Dunlap, c1920
x, 341 p. ;19 cm.

I712.45/W819F471
Fighting Blood/H. C. Witwer. —New York: G. P. Putnam's Sons, c1923
vi, 377 p. ;19 cm.

I712.45/W837
Aurora Dawn, or, The True History of Andrew Reale/Herman Wouk. —New York: Simon and Schuster, c1947
xi, 241 p. ;21 cm.

I712.45/W838
Uncle Fred in the Springtime/P. G. Wodehouse. —Shanghai: The Far Easter Book Co. , [?]
311 p. ;17 cm.

I712.45/W853
American Guerrilla in the Philippines/Ira Wolfert. —New York: Simon and Schuster, c1945
ix, 301 p. ;21 cm.

I712.45/W853H655
The Hills Beyond/Thomas Wolfe. —New York: The Sun Dial Press, c1943
386 p. ;20 cm.

I712.45/W853L847
The Lonely Steeple/Victor Wolfson. —New York: A Venture Press Book, 1945
260 p. ;20 cm.

I712.45/W853Y
You Can't Go Home Again/Thomas Wolfe. —New York: The Sun Dial Press, c1942
viii, 743 p. ;22 cm.

I712.45/W863
The Portable Noels of Science/Donald A. Wollheim. —New York: The Viking Press, c1945
xiii, 737 p. ;17 cm.

I712.45/W873
The Presence of Everett Marsh/Playsted Wood. —Indianapolis: The Bobbs-Merrill Company, c1937
387 p. ;21 cm.

I712.45/W924
"Wildcats" over Casablanca/M. T. Wordell, E. N. Seiler. —Boston: Little, Brown, and Company, c1943
309 p. ;20 cm.

I712.45/W947
The Great Horn Spoon/Eugene Wright. —New York: New York Publishing Co. , Inc. , c1928
320 p. ;21 cm.

I712.45/W947B627
Black Boy: A Record of Childhood and Youth/Richard Wright. —New York and London: Harper & Brothers Publishers, c1945
228 p. ;21 cm.

I712.45/W985
Red Sun South/Oswald Wynd. —New York: Doubleday & Co. , Inc. , c1948
276 p. ;21 cm.

I712.45/W988
The Blue Vesuvius/Anthony Wynne. —Phila-

delphia: J. B. Lippincott Company, c1931
320 p. ;19 cm.

I712. 45/Y27
Crows Are Black Everywhere/Herbert O. Yardley, Carl Grabo. —New York: G. P. Putnam's Sons, c1945
247 p. ;21 cm.

I712. 45/Y31W638
The Widow's Walk/Margaret Yates, Paula Bramlette. —New York: E. P. Dutton & Company, Inc. , c1945
249 p. ;18 cm.

I712. 45/Y49A778
Arrogant Beggar/Anzia Yezierska. —New York: Doubleday, Page & Co. , c1927
279 p. ;20 cm.

I712. 45/Y64P478
Peter's People/Curtis Yorke. —London: Hutchinson & Co. , [?]
288 p. ;19 cm.

I712. 453/F533
The Mothers: An American Saga of Courage/Vardis Fisher. —New York: The Vanguard Press, c1943
viii, 334 p. ;21 cm.

I712. 455/N319
The World's Awakening/Navarchus. —London: Hodder and Stoughton Publishiers, c1908
vii, 463 p. ;18 cm.

I712. 456/D583
The Scarab Murder Case: A Philo Vance Story/S. S. Van Dine. —New York: Charles Scribner's Son, c1930
328 p. ;19 cm.

I712. 456/D583G218
The Canary Murder Case/S. S. Van Dine. —London: Ernest Benn Ltd. , c1930
288 p. ;19 cm.

I712. 456/Q3
The French Powder Mystery/Ellery Queen. —New York: Frederick A. Stokes Company, c1930
xviii, 127 p. ;17 cm.

I712. 456/W453
In the Tiger's Cage/Carolyn Wells. —Philadelphia, London: J. B. Lippincott Company, c1934
311 p. ;19 cm.

I712. 5/A437
Cheapjack/Allinghan, Philip. —New York: Frederick A. Stokes Company, c1934
xvii, 301 p. ;21 cm.

I712. 5/A939
More Merry-go-Round/By the Authors of Washing ton Merry-go-Round. —New York: Liveright, Inc. , Publishers, c1932
482 p. ;21 cm.

I712. 5/B111
Robbery by Mall: The Story of the U. S. Postal Inspectors/Karl Baarslag. —New York: Farrar & Rinehart, Inc. , c1938
324 p. ;21 cm.

I712. 5/B922
Other Gods: An American Legend/Pearl L. Buck. —New York: The John Day Company, c1940
381 p. ;22 cm.

I712. 5/F785
Good Night, Sweet Prince: The Life and Times of John Barrymore/Gene Fowler. —New York: The Viking Press, c1943, 1944

477 p. ;21 cm.

I712. 5/G549

The War of the Copper Kings: Builders of Butte and Wolves of Wall Steet/C. B. Glasscock. —New York: Grosset & Dunlap Publishers, c1935

ix, 314 p. ;21 cm.

I712. 5/G755

I, Claudius: From the Autobiography of Tiberius Claudius born B. C. 10 Murdered and Deified A. D. 54/Robert Garaves. —New York: The Modern Library, c1934

x, 427 p. ;18 cm.

I712. 5/J65

Queen of the Flat-Tops: The U. S. S. Lexington and the Coral Sea Battle/Stanley Johnston. —New York: E. P. Dutton & Co. , Inc. , c1942

280 p. ;22 cm.

I712. 5/L742

North to the Orient/Anne Morrow Lindbergh. —New York: Harcourt, Brace and Company, c1935

255 p. ;21 cm.

I712. 5/M329

Talking to the Moon/John Joseph Mathews. —Chicago: University of Chicago Press, c1945

243 p. ;23 cm.

I712. 5/M979

Pioneers of the Rocky Mountains and the West/Charles A. Mcmurry. —New York: The Macmillan Company, c1904

x, 248 p. ;19 cm.

I712. 5/McG771

I Was Condemned to the Chair/Edward F. McGrath. —New York: Frederick A. Stokes Company, c1934

vi, 312 p. ;21 cm.

I712. 5/P249-8

The Oregon Trail Sketches of Prairie and Rocky-Mountain Life/Francis Parkman. —8th ed.. —Boston: Little, Brown, and Company, c1911

xiv, 381 p. ;19 cm.

I712. 5/P374

The Polar Bear Hunt/C. V. A. Peel. —London: Old Royalty book Publishers, c1928

128 p. ;22 cm.

I712. 5/P615

The Pedagogues: A Story of the Harvard Summer School/Arthur Stanwood Pier. —Boston: Small, Maynard & Company, c1899

287 p. ;18 cm.

I712. 5/S616-2

The Brass Check: A Stydy of American Journalism/Upton Sinclair. —rev. ed.. —[S. l. : s. n.], c1936

446 p. ;21 cm.

I712. 5/T454

Count Luckner, the Sea Devil/Lowell Thomas. —New York: Doubleday, Doran & Company, Inc. , c1928

x, 308 p. ;21 cm.

I712. 5/T454E

European Skyways: The Story of a Tour of Europe by Airplane/Lowell Thomas. —Boston: Houghton Mifflin Company, c1927

xv, 524 p. ;21 cm.

I712. 5/T469

Presidents I've Known and Two Near Presidents/Charles Willis Thompson. —Indianapolis: The Bobbs-Merrill Company Publishers, c1929

386 p. ;22 cm.

I712. 5/T768

Mr. Tutt Finds a Way/Train, Arthur. —New York: Charles Scriber's Sons, c1945

241 p. ;20 cm.

I712. 5/T784

Guadalcanal Diary/Richard Tregaskis. —New York: Random House, c1943

263 p. ;21 cm.

I712. 5/W216

Turn of the Tide/Leo Walmsley. —New York: Doubleday, Doran and Company, Inc. , c1945

306 p. ;20 cm.

I712. 5/W582

Dog Days: Oter Times, Other Dogs/White, Stewart Edward. —New York: Doubleday, Doran & Company, Inc. , c1933

285 p. ;20 cm.

I712. 55/A211

We Stood Alone/Dorothy Adams. —London: Longmans, Green and Co. , c1944

284 p. ;21 cm.

I712. 55/A366

America ad I Saw it, or America revisited/Mrs. Alec-Tweedie. —New York: The Macmillan Company, c1913

ix, 475 p. ;20 cm.

I712. 55/A425

Our Fair City/Robert S. Allen. —New York: The Vanguard Press, Inc. , 1947

viii, 387 p. ;21 cm.

I712. 55/B288

East of Malta, West of Suez: The Official Admiralty Account of the Mediterranean Fleet 1939-1943/Bartimeus. —Boston: Little, Brown and Company, c1944

x, 221 p. ;20 cm.

I712. 55/B329

Spanish Highways and Byways/Katharine Lee Bates. —Chautauqua: The Chautauqua Press, c1905

xii, 448 p. ;20 cm.

I712. 55/B358

Last Man Off Wake Island/Walter L. J. Bayler. —Indianapolis: The Bobbs-Merrill Company, x1943

367 p. ;22 cm.

I712. 55/B955

Who Walk Alone/Perry Burgess. —New York: Henry Holt and Company, c1940

viii, 308 p. ;20 cm.

I712. 55/C321

Home Away from Home: The Story of the USO/Julia M. H. Carson. —New York: Harper & Brothers Publishers, c1946

xiv, 221 p. ;21 cm.

I712. 55/C789

Mount Royal: Chronicles of an American Town/Elizabeth Corbett. —New York: Reynal & Hitchcock, c1936

268 p. ;20 cm.

I712. 55/C899

Back to the Long Grass: My Link with Livingstons/Dan Crawford. —New York: George H. Doran Company, [?]

373 p. ;23 cm.

I712. 55/E13S615

Since Lenin Died/Max Eastman. —New York: Boni and Liveright Publisher, c1925

158 p. ;19 cm.

I712. 55/E44

On the Bottom/Commander Edward Ellsberg. —New York: Dodd, Mead & Company, c1943

x, 324 p. ;21 cm.

I712. 55/F352

Mink, Mary and Me: The Story of a Wilderness Trapline/Chick Ferguson. —New York: M. S. Mill Company, Inc. Pulisher, c1946

248 p. ;22 cm.

I712. 55/G489

The First Glencannon Omnibus: Including Scotch and Water Half-seas Over Three Sheets in the Wind/Guy Gilpatric. —New York: Dodd, Mead & Company, c1945

viii, 437 p. ;21 cm.

I712. 55/G696

Yankee Storekeeper/R. E. Gould. —New York: Whittlesey House, [1946]

vi, 195 p. ;21 cm.

I712. 55/G738

The Brooklyn Dodgers: An Informal History/Frank Graham. —New York: G. P. Putnam's Sons, c1945

248 p. ;21 cm.

I712. 55/G745

Free Men Are Fighting: The Story of World War II/Oliver Gramling, Associated Press Correspondents around the World. —New York: Farrar and Rinehart, Inc. , c1942

xvi, 488 p. ;23 cm.

I712. 55/H237

Gold Rush by Sea/Kenneth Haney. —Philadelphia: University of Pennsylvania Press, c1941

187 p. ;21 cm.

I712. 55/H361

Son of the Smoky Sea/Alden Hatch. —New York: Julian Messenr, Inc. , c1941

viii, 243 p. ;22 cm.

I712. 55/H434

A Statement for Non = Exclusion/Patrick J. Healy, NG Poon Chew. —San Francisco: November, c1905

255 p. ;24 cm.

I712. 55/H487

Men at War: The Best War Stories of All Time/Ernest Hemingway. —New York: Crown Publishers, c1942

xxxi, 1072 p. ;21 cm.

I712. 55/H567

Canadian Camp Life/Frances E. Herring. —London: T. Fisher Unwin, c1900

247 p. ;19 cm.

I712. 55/H645

Desert Conquest/Russell Hill. —New York: Alfred A. Knopf, c1943

viii, 340 p. ;20 cm.

I712. 55/J72

Ten-and Out!: The Complete Story of the Prize Ring in America/Alexander Johnston. —New York: Ives Washburn, Publisher, c1927, 1936, 1943

x, 390 p. ;22 cm.

I712. 55/K29

The Sportsman's Anthology/Robert F. Kelley. —New York: Howell, Soskin, Publishers, c1944

396 p. ;23 cm.

I712. 55/L274

I'll Take the High Road/Wolfgang Langewiesche. —New York: Harcourt, Brace and Compa-

ny, c1939

x, 254 p. ;21 cm.

I712. 55/L574

Aviation Cadet: Dick Hilton Wins His Wings at Pensacola/Henry B. Lent. —New York: The Macmillan Company, c1941

175 p. ;22 cm.

I712. 55/L716

The St. Louis Cardinals: The Story of A Great Baseball Club/Frederick G. Lieb. —New York: G. P. Putnam's Sons, c1945

218 p. ;21 cm.

I712. 55/L742

Listen! The Wind/Anne Morrow Lindbergh; with foreword and map drawing by Charles A. Lindbergh. —New York: Harcourt, Brace and Company, c1938

xii, 275 p. ;21 cm.

I712. 55/L848

Seven Seas on a Shoestring: Sailing all seas in "Idle Hour"/Dwight • Long. —New York: Harper & Brothers Publishers, c1938

x, 310 p. ;22 cm.

I712. 55/M481

Trap-Lines North: A True story of the Candian Woods/Stephen W. Meader. —New York: Dodd, Mead and Company, c1943

xviii, 268 p. ;21 cm.

I712. 55/M928

Combined Operations: The Official Story of the Commandos/Vice-Admiral Lord Louis Mountbatten. —New York: The Macmillan Company, c1943

xiii, 155 p. ;21 cm.

I712. 55/P792

Kabloona/Gontran De Poncins. —New York: Reynal & Hitchcock, Inc. , c1941

xii, 339 p. ;21 cm.

I712. 55/R454

The Sea Devi: The Story of Count Felix von Luckner, the German War Raider/Lowell Rhomas. —London: William Heinemann Ltd. , c1930

viii, 308 p. ;22 cm.

I712. 55/R561

Yankee Skippers to the Rescues: A Record of Gallant Rescues on the North Atlantic by American Seamen/Felix Riesenberg. —New York: Dodd, Mead & Company, c1943

xiii, 281 p. ;21 cm.

I712. 55/S649

Life in a Putty Knife Factory/H. Ellen Smith. —Philadelphia: The Blakiston Company, [c1943]

v, 218 p. ;19 cm.

I712. 55/T613

Pioneering Where the World is Old (Leaves from a manchurian note-book)/Alice Tisdale. —New York: Henry Holt and Company, c1917

xvi, 227 p. ;19 cm.

I712. 55/W526

Legends of Old Honolulu: Collected and Translated from the Hawaiian/W. D. Westervelt. —Boston: Press of GEO. H. Ellis Co. , c1915

ix, 282 p. ;19 cm.

I712. 55/W558

Prekaska's Wife: A Year in the Aleutians/Helen Wheaton. —New York: Dodd, Mead & Company, c1945

251 p. ;21 cm.

I712.55/W739

Alaska Holiday/Barrett Willoughby.—Boston: Little, Brown and Company, c1944

296 p.;22 cm.

I712.55/W776

Down the Stretch: The Story of Colonel Matt J. Win as Told to Frank G. Menke/Matt J. Winn.—New York: Simth & Surrell, c1945

xviii, 299 p.;23 cm.

I712.55/W913

Long, Long Ago/Alexander Woollcott.—New York: The Viking Press, c1943

vii, 280 p.;21 cm.

I712.6/A365

Crowding Memories/Thomas Bailey Aldrich.—Boston: Houghton Mifflin Company, c1920

viii, 295 p.;22 cm.

I712.6/B877

The Foe of Compromise and Other Essays/William Garrott Browm.—New York: The Macmillan Company, c1903

224 p.;18 cm.

I712.6/B915

Working for Democracy/Lyman Bryson, Kerry Smith.—New York: The Macmillan Company, c1941

xvi, 425 p.;21 cm.

I712.6/F247

Going Fishing/Negley Farson.—New York: Harcourt, Brace and Company, [?]

148 p.;25 cm.

I712.6/H399

Selections from Hawthorne/Hawthorne.—Tokyo: Keibundo, c1939

142, 27 p.;22 cm.

I712.6/H734

Every-Day Topics: A Book of Briefs/J. G. Holland.—New York: Scribner, Armstrong and Company, c1876

ix, 391 p.;20 cm.

I712.6/J75

Edgehill Essays/Adian Hoffman Joline.—Boston: Richard G. Badger, c1911

226 p.;23 cm.

I712.6/McK51

A School History of the Great War/Albert E. McKinley, Charles A. Coulomb, Armand J. Gerson.—New York: American Book Company, c1918

192 p.;17 cm.

I712.6/OS795

Essays of American Essayists/Chauncey C. Starkweather.—revised edition.—New York: The Colonial Press, c1900

viii, 456 p.;24 cm.

I712.6/P462

Roundup Time: A Collection of Southwestern Writing/George Sessions Perry.—New York: McGraw-Hill Book Company, Inc., c1943

xvi384 p.;24 cm.

I712.6/W913

As You Were: A Portable Library of American Prose and Poetry Assembled for Members of the Armed Forces and the Merchant Marine/Alexander Woollcott.—New York: The Viking Press, c1943

xiv, 657 p.;17 cm.

I712.6/W913L848

Long, Long Ago/Alexander Woollcott.—New York: The Viking Press, c1943

vii, 280 p.;21 cm.

I712.64/I72

The Sketch Book/Washington Irving. —London: Collins Clear-Type Press, [?]

410 p. ;15 cm.

I712.64/I72C

Selections from the Sketch-Book/Washington Irving. —Shanghai: The Commercial Press, c1929

xi, 200, 71 p. ;19 cm.

I712.64/I72C743

The Conquest of Granada/Washington Irving. —London and Toronto: J. M. Dent & Sons Ltd. , c1915

xiv, 351 p. ;17 cm.

I712.64/I72S625

The Sketch Book/Washington Irving. —New York: Literary Classics, Inc. , [?]

xix, 391 p. ;21 cm.

I712.64/L914(1)

Literary Essays. 1/James Russell Lowell. —Boston: Hughton, Mifflin and Company, c1864, 1871, 1876, 1890

vii, 381 p. ;20 cm.

I712.64/N274

Journal for Josephine/Robert Nathan. —New York: Alfred A. Knopf, c1943

142 p. ;20 cm.

I712.64/P612

Around the World Single-Handed: The Cruise of the "Islander"/Harry Pidgeon. —New York: D. Appleton-Century Company, c1932

ix, 233 p. ;22 cm.

I712.64/T488(O)

Walden, or, Life in the Woods and on the Duty of Civil Disobedience/Henry David Thoreau. —London: Penguin Books Ltd. , c1938

278 p. ;18 cm.

I712.64/T488W162K33

Walden/Henry David Thoreau. —Tokyo: Kenkyusha, c1928

xxi, 500 p. ;19 cm.

I712.65/B972(7)

The Writings of John Burroughs. xii, Ways of Nature/John Burroughs. —Boston: Houghton Mifflin Company, c1905

279 p. ;19 cm.

I712.65/B995

Alone/Richard E. Byrd. —London: Readers Union Ltd. , c1939

xiii, 302 p. ;20 cm.

I712.65/C278

Greenland Lies North/William S. Carlson. —New York: The Macmillan Company, c1944

306 p. ;21 cm.

I712.65/C672

A-Hiking we will go/Jack van Coevering. —Philadelphia: J. B. Lippincott Company, c1941

214 p. ;22 cm.

I712.65/C853

By the Sweat of the Brow/Rev. Chas. E. Coughlin. —Michigan: The Radio League of the Little Flower, c1931

191 p. ;23 cm.

I712.65/D994

Out-of-Doors in the Holy Land: Impressions of Travel in Body and Spirit/Henry Van Dyke. —New York: Charles Scribner's Sons, c1908

xii, 325 p. ;19 cm.

I712.65/L914

Lastest Literary Essays and Addresses/James Russell Lowell. —Boston: Houghton, Mifflin and Company, c1891

322 p. ;20 cm.

I712. 65/M391

Dream Life/Ik Marvel. —New York: H. M. Caldwell Co. , Publishers, [?]

265 p. ;16 cm.

I712. 65/M754

H. M. Corvette/Nicholas Monsarrat. —Philadelphia: J. B. Lippincott Company, c1943

169 p. ;21 cm.

I712. 65/P349

The Road of a Naturalist/Donald Culross Peattie. —Boston: Houghton Mifflin Company, c1941

viii, 314 p. ;21 cm.

I712. 65/P349J86

Journey into America/Donald Culross Peattie. —Boston: Houghton Mifflin Company, c1943

276 p. ;21 cm.

I712. 65/R498

Happy the Land/Louise Dickinson Rich. —Philadelphia: J. B. Lippincott Company, c1946

259 p. ;21 cm.

I712. 67/B868

Pleasant Valley/Louis Bromfield. —New York: Harper & Brothers Publishers, c1943

vii, 301 p. ;22 cm.

I712. 7/C978

Indian Days of the Long Ago/Edward S. Curtis. —New York: World Book Company, c1932

x, 221 p. ;21 cm.

I712. 73/B748

A Treasury of American Folklore: Stories, Ballads, and Traditions of the People/B. A. Botkin. —New York: Crown Publishers, c1944

xxvii, 932 p. ;22 cm.

I712. 73/B972

Tarzan Triumphant/Edgar Rice Burroughs. —New York: Grosset & Dunlap, c1932

318 p. ;19 cm.

I712. 73/C776

The Headsman: A Tale/J. Fenimore Cooper. —New York: D. Appletion & Company, [?]

466 p. ;20 cm.

I712. 73/C776H465

The Heidenmauer or, the Benedictines: A Legend of the Rhine/J. Fenimore Cooper. —New York: D. Appleton & Company, [?]

436 p. ;20 cm.

712. 73/C776T

The Two Admirals: A Tale/J. Fnimore Cooper. —New York: D. Appleton & Company, [?]

532 p. ;20 cm.

I712. 73/C776W

Wyandotte or, the Hutted Knoll/J. Fenimore Cooper. —New York: D. Appleton & Company, [?]

485 p. ;20 cm.

I712. 73/F251

The American: A Middle Western Legend/Howard Fast. —New York: Duell, Sloan and Pearce, c1946

337 p. ;21 cm.

I712. 73/G778

The New Anecdota Americana: Five Hundred Stories for America's Amusement/The Grayson Publishing Corp. —New York: The Grayson Publishing Corp. , c1944

v, 171 p. ;21 cm.

I712.73/H399

A Wonder Book and Tanglewood Tales/Nathaniel Hawthorne.—London: J. M. Dent & Sons, Ltd., c1914

404 p.;17 cm.

I712.73/L919

Ghosts That Still Walk: Real Ghosts of America/Marion Lowndes.—New York: Alfred A. Knopf, Inc., c1941

xvi, 147 p.;19 cm.

I712.73/M689

Bulfinch's Mythology: The age of Fable the age of Chivalry Legends of Charlemagne/Ther Modern Library.—New York: The Modern Library, c1934

778 p.;21 cm.

I712.73/S539

A Book of Short Stories/Stuart P. Sherman.—New York: Henry Holt and Company, c1914

xxxiv, 353 p.;17 cm.

I712.74/E49(3)

Cathedral Basic Readers. Book Three/John A. Elson.—Chicago: Sott, Forerman and Company, c1931

336 p.;20 cm.

I712.74/OB853(2)

Cathedral Basic Readers. Book Two/Rev. John A. O'Brien.—Chicago: Sott, Forerman and Company, c1931

174 p.;19 cm.

I712.74/OB853(5)

Cathedral Basic Readers. Book Five/Rev. John A. O'Brien.—Chicago: Sott, Forerman and Company, c1931

448 p.;19 cm.

I712.78/C411

Try and Stop Me: A Collection of Anecdotes and Stories, Mostly Humorous/Bennett Cerf.—New York: Simon and Schuster, c1944

378 p.;22 cm.

I712.78/F336

Time to Laugh: Funny Tales from Here and There/Phyllis R. Fenner.—New York: Alfred A. Knopf, c1942

240 p.;20 cm.

I712.78/S957

Irvin Cobb at His Best/The Sun Dial Press.—New York: The Sun Dial Press, c1940

341 p.;20 cm.

I712.8/B517

The Man Who Never Died/Gerald T. Brennan.—Chicago: The Bruce Publishing Company, c1946

96 p.;20 cm.

I712.82/T468

More Silver Pennies/Blanche Jennings Thompson.—New York: The Macmillan Company, c1938

155 p.;20 cm.

I712.83/M153

The House of the Heart and Other Plays for Children: Designed for Use in the Schools/Constance D'Arcy Mackay.—New York: Henry Holt and Company, c1909

226 p.;17 cm.

I712.84/A365

The Story of a Bad Boy/Thomas Bailey Aldrich.—Chicago: The Goldsmith Publishing Company, [?]

250 p.;21 cm.

I712. 84/B858
Caddie Woodlawn/Carol Ryrie Brink. —New York: The Macmillan Company, c1936
x, 270 p. ;21 cm.

I712. 84/B964L778
Little Lord Fauntleroy/Frances Hodgson Burnett. —New York: Charles Scribner's Sons, c1915
ix, 290 p. ;19 cm.

I712. 84/B964M389
Little Lord Fauntleroy/Frances Hodgson Burnett. —Tokyo: Maruzen Co. , Ltd. , [?]
242 p. ;19 cm.

I712. 84/D235
The Blue Book of Medal Stories/The Daughters of Charity Emmitsburg, Maryland. —Rainbow ed.. —Racine: Whitman Publishing Co. , c1934
140 p. ;18 cm.

I712. 84/D621
The Twisted Claw/by Franklin W. Dixon.. —New York: Grosset & Dunlap Publishers, c1939
217 p. ;20 cm.

I712. 84/D966
The Boy Scouts' Victory/George Durston. —Chicago: The Saalfield Publishing Company, [?]
1 v. ;19 cm.

I712. 84/F394
The X Bar X Boys at Nugget Camp/James Cody Ferris. —New York: Grosset & Dunlap Publishers, c1928
iv, 216 p. ;19 cm.

I712. 84/F453
Hitty: Her First Hundred Years/Rachel Field. —New York: The Macmillan Company, c1946
ix, 207 p. ;22 cm.

I712. 84/F855
Child-Story Readers/Frank N. Freeman, Eleanor M. Johnson. —New York: Lyons and Carnahan, Publisher, c1929-1930
480 p. ;19 cm.

I712. 84/F855(2)
Child-Story Readers. Second Reader /Frank N. Freeman, Eleanor M. Johnson. —New York: Lyons and Carnahan, c1927-30
296 p. ;19 cm.

I712. 84/F855(3)
Child-Story Readers. Third Reader /Frank N. Freeman, Eleanor M. Johnson. —New York: Lyons and Carnahan, c1927-30
413 p. ;19 cm.

I712. 84/F855(5)
Child-Story Readers. Fifth Reader /Frank N. Freeman, Eleanor M. Johnson. —New York: Lyons and Carnahan, c1927-30
280 p. ;19 cm.

I712. 84/F855(6)
Child-Story Readers. Sixth Reader/Frank N. Freeman, Eleanor M. Johnson. —New York: Lyons and Carnahan, c1929
480 p. ;19 cm.

I712. 84/F855(14)
Child-Story Readers. Vol. 14/Frank N. Freeman, Eleanor M. Johnson. —New York: Lyons and Carnahan, Publisher, c1929-1930
480 p. ;19 cm.

I712. 84/F855(3, 12)
Child-Story Readers. Book 3, vol. xii/Frank N. Freeman, Eleanor M. Johnson. —New York: Lyons and Carnahan, c1927-29
413 p. ;19 cm.

I712. 84/J72K778

The Little Colonet/Annie Fellows Johnston. —Shirlly Temple ed.. —Boston: L. C. Page and Company, c1922

145 p. ;21 cm.

I712. 84/K26

The Secret at Shadow Ranch/Carolyn Keene. —New York: Grosser & Dunlap Publishers, c1931

iv, 203 p. ;19 cm.

I712. 84/K26S578

The Sign of the Twisted Candles/Carolyn Keene. —New York: Grosset & Dunlap, c1933.

iv, 217 p. , [1] leaf of plates;20 cm.

I712. 84/L673

Young Fu of the Upper Yangtze/Elizabeth Foreman Lewis. —Chicago: The John C. Winston Company, c1932

265 p. ;22 cm.

I712. 84/McN595

Crazy Weather/Charles L. McNichols. —New York: The Macmillan Company, 1944

195 p. ;19 cm.

I712. 84/T969(O)

The Adventures of Tom Sawyer/Mark Twain. —New York: Harper & Brothers Publishers, c1903

290 p. ;20 cm.

I712. 84/W218

Jeremy/Hugh Walpole. —New York: Grosset & Dunlap, c1919

xii, 341 p. ;20 cm.

I712. 84/W655M887

Mother Carey's Chickens/Kate Douglas Wiggin. —Boston: Houghton Mifflin Company, c1911

v, 355 p. ;19 cm.

I712. 84/W995(O)

The Swiss Family Robinson, or, Adventures on a Desert Island/Johann Wyss. —London: Thomas Nelson and Sons, [?]

xvi, 565 p. ;19 cm.

I712. 84/W995S976(O)

The Swiss Family Robinson/Jean Rudolph Wyss. —Chicago: The Goldsmith Publishing Company, [?]

250 p. ;20 cm.

I712. 84/W995S976F198(O)

The Swiss Family Robinson, or, Adventures on a Desert Island/Johann Wyss. —Chicago: Rand McNally & Company, c1916

441 p. ;23 cm.

I712. 85/A545

The Austin Boys-Marooned/Ken Anderson. Grand Papids: Zondervan Publishing House, [?]

100 p. ;19 cm.

I712. 85/A841

Short Stories for Short People/Alicia Aspinwall. —New York: E. P. Dutton & Co. , Inc. , c1896

254 p. ;20 cm.

I712. 85/B954

The Adventures of Reddy Fox/Thornton W. Burgess. —Boston: Little, Brown and Company, c1918

vi, 120 p. ;18 cm.

I712. 85/C774

What Katy Did/Susan Coolidge. —London: Blackie and Son Ltd. , [?]

192 p. ;19 cm.

I712.85/D621

The Secret Warning/Franklin W. Dixon.—New York: Grosset & Dunlap Publishers, c1938

iv, 220 p.;19 cm.

I712.85/D621

The Sinister Sign Post/Franklin W. Dixon.—New York: Crosset & Dunlap Publishers, c1936

215 p.;19 cm.

I712.85/D621C

The Clue of the Broken Blade/by Franklin W. Dixon; illustrated by Paul Laune..—New York: Grosset & Dunlap, c1942.

vi, 218 p.;20 cm.

I712.85/D621G786

The Great Airport Mystery/Fanklin W. Dixon.—New York: Grosset & Dunlap Publisheres, c1930

ix, 210 p.;19 cm.

I712.85/D621H948

Hunting for Hidden Gold/Franklin W. Dixon.—New York: Grosset & Dunlap Publishers, c1928

iv, 214 p.;20 cm.

I712.85/D621M678

The Missing Chums/Franklin W. Dixon.—New York: Grosset & Dunlap Publishers, c1928

iv, 214 p.;19 cm.

I712.85/D621O196

Over the Ocean to Paris, or Ted Scott's Daring Long-Distance Flight/Franklin W. Dixon.—New York: Grosset & Dunlap Publishers, c1927

vi, 214 p.;20 cm.

I712.85/D621S559

The Shore Road Mystery/Franklin W. • Dixon.—New York: Grosset & Dunlap Publishers, c1928

iv, 212 p.;19 cm.

I712.85/D621W676

While the Clock Ticked/Franklin W. Dixon.—New York: Grosset & Dunlap Publishers, c1932

iv, 213 p.;19 cm.

I712.85/E49(3)

The Elson Basic Readers. Book Three/William Eison, William S. Gray.—Chicago: Scott, Foresman and Company, c1931

336 p.;19 cm.

I712.85/E49(6)

The Elson Basic Readers. Book Six/William Eison, William S. Gray.—Chicago: Scott, Foresman and Company, c1931

464 p.;19 cm.

I712.85/G347C356

Children of the Morning/W. L. Gforge.—New York: G. P. PutnaM's Sons, c1927

305 p.;19 cm.

I712.85/L765

Wilderness Champion: The Story of a Great Hound/Joseph Wharton Lippincott.—New York: J. B. Lippincott Company, c1944

195 p.;23 cm.

I712.85/L775

Told Under the Green Umbrella: Old Stories for New Children/Literature Committee of the International Kindergarten Union.—New York: The Macmillan Company, c1946

x, 188 p.;20 cm.

I712.85/M647(2)

Up One Pair of Stairs of My Bookhouse. 2/Olive Beaupre Miller.—Chicago: The Bookhouse for Children, c1920, 1925

448 p.;24 cm.

I712.85/M681

Another Here and Now Story Book/Lucy Sprague Mitchell.—New York: E.P. Dutton & Co., Inc., c1946

xxvi, 369 p.;19 cm.

I712.85/M681

Here and Now Story Book: Two-to Seven-Year-old/Lucy Sprague Mitchell.—New York: E.P. Dutton & Company, Inc., c1921

xii, 360 p.;19 cm.

I712.85/P448

The American Twins of 1812/Lucy Fitch Perkins.—Boston: Houghton Mifflin Company, c1925

194 p.;19 cm.

I712.85/P466

The Radio Boys in Gold Valley; The Mystery of the Deserted Mining Camp/Allen Chapman.—New York: Grosset & Dunlap Publishers, c1927

222 p.;20 cm.

I712.85/S245

The Human Comedy/William Saroyan.—Cleveland: The World Publishing Company, c1945

ix, 291 p.;21 cm.

I712.85/S562

Barefoot Boy with Cheek/Max Shulman.—Philadelphia: The Blakiston Company, c1944

207 p.;19 cm.

I712.85/S569

Five Little Peppers Midway/Margaret Sindney.—New York: Grosset & Dunlap Publishers, c1890

426 p.;21 cm.

I712.85/T486

Pirates in Oz/Ruth Plumly Thompson.—Chicago: The Reilly & Lee Co., c1931

280 p.;21 cm.

I712.85/W119

Second Reader/Joseph H. Wade, Emma Sylvester.—Boston: Ginn & Company, c1906

160 p.;19 cm.

I712.85/W187

Barington/Edward Tatum Wallace.—New York: Simon and Schuster, c1945

311 p.;20 cm.

I712.85/W577(O)

Mistress Masham's Repose/T. H. White.—New York: G.P. Putnam's Sons, c1946

254 p.;21 cm.

I712.85/W786

The Gingerbread Boy/Milo Winter.—Chicago: Merrill Publishing Co., c1938

1 v.;32 cm.

I712.85/W947

The Great Modern French Stories: A Chronological Anthology/Willard Huntington Wright.—New York: Boni and Liveright, c1917

xlii, 409 p.;20 cm.

I712.88/L829

The Story of Doctor Dolittle/Hugh Lofting.—New York: J. B. Lippingcott Co., c1920

xii, 180 p.;19 cm.

I712.88/M112

Legends That Every Child Should Know: A Selection of the Great Legends of All Times for Young People/Hamilton Wright Mabie.—New York: Grosset & Dunlap Publishers, c1906

265 p.;19 cm.

I712.935/S594

Thrillers: Seven New Non-Royalty Plays for

Men and Boys/S. Sylvan Simon. —New York: Samuel French, c1943
viii, 144 p. ;20 cm.

I712. 99/B974
A Harmony of the Synoptic Gospels for Historical and Critical Study/Ernest Dewitt Burton. —New York: Charles Scribner's Sons, c1917
xv, 275 p. ;22 cm.

I712. 99/H967
Sketches for the Exercises of An Eight Days' Retreat/Hugo Hurter. —3rd ed. . —St. Louis: B. Herder Book Co. , c1926
xii, 275 p. ;19 cm.

I712. 99/M283
Chronicles of "The Little Sisters"/Mary E. Mannix. —Indiana: Notre Dame, c1899
368 p. ;19 cm.

I712. 99/M626
The Conduct of Brief Devotional Meetings/Paul Micou. —New York: Association Press, c1917
vii, 100 p. ;17 cm.

I712. 99/P314
Up the Shining Path/Margaret Patrice. —Milwaukee: The Bruce Publishing Company, c1946
173 p. ;20 cm.

I712. 99/S559
Twice-Born Ministers/S. M. Shoemaker. —New York: Fleming H. Revell Company, [?]
198 p. ;19 cm.

I712. 99/S743
The Road to Victory/Francis J. Spellman. —New York: Charles Scribner's Sons, c1942
xi, 131 p. ;20 cm.

I712. 99/S743R595
The Risen Soldier/Francis J. Spellman. —New York: The Macmillan Company, c1944
39 p. ;19 cm.

I71245/B922
Dragon Seed/Pearl S. Buck. —New York: The John Day Company, c1941, 1942
378 p. ;21 cm.

IG633. 41/W256
Manual for the Junior Highway to English: Revised Books one and two/C. H. Ward, H. Y. Moffett. —Chical: Scott, Foresman and Company, c1923
iv, 282 p. ;19 cm.

J 艺术

J0-05/S722
The Useful Art of Economics/George Soule. —New York: The Macmillan Company, c1929
250 p. ;19 cm.

J01/G622-3
Art in Everyday Life/Harriet Goldstein, Vetta Goldstein. —3rd ed. . —New York: The Macmillan Company, c1946
xxxvi, 497 p. ;24 cm.

J120. 9/M821

A History of Chinese Art: From Ancient Times to the Present Day/George Soulie De Morant. —London: George G. Harrap & Co. , Ltd. , c1931

295 p. ;24 cm.

J2/R956(3)

Modern Painters. 3/John Ruskim. —London: J. M. Dent. & Co. , c1945

325 p. ;18 cm.

J2/R956(4)

Modern Painters. Volume Four/John Ruskim. —London: J. M. Dent. & Co. , c1945

x, 389 p. ;18 cm.

J2/R956(5)

Modern Painters. 5/John Ruskim. —London: J. M. Dent. & Co. , c1945

368 p. ;18 cm.

J215/R876

The Art of Landscape Painting in Water Colours. vol. 3/Thomas Rowbotham, Thomas L. Rowbotham. —London: Winsor & Newton, Ltd. , [?]

56, 7 p. ;19 cm.

J218. 2/J66

Barnaby/Crockett • Johnson. —New York: Henry Holt and Company, c1943

361 p. ;19 cm.

J31/J12

Wood-Carving Design and Workmanship/ George Jack. —New York: D. Appleton and Company, c1903

311 p. ;19 cm.

J314. 2/J12

Wood Carving: Design and Workmanship/ George Jack. —London: John Hogg 13 Paternoster Row, c1903

318 p. ;19 cm.

J314. 2/T161

Whittling and Woodcarving/E. J. Tangerman. —New York: Whittlesey House, c1936

x, 293 p. ;23 cm.

J4/T253

The Boys' Book of Photography/Edwin Way Teale. —New York: E. P. Dutton & Co. , Inc. , c1941

252 p. ;20 cm.

J403/N358

Elementary Photography for Club and Home Use/C. B. Neblette. —New York: The Macmillan Company, c1937

viii, 253 p. ;20 cm.

J525. 1/G622

Art in Every Day Life/Harriet Goldstein, Vetta Goldstein. —Revised Edision. —New York: The Macmillan Company, c1938

xxix, 527 p. ;21 cm.

J6/T174-2

Chats with Music Students, or, Talks About Music and Music Life/Thomas Tapper. —revised ed. . —Philadelphia: Theodore Presser Co. , c1901

340 p. ;17 cm.

J6-62/K81

New Guide to Recorded Music/Irving Kolodin. —New York: Doubleday & Company, Inc. , c1947

xxi, 382 p. ;22 cm.

J6-62/S571

The Music Lover's Handbook/edited by Elie Siegmeister. —New York: William Morrow and Company Morrow and Company, c1943.

xiii, 817 p. ;22 cm.

J6-62/U65

The Standard Concert Guide: A Handbook of the Standard Symphonies, Oratorios Cantatas, and Symphonic Poems for he Concert Goer/George P. Upton. —Chicago: A. C. Mcclurg & Co. , c1908

xvi, 502 p. ;18 cm.

J60/D553

The Eduction of a Music Lover: A Book for Those Who Study of Teach the Art of Listening/Edward Dickinson. —New York: Charles Scribner's sons, c1916

xi, 293 p. ;20 cm.

J60/F263

What We Hear in Music: A Course of Study in Music Appreciation and History/Anne Shaw Faulkner. —Camden: RCA Victor Co. , Inc. , c1931

628 p. ;21 cm.

J60/J76

Theory fo Music: Fundamentals of Music and Music Notation Elementary Harmony and Form the Instruments of the Orchestra/Robert Gomer Jones. —New York: Harper & Brother Publishers, c1936

vii, 131 p. ;22 cm.

J603/T222

Music on My Beat: An Intimate Volume of Shop Talk/Howard Taubman. —New York: Simon and Schuster, c1943

viii, 267 p. ;21 cm.

J605/McK51-2

Discovering Music: A Course in Music Appreciation/Howard D. McKinney, W. R. Anderson. —2nd ed.. —New York: American Book Company, c1943, 1934

xx, 470 p. ;23 cm.

J605/S732

The Art of Enjoying Music/Sigund Spaeth. —New York: New York Publishing Co. , Inc. , c1942

xiv, 451 p. ;20 cm.

J605/T238

The Well Tempered Listener/Deems Taylor. —New York: Simon and Schuster, c1940

xv, 333 p. ;21 cm.

J609. 1/B197

A Complete History of Music: For Schools, Clubs, and Private Reading/W. J. Baltzell. —Philadelphia: Theodore Presser Co. , c1905

564 p. ;20 cm.

J609. 1/C772

Young Folks' Picture-History of Music/James Francis Cooke. —Philadelphia: Theo. Presser Co. , c1925

82 p. ;23 cm.

J609. 1/W582

History of Music: A Text Book on Music of the Different Nations from Early Egyptians to the Present Day/Matilda P. White-Rudgers. —Cincinnati: The Willis Music Company, c1907

204 p. ;20 cm.

J61/G599

Exercises in Elementary Counterpoint/Percy Goetschius. —New York: G. Schirmer, Inc. , c1910

169 p. ;22 cm.

J613/T174

First Year Analysis: Musical Form/Thomas Tapper. —Boston: The Arthur P. Schmidt Co. , c1914

113 p. ;17 cm.

J613. 1/H432

Harmony for Ear, Eye, and Keyboard/Arthur Edward Heacox. —Boston: Oliver Ditson Company, [?]

x, 184 p. ;20 cm.

J615. 1/F514(1)

The Art of the Choral Conductor. Vol. one, Choral Technique/William J. Finn. —Boston: C. C. Birchard and Company, c1939

viii, 292 p. ;23 cm.

J65/D994

Twice 55 Plus Community Songs: The New Brown Songs/Peter W. Dykema, Will Earhart. —Boston: C. C. Birchard and Company. , [?]

1 v. ;21 cm.

J652/B223-5

The Service Song Book/Clarence A. Barbour. —5th ed.. —New York: Association Press, c1917

232 p. ;19 cm.

J652/B526

Song and Serbire Book for Ship and Field Armg and Nabg/Jban L. Bernett. —Washington: United States Government Printing Office, c1942

192 p. ;17 cm.

J652/B952

United States Navy Song Book/The Bureau of Naval Personnel. —[S. l. : s. n.], [c1945]

94 p. ;22 cm.

J652/R573

Tunes and Runes for the School Room/Alice C. D. Riley, Dorothy Riley Brown. —Chicago: Clayton F. Summy Co. , c1925

56 p. ;26 cm.

J652/S647

Songs We Sing/Fowler Smith, Harry Robert Wilson, Glenn H. Woods. —Chicago: Hall & Mccreary Company, c1941

120 p. ;24 cm.

J652. 1/S642

Songs We Sing/Fowler Smith. —Chicago: Hill & Mccreary Company, c1940

144 p. ;24 cm.

J652. 2/N113

Song and Serbice Book for Ship and Field/Armg and Nabg. —Washington: United States Government Printing Office, c1942

192 p. ;17 cm.

J652. 2(712)/G795

Northwestern Songs/Albert B. Green, Carl M. Beecher. —Dixon: Rogers Printing, c1909

91 p. ;26 cm.

J652. 6/B167

Songs for the Little Child/Clara Belle Baker. —New York: Abingdon-Cokesbury Press, c1921

100 p. ;21 cm.

J652. 6/G453

Introductory Music/Thaddeus P. Giddings, Will Earhart, Ralph L. Baldwin. —Boston: Ginn and Company, c1923

176 p. ;21 cm.

J652. 6/McC743(2)

New Music Horizons. Second Book/Osbourne Mcconathy, Russell V. Morgan. —New York: Silver Burdett Company, c1944

139 p. ;20 cm.

J652. 6/McC743(3)

New Music Horizons. Third Book/Osbourne Mcconathy. —New York: Silver Burdett Compa-

ny, c1944
163 p. ;20 cm.

J652. 6/McC743(4)
New Music Horizons. Fourth Book/Osbourne Mcconathy, Russell V. Morgan. —New York: Silver Burdett Company, c1945
188 p. ;20 cm.

J692. 4/M179-7
Instrumental Technique for Orchestra and Band: An Exhaustive and Practical Text-book for Teachers, Conductors and Students/J. E. Maddy, T. P. Giddings. —7th ed. , Revised and Enlarged. . —Cincinnati: The Willis Music Company, c1926
viii, 267 p. ;25 cm.

J732. 8/L477
Dancing/Betty Lee. —New York: Edward J. Clode, Inc. , c1934
x, 298 p. ;19 cm.

J732. 8/S587
Theory and Technique of Ballroom Dancing/Victor Silvester. —Revised and Enlarged ed. . —London: Herbert Jenkins Ltd. , c1932
153 p. ;19 cm.

J832/V642
The Victor Book of the Opera: Stories of Seventy Grand Operas with Three Hundred Illustrations & Descriptions of Seven Hundred Victor Opera Records/Victor Talking Machine Co. ,—Camden: Victor Talking Machine Co. , c1912
375 p. ;21 cm.

K 历史、地理

K/C495
Danger Zone: The Story of the Queenstown Command/E. Keble Chatterton. —Boston: Little, Brown and Company, c1934
437 p. ;23 cm.

K05/M117
Essays on Lord Clive and Warren Hastings/Thomas Babington • Macaulay. —New York: Charles E. Merrill Co. , c1910
339 p. ;17 cm.

K09/K21
Modern Languages for Modern Schools/Walter Vincent Kaulfers. —New York: McGraw-Hill Book Company, Inc. , c1942
xviii, 525 p. ;24 cm.

K1/B662(2)
World History. Volume 2/Arthur E. R. Boak, Preston Slosson, Howard R. Anderson. —Boston: Houghton Mifflin Company, c1944
279-554 p. ;24 cm.

K1/B662
World History/Arthur E. R. Boak, Preston Slosson. —Boston: Houghton Mifflin Company, c1946
554, xvi p. ;27 cm.

K1/E49
Modern Time and the Living Past/Henry W. Elson. —New York: American Book Company, c1930
viii, 730 p. , xxxviii;20 cm.

K1/H436

The Social and Political Ideas of Some Great Mediaeval Thinkers: A Series of Lectures Delivered at King's College, University of London/edited by F. J. C. Hearnshaw. —London: G. G. Harrap & Company, Ltd. , 1923.

223 p. ;23 cm.

K1/I58(4)

The History of the World. Volume IV/Arthur Donald Innes. —New York: J. A. Richards, Inc. , c1924

iii, 506 p. ;19 cm.

K1/R419

Outlines of General History: For Eastern Students/by Frank Moore Colby. —New York: American Book Company, c1900.

xxii, 485 p. ;22 cm.

K1/W453

The New and Revised Outline of History/H. G. Wells. —New York: New York Publishing Company, Inc. , c1920

xxi, 1255 p. ;21 cm.

K1/W453-3

The Outline of History: Being a Plain History of Life and Mankind/H. G. Wells. —3rd ed. . —New York: The Macmillan Company, c1922

xxi, 1171 p. ;22 cm.

K1/W721(1)

The Historian's History of the World. volume i, Introduction; Egypt, Mesopotamia/Henry Smith Williams. —London: The Encyclopaedia Briatnnica Co. , Ltd. , c1904, 1907, 1926

xii, 666 p. ;22 cm.

K1/W721(19)

The Historian's history of the world. volume xix, England, 1485-1642/Henry Smith Williams. —London: The Encyclopaedia Briatnnica Co. , Ltd. , c1904, 1907, 1926

xii, 663 p. ;22 cm.

K10/B395

Modern History: The Rise of a Democratic, Scientific, and Industrialized Civilization/Carl L. Becker. —New York: Silver Burdett Company, c1931

xiii, 889, xxiv p. ;21 cm.

K10/M996

General History/Philip Van Ness Myers. —Rebised ed. . —Boston: Ginn and Company, c1906

xv, 779 p. ;20 cm.

K10/M996-2

General History/Philip Van Ness Myers. —2nd Revised ed. . —Boston: Ginn and Company, c1921

xiv, 711, xxxiii p. ;20 cm.

K10/W721(3)

The Historians' History of the World. V. 3, Greece/Henry Smith Williams. —London: The Encyclopaedia Britannica Co. , Ltd. , c1904, 1907, 1926

xiv, 639 p. ;22 cm.

K10/W721(5)

The Historians' History of the World. V. 5, The Roman Republic/Henry Smith Williams. —London: The Encyclopaedia Britannica Co. , Ltd. , c1904, 1907, 1926

xii, 672 p. ;23 cm.

K10/W721(11)

The Historians' History of the World. V. 11, France/Henry Smith Williams. —London: The Encyclopaedia Britannica Co. , Ltd. , c1904, 1907, 1926

xiv, 653 p. ;22 cm.

K10/W721(21)

The Historians' History of the World. V. 21, Scotland and Ireland; England Since 1792/Henry Smith Williams. —London: The Encyclopaedia Britannica Co., Ltd., c1904, 1907, 1926

xiii, 654 p.; 22 cm.

K10/W874

A Popular History of the World/Clement Wood. —New York: Lantern Library Grosset & Dunlap, c1935

xi, 370 p.; 22 cm.

K103/H949

Mainsprings of Civilization/Ellsworth Huntington. —New York: John Wiley and Sons, Inc., c1945

xii, 660 p.; 22 cm.

K103/K37

Old Tartar Trails/A. S. Kent. —Shanghai: North-China Daily News and Herald, Ltd., c1919

153 p.; 24 cm.

K103/M996-2

Mediaeval and Modern History/Philip Van Ness Myers. —Revised ed.. —Boston: Ginn & Company, c1905

xvi, 751 p.; 20 cm.

K103/S225

Ther Pivot of Civilization/Margaret Sanger. —New York: Brentano's Publishers, c1922

xviii, 284 p.; 19 cm.

K105/B619

Famous Trials of History/Earl of Birkenhead. —New York: New York Publishing Co., Inc., c1926

319 p.; 21 cm.

K105/E93

Exciting Experiences in the Japanese-Russian War/Marshall Everett. —[S. l.]: Henry Nell, c1904

1 v.; 23 cm.

K106/B499

The History of Reparations/Carl Bergmann. —Boston: Houghton Mifflin Company, c1927

xx, 333 p.; 26 cm.

K107/P267-7

Some Lies and Errors of History/Rev. Peuben Parsons. —7th ed. Revised. —Indiana: Notre Dame, c1893

vii, 393 p.; 20 cm.

K109/W453(2)

Outline of History. Volume II/H. G. Wells. —New York: Triangle Books, c1940

xii, 413-803 p.; 19 cm.

K12/O91

A Brief History of Greece and Rome/The Rev. E. C. Everard Owen. —London: Blackie & Son Ltd., c1913

viii, 298 p.; 18 cm.

K125/R261

Herodotus: The Persian Warsd/George Rawlinson. —New York: The Modern Library, c1942

xxii, 714 p.; 18 cm.

K126/F828

A History of Rome/Tenney Frank. —New York: Henry Holt and Company, c1923

viii, 613 p.; 22 cm.

K13/A213

Civilization During the Middle Ages: Especially in Relation to Modern Civilization/George Burton Adams. —Revised ed.. —New York:

Charles Scribener's Sons, c1894, 1914
vi, 455 p. ;21 cm.

K14/M996
Outlines of Nineteenth Century History/Phlip Van Ness Myers. —London: Ginn & Company, c1885, 1905, 1906
v, 138 p. ;20 cm.

K143/F939
The Battle of Jutland/Holloway H. Frost. —London: United States Naval Institute, c1936
xiv, 571 p. ;23 cm.

K143/M654
Road to War: America: 1914-1917/Waite Millis. —[S. l. : s. n.], [?]
460 p. ;21 cm.

K152/E36
Crusade in Europe/Dwight D. Eisenhower. —New York: Doubleday, c1948.
xiv, 559 p. ;23 cm.

K152/I43
The World at War, 1939-1944: A Brief History of World War II/The Infantry Journal. —Washington: The Infantry Journal, c1945
416 p. ;17 cm.

K152/M654
This is Pearl: The United States and Japan-1941/Walter Millis. —New York: William Morrow & Company, c1947
xiii, 383 p. ;

K152/M665
Documents and Materials Relating to the Eve of the Second World War. Volume I/Ministry of Foreign Affairs of the U. S. S. R. . —[S. l. : s. n.], [?]
313 p. ;19 cm.

K18/K19
History and Destiny of the Jews/Josef Kastein. —New York: New York Publishing Co. , Inc. , 1936
viii, 464 p. ;21 cm.

K2/D731
China/Robert K. Douglas. —New York: G. P. Putnam's Sons, [?]
xv, 474 p. ;20 cm.

K20/B761(1)
History of China. Vol. 1/Demetrius Charles Boulger. —London: W. Thacker & Co. , c1898
734 p. ;21 cm.

K20/G654
A Short History of the Chinese People/L. Carrington Goodrich. —New York: Harper & Brothers Publishers, c1943
xv, 260 p. ;20 cm.

K203/P349
China: Collapse of a Civilization/Nathaniel Peffer. —New York: The John Day Company, c1930
vii, 306 p. ;24 cm.

K206/J66
A Study of Chinese Alchemy/Obed Simon Johnson. —Shanghai: The Commercial Press, Ltd. , c1928
xi, 156 p. ;21 cm.

K209/B495
The Story of China/R. Van Bergen. —New York: American Book Company, c1902
236 p. ;19 cm.

K25/B761(2)
The History of China. vol. II/Demetrius Charles Boulger. —London: W. Thacker & Co. , c1898

627, 31 p. ;21 cm.

K25/G517

Tsingtau Under Three Flags/Wilson Leon Godshall. —Shanghai: The Commercial Press, Ltd. , c1929

xi, 580 p. ;22 cm.

K25/G674

China/Harold E. Gorst. —London: Sands & Company, c1899

xx, 300 p. ;23 cm.

K25/H725

The Chinese Revolution: A Phase in the Regeneration of a World Power/Arthur N. Holcombe. —Cambrige: Harvard University Press, c1930

xiii, 401 p. ;23 cm.

K25/M379

The Siege in Peking: China against the World/W. A. P. Martin. —New York: Fleming H. Revell Company, c1900

190 p. ;20 cm.

K25/T482

China Revolutionized/John Stuart Thomson. —Indianapolis: The Bobbs-Merrill Company Publishers, c1913

590 p. ;22 cm.

K250. 6/S416

China: the Long-lived Empire/Eliza Ruhamah Scidmore. —New York: The Century Co. , c1900

xv, 466 p. ;21 cm.

K250. 6/W419

Russo-Chinese Diplomacy/Ken Shen Weigh. —Shanghai: Commercial Press, 1928.

xxi, 382 p. ;23 cm.

K254. 9/G662

Events in the Taeping Rebellion/General Gordon. —London: W. H. Allen and Co. , Ltd. , c1891

531 p. ;23 cm.

K258/B167

Explaining China/John Earl Baker. —London: A. M. Philpot Ltd. , c1927

xviii, 312 p. ;22 cm.

K258/B877

The Chinese Revolution/Arthur Judson Brown. —New York: Student Volunteer Movement, c1912

ix, 217 p. ;19 cm.

K258/Macm981(2)

Treaties and Agreements with and Concerning China 1894-1919. Vol. II, Republican Period (1912-1919)/John V. A. Macm. urray. —New York: Oxford University Press, c1921

930-1729 p. ;25 cm.

K258/T262

Affairs of China: a Survey of the Recent History and Present Circumstances of the Republic of China/Sir Eric Teichman. —London: Methuen, 1938.

311 p. ;23 cm.

K26/B724

News is My Job: A Correspondent in War-Torn China/Edna Lee Booker. —Shanghai: World Book Service, c1940

vii, 375 p. ;21 cm.

K26/C532

China: Shall Rise Again/May-Ling Song Chiang. —New York: Happer & Brothers Publishers, c1940

xv, 356 p. ;22 cm.

K263/A142

My Life in China: 1926-1941/Hallett Abend. —New York: Harcourt, Brace and Company, c1943

viii, 395 p. ;21 cm.

K263/A142R311

Reconquest Its Results and Responsibilities/Hallett Abend. —New York: Doubleday & Company, Inc. , c1946

305 p. ;20 cm.

K264/W632

The Truce in the East and Its Aftermath: Being the Sequel to The re-shaping of the Far East/by B. L. Putnam Weale [pseud.]. —New York: The Macmillan Company, 1907.

xv, 647 p. ;23 cm.

K265/T665

China Handbook, 1937-1945: A Comprehensive Survey of Major Developments in China in Eight Years of War/Compiled by Chinese ministry of information. —Rev. and enl. . —New York: Macmillan Co. , c1947.

xvi, 862 p. , 1 folded chart;22 cm.

K265.61/H825

Manchuria: Its People, Resources and Recent History/Alexander Hosie. —London: Methuen & Co. , c1901

xi, 293 p. ;22 cm.

K265.61-54/M151(1941)

The Manchoukuo Year Book/The Manchoukuo Year Book Co. ,—Hsinking: The Manchoukuo Year Book, c1940

xiv, 961 p. ;22 cm.

K266.1/T295

Chungking Listening Post/Mark Tennien. —New York: Creative Age Press, Inc. , [1945].

201 p. ;21 cm.

K293-54/T111-2(1931)

The Manchuria Year Book, 1931. /Tao-Keizai Chosakyoku (East-Asiatic Economic Investigation Bureau),. —2nd ed. . —Tokyo: Tao-Keizai Chosakyoku (East-Asiatic Economic Investigation Bureau), 1931.

xi, 347 p. ;23 cm.

K295.2/H459

On the Shantung Front: A History of the Shantung Mission of the Presbyterian Church in the U. S. A. 1861-1940 in ins Historical, Economic, and Political Setting/John J. Heeren. —New York: The Board of Foreign Missions of the Presbyterian Church in the United States of America, c1940

xiii, 264 p. ;23 cm.

K295.2/Z93

Tsingtao: A Historical, Political and Economic Survey/Kyi Zuh-Tsing. —Tsingtao: The Catholic Mission Press, c1930

xvi, 125 p. ;22 cm.

K3/K91

The Far East: Its History and Its Question/Alexis Krausse. —London: Richard Clay and Sons, Ltd. , c[1900]

372 p. ;22 cm.

K31/L419

War and Neutrality in the Far East/T. J. Lawrence. —London: Macmillan and Co. , Ltd. , c1904

xiii, 232 p. ;20 cm.

K31/P989

The Coming Struggle in Eastern Asia/B. L. Putnam. —London: Macmillan and Co. , Ltd. , c1909

xxvi, 656 p. ;23 cm.

K31/W223

The Sino-Japanese Conflict/Tom Walsh.—Sydney: Angus & Robertson Ltd., c1939

107 p.;22 cm.

K312.4/L154

In Korea with Marquis Ito/George Trumbull Ladd.—New York: Charles Scribner's Sons, c1908

x, 477 p.;21 cm.

K313.03/N731

Bushido: The Soul of Japan/Inazo Nitobe.—Tokyo: Kenkyusha, [?]

211 p.;19 cm.

K313.25/O56

Diaries of Court Ladies of Old Japan/Annie Shepley Omori.—Tokyo: Kenkyusha Co., c1935

xxix, 209 p.;23 cm.

K313.36/C683

With Perry in Japan: The Diary of Edwars Yorke Mccauley/Allan B. Cole.—Princeton: Princeton University Press, c1942

124 p.;24 cm.

K313.4/G971

Toward Understanding Japan: Constructive Proposals for Removing the Menace of War/Sidney L. Gulick.—New York: Macmillan, c1935

ix, 270 p.;21 cm.

K313.45/F949

The Great Earthquake of 1923 in Japan/The Bureau of Social Affairs, Home Office, Japan.—[S. l.: s. n.], c1926

xxvi, 615 p.;22 cm.

K342.41/V868

The Story of the Dutch East Indies/Bernard H. M. Vlekke.—Cambridge: Harvard University Press, c1945

xvii, 233 p.;22 vm

K351/D947

The Case for India/Will Durant.—[S. l.: s. n.], [?]

viii, 232 p.;18 cm.

K351.8/H361

The Land Pirates of India/W. J. Hatch.—London: Seeley, Service & Co., Ltd., c1928

272 p.;22 cm.

K37/H915

Twenty Years in the Near East/Ardern G. Hulme-Beaman.—London: Methuen & Co., c1898

viii, 315 p.;21 cm.

K381.98/V665

My First Two Thousand Years: The Autobiography of the Wandering Jew/George Sylvester Viereck, Paul Eldridge.—London: Duckworth, c1929

468 p.;22 cm.

K404/J66

A History of the Colonization of Africa by Alien Races/Sir Harry H. Johnston.—New ed., rev. throughout and Considerably enlarged..—Cambridge: University Press, 1930.

xvi, 505 p.;20cm.

K411.4/C727

The Making of Modern Egypt/Auckland Colvin.—London, Edinburgh, Dublin and New York: Thomas Nelson & Sons, [?]

384 p.;16 cm.

K421.53/N554

Italy's Conquest of Abyssinia/Major E. W. Polson Newman.—London: Thornton Butterworth Ltd., c1937

315 p. ;22 cm.

K5/A213

European History: An Outline of Its Development/George Burton Adams. —New York: The Macmillan Company, c1899

xxviii, 577 p. ;20 cm.

K5/C525

The End of the Armistice/G. K. Chesterton. — London: Sheed & Ward, c1940

223 p. ;19 cm.

K5/H815

Europe: The Mother of America/Charles F. Horne, Olive Bucks. —New York: Charles E. Merrill Company, c1930

xi, 294 p. ;19 cm.

K500/F533

A History of Europe/H. A. L. Fisher. —London: Edward Arnold & Co. , c1936

xiv, 1301 p. ;22 cm.

K500/R379

World History at A Glance/Joseph Reither. — New York: The New Home Library, c1942

xxi, 425 p. ;20 cm.

K500/R658(1)

Outlines of European History. part I, Robinson and Breasted/Robinson, Breasted. —Boston: Ginn and Company, [?]

xiii, 728 p. ;19 cm.

K500/R662(1)

Readings in European History. Vol. I, From the Breaking up of the Roman Empire to th Protestant Revolt/James Harvey Robinson. —Boston: Ginn & Company, c1904

xxxi, 551 p. ;19 cm.

K500/W744-7

Makers of Europe: Outlines of European History for the Middle Forms of Schools/E. M. Wilmot-Buxton. —7th ed. . —London: Methuen & Co. , c1906

xii, 260, 32 p. ;19 cm.

K503/D261

Medieval Europe/H. W. C. Davis. . —London: Williams and Norgate, c1930.

256 p. ;17 cm.

K503/H436

The Social & Political Ideas of Some Great Thinkers of the Renaissance and the Reformation: A Series of Lectures Delivered at King's College University of London/F. J. C. Hearnshaw. —London: George G. Harrap & Company Ltd. , c1925

215 p. ;22 cm.

K503/L213

The Crusades: The Whole Story of the Crusades Originally Published in Two Volumes as Iron Men and Saints and the Flame of Islam/Harold Lamb. —New York: Doubleday, Doran & Company, Inc. , c1930

xi, 490 p. ;22 cm.

K504/H429

Fifty Years of Europe (1870-1919)/Charles Downer Hazen. —London: G. Bell & Sons Ltd. , c1919

428 p. ;21 cm.

K504/H429-3

Modern European History/Charles Downer Hazen. —3rd ed. . —New York: Henry Holt and Company, c1919

xiv, 650 p. ;20 cm.

K504/H429E

Europe Since 1815/Charles Downer Hazen. —

New York: Henry Holt and Company, c1910
xxiv, 830 p. ;22 cm.

K504/H429F469
Fifty Years of Europe (1870-1919)/Charles Downer Hazen. —New York: Henry Holt and Company, c1919
428 p. ;21 cm.

K504/S398
A Political History of Modern Europe From the Reformation to the Present Day/Ferdinand Schwill. —New York: C. Scribner's Sons, 1907.
xiv, 607 p. ;21 cm.

K505/B395(2)
History of Modern Europe. Course Two, Democracy, Nationalism, and the Industrial Revolution/Carl L. Becker. —Washington: Silver Burdett Company, c1945
xii, 372, xiv p. ;19 cm.

K505/R658
History of Europe Our Own Times: The Eighteenth and Nineteenth Centuries: The opening of the Twentieth Century and the World War/ James Harvey Robinson, Charles A. Beard. —Boston: Ginn and Company, [?]
xii, 616, xxi p. ;20 cm.

K51/G295-6
Betrayal in Central Europe: Austria and Czechoslovakia: The Fallen Bastions/G. E. R. Gedye. —6th ed.. —New York and London: Harper & Brothers Publishers, c1939
ix, 499 p. ;22 cm.

K51/J13
The Post-War World: A Short Political History/J. Hampden Jackson. —London: Victor Gollance Ltd., c1938
520 p. ;19 cm.

K512/B362(1)
A History of the U. S. S. R.. Part One/K. V. Bazilevich, S. V. Bakhrushin, A. M. Pankratova. —Moscow: Foreign Languages Publishing House, c1947
254 p. ;22 cm.

K512/B362(3)
A History of the U. S. S. R.. Part three/K. V. Bazilevich, S. V. Bakhrushin, A. M. Pankratova. —Moscow: Foreign Languages Publishing House, c1948
427 p. ;22 cm.

K512/B363(2)
A History of the U. S. S. R.. Part Two/K. V. Bazilevich, S. V. Bakhrushin, A. M. Pankratova. —Moscow: Foreign Languages Publishing House, c1948
300 p. ;22 cm.

K512.0/S612
Russia and the Russian People/Simpkin, Marshall, Hamilton, Kent & Co., Ltd. —London: Simpkin, Marshall, Hamilton, Kent & Co., Ltd., c1914
128 p. ;18 cm.

K512.55/K95
The Life of Frederick the Great: Comprehending a Complete History of the Silesian Campaign and The Thirty Years' War/Francis Kugler. —New York: A. L. Burt Company, c1902
v, 453 p. ;19 cm.

K513.0/S959
Events and Personalities in Polish History/ Paul Super. —London: The Baltic Institute, c1936
115 p. ;17 cm.

K513.43/L265
I saw Poland Betrayed: an American Ambassa-

dor Reports to the American People/Arthur Bliss Lane. —Indianapolis: Bobbs-Merrill Co. , c1948.
344 p. ;23 cm.

K516. 44/K77
Inside the Gestapo: Hitler's Shadow Over the World/Hansjurgen Koehler. —[S. l. : s. n.], c1940
287 p. ;20 cm.

K516. 44/R647-9
The House that Hitler Built/Stephen H. Roberts. —9th ed. . —London: Methuen Publishers, c1938.
xii, 408 p. ;24 cm.

K545/R795
A Popular History of Greece: From the Earliest Period to the Incorporation with the Roman Empire/D. Rose. —London: Ward, Lock and Co. , [?]
472 p. ;21 cm.

K545. 0/J88
Grecian History: An Outline Sketch/James Richard Joy. —New York: Chautauqua Press, c1892
298 p. ;19 cm.

K545. 0/S663
A History of Greece: From the Earliest Times to the Roman Conquest/William Smith. —New ed. . —New York: American Book Company, c1854
xxxiv, 704 p. ;20 cm.

K546/M149
History of Florence and of the Affairs of Italy/Niccolo Machiavelli. —New York: M. Walter Dunne, Publisher, c1901
xvii, 417 p. ;23 cm.

K546. 42/M496
Mussolini in the Making/Gaudens Megaro. —London: George Allen & Unwin Ltd. , c1938
347 p. ;22 cm.

K546. 42/N733
Bolshevism, Fascism and Democracy/Francesco Nitti. —New York: The Macmillan Company, c1927
223 p. ;20 cm.

K546. 9/C899(2)
Salve Venetia: Gleanings from Venetian History. Volume II/Francis Marion Crawford. —New York: The Macmillan Company, c1905
x, 441 p. ;20 cm.

K551. 52/G198
Spain in Revolt: A History of the Civil War in Spain in 1936 and A Study of Its Social Political and Economic Causes/Harry Gannes, Theodore Repard. —London: Victor Gollancz Ltd. , c1936
287 p. ;18 cm.

K551. 52/P324
The Life and Death of a Spanish Town/Elliot Paul. —New York: Random house, c1937.
xii, 427 p. ;21 cm.

K56/R662
An Introduction to the History of Western Europe/James Harvey Robinson. —Boston: Ginn & Company, c1903
xi, 714 p. ;19 cm.

K56/R662(3)
An Introduction to the History of Western Europe. vol. III/James Harvey Robinson. —New Brief ed. . —Boston: Ginn and Company, c1931
xi, 829, xxxiv p. ;20 cm.

K561/C531
A Short History of England/Edward P.

Cheyney. —Boston: Ginn and Company, c1904
xvi, 695 p. ;19 cm.

K561/G224-2
Introduction to the Study of English History/Samuel R. Gardiner, J. Bass Mullinger. —2nd ed.. —London: Kegan Paul, Trench, & Co., c1882
xvii, 424, 38 p. ;20 cm.

K561/G738
The Mother of Parliaments/Harry Graham. —Boston: Little, Brown, & Company, c1911
xii, 314 p. ;22 cm.

K561/G795
A Short History of the Englishi People/John Richard Green. —London: Machillan ans Co., Ltd., c1911
xxxii, 872 p. ;19 cm.

K561/H974
The Oxford Movement: Being A Selection from Tracts for the Times/William G. Hutchison. —London: The Walter Scott Publishing Co., Ltd., [?]
xlix, 279 p. ;17 cm.

K561/M113(2)
The History of England from the Accession of James II. Vol. Two/Thomas Babington Macavlay. —London: J. M. Dent & Sons Ltd., c1912
856 p. ;18 cm.

K561/M113(3)
The History of England from the Accession of James II. Vol. Three/Thomas Babington Macavlay. —London: J. M. Dent & Sons Ltd., c1916
viii, 758 p. ;18 cm.

K561/M113
The History of England from the Accession of James II/Thomas Babington Macavlay. —London: J. M. Dent & Sons Ltd., c1906
xii, 804 p. ;18 cm.

K561/S467
1066 and all That: A Memorable History of England/Walter Carruthers Sellar, Robert Julian Yeatman. —New York: E. P. Dutton & Co., Inc., c1931
115 p. ;19 cm.

K561/S787(2)
In Darkest Africa, or, The Quest, Rescue, and Retreat of Emin Governor of Equatoria. Vol. II/Henry M. Stanley. —New York: Charles Scribner's Sons, c1891
xvi, 539 p. ;22 cm.

K561/T454
Highroads of History. Other Days and Other Ways(From the Earliest Times to 1485). IV/Thomas Nelson and Sons, Ltd.,—London: Thomas Nelson and Sons, Ltd., c1932
256 p. ;21 cm.

K561/W957
Britain's History/George M. Wrong. —Toronto: The Copp Clark Company, Ltd., c1929
vii, 396 p. ;19 cm.

K561.0/D261
Life in Elizabethan Days: A Picture of a Typical English Community at the End of the Sixteenth Century/William Stearns Davis. —New York: Harper & Brothers Publishers, c1930
xii, 376 p. ;21 cm.

K561.0/G221(1)
A Student's History of England from the Earliest Times to the Death of Queen Victoria. vol. I, B. C. 55-A. D. 1509/Samuel R. Gardiner. —London: Longmans, Green and Co., c1908
xxxii, 378 p. ;20 cm.

K561. 0/G795

A Short History of the English People/John Richard Green. —New York: Ameican Book Comany, c1902.

xlvii, 872 p. ;20 cm.

K561. 4/G793

The English Revolution: 1688-89/A. Greeff. —Leipzig: [s. n.], [?]

164, 23 p. ;19 cm.

K561. 4/McC326(6)

A History of Our Own Times. 6, Form 1897 to the Accession of King Enward VII/Justin Mccarthy. —London: Caxton Publishing Company, c1908

409 p. ;22 cm.

K561. 4/T812

British History in the Nineteenth Century (1782-1901)/George Macaulay Trevelyan. —London: Longmans, Green and Co. , Ltd. , c1928

xvi, 445 p. ;23 cm.

K561. 4/W279(3)

The Groundwork of British History. Section III, 1714-1921/George Townsend Warner, C. H. K. Marten. —London: Blackie & Son Ltd. , c1930

viii, 459-783 p. ;20 cm.

K561. 4/W365

The Consumers' Cooperative Movement/Sidney Webb, Beatrice Potter. —London: Longmans, Green and Co. , c1921

xv, 504 p. ;21 cm.

K561. 43/A628

The Saga of the Bounty: Its Strange History as Related by Participants Themselves/Irvin Anthony. —New York: G. P. Putnam's Sons, c1935

xiv, 358 p. ;21 cm.

K561. 43/G842(1)

Twenty-Five Years: 1892-1916. Volume I/Viscount Grey of Fallodon. —New York: Frederick A. Stokes Company, c1925

xxx, 331 p. ;24 cm.

K561. 43/G842(2)

Twenty-Five Years: 1892-1916. Volume II/Viscount Grey of Fallodon. —New York: Frederick A. Stokes Company, c1925

ix, 353 p. ;24 cm.

K561. 44/H145

The Last Boer War/H. Rider Haggard. —London: Kegan Paul, Trench, Truebner & Co. , Ltd. , c1899

xxx, 244 p. ;18 cm.

K563. 3/M919

The Rise of the Dutch Republic: A History/John Lothrop Motley. —A New Edition. —A New Edition London: Routledge, Warne and Routledge, Broadway, Ludgate Hill, c1865

xi, 930 p. ;18 cm.

K563. 4/H673

Netherlands America: The Dutch Territories in the West/Philip Hanson Hiss. —New York: Duell, Sloan and Pearce, c1943

xiii, 225 p. ;24 cm.

K564/W557(1)

Belgium: A Personal Narrative. Vol. I/Brand Whitlock. —New York: D. Appleton and Company, c1919

xi, 660 p. ;23 cm.

K564. 51/H844

The Pan-Germanic Crime: Impressions and Investigations in Belgium During the German Occupation/Paul Van Houtte. —London: Hodder and Stoughton, [?]

192 p. ;19 cm.

K565/P249

Pioneers of France in the New World: Huguenots in Florida Samuel de Champlain/Francis Parkman. —Boston: Little, Brown, and Company, c1907

xxi, 491 p. ;19 cm.

K565/S814

A Brief History of France/Joel Dorman Steele, Esther Barker Steele. —New York: American Book Company, c1903

viii, 301, xxx p. ;20 cm.

K565/Y57

History of France/Charlotte M. Yonge. —New York: A Merican Book Company, [?]

122 p. ;16 cm.

K565. 01/C278(1)

The French Revolution: A History. Volume I/Thomas Carlyle. —London: J. M. Dent & Sons, Ltd. , c1897

360 p. ;16 cm.

K565. 01/C278(2)

The French Revolution: A History. Volume II/Thomas Carlyle. —London: J. M. Dent & Sons, Ltd. , c1913

xii, 399 p. ;18 cm.

K565. 01/C286(O)

The French Revolution: A History/Thomas Carlyle. —New York: Random House, Inc. , [?]

xxix, 748 p. ;21 cm.

K565. 01/C286

The French Revolution: A History/Thomas Carlyle. —London: George Routledge & Sons, Ltd. , [?]

1 v. ;21 cm.

K565. 4/B772(2)

History of Modern France 1815-1913. Volume II 1852-1913/Emile Bourgeois. —Cambridge: Cambridge University Press, c1919

vii, 415 p. ;19 cm.

K565. 4/C286(1)

The French Revolution. Vol. 1/Thomas Carlyle. —London: Collins' Clear-Type Press, [?]

viii, 528 p. ;16 cm.

K565. 41/M623

A Historical View of the French Revolution from Its Earliest Indications to the Flight of the King in 1791/J. Michelet. —London: G. Bell & Sons, Ltd. , c1912

xxii, 621, 24 p. ;19 cm.

K565. 44/R888

The Double Heart: A Study of Julie de Lespinasse/Naomi Royde-Smith. —New York: Harper and Brothers, [?]

287 p. ;23 cm.

K712/A565

History of the United States/Matthew Page Andrews. —Philadelphia and London: J. B. Lippincott Company, c1914

xvii, 378, xlviii p. ;19 cm.

K712/C672

Makers of the Nation/Fanny E. Coe. —New York: American Book Company, c1914

382 p. ;19 cm.

K712/C734

America: Land of Opportunity/Brooklyn Community. —New York: The Bruce Publishing Company, c1938

x, 363 p. ;22 cm.

K712/D892

A History of the United States/Dwight Lowell Dumond. —New York: Henry Holt and Company, c1942

viii, 882 p. ;21 cm.

K712/E28

A First Book in American History/Edward Eggleston. —New York: American Book Company, c1899

vi, 207 p. ;19 cm.

K712/E92

First Lesson in American History/Lawt B. Evans. —Chicago: Benj. H. Sanborn & Co. , c1915

x, 292 p. ;18 cm.

K712/F263-3

America: Its History and People: A Unit Organization/Harold Underwood Faulkner, Tyler Kepner. —3rd ed. . —New York: Harper & Brothers Publishers, c1942

xiv, 890 p. ;24 cm.

K712/H223

The War Myth in United States History/C. H. Hamlin. —New York: Vanguard Press, c1927

93 p. ;18 cm.

K712/H325

Essentials in American History(From the Discover Present Day)/Albert Bushnell Hart. —New York: American Book Company, c1914

590, 125 p. ;21 cm.

K712/L848

Early Settlements in America/John A. Long. —Chicago: Row, Peterson and Company, c1925

428 p. ;19 cm.

K712/M994

A History of Our Country: A Textbook for High-School Students/David Saville Muzzey. —Boston: Ginn and Company, c1945

xii, 900, lviii p. ;19 cm.

K712/McL374

A History of the American Nation/Andrew C. McLaughlin. —New York: D. Appleton and Company, c1899

xvi, 562, xiv p. ;20 cm.

K712/N664

Following the Frontier: Stories of the Westward Movement/William L. Nida. —New York: The Macmillan Company, c1927

326 p. ;19 cm.

K712/R129

The Story of the American Indian/Paul Radin. —New York: Liveright Publishing Corporation, c1927

xiv, 391 p. ;22 cm.

K712/R262(1. 10)

Official Records of the Union and Confederate Navies in the War of the Rebellion. Series I-Volume 10/Edward K. Rawson. —Washington: Government Printing Office, c1900

xxiii, 902 p. ;23 cm.

K712/R262(1. 11)

Official Records of the Union and Confederate Navies in the War of the Rebellion. Series I-Volume 11/Edward K. Rawson. —Washington: Government Printing Office, c1900

xviii, 915 p. ;23 cm.

K712/R262(1. 16)

Official Records of the Union and Confederate Navies in the War of the Rebellion. Series I-Volume 16/Edward K. Rawson. —Washington: Government Printing Office, c1903

xxi, 973 p. ;23 cm.

K712/R262(1.17)

Official Records of the Union and Confederate Navies in the War of the Rebellion. Series I-Volume 17/Edward K. Rawson. —Washington: Government Printing Office, c1903

xix, 996 p. ;23 cm.

K712/R262(1.26)

Official Records of the Union and Confederate Navies in the War of the Rebellion. Series I-Volume 26, Naval Forces on Western Waters/Edward K. Rawson. —Washington: Government Printing Office, c1914

xviii, 915 p. ;24 cm.

K712/R262(1.9)

Official Records of the Union and Confederate Navies in the War of the Rebellion. Series I-Volume 9/Edward K. Rawson. —Washington: Government Printing Office, c1899

xxi, 915 p. ;23 cm.

K712/S728

American History: From the Discovery of America to the Present Day/Gertrude Van Duyn Southworth, John Van Duyn Southworth. —Syracuse: Iroquois Publishing Company, Inc., c1934

viii, 485 p. ;21 cm.

K712.0/N664

The Dawn of American History/William L. Nida. —New York: The Macmillan Company, c1932

xiii, 519 p. ;19 cm.

K712.03/S413

Sacrifice or Chaos? /R. R. Schweitzer. —Norfolk: Printcraft Publishing Co., c1933

155 p. ;20 cm.

K712.42/A425(1)

Only Yesterday. Volume one, An Informal History of the Nineteen-Twenties in America/Frederick Lewis Allen. —Norfolk: Penguin Books Ltd., c1931

xiii, 246 p. ;18 cm.

K712.42/A425(2)

Only Yesterday. Volume Two: An Informal History of the Nineteen-Twenties in America/Frederick Lewis Allen. —London: Penguin Books Ltd., c1931

265-503 p. ;18 cm.

K712.44/F241

The Development of the United States from Colonies to a World Power/Max Farrand. —Boston: Houghton Mifflin Company, c1918

335 p. ;19 cm.

K712.51/B726

Neutrality for the United States/Edwin Borchard, William Potter Lage. —New Haven: Yale University Press, c1937

xi, 380 p. ;23 cm.

K712.9/A799

The Barbary Coast: An Informal History of the San Francisco Underworld/Herbert Asbury. —New York: A. A. Knopf, 1933.

7 p. l., [3]-319, xi, [1] p. ;23 cm.

K712-49/F228

Makers of Our History/Hohn T. Faris. —Boston: Ginn And Company, c1917

xii, 387 p. ;19 cm.

K731/P929

History of the Conquest of Mexico and History of the Conquest of Peru/William H. Prescott. —New York: The Modern Library, [?]

xxxvi, 1288 p. ;20 cm.

K731.8/M338

The Development of Hispanic America/Marine

Corps Institute. —Washington, D. C. : Marine Corps Institute, c1941
xviii, 941 p. ;23 cm.

K778. 2/B617
Brothers of Doom: The Story of the Pizarros of Peru/Hoffman Birney. —New York: G. P. Putnam's Sons, c1942
x, 322 p. ;22 cm.

K784/H251
Chile: Land of Progress/Earl Parker Hanson. —New York: Reynal & Hitchcock, c1941
xx, 201 p. ;20 cm.

K810/M864
Biographical Studies/John Viscount Morley. —London: Macmillan and Co. , Ltd. , c1923
xii, 435 p. ;20 cm.

K811/S785
Guerilla Leaders of the World/Percy Cross Standing. —Boston: Houghton Mifflin Company, c1913
294 p. ;21 cm.

K815. 1/W746
Great Men of Science: Their Lives and Discoveries/Grove Wilson. —New York: New York Pub. Co. , c1929.
vi, ix-x, 1 l. , 397 p. ;22 cm.

K815. 6/D142(1)
Great Authors: From Chaucer to Pope. Part 1/W. Scott Dalgleish. —London: Thomas Nelson and Sons, c1905
272 p. ;19 cm.

K815. 6/S431
The Lives of the Novelists/Walter Scott. —London: J. M. Dent. & Sons Ltd. , [?]
xv, 408 p. ;18 cm.

K815. 7/L943
Memories of Eight Parliaments: 1868-1906/Henry W. Lucy. —New York: G. P. Putnam's Sons, c1908
416 p. ;23 cm.

K815. 7/L948
Three Titans/Emil Ludwig. —New York: Blue Ribbon Books, Inc. , c1930
xiii, 363 p. ;21 cm.

K815. 76/S368
The Complete Book of the Great Musicians: A Course in Appreciation for Young Readers/Percy A. Scholes. —London: Humphrey Milford Oxford University Press, [?]
1v. ;19 cm.

K815. 85/F841(1)
A Diplomatist's Wife in Many Lands. Vol. I/Hugh Fraser. —New York: Didd, Mead & Company, c1911
x, 324 p. ;23 cm.

K815. 85/F841(2)
A Diplomatist's Wife in Many Lands. Vol. II/Hugh Fraser. —New York: Didd, Mead & Company, c1911
x, 324 p. ;23 cm.

K815. 89/M681
Earth Conquerors: The Lives and Achievements of the Great Explorers/J. Leslie Mitchell. —New York: New York Publishing Company, Inc. , c1934
ix, 370 p. ;21 cm.

K819. 85/B268
The Laughing Queen/E. Barrington. —New York: Didd, Mead & Company, c1929
307 p. ;19 cm.

K827=52/B642

China Under the Empress Dowager: Being the History of the Life and Times of Tz'u Hsi/J. O. P. Bland, E. backhouse. —Peking: Henri Vetch, c1939

xxii, 470 p. ;23 cm.

K828. 5/C347

Marie-Therese Wang: Marie-Therese Wang 1917-1932/Rev. E. Castel. —New York: Benziger Brothers, c1934

x, 131 p. ;19 cm.

K831. 37/F949-3

The Autobiography of Fukuzawa Yukichi/translation by Eiichi Kiyooka; with an introduction by Shinzo Koizumi. . —3rd and revised ed. —Tokyo: The Hokuseido Press, c1940.

xx, 380 p. ;23 cm.

K832. 611/A628

Queen Elizabeth/Katharine Anthony. —New York: Alfred A. Knopf, c1929

623, ix p. ;22 cm.

K833. 512. 2/T858

The Life of Hodson of Hodson's Horse/by Captain Lionel J. Trotter. —London: J. M. Dent & Sons, Ltd. , c1912.

xi, 306 p. ;18 cm.

K833. 517/A565

Mahatma Gandhi-His Own Story/C. F. Andrews. —New York: The Macmillan Company, c1930

372 p. ;20 cm.

K834. 117/S484

Cleopatra of Egypt: Antiouity's Queen of Romance/Philip W. Sergeant. —London: Hutchinson & Co. , [?]

347 p. ;18 cm.

K834. 127=41/B181

Abraham Lincoln: A True Life/James Baldwin. —New York: American Book Company, c1904

288 p. ;18 cm.

K834. 75/C643

Against These Three: A Biography of Paul Kruger, Cecil Rhodes and Lobengula, Last King of the Matabele/Stuart Cloete. —Boston: Houghton Mifflin Company, c1945

472 p. ;20 cm.

K835. 125. 6/L759

The Stories of Anton Tchekov/Robert N. Linscott. —New York: The Modern Library, c1932

x, 448 p. ;18 cm.

K835. 127/A628

Catherine the Great/Katharine Anthony. —New York: New York Pub, c1925.

330 p. ;21 cm.

K835. 127/K43

The Life of Peter the Great/Henry Ketcham. —New York: A. L. Burt Company, c1903

xv, 405 p. ;19 cm.

K835. 127/W797

Ivan Grozny/R. Wipper. —Moscow: Foreign Languages Publishing House, c1947

252 p. ;22 cm.

K835. 128. 5/S877

Mart of Muscovy: The Fabulous life of Russia's first Empress/Phil Strong. —New York: Doubleday, Doran & Company, Inc. , c1945

viii, 274 p. ;22 cm.

K835. 128. 9/M864

Voltaire/John Viscount Morley. —London: Macmillan and Co. , Ltd. , c1923 xii，365 p. ;20 cm.

K835. 16/H674
Mein Kampf/Adolf Hitler. —[S. l. : s. n.], [?]
669 p. ;21 cm.

K835. 165. 2/H662
Out of My Life/Marshal von Hindenburg. —London：Cassell and Company，Ltd. , c1920
xii，458 p. ;24 cm.

K835. 166. 15/H133
The Story of The Development of A Youth：letters to His Parents 1852-1856/Ernst Haeckel. —New York：Harper & Brothers，c1923
xii，420 p. ;20 cm.

K835. 167/H674
My Struggle/Adolf Hitler. —London：The Pathernoster Library，c1938
285 p. ;22 cm.

K835. 167/L948
Bismarck：The Story of a Fighter/Emil Ludwig. —New York：Blue Ribbon Books，c1927
xvi，661 p. ;21 cm.

K835. 167/S894
Hitler and I/Otto Strasser. —[S. l. : s. n.], [?]
240 p. ;20 cm.

K835. 167/T815
The Last days of Hitler/H. R. Trevor-Roper. —New York：The Macillan Company，c1947
ix，254 p. ;21 cm.

K835. 215. 6/F763
The Portrait of a Politician：Stefan Zweig/Joseph Fouche. —New York：Blue Ribbon Booka，Inc. , c1930
xviii，327 p. ;21 cm.

K835. 217. 6/W673(1)
Mozart/Victor Wilder. —New York：Charles Scribner's Sons，[?]
xiii，222 p. ;20 cm.

K835. 46/G757
The Divine Comedy of Dante Alighieri/C. H. Grandgent. —New York：The Modern Library，c1932
xiii，584 p. ;18 cm.

K835. 46/S988
The Autobiography of Benvenuto Cellini/J. Addington. —New York：The Book League of America，c1937
506 p. ;20 cm.

K835. 460. 9/Y68
The Medici/by Colonel G. F. Young，C. B. . —New York：The Modern library，[?]
xxi，824 p. ;20 cm.

K835. 465. 7/C393(1)
The Life of Benvenuto Cellini. Vol. 1/Benvenuto Cellini. —New York：Brentano's，c1906
xxii，359 p. ;24 cm.

K835. 465. 7/C393(2)
The Life of Benvenuto Cellini Written By Himself/John Addington. —New York：Brentano's，c1906
vii，386 p. ;24 cm.

K835. 465. 78/C257
Enrico Caruso：His Life and Death/Dorothy Caruso. —New York：Simon and Schuster，c1945
303 p. ;21 cm.

K835. 467/M951
Ciano's Diary/Sumner Welles. —London：William Heinemann Ltd. , c1947

xxii, 575 p. ;25 cm.

K835.467/M989

My Autobiography/Benito Mussolini. —New York: Charles Scribner's Sons, c1928

xix, 318 p. ;21 cm.

K835.517/P647

An Sickles: Hero of Gettysburg and "Yankee King of Spain"/Edgcumb Pinchon. —New York: Doubleday, Daoran and Company, Inc., c1945

xiii, 280 p. ;22 cm.

K835.52/McC649(1)

Essays, Speeches, and Memoirs of Field-Marshal Count Helmuth von Moltke. Vol. I/Charles Flint Mcclumpha, May Herms. —New York: Harper & Brothers, Franklin Square, c1893

viii, 308 p. ;23 cm.

K835.553.61/ON412

Prodigal Genius: the Life of Nikola Tesla/John J. O'nell. —New York: Ives Washburn, Inc., c1944

326 P. ;22 cm.

K835.61/A263

Ego: The Autobiography of James Agate/James Agate. —London: Hamish Hamilton, c1935

388 p. ;24 cm.

K835.61/C187

Livingstone/R. J. Campbell. —New York: Dodd, Mead & Company, c1930

x, 295 p. ;22 cm.

K835.61/C224

When Fleet Street Calls: Being the Experiences of a London Journalist/J. C. Cannell. —London: Jarrolds Publishers, [?]

286 p. ;23 cm.

K835.61/C294

Augustus Carp, Esq.: Being the Autobiography of A Really Good Man/Augustus Carp Carp. —London: William Heinemann, Ltd., c1924

xiii, 274 p. ;19 cm.

K835.61/D766

Music at Midnight/Muriel Draper. —London: William Heinemann Ltd., c1929

245 p. ;22 cm.

K835.61/G841

William Bentinck and William III: The Life of Bentinck Earl of Portland from the Welbeck Corresponence/Marion E. Grew. —London: John Murray, c1924

viii, 433 p. ;23 cm.

K835.61/H217

Some Further Adventures of Mr. P. J. Davenant/Lord Frederic Hamilton. —London: Eveleigh Nash Company Ltd., c1916

309 p. ;19 cm.

K835.61/H314

Bernard Shaw/Frank Harris. —New York: New York Publishing Company, c1931

xxvi, 441 p. ;21 cm.

K835.61/H813

The Life and Works of Alfred Aloysius Horn: An Old Visiter/Alfred Aloysius Horn. —London: Butler & Tanner Ltd., c1928

256 p. ;20 cm.

K835.61/M864(1)

The Life of William Ewart Gladstone. Vol. I/John Morley. —New York: The Macmillan Company, c1903

x, 661 p. ;23 cm.

K835.610.9/C699

Intimate Accounts of Royalty/Frederick L. Collins.—London: T. Werner Laurie, Ltd., c1928

218 p.;22 cm.

K835.612.6/C525

Autobiography/G. K. Chesterton.—London: Hutchinson & Co., (Publishers)Ltd., c1936

347 p.;22 cm.

K835.615/L735

Ben Jonson and King James: Biography and Portrait/Eric Linklater.—London: Jonathan Cape, c1931

328 p.;21 cm.

K835.615.2/H429(7.2)

A Library of Universal Literature: Comprising Science, Biography, Fiction and the Great Orations. Part Two, Biography/Oliver Cromwell.—New York: P. F. Collier and Son, [?]

696 p.;20 cm.

K835.615.2/L675

England's Sea-Officers: The Story of the Naval Profession/Michael Lewis.—London: George Allen & Unwin Ltd., c1939

307 p.;22 cm.

K835.615.2/M167

Into the Blue/Captain Norman Macmillan.—London: Duckworth, c1929

213 p.;22 cm.

K835.615.2/M864

Oliver Cromwell/John Viscount Morley.—London: Macmillan and Co., Ltd., c1923

533 p.;20 cm.

K835.615.2/W947

Portraits and Criticisms/Peter E. Wright.—London: Eveleigh Nash & Grayson, c1925

214 p.;21 cm.

K835.615.6/B185

The Life of Robert Louis Stevenson/Graham Balfour.—New York: Charles Scribner's Sons, c1911

364 p.;19 cm.

K835.615.6/C525

Robert Browning: English Men of Letters/G. K. Chesterton.—New York: The Macmillan Company, c1903

v, 207 p.;19 cm.

K835.615.6/C699

Lord Byron in His Letters: Selections From His Letters and Journals/V. H. Collins.—London: John Murray, Albemarle Street, W., c1927

xvi, 301 p.;22 cm.

K835.615.6/G248

The Life of Charlotte Bronte/E. C. Gaskell.—London: J. M. Dent, c1908

xxiii, 411 p.;17 cm.

K835.615.6/M135

Autobiography of a Cad/A. G. Macdonell.—London: Macmillan and Co., c1938

314 p.;19 cm.

K835.615.6/M454

The Du Mauriers/Daphne Du Maurier.—London: Victor Gollancz Ltd., c1937

334 p.;22 cm.

K835.615.6/M864

Critical Miscellanies/John Viscount Morley.—London: Macmillan and Co., Ltd., c1923

xiii, 424 p.;20 cm.

K835.615.6/R658

Lawrence: The Story of His Life/Edward

Robinson. —London: Oxford University Press, c1935
250 p. ;19 cm.

K835. 615. 6/W721
The Exquisite Tragedy and Intimate Life of John Ruskin/Amabel Williams-Ellis. —New York: Doubleday, Doran and Company, c1929
ix, 371 p. ;23 cm.

K835. 615. 6=41/B741(1)
The Life of Samuel Johnson. Volume I/James Boswell. —London: J. M. Dent and Sons Ltd. , c1906
xx, 638 p. ;18 cm.

K835. 615. 7/B871
The Log of A Rolling Stone/Henry Arthur Broome. —London: T. Werner Laurie Ltd. , [?]
xv, 325 p. ;21 cm.

K835. 615. 7/H198
Laughing Torso: Reminiscences of Nina Hamnett/Nina Hamnett. —London: Constable & Co Ltd. , c1932
326 p. ;23 cm.

K835. 615. 76/M398
Memories of a Musical Life/William Mason. —New York: The Century Co. , c1900
xii, 306 p. ;21 cm.

K835. 615. 78/B181
Muriel and Her Aunt Lu or School and Art Life in Paris/May Baldwin. —London: W. & R. Chambers, Ltd. , c1909
412 p. ;20 cm.

K835. 616. 1/A131-3(2)
The Life and Letters of Benjamin Jowett, M. A. Master of Balliol College, Oxford. Vol. II/Evelyn Abbott, Lewis Campbell. —3rd ed. —London: John Murray, Albemarle Street, c1897
viii, 499 p. ;21 cm.

K835. 616. 15/H986(2)
Life and Letters Thomas Henry Huxley. Vol. II/Leonard Huxley. —New York: D. Appleton and Company, c1901
vii, 541 p. ;21 cm.

K835. 616. 2/L319
First, The Kingdom!: The Story of Robert Fletcher Moorshead Physician/H. V. Larcombe. —London: Carey Press, [?]
iv;21 cm.

K835. 617/B474(3)
The Letters of Queen Victoria: A Selection from her Majesty's Correspondence Between the Years 1837 and 1861. Vol. III (1854-1861)/Arthur Christopher Benson, M. A. . —New York: Longmans, Green, and Co. , c1907
ix, 657 p. ;23 cm.

K835. 617/B474(3)
The Letters of Queen Victoria: A Selection from her Majesty's Correspondence Between the Years 1837 and 1861. Vol. III/Arthur Christopher Benson, Viscount Esher. —London: John Murray, Albenarle Street, W. , c1908
vii, 520 p. ;19 cm.

K835. 617/B561
The Druce-Portland Case/Theodore Besterman. —London: Duckworth, c1935
308 p. ;22 cm.

K835. 617/B617
Gladstone/Francis Birrell. —London: Duckworth, c1933
144 p. ;19 cm.

K835. 617/B786
Mary Queen of Scots: Daughter of Debate/Marjorie Bowen. —London: John Lane the Bod-

ley Head Ltd. , c1934
477 p. ;22 cm.

K835. 617/C563
The Gathering Storm: the Second World War/ W. S. Churchill. —Boston: Houghton Mifflin, c1948.
xvi, 784 p. ;21 cm.

K835. 617/C821
The Reminiscences of Lady Randolph Churchill/Mrs. George Cornwallis-West. —New York: The Century Co. , c1909
xii, 470 p. ;23 cm.

K835. 617/D552(2)
The life of Sir Harry Parkes. Vol. II, Minister Plenipotentiary to China ang Japan/F. V. Dickins, S. Lane-Poole. —London: Macmillan and Co. , c1894
xxi, 477 p. ;23 cm.

K835. 617/D781
Cromwell: A Character Study/John Drinkwater. —London: Hodder and Stoughton Publishers, [?]
261 p. ;18 cm.

K835. 617/E22
Portrait of Churchill/Guy Eden. —London: Hutchison & Co. , (Publishers)Ltd. , [?]
144 p. ;18 cm.

K835. 617/F485
Pendower: A Story of Cornwall in the Reign of Henry -VIII/M. Filleul. —[S. l. : s. n.], [?]
336 p. ;21 cm.

K835. 617/G442
The Books of the King's Jubilee: The Life and Times of Our King and Queen and Their People 1865-1935/Philip Gibbs. —London: Hutchinson & Co. , (Publishers) Ltd. , [?]
512 p. ;22 cm.

K835. 617/G442
King's Favourite: The Love Story of Robert Carr and Lady Essex/Philip Gibbs. —London: Hutchinson & Co. , (Publishers)Ltd. , [?]
320 p. ;22 cm.

K835. 617/H599
The Life and Death of Richard Yea-and-Nay/ Maurice Hewlett. —London: Macmillan and Co. , Ltd. , c1900
xi, 429 p. ;18 cm.

K835. 617/H921-4
The Wives of Henry the Eighth: And the Parts They Played in History/Martin Hume. — 4th ed. . —London: Eveleigh Nash & Grayson, [?]
x, 464 p. ;22 cm.

K835. 617/I65
Elizabeth: Captive Princess/Margaret Irwin. —London: Chatto & Windus, c1948
236 p. ;21 cm.

K835. 617/J65
Kings' Masque: Scenes from an Historical Tragedy/Evan John. —London: William Heinemann Ltd. , c1941
503 p. ;20 cm.

K835. 617/J72
Oliver Cromwell and his Times/Hilda Johnstone. —London: T. C. & E. C. Jack, [?]
92 p. ;17 cm.

K835. 617/K91
Winston Churchill/Rene Kraus. —Shanghai: Popular Book Company, c1940
366 p. ;20 cm.

K835. 617/L816

Memoirs of a British Agent: Being an Account of the Author's Early life in Many lands and of His Official Mission to Moscow in 1918/R. H. Bruce Lockhart. —London: Putnam, c1933

xi, 355 p. ;22 cm.

K835. 617/M156

The Windsor Tapestry: Being A Study of the Life, Heritage and Abdication ot H. R. H. the Duke of Windsor, K. G/Compton Mackenzie. —London: Rich & Cowan, Ltd. , c1938

ix, 584 p. ;23 cm.

K835. 617/M864

Burke/John Visount Morley. —London: Macm. aillan and Co. , Ltd. , c1923

318 p. ;20 cm.

K835. 617/S215

Edward Prince of Wales: An Authentic Biography/G. Ivy Sanders. —London: Nisbet & Co. , Ltd. , c1921

176 p. ;19 cm.

K835. 617/S894

Queen Victoria/Lytton Strachey. —London: Chatto & Windus, c1921

314 p. ;22 cm.

K835. 617/S894Q3

Queen Victoria/Lytton Strachey. —London: Chatto & Windus, c1924

274 p. ;19 cm.

K835. 617/S894Q3C

Queen Victoria/Lytton Strachey. —London: The Continental Book Company AB, c1945

274 p. ;19 cm.

K835. 617/W562

The History of the King's Messengers/V. Wheeler-Holohan. —London: Grayson & Grayson, c1935

xi, 291 p. ;21 cm.

K835. 617/W939(2)

Pilgrims and Adventurers. Part II/Phyllis Wragge. —London: Thomas Nelson and Sons, Ltd. , [?]

291 p. ;19 cm.

K835. 618/M252

Lord Clive: and the Establishment of the English in India/Colonel G. B. Malleson. —Oxford: The Clarendon Press, [?]

229 p. ;20 cm.

K835. 618. 5/B974

Sir Richard Burton's Wife/Jean Burton. —New York: Alfred A. Knopf, c1941

vi, 365, xiii p. ;22 cm.

K835. 618. 5/K52

Sunrise to Evening Star: My Seventy years in south Africa/Marina King. —London: George G. Harrap & Co. , Ltd. , c1935

314 p. ;22 cm.

K835. 618. 5/R482

Stray Pearls: Memoirs of Margaret de Ribaumont/Margaret de Ribaumont. —[S. l. : s. n.], [?]

xvi, 424, 44 p. ;19 cm.

K835. 618. 9/M398

The Life of Francis Drake/A. E. W. Mason. —New York: Doubleday, Doran & Company, Inc. , c1942

349 p. ;23 cm.

K835. 62/C388

Essays by the Late Marquess of Salisbury K. G. : Biographical/Lord Robert Cecil. —New York: E. P. Dutton & Co. , c1905

212 p. ;20 cm.

K835. 627/S745-8(2)

Memoirs of William Hickey. Vol. II/Alfred Spencer. —8th ed.. —London: Hurst & Blckett, Ltd. , [?]

x, 406 p. ;22 cm.

K835. 637/V292

Laughing Diplomat/Danele Vare. —[S. l. : s. n.], [?]

xii, 448 p. ;20 cm.

K835. 65/V184

The Life of Pasteur/Rene Vallery-Radot. —New York: Doubleday, Page & Company, c1923

xxi, 484 p. ;22 cm.

K835. 651=41/G442

Military Career of Napoleon the Great/Montcomery B. Gibbs. —New York: The Saalfield Publishing Co. , c1895

514 p. ;20 cm.

K835. 655. 15/T426

Abbot Columba Marmion: A Master of the Spiritual Life 1858-1923/Dom Raymund Thibaut. —London: Sands & Co. , c1932

488 p. ;22 cm.

K835. 655. 6/F568

The Marquis De Sade/Otto Flake. —London: Peter Dvies, c1931

230 p. ;21 cm.

K835. 655. 6/J83

Stendhal: or The Pursuit of Happiness/Matthew Josephson. —New York: Doubleday & Company, Inc. , c1946.

xiii, 489 p. ;23 cm.

K835. 655. 7/C855

Mata Hari: Courtesan and Spy/Major Thomas Coulson. —New York: Harper & Brothers Publishers, c1930

xi, 312 p. ;22 cm.

K835. 656. 1/C975

Madame Curie: A Biography by Eve Curie/Eve Curie. —New York: New York, c1943

393 p. ;20 cm.

K835. 656. 1/C975

Madame Curie/Eve Curie. —New York: Doubleday, Doran & Company, Inc. , 1938

xi, 412 p. ;23 cm.

K835. 656. 1/C975M178

Madame Curie: A Biography by Eve Curie/Eve Curie. —New York: Doubleday, Doran & Company, Inc. , c1938

xi, 412 p. ;23cm.

K835. 657/B776(2)

Memoirs of Napoleon Bonaparte. Vol. II/Louis Antoine Fauvelet De Bourrienne. —New York: Charles Scribner's Sons, c1891

xvi, 440 p. ;20 cm.

K835. 657/B776(3)

Memoirs of Napoleon Bonaparte. Vol. III/Louis Antoine Fauvelet De Bourrienne. —New York: Charles Scribner's Sons, c1891

xvii, 459 p. ;19 cm.

K835. 657/B776(4)

Memoirs of Napoleon Bonaparte. Vol. IV/Louis Antoine Fauvelet De Bourrienne. —New York: Charles Scribner's Sons, c1891

ix, 444 p. ;19 cm.

K835. 657/G855

Life of Napoleon/Arthur Griffiths. —London: Anthony Treherne & Co. , c1902

viii, 325 p. ;20 cm.

K835.657/H353

Louis XIV and the Zenith of the French Monarchy/Arthur Hassall.—New York: G. P. Putnam's Sons, c1901

xvi, 444 p.;20 cm.

K835.657/K93

Memoirs of a Revolutionist/Peter Kropotkin.—Boston: Houghton Mifflin Company, c1930

xiv, 502 p.;21 cm.

K835.657/L822

The Life of Cardinal Richelieu/Richard Lodge.—New York: A. L. Burt Company Publishers, c1903

viii, 328 p.;19 cm.

K835.657/L888(1)

Memoirs of Napoleon Bonaparte. Vol. 1/Louis Antoine Fauvelet De Bourrienne.—New York: Charles Scribner's Sons, c1891

lii, 422 p.;19 cm.

K835.657/L914

Joan of Arc/Francis C. Lowell.—Boston: Houghton, Mifflin and Company, c1896

382 p.;21 cm.

K835.657/L948

Napoleon/Emil Ludwig.—New York: Boni & Liveright, c1926

xii, 707 p.;24 cm.

K835.657/L948N195

Napoleon/Emil Ludwig.—New York: Modern Library, c1915

xi, 703 p.;18 cm.

K835.657/P641

The Real Martyr of ST. Helena/T. Dundas Pillans.—New York: McBride, Nast & Company, c1913

320 p.;21 cm.

K835.657/W928

The Ruin of a Princess: As Told by the Duchesse d'Angouleme, Madame Elizabeth, Sister of Louis XVI, and Clery, the King's Valet de Chambre/Katharine Prescott Wormeley.—New York: The Lamb Publishing Co., c1912

329 p.;22 cm.

K835.658/M717(2)

Essays, Speeches and Memoirs of Field-Marshal Count Helmuth von Moltke. Vol. II/Count Helmuth von Moltke.—New York: Harper & Brothers, Franking Square, c1893

ix, 237 p.;23 cm.

K835.658.5/A935

The Immortal Ninon: A Character-Study of Ninon De L'enclos/Cecll Austin.—New York: Publishers Brentano's, c1927

viii, 261 p.;22 cm.

K837.12/A214

The Adams Family/James Truslow Adams.—New York: Blue Ribbon Books, c1930

364 p.;21 cm.

K837.12/A737

Trelawny: A Man's Life/Margaret Armstrong.—New York: The Macmillan Company, c1940

379 p.;24 cm.

K837.12/B167

Daniel Boone/John Bakeless.—New York: William Morrow & Company, c1939

480 p.;22 cm.

K837.12/B715

Haunch Paunch and Jowl: An Anonymous Autobiography/Boni and Liveright Publishers.—New York: Boni and Liveright Publishers, c1923

300 p. ;21 cm.

K837. 12/B922

All in a Lifetime/Frank Buck. —New York: Robert M. McBride & Company, c1941

277 p. ;24 cm.

K837. 12/C563

Richard Carvel/Winston Churchill. —New York: The Macmillan Company, c1899

xi, 537 p. ;20 cm.

K837. 12/C563R511

Richard Carvel/Winston Churchill. —London: Macmillan and Company, Ltd. , c1906

xi, 538 p. ;20 cm.

K837. 12/C776

Lionel Lincoln: The Leaguer of Boston/J. Fenimore Cooper. —New York: D. Appleton & Company, [?]

460 p. ;20 cm.

K837. 12/D273

Life with Mother/Clarence Day. —New York: Alfred A. Knopf, c1944

xiii, 250 p. ;19 cm.

K837. 12/D273

Life With Father & Mother/Clarence Day. —New York: Alfred A. Knopf, c1943

374 p. ;21 cm.

K837. 12/F499

American Spiritual Autobiographies: Fifteen Self-Portraits/Louis Finkelstein. —New York: Harper & Brothers, c1948

xvi, 276 p. ;21 cm.

K837. 12/H496

Stonewall Jackson and the American Civil War/G. F. R. Henderson. —London: Longmans, Green, and Co. , c1945

xix, 737 p. ;20 cm.

K837. 12/H496(1)

Stonewall Jackson and the American Civil War. Vol. I. /G. F. R. Henderson. —London: Longmans, Green, and Co. , c1905

xxiii, 447 p. ;20 cm.

K837. 12/H857(1)

The Life and Letters of George Bancroft. Volume I/M. A. DeWolfe Howe. —New York: Charles Scribner's Sons, c1908

364 p. ;21 cm.

K837. 12/H857(2)

The Life and Letters of George Bancroft. Volume II/M. A. DeWolfe Howe. —New York: Charles Scribner's Sons, c1908

364 p. ;21 cm.

K837. 12/K55

Four American Explores: Captain Meriwether Lewis, Captain William Clark, General John C. Frenmont, Dr. Elisha K. Kane: A Book for Young Americans/Nellie F. Kingsley. —New York: American Book Company, c1902

271 p. ;19 cm.

K837. 12/L897

Many Happy Days I've Squandered/Arthur Loveridge. —New York: Harper & Brother Publishers, c1944

viii, 278 p. ;21 cm.

K837. 12/M143

Manhood and Marriage/Bernarr Macfadden. —New York: Physical Culture Publishing Co. , c1916

x, 364 p. ;19 cm.

K837. 12/P238

The Seats of the Mighty: Being the Memoirs of Captain Robert Moray, Sometime An Officer in the Virginia Regiment, and Afterwards of Amherst's Regiment/Gilbert Parker. —New York: A. L. Burt Company, c1905

x, 376 p. ;19 cm.

K837.12/P274

Captains of Industry/James Parton. —Boston: Houghtion, Mifflin & Company, c1884

xii, 399, 26 p. ;18 cm.

K837.12/P274(2)

Captains of Industry. Second Series/James Parton. —Boston: Houghtion, Mifflin & Company, c1891

xii, 393, 26 p. ;18 cm.

K837.12/P844

Just David/Eleanor H. Porter. —New York: The Christian Herald, c1916.

323 p. ;21 cm.

K837.12/V583

Kit Carson: The Happy Warrior of the Old West: A Biography/Stanley Vestal. —Boston: Houghton Mifflin Company, c1928

297 p. ;21 cm.

K837.12/W473

Lords of the Levee: The Story of Bathhouse John and Hinky Dink/Lloyd Wendt, Herman Kogan. —New York: Garen City Publishing Co., Inc., c1944

384 p. ;20 cm.

K837.12/W582

Texas: An Informal Biography/Owen P. White. —New York: G. P. Putnam's Sons, c1945

ix, 267 p. ;21 cm.

K837.12/Z77

As I Remember Him: The Biography of R. S. / Hans Zinesser. —Boston: Little, Brown and Company, c1940

ix, 443 p. ;22 cm.

K837.122.7/F831

The Autobiography of Benjamin Franklin: Poor Richard's Almanac and Other Papers/Benjamin Franklin. —U. S. A.: The Spencer Press, [?]

viii, 311 p. ;21cm.

K837.125.1/H758

I Haven't Unpacked/William Holt. —London: George G. Harrap & Co., Ltd, c1939

287 p. ;21 cm.

K837.125.19/D225

The Story of My Life/Clarence Darrow. —New York: Charles Scribner's Sons, c1932

viii, 465 p. ;23 cm.

K837.125.2/B763

The Life of General Gordon/Demktrius C. Boulger. —New York: Thomas Nelson & Sons, [?]

479 p. ;16 cm.

K837.125.2/B799

Lee the American/Gamaliel Bradford. —Boston: Houghton Mifflin Company, c1912

xiii, 324 p. ;23 cm.

K837.125.2/B983

My Three Years with Eisenhower/Harry C. Butcher. —New York: Simon and Schuster, c1946

xvii, 911 p. ;22 cm.

K837.125.2/H196

Admiral Halsey's Story/William F. Halsey. —New York: Whittlesey House McGraw Hill Book Co., Inc., c1947

xvii, 310 p. ;23 cm.

K837.125.2/H433

The Life of Ulysses S. Grant/J. T. Headley. —New York: A. L. Burt Company, c1885

590 p.;19 cm.

K837.125.2/H521

"First with the Most" Forrest/Robert Selph Henry. —Indianapolis: The Bobbs-Merrill Company, c1944

558 p.;21 cm.

K837.125.2/K77

The Three Musketeers of the Air: Their Conquest of the Atlantic from to West/Captain Hermann Koehl. —New York: G. P. Putnam's Sons, c1928

xi, 330 p.;21 cm.

K837.125.2/M214

From Sall to Steam: Recollections of Naval / A. T. Mahan. —New York: Harper & Brothers Publishers, c1906, 1907

xvi, 325 p.;21 cm.

K837.125.2/P132

Robert E. Lee: The Southerner/Thomas Nelson Page. —New York: Charles Scribner's Sons, c1908

xiii, 312 p.;19 cm.

K837.125.2/P322

War as I Knew It/George S. Patton, Jr.; annotated by Paul D. Harkins; with a new introduction by Rick Atkinson. —Boston: Houghton Mifflin Co., c1947.

xix, 425 p.;21 cm.

K837.125.2/S218

Crazy Horse, the Strange Man of the Oglalas: A biography/Mari Sandoz. —New York: A. A. Knopf, c1944

x, 428 p.;21 cm.

K837.125.2/S727

The Life of Admiral Horatio Nelson/Robert Southey. —New York: The Perkins Book Company, c1902

xii, 357 p.;19 cm.

K837.125.2/S856

The Stilwell Papers/Joseph W. Stilwell. —New York: William Sloane Associates, Inc. Publishers, c1948

xvi, 357 p.;21 cm.

K837.125.2/W516

Gideon Welles: Lincoln's Navy Department/Richards S. Department. —New York: The Bobbs-Merrill Company Publishers, c1943

379 p.;24 cm.

K837.125.3/J83

The Robber Barons: the Great American Capitalists, 1861-1901/Matthew Josephson. —New York: Harcourt, Brace and Company, c1934.

viii, 474 p.;21 cm.

K837.125.381/D994

Autobiography of Andrew Carnegie/John C. Van Dyke. —Boston: Houghton Mifflin Company, c1920

xii, 385 p.;23 cm.

K837.125.4/A193

A Woollcott: His Life and His World/Samuel Hopkins Adams. —New York: Reynal & Hitchcock, c1945

386 p.;21 cm.

K837.125.4/K21

The Letters of Alexander Woollcott/Beatrice Kaufman, Joseph Hennessey. —New York: The Viking Press, c1944

xxiv, 410 p.;22 cm.

K837. 125. 42/W344(2)

Marse Henry: An Autobiography. Vol. II/ Henry Watterson. —New York: George H. Doran Company, c1919

ix, 314 p. ;22 cm.

K837. 125. 46/H564

Stephen Girard Founder/Cheesman A. Herrick. —Philadelphia: Girard College, c1923

ix, 203 p. ;21 cm.

K837. 125. 46/S545

John Harvard and his Times/Henry C. Shelley. —Boston: Little, Brown and Company, c1908

xiv, 331 p. ;21 cm.

K837. 125. 47/J76

Down the Fairway: The Golf Life and Play of Robert T. Jones, Jr. /Robert T. Jones, O. B. Keeler. —New York: Blue Ribbon Books, c1927

239 p. ;21 cm.

K837. 125. 6/D888

An Amazing Journey: Isadora Duncan in South America/Maurice Dumesnil. —London: Jarrolds Publishers, [?]

288 p. ;23 cm.

K837. 125. 6/E77

Minor Heresies/John J. Espey. —New York: Alfred A. Knopf, Inc. , c1945

202 p. ;19 cm.

K837. 125. 6/F346

A Peculiar Treasure/Edan Ferber. —[S. l. : s. n.], [?]

398 p. ;23 cm.

K837. 125. 6/F553

The Crack-up/F. Scott Fitzgerald. —[S. l.]: New Directions, c1945

347 p. ;23 cm.

K837. 125. 6/J60

Remembered Yesterdays/Robert Underwood Johnson. —Boston: Little, Brown, Company, c1923

xxi, 624 p. ;22 cm.

K837. 125. 6/L743

"We"/Charles A. Lindbergh. —New York: Grosset & Dunlap Publishers, c1927

318 p. ;20 cm.

K837. 125. 6/L795

Gentlemen Prefer Blondes: the Illumingation Diary of a Professional Lady/Anita Loos. —New York: Grosset & Dunlap, publishers, c1925

216 p. ;20 cm.

K837. 125. 6/M536

Newspaper Days 1899-1906/H. L. Mencken. —New York: Alfred a Knopf, c1943

xi, 313 p. ;23 cm.

K837. 125. 6/M911

Louisa may Alcott: Dreamer and worker: story of Achievement/Belle Moses. —New York: D. Appleton and Company, c1909

334 p. ;19 cm.

K837. 125. 6/S892

Harriet Beecher Stowe: The Story of her life/ Charles Edward Stowe, Lyman Beecher Stowe. —Boston: Houghton Mifflin Company, c1911

vi, 313 p. ;21 cm.

K837. 125. 6/Y54

New Selections from Irving's Sketch-Book/ Kiyoshi Yoshida. —Tokyo: Kairyudo, c1940

170 p. ;18 cm.

K837. 125. 7/B478

Tom Benton's America: An Artist in America/

Thomas Hart Benton. —New York: Robert M. McBride & Company, c1937
xi, 276 p. ;24 cm.

K837. 125. 7/G282
There's Laughter in the Air: Radio's top Comedians and Theie Best Shows/Jack Gaver, Dave Stanley. —New York: Greenberg, c1945
291 p. ;21 cm.

K837. 125. 76/I65
The Proud Servant: the Story of Montrose/Margaret Irwin. —London: Chatto & Windus, c1936
526 p. ;21 cm.

K837. 125. 76/S734
Rise to Follow: An Autobiography/Albert Spalding. —New York: Henry Holt and Company, c1943
351 p. ;12×17 cm.

K837. 125. 78/E28
The Success of Patrick Desmond/Maurice Francis Egan. —[S. l.]: Notre Dame, Ind., c1893
412 p. ;19 cm.

K837. 125. 8/S539
Personal History/Vincent Sheean. —New York: The Literary Guild, c1934
403 p. ;22 cm.

K837. 125. 81/N994
George Bancroft: Brahmin Rebel/Russel B. Nye. —London: Alfred A. Knopf, c1944
x, 340, xii p. ;22 cm.

K837. 126. 1/B915
Edison: The Man and His Work/George S. Bryan. —London: Alfred A. Knopf Publisher, [?]
viii, 303 p. ;22 cm.

K837. 126. 1/C945
Famous American Men of Science/J. G. Crowther. —New York: W. W. Norton & Company Inc. c1937
xvi, 414 p. ;22 p.

K837. 126. 11/O63
Wallace Clement Sabine: A Study in Achievement/William Dana Orcutt. —Massachusetts: Privately Printed by the Plimpton Press, c1933
xiv, 376 p. ;24 cm.

K837. 126. 14/P989
High Journey: a Decade in the Pilgrimage of an Air Line Pioneer/Carleton Putnam. —New York: Charles Scribner's Sons, c1945
viii p., 1 l., 308 p. ;21 cm.

K837. 126. 15/R852
Audubon/Constance Rourke. —New York: Harcourt, Barace and Company, c1936
342 p. ;23 cm.

K837. 126. 2/H576
The Horse & Buggy Doctor/Arthur E. Hertzler. —London: John Lane the Bodley Head, c1939
355 p. ;23 cm.

K837. 126. 3/P349
Green Laurels: The lives and Achievements of the Great Naturalists/Donald Culross Peattie. —New York: Simon and Schuster, c1936
xxiii, 368 p. ;22 cm.

K837. 127/A131
Impressions of Theodore Roosevelt/Lawrence F. Abbott. —New York: Doubleday, Page & Company, c1920
xvii, 315 p. ;24 cm.

K837.127/B181

Abraham Lincoln: A True Life/James Baldwin. —New York: American Book Company, c1904

288 p.;18 cm.

K837.127/B268

Our Friend John Burroughs/Clara Barrus. —Boston and New York: Houghton Mifflin Company, c1914

286 p.;22 cm.

K837.127/B293

The Soul of Abraham Lincoln/William E. Barton. —New York: George H. Doran Company, c1920

405 p.;23 cm.

K837.127/B293(O)

The Soul of Abraham Lincoln/William E. Barton. —New York: George H. Doran Company, c1920

xiv, 407 p.;23 cm.

K837.127/B474

Abraham Lincoln/Godfrey Rathbone Benson. —New York: Pocket Books, Inc., c1917

495 p.;16 cm.

K837.127/C321

Son of Thunder: Patrick Henry/Julia M. H. Carson. —London: Longmans, Green and Co., Inc., c1945

244 p.;21 cm.

K837.127/C483

Abraham Lincoln/Lord Charnwood. —New York: New York Publishing Co., Inc., c1938

vi, 482 p.;21 cm.

K837.127/C563

The Celebrity: An Episode/Winston Churchill. —New York: The Macmillan Company, c1905

302 p.;18 cm.

K837.127/C776

Ten Thousand Public Enemies/Courtney Ryley Cooper. —Boston: Little, Brown, and Company, c1935

ix, 356 p.;22 cm.

K837.127/C858

Unlocking Adventure/Charles Courtney. —New York: Whittlesey House, c1942

v, 335 p.;21 cm.

K837.127/C944

Willard Straight/Herbert Croly. —New York: The Macmillan Company, c1924

xvi, 569 p.;23 cm.

K837.127/D695

Benjamin Franklin/Carl Van Doren. —New York: Overseas Editions, Inc., c1938

xii, 496 p.;16 cm.

K837.127/F837

Benjamin Franklin: His Life/Benjamin Franklin. —Boaton: Ginn and Company, c1888, 1906

xvii, 311 p.;17 cm.

K837.127/G295

Franklin Delano Roosevelt: A Memorial/Donald Porter Geddes. —New York: Pocket Books, Inc., c1945

249 p.;17 cm.

K837.127/G763(1857-78)

Letters of Ulysses S. Grant to His Father and His Youngest Sister. 1857-78/Ulysses S. Grant. —New York and London: The Rnickerbocker Dress, c1912

182 p.;23 cm.

K837.127/H141

Roosevelt in the Bad Lands/Hermann Hagedorn.—Boston: Houghton Mifflin Company, c1921

xxvi, 491 p. ;22 cm.

K837.127/H325

Selected Addresses and Public Papers of Woodrow Wilson/Albert Bushneil Hart.—New York: Boni and Liberight Publishers, c1918

v, 316 p. ;17 cm.

K837.127/J67

Woodrow Wilson: The Unforgettable Figure Who Has Returned to Haunt Us/Gerald W. Johnson.—New York: Happer & Brothers, c1944

vii, 293 p. ;25 cm.

K837.127/L299

The Writings of Abraham Lincoln/Arthur Brooks Lapsley.—New York: The Lamb Publishing Company, [?]

v, 377 p. ;21 cm.

K837.127/L299(2)

The Writings of Abraham Lincoln. Volume two(1843-1858)/Arthur Brooks Lapsley.—New York: The Lamb Publishing Company, [?]

vii, 323 p. ;21 cm.

K837.127/L299(5)

The Writings of Abraham Lincoln. Volume Five(1858-1862)/Arthur Brooks Lapsley.—New York: The Lamb Publishing Company, [?]

xiv, 471 p. ;21 cm.

K837.127/L299(7)

The Writings of Abraham Lincoln. Volume seven (1863-1868)/Arthur Brooks Lapsley.—New York: The Lamb Publishing Company, c1906

xxi, 435 p. ;21 cm.

K837.127/L736(2)

The Life of Abraham Lincoln: drawn from original sources and Containing many speeches, letters and telegrams hitherto unpublished. Second Volume/Abraham Lincoln.—New York: Lincoln Memorial Association, c1900

220 p. ;23 cm.

K837.127/N641(1)

Abraham Lincoln: A History. Volume one/ John G. Nicolay, John Hay.—New York: The Century Co., c1909

xviii, 456 p. ;23 cm.

K837.127/N641(2)

Abraham Lincoln: A History. vol. 2/John G. Nicolay, John Hay.—New York: The Century Co., c1909

xiv, 447 p. ;23 cm.

K837.127/N641(5)

Abraham Lincoln: A History. Volume Five/ John G. Nicolay, John Hay.—New York: The Century Co., c1909

xvi, 460 p. ;23 cm.

K837.127/N641(8)

Abraham Lincoln: A History. Volume Eight/ John G. Nicolay, John Hay.—New York: The Century Co., c1909

xviii, 486 p. ;23 cm.

K837.127/N641(9)

Abraham Lincoln: A History. vol. 9/John G. Nicolay, John Hay.—New York: The Century Co., c1909

xviii, 496 p. ;23 cm.

K837.127/P244

Letters and Addresses of Thomas Jefferson/ William B. Parker, Jonas Viles.—New York: The Unit Book Publishing Co., c1905

323 p. ;18 cm.

K837. 127/R211

Intimate Character Sketches of Abraham Lincoln/Henry B. Rankin. —Philadelphia: J. B. Lippincott Company, c1924

344 p. ;21 cm.

K837. 127/R949

Selections from Roosevelt/C. Ruse. —Tokyo: Uchida Rokakuho, 1906

160, 2 p. ;19 cm.

K837. 127/S213

Abraham Lincoln: The Prairie Years/Carl Sandburg. —New York: Harcourt, Brace and Company, c1926

xiv, 604 p. ;24 cm.

K837. 127/U58

Letters and Addresses of Abraham Lincoln/Unit Book Publishing Co. ,—New York: Unit Book Publishing Co. , c1905

389 p. ;18 cm.

K837. 127/V691

Letters and Addresses of George Washington/Jonas Viles. —New York: The Unit Book Publishing Co. , c1908

489 p. ;18 cm.

K837. 127/W582

A Puritan in Babylon: The Story of Calvin Coolidge/William Allen White. —New York: The Macmillan Company, c1940

xvi, 460 p. ;24 cm.

K837. 127/W698

Inside History of the White House: The Complete history of the domestic and official life in Washington of the Nation's presidents and their families/Cilson Willets. —New York: The Christian Herald, c1908

492 p. ;20 cm.

K837. 127/W721

Anson Burlingame and the First Chinese Mission to Foreign Powers/Frederick Wells Williams. —New York: Russell & Russell, c1972

x, 370 p. ;22 cm.

K837. 127=52/B622

Theodore Roosevelt's Letters to His Childern/Joseph Bucklin Bishop. —New York: Charles Scribner's Sons, c1923

x, 240 p. ;19 cm.

K837. 127=533/K29

The Story of My Life/Helen Keller. —New York: Grosset & Dunlap, c1905

441 p. ;19 cm.

K837. 128/453

All This, and Heaven too/Rachel Field. —New York: The Macmillan Company, c1943

596 p. ;21 cm.

K837. 128/A362

Andrew Carnegie: From Telegraph Boy to Millionaire/Bernard Alderson. —London: C. Arthur Pearson, 1902

ix, 223 p. ;20 cm.

K837. 128/B365

The Boy's Story of Lindbergh the Lone Eagle/Richard J. Beamish. —Chicago: The John C. Winston Company, c1928

320 p. ;22 cm.

K837. 128/B786

Yankee from Olympus: Justice Holmes and His Family/Catherine Drinker Bowen. —Boston: Little, Brown and Company, c1945 [c1944]

xiii, 465 p. ;22 cm.

K837. 128/B786Y21

Yankee from Olympus: Justice Homes and Family/Catherine Drinker Bowen. —New York: Overseas Editions, Inc. , c1943, 1944

xi, 434 p. ;16 cm.

K837. 128/T138-3

Saint Among Savages: The Life Of Isaac Jogues/Francis Talbot. —3rd ed. . —New York: Harper & Brothers Publishers, c1935

466 p. ;22 cm.

K837. 128. 2/M819

With Japan's Leaders: An Intimate Record of Fourteen years as Counsellor to the Japanese Government, Ending December 7, 1941/Frederick Moore. —New York: Charles Scribner's Sons, c1942

365 p. ;21 cm.

K837. 128. 5/N458

White House Diary/Henrietta Nesbitt. —New York: Doubleday & Co. , Inc. , c1948

314 p. ;20 cm.

K837. 128. 7/W314

Up from Slavery: An Autobiography/Booker T. Washington. —New York: Doubleday, Page & Co. , c1901

330p. ;21cm.

K837. 128. 9/E44

Men Under the Sea/Edward Ellsberg. —New York: Dodd, Mead & Company, c1941

xii, 365 p. ;22 cm.

K837. 128. 9/G794

Reminiscences of Adventure and Service/Major-General A. W. Greely. —New York: Charles Scribner's Sons, c1927

xi, 356 p. ;22 cm.

K837. 128. 9/H283

Marion Harland's Autobiography: the Story of a Long Life/Marion arland. —New York: Harper & Brothers Publishers, c1910

ix, 497 p. ;22 cm.

K837. 31/B638

The Journey of the Flame/Antonio de Fiero Blanco. —Boston: Houghton Mifflin Company, c1933

xvii, 295 p. ;21 cm.

K837. 37/R852

Man of Glory: Simon Bolibar/Thomas Rourke. —New York: William Morrow & Company, c1942

x, 385 p. ;21 cm.

K85/A752

An Introduction to Paleobotany/Chester A. Arnold. —New York: McGraw-Hill Book Company, Inc. , c1947

ix, 433 p. ;23 cm.

K851. 2/S877

Marta of Muscovy: The Fabulous Life of Russia's First Empress/Phil Stong. —New York: Doubleday, Doran & Company, Inc. , c1945

vii, 274 p. ;21 cm.

K851. 285/D829

Education of A Princess: A Memoir by Marie, Grand Duchess of Russia/Marie. —New York: The Viking Press, c1930

xii, 388 p. ;22 cm.

K851. 685/N633

Recollections of A Great Lady being more Memoirs of the Comtesse de Boigne/M. Charles Nicoullaud. —New York: Charles Scribner's sons, c1912

x, 359 p. ;22 cm.

K853.289/H432

My Life as an Explorer/Sven Hedin. —New York: New York Pubulishing Co., Inc., [?]

xi, 544 p.;23 cm.

K856.1/M864(2)

The Life of William Ewart Gladstone. Vol. II/John Morley. —New York: The Macmillan Company, c1903

666 p.;23 cm.

K856.1/M864(3)

The Life of William Ewart Gladstone. Vol. III/John Morley. —New York: The Macmillan Company, c1903

641 p.;23 cm.

K856.128.9/R785

Lady May Wortley Montagu: Selct Passages from Her Letters/Arthur R. Ropes. —London: Seeley and Co., Ltd., c1892

308 p.;21 cm.

K856.152/S727

The Life of Nelson/Robert Southey. —London: Collins'Clear-Type Press, [?]

376 p.;16 cm.

K856.156/A828

Parson Austen's Daughter/Helen Ashton. —Collins: St. James's Place, c1949

352 p.;20 cm.

K856.156/D548

The Life and Adventures of Martin Chuzzilewit: His Relatives, Friends, and Enemies/Charles Dickens. —Copyright ed.. —[S. l.: s. n.], c1844

463 p.;16 cm.

K856.157.6/J65

Ellen Terry and Bernard Shaw/Christopher St. John. —New York: G. P. Putnam's Sons, c1931

xxx, 333 p.;24 cm.

K856.185/S983

Mary Anne Disraeli: The Story of Viscountess Beaconsfield/James Sykes. —London: Ernest Benn Ltd., c1928

155 p.;22 cm.

K856.57/M376

Petain: Verdun to Vichy/Francis Martel. —New York: E. P. Dutton & Company, Inc., c1943

226 p.;21 cm.

K871.2/S617(2)

The Story of the White House. Vol. II/Esther Singleton. —New York: The Mcclure Company, c1907

xiii, 340 p.;21 cm.

K871.2/T557(1)

Life, Letters, and Journals of George Ticknor. Volume I/George Ticknor. —Boston: Houghton Mifflin Company, c1909

xvii, 524 p.;22 cm.

K871.2/T557(2)

Life, Letters, and Journals of George Ticknor. Volume II/George Ticknor. —Boston: Houghton Mifflin Company, c1909

viii, 533 p.;22 cm.

K871.2/W473

Lords of the Levee: The Story of Bathhouse John and Hinkydink/Lloyd Wendt, Herman Kogan. —New York: New York Publishing Co., Inc., c1944

384 p.;20 cm.

K871.22/P378

Foreign Relations of the United States 1902:

Whaling and Sealing Claims Against Russia on Account of Arrest and Seizure of the American Vessels "Cape Horn pigeon", "James Hamilton Lewis", "C. H. White", and "kate and anna"/Herbert H. D. Peirce. —Washington: Government Printing Office, c1903
504 p. ;23 cm.

K871.25/C749-3
Letters from China: With Particular Reference to the Empress Dowager and the Women of China/Sarah Pike Conger. —3th. ed.. —Chicago: A. C. McClurg & Co., c1910
xv, 392 p. ;22 cm.

K871.254.2/B662
The Americanization of Edward bok: The Autobiography of a Dutch boy fifty years after/Edward Bok. —New York: Charles Scribner's Sons, c1923
xxiii, 562 p. ;19 cm.

K871.282/A589
The Lincoln Reader/Angle, Paul M.. —New Brunswick: Rutgers University Press, c1947
xii, 564 p. ;22 cm.

K877.4/Y36
Young Man of Caracas/T. R. Ybarra. —New York: Ives Washburn, Inc., c1941
xiii, 323 p. ;22 cm.

K89/B864
I Discover the Orient/Fietcher S. Brockman. —New York: Harper& Brothers Publishers, c1935
xii, 211 p. ;20 cm.

K891/Z93
The Splendour of the Liturgy/Maurice Zundel. —New York: Sheed & Ward, c1940
xii, 308 p. ;21 cm.

K892/K29
The Moon Dear/Kelly & Walsh, Ltd.,—Shanghai: Kelly & Walsh, Ltd., c1927
xi, 514, xx p. ;22 cm.

K892.2/C811
Chinese Birthday, Wedding, Funeral and other Customs/J. G. Cormack. —Shanghai: The Commercial Press, c1923
209 p. ;20 cm.

K894.7/S386
The Flying Missionary/Rev. Paul Schulte. —New York: Benziger Brothers, c1936
ix, 257 p. ;20 cm.

K897.12/V583
Short Grass Country/Stanley Vestal. —New York: Duell Sloan & Pearce, c1941
x, 304 p. ;22 cm.

K90/B855(2)
Essentials of Geography. Second Book/Albert Perry Brigham, Charles T. McFarlane. —New York: American Book Company, c1916
426, xxiii p. ;26 cm.

K90/G347
The Oxford and Cambridge Geography/George Gill & Sons, Ltd. —London: George Gill & Sons, Ltd., [?]
192 p. ;19 cm.

K90/N533
Modern Geography/Marion I. Newbigin. —New York: Henry Holt and Company, c1911
256 p. ;17 cm.

K91/B811
World Geography/John Hodgdon Bradley. —Boston: Ginn and Company, c1945
vii, 486 p. ;25 cm.

K91/D261

Elementary Physical Geography/Wilelam Morris Davis. —Boston: Ginn and Company, c1926, 1930

xviii, 401 p. ;19 cm.

K91/F165-4(5)

The Human Geographies. Book v, In the old World/Fairgrieve, J; Young, Ernest. —London: George Philip & Son, Ltd. , c1933

viii, 170 p. ;20 cm.

K91/F948

Complete Geography/Alexis Everett Frye. —Boston: Ginn & Company, Publishiers, c1919

1 v. ;30 cm.

K91/R845

Living in the Peoples' World/Lawrence V. Roth, Stiliman M. Hobbs. —Chicago: Laidlaw Brothers Publishers, c1944

704 p. ;23 cm.

K91/S698-2

A Geography of China and the World/The Society for the Diffusion of Christian and General Knowledge. —rev. ed. . —Shanghai: The Society for the Diffusion of Christian and General Knowledge, c1905

vii, 376 p. ;18 cm.

K91/S783-9

The World: A General Geography/L. Dufley Stamp. —9th ed. . —London: Longmans, Green and Co. , c1936

682 p. ;19 cm.

K91/S929

Our World Today: A Textbook in the New Geography/De Forest Stull, Roy W. Hatch. —Boston: Allyn and Bacon, c1931

vi, 704, 20 p. ;26 cm.

K91/T192(1)

First Book Home Geography And the Earth as A Whole/Ralph S. Tarr. —New York: The Macmillan Company, c1906

xv, 279 p. ;19 cm.

K91/T544

World Geography/E. L. Thurston, E. H. Faigle. —New York: Iroquois Publishing Company, Inc. , c1947

viii, 358 p. ;27 cm.

K91/W849

Geography of the World/Roger D. Wolcott. —Shanghai: The Commercial Press, Ltd. , c1927

474, xviii p. ;22 cm.

K912/W627

The Earth and the State: A Study of political Geography/Derwent Whittlesey. —New York: Henry Holt and Company, c1939

xvii, 618 p. ;22 cm.

K915/H274

Cities of Southern Italy and Sicily/Augstus J. C. Hare. —Philadelphia: Davis Mckay, Publisher, [?]

535 p. ;19 cm.

K918. 44/K57(1)

The Seven Seas. Vol. I/Rudyard Kipling. —[S. l. : s. n.], [?]

xiv, 135 p. ;17 cm.

K919/B414

A Macdougal Duff Mystery/William Beebe. —New York: Henry Holt and Company, c1918

xi, 297 p. ;19 cm.

K919/B652

The Drama of the Pacific: Being a Treatise on the Immediate Problems Which Face Japan in the

Pacific/Major R. V. Bodley. —Tokyo: The Hokuseido Press, c1934
xiv, 210 p. ;20 cm.

K919/B656
Told at the Explorers Club: true Tales of Modern Exploration/Frederick A. Blossom. —[S. l.]: Albert & Charles Boni, c1935
viii, 425 p. ;21 cm.

K919/B851
Heroes of Modern Adventure/T. C. Bridges, H. Hessell Tiltman. —London: George G. Harrap & Company Ltd. , c1927
x, 277 p. ;21 cm.

K919/C141
The Gobi Desert/Mildred Cable, Francesca French. —New York: The Macmillan Company, c1944
301 p. ;22 cm.

K919/D228(29)
The Voyage of the Beagle. vol. 29/Charles Darwin. —New York: P. F. Collier & Son Co. , c1909
524 p. ;22 cm.

K919/D695
The Travels of Marco Polo/Carl Van Doren. —New York: The Book League of America, c1936
xvii, 340 p. ;20 cm.

K919/G954
Over the Ocean; or, Sights and Scenes in Foreign Lands/Curtis Guild. —Boston: Lee and Shepard, Publishers, c1882
viii, 558 p. ;20 cm.

K919/H174
The Royal Adventures of Richard Halliburton/Richard Halliburton. —New York: The Bobbs Merrill Company Publishers, c1925
571 p. ;22 cm.

K919/H188
The Royal Road to Romance/Richard Halliburton. —New York: New York Publ. Co. , c1925.
399 p. ;20 cm.

K919/J66
I Married Adventure: The Lives and Adventures of Martin and Osa Johnson/Osa Johnson. —New York: New York Publishing Co. , Inc. , c1940
376 p. ;23 cm.

K919/N188
Farthest North: Being the Record of a Voyage of Exploration of the Ship "Fran" 1893-96 and of a Fifteen Month's Sleigh Journey by Dr. Nansen and Lieut Johansen/Fridtjof Nansen. —London: Archibald Constable and Co. , Ltd. , c1904
679 p. ;22 cm.

K919/P778
The Travels of Marco Polo/Marco Polo. —New York: Grosset & Dunlap, [?]
xvii, 340 p. ;21 cm.

K919/P778T779(O)
The Travels of Marco Polo: The Venetian/Marco Polo. —New York: Liveright Publishing Corp. , c1926
xxxii, 370 p. ;22 cm.

K919/R666
10000 Leagues Over the Sea/William Albert Robinson. —New York: Harcourt, Brace and Company, c1932
379 p. ;22 cm.

K919/S372
Through Europe on Two Dollars a Day/Frank Schoonmaker. —New York: Robert M. McBride

& Company, c1930
xii, 225 p. ;20 cm.

K919/S438
The Magic Island/W. B. Seabrook. —London: George G. Harrap & Company Ltd. , c1929
319 p. ;20 cm.

K919/S667
The Kangchenjunga Adventure/F. S. Smythe. —London: Victor Gollancz Ltd, c1931
464 p. ;21 cm.

K919/T742
Travels and Adventures of Marco Polo/George M. Towle. —[S. l: s. n.], [?]
vi, 274 p. ;19 cm.

K919/W187
The Big Game of Central and Western China: Being an Account of a Journey from Shanghai to London Overland Across Gobi Desert/Harols Frank Wallace. —Londom: John Murray, Albemarle Street, W, c1913
xviii, 318 p. ;22 cm.

K919/W362
Manchu and Muscovite/B. L. Putnam Weale. —London: Macmillan and Co. , Ltd. , c1904
xx, 564 p. ;22 cm.

K919/W477
Greater Britain: A Record of Travel in English-speaking Countries/Sir Charles Wentworth. —London: Macmillan and Co. , c1890
x, 633, 55 p. ;19 cm.

K919/Y37
European Jungle/F. Yeats-Brown. —[S. l. : s. n.], c1939.
vii, 11-409 p. ;22 cm.

K928. 3/B167
T'ai Shan: An Account of the Sacred Eastern Peak of China/Dwight Condo Baker. —Shanghai: The Commercial Press, Ltd. , c1925
xx, 225 p. ;20 cm.

K928. 42/P713-2
Glimpses of the Yangtze Gorges/Cornell Plant. —2th ed. . —Shanghai: Kelly & Walsh, Ltd. , c1936
xv, 86 p. ;22 cm.

K928. 5/N176
Soochow, the New York/F. R. Nance. —Shanghai: Kelly & Walsh, Ltd. , c1936
76 p. ;18 cm.

K928. 5/T877
Chinese Cities a Geographical Reader/Tsao Lien En. —Shanghai: Chung Hwa Book Co. , Ltd. , c1931
165 p. ;19 cm.

K928. 6/G464
What's Wrong with China/Rodney Gilbert. —London: John Murray, Albemarle Street, W. , c1926
315 p. ;22 p.

K928. 6/K91-3
China in Decay: The Story of a Disappearing Empire/Alexis Krausse. —3rd ed. . —London: George Bell & Sons, c1900
xiv, 418 p. ;21 cm.

K928. 7/F544
Hangchow-Chekiang Itineraries/Robert F. • Fitch. —Fourth Revised and Enlarged Edition. —Shanghai: Kelly & Walsh, Ltd. , [?]
v, 132 p. ;18 cm.

K928. 9/F597
News from Tartary: A Fourney for Peking to

Kashmir/Peter Fleming. —London: Jonathan Cape Thirty Bedford Square, c1936
381 p. ;20 cm.

K928. 9/H148
Hong Kong Holiday/Emily Hahn. —New York: Doubleday & Company, Inc. , c1946
viii, 305 p. ;19 cm.

K928. 9/S877
Historic Lushan: The Kuling Mountains/Albert H. Stone, J. Hammond Reed. —Hankow: Arthington Press, c[?]
106 p. ;24 cm.

K928. 9-62/C953-3
The Travelers' Handbook for China/Carl Crow. —3rd ed. —Shanghai: Ch'eng Wen, [?]
v, 314 p. ;17 cm.

K928. 91/P349
A Guide to Peiping and Its Environs/The Peking Bookshop. —Peking: The Peking Bookshop, c1946
viii, 143 p. ;18 cm.

K928. 926/C311-2(2)
Unknown Mongolia: A Record of Travel and Exploration in North-West Mongolia and Dzungaria. vol. II/Douglas Carruthers. —2nd ed. . —London: Hutchinson & Co. , c1914
x, 319-659 p. ;24 cm.

K928. 951/M648
Shanghai, the Paradise of Adventurers/G. E. Miller. —New York: Orsay Publishing House Inc. , c1937
307 p. ;24 cm.

K928. 951/N864
Landing at Shanghai/The North-China Daily News & Herald Ltd. —Shanghai: The North-China Daily News & Herald Ltd. , c1911
72 p. ;18 cm.

K93/U58-3(3)
Asiatic Pilot. Volume III, Coast of China Yalu River to Hong Kong Entrance Including the Coasts of Taiwan(Formosa)/United States Government Printing Office. —3rd ed. . —Washington: United States Government Printing Office, c1929
viii, 596 p. ;23 cm.

K931. 3/C443-7
A Handbook for Travellers in Japan: Including the Whole Empire from Yezo to Formosn/Basil hall Chamberlain, W. B. Mason. —7th ed. , Revised. —London: John Murray, c1903
586, 67 p. ;19 cm.

K931. 3/C443-8
A Handbook for Travellers in Japan: Including the Whole Empire from Yezo to Formosn/Basil hall Chamberlain, W. B. Mason. —8th ed. , Revised. —London: John Murray, c1907
570, 28 p. ;19 cm.

K931. 3/P945
Japan's Islands of Mystery/Willard Price. —New York: The John Day Company, c1944
vii, 264 p. ;21 cm.

K937-62/B139
Palestine and Syria with Routes Through Mesopotamia and Babylonia and the Island of Cyprus: Handbook for Travellers/Karl Baedeker. —Leipzig: Karl Baedeker, Publisher, c1912
civ, 462 p. ;16 cm.

K94/C536
Mumbo Jumbo, Esquire: A Book About the Two Africas/James Saxon Childers. —New york: D. Appleton-Century Company, c1941
xii, 421 p. ;23 cm.

K941.39/Y68

Liberia Rediscovered/James C. Young.—New York: Doubleday, Doran & Company, Inc., c1934

x, 212 p.;21 cm.

K95/B278

Europe and Asia/Harlan H. Barrows, Edith Putnan Parker, Margaret Terrell Parker.—New York: Silver Burdett Company, c1927

vii, 280 p.;26 cm.

K953.19/C466

Across Lapland: With Sledge and Reindeer/Olive Murray Chapman.—England: Penguin Books Ltd., c1939

183 p.;18 cm.

K955.19/F699

Gatherings from Spain/Richard Ford.—London: J.M. Dent & Co., [?]

xvi, 370 p.;18 cm.

K956.1/A219

Photographing in Old England with Some Snap Shots in Scotland and Wales/W. I. Lincoln Adams.—New York: The Baker & Taylor Company, c1910

111 p.;26 cm.

K956.15/D615

The City of London/P. H. Ditchfield.—London: Society for Promoting Christian Knowledge, c1921

vi, 126, 15 p.;19 cm.

K956.15/K93-16

The Little Londoner: A Concise Account of the Life and Ways of the English with Special Reference to London/R. Kron.—16th ed..—Freiburg: J. Bielefelds Verlag, c1921

238 p.;17 cm.

K956.17/T284(2)

Old World Memories. Volume II/Edward Lowe Temple.—Boston: L. C. Page and Company, c1900

327 p.;18 cm.

K956.19/E57

The Travels and Surprising Adventures of Baron Munchausen/Twelve Curious Engravings.—London: Greening & Co., [?]

xxvii, 239 p.;18 cm.

K956.19/M889

When You Go to London/H. V. Morton.—New York: Robert M. McBride & Company, c1931

xix, 319 p.;20 cm.

K96/C592

Westward to the Pacific/Marion G. Clark.—New York: Charles Scribner's Sons, c1932

xii, 498 p.;19 cm.

K96/O81

The Pacific World: Its Was Distances, Its Lands and the Life upon Them, and Its Peoples/Fairfield Osborn.—New York: W. W. Norton & Company, Inc., c1944

218 p.;22 cm.

K966.09/M999

Headhunting in the Solomon Islands Around the Coral Sea/Caroline Mytinger.—New York: The Macmillan Company, 1942.

xi p., 1 l., 416 p.;22 cm.

K971.2/B816

Social Geography Series/Frederick K. Branom, Helen M. Ganey.—New York: [s. n.], [?]

298 p.;26 cm.

K971.2/B816G

Geography of New York and North America/

Frederick K. Branom, Helen M. Ganey. —New York: William H. Sadlier, Inc. , [?]
300 p. ;26 cm.

K971. 2/C443
How We are Fed: A Geographical Reader/ James Franklin Chamberlain. —New York: The Macmillan Company, c1907
xii, 214 p. ;17 cm.

K971. 2/G924
Conquistador: American Fantasia/Philip Guedalla. —London: Ernest Benn Ltd. , c1927
xiii, 276 p. ;22 cm.

K971. 2/M379
Call It North Country: The Story of Upper Michigan/John Bartlow Martin. —New York: Alfred A. Knopf, c1944
281, ix p. ;22 cm.

K971. 2/McC743
The United States in the Modern World/W. R. Mcconnell. —New York: Rand McNally & Company, c1932
viii, 305 p. ;25 p.

K971. 2/P637
Sodom by The Sea: An Affectionate History of Coney Island/Oliver Pilat, Jo Ranson. —New York: New York Publishing Co. , Inc. , c1943
ix, 334 p. ;21 cm.

K971. 25/D261
Jamestown and Her Neighbors on Virginia's Historic Peninsula/J. E. Davis. —Richmond: Garrett and Massie, Inc. , c1928
ix, 99 p. ;23 cm.

K971. 25/D994
The New New York: A Commentary on the Place and the People/John C. Van Dyke. —New York: The Macmillan Company, c1909
xv, 425 p. ;21 cm.

K971. 26/B614
Northwest Gateway: The Story of the Port of Seattle/Archle Binns. —New York: Doubleday, Doran & Company, Inc. , c1945
ix, 313 p. ;23 cm.

K971. 29/E56
Adventures in Alaska and Along the Trail/ Wendell Endicott. —New York: Frederick A. Stokes Company, c1928
343 p. ;22 cm.

K971. 29/H188
The Glorious Adventure/Richard Halliburton. —Indianapolis: The Bobbs-Merrill Company, c1927
354 p. ;22 cm.

K971. 29/H875
Cradle of the Storms/Bernard R. Hubbard. —New York: Dodd, Mead & Company, c1935
xi, 285 p. ;22 cm.

K971. 29/W746
Tidewater Maryland/Paul Wilstach. —New York: Tudor Publishing Co. , [?]
383 p. ;22 cm.

K9712. /F164
Fairbanks' new Geography of California, the United States and the World from the Point of view of California Children/Harold W. Fairbanks. —San Francisco: Harr Wagner Publishing Company, c1923
203 p. ;23 cm.

K9712. 29/C525
St. Francis of Assisi/G. K. Chesterton. —New York: Mcm. xlii, c1924
234 p. ;19 cm.

K977/A555

A Naturalist in the Guianas/Eugene Andre. —London: Thomas Nelson & Sons, [?]

382 p. ;16 cm.

K977/B916

South America: Observations and Impressions/James Bryce. —London: Macmillan and Co. , Ltd. , c1912

xxiv, 611 p. ;22 cm.

K977/F164(2)

South America: New Progressive Series of Geographies Developed According to the Problem Method. Vol. II/Harold W. Fairbanks. —San Francisco: Harr Wagner Publishing Company, c1927

274 p. ;23 cm.

K977.79/F597

Brazilian Adventure/Peter Fleming. —New York: Charies Scriber's Sons, c1933

412 p. ;21 cm.

K977.79/F597B794

Brazilian Adventure/Peter Fleming. —London: The Reprint Society, c1940

376 p. ;20 cm.

K991/B287

A Literary of Historical Atlas of Africa and Australasia/J. G. Bartholomew. —London: J. M. Dent. & Co. , [?]

218 p. ;18 cm.

K991/M268

"Holborn" Clear School Atlas: 48 Pages Political and Orographical Maps/E. A. Manchester. —London: Educational Supply Association Ltd. , [?]

40, 23 p. ;23 cm.

K991/McN172

Standard Atlas of the World/Rand McNally. —New York: Rand McNally & Company, c1939

381 p. ;26 cm.

K993/G441

The New Map of Asia (1900-1919)/Herbert Adams Gibbons. —New York: The Century Co. , c1919

571 p. ;21 cm.

K995.61/B139-7

Great Britain: Handbook for Travellers/Karl Baedeker. —7th ed.. —London: T. Fisher Unwin, c1910

xlix, 624 p. ;16 cm.

自然科学总论

N0/R473

New Frontiers of the Mind: The Story of the Duke Experiments/J. B. Rhine. —New York: Farrar & Rinehart, c1937

275 p. ;21 cm.

N02/J62

Guide to Modern Thought/C. E. M. Joad. —London: Faber & Faber, c1933

268 p. ;19 cm.

N1/W655

The New Decalogue of Science/Albert Edward Wiggam. —New York: New York Publishing Co. , Inc. , c1925

303 p. ;21 cm.

N49/A126

Everyday Mysteries: Secrets of Science in the Home/Charles Greeley Abbot. —New York: The Macmillan Company, c1923

vi, 198 p. ;20 cm.

N49/C147

Everday Science/Otis W. Caldwell, Francis D. Curtis. —Boston: Ginn and Company, c1943

xiii, 664 p. ;24 cm.

N49/C147SD

Science Remaking the World/edited by Otis W. Caldwell and Edwin E. Slosson. —New York: Doubleday, Page & Company, c1922, 1923

x p. , 2 l. , 292 p. ;22 cm.

N49/C147SG

Science fot Today/Otise W. Caldwell, Francis D. Curtis. —Boston: Ginn and Company, c1936

xvi, 737, xxii p. ;19 cm.

N49/C886

Learning About Our World/Gerald S. Craig. —Boston: Ginn and Company, c1932

viii, 396 p. ;19 cm.

N49/F785

The Modern Life Arithmetics/John Guy Fowlkes, Thomas Theodore Goff. —New York: The Macmillan Company, c1929

xiii, 240 p. ;20 cm.

N49/H546

The Story of Force and Motion: The Science of Physics-Our World in terms of Energy, Matter, and Molecular Attraction/D. W. Hering. —New York: P. F. Collier & Son Corporation Publishers, c1922, 1930, 1933

viii, 418 p. ;20 cm.

N49/H991

Scientific and Technological Reader/Jinsun K. Hwoo. —Shanghai: The Commercial Press, c1925

161 p. ;19 cm.

N49/I27

Science in Public Affairs/J. E. Iland. —London: George Allen, c1906

xxiii, 290 p. ;19 cm.

N49/J43

Man and His Physical Universe/Frank Covert Jean. —Boston: Ginn and Company, [?]

viii, 607 p. ;24 cm.

N49/K29

Other Lands and Other Times: Their Gifts to American Life/Mary G. Kelty. —Boston: Ginn and Company, c1942

vii, 414 p. ;21 cm.

N49/K67(5)

The Wonderworld of Science. 5/Warren Knox, George Stone, Morris Meister. —New York: Charles Scribner's Sons, [?]

256 p. ;20 cm.

N49/K74(1)

The Wonderworld of Science. 1/Warren Knox, George Stone, Morris Meister. —New York: Charles Scribner's Sons, [?]

128 p. ;20 cm.

N49/K74(2)

The Wonderworld of Science. 2/Warren Knox, George Stone, Morris Meister. —New York: Charles Scribner's Sons, [?]

160 p. ;20 cm.

N49/K74(3)
The Wonderworld of Science. 3/Warren Knox, George Stone, Morris Meister. —New York: Charles Scribner's Sons, [?]
192 p. ;20 cm.

N49/K74(6)
The Wonderworld of Science. Book 6/Warren Knox. —New York: Charles Scribner's Sons, c1941
288 p. ;21 cm.

N49/L192
General Science/Charles H. Lake. —Boston: Silver, Burdett and Company, c1917
xv, 446 p. ;19 cm.

N49/L668
Science in an Irrational Society/H. Levy. —London: Watts & Co. , c1934
vii, 82 p. ;17 cm.

N49/M512-2
Coal; and What We get from It/Raphael Meldola. —2nd ed.. —London: Northumberland Avenue, W. C. , c1897
210, 6 p. ;17 cm.

N49/N664
Following Columbus: Stories of Exploration And Settlement/William L. Nida. —New York: The Macmillan Company, c1927
viii, 288 p. ;19 cm.

N49/P888
Our World and Science/Samuel Ralph Powers. —New ed.. —Boston: Ginn and Company, c1946
vii, 683 p. ;22 cm.

N49/S679
Matter and Energy/F. Soddy. —London: Williams and Norgate, [?]
255 p. ;17 cm.

N49/T482(1)
The Outline of Science: a Plain Story Simply Told. Tird Volumes/edited by J. Arthur Thomson. —New York: G. P. Putnam's Sons, c1922
xix, 567-864 p. ;27 cm.

N49/W256
Great Inventors: The Sources of Their Usefulness, and the Results of their Efforts/Ward, Lock, and Co. ,—London: Ward, Lock, and Co. , [?]
xii, 308 p. ;18 cm.

N49/W582
Science and the Modern World/A. N. Whitehead. —London: Penguin Books Ltd. , c1938
246 p. ;18 cm.

N49/W642
Home Folks: A Geography for Beginners/J. Russell Smith. —Chicago: The John C. Winston Company, c1939
viii, 260 p. ;25 cm.

N56/T859
A Book about a Thousand Things/George Stimpson. —New York: Harper & Brothers Publishers, c1946
x, 552 p. ;22 cm.

N8/K34
Tent Life in Siberia: A New Account of an Old Undertaking: Adventures among the Koraks and Other Tribes in Kamchatka and Northern Asia/George • Kennan. —New York: G. P. Putnam's Sons, c1910
xix, 482 p. ;24 cm.

N81/D228

A Naturalist's Voyage: Journal of Researches into the Natural History and Geology of the Countries Visited during the Voyage of H. M. S. 'Beagle' Round the World/Charles Darwin. —London: John Murray, c1889

x, 519 p. ;19 cm.

N81/R559

Treasure Hunter/Harry E. Risesberg. —New York: Robert M. McBride & Company, c1945

260 p. ;21 cm.

N816.6/W919

Endurance: An Epic of Polar Adventure/Prank Arthur Worsley. —London: Philip Allan & Co., Ltd., c1931

xii, 316 p. ;23 cm.

N816.61/E92

South With Scott/Edward R. G. R. Evans. —London: Collins, [?]

xii, 283 p. ;22 cm.

N871.2/B366

Kit Carson/Frank L. Beals. —Chicago: Wheelr Publishing Company, c1941

187 p. ;19 cm.

N91/B414

The Book of Naturalists: An Anthology of the Best Natural History/William Beebe. —New York: Alfred A. Knopf, c1945

xiv, 499 p. ;21 cm.

N917.12/P349

Audubon's America: The Narratives and Experiences of John James Audubon/Donald Culross Peattie. —Boston: Houghton Mifflin Company, c1940

vii, 329 p. ;29 cm.

数理科学和化学

O1/D554

Introduction to the Theory of Numbers/Leonard Eugene Dickson. —Chicago: The University of Chicago Press, c1929

viii, 183 p. ;20 cm.

O1/E57

First Course in Algebra/Fred Engelhardt, Leonard D. Haertter. —Revised ed.. —Chicago: The John C. Winston Company, c1935

ix, 448 p. ;19 cm.

O1/H714

Mathematics for the Million/Lancelot Hogben. —New, Revised and Enlarged ed.. —New York: W. W. Norton & Company Inc., c1937, 1940, 1943

xiv, 690 p. ;21 cm.

O1/M647

Popular Mathematics: The Understanding and Enjoyment of Mathematics/Denning Miller. —New York: Coward-Mccann, Inc., c1942

xi, 616 p. ;22 cm.

O1-49/L716

The Education of T. C. Mits/Hugh Gray Lieber. —New York: W. W. Norton & Company, Inc., c1942, 1944

230 p. ;21 cm.

O1-64/P973

Chambers's Seven-figure Mathematical Tables/edited by James Pryde. —New Edition. —London: W. & R. Chambers, Ltd., c1936

2 p.;20 cm.

O12/M332-5

Elementary Arithmetic/The Marist Brothers. —5th ed.. —Shanghai: The Centurion Printing Co., c1931

xiii, 298 p.;19 cm.

O12/T638

Mensuration for Beginners with Numerous Examples/I. Todhunter. —London: Macmillan and Co., Ltd., c1907

vi, 296 p.;15 cm.

O121/B889(5)

The New Curriculum Arithmetics (Triangle Series). Grade Five/Leo J. Brueckner, C. J. Anderson, G. O. Banting. —Chicago: The John C. Winston Company, c1935

ix, 277 p.;20 cm.

O121/B889(6)

The New Curriculum Arithmetics (Triangle Series). Grade Six/Leo J. Brueckner, C. J. Anderson, G. O. Banting. —Chicago: The John C. Winston Company, c1935

277 p.;19 cm.

O121/B889(7)

The New Curriculum Arithmetics (Triangle Series). Grade seven/Leo J. Brueckner, C. J. Anderson, G. O. Banting. —Chicago: The John C. Winston Company, c1935

280 p.;19 cm.

O121/B976(1)

Review Arithmetic. Textbook I, Whole Numbers and Fractions/Guy T. Buswell, William A. Brownell, Lenore John. —[Washington]: Ginn and Company, c1944

v, 172 p.;20 cm.

O121/B976(2)

Review Arithmetic. Textbook II, Decimals, Per Cents and Applications of Arithmetic/Guy T. Buswell, William A. Brownell, Lenore John. —Boston: Ginn and Company, c1944

215 p.;19 cm.

O121/F532

The Complete Arithmetic: Oral and Written/Daniel W. Fish. —New York: American Book Company, c1873

x, 516 p.;17 cm.

O121-43/B976(2)

Review Arithmetic: Decimals, Per Cents and Applications of Arithmetic. Vol. 2/Guy T. Buswell. —Boston: Ginn and Company, c1943

v, 214 p.;20 cm.

O122/E23

Elementary Algebra/Edward I. Edgerton, Perry A. Carpenter. —Boston: Allyn and Bacon, c1929

xli, 498 p.;19 cm.

O122/M659

Elements of Algebra/William J. Milne. —New York: American Book Company, c1894

199 p.;19 cm.

O122/S877

Second Course in Algebra/John C. Stone, Virgil S. Mallory. —Chicago: Benj. H. Sanborn & Co., c1937

504 p.;19 cm.

O122/S878

A First Course in Algebra/John C. Stone. —Chicago: Benj. H. Sanborn & Co., c1936

vii, 510 p. ;19 cm.

O122/S878S

A Second Course in Algebra/John C. Stone, Vircil S. Mallory. —Chicago: Benj. H. Sanborn & Co. , c1937

vii, 504 p. ;19 cm.

O122/W477

Elements of Algebra/G. A. Wentworth. —Complete ed.. —Boston: Ginn and Company, c1881

xvi, 510 p. ;19 cm.

O122/W477(3)

New School Algebra. vol. III/G. A. Wentworth. —Boston: Ginn & Company, c1898

iv, 424 p. ;18 cm.

O122. 2/D554

Elementary Theory of Equations/Leonard Eugene Dickson. —[S. l. : s. n.], [?]

iii, 183 p. ;22 cm.

O123/T638

The Elements of Euclid for the Use of Schools and Colleges/Todhunter. —London: Macmillan and Co. , Ltd. , c1903

xi, 400 p. ;15 cm.

O123/W477

Plane and Solid Geometry/George Wentworth, David Eugene Smith. —Boston: Ginn and Company, c1888

viii, 480 p. ;19 cm.

O123. 1/S387

Plane Geometry/Arthur Schultze, Frank L. Sevenoak. —New York: [S. n.], [?]

xiv, 313 p. ;19 cm.

O123. 1/W439

Plane Geometry/A. M. Welchons, W. R. Krickenberger. —Revised ed.. —Boston: Ginn and Company, c1943

ix, 544 p. ;20 cm.

O123. 1/W477

Solid Geometry/G. A. Wentworth. —Revised ed.. —Boston: Ginn & Company, c1899

xvii, 251-468 p. ;19 cm.

O123. 2/W439

Solid Geometry: A Self-teaching Coure/A. M. Welchons. —Revised ed. —Boston: Ginn and Company, c1944

v, 317 p. ;19 cm.

O123. 2/W478-2

Solid Geometry/G. A. Wentworth. —revised ed.. —Boston: Ginn and Company, c1899

xvii, 251-468 p. ;19 cm.

O124/B842

Trigonometry: Plane and Spherical/Ernst R. Breslich. —Chicago: Laidlaw Brothers, c1936

viii, 108 p. ;19 cm.

O124/B842

Trigonometry: Plane and Spherical/Ernst R. Breslich. —Revised ed.. —Chicago: Laidlaw Brothers Publishers, 1928, 1936

1 v. ;19 cm.

O141. 2/D554

First Course in the Theory of Equations/Leonard Eugene Dickson. —New York: John Wiley & Sons, Inc. , c1922

vi, 168 p. ;22 cm.

O15/B289

Algebra Review Exercises: Especially Adapted to Preparation for College-Entrance Examinations/Josiah Bartlett, George W. Creelman, Ernest E. Rich. —Boston: Ginn and Company, c1930

vi, 171 p. ;18 cm.

O15/F495

A College Algebra/Henry Burchard Fine. —[S. l. : s. n.], c[1905]

595, 53 p. ;19 cm.

O15/H174-4

Higher Algebre: A Sequel to Elemntary Algebra for Schools/H. S. Hall, S. R. Knight. —4th ed. . —London: Macmillan and Co. , Ltd. , c1919

xxii, 557 p. ;19 cm.

O15/S878

A First Course in Algebra/John Stone, Virgil S. Mallory. —Chicago: Benj. H. Sanborn & Co. , c1936

vii, 510 p. ;19 cm.

O15/T943

Theory of Equations/H. W. Turnbull. —Edinburgh: Oliver and Boyd Ltd. , 1947

xii, 166 p. ;18 cm.

O15-43/C558(2)

Algebra: An Elementary Text-Book for the Higher Clases of Secondary Schools and for Colleges. Part II/G. Chrystal. —Edinburgh: Adam and Charles Black, [?]

xxiii, 588 p. ;19 cm.

O15-44/S645

Exercises and Tests in Intermediate Algebra/David Eugene Smith, William David Reeve, Edward Longworth Morss. —Boston: Ginn and Company, [?]

111 p. ;24 cm.

O151/D989

Linear Computations/Paul S. Dwyer. —New York: John Wiley & Sons, Inc. , [?]

viii, 344 p. ;22 cm.

O153-43/S878

A First Course in Algebra/John C. Stone, Virgil S. Mallory. —Chicago: Benj. H. Sanborn & Co. , c1936

vii, 510 p. ;19 cm.

O172/F946-2

Elementary Differential Equations/Thornton C. Fry. —2nd ed. . —New York: D. Van Nostrand Company, Inc. , c1929

x, 255 p. ;23 cm.

O172/G765

Elements of the Differential and Integral Calculus/William Anthony Granville. —Boston: Ginn and Company, c1929

xi, 516 p. ;19 cm.

O172/O82

Advanced Calculus/William F. Osgood. —New York: The Macmillan Company, c1928

xvi, 529 p. ;22 cm.

O172/W729-8

An Elementary Treatise on The Integral Calculus/Benjamin Williamson. —8th ed. . —Tokyo: The Maruzen-Kabushiki-Kaisha, c1913

xvii, 520 p. ;19 cm.

O172/W894

Advanced Calculus: A Course Arranged with Special Reference to the Needs of Students of Applied Mathematics/Frederick S. Woods. —New ed. . —Boston: Ginn and Company, c1926, 1932, 1934

ix, 397 p. ;24 cm.

O172/W894E

Elementary Calculus/Frederick S. Woods, Frederick H. Bailey. —Boston: Ginn and Company, c1928

x, 385 p. ;21 cm.

O172. 1/W729

An Elementary Treatise on the Differential Calculus: Containing the Theory of Plane Curves with Numerous Examples/Benjamin Williamson. —Tokyo: [s. n.], c1904

xvi, 472 p. ;19 cm.

O172. 2/P615

A Short Table of Integrals/by B. O. Pierce. —Boston: Ginn, [c1929]

156 p. ;22 cm.

O173/K72

Theory and Application of Infinite Series/Konrad Knopp. —[S. l. : s. n.], c1928

xii, 571 p. ;23 cm.

O174/B889(3)

The Triangle Arithmetics. Book Three/Leo J. Brueckner. —Philadelphia: The John C. Winston Company, c1928

1 v. ;19 cm.

O18/N274

College Geometry: A Second Course in Plane Geometry for Colleges and Normal Schools/Nathan Altshiller-Court, D. Sc.. —[S. l.]: University of Oklahoma, [?]

x, 254 p. ;19 cm.

O18/S651

Elements of Geometry/J. Hamblin Smith. —New York: Longmans, Green, c1908

xv, 349 p. ;17 cm.

O181/B167(2)

Principles of Geometry. Volume II/H. F. Baker. —[S. l. : s. n.], c1930

xv, 259 p. ;23 cm.

O181/B167(3)

Principles of Geometry. Volume III, Solid Geometry/H. F. Baker. —[S. l. : s. n.], c1934

xix, 230 p. ;23 cm.

O181/B167(5)

Principles of Geometry. Volume v/H. F. Baker. —[S. l. : s. n.], c1930

xv, 259 p. ;23 cm.

O181/B167(6)

Principles of Geometry. Volume VI, Introduction to the Theory of Algebraic Surfaces and Higher Loci/H. F. Baker. —[S. l. : s. n.], c1933

ix, 308 p. ;23 cm.

O182/L897-2

Analytic Geometry/Clyde E. Love. —revised ed.. —New York: The Macmillan Company, c1937

xiv, 257 p. ;20 cm.

O182/S565

Analytic Geometry/Lewis Parker Siceloff, George Wentworth, David Eugene Smith. —Boston: Ginn and Company, c1922

vi, 290 p. ;21 cm.

O182/S642

The Elements of Analytic Geometry/Percey F. Smith and Arthur Sullivan Gale. —Boston: Ginn, c1904.

xii, 424 p. , 2 leaves of plates;22 cm.

O182/S642I

Introduction to Analytic Geometry/Percey F. Smith, Arthur Sullivan Gale. —Boston: Ginn and Company, c1905

viii, 217 p. ;21 cm.

O182. 2/S675

Analytic Geometry of Space/Virgil Snyder, C. H. Sisam. —New York: Henry Holt and Company, c1914.

xi, 289 p. ;20 cm.

O185. 1/Y73

Projective Geometry/John Wesley Young. —Chicago: The Open Court Publishing Company, c1930

ix, 185 p. ;19 cm.

O185. 2/K33

Descriptive Geometry: Enlarged Edition/Ervin Kenison, Harry Cyrus Bradley. —New York: The Macmillan Company, c1923

xviii, 405 p. ;20 cm.

O29/F797

Differential Equations for Electrical Engineers/Ihilir, Franklin. —New York: John Wiley & Sons, c1947.

299 p. ;20 cm.

O29/S619

Complete Commercial Arithmetic/SIR Isaac Pitman&Sons, Ltd. ,—London: SIR Isaac Pitman & Sons, Ltd. , [?]

264 P. ;19 cm.

O3/B697

The Story of Mechanics: The Science of Captives Force or Development of Machine Power in this Industrial Age/A. Russell Bond. —New York: P. F. Collier & Son Corporation Publishers, c1939

viii, 421 p. ;20 cm.

O3/L847

Mechanics and Hydrostatics for Beginners/S. L. Loney. —Cambridge: Cambridge University Press, c1927

viii, 309, xv p. ;17 cm.

O31/L847-4

Solutions of the Examples in the Elements of Statics and Dynamics/S. L. Loney. —4th ed. . —London: Cambridge University Press, c1906

391 p. ;17 cm.

O31/L847-5(1)

The Elements of Staticsand Dynamics. Part I, Statics/S. L. Loney. —5th ed. . —[S. l. : s. n.], c[1890]

viii, 240, xiv p. ;19 cm.

O31/Macm645

Theoretical Mechanic: Statics and The Dynamics of a Particle/William Duncan Macmillan. —London: McGraw-Hill Book Company, Inc. , c1927

xviii, 430 p. ;23 cm.

O313/L847

An Elementary Treatise on the Dynamics of a Particle and of Rigid Bodies/S. L. Loney. —Cambridge: The University Press, c1927

viii, 395, vi p. ;22 cm.

O315/H564

Exterior Ballistics 1935/Ernest E. Hermann. —Annapolis: The U. S. Naval Institute, c1935

viii, 305 p. ;26 cm.

O322/M666

Introduction to Non-linear Mechanics: Topelegical Metheds; Analytical; Mon-linear Aresonance; Relaxation Oscilations/N. Minorsky. —[S. l]: Edwards, c1947

464 p. ;26 cm.

O343/G795

Theoretical Elasticity/A. E. Green, W. Zerna. . —[S. l. : s. n.], [?]

xiii, 442 p. ;22 cm.

O39/PP823-2

Applied Mechanics/Alfred P. Poorman. —2nd ed. . —New York: McGraw-Hill Book Company, Inc. , c1923

xiv, 293 p. ;24 cm.

O4/A955

Elementary Physics/Elroy M. Avery. —New York: American Book Company, c1897

317 p. ;19 cm.

O4/B627

Elementary Practical Physics/Newton Henry Black, Harvey Nathaniel Davis. —New York: The Macmillan Company, c1947

viii, 710 p. ;21 cm.

O4/D855-7

Physics: For Students of Science & Engineering/A. Wilmer Duff. —7th Revised ed.. —[S. l. : s. n.], [?]

xi, 681 p. ;22 cm.

O4/D883

Modern Physics/Charles E. DUll. —New York: Henry Holt and Company, c1945

x, 598, xxv p. ;24 cm.

O4/D883(1)

Physics. Course 1/Charles E. Dull. —New York: Henry Holt and Company, Inc. , c1943

vi, 352 p. ;19 cm.

O4/D883(2)

Physics: Heat, Sound, and Light. Course 2/Charles E. Dull. —Washington: Henry Holt and Company. Inc. , c1943

ix, 345 p. ;19 cm.

O4/D883(3)

Physics: Electricity. Course 3/Charles E. Dull. —Washington: Henry Holt and Company. Inc. , c1943

vii, 314 p. ;19 cm.

O4/E15

The Physical Sciences/Eby... [et al]. —Boston: Ginn and Company, c1943

484 p. ;23 cm.

O4/M654

New Elementary Physics/Robert Andrews Millikan. —Boston: Ginn and Company, c1941

xiv, 637 p. ;20 cm.

O4/M654F

A First Course in Physics/Robert Andrews Millikan, Henry Gordon Gale. —Shanghai: Commercial Press, Ltd. , c1913

viii, 570 p. ;19 cm.

O4/M654P

Practical Physics/Robert Andrews Millikan, Henry Gordon Gale. —Boston: Ginn and Company, c1906, 1913

x, 461 p. ;19 cm.

O4/R323

College Physics/John Oren Reed, Karl Eugen Guthe. —New York: The Macmillan Company, c1915

xxviii, 622 p. ;21 cm.

O4/S257-3

A Survey of Physics for College Students/Frederick A. Saunders. —3rd ed.. —New York: Henry Holt and Company, c1930

xii, 724 p. ;22cm.

O4/S546

A First Course in Physics/B. Shen. —Shanghai: The Commercial Press, Ltd. , c1927

ix, 404 p. ;21 cm.

O4/S849-4

Physics: A Textbook for Colleges/Oscar M. Stewart. —4th ed.. —Boston: Ginn and Company, c1944

x, 785 p. ;24 cm.

O4/W715

Experiences in Physics/Lester R. Williard. —Boston: Ginn and Company, c1940

iv, 60 p. ; 24 cm.

O4-33/R498

Physics Laboratory Manual/Daniel L. RIch. —Michigan: George Wahr, Publisher, c1923

201 p. ; 23 cm.

O4-33/W715

Experiences in Physics/Lester R. Williard. —Boston: Ginn and Company, c1939

x, 662 p. ; 24 cm.

O41/C592

Physics of Today/John A. Clark. —Boston: Houghton Mifflin Company, c1938

v, 632, x p. ; 20 cm.

O41/C953-3

Ions, Electrons and Ionizing Radiations/James Arnold Crowther. —3rd ed.. —London: Longmans, Creen & Co., c1922

xii, 292 p. ; 22 cm.

O412/B499

An Introduction to the Theory of Relativity/Peter Gabriel Bergmann. —[S. l. : s. n.], c1947

287 p. ; 22 cm.

O43/B794

The Universe of Light/William Bragg. —London: G. Bell & Sons Ltd., c1933

x, 283 p. ; 22 cm.

O43/E21

Light for Students/Edwin Edser. —London: Macmillan and Co., Ltd., c1911

vi, 579 p. ; 18 cm.

O432.3/S971-3(2)

Colorimetric Methods of Analysis, Including Some Turbidimetric and Nephelometric Methods; V. 2 /Foster Dee Snell and Cornelia T. Snell.. —3rd ed.. —New York: D. Van Nostrand Co., c1942

x, 950 p. ; 24 cm.

O44/B365

The Story of Electricity and Magnetism: Harnessing Invisible Energy for the Service of Mankind/Robin Beach. —New York: P. F. Collier & Son Corporation, c1939, 1941

viii, 452 p. ; 20 cm.

O44/L736

Electricity for Home Study with Questions and Answers/John C. Lincoln. —New and Enlarged ed.. —New York: Montgomery Ward & Co., c1917

471 p. ; 17 cm.

O441/H131

Magnetism and Electricity for Students/H. E. Hadley. —London: Macmillan and Co., Ltd., c1912

x, 581 p. ; 18 cm.

O441/S795

Electricity and Magnetism: For Advanced Students/Sydney G. Starling. —[S. l. : s. n.], [?]

vi, 612 p. ; 19 cm.

O441.1-43/D883(3)

Physics: Electricity. Course 3/Charles E. Dull. —New York: Henry Holt and Company. Inc., c1943

viii, 314 p. ; 19 cm.

O56/G861(5)

A Textbook of Physics. vol. v, Physics of the Atom/E. Grimsehl. —[S. l. : s. n.], c1935

ix, 474 p. ; 23 cm.

O561/M654

Mechanics Molecular Physics and Heat: A Twelve Weeks' College Course/Robert Andrews Millikan. —Boston: Ginn and Company, c1902

242 p. ;21 cm.

O562. 6/C168

Isotopic Carbon: Techniques in Its Measurement and Chemical Manipulation/Melvin Calvin. —New York: John Wiley & Sons, Inc., c1949

xiii, 376 p. ;22 cm.

O571. 1/H289

Experimental Atomic Physics/G. P. Harnwell, J. J. Livingood. —New York: McGraw-Hill Book Company, Inc., c1933

xiii, 472 p. ;23 cm.

O572. 3/M654-2

Electrons, Protons, Photons, Neutrons, Mesotrons, and Cosmic Rays/Robert Andrews Millikan. —Revised ed.. —Chicago: The University of Chicago Press, c1937

x, 642 p. ;19 cm.

O59/B627

New Practical Physics: Fundamental Principles and Applications to Daily Life/by Newton Henry Black and Harvey Nathaniel Davis.. —Special China ed.. —Shanghai: The Commercial Press, Ltd., c1929.

x, 645 p. ;19 cm.

O6/A287

Living Chemistry/Maurice R. Ahrens. —Boston: Ginn and Company, [?]

iv, 536, xvii p. ;26 cm.

O6/C648(1)

Elementary Practical Chemistry. Part I, General Chemistry/Frank Clowes. —London: J. & A. Churchill, c1903

xiv, 198 p. ;20 cm.

O6/D378-3

General Chemistry: An Elementary Survey: Emphasizing Industrial Applications of Fundamental Principles/Horace G. Deming. —3rd ed.. Rewritten and Revised. —[S. l. : s. n.], c1930

ix, 715, iii p. ;22 cm.

O6/D379

Introductory College Chemistry: An Elementary Course Developed Historically/Horace G. Deming. —[S. l. : s. n.], c1933

xii, 590 p. ;21 cm.

O6/H424

This Chemical Age: The Miracle of Man Made Materials/Williams Haynes. —New York: Alfred A. Knopf, c1945

401, xxii p. ;22 cm.

O6/H749

Introductory College Chemistry/Harry N. Holmes. —New York: The Macmillan Company, c1932

viii, 550 p. ;23 cm.

O6/J23-2

Chemical Calculations: A Systematic Presentation of the Solution of Type Problems, with 1000 Chemical Problems Arranged Progressively According to Lesson Assignments/Bernard Jaffe. —rev. ed.. —Chicago: World Book Company, c1947

xii, 180 p. ;19 cm.

O6/P945

Chemistry and Human Affairs/William E. Price, George H. Bruce. —New York: World Book Company, c1946

788 p. ;22 cm.

O6/S642

General Chemistry for Colleges/Alexander Smith. —New York: The Century Co., c1905, 1906, 1908

xiii, 529 p.;21 cm.

O6-0/H642-4

Principles of Chemistry/Joel H. Hildebrand..—4th ed..—New York: The Macmillan Company, c1940

xii, 313 p.;22 cm.

O6-09/B977

A History of Chemistry from the Earliest Times Till the Present Day/James Campbell Brown. —London: J. &A. Churchill, c1913

xxix, 543, 22 p.;23 cm.

O6-1/J23

New World of Chemistry: Science in the Service of Man/Bernard Jaffe. —New York: Silver Burdett Company, c1940

xi, 691 p.;20 cm.

O6-3/B627

New Laboratory Experiments in Practical Chemistry: To Accompany Black and Conant's " New Practical Chemistry "/Newton Henry Black. —New York: The Macmillan Company, c1939

ix, 193 p.;20 cm.

O6-3/C348-4

A New Course of Experimental Chemistry: Including the Principles of Qualitative and Quantitative Analysis Being a Systematic Series of Experiments and Problems for the Laboratory and Class Room/John Castell-Evans. —4th ed..—London: Thomas Murby, 3 Ludgete Circus Buidings, E. C., [?]

1 v.;18 cm.

O6-3/D411

Laboratory Manual: To Accompany Clarke and Dennis's Elementary Chemistry/L. M. Dennis, F. W. Clarke. —New York: American Book Company, c1902

254 p.;19 cm.

O6-3/E19

Discovery Problems in Chemistry: A Workbook and Laboratory Manual for Use with Any Chemistry Text/Theodore E. Eckert. —New York: College Entrance Book Company, c1942

vii, 344 p.;22 cm.

O6-3/K12

Laboratory Exercises in General Chemistry/Louis Kahlenberg. —[S. l.]: Cantwell Printing Company, c1913

216 p.;19 cm.

O6-61/C853

A Dictionary of Chemical Terms/James F. Couch. —New York: D. Van Nostrand Company, c1920

iii, 203 p.;17 cm.

O6-61/P315

A German-English Dictionary for Chemists/Austin M. Patterson. —[S. l.: s. n.], c1917

xvi, 343 p.;18 cm.

O6-61/T518(1)

A Dictionary of Applied Chemistry. vol. 1, A-CHE/Sir Edward Thorpe. —revised and enlarged ed..—London: Longmans, Green, and Co., c1912

viii, 758 p.;23 cm.

O6-62/L274

Handbook of Chemistry: A Reference Volume for all Requiring Ready Access to Chemical and Physical Data Used in Laboratory Work and Manufacturing/Norbery Adolph Lange. —San-

dusky: Handbook Publishers, INC., c1946
xvi, 1767, 271, 28 p.;20 cm.

O61/B871
First Principles of Chemistry/Raymond B. Broenlee, Robert W. Fuller, William J. Hancock.—Boston: Allyn and Bacon, c1907, 1915
ix, 526 p.;19 cm.

O61/B873(1931)
First Principles of Chemistry/Raymond B. Broenlee, Robert W. Fuller, William J. Hancock.—Boston: Allyn and Bacon, c1931
vii, 777, 24 p.;19 cm.

O61/H733-4
A Text-Book of Inorganic Chemistry/A. F. Holleman, Hermon Charles Cooper.—4th English ed..—New York: John Wiley & Sons, c1912
viii, 505 p.;23 cm.

O61/J76
Practical Inorganic Chemistry for Advanced Students/Chapman Jones.—London: Macmillan and Co., Ltd., c1906
x, 239 p.;18 cm.

O61/O81
Inorganic Chemistry for Upper Forms/P. W. Oscroft.—London: G. Bell and Sons, Ltd., c1935
viii, 547 p.;19 cm.

O61/T241
Inorganic and Theoretical Chemistry/F. Sherwood, Taylor.—London: William Heinemann, c1936.
832 p.;21 cm.

O61-3/B627
Laboratory Experiments in Chemistry: Black and Conant's "Practical Chemistry"/N. Henry Black.—New York: The Macmillan Company, c1924
ix, 167 p.;19 cm.

O611/B135
Elements of Chemical Engineering/Walter L. Badger.—[S. l.: s. n.], [?]
xvii, 625 p.;23 cm.

O611/L488
Elements of Chemistry/Henry Leffmann.—Philadelphia: E. H. Butler & Co., c1882
227 p.;19 cm.

O613.2/C592-2
The Determination of Hydrogen Ions: An elementary treatise on the hydrogen electrode, indicator and supplementary methods with an indexed bibliography on applications/W. Mansfield Clark.—2nd ed..—Baltimore: Williams & Wilkins Company, c1925
480 P.;23 cm.

O62/C678
Theoretical Organic Chemistry/Julius B. Cohen.—London: Macmillan and Co., Ltd., c1910
xv, 578 p.;18 cm.

O62/K18-2
Organic Chemistry/Paul Karrer.—2nd English ed..: [S. l. s. n.], c1946
xx, 953 p.;23 cm.

O62/K61
Fats and Oils: An Outing of Their Chemisty and Technology/H. G. Kirschenbauer.—New York: Reinhold Publishing Corporation, c1944
154 p.;23 cm.

O622.7/S965
The Organic Chemistry of Sulfur: Tetracovalent Sulfur Compounds/Chester Merle Suter.—

[S. l. : s. n.], c1945
858 p. ;22 cm.

O63/B111
The Chemistry of High Polymers/C. E. H. Bawn. —[S. l. : s. n.], c1948
249 p. ;21 cm.

O64/F494
Practical Physical Chemistry/Alex Findlay. —London: Longmans, Green and Co. , c1911
xii, 288 p. ;19 cm.

O64/T238-2(1)
A Treatise on Physical Chemistry. vol. one, States of Matter/Hugh S. Taylor, Samuel Glasstone. —2nd ed. . —New York: D. Van Nostrand Company, c1931
xv, 852, 48 p. ;23 cm.

O64/T238-3(2)
A Treatise on Physical Chemistry. vol. Two, States of Matter/Hugh S. Taylor, Samuel Glasstone. —3rd ed. . —New York: D. Van Nostrand Company, c1924
v, 701 p. ;23 cm.

O64/W177-6
Introduction to Physical Chemistry/James Walker. —6th ed. . —London: Macmillan and Co. , Ltd. , c1910
xii, 417 p. ;22 cm.

O641. 6/S849-2
Stereochemistry/Alfred W. Stewart. —2nd ed. . —London: Longmans, Green and Co. , c1919
xvi, 277 p. ;22 cm.

O642. 1/L673-3(2)
A System of Phsical Chemistry. Vol. II, Thermodynamics/William C. McC. Lews. —3rd ed. . —New York: Longmans, Green and Co. , c1922
viii, 454 p. ;22 cm.

O65/A512
Symposium on pH Measurement/American Society for Testing Materials. —Philadephia: American Society for Testing Materials, c1916
iii, 101 p. ;23 cm.

O65/S553-2
Methods of Organic Analysis/Henry C. Sherman. —2nd ed. . —New York: The Macmillan Company, c1912
Xiii, 407 p. ;22 cm.

O65/V727(1)
Treatise on Applied Analytical Chemistry. Vol. 1/Vittorio Villavecchia. —London: J. & A. Churchill, 1918
xvi, 475 p. ;25 cm.

O652/K24-2
Lunge and Keane's Technical Methods of Chemical Analysis/Charles A. Keane, P. C. L. Thorne. —2nd ed. . —London: Gurney and Jackson, c1924
xx, 704 p. ;24 cm.

O655/O42-4
A Textbook of Quantitative Chemical Analysis/J. C. Olsen. —4th ed, Revised and Enlarged. —New York: D. Van Nostrand Company, c1910
xxi, 555, 12 p. ;23 cm.

O656. 2/K15-2
Qualitative Organic Analysis: An Elementary Course in the Identification of Organic Compounds/Oliver Kamm. —2nd ed. . —[S. l. : s. n.], c1932
ix, 210 p. ;22 cm.

O657.3/M621

Report on Standard Samples and Related Materials for Spectrochemical Analysis. 1955/Robert E. Michaelis. —Philadelphia: American Society for Testing Materials, c1916

v, 87 p. ;22 cm.

O661.1/W873

Standard Methods of Water Analysis: Standard Methods for the Examination of Water and Sewage/Koksan J. Woo. —2nd ed.. —New York: American Public Health Association, c1912

vi, 144 p;24 cm.

O69/B471

The Chemical Fomulary: A Collection of Valuable, Timely, Practical Commercial Formulae and Recipes for Making Thousand of Products in Many Fields of Industry/H. Bennett. —[S. l. : s. n.], c1939

632 p. ;23 cm.

O69/B627

Practical Chemistry: Fundamental Facts and Applications to Modern Life/Newton Henry Black, James Bryant Conant. —New York: The Macmillan Company, c1924

x, 474 p. ;19 cm.

O69/F494

Chemistry in the Service of Man/Alexander Findlay. —London: Green and Co. , c1916

247 p. ;22 cm.

O69/K12

Chemistry and Its Relations to Daily Life: A Textbook for Students of Agriculture and Home Economics in Secondary Schools/Louis Kahlenberg, Edwin B. Hart. —New York: The Macmillan Company, c1927

vii, 393 p. ;19 cm.

O69/L671

Service Chemistry: Being a short manual of chemistry and its applications in the naval and military services/Vivian B. Lewes, J. S. S. Brame. —London: Hernry Glaisher, c1906

675 p. ;22 cm.

O69/McP542

Chemistry for Today: A Textbook for Secondary Schools/William McPherson, William Edwards Henderson. —Boston: Ginn and Company, c1930

xi, 588 p. ;19 cm.

O69/P945

Chemistry and Human Affairs/William E. Price, George H. Bruce. —Great Britain: World Book Company, c1946

xii, 788 p. ;23 cm.

O69/R554

Indutrial Chemistry/Emil Raymond Riegel. —[S. l: s. n.], c1942

861 p. ;23 cm.

O69: TQ/H855

Chemistry in the World's Work/Harrison E. Howe. —New York: D. Van Nostrand Company, c1926

vii, 244 p. ;21 cm.

O71/B366

An Amateur's Introduction to Crystallography (from Morphological Observations)/William Phipson Beale. —London: Longmans, Green and Co. , c1915

vii, 220 p. ;23 cm.

P 天文学、地球科学

P1/A427

Astronomy: What Everyone Should Know/John Stuart Allen. —New York: The Bosss-Merrill Company Publishers, c1945

199 p. ;21 cm.

P1/H927

Ways of the Weather: A Cultural of Meteorology/Humphreys, W. J.. —Lancaster: The Jaques Cattell Press, c1942

400 p. ;23 cm.

P1/M927I

An Introduction to Astronomy/Forest Ray Moulton. —New York: The Macmillan Company, c1912

xviii, 57 p. ;19 cm.

P1/S491

Astronomy/Garrett P. Serviss. —New York: P. F. Collier and Son Corporation, c1941

viii, 368 p. ;20 cm.

P1-49/F939

Let's Look at the Stars/Edwin Brant Frost. —Boston: Houghton Mifflin Company, c1935

118 p. ;21 cm.

P128/V531

From the Earth to the Moon and Round the Moon/Jules Verne. —New York: A. L. Jules Verne, [?]

339 p. ;19 cm.

P183/S167

The Elements of Geography/Rollin d. Salisbury, Harlan H. Barrows, Walter S. Tower. —New York: Henry Holt and Company, c1912

1 v;21 cm.

P3/M646

The Story of our Earth: The Science of Geology, the history of the world can be reade form rocks and mineral deposits/William J. Miller. —New York: P. F. Collier & Son Corporation, c1939, 1941

viii, 384 p. ;20 cm.

P4/B894

Weather Study/David Brunt. —New York: The Ronald Press Company, c1942

xi, 215 p. ;20 cm.

P4/F492

Elementary Meteorology/Vernor C. Finch, Gienn T. Trewartha. —Washington D C: The McGraw-Hill Book Company, Inc. , c1942

301 p. ;21 cm.

P44/B873

Why the Weather? /Charles Franklin Brooks. —New York: Harcourt, Brace and Company, c1938

xvii, 295 p. ;21 cm.

P44/S534-2

The Drama of Weather/Sir Napier Shaw. —2nd ed.. —Cambridge: The University Press, c1939

xiv, 307 p. ;21 cn

P46/E48

Weather and Why/Captain Ienar E. Elm. —Philadelphia: David McKay Company, c1929

109 p. ;21 cm.

P48/C316

The Story of Manufactured Weather/Carrier Fngineering Corporation. —Boston: Carrier Fngineering Corporation, c[1919]

61 p. ;23 cm.

P49/T151

The Story of our Weather: Agricultural, Commercial, Aeronautical, Medical, Military, and Marine Meteorology/Charles Fitzhugh Talman. —New York: P. F. Collier & Son Corporation Piblishers, c1940

408 p. ;20 cm.

P5/B848

This Puzzling Planet: An Introduction to Geology/Edwin Tenney Brewster. —Revised ed.. —New York: The New Home Library, c1943

xiv, 280 p. ;20 cm.

P53/W899

History of Geology/Horace B. Woodward. —London: Watts & Co., c1911

vi, 154 p. ;18 cm.

P57/F699

Dana' Manual of Mineralogy/William E. Ford. —14th ed.. —New York: John Willey & Sons, Inc., c1912

x, 476 p. ;19 cm.

P57/L742

Mineral Deposits/Waldemar Lindgren. —New York: MaGraw-Hill Book Company, Inc., c1913

xv, 883 p. ;23 cm.

P624-62/B815

The A B C of Mining: A Handbook for Prospectors/Charles A. Bramble. —Chicago: Rand. McNally & Company, c1898

183 p. ;17 cm.

P7/K26

The South Seas in the Modern World/Felix M. Keesing. —New York: The John Day Copany, c1941

xv, 391 p. ;22 cm.

P717.01/B414

Half Mile Down/William Beebe. —New York: Harcourt, Brace and Company, c1934

xix, 344 p. ;24 cm.

P754/S425

Seventy Fathoms Deep: with the Divers of the Salvage Ship Artiglio/David Scott. —London: Faber & Faber Ltd., [?]

288 p. ;21 cm.

P9/M459

Physical Geography/M. F. Maury. —New York: American Book Company, c1908

347 p. ;21 cm.

Q 生物科学

Q/M818-2

Biology for Beginners/Truman J. Moon. —rev. ed.. —New York: Henry Holt and Company, c1926 viii, 647, xvii p. ;20 cm.

Q/R333

Biology/Regents Publishing Co. ,—New York: Regents Publishing Co. , [?]

126 p. ;17 cm.

Q-0/C978

Everyday Biology/Francis D. Curtis, Otis W. Caldwell. —Boston: Ginn and Company, c1946

xi, 698 p. ;24 cm.

Q-0/M519

Essentials of Biology/W. H. D. Meler, Lois Meler. —[S. l: s. n.], [?]

vii, 529 p. ;19 cm.

Q-0/M519E78

Essentials of Biology/W. H. D. Meier, Lois Meier Shoemaker. —New Editon. —Boston: Ginn and Company, c1948

vii, 725 p. ;19 cm.

Q-49/J67

Nature's Program/Gaylord Johnson. —New York: Doubleday, Page & Company, c1926

181 p. ;21 cm.

Q1/A987

Civic and Economic Biology/Wm. H. Atwood. —Philadelphia: P. Blakiston's Son & Co. , c1922

xv, 486 p. ;20 cm.

Q1/G886

Elementary Biology: An Introduction to the Science of Life/Benjamin C. Gruenberg. —Boston: Ginn and Company, [c1919]

x, 528 p. ;20 cm.

Q1/McF231-5

Biology: General and Medical/Joseph McFarland. —5th ed. Thoroughly Revised. —Philadelphia and London: W. B. Saunders Company, c1927

475 p. ;20 cm.

Q1/S635

New General Biology/W. M. Smallwood, Ida L. Reveley, Guy A. Bailey. —Boston: Allyn and Bacon, c1929

xx, 788p. ;19 cm.

Q1/S635N532

New Biology/W. M. Smallwood, Ida L. Reveley, Guy A. Bailey. —Boston: Allyn and Bacon, c1924

xxi, 704, 37 p. ;19 cm.

Q1/W447

A Brief Course in Biology/Walter H. Wellhouse, George O. Hendrickson. —New York: The Macmillan Company, c1935

xii, 200 p. ;21 cm.

Q1-0/L563

The Situation in Biological Science: Proceeding of the Lenin Academy of Agricultural Sciences of the U. S. S. R. . July31-August7, 1948/Lenin Academy of Agricultural Scienes of th U. S. S. R. —Moscow: Foreign Languages Publishing House, c1948

631 p. ;23 cm.

Q1-0/M681

The Lives and Achievements of the Great Explorers/J. Leslie Mitchell. —New York: The New Home Library, c1942

370 p. ;21 cm.

Q1-49/G297

Introduction to Biology/N. Gist Gee. —Shanghai: The Commercial Press, c1928

372 p. ;19 cm.

Q111. 2/D213O69

The Origin of Species: By Means of Natural Selection or the Preservation of Favoured Races in the Struggle for Life/Charles Darwin. —London: John Murray, Albemarle Atreet, c1900

xxxi, 703 p. ;20 cm.

Q111. 2/R599

Darwinism and Politics: With Two Additional Essays on Human Evolution/David G. Ritchie. —London: Swan Sonnenschein & Co. , c1901

vii, 141 p. ;19 cm.

Q148/B613

Biology and Man/Gruenberg Bingham. —Boston: Ginn and Company, [?]

718 p. ;23 cm.

Q178. 53/B414

Beneath Tropic Seas: A Record of Diving among the Coral Reefs of Haiti/William Beebe. —New York: G. P. Putnam's Sons, c1928

xiii, 234 p. ;22 cm.

Q178. 53/B414B461

Beneath Tropic Seas: A Record of Diving among the Coral Reefs of Haiti/William Beebe. —New York: Blu Ribbon Books, c1928

viii, 234 p. ;21 cm.

Q178. 53/U58(24. 2)

Journal of the Marine Biological Association of the United Kingdom. volme XXIV, No. 2/The University Press. —Cambridge: The University Press, c1940

1 v. ;24 cm.

Q3-02/P984-5

Mendelism/Reginald Crundall Punnett. —5th ed. . —London: Macmillan and Co. , c1919

xv, 219 p. ;18 cm.

Q4/G861(1)

A Textbook of Physics. Vol. I/E. Grimsehl. —[S. l. : s. n.], [?]

vi, 433 p. ;23 cm.

Q4/G861(2)

A Textbook of Physics. Vol. II, Heat and Sound/E. Grimsehl. —[S. l. : s. n.], c1933

vii, 310 p. ;23 cm.

Q4/G861(4)

A Textbook of Physics. Vol. IV/E. Grimsehl. —[S. l. : s. n.], [?]

viii, 301 p. ;23 cm.

Q427/P497(1)

Lectures on Conditioned Reflexes: Twenty-five Years of Objective Study of the Higher Nervous Activity(Behaviour)of Animals. Vol. 1/ Ivan Petrovitch Pavlov. —Shanghai: [s. n.], [?]

414, 199 p. ;23 cm.

Q5/B666-4

Introduction to Physiological Chemistry/Meyer Bodansky. —4th ed. . —[S. l. : s. n.], c1938

ix, 686 p. ;21 cm.

Q5/H392-8

Practical Physiological Chemistry: A Book Designed for Use in Courses in Practical Physiological Chemistry in Schools of Medicine and of Science/Philip B. Hawk. —8th ed. , Revised. —Philadelphia: P. Blakiston's Son & Co. , c1923.

xvi. 698 p. ;24 cm.

Q5/S553

Crashing Through! /Harold M. Sherman. —New York: Grosset & Dunlap, c1932

v, 266 p. ;19 cm.

Q50/P511

An Intermediate Textbook of Physiological

Chemistry with Experiments/C. J. V. Pettiebone. —St. Louis：C. V. Mosby Company，c1917
328 p. ;22 cm.

Q93/F529
The Structure and Functions of Bacteria/Alfred Fischer. —Oxford：Clarendon Press，c1900
198 p. ;25 cm.

Q93/G787-5
Elementary Bacteriology/Joseph E. Greaves. —5th ed.. —Philadelphia：W. B. Saunders Company，c1946
xvii，613 p. ;20 cm.

Q93/K94
Microbe Hunters/Paul De Kruif. —New York：Harcourt，Brace and Company，[c1926]
6 p. l. ，3-363 p. ;23 cm.

Q93-335/C734
Manual of Methods for Pure Culture Study of Bacteria/Commiattee on Bacteriological Techinc of the Society of American Bacteriologists. —[S. l. : s. n.]，[?]
1 v. ;23 cm.

Q939. 1/C743-3
Bacteria，Yeasts，and Molds in the Home/H. W. Conn. —3rd revised ed.. —Boston：Ginn and Company，c1912
viii，320 p. ;20 cm.

Q939. 1/J82--8
A Text-book of General Bacteriology/Edwin O. Jordan. —8th ed. ，Thoroughly Revised：W. B. Saunders Company，c1925
750 p. ;23 cm.

Q94/B495
Sentials of Botany/Joseph Y. Bergen. —[S. l. : s. n.]，[?]
ix，267 p. ;19 cm.

Q94/C855(1. 2)
A Textbook of Botany for Colleges and Universities. Vol. I. ，Part II，Physiology/John Merle Coulter，Charles Reid Barnes，Henry Chandler Cowles. —New York：American Book Company，c1910
1 v;21 cm.

Q94/C875
A Spring Flora/Henry C. Cowles，John G. Coulter. —New York：American Book Company，c1915
144 p. ;19 cm.

Q94/F919
Elementary Studies in Plant Life/F. E. Fristch，E. J. Salisbury. —London：G. Bell and Sons，Ltd. ，c1932
xv，194 p. ;19 cm.

Q94/H747-4
A Textbook of General Botany for Colleges and Universities/Richard M. Holman，Wilfred W. Robbins. —4th ed.. —New York：John Wiley & Sons，Inc. ，c1938，1939
xvii，664 p. ;22 cm.

Q94/P821
Frist Course in Botany：An Introduction to the Study of Plants as Related to the Development of a Knowledge of the Universe in Which We Live and as a Phase of Modern Science/Raymond J. Pool，Arthur T. Evans，Otis W. Caldwell. —Boston：Ginn and Company，c1941
ix，422 p. ;19 cm.

Q94/T238
The Story of Our Plants：The Science of Botany—The Forms，Functions and Economic Importance of Vegetable Life/Norman Taylor. —New York：P. F. Collier & Son Corporation，c1940

407 p. ;20 cm.

Q946/J32-2
Vegetable Fats and Oils: Their Chemistry, Production, and Utilization for Edible, Medicinal and Technical Purposes/George S. Jamieson. —2nd ed. : Reinhold Publishing Corporation, c1943
508 p. ;23 cm.

Q946. 1/O81
The Vegetable Proteins/Thomas B. Osborne. —London: Longmans, Green, and Co. , c1912
xiii, 125 p. ;26 cm.

Q949. 777. 5/P377
The Verbenaceae of China/P'ei Chien. —Shanghai: The Science Society of China, c1932
188 p. ;26 cm.

Q95/B414
Book of Bays/William Beebe. —New York: Harcourt, Brace and Company, c1942
xviii, 302 p. ;22 cm.

Q95/D615
Strange Animals I Have Known/Raymond L. Ditmars. —New York: Harcourt, Brace and Company, c1931
375 p. ;20 cm.

Q95/H462-5
College Zoology/Robert W. Hegner. —5th ed. . —New York: The Macmillan Company, c1947
xvii, 817 p. ;24 cm.

Q95/I47
The Story of Our Animals: The Science of Zoology—the Animal Life of Today and of Past Ages, Its Varied Forms and Changes/Ernest Ingersoll. —New York: P. F. Collier & Son Corporation, c1940
392 p. ;20 cm.

Q95/N747
The Nature of the Beast: A Popular Account of Animal Psychology from the Point of View of a Naturalist/Ruth Crosby Noble. —New York: Doubleday, Doran and Company, Inc. , c1945
viii, 224 p. ;22 cm.

Q95/P238-6(1)
A Text-Book of Zoology. Vol. 1/T. Jeffery Parker, William A. Haswell. —6th ed. . —London: Macmillan and Co. , Ltd. , c1943
xxxii, 770 p. ;25 cm.

Q95-49/S495
Lives of the Hunted/Ernest Thompson Seton. —[S. l. : s. n.], [?]
360 p. ;20 cm.

Q958. 5/C323
Mammals of the Pacific World/T. D. Carter, J. E. Hill, G. H. H. Tate. —New York: The Macmillan Company, c1945
xvi, 227 p. ;21 cm.

Q958. 571. 2/D715
The Animal Book: American Mammals North of Mexico/Dorothy Childs Hogner and Nils Hogner. —London: Oxford University Press, c1942
223 p. ;27 cm.

Q959. 7/M474
Birds of the Southwest Pacific: A Field Guide to the Birds of the Area between Samoa, New Caledonia, and Micronesia/Ernst Mayr. —New York: The Macmillan Company, c1945
xix, 316 p. ;19 cm.

Q959. 8/C132
Meeting the Mammals/Victor H. Cahalane. —

New York: The Macmillan Company, c1945
ix, 133 p. ;25 cm.

Q96/C976
Insects of the Pacific World/C. H. Curran.—New York: The Macmillan Company, c1945
xv, 317 p. ;21 cm.

Q98/H383
The Story of Mankind: Science of anthropology-man's evolution-his physical, mental and moral development/Loomis Havemeyer.—New York: P. F. Collier & Son Corporation Publishers, c1940
388 p. ;20 cm.

Q98/S347
Why We Misbehave/Samuel D. Schmalhausen.—New York: New York Publishing Co., Inc., c1928
312 p. ;21 cm.

Q98-49/L863
The Story of Mankind/Hendrik Van Loon.—New York: New York Publishing Company, Inc., c1926
xxviii, 482 p. ;21 cm.

R 医学、卫生

R-0/C883
In Sickness and in Health: A Manual of Domestic Medicine and Surgery, Hygiene Dietetics, and Nursing/George Waldo Crary, Frederic S. Lee.—New York: D. Appletion and Company, c1912
xvi, 991 p. ;24 cm.

R11/R813-3
Preventive Medicine and Hygiene/Milton J. Rosenau.—3rd ed..—New York: D. Appleton and Company, c1918
xxxvi, 1374 p. ;24 cm.

R126.6/A242
The Healthy Home and Community/J. mace Andress.—Boston: Ginn and Company, c1945
338 p. ;21 cm.

R151/B111
Food Facts: Practical Information on the Science of Eating/Arthur T. Bawden.—Shanghai: Shanghai Times, c1931.
255 p;23 cm.

R151.2/B738
Vitamins: What They Are and How They Can Bennefit You/Henry Borsook.—[S. l.: s. n.], c1940
xiii, 212 p. ;21 cm.

R151.3/S553
Chemistry of Food and Nutrition/Henry C. Sherman.—New York: The Macmillan Company, c1916
viii, 355 p. ;19 cm.

R151.3/S553(O)
Chemistry of Food and Nutrition/Henry C. Sherman.—New York: The Macmillan Company, c1912
viii, 355 p. ;19 cm.

R151. 3/S553-7

Chemistry of Food and Nutrition/Henry C. Sherman. —7th ed.. —New York: The Macmillan Company, c1946

viii, 675 p. ;22 cm.

R151. 4/H412

Health Via Food/William Howard Hay. —New York: Sun-Diet Health Foundation, c1934

317 p. ;21 cm.

R16/A561

Helping the Body in Its Work/J. Mace Andress, I. H. Goldberger, Grace T. Hallock. —New ed.. —Boston: Ginn and Company, c1945

viii, 313 p. ;21 cm.

R16/S613

The Principles of Hygiene: As Applied to Tropical and Sub-Tropical Climates and the Principies of Personal Hygiene in Them as Applied to Europeans/W. J. R. Simpson. —New York: William Wood and Company, c1908

xii, 396 p. ;22 cm.

R161/A561

Doing Your Best for Health: New Edition/J. Mace Andress, I. H. Goldberger, Grace T. Hallock. —Boston: Ginn and Company, c1945

viii, 298 p. ;20 cm.

R161/A561B932

Building Good Health: New Edition/J. Mace Andress, I. H. Goldberger, Grace T. Hallock. —Boston: Ginn and Company, c1945

viii, 298 p. ;21 cm.

R161/A561D657

Doing Your Best for Health/J. Mace Andress, I. H. Goldberger, Grace T. Hallock. —Boston: Ginn and Company, c1941

viii, 279 p. ;21 cm.

R161/G618

Health and Physical Fitness/I. H. Goldberger, Grace T. Hallock. —Boston: Ginn and Company, c1946

x, 595 p. ;23 cm.

R161/S544(2)

A Health Reader. Book 2/C. E. Shelly, E. Stenhouse. —London: Macmillan and Co., Ltd., c1925

viii, 196 p. ;17 cm.

R161/W778

The Home Medical Adviser/Kenelm Winslow. —New York: D. Appleton and Company, c1917

xx, 749 p. ;24 cm.

R161. 1/C666

Health and Achievement: A Textbook of Health with A Physiological Background/Edgar A. Cockefair, Ada Milam Cockefair. —Boston: Ginn and Company, c1940

ix, 558 p. ;20 cm.

R161. 5/R643

Nutrition Work with Children/Lydia J. • Roberts. —Chicago: The University of Chicago Press, c1927

xiv, 394 p. ;21 cm.

R161. 7/G971

The Efficient Life/Luther H. Gulick. —New York: Doubleday, Page & Company, c1913

xvi, 195 p. ;19 cm.

R167/W423

Sex and Character/Otto Weininger. —New York: A. L. Burt Company, [?]

xxii, 356 p. ;21 cm.

R169. 4/S883

Wise Parenthood: A Practical Sequel to "Mar-

ried Love"/Marie Carmichael Stopes. —London: G. P. Putnam's Sons, Ltd. , c1927
xiv, 67 p. ;19 cm.

R169. 41/H149
Birth-Control Methods (Contraception, Abortion, Sterilisation)/Norman Haire. —London: George Allen & Unwin Ltd. , [?]
212 p. ;19 cm.

R174/H645
Clinical Lectures on Infant Feeding/Lewis Webb Hill. —Philadelphia: W. B. Saunders Company, c1917
367 p. ;20 cm.

R174/H758
The Care and Feeding of Children: a Catechism for the Use of Mothers and Children's Nurses/L. Emmett Holt. —New York: D. Appleton and Company, 1894, 1923.
252 p. ;18 cm.

R179/G448
Boyology or Boy Analysis/H. W. Gibson. —New York: Association Press, c1918
x, 294 p. ;17 cm.

R18/J45
The Diseases of China: Including Formosa and Korea/W. Hamilton Jefferys, James L. Maxwell. —Philadelphia: P. Blakiston's Son & Co. , c1911
xvi, 716 p. ;24 cm.

R199. 712/McC731
City Health Administration/Carl E. Mccombs. —New York: The Macmillan Company, c1927
x, 524 p. ;22 cm.

R28/O81-8
The Principles and Practice of Medicine: Designed for the Use of Practitioners and Students of Medicine/Sir William Osler. —8th ed. . —New York: D. Appleton and Company, c1919
xxiv, 1225 p. ;23 cm.

R32/M379
The Story of Our Bodies/Ernest G. Martin. —New York: P. F. Collier & Son Corporation, c1940
382 p. ;20 cm.

R322/D261-6
Applied Anatomy: The Construction of the Human Body/Gwilym G. Davis. —6th ed. . —Philadelphia: J. B. Lippincott Company, c1924
xii, 638 p. ;26 cm.

R33/B634
Our Bodies and How We Live: An Elementary Text-Book of Physiology and Hygiene for Use in Schools/Albert F. Blaisdell. —Boston: Ginn and Company, c1921
vii, 369 p. ;19 cm.

R331. 1/T918
Blood Cells and Plasma Proteins: Their State in Nature/James L. Tullis. —[S. l. : s. n.], [?]
436 p. ;22 cm.

R38/C455-4
Introduction to Human Parasitology/Asa C. Chandler. —4th ed. . —New York: John Wiley & Sons, Inc. , c1930
xiv, 655 p. ;23 cm.

R394/S318
You and Heredity/Amram Scheinffeld. —New York: J. B. Lippincott Company, c1939
xvii, 434 p. ;22 cm.

R39536-49/L716
Peace of Mind/Joshua Loth Liebman. —New York: Simon and Schuster, c1946

xiv, 203 p. ;21 cm.

R459. 7/A512-2

American Red Cross First Aid Text-Book/The American Red Cross for the Instruction of First Aid Classes. —Rev. ed.. —Philadelphia: The Blakiston Company, c1937

xi, 256 p. ;20 cm.

R47/H287

Text-Book of the Principles and Practice of Nursing/Bertha Harmer. —New York: The Macmillan Company, c1922

xiv, 695 p. ;22 cm.

R472. 2/M338

First Aid and Field Sanitation/Marine Corps Schools. —Virginia: Marine Corps Schools, c1943

88 p. ;23 cm.

R51/D817

Bacterial and Mycotic Infections of Man/edited by Rene J. Dubos. —Shanghai: The Honvan Book Company, c1949

xii, 785 p. ;25 cm.

R521. 05/P119

Artifical Pneumothorax: Its Practical Application in the Treatment of Pulmonary Tuberculosis/Edward N. Packard, John N. Hayes, Sidney F. Blanchet. —Philadelphia: Lea & Febiger, c1940

300 p. ;24 cm.

R6/C556-5

Minor Surgery/Frederick Christorpher. —5th ed.. —Philadelphia: W. B. Saunders Company, c1945

viii, 1006 p. ;24 cm.

R61/W253(1)

Surgical Treatment: A Practical Treatise on the Therapy of Surgical Diseases for the Use of Practitioners and Student of Surgery. Volume I/James Peter Warbasse. —Philadelphia: W. B. Saunders Company, c1920

947 p. ;24 cm.

R61/W253(2)

Surgical Treatment: A Practical Treatise on the Therapy of Surgical Diseases for the Use of Practitioners and Student of Surgery. Volume II/James Peter Warbasse. —Philadelphia: W. B. Saunders Company, c1920

829 p. ;24 cm.

R61/W253(3)

Surgical Treatment: A Practical Treatise on the Therapy of Surgical Diseases for the Use of Practitioners and Student of Surgery. Volume III/James Peter Warbasse. —Philadelphia: W. B. Saunders Company, c1920

861 p. ;24 cm.

R614. 3/B825-2

Local anesthesia: Its scientific basis and practical use/Heinrich Braun. —2nd American from the sixth revised German ed. —Philadelphia: Lea & Febiger, c1924

xi, 411 p. ;c25 cm.

R655/L728

Thoracic Surgery: The Surgical Treatment of Thoracic Disease/Howard Lilienthal. —Philadelphia: W. B. Saunders Company, c1925

iv, 600 p. ;24 cm.

R655/L728T487(1)

Thoracic Surgery: The Surgical Treatment of Thoracic Disease. Vol. 1/Howard Lilienthal. —Philadelphia: W. B. Saunders Company, c1925

vii, 694 p. ;24 cm.

R655. 802/H576

Surgical Pathology of the Mammary Gland/

Arthur E. Hertzler, Irene A. Koeneke. —Philadelphia: J. B. Lippincott Company, [?]
xviii, 283 p. ;25 cm.

R656/M938-4(1)
Abdominal Operations. vol. 1/Berkeley Moynihan. —4th ed.. —Philadelphia: W. B. Saunders Company, c1926
575 p. ;24 cm.

R656/M938-4(2)
Abdominal Operations. vol. II/Berkeley Moynihan. —4th ed.. —Philadelphia: W. B. Saunders Company, c1926
642 p. ;24 cm.

R69/C116(2)
Modern Urology. vol. II/Hugh Cabot. —Philadelphia and New York: Lea & Febiger, c1924
viii, 744 p. ;25 cm.

R76/B191
Diseases of the Nose, Throat and Ear/William Loncoln Ballenger, Howard Charles Ballenger. —[S. l. : s. n.], c1947
993 p. ;21 cm.

R77/M143
Strengthening the Eyes: A System of Scientific Eye Training/Bernarr Macfadden. —New York: Macfadden Book Company, Inc. , c1936
xiv, 210 p. ;19 cm.

R778. 1/B468
Better Sight Without Glasses/Harry Benjamin. —London: Health For All Publishing Company, c1935
1 v;21 cm.

R82-62/S636-3
Handbook for the Hospital Corps of the U. S. Army and State Millitary Forces/—3rd ed. (revised and enlarged). —New York: William Wood and Company, c1902
vii, 413 p. ;19 cm.

R821. 89/U58
Handbook of the Hospital Corps United States Navy 1939/United States Government Printing Office. —Washington: The Bureau of Medicine and Surgery under the Auathority of the Secretary of the Navy, c1939
vi, 1015 p. ;23 cm.

R83-62/L434-13
The Ship Captain's Medical Guide/Harry Leach. —13th ed.. —London: Simpkin, Marshall, Hamilton, Kent & Co. , Ltd. , c1901
xvi, 190 p. ;19 cm.

R921. 712/A939
The Pharmacopoeia of the United States of America: Ninth Decennial Revision (Official from September 1, 1916)/Authoripy of the United States Pharmacopoeia Convention. —New York: P. Blackiston's Son & Company, c1916
lxxx, 728 p. ;23 cm.

R96/A939
Laboratory Manual for the Detection of Poisons and Powerful Drugs/Wilhelm Autenrieth, William H. Warren. —Philadelphia: P. Blakiston's Son & Co. , c1915
xv, 320 p. ;23 cm.

S 农业科学

S15/H174

The Soil: An Introduction to the Scientific Study of the Growth of Crops/A. D. Hall. —New York: E. P. Dutton and Company, c1910

xv, 311 p. ;20 cm.

S5/C443

Pitman's Commercial Readers Our Food Supplies. Junior Book/F. W. Chambers. —London: Sir Isaac Pitman & Sons, [?]

238 p. ;19 cm.

S5/C877

Crops: A Self-Teaching Course, Based on Crop Management and Soil Conservation/Joseph F. Cox, Lyman E. Jackson. —Washington: John Wiley & Sons, Inc. , c1937

ix, 307 p. ;19 cm.

S562/B959

Cotton: Its Cultivation, Marketing, Manufacture, and the Problems of the Cotton World/Charles William Burkett, Clarence Hamilton Poe. —New York: Doubleday, Page & Company, c1906

ix, 329 p. ;23 cm.

S572/K46

Tabacco Leaf: /J. B. Killebrew, Herbert Myrick. —New York: Orang Jud Copany, c1918

xiv, 506 p. ;19 cm.

S63/W348

The Vegetable Growing Business/Ralph L. Watts, Gilbert Searle Watts. —[S. l.]: Orange Judd Publishing Company, Inc. , c1940

x, 520 p. ;21 cm.

S652/B878

Cotton: History, Species, Varieties, Morphology, Breeding, Culture, Diseases, Marketing, and Uses/Harry Bates Brown. —[S. l. : s. n.], [?]

xi, 517 p. ;23 cm.

S66/R727

Trees That Every Child Should Know/Julia Ellen Rogers. —New York: Doubleday, Page & Company, c1913

ix, 263 p. ;19 cm.

S68/M178

Simple Gardening/A. J. Macself. —London: W. H. & L. Collingridge Ltd. , [?]

xi, 126 p. ;18 cm.

S68/P349

Flowering Earth/Donal Culross Peattie. —New York: G. P. Putnam's Sons, c1939

260 p. ;21 cm.

S68/S967

The Cool Greenhouse/L. N. Sutton. —London: Putnam, c1935

xii, 186 p. ;19 cm.

S68-62/B153

Gardener's Handbook: Successor the Gardener/L. H. Bailey. —New York: The Macmillan Company, c1947

292 p. ;24 cm.

S737.12/B672

Behold Our Green Mansions: A Book About

American Forests/Richard H. D. Boerker. —Chicago: The University of North Carolina Press, c1945

xv, 313 p. ;23 cm.

S79/E53-5

Our Trees How to Know Them/Artur I. Emerson. —5th ed.. —New York: Gardern City Publishing Co. , Inc. , c1946

xx, 295 p. ;25 cm.

S8/J12

Livestock Farming: A Self-teaching Course/William Jackson. —Washington: War Department, c1944

ix, 310 p. ;19 cm.

S829. 1/S551

The Care and Management of Rabbits/Chesla C. Sherlock. —Washington D. C. : [s. n.], [?]

253 p. ;19 cm.

S85/W328

The Farmers Short Courses in Live Stock/George A. Waterman. —[S. l: s. n.], [?]

67-960 p. ;23 cm.

S978/C495

Whalers and Whaling/E. Keble Chatterton. —London: Philip Allan & Co. , Ltd. , c1930

251 p. ;17 cm.

T 工业技术

T/I61

International Library of Technology: Ring Farmes, Cotton Mules, Twisters, Spoolers, Beam Warpers, Slashers, Chain Warping/International Textbook Company. —Scranton: International Textbook Company, c1906

1 v. ;23 cm.

T-61/C156

Russian-English Technical and Chemical Dictionary/Ludmilla Ignatiev Callaham. —2nd ed.. —[S. l. : s. n.], c1947

xv, 794 p. ;19 cm.

T-62/H674

Hitchcock's Industrial Refrence: 1946 Edition/Hitchcock Publishing Company. —Chicago: Hitchcock Publishing Company, c1946

678 p. ;18 cm.

TB11/G259(1)

Pure Mathematics for Engineers. Part 1/S. B. Gates, H. A. Webb. —London: Hodder and Stoughton Ltd. , [?]

xi, 191 p. ;19 cm.

TB12/L847-5

The Elements of Statics and Dynamics/S. L. Loney. —5th. ed.. —Cambridge: The University Press, c1932

viii, 332 p. , xx, 240 p. , xiv;17 cm.

TB301/M568-11

Mechanics of Materials/Mansfield Merriman. —11th ed.. —New York: John Wiley & Sons, Inc. , c1916

xi, 524 p. ;22 cm.

TB301/T585-2

Elements of Strength of Materials/S. Timosh-

enko, Gleason H. Maccullough. —2nd ed.. —[S. l. : s. n.], [?]
xii, 371 p. ;23 cm.

TB302/A512(2)
American Society for Testing Materials: A. S. T. M. Standards (Issued Triennially) 1930. Part II, Non-Metallic Materials/American Society for Testing Materials. —Philadelphia: American Society for Testing Materials, c1930
1214 p. ;23 cm.

TB302-532/A512(28. 1)
American Society for Testing Materials: Proceedings of the Thirty-First Annual Meeting Held at Atlantic City, New Jersey June 25-29, 1928. Vol. 28 Part I. Committee Reports New and Revised Tentative Standards/American Society for Testing Materials. —Philadelphia: American Society for Testing Materials, c1928
1184 p. ;23 cm.

TB302-532/A512(29. 2)
American Society for Testing Materials: Proceedings of the Thirty-Second Annual Meeting Held at Atlantic City, New Jersey Jun 24-28, 1929. Vol. 29 Part II. Technical Papers/American Society for Testing Materials. —Philadelphia: American Society for Testing Materials, c1929
1016 p. ;23 cm.

TB302-532/A512(31. 1)
American Society for Testing Materials: Proceedings of the Thirty-Fourth Annual Meeting. Volume 31. Part I, Technical Papers/American Society for Testing Materials. —Philadelphia: American Society for Testing Materials, c1931
1119 p. ;23 cm.

TB302-532/A512(31. 2)
American Society for Testing Materials: Proceedings of the Thirty-Fourth Annual Meeting. Volume 31. Part I, Technical Papers/American Society for Testing Materials. —Philadelphia: American Society for Testing Materials, c1931
1067 p. ;23 cm.

TB302-532/A512(32. 2)
American Society for Testing Materials: Proceedings of the Thirty-Fifth Annual Meeting. Volume 32. Part II, Technical Papers/American Society for Testing Materials. —Philadelphia: American Society for Testing Materials, c1931
827 p. ;23 cm.

TB324/S349
Principles of High-polymer Theory and Practice: Fibers. Plastics. Rubbers. Coatings. Adhesives /Alois X. Schmidt and Charles A. Marlies. —[S. l. : s. n.], 1948.
xii, 742 p. ;22 cm.

TB6/H376-2
Evaporating, Condensing and Cooling Apparatus: Explanations, Formule and Tables for Use in Practice/E. Hausbrand. —2nd ed.. —London: Scott, Greenwood & Son, c1916
xxiii, 401 p. ;22 cm.

TB657/A425-6
Heating and Air Conditioning/John R. Allen, James Herbert Walker, John William James. —6th ed.. —[S. l. : s. n.], c1946
vii, 667 p. ;21 cm.

TB657/A545
Audels Refrigeration and Air Conditioning Guide/Anderson, Edwin P. —New York: Theo. Audel & Co. , Publishers, c1944
1242 p. ;17 cm.

TB71/D971
Scientific Foundations of Vacuum Techinque/Saul Dushman. —New York: John Wiley & Sons, Inc. , c1949
882 p. ;20 cm.

TD-54/A512(1939)

1939 Year Book on Coal Mine Mechanization/The American Mining Congress. —Washington: The American Mining Congress, c1939

366 p. ;23 cm.

TD872/B787

The Stone Industries: Dimension Stone, Croushed Stone, Geology Technology, Distribution Utilization/Oliver Bowles. —New York: McGRaw-Hill Book Company, Inc. , c1939

xiii, 519 p. ;23 cm.

TD91/W631

The Theory and Practice of Ore Dressing/Edward S. Wiard. —New York: McGraw-Hill Book Company, Inc. , c1915

ix, 426 p. ;23 cm.

TE626/C166

Petroleum Products/CALTEX. —[U. S. A.]: The Texas Company, c1944

154 p. ;23 cm.

TF051/R516(1)

Metallurgical Calculations/Joseph W. Richards. —New York: McGraw-Hill Book Company, Inc. , c1918

xxiii, 675 p. ;24 cm.

TF1/S645

Hydrogen in Metals/Donald P. Smith. —Chicago: The University of Chicago Press, c1948

ix, 366 p. ;22 cm.

TF80/B827-2

Non-Ferrous Production Metallurgy/John L. Bray. —2nd ed. . —New York: Jonhn Wiley & Sons, Inc. , c1947

xi, 587 p. ;22 cm.

TG-65/A512(1933. 1)

Books of A. S. T. M. Standards (Issued Trienially). Part 1, Metals/American Society for Testing Meterials. —Philadelphia: American Society for Testing Meterials, c1933

xx, 1002 p. ;23 cm.

TG143/D792

The Structure of Cast Iron/Alfred Boyles. —Cleveland: American Society for Metals, c1949

154 p. ;22 cm.

TG146/E47

Copper and Copper Alloys/Owen W. Ellis. —Cleveland: American Society for Metals, c1948

184 p. ;21 cm.

TG146. 2/M741

Metallography of Aluminum Alloys/Lucio F. Mondolfo. —New York: John Wiley & Sons, Inc. , c1943

vii, 351 p. ;22 cm.

TG22/W473-4

Sea Level: A Text on Molding, Dry-sand Coremaking, Melting and Mixing of Metals and Problems in Foundry Management/R. E. Wendt. —4th ed. . —New York: McGraw-Hill Book Company, Inc. , c1942

xii, 261 p. ;19 cm.

TG333. 15/D249

Bridge's Modern Mill Gearing/David Bridge & Co. , Ltd. ,—London: David Bridge & Co. , Ltd. , c1923

132 p. ;20 cm.

TG4-62/P558-4(1)

Welding Handbook BasicPrinciples & Data/Arthur L. Phillips. —4th ed. . —London: Cleaver-Hume Press Ltd. , [?]

1 v. ;23 cm.

TG502/W492

The Machine Tool and Small Toll Industry: An outline of its development and modern organisation/Fritz Werner. —Berlin: Organization Verlagsgesellachaft M. B. H. , c1931

74 cm. ;23 cm.

TH-49/P825(61. 1)

Popular Mechanics Magazine. Vol. 61, No. 1, January, 1934. /Popular Mechanics Co. ,—Chicago: Popular Mechanics Co. , c1934

960 p. ;24 cm.

TH-61/H816-8

Dictionary of Terms Used in the Theory and Practice of Mechanical Engineering/J. G. • Horner. —8th ed. . —London: The Technical Press, c1936

iv, 417 p. ;18 cm.

TH-62/M269

Mechanical World Year Book 1937/Manchester Emmott & Company, Ltd. ,—London: Manchester Emmott & Company, Ltd. , c1937

359 p. ;16 cm.

TH11/S657-11

Text-Book of Advanced Machine Work/Robert H. Smith. —11th ed. . —[S. l. : s. n.], c1917

1619, 16 p. ;19 cm.

TH111/K24-3

Mechanism/Robert McArdle Keown, Virgil Moring Faires. —3rd ed. . —[S. l. : s. n.], c1931

xiii, 242 p. ;23 cm.

TH18/B275

Machine Shop Operations/by John Willard Barritt and Enfried Torsten Larson. . —Chicago: American Technical Society, c1945

1 v. ;25 cm.

TH21/H537-56

Modern Lifting/Herbert Morris, Ltd. ,—56th ed. . —Loughborough: Herbert Morris, Ltd. , c1933

1124 p. ;23 cm.

TH742/G132-12

The Microscope: An Introduction to Microscopic Methods and to Histology/Simon Henry Gage. —12th ed. . —[S. l.]: The Comstock Publishing Company, c1917

ix, 472 p. ;23 cm.

TJ760. 2/J55

Systems Preliminary Design/Joseph J. Jerger. —New York: D. Van Nostrand Company, Inc. , [?]

xii, 625 p. ;22 cm.

TK1/G293-6

Steam Power Plant Engineering/G. F. Gebhardt. —6th ed. . —New York: John Wiley & Sons, Inc. , c1928

v, 1036 p. ;23 cm.

TK1/O81

Induction Heating/H. B. Osborn, P. H. Brace, W. G. Johnson. —[S. l. : s. n.], c1946

172 p. ;21 cm.

TK16/W582-2

Technical gas and fuel Analysis/Alfred H. White. —2nd ed. . —London: McGraw-Hill Book Company, Inc. , c1920

xiii, 319 p. ;21 cm.

TK22/B112-36

Steam: its generation and use. /Babcock and Wilcox Company. —36th ed. . —New York: Babcock and Wilcox Company, c1923

383 p. ;26 cm.

TK22/C652

Coatesville Boiler Works: Manufacturers of Steel Tanks, A. S. M. E. Boilers and Heavy Steel Plate Work/Coatesville Boiler Works.—New York: Coatesville, Pa., [?]

96 p.;23 cm.

TK26/C561-2

Steam Turbines/Edwin F. Church.—2nd ed..—[S. l.: s. n.], [?]

327 p.;20 cm.

TK4/L699

Internal Combustion Engines/Lester C. Lichty.—5th ed..—[S. l.: s. n.], c1939

vii, 603 p.;21 cm.

TK4/L912

Heat Engines: The Theory, Constrution, and Performance of Steam Boilers Reciprocating Steam Engines Steam Turbines and Internal Combustion Engines/David Allan Low.—London: Longmans, Green and Co., Ltd, c1924, 1930

vii, 592 p.;22 cm.

TK4/P762

Internal Combustion Engines/J. A. Polson.—[S. l.: s. n.], c1931

475 p.;23 cm.

TM1/C685-6

Electrical Technology/H. Cotton.—6th ed..—Shanghai: Van Chong Book Company, c1949

xiv, 600 p.;19 cm.

TM13/C738

Electric Circuitsl a First Course in Circuit Analysis for Electrical Engineers/Karl T. Compton.—New York: John Wiley & Sons, c1943

xxxiii, 782 p.;23 cm.

TM3/K18-4(2)

Experimental Electrical Engineering and Manual for Electrical Testing/V. Karapetoff.—4th ed..—[S. l.: s. n.], c1941

xxxii, 814 p.;23 cm.

TM33/L269-5

Principles of Direct-Current Machines/Alexander S. Langsdorf.—5th ed..—St. Louis: Washington University, c1940

xxi, 746 p.;20 cm.

TM34/L419-3

Alternating-Current Machinery/Ralph R. Lawrence.—3rd ed..—[S. l.: s. n.], c1940

xix, 678 p.;23 cm.

TM343/H793

Induction Motor Practice/R. E. Hopkins.—[S. l.: s. n.], 1932

367 p.;22 cm.

TM4/D419

Magnetic Circuits and Transformers: A First Course for Power and Communication Engineers/Department of Electrical Engineering.—New York: John Wiley & Sons, Inc., c1944

xxiv, 718 p.;23 cm.

TM6/S187-2

Power Unleashed: The story of electricity and power/M. M. Samuels.—2nd ed..—New York: Dorset House Inc., c1943

xii, 301 p.;22 cm.

TM64/M664

Insulation of Electrical Apparatus/Douclas F. Miner.—[S. l.: s. n.], c1941

viii, 452 p.;20 cm.

TM712/K49(1)

Power System Stability. Volume I, Elements of stability calculations/Edward Wilson Kim-

bark. —[S. l：s. n.], c1948
viii, 355 p. ;21 cm.

TM721. 1/D269-3(1)
A Course in Electrical Engineering. vol. I, Direct Currents/Chester L. Daews. —3rd ed.. —[S. l. : s. n.], c1937
xix, 751 p. ;20 cm.

TM721. 1/D269-3(2)
A Course in Electrical Engineering. vol. II, Alternating Currents/Chester L. Daews. —3rd ed.. —[S. l. : s. n.], c1934
xxi, 705 p. ;20 cm.

TM912/A681
Storage Batteries：Theory, Manufature, Care and Application/Morton Arendt. —New York：[s. n.], c1928
v, 285 p. ;22 cm.

TM923/M818
The Scientific Basis of Illuminating Engineering/Parry Moon. —[S. l. : s. n.], c1936
xii, 608 p. ;22 cm.

TM93/F234
Electrical Measurements in Practice/F. M. Farmer. —New York：F. M. Farmer, c1917
259 p. ;22 cm.

TN-62/H432-23
The Radio Amateur's Handbook/The Headquarters Staff of the American Radio Relay League. —23rd ed.. —Connecticut：The American Radio Relay League, Inc., c1946
460, 205 p. ;24 cm.

TN01/G548
Principles of Radio Engineering/R. S. Glasgow. —[S. l. : s. n.], c1936
xii, 520 p. ;c1936

TN916/M647
Telephone Theory and Practice：Automatic Switching and Auxillary Equipment/Kempster B. Miller. —[S. l. : s. n.], c1932
xi, 494 p. ;22 cm.

TN92/M835-3
Principles of Radio Communication/John H. Morecroft. —3rd ed.. —[S. l. : s. n.], c1933
1084 p. ;23 cm.

TQ/B657-6(2)
Chemistry for Engineers and Manufacturers：A Practical Text-Book. Volume II., Chemistry of Maufacturing Processes/Bertram Blount, A. G. Bloxam. —6th ed.. —London：Charles Criffin & Company, Ltd., c1921
xv, 513 p. ;22 cm.

TQ/G886
The Story of Chemistry：The Nature and Structure of Matter-How Chemistry Is Utilized in Our Present Day Economic and Industrial Development. vol. 6/Hippolyte Gruener. —New York：P. F. Coller & Son Corporation, c1941
viii, 429 p. ;20 cm.

TQ/M381
Industrial and Manufacturing Chemistry. Part I, Organic：A Practical Treatise/Geoffrey Martin. —London：Crosby Lockwood and Son, c1922
xx, 744, xvi p. ;25 cm.

TQ-62/W132
Manual of Chemical Technology/Rudolf Von Wagner. —New York：D. Appleton & Co., c1900
xxiii, 968 p. ;26 cm.

TQ013. 1/G549
Thermodynamics for Chemists/Samuel Glasstone. —Toronto, London, New York：D. Van

Nostrand Company, c1947
522 p. ;22 cm.

TQ014/R722
Industrial Chemistry: A Manual for the Student and Manufacturer/Allen Rogers, Alfred B. Aubert. —New York: D. Van Nostrand Company, c1913
xiv, 854 p. ;25 cm.

TQ015/C597
Manual for Process Engineering Calculations/Loyal Clarke. —New York: McGraw-Hill Book Company, Inc., c1947
ix, 438 p. ;23 cm.

TQ062/B471(1)
The Chemical Formulary: A Condensed Collection of Valuable, Timely, Practical Formulae for Making Thousands of Products in All Fields of Industry. Volume I/H. Bennett. —[S. l. : s. n.], [?]
x, 604 p. ;23 cm.

TQ062/B471(2)
The Chemical Formulary: A Condensed Collection of Valuable, Timely, Practical Formulae for Making Thousands of Products in All Fields of Industry. Volume II/H. Bennett. —[S. l. : s. n.], [?]
ix, 570 p. ;23 cm.

TQ062/B471(3)
The Chemical Formulary: A Condensed Collection of Valuable, Timely, Practical Formulae for Making Thousands of Products in All Fields of Industry. Volume III/H. Bennett. —[S. l. : s. n.], [?]
xi, 566 p. ;23 cm.

TQ111. 1/F172
Sulfuric Acid Manufacture/Andrew M. Fairlie. —[S. l. : s. n.], 1936
669 p. ;23 cm.

TQ114/P273-2
The Alkali Industry/J. R. Partington. —2nd ed.. —New York: D. Van Nostrand Company, c1925
xi, 344 p. ;22 cm.

TQ125. 1/T355
Sulphur: An Essential to Industry and Agriculture/Texas Gulf Sulphur Company. —New York: Texas Gulf Sulphur Company, c1942
v, 45 p. ;23 cm.

TQ171. 11/M835
The Properties of Glass /Morey, George W.. —New York: Reinhold Publishing Corporation, 1938.
561 p. ;24cm.

TQ176/J76
Asbestos: Its Properties Occurrence and Uses: With Some Account of the Mines of Italy and Canada/Robert H. Jones. —London: Crosby Lockwood and Son, c1890
xii, 236 p. ;19 cm.

TQ32/D917
Working with Plastics/Arthur Dunham. —New York: McGraw-Hill Book Company, Inc., c1948
ix, 225 p. ;25 cm.

TQ32/P888
Synthetic Resins and Rubbers/Paul O. Powers. —New York: John Wiley & Sons, Inc., c1945
296 p. ;22 cm.

TQ32/R521
Fundamentals of Plastics/Henry M. Richardson. —New York: McGraw-Hill Book Company, Inc., c1946

viii, 483 p. ;23 cm.

TQ320/S597-2

Industrial Plastics/Herbert R. Simonds. —2nd ed.. —New York: Pitman Publishing Corporation, c1941

x, 396 p. ;21 cm.

TQ330/T137

Synthetic Rubber From Alcohol: A Survey Based on the Russian Literature/Anselm Talalay, Michel Magat. —Shanghai: Van Chong Book Company, [?]

xiii, 298 p. ;21 cm.

TQ520.11/L921(1)

Chemistry of Coal Utilization. Volume I/H. H. Lowry. —New York: John Wiley & Sons, Inc., c1945

xiii, 920, cv p. ;22 cm.

TQ520.11/L921(2)

Chemistry of Coal Utilization. Volume II/H. H. Lowry. —New York: John Wiley & Sons, Inc., c1945

xiii, 921-1868, cv p. ;22 cm.

TQ63/M444(1)

Protective and Decorative Coatings: Coatings: Paints, Varnishes, Lacquers, and Inks. Vol. 1, Raw Materials for Varnishes and Vehicles/Joseph J. Mattiello. —New York: John Wiley & Sons, Inc., c1941

xii, 819 p. ;23 cm.

TQ63/M444(3)

Protective and Decorative Coatings. volume III, Manufacture and Uses, Colloids, Oleoresinous Vehicles and Paints, Water and Emulsion Paints, Lacquers, Printing Inks Lumineschent Paints, and Stains/Joseph J. Mattiello. —New York: John Wiley & Sons Inc., c1946

XIV, 830 p. ;23 cm.

TQ63/M444(4)

Protective and Decorative Coatings. volume IV, Special Studies/Joseph J. • Mattiello. —New York: John Wiley & Sons Inc., c1944

x, 419 p. ;23 cm.

TQ63/M444(5)

Protective and Decorative Coatings. volume V, Analysis and Testing Methods/Joseph J. Mattiello. —New York: John Wiley & Sons Inc., c1946

ix, 662 p. ;23 cm.

TQ65/P872-5(2)

Perfumes Cosmetics & Soaps: With Especial Reference to Synthetics. Vol. II, Being A Treatise on Mondern Cosmetic/William A. Poucher. —5th ed.. —[S. l. : s. n.], c1936

xiii, 426 p. ;20 cm.

TQ65/P872-5(3)

Perfumes Cosmetics & Soaps: With Especial Reference to Synthetics. Vol. III, Being A Treatise on Mondern Cosmetic/William A. Poucher. —5th ed.. —[S. l. : s. n.], c1936

xi, 227 p. ;20 cm.

TQ98-49/L863S887

The Story of Mankind/Hendrik Willem Van Loon. —Black & Gold ed.. —[S. l.]: Citadel Press, c1943

xxiv, 500 p. ;22 cm.

TS03/I32

Auxiliary Products for the Textile and Allied Industries/Imperial Chemical Industries Ltd., —Brimingham: The Kynoch Press, c1940

103 p. ;26 cm.

TS102.9/T496-2

Cotton Waste: Its Production, Manipulation and Uses/Thomad Thornley. —2nd ed.. —London: Scott, Greenwood & Son, c1921 xii，400 p. ;22 cm.

TS12/W873

Jute and Linen Weaving/Thomas Woodhouse, Thomsa Milne. —[S. l. : s. n.], [?]

xxvii, 590 p. ;19 cm.

TS13/B798

Wool Carding/James Bradley. —London: Manchester Emmott & Co. , Ltd. , c1921

viii, 344 p. ;22 cm.

TS201/L434-3

Food Inspection and Analysis: For the Use of Public Analysts, Health Officers, Sanitary Chemists, and Food Economists/Albert E. Leach. —3rd ed. . —New York: John Wiley & Sons, Inc. , c1913

xix, 1001 p. ;24 cm.

TS202/S553

Food Products/Henry C. Sherman. —New York: The Macmillan Company, c1917

ix, 594 p. ;20 cm.

TS207. 3/B285

Methods Used in the Examination of Milk and Dairy Products/Chr. Barthel. —London: Macmillan and Co. , Ltd. , c1910

xi, 260 p. ;22 cm.

TS252/F246

Testing Milk and Its Products: A Manual for Dairy Students, Creamery and Cheese-factory and Dairy Famers/E. H. Farrington, F. W. Woll. —Madison: Mendota Book Company, c1897

viii, 236 p. ;20 cm.

Ts252. 7/S365

Milk Testing: Instructions for Testing Milk and Dividing Money for Creameries, Cheese Factories and Dairymen/Adolph Schoenman. —2nd ed. . —Madison: Tracy, Gibbs and Co. , c1895

iv, 42 p. ;20 cm.

TS27/B978

Recipes for the Manufacture of Aerated Beverages and Carbonated Mineral Waters, Non-alcoholic Brewed Beers, Cordials, etc. /W. J. Bush and Co. , Ltd. ,—6th ed. . —London: W. J. Bush and Co. , Ltd. , c1903

vi, 125 p. ;21 cm.

TS3/M329

The Salt and Alkali Industy: Including Potassium Salts and the Stassfurt Industy/Martin. —London: Crosby Lockwood and Son, c1916

viii, 100 p. ;25 cm.

TS4-49/Y78

The Story of the Cigarette/William W. Young. —New York: D. Appleton and Company, c1916

ix, 281 p. ;19 cm.

TS513/McL374

The Chemistry of Leather Manufacture/George D. McLaughlin, Edwin R. Theis. —New York: Reinholp Publishing Coproations, c1945

x, 800 p. ;23 cm.

TS6/G853

Essentials of Wood Working: A Textbook for Schools/Ira Samuel Griffith. —15th ed. . —Peoria: The Manual Arts Press, c1917

190 p. ;20 cm.

TS656/S464

Elementary Turing for Use in Manual Training Classes/Frank Henry Selden. —Chicago: Rand, McNally & Co. , c1907

197 p. ;18 cm.

TS71/S965-3

Chemistry of Pulp and Paper Making/Edwin

Sutermeister. —3rd ed.. —New York: J. Wiley, [c1941]

xii, 529 p., [9] leaves of plates; 24 cm.

TS879/S649

Typewriting Technique: College Course/Harold H. Smith. —New York: The Gregg Publishing Company, c1938

173 p.; 28 cm.

TS941.5/D947

Special Sewing Machines for White Goods, Clothing, Overalls, Knit Goods and Hosiery, Boot and Shoe Industries etc./Durkoppwerke Aktiengesellschaft. —Bielefeld: [Durkoppwerke Aktiengesellschaft], [?]

194 p.; 22 cm.

TS941.5/S617

Machine Sewing: A Treatise on the Care and Use of Family Sewing Machines and Their Attachments/Singer Sewing Machine Co., —New York: Singer Sewing Machine Co., Inc., c1923, 1924

159 p.; 22 cm.

TS97/H283

Marion Harland's Complete Cook Book: A Practical and Exhaustive manual of Cookery and Housekeeping/Marion Harland. —New ed., Revised and enlarged. —Indianapolis: The Bobbs-Mierrill Company Publishers, c1903

viii, 781 p.; 21 cm.

TS971/C774(2)

Household arts for Home and School. Volume II, Care of the home Cooking and serving selection of food laundering hospitality/Anna M. Cooley, Wilhelmina H. Spohr. —New York: The Macmillan Company, c1927

viii, 436 p.; 19 cm.

TS972.1/B154-11

Foods: Preparation and Serving/Pearl L. Bailey. —11th ed.. —St. Paul: Webb Book Publishing Co., c1928

486 p.; 19 cm.

TS972.1/S393-2

Chinese Chopsticks: A Manual of Chinese Cookery and Guide to Peking Restaurants/Mary II Sia. —2nd ed.. —Peking: Peking International Women's Club, c1938

xvii, 144 p.; 19 cm.

TS972.1/W873

The Pocket Cook Book/Elizabeth Woody, Mccall's Food Staff. —Rockefeller Center, New York: Pocket Books. Inc., c1942

vii, 376 p.; 16 cm.

TS972.183/T238

Menu And Recipe Book/D. D. Cottington Taylor. —London: Good Housekeeping Magazine, c1926

256 p.; 19 cm.

TS972.183/W256

Mrs. Beeton's Cookery Book: All about Cookery, household work, marketing, trussing, carving, etc/Ward, Lock & Co., Limitied. —London: Ward, Lock & Co., Limitied, c1909

380 p.; 19 cm.

TS972.187.12/F233

The Boston Cooking-School Cook Book/Fannie Merritt Farmer. —New ed, Revised and Enlarged.. —Boston: Little, Brown, and Company, c1924

xvi, 806 p.; 21 cm.

TS976/P668

The Science of Home Making: A Textbook in Home Economics/Emma E. Pirie. —Chicago: Scott, Foresman and Company, c1915

404 p. ;19 cm.

TS976.8/F596-28

The Buyers' Guide through Germany, Bohemia etc. /Julius Fleischmann. —28th. ed.. —Germany: Julius Fleischmann, [?]

436 p. ;15 cm.

TS976.8/P825(1941)

Popular Mechanics Home Kinks: Money-Saving Ideas for Everybody. 1941/Popular Mechanics Company. —Chicago: Popular Mechanics Company, c1940

104 p. ;24 cm.

TU/N561

The Builders: A Story & Study of Masonry/Joseph Fort Newton. —London: George Allen & Unwin Ltd. , c1918

224 p. ;23 cm.

TU-098.154.6/R956(3)

The Stones of Venice. volume III/John Ruskin. —London: George Allen, Sunnyside, Orpington, c1900

vii, 538 p. ;18 cm.

TU-098.154.6/R965(1)

The Stones of Venice. volume 1/John Ruskin. —London: George Allen, Sunnyside, Orpington, c1900

xvi, 414 p. ;18 cm.

TU-098.2/L776

Ancient Landmarks of Pembroke/Henry Wheatland Litchfield. —Pembroke: George Edward Lewis, c1909

188 p. ;22 cm.

TU-851/C387

The Practical Painter & Decorator: An Authoritative work on the decoration of building/Alfred G. Ceeson. —London: Virtue and Company Ltd. , c1921

xiii, 306 p. ;25 cm.

TU3-62/K43-3

Structural Engineer's Handbook: Data for the Design and Construction of Steel Bridges and Buildings/Milo S. Ketchum. —3rd ed.. —New York: McGraw-Hill Book Company, c1924

xv, 316 p. ;23 cm.

TU43/T334

Soil mechanics in Engineering Practice /Karl Terzaghi and Ralph B. Peck. —[S. l. : s. n.], c1948.

566 p. ;22 cm.

TU528/B344

Plain Concrete/Edward E. Bauer. —New York: McGraw-Hill Book Company, Inc. , c1928

xi, 346 p. ;23 cm.

TU528/H656

The Concrete House/G. W. Hilton. —London: E. & F. N. Spon, Ltd. , c1919

1 v. ;19 cm.

TU7/M681-9(1)

Building Construction and Drawing: A Text Book on the Principles and Details of Modern Construction. Part 1, First Stage/Charles F. Mitchell. —9th ed.. —London: B. T. Batsford Ltd. , c1921

473 p. ;18 cm.

TU7/M681-9(2)

Building Construction and Drawing: A Text Book on the Principles and Details of Modern Construction. Part 2, Advance Course/Charles F. Mitchell. —9th ed.. —London: B. T. Batsford Ltd. , c1921

vi, 932 p. ;18 cm.

TU81/G442

Description and Instructions for Operation of Principal Engineering Piping Systems and Related Equipment/Gibbs & Cox, Inc. ,—New York: Gibbs & Cox, Inc. , [?]

1 v. ;27 cm.

TU83/M511

Mechanics of Heating and Ventilating/Konrad Meier. —New York: McGraw-Hill Book Company, c1912

161 p. ;23 cm.

TU984/L673-2

The Planning of The Modern City: A Review of the Principles Governing City Planning/Nelson P. Lewis. —2th ed. . —New York: John Wiley & Sons, Inc. , c1916

xvii, 457 p. ;23 cm.

TU986. 4/H875

An Introduction to the Study of Landscape Design/Henry Vincent Hubbard, Theodora Kimball. —New York: The Macmillan Company, c1917

xx, 406 p. ;29 cm.

TV21/H835

Fountains of Joy; or "By Water and Blood"/ Frederick A. Houck. —London: B. Herder Book Co. , c1931

ix, 277 p. ;19 cm.

TV21/H835-5

Fountains of Joy; or "By Water and Blood"/ Frederick A. Houck. —5th. ed. . —London: B. Herder Book Co. , c1931

ix, 277 p. ;19 cm.

U 交通运输

U1/W377

Travel by Air, Land, and Sea/Hanson Hart Webster. —Boston: Houghton Mifflin Company, c1933

432 p. ;20 cm.

U173-62/C938-4

Piping Handbook/Sabin Crocker. —4th ed. . —New York: McGraw-Hill Book Company, Inc. , c1945

xiv, 1376 p. ;18 cm.

U2-62/W516-8

"Saxby" Railway Safety Applliances/The Westinghouse Brake & Saxby Signal Co. , Ltd. ,—8th ed. . —London: The Westinghouse Brake & Saxby Signal Co. , Ltd. , c1924

168 p. ;25 cm.

U22/H263-3

Electric Railway Engineering/C. F. Harding and D. D. Ewing. —3rd ed. . —[S. l. : s. n.], [?]

xvii, 489 p. ;23 cm.

U26/H526

The Present Catalogue Will Give You An Idea of the Importance and Capacity of Our Locomotive Works/Henschel, Sohna. G. Kassel. —[S. l. : s. n.], c1931

159 p. ;29 cm.

U26/R323

Railway Engines of the World/Brian Reed. —

London: Oxford University Press, c1934
159 p. ;22 cm.

U261/J32-11
Elementary Manual on Steam and the Steam Engine: Specially Arranged for the Use of First-year Board of Education, South Kensington, City and Guilds of London/Abdrew Jamieson. —11th ed., Rvised and enlarged. —London: Charles Griffin and Company, Ltd., c1906
xiv, 355 p. ;18 cm.

U46/E46
The Gasoline Automobile/Ben G. Elliott, Earl L. Consoliver. —4th ed.. —[S. l. : s. n.], c1932
xi, 605 p. ;23 cm.

U46/F841-3
Motor Vehicles and Their Engines: A Practical handbook on care, repair and management of motor trucks and automobiles, for owners, chauffeurs, garagemen and schools/Edward B. Fraser, Ralph B. Jones. —3rd ed.. —New York: D. Van Nostran Company, Inc., c1919, 1922
434 p. ;23 cm.

U464. 172/B977
Instructions for the Care And Operation of Main Propulsion Engines/Busch-sulzer Bros. —Diesel Engine Co., —St. Louis: Busch-sulzer Bros. —Diesel Engine Co., c1942
1 v. ;27 cm.

U469. 209/C558
Truck Operator Manual: 1946/Chrysler Corporation Export Division. —Detroit: Chrysler Corporation Export Division, c1946
67 p. ;22 cm.

U471/P913-2
Pratt's Automobile Instructor: A Home-Study Course and Reference Work for Amateur and Expert/Clyde H. Pratt. —new and revised ed.. —Chicago: Shrewesbury Publishing Co., c1917
250 p. ;22 cm.

U471/V516
How to Operate A Motor Car/A. Hyatt Verrill. —Philadelphia: David McKay, Publisher, c1918
136 p. ;19 cm.

U6/M379
Cruising/E. G. Martin, John Irving, J. R. Barnett. —London: Seeley Service & Co., Ltd., [?]
592 p. ;21 cm.

U6/U58-6
United States Coast Pilot. Pacific Coast: California, Oregon, and Washington/United States Government Printing Office. —6th ed.. —Washington: United States Government Printing Office, c1943
xii, 415 p. ;26 cm.

U66/B748
Ships we See/Frank G. Bowen. —London: Sampson Low, Marston & Co., Ltd., [?]
viii, 311 p. ;21 cm.

U66/C287-2
Practical Ship Production/A. W. Carmichael. —2nd ed.. —New York: McGraw-Hill Book Company, Inc., c1941
xiv, 283 p. ;23 cm.

U66/D685-3
Chinese Junks and Other Native Craft/Ivon A. Donnelly. —3rd ed.. —Shanghai: Kelly & Walsh, Ltd., c1939
142 p. ;25 cm.

U664. 14/U58
Turbine-Electric Propulsion Equipment/United States Navy. —Schenectady: General Electric,

c1943

ix, 153 p. ;29 cm.

U666. 13/N316(c)

Astronomical Navigation Tables: Latitudes 10°—14°, North and South. vol. C/United States Navy Department, U. S. Hydrographic Office. —Washington: United States Government Printing Office, c1941

231 p. ;26 cm.

U672/H172

Ship Repair and Alteration/George V. Haliday, W. E. Swanson. —New York: Cornell Maritime Press, c1942

378 p. ;19 cm.

U674. 91/M312

Corinthian Yacht Club/Marblehead. —[S. l]: The Secretary, c1915

282 p. ;16 cm.

U675/1

On Going to Sea in Yachts/Conor O'Brien. —London: Oxford University Press, c1933

161 p. ;19 cm.

V 航空、航天

V-61/L297

Lanz Aviation Dictionary in nine Languages/John E. Lanz. —California: P. D. and Lone Perkins, c1944

430 p. ;23 cm.

V235/F492

Jet Propulsion-Turbojets/Volney C. Finch. —Revised ed.. —Palo Alto: The National Press, c1948

xv, 327 p. ;21 cm.

V275/G822

Anything a Horse Can Do: The Story of the Helicopter/Colonel H. F. Gregory. —New York: Reynal & Hitchcock, c1944

243 p. ;21 cm.

X 环境科学、劳动保护科学(安全科学)

X2/C295(1)

Our Environment: Its Relation to Us. Book 1/Harry A. Carpenter, George C. Wood. —Revised ed.. —Boston: Allyn and Bacon, c1933

vii, 348, 33, 11 p. ;19 cm.

X52/C734-3

Standard Methods for the Examination of Water and Wewage/Committees of the American Public Health Association. —3rd ed.. —Boston: American Public Health Association, c1917

xvi, 111 p. ;25 cm.

Z 综合性图书

Z1/M864(2)

Diderot and the Encyclopaedists. Vol. II/John Visounat Morley. —London: Macmillan and Co., Ltd., c1923

xii, 337 p.; 20 cm.

Z2/B792(1)

The Everyman Encyclopaedia. A=BAC. Vol. 1/Andrew Boyle. —London: J. M. Dent & Sons Ltd., [?]

628 p.; 17 cm.

Z2/B792(2)

The Everyman Encyclopaedia. Vol. 2/Andrew Boyle. —London: J. M. Dent & Sons Ltd., [?]

640 p.; 17 cm.

Z2/B792(3)

The Everyman Encyclopaedia. Vol. 3/Andrew Boyle. —London: J. M. Dent & Sons Ltd., [?]

639 p.; 17 cm.

Z2/B792(4)

The Everyman Encyclopaedia. Vol. 4/Andrew Boyle. —London: J. M. Dent & Sons Ltd., [?]

640 p.; 17 cm.

Z2/B792(6)

The Everyman Encyclopaedia. Vol. 6/Andrew Boyle. —London: J. M. Dent & Sons Ltd., [?]

640 p.; 17 cm.

Z2/B792(7)

The Everyman Encyclopaedia. Vol. 7/Andrew Boyle. —London: J. M. Dent & Sons Ltd., [?]

639 p.; 17 cm.

Z2/B792(8)

The Everyman Encyclopaedia. Vol. 8/Andrew Boyle. —London: J. M. Dent & Sons Ltd., [?]

640 p.; 17 cm.

Z2/B792(9)

The Everyman Encyclopaedia. Vol. 9/Andrew Boyle. —London: J. M. Dent & Sons Ltd., [?]

640 p.; 17 cm.

Z2/B792(10)

The Everyman Encyclopaedia. Vol. 10/Andrew Boyle. —London: J. M. Dent & Sons Ltd., [?]

vii, 640 p.; 18 cm.

Z2/B792(11)

The Everyman Encyclopaedia. Vol. 11/Andrew Boyle. —London: J. M. Dent & Sons Ltd., [?]

640 p.; 17 cm.

Z2/C344

The World of Wonders: A Record of Things Wonderful in Nature, Science, and Art/Cassell and Company, Ltd.,—London: Cassell and Company, Ltd., c1896

viii, 416, 8 p.; 26 cm.

Z2/C387(H351)

A Catalog of Scientific Apparatus Instruments and Supplies for the Teaching of Physics, Chemistry and the Natural Sciences in the Laboratory and Classroom. Catalog H351/Central Scientific Company. —Boston: Central Scientific Company, c1889

768 p.; 27 cm.

Z2/D639-2(1)

The New International Encyclopaedia. Volume I/Dodd, Mead and Company. —2nd ed.. —New York: Dodd, Mead and Company, c1920

xxxii, 806 p. ;25 cm.

Z2/D639-2(2)

The New International Encyclopaedia. Volume II/Dodd, Mead and Company. —2nd ed.. —New York: Dodd, Mead and Company, c1920

794 p. ;26 cm.

Z2/D639-2(3)

The New International Encyclopaedia. Volume III/Dodd, Mead and Company. —2nd ed.. —New York: Dodd, Mead and Company, c1920

794 p. ;26 cm.

Z2/D639-2(5)

The New International Encyclopaedia. Volume V/Dodd, Mead and Company. —2nd ed.. —New York: Dodd, Mead and Company, c1920

810 p. ;25 cm.

Z2/D639-2(7)

The New International Encyclopaedia. Volume VII/Dodd, Mead and Company. —2nd ed.. —New York: Dodd, Mead and Company, c1920

xxxii, 794 p. ;25 cm.

Z2/D639-2(8)

The New International Encyclopaedia. Volume VIII/Dodd, Mead and Company. —2nd ed.. —New York: Dodd, Mead and Company, c1920

794 p. ;25 cm.

Z2/D639-2(10)

The New International Encyclopaedia. Volume X/Dodd, Mead and Company. —2nd ed.. —New York: Dodd, Mead and Company, c1920

vi, 789 p. ;25 cm.

Z2/D639-2(15)

The New International Encyclopaedia. Volume XV/Dodd, Mead and Company. —2nd ed.. —New York: Dodd, Mead and Company, c1920

vi, 783 p. ;25 cm.

Z2/D639-2(18)

The New International Encyclopaedia. Volume XVIII/Dodd, Mead and Company. —2nd ed.. —New York: Dodd, Mead and Company, c1920

vi, 826 p. ;26 cm.

Z2/D639-2(21)

The New International Encyclopaedia. Volume XXI/Dodd, Mead and Company. —2nd ed.. —New York: Dodd, Mead and Company, c1920

858 p. ;26 cm.

Z2/D639-2(22)

The New International Encyclopaedia. Volume XXII/Dodd, Mead and Company. —2nd ed.. —New York: Dodd, Mead and Company, c1920

826 p. ;26 cm.

Z2/D639-2(24)

The New International Encyclopaedia. Volume XXIV/Dodd, Mead and Company. —2nd ed.. —New York: Dodd, Mead and Company, c1920

312 p. ;26 cm.

Z2/F792(5)

The Everyman Encyclopaedia. Vol. 5, DEC-FAT/Andrew Boyle. —London: J. M. Dent & Sons Ltd., [?]

640 p. ;17 cm.

Z2/F792(12)

The Everyman Encyclopaedia. Vol. 12, STE=ZYM/Andrew Boyle. —London: J. M. Dent & Sons Ltd., [?]

640 p. ;17 cm.

Z2/P426(1)

The Source Book: An International Encyclopedic Authority Written from the New World Viewpoint. Vol. I/Perpetual Encyclopedia Corporation. —Chicago: Perpetual Encyclopedia Corporation, [?]

488 p. ;24 cm.

Z2/P426(2)

The Source Book: An International Encyclopedic Authority Written from the New World Viewpoint. Vol. 2/Perpetual Encyclopedia Corporation. —Chicago: Perpetual Encyclopedia Corporation, [?]

489-968 p. ;24 cm.

Z2/P426(3)

The Source Book: An International Encyclopedic Authority Written from the New World Viewpoint. Vol. III/Perpetual Encyclopedia Corporation. —Chicago: Perpetual Encyclopedia Corporation, [?]

969-1432 p. ;24 cm.

Z2/P426(4)

The Source Book: An International Encyclopedic Authority Written from the New World Viewpoint. Vol. IV/Perpetual Encyclopedia Corporation. —Chicago: Perpetual Encyclopedia Corporation, [?]

1433-1896 p. ;24 cm.

Z2/P426(5)

The Source Book: An International Encyclopedic Authority Written from the New World Viewpoint. Vol. V/Perpetual Encyclopedia Corporation. —Chicago: Perpetual Encyclopedia Corporation, [?]

1897-2360 p. ;24 cm.

Z2/P426(6)

The Source Book: An International Encyclopedic Authority Written from the New World Viewpoint. Vol. VI/Perpetual Encyclopedia Corporation. —Chicago: Perpetual Encyclopedia Corporation, [?]

2361-2824 p. ;24 cm.

Z2/P426(7)

The Source Book: An International Encyclopedic Authority Written from the New World Viewpoint. Vol. VII/Perpetual Encyclopedia Corporation. —Chicago: Perpetual Encyclopedia Corporation, [?]

2825-3200, Lxxxv p. ;24 cm.

Z2/P426(8)

The Source Book: An International Encyclopedic Authority Written from the New World Viewpoint. Volume VIII/Perpetual Encyclopedia Corporation. —Chicago: Perpetual Encyclopedia Corporation, [?]

3221-3648 p. ;24 cm.

Z2/P426(10)

The Source Book: An International Encyclopedic Authority Written from the New World Viewpoint. Vol. x/Perpetual Encyclopedia Corporation. —Chicago: Perpetual Encyclopedia Corporation, [?]

4120-4696 p. ;24 cm.

Z2/R516(6)

The Outline of Knowledge. Volume VI, Geology, Biology, Zoology/James A. Richards. —New York: J. A. Richards, Inc. , c1924

iv, 508 p. ;19 cm.

Z2/R516(8)

The Outline of Knowledge: Chemistry, Physics, Electricity, Medicine, Mathematics. Volume VIII/James A. Richards. —New York: J. A. Richards, Inc. , c1924

iv, 498 p. ;19 cm.

Z2/R516(9)

The Outline of Knowledge: Sacred Writings. Vol. ix/James A. Richards. —New York: J. A. Richards, Inc. , c1924

598 p. ;20 cm.

Z2/W873

The Nuttall Encyclopaedia: A Concise and Comprehensive Dictionary of General Knowledge/Rev. James Wood. —Boston: Frederick Warne and Co. , c1901

699 p. ;20 cm.

Z22/P614(10)

The Chinese Repository. X/Pill Shin Corp. —Tokyo: Pill Shin Corp, c1942

viii, 688 p. ;20 cm.

Z22/P641(3)

The Chinese Repository. Vol. III/Pill Shin Corp. —Tokyo: Pill Shin Corp, c1835

viii, 584 p. ;21 cm.

Z22/P641(4)

Chinese Repository. Vol IV: from May 1835, to April 1836/Pill Shin Corp. —Tokyo: Pill Shin Corp, c1931

vii, 584 p. ;21 cm.

Z22/P641(5)

The Chinese Repository. Vol. V/Pill Shin Corp. —Tokyo: Pill Shin Corp, c1937

viii, 576 p. ;20 cm.

Z22/P641(6)

The Chinese Repository. Vol. Vi/Pill Shin Corp. —Tokyo: Pill Shin Corp, c1938

viii, 608 p. ;20 cm.

Z22/P641(7)

Chinese Repository. Vol VII: from May 1838, to April 1839/Pill Shin Corp. —Canton: Pill Shin Corp, c1839

vii, 654 p. ;21 cm.

Z22/P641(8)

The Chinese Repository. Vol. VIII/Pill Shin Corp. —Tokyo: Pill Shin Corp, c1942

viii, 648 p. ;20 cm.

Z22/P641(9)

The Chinese Repository. IX/Pill Shin Corp. —Tokyo: Pill Shin Corp, c1947

viii, 648 p. ;21 cm.

Z22/P641(11)

Chinese Repository. Vol XI: from January to December, 1842/Pill Shin Corp. —Canton: Pill Shin Corp, c1842

viii, 688 p. ;21 cm.

Z22/P641(13)

The Chinese Repository. Vol. XIII/Pill Shin Corp. —Tokyo: Pill Shin Corp, c1844

viii, 656 p. ;20 cm.

Z22/P641(14)

The Chinese Repository. Vol. XIV/Pill Shin Corp. —Tokyo: Pill Shin Corp, c1845

viii, 592 p. ;21 cm.

Z22/P641(15)

The Chinese Repository. Vol. XV/Pill Shin Corp. —Tokyo: Pill Shin Corp, c1846

viii, 624 p. ;21 cm.

Z22/P641-2(1)

Chinese Repository. Vol. 1/Pill Shin Corp. —2nd ed. . —Tokyo: Pill Shin Corp, c1833

vii, 512 p. ;21 cm.

Z22/P641-2(2)

Chinese Repository. Vol. 2/Pill Shin Corp. —2nd ed. . —Tokyo: Pill Shin Corp, c1833

vii, 576 p. ;21 cm.

Z228/B433(7)

The Book of Ural Life Knowledge and Inspiration: A Guide to the Best in Modern Living. vol. VII/The Bellows-Durham Company. —Chicago: The Bellows-Durham Company, c1925

3813-4423 p. ;25 cm.

Z256. 1/A193-9(11)

Encyclopaedia Britannica. Vol. IX/Adam and Charles Black. —9th ed.. —Edinburgh: Adam and Charles Black, c1879

856 p. ;28 cm.

Z256. 1/E56(1)

The Boys' and Girls' Encyclopaedia Britannica Junior. Vol. 1/Walter Yust. —Chicago: Encyclopaedia Britannica, Inc. , c1945

xiv, 492 p. ;26 cm.

Z256. 1/E56(12)

The Boys' and Girls' Encyclopaedia Britannica Junior. Vol. XII/Walter Yust. —Chicago: Encyclopaedia Britannica, Inc. , c1945

xiv, 300, Plate 80 p. ;26 cm.

Z256. 1/P361-9

Pears' Shilling Cyclopaedia/A. and F. Pears, Ltd. ,—9th ed. . —London: A. and F. Pears, Ltd. , [?]

776 p. ;17 cm.

Z256. 1/U58(1)

Encyclopaedia Britannica: A new survey of uniersal knowledge. vol. 1, A to Annoy/The Universty of Chicago. —Chicago: Encyclopaedia Britannica, Inc. , c1929

civ, 999 p. ;30 cm.

Z256. 1/U58(2)

Encyclopaedia Britannica: A New Survey of Univeral Knowledge. Vol. 2, Annual register to Baltic Sea/The University of Chicago. —Chicago: Encyclopaedia Britannica, Inc. , c1947

1016 p. ;28 cm.

Z256. 1/U58(4)

Encyclopaedia Britannica: A New Survey of Univeral Knowledge. Vol. 4, Brain to Casting/The University of Chicago. —Chicago: Encyclopaedia Britannica, Inc. , c1947

990 p. ;28 cm.

Z256. 1/U58(5)

Encyclopaedia Britannica: A New Survey of Univeral Knowledge. Vol. 5, Cast-Iron to Cole/The University of Chicago. —Chicago: Encyclopaedia Britannica, Inc. , c1947

992 p. ;28 cm.

Z256. 1/U58(6)

Encyclopaedia Britannica: A New Survey of Univeral Knowledge. Vol. 6, Colebrooke to Damascius/The University of Chicago. —Chicago: Encyclopaedia Britannica, Inc. , c1947

998 p. ;28 cm.

Z256. 1/U58(7)

Encyclopaedia Britannica: A New Survey of Univeral Knowledge. Vol. 7, Damadcus to education in animals/The University of Chicago. —Chicago: Encyclopaedia Britannica, Inc. , c1947

1012 p. ;28 cm.

Z256. 1/U58(8)

Encyclopaedia Britannica: A New Survey of Univeral Knowledge. Vol. 8, Edward to Extract/The University of Chicago. —Chicago: Encyclopaedia Britannica, Inc. , c1947

1000 p. ;28 cm.

Z256. 1/U58(9)

Encyclopaedia Britannica: A New Survey of Univeral Knowledge. Vol. 9, Extraction to Gambrinus/The University of Chicago. —Chicago: Encyclopaedia Britannica, Inc. , c1947

999 p. ;28 cm.

Z256. 1/U58(10)

Encyclopaedia Britannica: A New Survey of Univeral Knowledge. Vol. 10, Game to Gunmetal/The University of Chicago. —Chicago: Encyclopaedia Britannica, Inc. , c1947

988 p. ;28 cm.

Z256. 1/U58(11)

Encyclopaedia Britannica: A New Survey of Univeral Knowledge. Vol. 11, Gunnery to Hydroxulamine/The University of Chicago. —Chicago: Encyclopaedia Britannica, Inc. , c1947

1000 p. ;28 cm.

Z256. 1/U58(12)

Encyclopaedia Britannica: A New Survey of Univeral Knowledge. Vol. 12, Hydrozoa to Jeremy, Epistle of/The University of Chicago. —Chicago: Encyclopaedia Britannica, Inc. , c1947

1005 p. ;28 cm.

Z256. 1/U58(13)

Encyclopaedia Britannica: A New Survey of Univeral Knowledge. Vol. 13, Jerez de frontera to liberty, statue of/The University of Chicago. —Chicago: Encyclopaedia Britannica, Inc. , c1947

1006 p. ;28 cm.

Z256. 1/U58(14)

Encyclopaedia Britannica: A New Survey of Univeral Knowledge. Vol. 14, Libido to mary, duchess of burgundy/The University of Chicago. —Chicago: Encyclopaedia Britannica, Inc. , c1947

1006 p. ;28 cm.

Z256. 1/U58(15)

Encyclopaedia Britannica: A New Survey of Univeral Knowledge. Vol. 15, Maryborough to mushet steel/The University of Chicago. —Chicago: Encyclopaedia Britannica, Inc. , c1947

1006 p. ;28 cm.

Z256. 1/U58(16)

Encyclopaedia Britannica: A New Survey of Univeral Knowledge. Vol. 16, Mushroom to Ozonides/The University of Chicago. —Chicago: Encyclopaedia Britannica, Inc. , c1947

1005 p. ;28 cm.

Z256. 1/U58(17)

Encyclopaedia Britannica: A New Survey of Univeral Knowledge. Vol. 17, P to planting of trees/The University of Chicago. —Chicago: Encyclopaedia Britannica, Inc. , c1947

1010 p. ;28 cm.

Z256. 1/U58(20)

Encyclopaedia Britannica: A New Survey of Univeral Knowledge. Vol. 20, Sarsaparilla to Sorcery/The University of Chicago. —Chicago: Encyclopaedia Britannica, Inc. , c1947

1006 p. ;28 cm.

Z256. 1/U58(22)

Encyclopaedia Britannica: A New Survey of Univeral Knowledge. Vol. 22, Textiles to Vasular system/The University of Chicago. —Chicago: Encyclopaedia Britannica, Inc. , c1947

1010 p. ;28 cm.

Z256. 1/U58(23)

Encyclopaedia Britannica: A New Survey of Univeral Knowledge. Vol. 23, Vase to Zyagote/The University of Chicago. —Chicago: Encyclopaedia Britannica, Inc. , c1947

998 p. ;28 cm.

Z256. 1/U58(24)

Encyclopaedia Britannica: A New Survey of Univeral Knowledge. Vol. 24, Atlas, index to atlas index to volumes 1 to 23 list of Contributors/The University of Chicago. —Chicago: Encyclopaedia Britannica, Inc. , c1947

959 p. ;28 cm.

Z256. 1/U58-9(8)

The Encyclopaedia Britannica: A Dictionary of Arts, Sciences, and General Literature. Volume VIII/The University of Cambridge. —9th ed.. —Edinburgh: Adam and Charles Black, [?]

856 p. ;27 cm.

Z256. 1/U58-11(2)

The Encyclopaedia Britannica: A Dictionary of Arts, Sciences, Literature and General Information. Volume II(Andros to Austria)/The University of Cambridge. —11th ed.. —Cambridge: Cambridge University Press, c1910

xii, 976 p. ;30 cm.

Z256. 1/U58-11(3)

The Encyclopaedia Britannica: A Dictionary of Arts, Sciences, Literature and General Information. Volume III(Austria Lower to Bisectrix)/The University of Cambridge. —11th ed.. —Cambridge: Cambridge University Press, c1910

xiv, 992 p. ;30 cm.

Z256. 1/U58-11(4)

The Encyclopaedia Britannica. Volume IV (Bisharin to Calgary), A Dictionary of Arts, Sciences, Literature and General Information/The University of Cambridge. —11th ed.. —Cambridge: Cambridge University Press, c1911

xiii, 1004 p. ;30 cm.

Z256. 1/U58-11(5)

The Encyclopaedia Britannica: A Dictionary of Arts, Sciences, Literature and General Information. Volume VI(Tonalite toVesuvius)/The University of Cambridge. —11th ed.. —New York: Encyclopedia Britannica, Inc. , c1910

xiii, 964 p. ;30 cm.

Z256. 1/U58-11(6)

The Encyclopaedia Britannica: A Dictionary of Arts, Sciences, Literature and General Information. Volume VI/The University of Cambridge. —11th ed.. —Cambridge: Cambridge University Press, c1910

xiii, 992 p. ;30 cm.

Z256. 1/U58-11(8)

The Encyclopaedia Britannica. Volume VIII (Demijohn to Edward), A Dictionary of Arts, Sciences, Literature and General Information/The University of Cambridge. —11th ed.. —Cambridge: Cambridge University Press, c1911

xiv, 1000 p. ;30 cm.

Z256. 1/U58-11(11)

The Encyclopaedia Britannica. Volume XI (Franciscans to Gibson), A Dictionary of Arts, Sciences, Literature and General Information/The University of Cambridge. —11th ed.. —Cambridge: Cambridge University Press, c1910

xii, 960 p. ;30 cm.

Z256. 1/U58-11(12)

The Encyclopaedia Britannica: A Dictionary of Arts, Sciences, Literature and General Information. Volume XII(Gichtel to Harmonium)/The University of Cambridge. —11th ed.. —Cambridge: Cambridge University Press, c1911

xiii, 960 p. ;30 cm.

Z256. 1/U58-11(13)

The Encyclopaedia Britannica: A Dictionary of Arts, Sciences, Literature and General Information. Volume XIII/The University of Cambridge. —11th ed.. —New York: Encyclopaedia Britannica, Inc. , c1910

xiii, 920 p. ;30 cm.

Z256. 1/U58-11(16)

The Encyclopaedia Britannica: A Dictionary of Arts, Sciences, Literature and General Information. Volume XVI(L to Lord Advocate)/The University of Cambridge. —11th ed.. —Cam-

bridge: Cambridge University Press, c1911
xiv, 992 p. ;30 cm.

Z256. 1/U58-11(17)
The Encyclopaedia Britannica: A Dictionary of Arts, Sciences, Literature and General Information. Volume XVII(Lord Chamberlain to Mecklenburg)/The University of Cambridge. —11th ed.. —Cambridge: Cambridge University Press, c1911
xvii, 1020 p. ;30 cm.

Z256. 1/U58-11(17-18)
The Encyclopaedia Britannica. Volume XVII-XVIII/The University of Cambridge. —11th ed.. —Cambridge: Cambridge University Press, c1911
968 p. ;28 cm.

Z256. 1/U58-11(18)
The Encyclopaedia Britannica. Volume XVIII (Mesal to Mumps), A Dictionary of Arts, Sciences, Literature and General Information/The University of Cambridge. —11th ed.. —Cambridge: Cambridge University Press, c1911
968 p. ;30 cm.

Z256. 1/U58-11(19)
The Encyclopaedia Britannica. Volume XIX (Mun to Oddfellows), A Dictionary of Arts, Sciences, Literature and General Information/The University of Cambridge. —11th ed.. —Cambridge: Cambridge University Press, c1911
996 p. ;30 cm.

Z256. 1/U58-11(20)
The Encyclopaedia Britannica. Volume XX, A Dictionary of Arts, Sciences, Literature and General Information/The University of Cambridge. —11th ed.. —Cambridge: Cambridge University Press, c1911
980 p. ;30 cm.

Z256. 1/U58-11(22)
The Encyclopaedia Britannica: A Dictionary of Arts, Sciences, Literature and General Information. Volume XXII/The University of Cambridge. —11th ed.. —Cambridge: Cambridge University Press, c1911
xiv, 975 p. ;30 cm.

Z256. 1/U58-11(23)
The Encyclopaedia Britannica. Volume XXIII (Reffctory to Sainte-Beuve), A Dictionary of Arts, Sciences, Literature and General Information/The University of Cambridge. —11th ed.. —Cambridge: Cambridge University Press, c1911
xiii, 1024 p. ;30 cm.

Z256. 1/U58-11(23)
The Encyclopaedia Britannica: A Dictionary of Arts, Sciences, Literature and General Information. Volume XXII(Refectory to Sainte-Beuve))/The University of Cambridge. —11th ed.. —Cambridge: Cambridge University Press, c1911
xiii, 1024 p. ;30 cm.

Z256. 1/U58-11(24)
The Encyclopaedia Britannica: A Dictionary of Arts, Sciences, Literature and General Information. Volume XXIV (Sainte-Claire Deville to Shuttle)/The University of Cambridge. —11th ed.. —Cambridge: Cambridge University Press, c1911
xiii, 1024 p. ;30 cm.

Z256. 1/U59-11(27)
The Encyclopaedia Britannica. Volume XXVII (Tonalite to Vesuvius), A Dictionary of Arts, Sciences, Literature and General Information/The University of Cambridge. —11th ed.. —Cambridge: Cambridge University Press, c1911
1064 p. ;30 cm.

Z256. 1/U59-9(19)

The Encyclopaedia Britannica: A Dictionary of Arts, Sciences, and General Literature. Volume XIX/The University of Cambridge. —9th ed. . —Edinburgh: Adam and Charles Black, [?]

886 p. ;27 cm.

Z256. 1/W164

The Omnibus Book of Travellers' Tales: Being the History of Exploration Told by the Explorers/Milton Waldman. —London: Victor Gollancz Ltd. , c1931

864 p. ;19 cm.

Z271. 2/A512(2)

The Encyclopedia Americana: 1944 Edition. Volume 2/Americana Corporation. —New York: Americana Corporation, c1944

692 p. ;26 cm.

Z271. 2/A512(6)

The Encyclopedia Americana: 1944 Edition. Volume 6/Americana Corporation. —New York: Americana Corporation, c1944

736 p. ;26 cm.

Z271. 2/A512(15)

The Encyclopedia Americana: 1944 Edition. Volume 15/Americana Corporation. —New York: Americana Corporation, c1944

772 p. ;25 cm.

Z271. 2/A512(16)

The Encyclopedia Americana: 1944 Edition. Volume 16/Americana Corporation. —New York: Americana Corporation, c1944

767 p. ;25 cm.

Z271. 2/A512(17)

The Encyclopedia Americana: 1944 Edition. volume 17/Americana Corporation. —New York: Americana Corporation, c1944

752 p. ;25 cm.

Z271. 2/A512(19)

The Encyclopedia Americana: 1944 Edition. Volume 19/Americana Corporation. —New York: Americana Corporation, c1944

809 p. ;25 cm.

Z271. 2/A512(20)

The Encyclopedia Americana: 1944 Edition. volume 20/Americana Corporation. —New York: Americana Corporation, c1944

516 p. ;25 cm.

Z271. 2/A512(21)

The Encyclopedia Americana: 1944 Edition. Volume 21/Americana Corporation. —New York: Americana Corporation, c1944

805 p. ;26 cm.

Z271. 2/A512(22)

The Encyclopedia Americana: 1944 Edition. Volume 22/Americana Corporation. —New York: Americana Corporation, c1944

800 p. ;25 cm.

Z271. 2/A512(24)

The Encyclopedia Americana: 1944 Edition. Volume 24/Americana Corporation. —New York: Americana Corporation, c1944

812 p. ;26 cm.

Z271. 2/A512(30)

The Encyclopedia Americana: 1944 Edition. Volume 30/Americana Corporation. —New York: Americana Corporation, c1944

824 p. ;25 cm.

Z271. 2/A512(1944)

The Encyclopedia Americana: 1944 Edition/Americana Corporation. —New York: Americana Corporation, c1944

719 p. ;25 cm.

Z271. 2/H673

Henley's Twentieth Century Book of Formulas, Processes and Trade Secrets: A Valuable reference book for the home, factory, office, laboratory and the workshop/Gardner D. Hiscox. —New York: The Norman W. Henley Publishing Company, c1937

xiv883, 40 p. ;22 cm.

Z271. 2/H673-1921

Henley's Twentieth Century Formulas, Recipes and Processes: Containing ten thousand selected household and workshop formulas, recipes, processes and moneysaving methods for the practical use of manufacturers, mechanics, housekeeppers and home workers/Gardner D. Hiscox. —1921 ed, Revised and Englarged. —New York: The Norman W. Henley Publishing Company, c1921

807, 40 p. ;22 cm.

Z271. 2/M647(3)

The Standard American Encyclopedia. 3/Walter Miller. —Chicago: Standard American Corporation, c1937

1 v. ;24 cm.

Z271. 2/M647(4)

The Standard American Encyclopedia. 4/Walter Miller. —Chicago: Standard American Corporation, c1937

1 v. ;24 cm.

Z271. 2/M647(11)

The Standard American Encyclopedia. 11/Walter Miller. —Chicago: Standard American Corporation, c1937

1 v. ;24 cm.

Z271. 2/M647(13)

The Standard American Encyclopedia. 13/Walter Miller. —Chicago: Standard American Corporation, c1937

1 v. ;24 cm.

Z271. 2/M647(15)

The Standard American Encyclopedia. 15/Walter Miller. —Chicago: Standard American Corporation, c1937

1 v. ;24 cm.

Z271. 2/P739

The Frontiersman's Pocket-Book/Roger Pocock. —London: John Murray, c1909

xx, 463, 20 p. ;15 cm.

Z3/I72

The World Almanac and Book of Facts for 1948/edited by E. E. Irvine. . —63rd year of publication. . —New York: New York World-Telegram, c1948.

912 p. ;21 cm.

Z4/S111(1)

The History of Don Quixote De La Mancha. Volume I/Miguel De Cervantes Saavedra. —London: J. M. Dent & Sons Ltd. , c1916

xxxii, 424 p. ;18 cm.

Z52/W888(1913)

The China Year Book 1913/H. G. W. Woodhead. —London: George Routledge & Sons, Ltd. , c1913

xv, 728 p. ;22 cm.

Z52/W888(1921-2)

The China Year Book 1921-2/H. G. W. Woodhead. —London: Simpkin, Marshall, Hamilton, Kent & Co. , Ltd. , c[1921]

xxx, 1063 p. ;23 cm.

Z52/W888(1923)

The China Year Book 1923/H. G. W. Woodhead. —Tientsin: The Tientsin Press, Ltd. , c1923

xxxviii, 1243 p. ;22 cm.

Z52/W888(1924.5)

The China Year Book 1924.5/H. G. W. Woodhead. —Tientsin: The Tientsin Press, Ltd., c1924

xxxiii, 1249 p.;22 cm.

Z52/W888(1925-26)

The China Year Book 1925-6/H. G. W. Woodhead. —London: Simpkin, Marshall, Hamilton, Kent & Co., Ltd., c[1926]

xxx, 1349 p.;23 cm.

Z52/W888(1926-27)

The China Year Book 1926-7/H. G. W. Woodhead. —London: Simpkin, Marshall, Hamilton, Kent & Co., Ltd., c[1927]

xxix, 1335 p.;21 cm.

Z52/W888(1929-30)

The China Year Book 1929-30/H. G. W. Woodhead. —London: Simpkin, Marshall, Hamilton, Kent & Co., Ltd., c[1926]

xxx, 1267 p.;23 cm.

Z52/W888(1936)

The China Year Book 1936/H. G. W. Woodhead. —Tientsin: The Tientsin Press, Ltd., c1936

xxiv, 511 p.;22 cm.

Z52/W888(1938)

The China Year Book 1938/H. G. W. Woodhead. —Tientsin: The Tientsin Press, Ltd., c1938

xxiv, 595 p.;22 cm.

Z531.3/T136(1945)

The Japan year book, 1945/edited by Sekijiro Takagaki. —Tokyo: Foreign Affairs Association of Japan, c1943.

xiv, 1380 p., 3 p.;20 cm.

Z531.3/T136(1943-1-44)

The Japan year book, 1943-1944/edited by Sekijiro Takagaki. —Tokyo: Foreign Affairs Association of Japan, c1943.

xiv, 1099 p., 3 p.;20 cm.

Z815.61/M592

A Complete Catalogue of Books/Methuen & Co., Ltd.,—London: Methuen & Co., Ltd., c1936

325 p.;22 cm.

Z815.61/S699-3(1)

The Best Books: A Reader's Guide. Part I/ William Swan Sonnenschein. —3rd ed.. —London: George Routledge & Sons, Ltd., c1910

458 p.;24 cm.

Z822.01/N277(1)

Union Catalogue of Books in European Languages in Peiping Libraries.. V. 1, A-G. /National Library of Peiping. —Peiping: National Library of Peiping, c1931

930 p.;19 cm.

Z822.01/N277(2)

Union Catalogue of Books in European Languages in Peiping Libraries.. V. 2, H-O. /National Library of Peiping. —Peiping: National Library of Peiping, c1931

931-1741 p.;26 cm.

Z822.01/N277(3)

Union Catalogue of Books in European Languages in Peiping Libraries.. V. 3, p-z. /National Library of Peiping. —Peiping: National Library of Peiping, c1931

1743-2562 p.;25 cm.

Z825.61/J66-8

Oxford University Press General Catalogue/ John Johnson. —8th ed.. —London: The University Press, Oxford, c1937

viii，460 p. ;22 cm.

Z825. 61/O98

Select Catalogue 1935：Being a Selection of Oxford Books offered for General Reading/Oxford University Press. —[S. l.]：Humphrey Milford，c1935

176 p. ;19 cm.

Z825. 61/S992

A Catalogue of Books/The Syndics of the Cambridge University Press. —London：Fetter Lane，c1936

xiv，337 p. ;21 cm.

Z857. 12/J65

Wiley Books/John Wiley & Sons，Inc. —New York：John Wiley & Sons，Inc. ，[?]

262 p. ;21 cm.

题名索引

—B—

—C—

—D—

—E—

—F—

—G—

—H—

—I—

—J—

—K—

—L—

—M—

—N—

—O—

—P—

—Q—

—R—

—S—

—T—

—U—

—V—

—Y—

—Z—

《中国图书馆分类法》类目

德语专辑

A 马克思主义、列宁主义……

A226/L563-2

Der Imperialismus als juengste Etappe des Kapitalismus/N. Lenin. —2. Aufl.. —Wien: Verlag fuer Literatur und Politik, c1926

132 S. ;21 cm.

B 哲学、宗教

B024/G914

Der Gegensatz: Versuche zu einer Philosophie des Lebendig-konkreten/Romano Guardini. —Mainz: Der Werkkreis im Matthias Gruenewald Verlag, 1925

16,257 S. ;22 cm.

B081. 1/J35

Aufstiege zur Metaphysik: Heute und Ehedem/Bernhard Jansen. —Freiburg im Breisgau: Herder & Co. G. m. b. H. Verlagsbuchhandlung, 1933

8,537 S. ;24 cm.

B2/H123(5)

Chinesische Philosophie. Band 5/Heinrich Hackmann. —Muenchen: Verlag Ernst Reinhardt, c1927

406 S. ;20 cm.

B222. 2/W678

Kung-tse: Leben und Werk/Richard Wilhelm. —Stuttgart: Fr. Frommanns Verlag (H. Kurtz), c1925

210 S. ;21 cm.

B5/M685(1)

Wandel des Weltbildes von Thomas auf Heute. Band I, Das Ringen der alten Stoff-Form-Metaphysik mit der heutigen Stoff-Physik/Albert Mitterer. —Innsbruck: Tyrolia Verlag, 1935

160 S. ;23 cm.

B504/D389

Goerres Spricht zu unserer Zeit: Der Denker und sein Werk/Alois Dempf. —Freibug im Breisgau: Herder & Co. G. m. b. H. Verlagsbuchhandlung, 1933

11,224 S. ;21 cm.

B516. 31/K91-2

Populaere Darstellung von Immanuel Kant's Kritik der reinen Vernunft/Albrecht Krause. —2. Aufl.. —Lahr: Verlag von Moritz Schauenburg, 1882

16,211 S. ;19 cm.

B516. 59-53/K63-4

Mensch und Erde: Sieben Abhandlungen/Ludwig Klages. —4. Aufl.. —Jena: Eugen Diederichs Verlag, c1929

181 S. ;21 cm.

B821/H133-3

Was ist der Mensch? /Theodor Haecker. —3. Aufl.. —Leipzig: MCMXXXV bei Jakob Hegner,1935

191 S. ;19 cm.

B821/K38-2

Mehr Freude/Paul Wilhelm von Keppler, Bischof von Rottenburg. —2. Aufl.. —Freiburg im Breisgau: Herdersche Verlagshandlung,1911

260 S. ;19 cm.

B821/K95-11

Schafft anstaendige Kerle!:Zeitlose Zeitgedanken /Erich Kuehn. —11. Aufl.. —Berlin: Theodor Weicher Verlag,c1938

170 S. ;20 cm.

B821/M561

Leben nicht nur Dasein: 365 deutsche Gedanken, auch Geschichte/Gerhard Merian. —Stuttgart: Verlag Gerhard Merian,[?]

126 S. ;16 cm.

B823. 4/S334

Um die Reinheit der Jugend: Ein Buch ueber die Erziehung zur Keuschheit fuer Eltern, Seelsorger und Erzieher/Hardy Schilgen. —Duesseldorf: Verlag von L. Schwann,[?]

18 S. ;20 cm.

B84/K63-6

Die Tiefen der Seele: Moralpsychologische Studien/I. Klug. —6. Aufl.. —Paderborn: Ferdinand Schoeningh Verlag,c1926

455 S. ;23 cm.

B842. 3/J91

Die Kunst des Behaltens: Kleine Gedaechtnisschule/Hans Juenemann. —Hamburg: Hanseatische Verlagsanstalt Hamburg,[?]

44 S. ;21 cm.

B844. 5/W375

Die Frauen und die Liebe/Marianne Weber. —Koenigstein im Taunus: Karl Robert Langewiesche Verlag,[?]

285 S. ;19 cm.

B848. 4/M847

Nicht warten-wirken!: Amerikas Glaube an Deutschland/K. Phillips Morgan. —Muenchen: Georg Mueller,c1931

292 S. ;21 cm.

B848. 4/P613-2

Vom Sinn der Tapferkeit/Josef Pieper. —2. Aufl.. —Leipzig: Verlag Jakob Hegner,[?]

92 S. ;19 cm.

B848. 6/H476-4

Vier Temperamente der Erwachsenen: Eine Anleitung zur Selbst- und Menschenkenntnis und ein praktischer Fuehrer und Ratgeber im Umgang mit der Welt/Bernhard Hellwig. —4. Aufl.. —Paderborn: Verlag von J. Esser,1899

99 S. ;20 cm.

B848. 6/K63-4

Handschrift und Charakter: Gemeinverstaendlicher Abriss der graphologischen Technik/Ludwig Klages. —3. und 4. Aufl.. —Barth: Verlag von Johann Ambrosius,c1921

11,254 S. ;24 cm.

B848. 6/R918-2

Die Arbeit am Charakter: Die neuere Psychotherapie in ihrer Anwendung auf Erziehung, Selbsterziehung und seelische Hilfeleistung/Fritz Ruenkel. —2. Aufl.. —Schwerin i. Mecklb.: Verlag Friedrich Bahn,c1929

167 S. ;22 cm.

B9/W828

Die ostasiatischen Kulturreligionen/J. Witte. —Leipzig: Verlag von Quelle & Meyer,[?]

8,183 S. ;18 cm.

B921/S314

Natur und Gnade: Versuch einer systematischen, wissenschaftlichen Darstellung der natuerlichen und uebernatuerlichen Lebensordnung im Menschen/M. Jos. Scheeben. —Muenchen: Theatiner Verlag,1922

345 S. ;24 cm.

B94/S386

Die Botschaft des Buddha vom Lotos des guten Gesetzes/Guenther Schulemann. —Freiburg im Breigau: Herder & Co. G. m. b. H. Verlagsbuchhandlung,1937

197 S. ;23 cm.

B97/A182-5

Lebensschule fuer Ordensfrauen/Bernhard van Acken. —4. und 5. Aufl.. —Paderborn: Verlag Ferdinand Schoeningh,c1935

432 S. ;17 cm.

B97/A193

Jesus Christus/Karl Adam. —Augsburg: Haas und Grabherr,c1933

351 S. ;22 cm.

B97/A193-3

Jesus Christus/Karl Adam. —3. Aufl.. —Augsburg: Haas und Grabherr,c1933

327 S. ;22 cm.

B97/A193-4

Jesus Christus/Karl Adam. —4. Aufl.. —Augsburg: Haas und Grabherr,c1935

327 S. ;22 cm.

B97/A193-4(6)

Seele-Buecherei: Zur Auferbauung gefunden Christenlebens. Band 6, Christus unser Bruder/Karl Adam. —4. Aufl.. —Regensburg: Verlag von Josef Habbel,[?]

280 S. ;18 cm.

B97/A313-2

Ich lebe und ihr lebet: Vom Strom des Lebens in der Kirche/Die Akademische Bonifatius-Einigung. —2. Aufl.. —Paderborn: Verlag der Bonifacius Druckerei GmbH. ,c1937

218 S. ;23 cm.

B97/A612-7

Comes pastoralis confessarii praesertim religiosi: Fuer die seelsorgliche Praxis aus Pastoral und Kirchenrecht zusammengestellt/Ludwig Anler. —7. Aufl.. —Fulda: Fuladaer Actiendruckerei,1933

8,308 S. ;19 cm.

B97/A657

Das Wort/Thomas von Aquin. —Leipzig: MCMXXXV bei Jakob Hegner,[?]

102 S. ;19 cm.

B97/A923

Ueber die Psalmen/Aurelius Augustinus. —Leipzig: MCMXXXVI im Verlag Jakob Hegner,[?]

366 S. ;19 cm.

B97/B118

Mutterrecht und Urreligion/Johann Jakob Bachofen. —Leipzig: Alfred Kroener Verlag,[?]

19,280,40 S. ;18 cm.

B97/B283-4

Maria/Bernhard Bartmann. —3. und 4. Aufl.. —Paderborn: Verlag der Bonifacius Druckerei,c1925

13,447 S. ;21 cm.

B97/B284-6

Der Roemerbrief/Karl Barth. —6. Aufl.. —Muenchen: Chr. Kaiser Verlag,c1922

28,528 S. ;23 cm.

B97/B337

Die Heimholung der Welt: Von der sakramentalen Lebensordnung/Oskar Bauhofer. —Freiburg im Breisgau: Herder & Co. G. m. b. H. Verlagsbuchhandlung, c1936

10,271 S. ;20 cm.

B97/B347-2

Herz Jesu und Priestertum/Ferdinand Baumann. —2. Aufl.. —Freiburg im Breisgau: Herder & Co. G. m. b. H. Verlagsbuchhandlung, 1936

19,205 S. ;18 cm.

B97/B474

Christus in der Kirche/Robert Hugh Benson. —Muenchen: Verlag Koesel Pustet, [?]

153 S. ;19 cm.

B97/B512

Deutsche Synopse: Der vier Evangelien/P. Johann Berk. —Osnabrueck: Druck und Komissionaverlag der Handelsdruckerei A. Fromm, 1933

31,152 S. ;21 cm.

B97/B524

Maria und ich/M. V. Bernadot. —Basel: Verlag Nazareth, [?]

167 S. ;20 cm.

B97/B548-3

Der heilige Augustin/Louis Bertrand. —3. Aufl.. —Paderborn: Ferdinand Schoeningh Verlag, 1932

16,328 S. ;21 cm.

B97/B586(2)

Pusillum: Buendige Priesterbetrachtungen fuer Reise und Haus. 2. Baendchen, Vom Sonntag Septuagesima bis zum dritten Sonntag nach Ostern/P. Athanasius Bierbaum. —Werl i. W.: Franziskus, 1928

194 S. ;17 cm.

B97/B586(3)

Pusillum: Buendige Priesterbetrachtungen fuer Reise und Haus. 3. Baendchen, Vom dritten Sonntag nach Ostern bis zum zwoelften Sonntag nach Pfingsten/P. Athanasius Bierbaum. —Werl i. W.: Franziskus, 1928

263 S. ;17 cm.

B97/B586-4(2)

Pusillum: Buendige Priesterbetrachtungen fuer Reise und Haus. 2. Baendchen, Vom Sonntag Septuagesima bis zum dritten Sonntag nach Ostern/P. Athanasius Bierbaum. —4. Aufl.. —Werl i. W.: Franziskus, 1935

198 S. ;17 cm.

B97/B746(10)

Buecher der Geisteserneuerung. 10. Band, Das Hohepriesterliche Gebet unseres Herrn/Jacques Benigne Bossuet. —Salzburg: Verlag Anton Pustet, [?]

180 S. ;19 cm.

B97/B828

Breviloquium des Hl. Bonaventura: Ein Abriss der Theologie/Breviloquium. —Werl i. Westf.: Franziskus Druckerei, 1931

8,290 S. ;17 cm.

B97/B888-7

Die Lehre des Hl. Franz von Sales von der wahren Froemmigkeit/Jakob Brucker. —6. und 7. Aufl.. —Freiburg im Breigau: Herder & Co. G. m. b. H. Verlagsbuchhandlung, 1921

20,470 S. ;16 cm.

B97/C434-7(2)

Betrachtung fuer Priester oder der Priester geheiligt durch die Uebung des betrachtenden Gebetes. 2. Band/P. Chaignon. —7. Aufl.. —Tri-

er: Verlag der Fr. Lintz'schen Buchhandlung, 1896
324 S. ;20 cm.

B97/C583-3
Als die Zeit erfuellt war: Das Evangelium des Hl. Matthaeus/Hermann J. Cladder. —2. und 3. Aufl.. —Freiburg im Breisgau: Herder & Co. G. m. b. H. Verlagsbuchhandlung, [?]
12,268 S. ;17 cm.

B97/C585(3)
Die Schriften des sonigfliessenden Lehrers Bernhard von Clairvaux. Band 3, Ansprachen auf Muttergottes- und Seiligenfeste/Bernhard von Clairvaux. —Wittlich: Georg Fischer Verlag, [?]
300 S. ;19 cm.

B97/C585(4)
Die Schriften des sonigfliessenden Lehrers Bernhard von Clairvaux. Band 4, Miszellen Ansprachen ueber verschiedene Gegenstaende/Bernhard von Clairvaux. —Wittlich: Georg Fischer Verlag, [?]
326 S. ;19 cm.

B97/C661
Das heilige Messopfer: Unterweisungen und Gebete/P. Martin von Cochem. —Einsiedeln: Verlagsanstalt Benziger & Co. A. —G. , [?]
339 S. ;21 cm.

B97/C678-2
Jesus Christus Der Koenig der Welt: Eine Werbeschrift zum neuen Fest unseres "Herrn Jesus Christus des Koenigs"/Otto Cohausz. —2. Aufl.. —Kaldenkirchen: Missionsdruckerei Steyl, [?]
158 S. ;17 cm.

B97/D148(2)
Ergaenzungen und Verbesserungen zu Jesus-Jeschua: Die drei Sprachen Jesu Kesusin der Synagoge, auf dem Berge beim Passahmahl, am Kreuz. 2. Band, Die Worte Jesu/Gustaf Dalman. —Leipzig: J. C. Hinrichs'sche Buchhandlung, 1929
222 S. ;23 cm.

B97/D324-3
Zitaten-Apologie oder christliche Wahrheiten im Lichte der menschlichen Intelligenz: Christliches Vademekum fuer die gebildete Welt/Theodor Deimel. —3. Aufl.. —Freiburg im Breisgau: Herdersche Verlagshandlung, 1912
15,355 S. ;16 cm.

B97/E65
In stiller Stunde: Andachten und Betrachtungen/Ernst Aller's Verlag. —Strehlen ScHl. : Ernst Aller's Verlag, 1892
12,300 S. ;20 cm.

B97/E97-2(3)
Die heilige Eucharistie. III. Serie, Geistliche Uebungen zu den Fuessen Jesu in der heiligen Eucharistie/P. Peter Julian Eymard. —2. Aufl.. —Schaan: Verlag des Emmanuel, 1914
8,287 S. ;16 cm.

B97/E97-2(4)
Die Hl. Eucharistie: Exerzitien-Vortraege. 4. Baendchen/P. Eymard. —2. Aufl.. —Rottweil: Verlag des Emmanuel, [?]
775 S. ;16 cm.

B97/F312
Jesus von Nazareth: Ein Christusbuch/Hilarin Felder. —Paderborn: Ferdinand Schoeningh, c1937
8,392 S. ;21 cm.

B97/F312-4
Die Ideale des Hl. Franziskus von Assisi/P. Hilarin Felder. —4. Aufl.. —Paderborn: Ferdinand Schoeningh Verlag, c1935

15,445 S. ;22 cm.

B97/F423

Unsere Kirche im Kommen: Begegnung von Jetztzeit und Endzeit/Georg Feuerer. —Freiburg im Breisgau: Herder & Co. G. m. b. H. Verlagsbuchhandlung,c1937

8,228 S. ;23 cm.

B97/G262

Die Weltmission der Kirche und wir Seelsorger/Michael Gatterer. —Innsbruck: Verlag von Felizian Rauch,1933

138 S. ;18 cm.

B97/G262(5)

Das Religionsbuch der Kirche (Catechismus Romanus). 5. Baendchen, Das vatikanische Konzil/Michael Gatterer. —Innsbruck: Verlag von Felizian Rauch,1931

206 S. ;18 cm.

B97/G262-2(3)

Das Religionsbuch der Kirche (Catechismus Romanus). 3. Teil, Von den Geboten/Michael Gatterer. —2. Aufl.. —Innsbruck: Verlag von Felizian Rauch,1933

156 S. ;18 cm.

B97/G462-19

Das heilige Messopfer: dogmatisch, liturgisch und aszetisch erklaert/Rikolaus Gihr. —17. bis 19. Aufl.. —Freiburg im Breisgau: Herder & Co. G. m. b. H. Verlagsbuchhandlung,1922

15,687 S. ;24 cm.

B97/G728

Christus in seinen heiligen Sakramenten/Rudolf Graber. —Muenchen: Verlag Koesel Pustet, [?]

182 S. ;20 cm.

B97/G864

Ganz schoen bist du, Maria!:Ein Lobpreis zu Ehren der unbefleckt empfangenen Gottesmutter Maria/Antonin Grimm. —Paderborn: Verlag Ferdinand Schoeningh,c1936

181 S. ;19 cm.

B97/G914

Vom lebendigen Gott/Romano Guardini. —Mainz: Matthias Gruenewald Verlag,1936

156 S. ;19 cm.

B97/G914J11

Der Engel in Dantes goettlicher Komoedie/Romano Guardini. —Leipzig: Verlag Jakob Hegner, [?]

134 S. ;19 cm.

B97/G914M443

Von heiligen Zeichen/Romano Guardini. —Mainz: Matthias Gruenewald Verlag,1936

98 S. ;18 cm.

B97/G914W484

Der Herr: Betrachtungen ueber die Person und das Leben Jesu Christi/Romano Guardini. —Burg Rothenfels am Main: Werkbund Verlag Wuerzburg, Abteilung die Burg,1937

13,762 S. ;22 cm.

B97/H169-6(1)

Huelfsbuch fuer den evangelischen Religionsunterricht an den hoeheren Lehranstalten. 1. Teil,Fuer Sexta bis Quarta aller Anstalten/H. Halfmann, J. Koester. —6. Aufl.. —Berlin: Verlag von Reuther & Neichard,1905

8,208 S. ;22 cm.

B97/H198

Der Bordesholmer Altar Meister Brueggemanns/Freerk Haye Hamkens. —Leipzig: Insel Verlag,[?]

56 S. ;21 cm.

B97/H249-2

Der heilige Geist: Kanzelvortraege, gehalten in der Kirche St. Martin zu Freiburg/Heinrich Hansjakob. —2. Aufl.. —Freiburg im Breisgau: Herdersche Verlagshandlung,1905

10,196 S. ;24 cm.

B97/H249-3

Jesus von Nazareth, Gott in der Welt und im Sakramente: Sechs Vortraege, gehalten in der Fastenzeit 1890 in der Kirche St. Martin zu Freiburg/Heinrich Hansjakob. —3. Aufl.. —Freiburg im Breisgau: Herdersche Verlagshandlung,1901

8,86 S. ;23 cm.

B97/H461

Des heiligen Augustin Bekenntnisse/Herman Hefele. —Jena: Eugen Diederichs,[?]

19,317 S. ;21 cm.

B97/H466(1)

Wege zum Glueck: Buecher fuer schoene Lebensgestaltung. 1. Band, Stunden der Stille/Alfons Heilmann. —Freiburg im Breisgau: Herder & Co. G. m. b. H. Verlagsbuchhandlung,[?]

8,238 S. ;18 cm.

B97/H573-28

Die Bekenntnisse des heiligen Augustinus: Buch I-X/Georg Grafen von Hertling. —28. Aufl.. —Freiburg im Breisgau: Herder & Co. G. m. b. H. Verlagsbuchhandlung,1936

10,519 S. ;15 cm.

B97/H581-4(4)

Ecclesia Orans: Zur Einfuehrung in den Geist der Liturgie. 4. Baendchen, Die Psalmen I/Ildefons Herwegen. —3. und 4. Aufl.. —Freiburg im Breigau: Herder & Co. G. m. b. H. Verlagsbuchhandlung,1920

12,295 S. ;17 cm.

B97/H685-2

Meister Eckharts deutsche Predigten und Traktate/Eckhart von Hochheim. —2. Aufl.. —Leipzig: Insel Verlag,[?]

449 S. ;22 cm.

B97/H693

Das Buch der Buecher: Gedanken ueber Lektuere und Studium der Heiligen Schrift/Hildebrand Hoepfl. —Freiburg im Breisgau: Herdersche Verlagshandlung,1904

13,284 S. ;20 cm.

B97/H887-5

Helden und Heilige: Januar bis Juni/Hans Huemmeler. —5. Aufl.. —Bonn a. Rhein: Verlag der Buchgemeinde,c1934

351 S. ;24 cm.

B97/H967-3

Exerzitien fuer Priester und Laien: Ausfuehrliche Entwuerfe zu Vortraegen und Betrachtungen/Hugo Hurter. —3. Aufl.. —Innsbruck: Verlag von Fel. Rauch,1925

407 S. ;21 cm.

B97/I58-4(1)

Kurzgefasster Kommentar zu den vier heiligen Evangelien. 1. Band, Kommentar zum Evangelium des Heiligen Matthaeus mit Ausschluss der Leidensgeschichte/Theodor Innitzer. —4. Aufl.. —Graz: Verlagsbuchhandlung Styria,1932

20,451 S. ;23 cm.

B97/K14(3.1)

Die Heilige Schrift: fuer das Leben erklaert. Band III, Die Samuelbuecher. 1. Teil/Edmund Kalt, Willibald Lauck. —Freiburg im Breisgau: Herder & Co. G. m. b. H. Verlagsbuchhandlung,c1940

10,319 S. ;23 cm.

B97/K14(6)

Die heilige Schrift: fuer das Leben erklaert. Band VI, Die Psalmen/Edmund Kalt. —Freiburg im Breisgau: Herder & Co. G. m. b. H. Verlagsbuchhandlung, 1935

14, 524 S. ; 23 cm.

B97/K14(8)

Die Heilige Schrift: fuer das Leben erklaert. Band VIII, Das Buch der Weisheit, Das Buch Isaias/Edmund Kalt, Willibald Lauck. —Freiburg im Breisgau: Herder & Co. G. m. b. H. Verlagsbuchhandlung, c1938

12, 430 S. ; 23 cm.

B97/K14-2(11. 1)

Die Heilige Schrift: fuer das Leben erklaert. Band XI, Das Evangelium des Hl. Matthaeus und des Hl. Markus/Edmund Kalt, Willibald Lauck. —2. Aufl.. —Freiburg im Breisgau: Herder & Co. G. m. b. H. Verlagsbuchhandlung, 1937

22, 317 S. ; 23 cm.

B97/K18-2

Das Religioese in der Menschheit und das Christentum/Otto Karrer. —2. Aufl.. —Freiburg im Breisgau: Herder & Co. G. m. b. H. Verlagsbuchhandlung, c1934

9, 264 S. ; 23 cm.

B97/K18-3

Das Religioese in der Menschheit und das Christentum/Otto Karrer. —3. Aufl.. —Freiburg im Breisgau: Herder & Co. G. m. b. H. Verlagsbuchhandlung, c1934

14, 264 S. ; 23 cm.

B97/K19-3

Marianische Christusgestaltung der Welt/ Ferdinand Kastner. —3. Aufl.. —Paderborn: Ferdinand Schoeningh, c1937

324 S. ; 22 cm.

B97/K19-4

Marianische Christusgestaltung der Welt/ Ferdinand Kastner. —4. Aufl.. —Paderborn: Ferdinand Schoeningh, c1937

324 S. ; 22 cm.

B97/K32

Vier Buecher von der Nachfolge Christi/ Thomas von Kempen. —Berlin: Deutsche Buch Gemeinschaft G. m. b. H. , [?]

12, 350 S. ; 19 cm.

B97/K47-4(1)

Evangelisches Religionsbuch. Teil 1, fuer die Grundschule/Hans Kiesbye[usw.]. —4. Aufl.. —Frankfurt a. M. : Verlag Moritz Diesterweg, 1933

104 S. ; 23 cm.

B97/K58(1)

Osterjubel der Ostkirche: Hymnen aus der fuenfzigtaegigen Osterfeier der Byzantinischen Kirche. 1. Teil, Des Pentekostarion/P. Kilian Kirchhoff. —Muenster: Regensbergsche Verlagsbuchhandlung, [?]

23, 309 S. ; 19 cm.

B97/K58-2(2)

Helden des Christentums: Heiligenbilder. Band II, Aus dem Mittelalter/Konrad Kirch. —1. und 2. Aufl.. —Paderborn: Verlag der Bonifacius, c1924

238 S. ; 18 cm.

B97/K58-2(3)

Helden des Christentums: Heiligenbilder. Band III, Aus der Neuzeit/Konrad Kirch. —1. und 2. Aufl.. —Paderborn: Verlag der Bonifacius, c1934

218 S. ; 18 cm.

B97/K58-2(3. 4)

Helden des Christentums: Heiligenbilder.

Band III, Aus der Neuzeit, Lieblinge des Volkes. 4. Teil/Konrad Kirch. —1. und 2. Aufl. . —Paderborn: Verlag der Bonifacius, c1934
242 S. ;18 cm.

B97/K58-3(1)
Helden des Christentums: 4. Moenchsgestalten. Band I, Aus dem christlichen Altertum/Konrad Kirch. —3. Aufl. . —Paderborn: Verlag der Bonifacius, c1932
230 S. ;18 cm.

B97/K58-3(2)
Helden des Christentums: Heiligenbilder. Band II, Aus dem Mittelalter/Konrad Kirch. —3. Aufl. . —Paderborn: Verlag der Bonifacius, c1933
286 S. ;18 cm.

B97/K58-3(3)
Helden des Christentums: Heiligenbilder. Band III, Aus der Neuzeit/Konrad Kirch. —3. Aufl. . —Paderborn: Verlag der Bonifacius, c1931
240 S. ;18 cm.

B97/K58-4(1. 2)
Helden des Christentums: Heiligenbilder. Band I, Aus dem christlichen Altertum. 2. Teil/Konrad Kirch. —4. Aufl. . —Paderborn: Bonifacius Druckerei, c1927
191 S. ;18 cm.

B97/K58-5(1. 1)
Helden des Christentums: Heiligenbilder. Band I, Aus dem christlichen Altertum. 1. Teil/Konrad Kirch. —5. Aufl. . —Paderborn: Bonifacius Druckerei, c1936
196 S. ;18 cm.

B97/K63(1)
Einkehr: Ein Jahrbuch der Seele. 1. Jahrgang/I. Klug. —Paderborn: Verlag von Ferdinand Schoeningh, 1927
304 S. ;18 cm.

B97/K63-2
Der Heiland der Welt: Ein Christusbuch/I. Klug. —2. Aufl. . —Paderborn: Verlag von Ferdinand Schoeningh, c1924
8, 696 S. ;19 cm.

B97/K63-3
Der Helfer Gott/I. Klug. —3. Aufl. . —Paderborn: Ferdinand Schoeningh Verlag, 1929
248 S. ;19 cm.

B97/K63P123(1)
Ein Sonntagsbuch. 1. Band/I. Klug. —Paderborn: Verlag von Ferdinand Schoeningh, c1911
8, 540 S. ;18 cm.

B97/K76-2(1)
Homiletisches Quellenwerk: Stoffquellen fuer Predigt und christliche Unterweisung. 1. Band/Anton Koch. —2. Aufl. . —Freiburg im Breisgau: Herder & Co. G. M. B. H. Verlagsbuchhandlung, c1937
13, 488 S. ;23 cm.

B97/K76-2(2)
Homiletisches Quellenwerk: Stoffquellen fuer Predigt und christliche Unterweisung. 2. Band/Anton Koch. —1. und 2. Aufl. . —Freiburg im Breisgau: Herder & Co. G. M. B. H. Verlagsbuchhandlung, c1938
8, 492 S. ;23 cm.

B97/K76-2(3)
Homiletisches Quellenwerk: Stoffquellen fuer Predigt und christliche Unterweisung. 3. Band/Anton Koch. —1. und 2. Aufl. . —Freiburg im Breisgau: Herder & Co. G. M. B. H. Verlagsbuchhandlung, c1938
8, 484 S. ;23 cm.

B97/K76-2(4)
Homiletisches Quellenwerk: Stoffquellen fuer

Predigt und christliche Unterweisung. 4. Band/Anton Koch. —1. und 2. Aufl.. —Freiburg im Breisgau: Herder & Co. G. M. B. H. Verlagsbuchhandlung, c1939
8,503 S. ;23 cm.

B97/K76-3
Das Religionsbuch der Kirche: Einfuehrung und vom Glaubensbekenntnis/Anton Koch. —3. Aufl.. —Innsbruck/Leipzig: Verlag Felizian Rauch, 1940
275 S. ;17 cm.

B97/K76-3(3)
Homiletisches Quellenwerk: Stoffquellen fuer Predigt und christliche Unterweisung. 3. Band/Anton Koch. —3. Aufl.. —Freiburg im Breisgau: Herder & Co. G. M. B. H. Verlagsbuchhandlung, c1939
8,481 S. ;23 cm.

B97/K76F313-2(1)
Das Religionsbuch der Kirche. 1. Teil, Einfuehrung und vom Glaubensbekenntnis/Anton Koch. —2. Aufl.. —Innsbruck: Verlag Felizian Rauch, 1932
272 S. ;17 cm.

B97/K93
Licht von seinem Lichte: Worte aus Ewigkeit und Vergaenglichkeit/Jakob Kroeker. —Giessen: Brunnen Verlag, c1935
104 S. ;18 cm.

B97/K95
Der Blumenstrauss des Hl. Franz von Assisi/Otto Kunze. —Tyrolia, Innsbruck, Wien, Muenchen, Bozen: Verlagsanstalt Tyrolia, Innsbruck, Wien, Muenchen, Bozen, 1921
134 S. ;23 cm.

B97/L274
Das apostolische Vikariat Tsinanfu: Franziskanische Missionsarbeit in China/Vitalis Lange. —Werl: Verlag der Provinzial Missionsverwaltung, 1929
210 S. ;24 cm.

B97/L326(4)
Evangelium hier und heute. 4. Band, Der religioese Sinn/Matthias Laros. —Regensburg: Verlag Friedrich Pustet, 1940
261 S. ;20 cm.

B97/L326-2
Pfingstgeist ueber uns: Die heilige Firmung als Sakrament der Persoenlichkeit, des allgemeinen Priestertums und des apostolischen Geisters hier und heute/M. Laros. —2. Aufl.. —Regensburg: Verlag Friedrich Pustet, [?]
219 S. ;19 cm.

B97/L326-3(1)
Evangelium hier und heute. 1. Teil, Frage und Antwort/M. Laros. —3. Aufl.. —Regensburg: Verlag Friedrich Pustet, 1937
247 S. ;20 cm.

B97/L366(11)
Die Heilige Schrift: fuer das Leben erklaert. Band XI, Das Evangelium des Hl. Matthaeus und des Hl. Markus/Willibald Lauck. —Freiburg im Breisgau: Herder & Co. G. m. b. H. Verlagsbuchhandlung, 1936
12,332 S. ;23 cm.

B97/L727(1)
Die wahre Braut Jesu Christi. 1. Theil/Alfons Maria von Liguori. —Regensburg: Verlag von Georg Joseph Manz, 1874
499 S. ;17 cm.

B97/L727-12
Die wahre Braut Jesu Christi: oder die durch Uebung der kloesterlichen Tugenden geheiligte Ordensperson/Alfons Maria von Liguori. —12.

Aufl..—Regensburg: Verlag Josef Koesel & Friedrich Pustet, c1923
16,696 S. ;17 cm.

B97/L765
Unseres Leidenden Herrn Reden und Schweigen vor den Menschen/Peter Lippert. —Freiburg im Breisgau: Herder & Co. G. m. b. H. Verlagsbuchhandlung, c1938
300 S. ;18 cm.

B97/L765-8
Der dreipersoenliche Gott/Peter Lippert. —8. Aufl..—Freiburg im Breisgau: Herder & Co. G. m. b. H. Verlagsbuchhandlung, 1939
136 S. ;17 cm.

B97/L923(2)
Hochschule der Gottesliebe: Die Exerzitien des heiligen Ignatius von Loyola. II. Band/Ignatius von Loyola. —Warendorf i. W. : J. Schnellsche Verlagsbuchhandlung, 1937
654 S. ;21 cm.

B97/M111
Von der Herrlichkeit christlichen Lebens/Johannes Maassen. —Freiburg im Breisgau: Verlag Herder, c1937
292 S. ;23 cm.

B97/M351
Christus unser Ideal/D. Columba Marmion. —Paderborn: Ferdinand Schoeningh Verlag, 1929
539 S. ;19 cm.

B97/M479
Das Urchristentum: Apologetische Abhandlungen/Franz Meffert. —Berlin: Verlag Gotthard Roll & Co., c1920
12,781 S. ;20 cm.

B97/M515
Die Vollendung der Welt im Opfer des Gottmenschen/Franz Meister. —Freiburg im Breisgau: Herder & Co. G. m. b. H. Verlagsbuchhandlung, c1938
248 S. ;23 cm.

B97/M515H877
Durch's Heilige Land: Fuehrer fuer Pilger und Reisende/Barnabas Meistermann. —Trier: Kunst- und Verlagsanstalt Schaar & Dathe, [?]
16,739 S. ;17 cm.

B97/M578-5(1)
Das Leben unseres Herrn Jesu Christi des Sohnes Gottes. Band I/Moritz Meschler. —5. Aufl..—Freiburg im Breisgau: Herder'sche Verlags-handlung, 1902
22,653 S. ;20 cm.

B97/M578-5(2)
Das Leben unseres Herrn Jesu Christi des Sohnes Gottes. Band II/Moritz Meschler. —5. Aufl..—Freiburg im Breisgau: Herder'sche Verlagshandlung, 1902
10,586 S. ;20 cm.

B97/M578-5(3)
Das Leben unseres Herrn Jesu Christi des Sohnes Gottes in Betrachtungen. Band III/Moritz Meschler. —5. Aufl..—Freiburg im Breisgau: Herder & Co. G. m. b. H. Verlagshandlung, 1932
453 S. ;17 cm.

B97/M578-13(2)
Das Leben unseres Herrn Jesu Christi des Sohnes Gottes in Betrachtungen. Band II/Moritz Meschler. —12. und 13. Aufl..—Freiburg im Breisgau: Herder & Co. G. m. b. H. Verlagshandlung, 1922
9,584 S. ;17 cm.

B97/M612-2(3)
Die Psalmen des Priesters Betrachtungsbuch.

3. Band/Wendelin Meyer.—2. Aufl..—Paderborn: Verlag der Bonifacius,1927
13,233 S.;18 cm.

B97/M612-2(4)
Die Psalmen des Priesters Betrachtungsbuch. 4. Band/Wendelin Meyer.—2. Aufl..—Paderborn: Verlag der Bonifacius,1932
13,246 S.;18 cm.

B97/M612-3
Mit ganzer Seele Ordensfrau: Schwestern-Konferenzen des Hochseligen Bischofs von Leitmeritz Dr. Josef Gross/P. Wendelin Meyer.—3. Aufl..—Kevelaer: Butzon & Bercker,1935
227 S.;20 cm.

B97/M612-4(1)
Die Psalmen des Priesters Betrachtungsbuch. 1. Band/Wendelin Meyer.—4. Aufl..—Paderborn: Verlag der Bonifacius,1923
23,286 S.;18 cm.

B97/M989-6(27)
Wissenschaftliche Handbibliothek. 27. Band, Christliche Aszetik/Franz Haver Muss.—6. Aufl..—Paderborn: Verlag von Ferdinand Schoeningh,1923
16,491;22 cm.

B97/O12
Drei Herrgottsbuben/Joseph Georg Oberkofler.—Innsbruck: Tyrolia Verlag,1937
234 S.;19 cm.

B97/O12(3)
Der heiligen Eucharistie geweihtes Jahr. III. Band, Im Feuer des Hl. Geistes/Clem. Oberhammer.—Innsbruck: Verlagsanstalt Tyrolia, 1923
332 S.;15 cm.

B97/P266-10(3)
Das Jahr des Heiles: Klosterneuburger Liturgiekalender fuer immerwaehrenden Gebrauch. 3. Band,Nachpfingstzeit/Pius Parsch.—10. Aufl..—klosterneuburg: Verlag Volksliturgisches Apostolat Klosterneuburg,1932
760,59,13 S.;17 cm.

B97/P266-11(1)
Das Jahr des Heiles: Klosterneuburger Liturgiekalender fuer immerwaehrenden Gebrauch. 1. Band,Weihnachtsteil/Plus Parsch.—11. Aufl..—Klosterneuburg: Verlag Volksliturgisches Apostolat,c1933
488,32 S.;18 cm.

B97/P266-12(1)
Das Jahr des Heiles: Klosterneuburger Liturgiekalender. 1. Band, Weihnachtsteil/Plus Parsch.—12. Aufl..—Klosterneuburg bei Wien: Verlag Volksliturgisches Apostolat,c1938
528 S.;18 cm.

B97/P266-12(2)
Das Jahr des Heiles: Klosterneuburger Liturgiekalender. 2. Band, Osterteil/Plus Parsch.—12. Aufl..—Klosterneuburg bei Wien: Verlag Volksliturgisches Apostolat,c1938
728,40 S.;18 cm.

B97/P266-12(3)
Das Jahr des Heiles: Klosterneuburger Liturgiekalender. 3. Band, Nachpfingstteil/Plus Parsch.—12. Aufl..—Klosterneuburg bei Wien: Verlag Volksliturgisches Apostolat,c1938
855,47,36 S.;18 cm.

B97/P481
Das Buch der Psalmen/Norbert Peters.—Paderborn: Verlag der Bonifacius-Druckerei,c1930
12,384 S.;20 cm.

B97/P531(6)

Buecher der Geisteserneuerung. 6. Band, Geister, die um Christus ringen/Karl Pfleger. —Leipzig: Verlag Anton Pustet, c1934

313 S. ; 19 cm.

B97/P594-2

Messiaskoenig Jesus: In der Auffassung seiner Zeitgenossen/Josef Pickl. —2. Aufl.. —Muenchen: Verlag Josef Koesel & Friedrich Pustet, c1935

286 S. ; 24 cm.

B97/P594-3

Messiaskoenig Jesus: In der Auffassung seiner Zeitgenossen/Josef Pickl. —3. Aufl.. —Muenchen: Verlag Josef Koesel & Friedrich Pustet, c1935

286 S. ; 24 cm.

B97/P658

Die Sakramentale Welt/Johannes Pinsk. —Freiburg im Breisgau: Herder & Co. G. M. B. H. Verlagsbuchhandlung, 1938

14, 214 S. ; 19 cm.

B97/P733-2

In Christus Jesus/Raoul Plus. —2. Aufl.. —Regensburg: Verlag von Josef Habbel, [?]

271 S. ; 19 cm.

B97/P733-3

Christus in unseren Bruedern/Raoul Plus. —3. Aufl.. —Regensburg: Hosef Habbel Verlag, [?]

277 S. ; 18 cm.

B97/R312(4)

Buecher der Geisteserneuerung. 4. Band, Liturgie und Persoenlichkeit/Virgil Redlich. —Leipzig: Verlag Anton Pustet, c1933

197 S. ; 19 cm.

B97/R559(1)

Die heilige Schrift des Alten Bundes: nach dem Grundtext uebersetzt. 1. Band, Geschichtliche Buecher/Paul Riessler. —Mainz: Matthias Gruenewald Verlag, 1924

16, 990 S. ; 22 cm.

B97/R559(2)

Die heilige Schrift des Alten Bundes: nach dem Grundtext uebersetzt. 2. Band, Weisheitsbuecher, Psalmen Propheten/Paul Riessler. —Mainz: Matthias Gruenewald Verlag, 1924

1168 S. ; 22 cm.

B97/R918

Vom Reichtum der Seele: Religioese Betrachtungen/Josef Ruehnel. —Mainz: Matthias Gruenewald Verlag, 1921

168 S. ; 18 cm.

B97/S163(1)

Theotimus: Abhandlung von der Gottesliebe. Band I/Franz von Sales. —Regensburg: Verlagsanstalt vorm. G. J. Manz A. G., 1931

20, 514 S. ; 18 cm.

B97/S163(2)

Theotimus: Abhandlung von der Gottesliebe. Band II/Franz von Sales. —Regensburg: Verlagsanstalt vorm. G. J. Manz A. G., 1931

12, 515 S. ; 18 cm.

B97/S291

Botschaft Jesu an seine Priester: Exerzitiengedanken/Joseph Schryvers. —Baden: Verlag der Schulbrueder, 1939

146 S. ; 17 cm.

B97/S294-2

Die Apokalypse des Hl. Johannes/Jakob Schaefer. —2. Aufl.. —Wien: Verlag Volksliturgisches Apostolat, c1938

130 S. ; 19 cm.

B97/S314

Die Mysterien des Christentums: Wesen, Bedeutung und Zusammenhang derselben nach der in ihrem uebernatuerlichen Charakter gegebenen Perspective dargestellt/M. J. Scheeben. —Freiburg im Breisgau: Herder'sche Verlagshandlung, 1865

16,772 S. ;22 cm.

B97/S314-3

Die Mysterien des Christentums nach Wesen, Bedeutung und Zusammenhang/Matthias Joseph Scheeben. —3. Aufl.. —Freiburg im Breisgau: Ferder & Co. G. m. b. H. Verlagsbuchhandlung, 1912

24,691 S. ;23 cm.

B97/S314-14

Die Herrlichkeiten der goettlichen Gnade/Matth. Joseph Scheeben. —13. und 14. Aufl.. —Freiburg im Breisgau: Herder & Co. G. m. b. H. Verlagsbuchhandlung, 1925

10,684 S. ;17 cm.

B97/S314F291

Die braeutliche Gottesmutter/Matthias Joseph Scheeben. —Freiburg im Breisgau: Herder & Co. G. m. b. H. Verlagsbuchhandlung, c1936

16,202 S. ;20 cm.

B97/S334-2

In der Schule Loyolas: Der Gedankengang der Ignatianischen Exerzitien/Hardy Schilgen. —2. Aufl.. —Freiburg im Breisgau: Herder & Co. G. m. b. H. Verlagsbuchhandlung, 1934

12,271 S. ;21 cm.

B97/S349-3

Organische Aszese: Ein zeitgemaesser, psychologisch orientierter Weg zur religioesen Lebensgestaltung/Hermann Schmidt. —3. Aufl.. —Paderborn: Ferdinand Schoeningh, c1938

478 S. ;22 cm.

B97/S358

Las Casas Vor Karl V: Szenen aus der Konquistadorenzeit/Reinhold Schneider. —Leipzig: Insel Verlag, [?]

203 S. ;20 cm.

B97/S383

Die Priestersorge: Weisungen der Vaetermystik zu der priesterlichen Doppelaufgabe: "Gehet hin" (Matth. 28, 19) und "Bleibet in mir" (Joh. 15, 4)/Johannes Schuck. —Paderborn: Ferdinand Schoeningh Verlag, c1929

229 S. ;19 cm.

B97/S385

Christus mit uns: Geist und Kraft der eucharistischen Wirklichkeit/Anton Schuetz. —Muenchen: Verlag Koesel Pustet, [?]

288 S. ;18 cm.

B97/S411-6

Erst-Kommunion-Unterricht: Zugleich ein Beitrag fuer die religioese Erziehung in der Schule/Jos. Schwarz. —6. Aufl.. —Rottenburg a. N.: Bader'sche Verlagsbuchhandlung, 1928

12,167 S. ;21 cm.

B97/S467

Der Priester in der Welt/Josef Sellmair. —Regensburg: Verlag Friedrich Pustet, c1939

284 S. ;22 cm.

B97/S479

Papstgeschichte/Franz Xaver Seppelt, Klemens Loeffler. —Muenchen: Verlag Koesel Pustet, c1933

14,441 S. ;24 cm.

B97/S565

Leben Jesu nach den vier Evangelien: Kurzgefasste Erklaerung/Joseph Sickenberger. —Muenster i. W. : Verlag der Aschendorffschen Verlagsbuchhandlung, [?]

12,211 S. ; 22 cm.

B97/S571(3)

Ad Majora. III. Teil, Rekollektionen fuer Priester/Joseph Siepe. —Kevelaer: Verlag Butzon & Bercker, 1936

125 S. ; 20 cm.

B97/S683

Das Geheimnis des Gebetes: Betrachtungen zu seiner theologischen Sinndeutung/Thaddaeus Soiron. —Freiburg im Breisgau: Herder & Co. G. m. b. H. Verlagsbuchhandlung, 1937

8,200 S. ; 19 cm.

B97/S864

Das Priestertum: Gedanken und Erwaegungen fuer Theologen und Priester/Wilhelm Stockums. —Freiburg im Breisgau: Herder & Co. G. m. b. H. Verlagsbuchhandlung, 1934

8,223 S. ; 20 cm.

B97/T365

Jenseitige Menschen: Eine Sinndeutung des Ordensstandes/Dominikus Thalhammer. —Freiburg im Breisgau: Herder & Co. G. m. b. H. Verlagsbuchhandlung, c1937

8,98 S. ; 20 cm.

B97/T584

Das Jesuskind in Flandern/Felix Timmermans. —Leipzig: Insel Verlag, [?]

231 S. ; 20 cm.

B97/T717

Christus und die Jugend/Tihamer Toth. —Freiburg im Breisgau: Herder & Co. G. m. b. H. Verlagsbuchhandlung, 1929

146 S. ; 20 cm.

B97/T717-3

Mit offenen Augen durch Gottes Natur/Tihamer Toth. —3. Aufl.. —Freiburg im Breisgau: Herder & Co. G. m. b. H. Verlagsbuchhandlung, 1937

176 S. ; 20 cm.

B97/T717-5(1)

Die zehn Gebote. I. Band/Tihamer Toth. —5. Aufl.. —Paderborn: Ferdinand Schoeningh Verlag, 1936

312 S. ; 21 cm.

B97/T717-5(2)

Die zehn Gebote. II. Band/Tihamer Toth. —5. Aufl.. —Paderborn: Ferdinand Schoeningh Verlag, 1936

334 S. ; 21 cm.

B97/V243

Das heilige Messopfer: Fuehrer zur Heiligkeit Geisteserhebungen/Dom Eugen Vandeur. —Regensburg: Verlag Friedrich Pustet, 1933

347 S. ; 15 cm.

B97/V742

Aszese und Mystik in der Vaeterzeit: Ein Abriss/Marcel Viller, Karl Rahner. —Freiburg im Breisgau: Herder & Co. G. m. b. H. Verlagsbuchhandlung, 1939

16,322 S. ; 24 cm.

B97/V982

Denken und Sein: Ein Aufbau der Erkenntnistheorie/Joseph de Vries. —Freiburg im Breisgau: Herder & Co. G. m. b. H. Verlagsbuchhandlung, c1937

8,304 S. ; 23 cm.

B97/W231-2

Die Herrlichkeit des christlichen Sterbens: Die heilige Oelung als letzte Vollendung der Taufherrlichkeit/Eugen Walter. —2. Aufl.. —

Freiburg im Breisgau: Herder & Co. G. m. b. H. Verlagsbuchhandlung, 1939
88 S. ;19 cm.

B97/W423
Zwischen Goettern und Daemonen: Vierzig Oden/Josef Weinheber. —Muenchen: Albert Langen/Georg Mueller Verlag, c1938
68 S. ;20 cm.

B97/W426
Eines nur ist notwendig: Exerzitien zur Umgestaltung in Christus durch Maria in vollkommener Liebe/Franz X. Weis. —Paderborn: Ferdinand Schoeningh, c1937
304 S. ;19 cm.

B97/W429(1)
Danken und Dienen: Schriften zur religioesen Bewaehrung und Betaetigung. 1. Band, Aus Liebe zur Jugend/Franz Weiss. —Einsiedeln: Verlagsanstalt Benziger & Co. A. —G. ,[?]
154 S. ;17 cm.

B97/W429(2)
Danken und Dienen: Schriften zur religioesen Bewaehrung und Betaetigung. 2. Band, Aus Liebe zur Familie/Franz Weiss. —Einsiedeln: Verlagsanstalt Benziger & Co. A. —G. ,[?]
143 S. ;17 cm.

B97/W689(4)
Mensch, Welt, Gott. Ein Aufbau der Philosophie in Einzeldarstellungen. 4. Band, Seele und Geist/Alexander Willwoll. —Freiburg im Breisgau: Herder & Co. G. m. b. H. Verlagsbuchhandlung, c1938
8,258 S. ;23 cm.

B97/W689-3
Das Leben Jesu im Lande und Volke Israel/Franz Michael Willam. —3. Aufl.. —Freiburg im Breisgau: Herder & Co. G. m. b. H. Verlagsbuchhandlung, c1932
12,529 S. ;20 cm.

B97/W689-7
Das Leben Jesu im Lande und Volke Israel/Franz Michael Willam. —6. und 7. Aufl.. —Freiburg im Breisgau: Herder & Co. G. m. b. H. Verlagsbuchhandlung, c1932
12,552 S. ;20 cm.

B97/W799
Das grosse Aergernis: Christus und die Christen/Hans Wirtz. —Innsbruck: Tyrolia Verlag, 1936
326 S. ;19 cm.

B97/W846
Das Koenigliche Gebot: Kleine Kapitel von der Naechstenliebe/Bonifaz Wohrmueller. —Muenchen: Josef Koesel & Friedrich Pustet Verlag, c1921
324 S. ;19 cm.

B97: D9-43/E34-4(2)
Lehrbuch des Kirchenrecht auf Grund des Codex Iuris Canoniel. II. Band, Sachenrecht II-VI, Prozessrecht, Strafrecht/Eduard Eichmann. —4. Aufl.. —Paderborn: Verlag Ferdinand Schoeningh, c1933
493 S. ;23 cm.

B97-43/Z73-2
Lehrbuch der Aszetik/Otto Zimmermann. —2. Aufl.. —Freiburg im Breisgau: Herder & Co. G. m. b. H. Verlagsbuchhandlung, 1932
16,700 S. ;23 cm.

B97-61/S632-2
Kirchenlateinisches Woerterbuch: Ausfuehrliches Woerterverzeichnis zum Roemischen Missale, Breviarium, Rituale, Graduale, Pontificale, Caeremoniale, Martyrologium, sowie zur Vulgata und zum Codex juris canonici/Albert

Sleumer. —2. Aufl.. —Limburg a. d. Lahn: Verlag von Gebrueder Steffen, 1926
840 S. ;24 cm.

B97-62/H641-2(1)
Handbuch zum Einheitskatechismus. 1. Hauptstueck, Die Wahrheit/Otto Hilker. —2. Aufl.. —Paderborn: Ferdinand Schoeningh Verlag, 1928
16,191 S. ;23 cm.

B97-62/H641-2(2)
Handbuch zum Einheitskatechismus. 2. Hauptstueck, Das Weg/Otto Hilker. —2. Aufl.. —Paderborn: Ferdinand Schoeningh Verlag, 1928
12,221 S. ;23 cm.

B97-62/H641-3(1)
Handbuch zum Einheitskatechismus. 1. Hauptstueck, Vom Glauben/Otto Hilker. —3. Aufl.. —Paderborn: Ferdinand Schoeningh Verlag, 1938
191 S. ;23 cm.

B97-62/P874-3
Handbuch der Mystik/August Poulain. —2. und 3. Aufl.. —Freiburg im Breisgau: Herder & Co. G. m. b. H. Verlagsbuchhandlung, 1925
23,564 S. ;17 cm.

B971/H476
Worte Gottes/Ernst Hello. —Leipzig: MCMXXXV bei Jakob Hegner, [?]
289 S. ;19 cm.

B971/K14(12)
Die helige Schrift: fuer das Leben erklaert. Band XII. /Edmund Kalt, Willibald Lauck. —Freiburg im Breisgau: Herder & Co. G. m. b. H. Verlagsbuchhandlung, c1936
16,453 S. ;23 cm.

B971/K14(14)
Die Heilige Schrift: fuer das Leben erklaert. Band XIV, Der Roemerbrief, Die beiden Korintherbriefe/Edmund Kalt, Willibald Lauck. —Freiburg im Breisgau: Herder & Co. G. m. b. H. Verlagsbuchhandlung, c1937
14,460 S. ;23 cm.

B971/K14-2
Biblische Archaeologie/Edmund Kalt. —2. Aufl.. —Freiburg im Breisgau: Herder & Co. G. m. b. H. Verlagsbuchhandlung, 1934
12,147 S. ;23 cm.

B971/K68-20
Praktischer Kommentar zur Biblischen Geschichte: mit einer Anweisung zur Erteilung des biblischen Geschichtsunterrichts und einer Konkordanz der Biblischen Geschichte und des Katechismus/Friedrich Justus Knecht. —20. Aufl.. —Freiburg im Breisgau: Herdersche Verlagshandlung, 1904
14,815 S. ;22 cm.

B971/P481-2
Unsere Bibel: Die Lebensquellen der Heiligen Schrift/Norbert Peters. —2. Aufl.. —Paderborn: Verlag von der Bonifacius, c1929
16,528 S. ;21 cm.

B971/R421-7(1)
Lebensvoller biblischer Unterricht: Hilfsbuch zur kath. Einheitsschulbibel. I. Band, Altes Testament/Gregor Rensing. —7. Aufl.. —Duesseldorf: Verlag von L. Schwann, [?]
15,262 S. ;22 cm.

B971/R421-8(2)
Lebensvoller biblischer Unterricht: Hilfsbuch zur kath. Einheitsschulbibel. II. Band, Neues Testament/Gregor Rensing. —8. Aufl.. —Duesseldorf: Verlag von L. Schwann, [?]
24,378 S. ;22 cm.

B971/R718-2

Auf biblischen Pfaden: Reiseerinnerungen/Konstantin Roesch. —2. Aufl.. —Paderborn: Ferdinand Schoeningh Verlag, 1933

254 S. ; 19 cm.

B971-61/G383

Kurze biblische Realkonkordanz/P. Thomas Villanova Gerster. —Paderborn: Ferdinand Schoeningh, c1937

611 S. ; 17 cm.

B971-61/K14-2(1)

Biblisches Reallexikon. 1. Band, A-K/Edmund Kalt. —2. Aufl.. —Paderborn: Ferdinand Schoeningh, 1938

8, 1084 S. ; 26 cm.

B971-61/K14-2(2)

Biblisches Reallexikon. 2. Band, L-Z/Edmund Kalt. —2. Aufl.. —Paderborn: Ferdinand Schoeningh, 1939

1076 S. ; 26 cm.

B971-61/L926-11(2)

Biblische Realkonkordanz: Repertorium fuer Prediger, Religionslehrer, Seelsorger und Theologen. 2. Band, K-Z/Sev. Luegs. —10. und 11. Aufl.. —Regensburg: Verlagsanstalt vorm. G. J. Manz, 1928

735 S. ; 24 cm.

B971-61/M228-5(1)

Biblische Realkonkordanz: Repertorium fuer Prediger, Religionslehrer, Seelsorger und Theologen. 1. Band, A-J/Bernhard Mairhofer. —5. Aufl.. —Regensburg: Verlagsanstalt vorm. G. J. Manz, 1900

12, 743 S. ; 24 cm.

B971-61/W132

Biblisches Beispiellexikon: Die heilige Schrift in Leben und Lehre fuer Katechese und Predigt/Alexander Wagner. —Paderborn: Ferdinand Schoeningh, c1938

8, 1520 S. ; 26 cm.

B971-62/F249(1)

Methodisches Handbuch zur mitteleren Ausgabe der katholischen Schulbibel von Ecker. 1. Band, Altes Testament/Nikolaus Fassbinder, Heinrich Fassbinder. —Trier: Mosella Verlag, c1922

435 S. ; 20 cm.

B971-62/F249(2)

Methodisches Handbuch zur mitteleren Ausgabe der katholischen Schulbibel von Ecker. 2. Band, Neues Testament/Nikolaus Fassbinder, Heinrich Fassbinder. —Trier: Mosella Verlag, c1924

682 S. ; 20 cm.

B971-62/K19

Handbuch zur Schulbibel/Karl Kastner. —Freibug im Breisgau: Herder & Co. G. m. b. H. Verlagsbuchhandlung, c1937

25, 506 S. ; 22 cm.

B971. 1/A416(6. 2)

Die heilige Schrift des Alten Testamentes. VI. Band, 2. Abteilung, Das Buch des Predigers oder Koheleth/Arthur Allgeier. —Bonn: Verlag von Peter Hanstein, c1925

56 S. ; 25 cm.

B971. 1/D853

Wollen und Wirken der alttestamentlichen Propheten/Lorenz Duerr. —Duesseldorf: L. Schwann Verlag, 1926

176 S. ; 22 cm.

B971. 1/D853H541

Religioese Lebenswerte des Alten Testaments/Lorenz Duerr. —Freiburg im Breisgau: Herder

& Co. G. m. b. H. Verlagsbuchhandlung, 1928
155 S. ; 20 cm.

B971. 1/F312(2. 2)
Die heilige Schrift des Alten Testamentes. II. Band, 2. Abteilung, Das Buch Deuteronomium/Franz Feldmann, Heinr. Herkenne. —Bonn: Peter Hanstein Verlagsbuchhandlung, c1933
10, 144 S. ; 25 cm.

B971. 1/F312(2. 3)
Die heilige Schrift des Alten Testamentes. II. Band, 3. Abteilung, Das Buch Josue/Franz Feldmann, Heinr. Herkenne. —Bonn: Peter Hanstein Verlagsbuchhandlung, 1924
78 S. ; 25 cm.

B971. 1/F312(2. 5)
Die heilige Schrift des Alten Testamentes. II. Band, 4. und 5. Abteilung, Das Buch der Richter und das Buch Ruth/Franz Feldmann, Heinr. Herkenne. —Bonn: Peter Hanstein Verlagsbuchhandlung, c1926
12, 129 S. ; 25 cm.

B971. 1/F312(6)
Die heilige Schrift des Alten Testamentes. VI. Band, Das Buch der Sprueche/Franz Feldmann, Heinr. Herkenne. —Bonn: Peter Hanstein Verlagsbuchhandlung, 1923
8, 100 S. ; 25 cm.

B971. 1/F312(7. 1)
Die heilige Schrift des Alten Testamentes. VII. Band, 1. Abteilung Das Buch Isaias/Franz Feldmann, Heinr. Herkenne. —Bonn: Peter Hanstein Verlagsbuchhandlung, c1937
9, 262 S. ; 25 cm.

B971. 1/F312(8. 1)
Die heilige Schrift des Alten Testamentes. VIII. Band, Das Buch Ezechiel, I. Haelfte/Franz Feldmann, Heinr. Herkenne. —Bonn: Peter Hanstein Verlagsbuchhandlung, 1923
236 S. ; 25 cm.

B971. 1/F312(8. 2)
Die heilige Schrift des Alten Testamentes. VIII. Band, Die zwoelf kleinen Propheten, II. Haelfte, NAHUM HABAKUK SOPHONIAS AGGAEUS ZACHARIAS MALACHIAS/Franz Feldmann, Heinr. Herkenne. —Bonn: Peter Hanstein Verlagsbuchhandlung, 1938
14, 229 S. ; 25 cm.

B971. 1/G599(8)
Die heilige Schrift des Alten Testamentes. VIII. Band, Das Buch Daniel/Johann Goettsberger. —Bonn: Peter Hanstein Verlagsbuchhandlung, c1928
8, 104 S. ; 25 cm.

B971. 1/G832-2
Altorientalische Bilder zum Alten Testament/Hugo Gressmann. —2. Aufl.. —Berlin: Verlag Walter De Gruyter & Co., 1927
11, 224, 260 S. ; 25 cm.

B971. 1/H468(1. 2)
Die heilige Schrift des Alten Testamentes. I. Band, 2. Abteilung, Das Buch Exodus/Paul Heinisch. —Bonn: Peter Hanstein Verlagsbuchhandlung, c1934
15, 297 S. ; 25 cm.

B971. 1/H468(2)
Die heilige Schrift des Alten Testamentes. II. Band, Das Buch Numeri/Paul Heinisch. —Bonn: Peter Hanstein Verlagsbuchhandlung, c1936
13, 141 S. ; 25 cm.

B971. 1/L525(3)
Die heilige Schrift des Alten Testamentes. III. Band, Die Buecher Samuel/Karl A. Leimbach. —Bonn: Peter Hanstein Verlagsbuchhandlung, c1936

13,234 S. ;25 cm.

B971. 1/S886

Die Froemmigkeit im Alten Testament/Rupert Storr. —M. Gladbach: Volksvereins Verlag, c1928

295 S. ;24 cm.

B971. 1-61/B917-17

Wilhelm Gesenius' hebraeisches und aramaeisches Handwoerterbuch ueber das Alte Testament/Frants BuHl. —17. Aufl.. —Leipzig: Verlag von F. C. W. Vogel, 1921

19,1013 S. ;24 cm.

B971. 2/D244-3(1)

Die heilige Schrift des Neuen Testamentes. I. Band, Die drei Aelteren Evangelien/Petrus Dausch. —3. Aufl.. —Bonn: Verlag von Peter Hanstein, 1923

548 S. ;24 cm.

B971. 2/D543-2

Die Pastoralbriefe: Handbuch zum neuen Testament/Martin Dibelius. —2. Aufl.. —Tuebingen: Verlag von J. C. B. Mohr, 1931

101 S. ;25 cm.

B971. 2/G914-3

Das Bild von Jesus dem Christus im Neuen Testament/Romano Guardini. —3. Aufl.. —Wuerzburg: Werkbund Verlag, 1939

126 S. ;22 cm.

B971. 2/K66-3

Das Markusevangelium/Erich Klostermann. —3. Aufl.. —Tuebingen: Verlag von J. C. B. Mohr (Paul Siebeck), 1936

174 S. ;24 cm.

B971. 2/L716-4

An die Roemer: Einfuehrung in die Textgeschichte der Paulusbriefe/Hans Lietzmann. —4. Aufl.. —Tuebingen: Verlag von J. C. B. Mohr (Paul Siebeck), 1933

136 S. ;24 cm.

B971. 2/S565-4(1)

Die heilige Schrift des Neuen Testamentes. I. Band, Die Geschichte des Neuen Testamentes/Joseph Sickenberger. —4. Aufl.. —Bonn: Peter Hanstein Verlagsbuchhandlung, c1934

8,91 S. ;24 cm.

B971. 2/S565-4(6)

Die heilige Schrift des Neuen Testamentes. VI. Band, Die Briefe des heiligen Paulus an die Korinther und Roemer/Joseph Sickenberger. —4. Aufl.. —Bonn: Peter Hanstein Verlagsbuchhandlung, 1932

18,333 S. ;24 cm.

B971. 2/S823

Die Apostelgeschichte/Alphons Steinmann. —Bonn: Verlag von Peter Hanstein, 1916

12,244,124,12,291,143 S. ;24 cm.

B971. 2/S823-3(4-6)

Die heilige Schrift des Neuen Testamentes. IV. —VI. Band/Alphons Steinmann. —3. Aufl.. —Bonn: Peter Hanstein Verlagsbuchhandlung, c1923

124,12,291,143,101 S. ;24 cm.

B971. 2/S894(4. 1)

Kommentar zum Neuen Testament: Aus Talmud und Midrasch. 4. Band, Exkurse zu einzelnen Stellen des Neuen Testaments. 1. Teil/Hermann L. Strack, Paul Billerbeck. —Muenchen: C. H. Beck'sche Verlagsbuchhandlung Oskar Beck, 1928

610 S. ;23 cm.

B971. 2/T574-4(3)

Die heilige Schrift des Neuen Testamentes. III. Band, Das Johannesevangelium/Fritz Till-

mann. —4. Aufl.. —Bonn: Peter Hanstein Verlagsbuchhandlung, c1931
12, 364 S.; 24 cm.

B971. 2/T574-4(4)
Die heilige Schrift des Neuen Testamentes. IV. Band, Die Apostelgeschichte/Fritz Tillmann, Alphons Steinmann. —4. Aufl.. —Bonn: Peter Hanstein Verlagsbuchhandlung, c1934
15, 329 S.; 24 cm.

B971. 2/T574-4(5)
Die heilige Schrift des Neuen Testamentes. V. Band, Die Briefe an die Thessalonicher und Galater/Fritz Tillmann, Alphons Steinmann. —4. Aufl.. —Bonn: Peter Hanstein Verlagsbuchhandlung, c1935
8, 179 S.; 24 cm.

B971. 2/T574-4(8)
Die heilige Schrift des Neuen Testamentes. VIII. Band, Die Pastoralbriefe des heiligen Paulus/Fritz Tillmann, Max Meinertz. —4. Aufl.. —Bonn: Peter Hanstein Verlagsbuchhandlung, c1931
8, 128 S.; 24 cm.

B971. 2/T574-4(9)
Die heilige Schrift des Neuen Testamentes. IX. Band, Die katholischen Briefe/Fritz Tillmann, Max Meinertz, Wilhelm Vrede. —4. Aufl.. —Bonn: Peter Hanstein Verlagsbuchhandlung, c1932
8, 200 S.; 24 cm.

B971. 2/T574-4(10)
Die heilige Schrift des Neuen Testamentes. X. Band, Der Hebraeerbrief und die Geheime Offenbarung des heiligen Johannes/Fritz Tillmann, Ignaz Rohr. —4. Aufl.. —Bonn: Peter Hanstein Verlagsbuchhandlung, c1932
8, 142 S.; 24 cm.

B971. 2-61/B344-3
Griechisch-Deutsches Woerterbuch zu den Schriften des Neuen Testaments und der uebrigen urchristlichen Literatur/Walter Bauer. —3. Aufl.. —Berlin: Verlag Alfred Toepelmann, c1937
12, 1490 S.; 27 cm.

B971. 2-61/K62(2)
Theologisches Woerterbuch zum Neuen Testament. 2. Band/Gerhard Kittel. —Stuttgart: Verlag von W. Kohlhammer, 1935
12, 958 S.; 30 cm.

B971. 2-61/P943-3
Griechisch-deutsches Woerterbuch zum Neuen Testament/Erwin Preuschen. —3. Aufl.. —Berlin: Verlag Alfred Toepelmann, c1937
188 S.; 19 cm.

B972/A923(3. 3)
Die Hauptwerke des Aurelius Augustinus. III. Band, Ueber den Gottesstaat. 3. Teil/Aurelius Augustinus. —Muenchen: Verlag Koesel Pustet, [?]
522 S.; 19 cm.

B972/A923(7)
Die Hauptwerke des Aurelius Augustinus. VII. Band, Augustinus Bekenntnisse/Aurelius Augustinus. —Muenchen: Verlag Koesel Pustet, [?]
9, 378 S.; 19 cm.

B972/A923(8)
Die Hauptwerke des Aurelius Augustinus. VIII. Band, Ausgewaehlte Schriften/Aurelius Augustinus. —Muenchen: Verlag Koesel Pustet, [?]
502 S.; 19 cm.

B972/B918-2(2)
Lexikon fuer Theologie und Kirche. 2. Band,

Bartholomaeus bis Colonna/Michael Buchberger. —2. Aufl.. —Freiburg im Breisgau: Herder & Co. G. M. B. H. Verlagsbuchhandlung, c1930
16, 1024 S. ; 26 cm.

B972/B918-2(3)
Lexikon fuer Theologie und Kirche. 3. Band, Colorbasus bis Filioque/Michael Buchberger. —2. Aufl.. —Freiburg im Breisgau: Herder & Co. G. M. B. H. Verlagsbuchhandlung, c1931
8, 1040 S. ; 26 cm.

B972/B918-2(4)
Lexikon fuer Theologie und Kirche. 4. Band, Filippini bis Heviter/Michael Buchberger. —2. Aufl.. —Freiburg im Breisgau: Herder & Co. G. M. B. H. Verlagsbuchhandlung, c1932
8, 1040 S. ; 26 cm.

B972/B918-2(6)
Lexikon fuer Theologie und Kirche. 6. Band, Kirejewski bis Maura/Michael Buchberger. —2. Aufl.. —Freiburg im Breisgau: Herder & Co. G. M. B. H. Verlagsbuchhandlung, c1934
8, 1040 S. ; 26 cm.

B972/B918-2(8)
Lexikon fuer Theologie und Kirche. 8. Band/Michael Buchberger. —2. Aufl.. —Freiburg im Breisgau: Herder & Co. G. M. B. H. Verlagsbuchhandlung, c1936
13, 1040 S. ; 26 cm.

B972/F291
Das Mysterium der heiligen Kirche: Dogmatische Untersuchungen zum Wesen der Kirche/Carl Feckes. —Paderborn: Verlag Ferdinand Schoeningh, c1933
222 S. ; 23 cm.

B972/F452
In jener Zeit... : Wege ins unbekannte Evangelium/Emil Fiedler. —Salzburg: Verlag Anton Pustet, c1938
295 S. ; 20 cm.

B972/J76-5
Katholische Moraltheologie: Unter besonderer Beruecksichtigung des Codex Iuris Canonici sowie des deutschen, oesterreichischen und schweizerischen Rechts/Heribert Jone. —5. Aufl.. —Paderborn: Verlag Ferdinand Schoeningh, c1929
687 S. ; 16 cm.

B972/J91-2
Der mystische Leib Christi als Grundprinzip der Aszetik: Aufbau des religioesen Lebens und Strebens aus dem Corpus Christi mysticum/Friedrich Juergensmeier. —2. Aufl.. —Paderborn: Ferdinand Schoeningh, c1933
381 S. ; 23 cm.

B972/J91-7
Der mystische Leib Christi als Grundprinzip der Aszetik: Aufbau des religioesen Lebens und Strebens aus dem Corpus Christi mysticum/Friedrich Juergensmeier. —7. Aufl.. —Paderborn: Ferdinand Schoeningh, c1935
346 S. ; 23 cm.

B972/K77
Die Kirche unseres Glaubens: Eine theologische Grundlegung katholischer Weltanschauung/Ludwig Koesters. —Freiburg im Breisgau: Herder & Co. G. m. b. H. Verlagsbuchhandlung, 1935
10, 264 S. ; 23 cm.

B972/K77-3
Die Kirche unseres Glaubens: Eine theologische Grundlegung katholischer Weltanschauung/Ludwig Koesters. —3. Aufl.. —Freiburg im Breisgau: Herder & Co. G. m. b. H. Verlagsbuchhandlung, 1938
12, 264 S. ; 23 cm.

B972/M447-2(2)

Die Ethik des heiligen Augustinus. 2. Band, Die sittliche Befaehigung des Menschen und ihre Verwirklichung/Joseph Mausbach. —2. Aufl.. — Freiburg im Breisgau: Herder & Co. G. m. b. H. Verlagsbuchhandlung, 1929

8,431 S. ;23 cm.

B972/M784(1)

Gesammelte Werke des seligen Ludwig Maria Grignion von Montfort. 1. Band, Abhandlung ueber die vollkommene Andacht zu Maria/Ludwig Maria Grignion von Montfort. —Freiburg: Verlag der paepstlichen Kanisiusdruckerei, 1925

46,308 S. ;20 cm.

B972/P895(2)

Deus Semper Maior: Theologie der Exerzitien. II. Band, Zweite Woche/Erich Przywara. — Freiburg im Breisgau: Herder & Co. G. m. b. H. Verlagsbuchhandlung, 1939

24,355 S. ;22 cm.

B972/P895(3)

Deus Semper Maior: Theologie der Exerzitien. III. Band/Erich Przywara. —Freiburg im Breisgau: Herder & Co. G. m. b. H. Verlagsbuchhandlung, 1940

22,442 S. ;22 cm.

B972/S683

Heilige Theologie: Grundsaetzliche Darlesungen/Thaddaeus Soiron. —Regensburg: Verlag Friedrich Pustet, [?]

178 S. ;19 cm.

B972/T161

Grundriss der aszetischen und mystischen Theologie/Ad. Tanquerey. —Paris: Societe de Saint Jean L'evangeliste Desclee & Cie, c1931

55,1104,32 S. ;17 cm.

B972/W848(1)

Fuenf Minuten Christenlehre: Drei Reihen Katechismuslesungen. 1. Band/Leo Wolpert. — Regensburg: Verlag Friedrich Pustet, 1938

168 S. ;19 cm.

B972/W848(2)

Fuenf Minuten Christenlehre: Drei Reihen Katechismuslesungen. 2. Band/Leo Wolpert. — Regensburg: Verlag Friedrich Pustet, 1938

182 S. ;19 cm.

B972/W848(3)

Fuenf Minuten Christenlehre: Drei Reihen Katechismuslesungen. 3. Band/Leo Wolpert. — Regensburg: Verlag Friedrich Pustet, 1937

203 S. ;19 cm.

B972-43/B283-5(2)

Lehrbuch der Dogmatik. 2. Band/Bernhard Bartmann. —4. und 5. Aufl.. —Freiburg im Breisgau: Herder & Co. G. m. b. H. Verlagsbuchhandlung, 1921

9,544 S. ;24 cm.

B972-43/B283-6(2)

Lehrbuch der Dogmatik. 2. Band/Bernhard Bartmann. —6. Aufl.. —Freiburg im Breisgau: Herder & Co. G. m. b. H. Verlagsbuchhandlung, 1923

9,547 S. ;24 cm.

B972-43/G454-9(2)

Lehrbuch der Dogmatik. 2. Band/Michael Gierens. —9. Aufl.. —Paderborn: Verlag Ferdinand Schoeningh, c1937

599 S. ;22 cm.

B972-62/S385-20

Handbuch der Pastoraltheologie: Allgemeine und spezielle Liturgik/P. Ignaz Schuech, P. Amand Polz. —19. und 20. Aufl.. —Innsbruck: Verlag von Felizian Rauch, 1925

917 S. ;24 cm.

B972-62/S385P762-20

Handbuch der Pastoraltheologie: Person der Hirten. Homiletik, Katechetik/P. Ignaz Schuech, P. Amand Polz.—19. und 20. Aufl..—Innsbruck: Verlag von Felizian Rauch, 1924

304 S. ;24 cm.

B975/A243

Menschenweisheit und Gottesweisheit im Laufe der Jahrtausende: Jugendfuehrer ins Land der Philosophie fuer Jugend und Jugendfuehrer mit Anschauungstafeln und Zeichnungen/Joseph Adrian.—Limburg a. d. Lahn: Verlag Gebr. Steffen,1937

311,15 S. ;17 cm.

B975/A465

Zeit fuer Gott: Vom Leben und Wirken des Vereinigten Gottes in uns/Odilo Altmann.—Innsbruck: Tyrolia Verlag,1937

214 S. ;19 cm.

B975/B139(6)

Buecher der Weltmission. 6. Band, Helden der Weltmission/Franz Baeumker.—Aachen: Xaverius Verlagsbuchhandlung A. G. ,1923

24,372 S. ;26 cm.

B975/B284(1. 1)

Die kirchliche Dogmatik. 1. Band, Die Lehre vom Wort Gottes. 1. Teil/Karl Barth.—Muenchen: Chr. Kaiser Verlag,1932

14,528 S. ;24 cm.

B975/B351-3(3)

Werde Licht!: Liturgische Betrachtungen an den Sonn- und Wochentagen des Kirchenjahres. III. Teil, Osterfestkreis die Nachpfingstzeit/Benedikt Baur.—3. Aufl..—Freiburg im Breisgau: Herder & Co. G. m. b. H. Verlagsbuchhandlung,c1937

15,691 S. ;16 cm.

B975/B548-2

Charismen priesterlicher Gesinnung und Arbeit: Skizzen und Winke fuer Tage der Recollectio/Adolf Kardinal Bertram.—2. Aufl..—Freiburg im Breisgau: Herder & Co. G. m. b. H. Verlagsbuchhandlung,1933

9,207 S. ;23 cm.

B975/B662

Missa Est: Buch der messliturgischen Bildungswerte/Linus Bopp.—Freiburg im Breisgau: Herder & Co. G. m. b. H. Verlagsbuchhandlung,1938

244 S. ;18 cm.

B975/B828-8

Wenn es in der Seele dunkelt: Ein Buch fuer die Muehseligen und Beladenen/Henriette Brey.—7. und 8. Aufl..—Freiburg im Breisgau: Herder & Co. G. m. b. H. Verlagsbuchhandlung,1929

225 S. ;17 cm.

B975/B836

Das wesentliche Gebet/Henri Bremond.—Regensburg: Verlag Friedrich Pustet,1936

291 S. ;22 cm.

B975/B858

Die heilige Messe: in ihrem Werden und Wesen/Johannes Brinktrine.—Paderborn: Ferdinand Schoeningh Verlag,1931

288 S. ;21 cm.

B975/B899-2(1)

Lehrbuch der Apologetik. 1. Band, Religion und Offenbarung/Johannes Brunsmann.—2. Aufl..—St. Gabriel bei Wien: Verlag der Missionsdruckerei,1930

16,459 S. ;23 cm.

B975/B928

Hundert Tage Sonnenschein: Ein Buch vom Sonntag und Alltag des Lebens/Bruno H. Buergel. —Berlin: Im Deutschen Verlag, c1940

229 S. ; 21 cm.

B975/C475

Unser Wandel mit Gott: Dreiunddreissig Betrachtungen/J. Clemens. —Paderborn: Verlag Ferdinand Schoeningh, 1931

252 S. ; 17 cm.

B975/D299

Predigt-Gedanken: Skizzen zu kurzen Ansprachen fuer alle Sonn- und Feiertage des Kirchenjahres/Wilhelm Dederichs. —Freiburg im Breisgau: Herder & Co. G. m. b. H. Verlagsbuchhandlung, 1926

11, 104 S. ; 19 cm.

B975/D578

Das Wort vom Logos: Vorlesungen ueber den Johannes-Prolog/Josef Dillersberger. —Salzburg: Verlag Anton Pustet, c1935

213 S. ; 21 cm.

B975/D652

Neue Stunde des Kindes: Kinderpredigten und Anregungen zur Gestaltung des Kindergottesdienstes/Karl Doerner. —Freiburg im Breisgau: Herder & Co. G. m. b. H. Verlagsbuchhandlung, 1936

13, 236 S. ; 20 cm.

B975/E16-3(1)

Sonn- und Festtagsklaenge aus dem Kirchenjahr: Ein Jahrgang Predigten. 1. Band/Franz Xaver Eberle. —2. und 3. Aufl.. —Freiburg im Breisgau: Herdersche Verlagsbuchhandlung, 1919

8, 396 S. ; 18 cm.

B975/E33-4(2)

Kanzel-Reden. 2. Band, Das Kirchenjahr/Joseph Georg von Ehrler. —4. Aufl.. —Freiburg im Breisgau: Herdersche Verlagshandlung, 1913

775 S. ; 24 cm.

B975/E33-4(4-5)

Kanzel-Reden. 4. und 5. Band, Das Kirchenjahr/Joseph Georg von Ehrler. —4. Aufl.. —Freiburg im Breisgau: Herdersche Verlagshandlung, 1916

524, 8, 325 S. ; 24 cm.

B975/E57(1)

Jahr des Heiles: Predigten fuer die Sonn- und Festtage des Kirchenjahres. 1. Teil, Sonntage von Advent bis Pfingsten/Joh. Engel. —Breslau: G. P. Aderholz' Buchhandlung, 1928

245 S. ; 19 cm.

B975/E57(2)

Jahr des Heiles: Predigten fuer die Sonn- und Festtage des Kirchenjahres. 2. Teil, Sonntage von Pfingsten bis Advent/Joh. Engel. —Breslau: G. P. Aderholz' Buchhandlung, 1929

229 S. ; 19 cm.

B975/F423-2

Ordnung zum Ewigen: Der Mensch in der religioesen Wirklichkeit seines Lebens/Georg Feuerer. —2. Aufl.. —Regensburg: Verlag Friedrich Pustet, [?]

229 S. ; 20 cm.

B975/F499(1)

Supra Petram. 1. Band, Festtags-Predigten/Stephan Fink. —Rottenburg a. N. : Bader'sche Verlagsbuchhandlung, 1930

8, 326, 16 S. ; 19 cm.

B975/F499(2)

Supra Petram. 2. Band, Sonntags-Predigten/Stephan Fink. —Rottenburg a. N. : Bader'sche

Verlagsbuchhandlung,1933
8,324 S. ;19 cm.

B975/G569(3)
Seelenbrot: Predigten, Ansprachen und Vortraege. 3. Band/Joseph Gmelch. —Rottenburg a. R. :Bader'sche Verlagsbuchhandlung,1934
307 S. ;19 cm.

B975/G569(4)
Seelenbrot: Predigten, Ansprachen und Vortraege. 4. Band/Joseph Gmelch. —Rottenburg a. R. :Bader'sche Verlagsbuchhandlung,1936
167 S. ;19 cm.

B975/G877-3
Ich glaube: Eine Auslegung des apostolischen Glaubensbekenntnisses/Robert Grosche. —3. Aufl.. —Paderborn: Bonifacius Druckerei GmbH. ,c1936
249 S. ;23 cm.

B975/H249-3
Kanzelvortraege fuer Sonn- und Feiertage: Gehalten in der Kirche St Martin zu Freiburg/Heinrich Hansjakob. —3. Aufl.. —Freiburg im Breisgau: Herdersche Verlagshandlung,1910
12,555 S. ;23 cm.

B975/H353
Vom Reiche Gottes: Sieben Predigten/Johannes Hassfeld. —Paderborn: Verlag der Bonlifacius Druckerei,1940
120 S. ;19 cm.

B975/H367
Heiliger Aufgang: Sonntagslesung/Johannes Hatzfeld. —Paderborn: Verlag der Bonifacius Druckerei,c1930
238 S. ;20 cm.

B975/H371
Vom Geheimnis der heiligen Messe/Donatus Haugg. —Muenchen: Verlag Koesel Pustet,[?]
168 S. ;19 cm.

B975/H469
Schwester Gertrud erzaehlt/Karl-Borromaeus Heinrich. —Muenchen: Verlagsanstalt vorm. G. J. Manz,[?]
230 S. ;20 cm.

B975/H641
Zum Altare Gottes: Vorbereitung der Kinder auf die Erstkommunion/Otto Hilker. —Paderborn: Ferdinand Schoeningh,c1938
139 S. ;19 cm.

B975/H699-2
Eins ist not!:Ein dritter Jahrgang Predigten, meistens ueber freie Texte/H. Hoffmann. —2. Aufl.. —Halle a. S. :Richard Muehlmann's Verlagshandlung,1903
9,403 S. ;22 cm.

B975/J22
Meine heilige Messe: Freundesbriefe/Rudolf Jaeger. —Paderborn: Verlag Bonifacius Druckerei,[?]
160 S. ;19 cm.

B975/K29-2
Salve Regina: Muttergottespredigten/E. Keller. —2. Aufl.. —Paderborn: Ferdinand Schoeningh Verlag,1937
112 S. ;21 cm.

B975/K92
Die Herrgottsseele/Martin Kreuser. —Einsiedeln: Verlagsanstalt Benziger & Co. A. G. , 1925
243 S. ;18 cm.

B975/K95
Ziele und Wege/Joseph Kuehnel. —Wiesbaden: Verlag Hermann Rauch,1925

176 S. ;18 cm.

B975/L727-2

Schule der christlichen Vollkommenheit fuer Welt- und Ordensleute/Alphons Maria von Liguori. —2. Aufl..—Regensburg: Verlag von Friedrich Pustet,1898

16,702 S. ;21 cm.

B975/L765

Der Mensch Job redet mit Gott/Peter Lippert. —Muenchen: Verlag Ars Sacra Josef Mueller,c1934

301 S. ;19 cm.

B975/L765-4(5)

Credo: Darstellungen aus dem Gebiet der christlichen Glaubenslehre. 5. Baendchen, Die Gnaden Gottes/Peter Lippert. —3. und 4. Aufl..—Freiburg im Breisgau: Herder & Co. G. m. b. H. Verlagsbuchhandlung,c1923

153 S. ;17 cm.

B975/L933

Die Reichtuemer des goettlichen Herzens Jesu: Gedanken und Erwaegungen zur Herz Jesu Litanei/Joseph Lucas. —Limburg: Pallottiner Verlag,1936

428 S. ;19 cm.

B975/M184

Zurueck zur Messe! /Robert Maeder. —Basel: Verlag Nazareth,1937

141 S. ;19 cm.

B975/M332

Die betende Kirche: Ein liturgisches Volksbuch/Abtei Marialaach. —Berlin: Sankt Augustinus Verlag,c1924

14,510,25 S. ;27 cm.

B975/M946-9

Zeremonienbuechlein fuer Priester und Kandidaten des Priestertums/Joh. Vapt Mueller. —9. Aufl..—Freiburg im Breisgau: Herder & Co. G. m. b. H. Verlagsbuchhandlung,c1926

16,299 S. ;16 cm.

B975/M946-15

Zeremonienbuechlein fuer Priester und Kandidaten des Priestertums/Joh. Vapt Mueller. —13. bis 15. Aufl..—Freiburg im Breisgau: Herder & Co. G. m. b. H. Verlagsbuchhandlung,1934

14,304 S. ;16 cm.

B975/N553

Die Kirche und die Welt: Predigten/John Henry Kardinal Newman. —Leipzig: Verlag Jakob Hegner,[?]

219 S. ;19 cm.

B975/N665

Das allgemeine Priestertum der Glaeubigen/Engelbert Niebecker. —Paderborn: Verlag von Ferdinand Schoeningh,c1936

173 S. ;19 cm.

B975/O12

Gottessaat und Seelenernte: Eine Sammlung von 52 Gelegenheits-Predigten und Vortraegen/Andreas Obendorfer. —Regensburg: Verlagsanstalt vorm. G. J. Manz,1928

8,354 S. ;21 cm.

B975/P266-2

Messerklaerung: Im Geister der liturgischen Erneuerung/Pius Parsch. —2. Aufl..—Klosterneuburg bei Wien: Verlag Volksliturgisches Apostolat,1935

359 S. ;18 cm.

B975/R312

Lehre mich Deine Wege! /Virgil Redlich. —Innsbruck: Verlagsanstalt Tyrolia,c1932

292 S. ;21 cm.

B975/R393

Das Hochzeitsmahl: Kommunionpredigten im Anschluss an das sonntaegliche Kommuniongebet der Kirche/Aloys Renkel. —Paderborn: Ferdinand Schoeningh Verlag, 1931

207 S. ;21 cm.

B975/R554(1)

Reifende Saaten: Auf Gottes Ackerfeld/Neue Folge. 1. Teil, Von Advent bis Pfingsten/Julius Rieger. —Rottenburg a. N. :Bader'sche Verlagsbuchhandlung, 1934

12,235 S. ;18 cm.

B975/R554(3)

Gedenkblaetter aus dem Leben und schriftlichen Nachlasse des Domkapitulars Paul Stiegele. III. Band, Ausgewaehlte Predigten/B. Rieg. —Rottenburg a. N. :Wilhelm Bader, 1905

494 S. ;23 cm.

B975/S291

Die Hingabe an Gott: Ein Wegbereiter zu den Hoehenpfaden seelischen Friedens/P. Joseph Schryvers. —Baden: Schulbrueder Verlag, 1935

13,176 S. ;19 cm.

B975/S348(1)

Konferenzen fuer die monatliche Geisteserneuerung. 1. Band, Hindernisse des geistlichen Fortschrittes/P. Max Schmid. —Muenchen: Verlag Josef Koesel & Friedrich Pustet, 1929

346 S. ;17 cm.

B975/S348(5)

Konferenzen fuer die monatliche Geisteserneuerung. 5. Band, Die geistlichen Uebungen/P. Max Schmid. —Regensburg: Verlagsanstalt vorm. G. J. Manz, 1934

302 S. ;17 cm.

B975/S358-16

Das andere Leben: Ernst und Trost der christlichen Welt- und Lebensanschauung/Wilhelm Schneider. —15. und 16. Aufl.. —Paderborn: Verlag von Ferdinand Schoeningh, 1923

15,540 S. ;19 cm.

B975/S364-3

Die Verwaltung der heiligen Sakramente: Unter pastoralen Gesichtspunkten/Otto Schoellig. —3. Aufl.. —Freiburg im Breisgau: Verlag Herder, 1946

9,442 S. ;22 cm.

B975/S395(1)

Liber Sacramentorum: Geschichtliche und liturgische Studien ueber das roemische Messbuch. I. Band/Ildefons Schuster. —Regensburg: Verlag Friedrich Pustet, [?]

217 S. ;20 cm.

B975/S395(3)

Liber Sacramentorum: Geschichtliche und liturgische Studien ueber das roemische Messbuch. III. Band/Ildefons Schuster. —Regensburg: Verlag Friedrich Pustet, [?]

243 S. ;20 cm.

B975/S395(5)

Liber Sacramentorum: Geschichtliche und liturgische Studien ueber das roemische Messbuch. V. Band/Ildefons Kardinal Schuster. —Regensburg: Verlag Friedrich Pustet, [?]

204 S. ;20 cm.

B975/S395(6)

Liber Sacramentorum: Geschichtliche und liturgische Studien ueber das roemische Messbuch. VI. Band/Ildefons Kardinal Schuster. —Regensburg: Verlag Friedrich Pustet, [?]

225 S. ;20 cm.

B975/S395(9)

Liber Sacramentorum: Geschichtliche und liturgische Studien ueber das roemische Mess-

buch. IX. Band/Ildefons Kardinal Schuster. —Regensburg：Verlag Friedrich Pustet，[?]
220 S. ；20 cm.

B975/S395(10)
Liber Sacramentorum. X. Band，Sachregister/Ildefons Kardinal Schuster. —Regensburg：Verlag Friedrich Pustet，[?]
180 S. ；20 cm.

B975/S398
Von Fest zu Fest durch das Kirchenjahr：Kurze Predigtentwuerfe/W. Fr. Schwierholz. —Regensburg：Verlag Friedrich Pustet，1935
153 S. ；20 cm.

B975/S683
Die Predigt Heute/Thaddaeus Soiron. —Paderborn：Ferdinand Schoeningh，c1937
125 S. ；19 cm.

B975/S798
Jesus und sein Priester：Gedanken ueber die Groesse und die Heiligkeit des Priestertums/Josef Staudinger. —Freiburg im Breisgau：Herder & Co. G. m. b. H. Verlagsbuchhandlung，1936
8，296 S. ；20 cm.

B975/S855-3(2)
Gedenkblaetter aus dem Leben und schriftlichen Nachlasse des Domkapitulars Paul Stiegele. II. Band，Fastenpredigten/Paul Stiegele. —3. Aufl.. —Rottenburg a. N. ：Wilhelm Bader，1907
8，370 S. ；23 cm.

B975/S961-2
Geistliche Zwiegespraeche：Unterricht ueber die christliche Vollkommenheit/Joseph Surin. —2. Aufl.. —Paderborn：Verlag der Bonifacius Druckerei，c1929
427 S. ；16 cm.

B975/T539
Das helle Segel/Georg Thurmair，Josef Rick. —Freiburg im Breisgau：Verlag Herder，[?]
231 S. ；20 cm.

B975/T665(2)
Im Geiste des Evangeliums：Homilien und Predigten auf alle Sonn- und Festtage des Kirchenjahres. II. Teil，Der Osterkreis/Jos. Tongelen. —Innsbruck：Verlagsanstalt Tyrolia A. G. ，c1927
162 S. ；23 cm.

B975/V523(1)
Die Verehrung des hlst. Herzens Jesu. 1. Band，Uebung der Herz-Jesu-Verehrung/A. Vermeersch. —Innsbruck：Verlag von Fel. Rauch，1925
560 S. ；19 cm.

B975/V523(2)
Die Verehrung des hlst. Herzens Jesu. 2. Band，Lehre und Liturgie der Herz-Jesu-Verehrung/A. Vermeersch. —Innsbruck：Verlag von Fel. Rauch，1925
335 S. ；19 cm.

B975/W231
Die Eucharistie：Das Sakrament der Gemeinschaft/Eugen Walter. —Freiburg im Breisgau：Herder & Co. G. m. b. H. Verlagsbuchhandlung，c1939
8. 92 S. ；18 cm.

B975/W231-7
Die heilige Messe der groesste Schatz der Welt und die Weile，ihn zu benuetzen：Ein Belehrungs- und Erbauungsbuch fuer das christliche Volk/Josef Walter. —7. Aufl.. —Innsbruck：Verlagsanstalt Tyrolia，[?]
556 S. ；16 cm.

B975/W423

O Mensch, gib acht: Ein erbauliches Kalenderbuch fuer Stadt- und Landleut/Josef Weinheber. —Muenchen: Albert Langen, Georg Mueller, c1937

131 S. ;19 cm.

B975/W859

Neue Sammlung von Vortraegen fuer christliche Vereine/G. Wolfgarten. —Freiburg im Breigau: Herder'sche Verlagshandlung, 1896

11,538 S. ;16 cm.

B976/A395

Konfessionskunde/Konrad Algermissen. —Hannover: Verlag Joseph Giesel, 1939

15,890 S. ;25 cm.

B976.1/A193-6

Das Wesen des Katholizismus/Karl Adam. —6. Aufl.. —Duesseldorf: Verlag von L. Schwann, 1931

294 S. ;24 cm.

B976.1/A193-8

Das Wesen des Katholizismus/Karl Adam. —8. Aufl.. —Duesseldorf: Verlag von L. Schwann, 1936

295 S. ;24 cm.

B976.1/B357

Der Prediger und Katechet: Eine praktische katholische Monatschrift fuer Prediger und Katecheten/Bayerische Ordensprovinz der Kapuziner. —Regensburg: Verlagsanstalt vorm G. J. Manz, 1923

8,584 S. ;22 cm.

B976.1/B357(70)

Der Prediger und Katechet: Eine praktische katholische Monatschrift fuer Prediger und Katecheten. 70. Jahrgang/Bayerische Ordensprovinz der Kapuziner. —Regensburg: Verlagsanstalt vorm G. J. Manz, 1920

8,548 S. ;22 cm.

B976.1/B858

Das Roemische Brevier/Johannes Brinktrine. —Paderborn: Ferdinand Schoeningh Verlag, 1932

141 S. ;21 cm.

B976.1/C583(1)

Unser Evangelien: Akademische Vortraege. 1. Reihe, Zur Literaturgeschichte der Evangelien/Hermann J. Cladder. —Freiburg im Breisgau: Herdersche Verlagshandlung, 1919

8,262 S. ;22 cm.

B976.1/D322

Katholischer Katechismus/Jos. Deharbes. —Regensburg: Verlag von Friedrich Pustet, 1906

16,144 S. ;18 cm.

B976.1/D485(3)

Hilfsbuch zum Einheitskatechismus: bearbeitet nach dem Prinzip der religioesen Lebensschule. Band III, Von den Gnadenmitteln/Georg Deubig. —Limburg a. d. Lahn: Verlag Gebr. Steffen, 1927

375 S. ;18 cm.

B976.1/D485-2(2)

Hilfsbuch zum Einheitskatechismus: bearbeitet nach dem Prinzip der religioesen Lebensschule. Band II, Von den Geboten/Georg Deubig. —2. Aufl.. —Limburg a. d. Lahn: Verlag Gebr. Steffen, 1936

367 S. ;18 cm.

B976.1/D559-9(1)

Katholische Dogmatik: nach den Grundsaetzen des heiligen Thomas. 1. Band/Franz Diekamp. —9. Aufl.. —Muenster in Westfalen: Aschendorffsche Verlagsbuchhandlung, 1938

12,371 S. ;22 cm.

B976. 1/D578-2(3)

Markus: Das Evangelium des heiligen Markus, in theologisch und heilsgeschichtlich vertiefter Schau. 3. Band, Das Brot des Herrn/Josef Dillersberger. —2. Aufl.. —Salzburg: Otto Mueller, c1937

190 S. ;18 cm.

B976. 1/D578-3(1)

Markus: Das Evangelium des heiligen Markus, in theologisch und heilsgeschichtlich vertiefter Schau. 1. Band, Der Gottes- und Menschensohn/Josef Dillersberger. —3. Aufl.. —Salzburg: Otto Mueller, c1937

198 S. ;18 cm.

B976. 1/G727

Die Geschichte der katholischen Theologie seit dem Ausgang der Vaeterzeit/Martin Grabmann. —Freiburg im Breisgau: Herder & Co. G. m. b. H. Verlagsbuchhandlung, 1933

13,368 S. ;23 cm.

B976. 1/H535-5(1. 1)

Charakterbilder der katholischen Frauenwelt: Kirchengeschichtliche Studien. 1. Band, Charakterbilder der biblischen Frauenwelt. 1. Abteilung/Pauline Herber, Maria Grisar. —5. Aufl.. —Paderborn: Verlag von Ferdinand Schoeningh, [?]

16,282 S. ;18 cm.

B976. 1/K11-15

Katholisches Religionsbuechlein/Die katechetische Sektion der Oesterreichischen Leo-Gesellschaft. —15. Aufl.. —Wien: Tyrolia Verlag, 1937

180 S. ;19 cm.

B976. 1/K47

Christliche Ehe: Eine Darstellung des Eherechts und der Ehemoral der Katholischen Kirche fuer Seelsorger und Laien/Erwin Roderich von Kienitz. —Frankfurt am Main: Verlag Fr. Borgmeyer. Hessenbuchhandlung, 1938

8,402,26 S. ;23 cm.

B976. 1/K63(1)

Katechismusgedanken. 1. Band, Die ewigen Dinge: Gedanken ueber das erste Hauptstueck des Katechismus/J. Klug. —Paderborn: Verlag von Ferdinand Schoeningh, c1915

312 S. ;14 cm.

B976. 1/K66-2

Das Lukasevangelium/Erich Klostermann. —2. Aufl.. —Tuebingen: Verlag von J. C. B. Mohr Paul(Siebeck), 1929

247 S. ;25 cm.

B976. 1/K77

Unser Christusglaube: Das Heilandsbild der katholischen Theologie/Ludwig Koesters. —Freiburg im Breislau: Herder & Co. G. m. b. H. Verlagsbuchhandlung, 1937

14,340 S. ;23 cm.

B976. 1/M537

Jugendmoral: An Beispielen erlaeuterte, praktisch-katholische Sittenlehre/Ludwig Mendigal. —Einsiedeln: Verlagsanstalt Benziger & Co. A. G., 1936

164 S. ;19 cm.

B976. 1/O12

Beispiele aus dem Leben: Fuer Kanzel und Schule/Klemens Oberhammer. —Innsbruck: Verlagsanstalt Tyrolia, 1931

410 S. ;21 cm.

B976. 1/S347(3. 1)

Katholische Dogmatik. 3. Band, 1. Teil, Kirche und Goettliches Leben im Menschen/Michael Schmaus. —Muenchen: Mac Hueber Verlag, c1940

11,444 S. ;24 cm.

B976. 1/S348

Katholische Missionsgeschichte/J. Schmidlin. —Kaldenkirchen: Missionsdruckerei Steyl, [?]

11,598 S. ;24 cm.

B976. 1/S683(11)

Der katholische Gedanke. Band XI,Das evangelium als Lebensform des Menschen/Thaddaeus Soiron. —Muenchen: Theatiner Verlag,c1925

82 S. ;18 cm.

B976. 1/S819-2(1)

Die philosophische Grundlegung der katholischen Sittenlehre. 1. Halbband/Theodor Steinbuechel. —2. Aufl.. —Duesseldorf: Mosella Verlag,1939

410 S. ;25 cm.

B976. 1-42/H641(1)

Gottes Lob aus Kindermund: Hilfsbuch fuer den katholischen Religionsunterricht im ersten und zweiten Schuljahr. 1. Schuljahr/Otto Hilker, Theo Gerber. —Paderborn: Verlag von Ferdinand Schoeningh,1931

14,113,8 S. ;23 cm.

B976. 1-42/H641(2)

Gottes Lob aus Kindermund: Hilfsbuch fuer den katholischen Religionsunterricht im ersten und zweiten Schuljahr. 2. Schuljahr/Otto Hilker, Theo Gerber. —Paderborn: Verlag von Ferdinand Schoeningh,1931

14,169 S. ;23 cm.

B976. 1-42/H641-2(1)

Methodisches Hilfsbuch zum neuen kleinen kathol. Katechismus: Mit ausgefuehrten Lektionen. 1. Teil, Das 3. Grundschuljahr/Otto Hilker. —2. Aufl.. —Paderborn: Verlag von Ferdinand Schoeningh,1932

174 S. ;22 cm.

B976. 1-42/H641-2(2)

Methodisches Hilfsbuch zum neuen kleinen kathol. Katechismus: Mit ausgefuehrten Lektionen. 2. Teil, Das 4. Grundschuljahr/Otto Hilker. —2. Aufl.. —Paderborn: Verlag von Ferdinand Schoeningh,c1936

188 S. ;22 cm.

B976. 1-43/S759

Lehrbuch der speciellen Methodik des kathlischen Religionsunterrichtes: Paedagogische Grundsaetze bei Erteilung des katholischen Religionsunterrichtes in der Volks- und Buergerschule/Franz Spirago. —Trautenau: Verlag von Professor Spirago,1900

230 S. ;21 cm.

B976. 1-62/S314(2)

Handbuch der katholischen Dogmatik. 2. Band/Matthias Joseph Scheeben. —Freiburg im Breisgau: Herder & Co. G. m. b. H. Verlagsbuchhandlung,1927

12,952 S. ;23 cm.

B976. 1-62/S314(3)

Handbuch der katholischen Dogmatik. 3. Band/Matthias Joseph Scheeben. —Freiburg im Breisgau: Herder & Co. G. m. b. H. Verlagsbuchhandlung,1933

10,1013 S. ;23 cm.

B976. 1-62/S819-2(1. 1)

Handbuch der katholischen Sittenlehre. Band I,Die philosophische Grundlegung der katholischen Sittenlehre. 1. Abteilung/Theodor Steinbuechel. —2. Aufl.. —Duesseldorf: Mosella Verlag,1939

410 S. ;25 cm.

B976. 3/P531-2(1)

An junge Menschen: Betrachtungen und Ansprachen im Anschluss an die Sonntagsevangelien. 1. Band, Advent bis Pfingsten/Michael Pfliegler. —2. Aufl.. —Salzburg: Verlag Anton Pustet, c1934

157 S. ;18 cm.

B976. 3/P531-2(2)

An junge Menschen: Betrachtungen und Ansprachen im Anschluss an die Sonntagsevangelien. 2. Band, Die Sonntage nach Pfingsten/Michael Pfliegler. —2. Aufl.. —Salzburg: Verlag Anton Pustet, c1934

152 S. ;18 cm.

B977/G889-2(3)

Exerzitien-Vortraege fuer weibliche Ordensgenossenschaften. 3. Band/Georg Grundlach. —2. Aufl.. —Regensburg: Verlag Josef Koesel & Friedrich Pustet Komm. Ges. , 1923

8,442 S. ;20 cm.

B977/K47

Die Gestalt der Kirche: Eine Einfuehrung in Geist und Form des kirchlichen Verfassungsrechts/Erwin Roderich von Kienitz. —Frankfurt am Main: Velag Fr. Borgmeyer Hessenbuchhanlung, 1937

288 S. ;24 cm.

B977/M392-9

Lehrbuch der Kirchengeschichte/J. Marx. —9. Aufl.. —Trier: Verlag der Paulinus, 1929

16,964 S. ;24 cm.

B977/W344-7

Ordensleben und Ordensgeist: Vierzig Vortraege zunaechst fuer Ordensschwestern/Ignaz Watterott. —6. bis 7. Aufl.. —Freiburg im Breisgau: Herder & Co. G. m. b. H. Verlagsbuchhandlung, 1921

8,413 S. ;19 cm.

B977. 546/Z73

Die Kirchen Roms/Franz Xaver Zimmermann. —Muenchen: R. Piper & Co. Verlag, c1935

343 S. ;25 cm.

B979/B576-11(1)

Kirchengeschichte auf Grund des Lehrbuches von F. X. von Funk. 1. Teil, Das christliche Altertum/Karl Bihlmeyer. —11. Aufl.. —Paderborn: Verlag Ferdinand Schoeningh, c1940

14,432 S. ;23 cm.

B979/F325-3(1)

Neutestamentliche Zeitgeschichte oder Judentum und Heidentum zur Zeit Christi und der Apostel. 1. Band/Joseph Felten. —2. und 3. Aufl.. —Regensburg: Verlagsanstalt vorm. G. J. Manz, 1925

8,643 S. ;22 cm.

B979/G463

Die Geschichte der christlichen Philosophie: von ihren Anfaengen bis Nikolaus von Cues/Etienne Gilson, Philotheus Boehner. —Paderborn: Ferdinand Schoeningh, c1937

29,619 S. ;23 cm.

B979/K78

Geschichte des Reiches Gottes: Bis auf Jesus Christus/Eduard Koenig. —Berlin: Verlag von Martin Warneck, 1908

8,330 S. ;19 cm.

B979/L878-6

Geschichte der Kirche in ideengeschichtlicher Betrachtung: Eine Sinndeutung der christlichen Vergangenheit in Grundzuegen/Joseph Lortz. —5. und 6. Aufl.. —Muenster in Westfalen: Aschendorffsche Verlagsbuchhandlung, 1937

22,88,121,116,94,42 S. ;23 cm.

B979/P855

Paenitentia secunda: Die kirchliche Busse im aeltesten Christentum bis Cyprian und Origenes/ Bernhard Poschmann. —Bonn: Peter Hanstein Verlagsbuchhandlung, c1940

10,496 S. ;24 cm.

B979.9/A634-2

Im Dienste Gottes und der Menschen: Ein Lebensbild des ehrwuerdigen Konrad Birndorfer von Parzham/P. Joseph Anton. —2. Aufl.. — Muenchen: Verlag Josef Koesel & Friedrich Pustet, 1929

232 S. ;17 cm.

B979.9/B347-2

Der heilige Paulus/Emile Baumann. —2. Aufl.. —Muenchen: Verlag Josef Koesel & Friedrich Pustet K. —G. ,1927

464 S. ;18 cm.

B979.9/C525

Der heilige Franziskus von Assisi/G. K. Chesterton. —Muenchen: Verlag Josef Koesel & Friedrich Pustet K. —G. ,1927

159 S. ;19 cm.

B979.9/C988

Der heilige Franz von Assisi/P. Cuthbert. — Colmar: Verlag Alsatia, 1927

575 S. ;21 cm.

B979.9/C988-2

Der heilige Franz von Assisi/P. Cuthbert. —2. Aufl.. —Colmar: Verlag Alsatia, 1927

10,586 S. ;21 cm.

B979.9/D325-2

Paulus: Eine kultur- und religionsgeschichtliche Skizze/Adolf Deissmann. —2. Aufl.. —Tuebingen: Verlag von J. C. B. Mohr (Paul Siebeck), c1925

15,292 S. ;24 cm.

B979.9/F293

Der heilige Franz von Assisi/Heinrich Federer, Fritz Kunz. —Muenchen: Gesellschaft fuer Christliche Kunst GmbH, [?]

98 S. ;20 cm.

B979.9/F535

Vater Arnolds Getreuen/Hermann Fischer. — Kaldenkirchen: Verlag der Missionsdruckerei in Steyl, [?]

8,413 S. ;24 cm.

B979.9/F899(6)

Bernhard von Clairvaux. 6. Band, Das Sohelied/Eberhard Friedrich. —Wittlich: Georg Fischer Verlag, [?]

324 S. ;19 cm.

B979.9/G411

Der Heilige Johannes Bosco/Henri Gheon. — Freiburg im Breisgau: Herder & Co. G. m. b. H. Verlagsbuchhandlung, 1937

16,221 S. ;20 cm.

B979.9/H758

Vater Renaldo oder die Macht des Evangeliums: Eine Erzaehlung aus der Glaubensverfolgung in Spanien unter Koenigin Isabella/G. Holtey-Weber. —Elberfeld: Verlag der Buchhandlung des Erziehungs-Vereins, [?]

220 S. ;17 cm.

B979.9/H762

Paulus: Ein Heldenleben im Dienste Christi in religionsgeschichtlichem Zusammenhang dargestellt/Josef Holzner. —Freiburg im Breisgau: Herder & Co. G. m. b. H. Verlagsbuchhandlung, c1937

10,458 S. ;23 cm.

B979.9/H762-2

Paulus: Ein Heldenleben im Dienste Christi in

religionsgeschichtlichem Zusammenhang dargestellt/Josef Holzner. —2. Aufl.. —Freiburg im Breisgau: Herder & Co. G. m. b. H. Verlagsbuchhandlung, c1937

12, 468 S. ; 23 cm.

B979. 9/H762-10

Paulus: Sein Leben und seine Briefe/Josef Holzner. —3. bis 10. Aufl.. —Freiburg im Breisgau: Herder & Co. G. m. b. H. Verlagsbuchhandlung, c1937

13, 501, 18 S. ; 23 cm.

B979. 9/J64-7

Der heilige Franz von Assisi: Eine Lebensbeschreibung/Johannes Joergensen. —7. Aufl.. —Muenchen: Verlag Josef Koesel & Friedrich Pustet, 1922

18, 637 S. ; 19 cm.

B979. 9/K63-2

Ringende und Reise: Lebensbilder vollendeter Menschen/J. Klug. —2. Aufl.. —Paderborn: Verlag von Ferdinand Schoeningh, 1922

475 S. ; 19 cm.

B979. 9/P293(4. 2)

Geschichte der Paepste seit dem Ausgang des Mittelalters. 4. Band, Geschichte der Paepste im Zeitalter der Renaissance und der Glaubenspaltung von der Wahl Leos X. bis zum Tode Klemens' VII. (1513-1534.). 2. Abteilung/Ludwig Pastor. —Freiburg im Breisgau: Herdersche Verlagsbuchhandlung, 1907

47, 799 S. ; 23 cm.

B979. 9/P293-4(3)

Geschichte der Paepste seit dem Ausgang des Mittelalters. 3. Band, Geschichte der Paepste im Zeitalter der Renaissance von der Wahl Innocenz' VIII. bis zum Tode Julius' II. /Ludwig Pastor. —3. und 4. Aufl.. —Freiburg im Breisgau: Herdersche Verlagsbuchhandlung, 1899

49, 956 S. ; 23 cm.

B979. 9/P293-4(4)

Geschichte der Paepste seit dem Ausgang des Mittelalters. 4. Band, Geschichte der Paepste im Zeitalter der Renaissance und der Glaubenspaltung von der Wahl Leos X. bis zum Tode Klemens' VII. (1513-1534)/Ludwig Pastor. —1. bis 4. Aufl.. —Freiburg im Breisgau: Herdersche Verlagsbuchhandlung, 1906

18, 609 S. ; 23 cm.

B979. 9/P293-4(6)

Geschichte der Paepste seit dem Ausgang des Mittelalters. 6. Band, Geschichte der Paepste im Zeitalter der katholischen Reformation und Restauration Julius III. , Marcellus II. und Paul IV. (1550-1559)/Ludwig von Pastor. —1. bis 4. Aufl.. —Freiburg im Breisgau: Herder & Co. G. m. b. H. Verlagsbuchhandlung, 1913

40, 723 S. ; 23 cm.

B979. 9/P293-4(8)

Geschichte der Paepste seit dem Ausgang des Mittelalters. 8. Band, Geschichte der Paepste im Zeitalter der katholischen Reformation und Restauration Pius V. (1566-1572)/Ludwig Freiherrn von Pastor. —1. bis 4. Aufl.. —Freiburg im Breisgau: Herder & Co. G. m. b. H. Verlagsbuchhandlung, 1920

36, 676 S. ; 23 cm.

B979. 9/P293-7(1)

Geschichte der Paepste seit dem Ausgang des Mittelalters. 1. Band, Geschichte der Paepste im Zeitalter der katholischen Reformation und Restauration: Klemens VIII. (1592-1605)/Ludwig Freiherrn von Pastor. —1. bis 7. Aufl.. —Freiburg im Breisgau: Herder & Co. G. m. b. H. Verlagsbuchhandlung, 1927

39, 804 S. ; 23 cm.

B979. 9/P293-7(14)

Geschichte der Paepste seit dem Ausgang des Mittelalters. 14. Band, Geschichte der Paepste im Zeitalter des fuerstlichen Absolutismus von der Wahl Innozenz' X. bis zum Tode Innozenz' XII. (1644-1700)/Ludwig Freiherrn von Pastor. —1. bis 7. Aufl.. —Freiburg im Breisgau: Herder & Co. G. m. b. H. Verlagsbuchhandlung, 1929

17, 665 S. ; 23 cm.

B979. 9/P293-7(16)

Geschichte der Paepste seit dem Ausgang des Mittelalters. 16. Band, Geschichte der Paepste im Zeitalter des fuerstlichen Absolutismus von der Wahl Benedikts XIV. bis zum Tode Pius' VI. (1740-1799)/Ludwig Freiherrn von Pastor. —1. bis 7. Aufl.. —Freiburg im Breisgau: Herder & Co. G. m. b. H. Verlagsbuchhandlung, 1931

21, 1011 S. ; 23 cm.

B979. 9/P293-7(16. 2)

Geschichte der Paepste seit dem Ausgang des Mittelalters. 16. Band, Geschichte der Paepste im Zeitalter des fuerstlichen Absolutismus von der Wahl Benedikts XIV. bis zum Tode Pius' VI. (1740-1799). 2. Abteilung/Ludwig Freiherrn von Pastor. —1. bis 7. Aufl.. —Freiburg im Breisgau: Herder & Co. G. m. b. H. Verlagsbuchhandlung, 1932

10, 440 S. ; 23 cm.

B979. 9/P613-3

Paulus: Seine missionarische Persoenlichkeit und Wirksamkeit/Karl Pieper. —2. und 3. Aufl.. —Muenster: Verlag der Aschendorffschen Verlagsbuchhandlung, 1929

292 S. ; 24 cm.

B979. 9/R894

Margarita von Cortona: Geschichte einer Liebenden/Maria Veronika Rubatscher. —Freiburg im Breisgau: Herder & Co. G. m. b. H. Verlagsbuchhandlung, 1938

278 S. ; 19 cm.

B979. 9/S565-19

Der Hochlandspfarrer/Ingeborg Maria Sick. — 19. Aufl.. —Stuttgart: Verlag von J. F. Steinkopf, 1926

224 S. ; 19 cm.

B979. 9/S875-32

Die heilige Elisabeth: Ein Buch fuer Christen/Alban Stolz. —31. bis 32. Aufl.. —Freiburg im Breisgau: Herder & Co. G. m. b. H. Verlagsbuchhandlung, 1934

12, 413 S. ; 20 cm.

B979. 9/Sv447-2

Guido, der kleine Bote Gottes/Jon Svensson. — 2. Aufl.. —Freiburg im Breisgau: Herder & Co. G. m. b. H. Verlagsbuchhandlung, 1935

9, 113 S. ; 18 cm.

B979. 951. 6/B736

Missionar in Neu-Guinea: P. Karl Morschheuser SVD. 1904-1934/Fritz Bornemann. — Moedling bei Wien: Verlag Missionsdruckerei St. Gabriel, 1938

175 S. ; 18 cm.

B979. 954. 6/K64

Forschungen zur Volkskunde. Heft 6-8, Antonius von Padua/P. Beda Kleinschmidt. —Duesseldorf: Verlag von L. Schwann, 1931

31, 410 S. ; 29 cm.

B979. 956. 5/T843

Der heilige Pfarrer von Ars: Johannes-Maria-Baptist Vianney 1786-1859/Francis Trochu. — Stuttgart: Otto Schloz Verlag, 1930

490 S. ; 22 cm.

B98/P481

Die Kirche aus Juden und Heiden: Drei Vorlesungen/Erik Peterson. —Salzburg: Verlag Anton

Pustet,[?]
72 S. ;22 cm.

B995. 162/K66-2(1)
Kursus der Astrologie. Band I, Lehrbuch der astrologischen Technik/H. Frhr. von Kloeckler. —2. Aufl.. —Leipzig: Astra Verlag, c1930
167 S. ;22 cm.

B995. 162/K66-2(2)
Kursus der Astrologie. II. Band, Grundlagen fuer die astrologische Deutung/H. Frhr. von Kloeckler. —2. Aufl.. —Leipzig: Astra Verlag, c1932
203 S. ;22 cm.

社会科学总论

C91/S334(7)
Ruestzeug der Gegenwart: Eine Sammlung von religioesen, philosophischen und apologetischen Tagesfragen. 7. Band, Die Staats- und Soziallehre des Papstes Leo XIII/Otto Schilling. —Koeln: Verlag J. P. Bachem G. m. b. H. ,[?]
188 S. ;20 cm.

C913. 13/B124
Das Geheimnis ist gross: Briefe an eine junge Braut von Heinrich Bachmann/Heinrich Bachmann. —Duesseldorf: Verbandsverlag weiblicher Vereine, 1939
144 S. ;16 * 23 cm.

C913. 13/D311-3
Verheiratet: Ein Buch von Mann und Frau/J. B. Deelen. —3. Aufl.. —Paderborn: Verlag der Bonifacius Druckerei G. m. b. H. ,c1933
187 S. ;20 cm.

C913. 14/K46-2(2)
Die sexuelle Untreue der Frau. 2. Teil, Das freie und das feile Weib/Heinrich Kisch. —2. Aufl.. —Bonn: A. Marcus & E. Webers Verlag, c1921
8,216 S. ;22 cm.

C913. 8/P856
Moderne Betrueger/Ulrich PosseHl. —Berlin: Bali Verlag Berger & Co. ,[?]
118 S. ;21 cm.

C95/B977
Illustrierte Voelkerkunde/Georg Buschan. —Stuttgart: Strecker Schroeder Verlag, [?]
97-686 S. ;22 cm.

C955. 2/E65
Chinesen/Eduard Erkes. —Leipzig: Duerr & Weber m. b. H. ,c1920
82 S. ;19 cm.

D 政治、法律

D0/S353

Repetitorium der praktischen Politik：Unter Beruecksichtigung der betreffenden Werke von Dahlmann，Waitz，Mohl，Escher，Bluntschli u. / Ludw. Heinr. Schmidt.—Leipzig：Verlag der Rossberg'schen Buchhandlung，1881

138 S.；17 cm.

D422.7/F959

Chinesisches Bauernleben：Drei Stuecke aus dem chinesischen Landleben/Hsiung Fu-Hsi.—Tokyo：Deutsche Gesellschaft fuer Natur- und Voelkerkunde Ostasiens，1938

161 S.；22 cm.

D75/L611(30.2)

Die Grosse Politik der Europaeischen Kabinette 1871-1914：Sammlung der Diplomatischen Akten des Auswaertigen Amtes. 30. Band，Der Italienisch-Tuerkische Krieg 1911-1912. 2. Haelfte/Johannes Lepsius [usw.].—Berlin：Deutsche Verlagsgesellschaft fuer Politik und Geschichte M. B. H.，c1926

341-593 S.；24 cm.

D75/L611(31)

Die Grosse Politik der Europaeischen Kabinette 1871-1914：Sammlung der Diplomatischen Akten des Auswaertigen Amtes. 31. Band，Das Scheitern der Haldane-Mission und ihre Rueckwirkung auf die Tripelententе 1911-1912/Johannes Lepsius[usw.].—Berlin：Deutsche Verlagsgesellschaft fuer Politik und Geschichte M. B. H.，c1926

556 S.；24 cm.

D75/L611(34.2)

Die Grosse Politik der Europaeischen Kabinette 1871-1914：Sammlung der Diplomatischen Akten des Auswaertigen Amtes. 34. Band，Die Londoner Botschafterreunion und der Zweite Balkankrieg 1912-1913. 2. Haelfte/Johannes Lepsius [usw.].—Berlin：Deutsche Verlagsgesellschaft fuer Politik und Geschichte M. B. H.，c1926

453-887 S.；24 cm.

D75/L611(37.1)

Die Grosse Politik der Europaeischen Kabinette 1871-1914：Sammlung der Diplomatischen Akten des Auswaertigen Amtes. 37. Band，Entspannungen unter den Maechten 1912-1913. 1. Haelfte/Johannes Lepsius [usw.].—Berlin：Deutsche Verlagsgesellschaft fuer Politik und Geschichte M. B. H.，c1926

470 S.；24 cm.

D75/L611-2(14.2)

Die Grosse Politik der Europaeischen Kabinette 1871-1914：Sammlung der Diplomatischen Akten des Auswaertigen Amtes. 14. Band，Weltpolitische Rivalitaeten. 2. Haelfte/Johannes Lepsius[usw.].—2. Aufl..—Berlin：Deutsche Verlagsgesellschaft fuer Politik und Geschichte M. B. H.，c1925

371-675 S.；24 cm.

D75/L611-2(16)

Die Grosse Politik der Europaeischen Kabinette 1871-1914：Sammlung der Diplomatischen Akten des Auswaertigen Amtes. 16. Band，Die Chinawirren und die Maechte 1900-1902/Johannes Lepsius[usw.].—2. Aufl..—Berlin：Deutsche Verlagsgesellschaft fuer Politik und Ge-

schichte M. B. H. ,c1925
491 S. ;24 cm.

D75/L611-2(18. 1)
Die Grosse Politik der Europaeischen Kabinette 1871-1914: Sammlung der Diplomatischen Akten des Auswaertigen Amtes. 18. Band, Zweibund und Dreibund 1900-1904. 1. Haelfte/Johannes Lepsius[usw.]. —2. Aufl.. —Berlin: Deutsche Verlagsgesellschaft fuer Politik und Geschichte M. B. H. ,c1925
481 S. ;24 cm.

D75/L611-2(18. 2)
Die Grosse Politik der Europaeischen Kabinette 1871-1914: Sammlung der Diplomatischen Akten des Auswaertigen Amtes. 18. Band, Zweibund und Dreibund 1900-1904. 2. Haelfte/Johannes Lepsius[usw.]. —2. Aufl.. —Berlin: Deutsche Verlagsgesellschaft fuer Politik und Geschichte M. B. H. ,c1925
482-935 S. ;24 cm.

D75/L611-2(19. 1)
Die Grosse Politik der Europaeischen Kabinette 1871-1914: Sammlung der Diplomatischen Akten des Auswaertigen Amtes. 19. Band, Der Russisch-Japanische Krieg. 1. Haelfte/Johannes Lepsius[usw.]. —2. Aufl.. —Berlin: Deutsche Verlagsgesellschaft fuer Politik und Geschichte M. B. H. ,c1925
350 S. ;24 cm.

D75/L611-2(19. 2)
Die Grosse Politik der Europaeischen Kabinette 1871-1914: Sammlung der Diplomatischen Akten des Auswaertigen Amtes. 19. Band, Der Russisch-Japanische Krieg. 2. Haelfte/Johannes Lepsius[usw.]. —2. Aufl.. —Berlin: Deutsche Verlagsgesellschaft fuer Politik und Geschichte M. B. H. ,c1925
353-674 S. ;24 cm.

D75/L611-2(20. 2)
Die Grosse Politik der Europaeischen Kabinette 1871-1914: Sammlung der Diplomatischen Akten des Auswaertigen Amtes. 20. Band, Entente cordiale und erste Marokkokrise. 2. Haelfte/Johannes Lepsius[usw.]. —2. Aufl.. —Berlin: Deutsche Verlagsgesellschaft fuer Politik und Geschichte M. B. H. ,c1925
293-696 S. ;24 cm.

D75/L611-2(22)
Die Grosse Politik der Europaeischen Kabinette 1871-1914: Sammlung der Diplomatischen Akten des Auswaertigen Amtes. 22. Band, Die Oesterreich-Russische Entente und der Balkan 1904-1907/Johannes Lepsius [usw.]. —2. Aufl.. —Berlin: Deutsche Verlagsgesellschaft fuer Politik und Geschichte M. B. H. ,c1925
522 S. ;24 cm.

D75/L611-2(23. 1)
Die Grosse Politik der Europaeischen Kabinette 1871-1914: Sammlung der Diplomatischen Akten des Auswaertigen Amtes. 23. Band, Die Zweite Haager Friedenskonferenz Nordsee- und Ostsee- Abkommen. 1. Haelfte/Johannes Lepsius[usw.]. —2. Aufl.. —Berlin: Deutsche Verlagsgesellschaft fuer Politik und Geschichte M. B. H. ,c1925
298 S. ;24 cm.

D75/L611-2(23. 2)
Die Grosse Politik der Europaeischen Kabinette 1871-1914: Sammlung der Diplomatischen Akten des Auswaertigen Amtes. 23. Band, Die Zweite Haager Friedenskonferenz Nordsee- und Ostsee- Abkommen. 2. Haelfte/Johannes Lepsius[usw.]. —2. Aufl.. —Berlin: Deutsche Verlagsgesellschaft fuer Politik und Geschichte M. B. H. ,c1925
299-568 S. ;24 cm.

D75/L611-2(28)

Die Grosse Politik der Europaeischen Kabinette 1871-1914: Sammlung der Diplomatischen Akten des Auswaertigen Amtes. 28. Band, England und die Deutsche Flotte 1908-1911/Johannes Lepsius [usw.]. —2. Aufl.. —Berlin: Deutsche Verlagsgesellschaft fuer Politik und Geschichte M. B. H., c1925

426 S.; 24 cm.

D75/L611-3(10)

Die Grosse Politik der Europaeischen Kabinette 1871-1914: Sammlung der Diplomatischen Akten des Auswaertigen Amtes. 10. Band, Das tuerkische Problem 1895/Johannes Lepsius [usw.]. —3. Aufl.. —Berlin: Deutsche Verlagsgesellschaft fuer Politik und Geschichte M. B. H., c1925

259 S.; 24 cm.

D75/L611-4(1)

Die Grosse Politik der Europaeischen Kabinette 1871-1914: Sammlung der Diplomatischen Akten des Auswaertigen Amtes. 1. Band, Frankfurter Friede und seine Nachwirkungen 1871-1877/Johannes Lepsius [usw.]. —4. Aufl.. —Berlin: Deutsche Verlagsgesellschaft fuer Politik und Geschichte M. B. H., 1927

16, 328 S.; 24 cm.

D75/L611-4(3)

Die Grosse Politik der Europaeischen Kabinette 1871-1914: Sammlung der Diplomatischen Akten des Auswaertigen Amtes. 3. Band, Das Bismarck'sche Buendnissystem/Johannes Lepsius [usw.]. —4. Aufl.. —Berlin: Deutsche Verlagsgesellschaft fuer Politik und Geschichte M. B. H., 1927

454 S.; 24 cm.

D751.6/H376-3

Der kleine Staatsbuerger: Ein Wegweiser durch's oeffentliche Leben fuer das deutsche Volk/Max Haushofer. —3. Aufl.. —Berlin: Verlag fuer Sprach- und Handelswissenschaft, 1902

8, 280 S.; 17 cm.

D751.6-55/D485

Deutsche Zukunft: Auslands- u. Uebersee-Ausgabe der Koelnischen Volkszeitung/Verlag der Deutschen Zukunft. —Koeln am Rhein: Verlag der Deutschen Zukunft, 1930

1 Heft; 31 cm.

D751.6-61/S121-5(2)

Staatslexikon: Im Auftrag der Goerres-Gesellschaft unter Mitwirkung zahlreicher Fachleute. 2. Band, Film bis Kapitalismus/Hermann Sacher. —5. Aufl.. —Freiburg im Breisgau: Herder & Co. G. M. B. H. Verlagsbuchhandlung, 1927

9, 1822 S.; 26 cm.

D751.6-61/S121-5(3)

Staatslexikon: Im Auftrag der Goerres-Gesellschaft unter Mitwirkung zahlreicher Fachleute. 3. Band, Kapitulationen bis Panslawismus/Hermann Sacher. —5. Aufl.. —Freiburg im Breisgau: Herder & Co. G. M. B. H. Verlagsbuchhandlung, 1929

10, 1932 S.; 26 cm.

D751.6-61/S121-5(5)

Staatslexikon: Im Auftrag der Goerres-Gesellschaft unter Mitwirkung zahlreicher Fachleute. 5. Band, Staatssozialismus bis Zwischenkirchenrecht Nachtraege/Hermann Sacher. —5. Aufl.. —Freiburg im Breisgau: Herder & Co. G. M. B. H. Verlagsbuchhandlung, c1937

12, 1796 S.; 26 cm.

D751.6-62/H699-2

Deutsche Buergerkunde: Kleines Handbuch des politisch Wissenswerten fuer jedermann/Georg Hoffmann, Ernst Groth. —2. Aufl.. —Leipzig: Fr. Wilh. Grunow, 1897

8, 360 S.; 18 cm.

D751.621/G593-3

Vom Kaiserhof zur Reichskanzlei: Eine historische Darstellung in Tagebuchblaettern (vom 1. Januar 1932 bis zum 1. Mai 1933)/Joseph Goebbels. —3. Aufl.. —Muenchen: Zentralverlag der N. S. D. A. P. Frz. Ehernachf. G. m. b. H., c1934

312 S. ;22 cm.

D751.638/F115-3

Weltwanderers letzte Fahrten und Abenteuer: Baltikum-Balkan-Suedsee-Japan-Korea-China-Sibirien-Moskau-Palaestina-Syrien-Kanada/Kurt Faber. —3. Aufl.. —Stuttgart: Robert Lutz Nachfolger Otto Schramm, c1930

332 S. ;20 cm.

D751.64/J64

Rassenhygienische Fibel: Der deutschen Jugend zuliebe geschrieben/Emil Joerns, Julius Scwab. —Berlin: Alfred Metzner verlag, c1933

112 S. ;22 cm.

D751.64-62/D485

Deutscher Jungendienst/Der Deutsche Jungendienst. —Potsdam: Ludwig Voggenreiter Verlag, c1933

388 S. ;20cm.

D751.68/M732

Soziale und wirtschaftspolitische Anschauungen in Deutschland: vom Beginn des neunzehnten Jahrhunderts bis zur Gegenwart/P. Mombert. —Leipzig: Verlag von Quelle & Meyer, 1919

110 S. ;18 cm.

D815/L772

Menschen und Maechte am Pazifik/Ivar Lissner. —Hamburg: Hanseatische Verlagsanstalt, c1937

382 S. ;21 cm.

D912.29/Z64

Wissenschaft bricht Monopole/Anton Zischka. —Leipzig: Wilhelm Goldmann Verlag, c1936

267 S. ;22 cm.

D951.6/F899-5

Die Handelsgesetzgebung des deutschen Reiches: Handelsgesetzbuch vom 10. Mai 1897 einschliesslich des Gerechtes. Allgemeine deutsche Wechselordnung. Die ergaenzenden Reichsgesetz/Emil Friedberg. —5. Aufl.. —Leipzig: Verlag von Breit & Comp, 1899

54,848 S. ;20 cm.

D951.63/S912

Die Miete nach dem buergerlichen Gesetzbuch: Ein Handbuechlein fuer Juristen, Mieter und Vermieter/Max Strauss. —Leipzig: Verlag von B. G. Teubner, 1908

8,150 S. ;18 cm.

D951.639.9/R347-39(2.1)

Deutsches Reichs-Gesetzbuch fuer Industrie, Handel und Gewerbe einschliesslich Handwerk und Landwirtschaft: Vollstaendige Sammlung aller einschlaegigen Reichsgesetze, Verordnungen, Ausfuehrungsbestimmungen. Band II. Teil 1./ Redaktion des Reichs-Gesetzbuchs fuer Industrie, Handel und Gewerbe. —39. Aufl.. —Berlin: Verlag von Bruer & Co., 1905

9,903,304 S. ;24 cm.

D951.64/S798-7

Strafgesetzbuch fuer das Deutsche Reich nach dem neuesten Stande: Nebst Anhang, enthaltend die wichtigsten Strafrechtlichen Nebengesetze/ Julius von Staudinger. —7. Aufl.. —Muenchen: C. H. Beck'sche Verlagsbuchhandlung, 1900

19,261 S. ;15 cm.

D995/B928

Neutralitaet, Blockade und U-Boot-Krieg in der Entwicklung des Modernen Voelkerrechts/

Ottmar Buehler. —Berlin：Junker und Duennhaupt Verlag，c1940

78 S. ；22 cm.

E 军事

E/S349

Anlagen zur Kriegs- Sanitaetsordnung：Auf Veranlassung der Medizinal-Abteilung des koeniglich preussischen Kriegsministeriums/Georg Schmidt. —Berlin：Ernst Giegfried Mittler und Sohn，1907

8，384，55 S. ；20 cm.

E19/B141(4)

Der Voelkerkrieg：Eine Chronik der Ereignisse seit dem 1. Juli 1914. 4. Band/C. H. Baer. —Stuttgart：Verlag von Julius Hoffmann，c1914

10，320 S. ；25 cm.

E516. 51/V971

Exerzir-Reglement fuer die Feld-Artillerie：Vom 23. August 1877/Vossische Buchhandlung. —Berlin：Vossische Buchhandlung，1877

23，309，30 S. ；19 cm.

E516. 53/D649

Die Fahrten der Breslau：im Schwarzen Meer/Doenitz. —Berlin：Ullstein & Co. ，c1917

157 S. ；16 cm.

E516. 53/U41

Skagerrak!：Der Ruhmestag der deutschen Flotte/[?]. —Berlin：Verlag Ullstein & Co. ，c1916

132 S. ；16 cm.

E516. 54/G727

Mit Bomben und MQs ueber Polen：PK-Kriegsberichte der Luftwaffe/Josef Grabler. —Guetersloh：Verlag C. Bertelsmann，c1940

294 S. ；19 cm.

E516. 9/O12

Der Sieg in Polen/Oberkommando der Wehrmacht. —Berlin：Zeitgeschichte-Verlag Wilhelm Andermann，c1939

175 S. ；24 cm.

E516. 9/S415

Ursachen des Zusammenbruchs：Entstehung，Durchfuehrung und Zusammenbruch der Offensive von 1918/Schwertfeger [usw.]. —Berlin：Verlag von Reimar Hobbing，1923

15，243 S. ；24 cm.

E516. 9/S559

Die Hoelle von Gallipoli：Der Heldenkampf an den Dardanellen /Walter von Schoen. —Berlin：Verlag Ullstein，c1937

243 S. ；20 cm.

E516. 9/W544(360)

Erinnerungsblaetter Deutscher Regimenter：Die Anteilnahme der Truppenteile der ehemaligen deutschen Armee am Weltkriege. 360. Band，Das III. aktive Bataillon des niedersaechsischen Fussartillerie-Regiment Nr. 10/Hermann Wetzel. —Oldenburg i. O. /Berlin：Verlag von Gerhard Stalling，1934

159 S. ；21 cm.

E824/S385

Luftkrieg bedroht Europa! /Lothar Schuet-

tel. —Muenchen: J. F. Lehmanns Verlag, c1938
182 S. ;23 cm.

E920.2/E65
Schiessvorschrift fuer die Infanterie/Ernst Siegfried Mittler und Sohn. —Berlin: Ernst Siegfried Mittler und Sohn, 1899
157 S. ;15 cm.

E929/M946-3
Die chemische Waffe: Im Weltkrieg und - Jetzt/Ulrich Mueller-Kiel. —3. Aufl.. —Berlin: Verlag Vhemie G. m. b. H. , c1932
8,152 S. ;21 cm.

F 经济

F032.2/K89-6
Zinstafeln: zur schnellen und fehlerlosen Berechnung der Zinsen aus 1 Mark bis 20000 Mark Kapital/E. L. Kraft. —6. Aufl.. —Stuttgart: J. B. Metzlersche Buchhandlung, [?]
16,382 S. ;20 cm.

F113.4-532/F828
Der Young-Plan: Der Schlussbericht der Pariser Sachverstaendigen-Konferenz im Wortlaut/ Frankfurter Societaets Druckerei G. m. b. H. Abteilung Buchverlag. —Frankfurt am Main: Frankfurter Societaets Druckerei G. m. b. H. Abteilung Buchverlag, 1929
120 S. ;22 cm.

F13-54/O85
Ost- und Suedostasien im Jahre 1930/Ostasiatischer Verein Hamburg-Bremen. —Hamburg: Ostasiatischer Verein Hamburg-Bremen, [?]
103 S. ;23 cm.

F13-54/O85-33
Ost- und Suedostasien im Jahre 1932/Ostasiatischer Verein Hamburg-Bremen. —33. Aufl. — Hamburg: Ostasiatischer Verein Hamburg-Bremen, [?]
144 S. ;23 cm.

F131.46/F652-2
Der ferne Osten: Macht- und Wirtschaftskampf in Ostasien/Gustav Fochler-Hauke. —2. Aufl.. —Leipzig: Verlag und Druck von B. G. Teubner, 1938
81 S. ;21 cm.

F151.6/G885-3
Deutsches Wirtschaftsleben: Auf geographischer Grundlage geschildert/Christian Gruber. — 3. Aufl.. —Leipzig: Verlag von B. G. Teubner, c1912
133,16 S. ;18 cm.

F151.6-61/S121-5(4)
Staatslexikon: Im Auftrag der Goerres-Gesellschaft unter Mitwirkung zahlreicher Fachleute. 4. Band, Papiergeld bis Staatsschulden/Hermann Sacher. —5. Aufl.. —Freiburg im Breisgau: Herder & Co. G. M. B. H. Verlagsbuchhandlung, 1931
8,1948 S. ;26 cm.

F151.652/L415-3
Technik und Wirtschaft im Dritten Reich: Ein Arbeitsbeschaffungsprogramm/Franz Lawaczeck. —3. Aufl.. —Muenchen: Verlag Frz. Eher Nachf. G. m. b. H. , 1933
95 S. ;22 cm.

F20/J51

Grundbegriffe und Grundsaetze der Volkswirtschaft: Eine populaere Volkswirtschftslehre/Carl Jentsch. —Leipzig: Fr. Wilh. Brunow,1895

8,446 S. ;18 cm.

F20/L619

Grundriss der Nationaloekonomie/Paul Leroy-Beaulien. —Frankfurt a. M. : J. D. Sauerlaender's Verlag,1896

8,255 S. ;21 cm.

F20/W974-5

Einfuehrung in die Volkswirtschaftslehre/W. Wygodzinski. —5. Aufl.. —Leipzig: Verlag von Quelle & Meyer,1922

149 S. ;18 cm.

F23/R122-6

Rackows Leitfaden zur Doppelten italienischen Buchfuehrung/Albrecht Rackow. —6. Aufl.. —Berlin: Lehrmittelverlag von Rackows Handels Akademien,1910

45 S. ;20 cm.

F279.516/K81(1)

Deutscher Fleiss: Wanderungen durch die Fabriken, Werkstaetten und Handelshaeuser Westdeutschlands. 1. Band/Karl Kollbach. —Koeln: Verlag von J. P. Bachem,1911

274 S. ;21 cm.

F451.64/D485(2)

Kurzberichte aus Deutschland: Aus Wirtschaft und Industrie. 2. Band/Die Deutsche Informations-Stelle Shanghai. —Shanghai: Verlag Max Noessler & Co. ,1943

62 S. ;21 cm.

F515.169/L885-3

Verkehrsentwicklung in Deutschland 1800-1900: fortgefuehrt bis zur Gegenwart/Walther Lotz. —3. Aufl.. —Leipzig: Verlag von B. G. Teubner,c1910

8,141,32 S. ;18 cm.

F595.16/R535-2

Das Wesergebirge und der Teutoburger Wald/Richters Reisefuehrer. —2. Aufl.. —Hamburg: Verlagsanstalt und Druckerei Gesellschaft m. b. H. ,1911

16,236,76 S. ;17 cm.

F595.16-62/B139-3

Deutschland in einem Band: Kurzes Reisehandbuch/Karl Baedeker. —3. Aufl.. —Leipzig: Verlag von Karl Baedeker,1913

26,446 S. ;16 cm.

F595.22/H459

Sommer in der Schweiz: Illustrierter Reisefuehrer/J. C. Heer. —Zuerich: Buergi & Co. , [?]

368 S. ;20 cm.

F595.22/K18-27

Die Schweiz nebst den Angrenzenden Teilen von Oberitalien, Savoyen und Tirol: Handbuch fuer Reisende/Verlag von Karl Baedeker. —27. Aufl.. —Leipzig: Verlag von Karl Baedeker, 1897

28,484 S. ;16 cm.

F714.1/B499

Die Preisberechnung fuer Handwerk, Handel und Industrie: eingehend erlaeutet und mit vielen der Praxis entnommenen Beispielen belegt. Ein Buch fuer Handwerker, Kaufleute und Industrielle, sowie fuer Fachschulen zu obigen Berufsarten/August Bergmann. —Leipzig: Verlag der modernen kaufmaennischen Bibliothek,[?]

8,116 S. ;22 cm.

F715/O14(2)

Das Buch des Kaufmanns. 2. Band/Georg

Obst. —Stuttgart: C. E. Poeschel Verlag,[?]
8,624 S. ;25 cm.

F715/O14-6(1)
Das Buch des Kaufmanns: Ein Handund Lehrbuch der gesamten Handelswissenschaften in gemeinverstaendlicher Darstellung. Band I/ Georg Obst. —6. Aufl.. —Stuttgart: C. E. Poeschel Verlag,c1922
671 S. ;25 cm.

F755.16/Z56
Merkbuch fuer den deutschen Aussenhandel/ Zentralstelle fuer Aussenhandel. —Berlin: Kontinent und Uebersee Verlagsgesellschaft m. b. H., 1931
114 S. ;21 cm.

F755.16-54/D485
Jahresbericht des Vorstandes fuer 1935/Deutsche Handelskammer Tientsin. —Tientsin: Peiyang Press,[?]
36 S. ;22 cm.

F83/O14-17(1)
Sammlung kaufmaennische Unterrichtswerke. 1. Band, Geld- Bank- und Boersenwesen/Georg Obst. —17. Aufl.. —Stuttgart: C. E. Poeschel Verlag,1922
12,427 S. ;21 cm.

G 文化、科学、教育、体育

G125/S386
Altes Erbe des neuen China: Ein Beitrag zur Verstaendigung von West und Ost/P. Bertram Schuler. —Paderborn: Ferdinand Schoeningh, c1937
319 S. ;21 cm.

G131.32/A138
Yamato: Der Sendungsglaube des japanischen Volkes/Lily Abegg. —Frankfurt am Main: Societaets Verlag Frankfurt am Main,c1936
285 S. ;21 cm.

G154.5/S316
Die Kultur der Griechen/Thassilo von Scheffer. —Wien: Phaidon Verlag,c1935
646 S. ;27 cm.

G154.62/B948
Die Kultur der Renaissance in Italien/Jacob Burckhardt. —Berlin: Verlag von Th. Knaur Nachf.,c1928
588 S. ;19 cm.

G424/K21(3)
Neubau des katholischen Religionsunterrichtes. 3. Band, Jesus, der Erloeser der Welt/Heinrich Kautz. —Kevelaer: Butzon & Bercker G. m. b. H.,1926
378 S. ;23 cm.

G424/K21-2(2)
Neubau des katholischen Religionsunterrichtes. 2. Band, Ein System der katholischen Religionspaedagogik/Heinrich Kautz. —2. Aufl.. —Kevelaer: Butzon & Bercker G. m. b. H.,1926
398 S. ;23 cm.

G424/K21-6(1)
Neubau des katholischen Religionsunterrichtes. 1. Band, Jesus, das goettliche Kind/Heinrich Kautz. —6. Aufl.. —Kevelaer: Butzon & Ber-

cker G. m. b. H. ,1928
398 S. ;23 cm.

G424. 1/S332-16
Methodik des gesamten Religionsunterrichts in der Volksschule unter Miteinbeziehung der Mittelschule/Josef Schieser. —12. bis 16. Aufl.. —Koeln: Verlag von J. P. Bachem,1921
186 S. ;22 cm.

G551. 69/K67
Geschichte des deutschen Schulwesens/Karl Knabe. —Leipzig: Verlag von B. G. Teubner, 1905
154 S. ;18 cm.

G633. 52/K77-9
Geschichts-Kursus fuer die oberen und mittleren Klassen hoeherer Lehranstalten und zum Selbstunterricht/H. Koepert. —9. Aufl.. —Leipzig: Georg Reichardt Verlag,1890
206 S. ;20 cm.

G633. 55/D184-200
Leitfaden fuer den Unterricht in der Geographie/H. A. Daniel. —200. Aufl.. —Halle a. S. :Verlag der Buchhandlung des Waisenhauses, 1895
20,219 S. ;19 cm.

G633. 55/S959-11
Deutsche Schulgeographie/A. Supan. —11. Aufl.. —Gotha: Justus Perthes,1914
8,242 S. ;22 cm.

G633. 6/L716(2)
Mathematisches Unterrichtswerk fuer hoehere Schulen. Band II,fuer Klasse 3 bis 5/Heye Lietzmann. —Leipzig: Verlag und Druck von B. G. Teubner,1939
320 S. ;23 cm.

G633. 92/H249
Geschlechtliche Erziehung des Kindes/Heinrich Hanselmann. —Erlenbach: Rotapfel Verlag, c1931
69 S. ;20 cm.

G634. 55/F533-7(1)
Erdkunde fuer hoehere Schulen. 1. Teil,Geographische Grundbegriffe. Uebersicht der Laenderkunde. Mitteleuropa, insbesondere das Deutsche Reich/Heinrich Fischer [usw.]. —7. Aufl.. —Berlin: Verlag von R. Oldenbourg,1913
90 S. ;22 cm.

G634. 55/K58-15(1)
Erdkunde fuer Schulen. 1. Teil, Unterstufe/Alfred Kirchhoff. —15. Aufl.. —Halle a. d. S. : Verlag der Buchhandlung des Waisenhauses,1909
68 S. ;22 cm.

G634. 55/K58-16(2)
Erdkunde fuer Schulen. II. Teil, Mittel- und Oberstufe/Alfred Kirchhoff. —16. Aufl.. —Halle a. d. S. : Verlag der Buchhandlung des Waisenhauses,1910
8,413 S. ;22 cm.

G634. 55/K58-17(2)
Erdkunde fuer Schulen. II. Teil, Mittel- und Oberstufe/Alfred Kirchhoff. —17. Aufl.. —Halle a. d. S. : Verlag der Buchhandlung des Waisenhauses,1912
8,417 S. ;22 cm.

G642. 302/T255(1926)
Technische Hochschule Hannover Vorlesungs-Verzeichnis fuer das Studienjahr 1926-1927: 1. Oktober 1926 bis 30. September 1927/Technische Hochschule Hannover. —Hannover: Berthold Pokrantz,1926
131 S. ;22 cm.

G775/F654

Jugendlehre：Ein Buch fuer Eltern，Lehrer und Geistliche/Fr. W. Foerster.—Berlin：Verlag von Georg Reimer，1906

14，724 S.；22 cm.

G775/K78

Saat und Ernte：Lebenkundliche Besprechungen zur Einstellung der jugendlichen Selbsterziehung auf den Familienberuf/Josef Koenn.—Einsiedeln：Verlagsanstalt Benziger & Co.，A.—G.，1926

169 S.；20 cm.

G83/Z27-3

Die Leibesuebungen und ihre Bedeutung fuer die Gesundheit/R. Zander.—3. Aufl..—Leipzig：Verlag von B. G. Teubner，c1911

8，151，32 S.；18 cm.

G863.11/Zd213

Fuer Skifahrer：Gesammelte Aufsaetze und Vortraege/M. Zdarsky.—Wien：Verlagsbuchhandlung Carl Konegen，1916

212 S.；16 cm.

G891.1/M631

Wie erlernt man schnell und leicht das Schachspiel?：Leichtfassliche Anleitung mit vielen Diagrammen/Jacques Mieses.—Berlin：Hugo Steinitz Verlag，1926

96 S.；20 cm.

G894.1-63/K95

Briefmarken-Spezial-Katalog Schweiz：7. Jahrgang 1929/Kuemin-Beul.—Zuerich：Kuemin-Beul，c1928

128，28 S.；19 cm.

G894.1-63/Z93-2

Kleiner Spezialkatalog ueber die Briefmarken der Schweiz：Bis auf die Neuzeit ergaenzter Auszug des Katalogteils vom grossen Handbuch und Spezial-Katalog/Zumstein & Cie..—2. Aufl..—Bern：Zumstein & Cie.，1927

197 S.；20 cm.

G894.1-63/Z93-3

Kleiner Spezialkatalog ueber die Briefmarken der Schweiz：Bis auf die Neuzeit ergaenzter Auszug des Katalogteils vom grossen Handbuch und Spezial-Katalog/Zumstein & Cie..—3. Aufl..—Bern：Zumstein & Cie.，c1928

205 S.；20 cm.

G894.1-63/Z93-4

Kleiner Spezialkatalog ueber die Briefmarken der Schweiz：Bis auf die Neuzeit ergaenzter Auszug des Katalogteils vom grossen Handbuch und Spezial-Katalog/Zumstein & Cie..—4. Aufl..—Bern：Zumstein & Cie.，1929

219 S.；20 cm.

G894.1-63/Z93-5

Kleiner Spezialkatalog ueber die Briefmarken der Schweiz：Bis auf die Neuzeit ergaenzter Auszug des Katalogteils vom grossen Handbuch und Spezial-Katalog/Zumstein & Cie..—5. Aufl..—Bern：Zumstein & Cie.，1930

220 S.；20 cm.

H 语言、文字

H019/M466

Der zeitgemaesse Redner：Ein Fuehrer zum Lebenserfolg/F. E. May. —Paderborn：Ferdinand Schoeningh Verlag，c1931

224 S. ；19 cm.

H313. 2/K66-3

Englische Synonymik：Kleine Ausgabe fuer hoehere Unterrichtsanstalten/C. Kloepper. —3. Aufl. . —Rostock：Wilh. Werthers Verlag，1891

124 S. ；23 cm.

H314/B124-10

Englische Konversations- und Korrespondenz-Grammatik fuer den Selbst-Unterricht/E. Bachmann. —10. Aufl. . —Berlin：August Schultze Verlag，1903

8，64，96，128，94，64 S. ；19 cm.

H314/B917-29

Englische Konversations-Grammatik/Aler Bubert. —29. Aufl. . —Heidelberg：Julius Groos Verlag，[?]

8，396 S. ；20 cm.

H314/G249-21

Englische Konversations-Grammatik zum Schul- und Privatunterricht/Thomas Gaspey. —21. Aufl. . —Heidelberg：Julius Groos' Verlag，1890

400 S. ；20 cm.

H314/G249-32

Englische Konversations-Grammatik fuer den Schul-，Privat- und Selbstunterricht/Thomas Gaspey. —32. Aufl. . —Heidelberg：Julius Groos Verlag，1938

411，8 S. ；20 cm.

H316/B347-16(2)

Muret-Sanders enzyklopaedisches englisch-deutsches und deutsch-englisches Woerterbuch：Mit Angabe der Aussprache nach dem phonetischen System der Methode Toussaint-Langenscheidt. Teil II，Deutsch-Englisch/H. Baumann. —Berlin：Langenscheidtische Verlagsbuchhandlung，c1910

40，1183，38，8 S. ；27 cm.

H316/K63(1)

Muret-Sanders enzyklopaedisches englisch-deutsches und deutsch-englisches Woerterbuch：Mit Angabe der Aussprache nach dem phonetischen System der Methode Toussaint-Langenscheidt. Teil 1，Englisch-Deutsch/B. Klatt. —Berlin：Langenscheidtische Verlagsbuchhandlung，c1910

32，1067 S. ；27 cm.

H316/K63-5(1)

Langenscheidts Taschenwoerterbuch der englischen und deutschen Sprache. 1. Teil，Englisch-Deutsch/Edmund Klatt. —5. Aufl. . —Berlin：Langenscheidtische Verlagsbuchhandlung，c1929

16，480，16 S. ；16 cm.

H316/L743-16(1)

Taschenwoerterbuch der englischen und deutschen Sprache：Mit Angabe der Aussprache nach dem phonetischen System der Methode Toussaint-Langenscheidt. 1. Teil，Englisch-Deutsch/Hermann Lindemann. —16. Aufl. . —Berlin：Langscheidtische Verlagsbuchhandlung，c1911

44，564，16 S. ；15 cm.

H32/R539-5

Lehrgang der franzoesischen Sprache/Wilhelm Ricken. —5. Aufl.. —Berlin: Verlag von Wilhelm Gronau, 1904

186 S. ;22 cm.

H326/S322-2(1)

Taschenwoerterbuch der franzoesischen und deutschen Sprache: Mit Angabe der Aussprache nach dem phonetischen System der Methode Toussaint-Langenscheidt. 1. Teil, Franzoesisch-Deutsch/Jacob Schellens. —2. Aufl.. —Berlin: Langscheidtische Verlagsbuchhandlung, c1911

52,512,24 S. ;15 cm.

H326/S322-11(2)

Taschenwoerterbuch der franzoesischen und deutschen Sprache: Mit Angabe der Aussprache nach dem phonetischen System der Methode Toussaint-Langenscheidt. 2. Teil, Deutsch-Franzoesisch/Jacob Schellens. —11. Aufl.. —Berlin: Langscheidtische Verlagsbuchhandlung, c1911

50,552,16 S. ;15 cm.

H329. 6/P729-3

Ploetz-Kares kurzer Lehrgang der franzoesischen Sprache: Uebungsbuch/Gustav Ploetz. —3. Auflage. —Berlin: F. A. Herbig Verlagsbuchhandlung, 1911

8,331 S. ;21 cm.

H329. 9-62/C858-37

Handbuch der franzoesischen Umgangssprache fuer Franzosen und Deutsche/Eduard Coursier. —37. Aufl.. —Berlin: Langenscheidtische Verlagsbuchhandlung, c1910

624,16 S. ;16 cm.

H329. 9-62/P729-16

Voyage A Paris: Sprachfuehrer fuer Deutsche in Frankreich: Praktisches Handbuch der franzoesischen Umgangssprache/Karl Ploetz. —16. Aufl.. —Berlin: Verlag von F. A. Herbig, 1903

126 S. ;15 cm.

H33/B283-9(1)

Dr. Friedrich Bartels Lern- und Uebungsbuch fuer die deutsche Sprachlehre und Rechtschreibung. 1. Heft/Friedrich Bartel. —9. Aufl.. —Leipzig: Verlag von Theodor Hofmann, 1904

60 S. ;21 cm.

H33/B297-11

Der grosse Duden: Rechtschreibung der deutschen Sprache und der Fremdwoerter/Otto Basler. —11. Aufl.. —Leipzig: Bibliographisches Institut, c1934

61,670 S. ;18 cm.

H33/B469

Die Schwierigkeiten unserer Muttersprache: Uebersichtliche Zusammenstellung der zweifelhaften Faelle im muendlichen und schriftlichen Sprachgebrauche, mit besonderer Beruecksichtigung der kaufmaennischen Sprache/A. Bennewitz, L. Link. —Leipzig: Verlag von G. A. Gloeckner, 1898

284 S. ;19 cm.

H33/G978-41

Gottfried Gurckes Hauptpunkte der deuschen Sprachlehre/Gottfried Gurcke. —Hamburg: Otto Meissner, 1900

8,112 S. ;19 cm.

H33/M443-10

Der grosse Duden: Rechtschreibung der deutschen Sprache und der Fremdwoerter/Theodor Matthias. —10. Aufl.. —Leipzig: Bibliographisches Institut, c1929

54,647 S. ;18 cm.

H33/T388-2

Sprachleben und Sprachschaeden: Ein Fuehrer durch die Schwankungen und Schwierigkeiten des deutschen Sprachgebrauchs/Theodor Matthias. —2. Aufl.. —Leipzig: Friedrich Brandstetter, 1897

14,484 S. ;21 cm.

H33-61/B864(2)

Der neue Brockhaus: Allbuch in vier Baenden und einem Atlas. 2. Band, F-K/F. A. Brockhaus. —Leipzig: F. A. Brockhaus, c1937

772 S. ;24 cm.

H33-61/B864-13(11)

Brockhaus' Conversations-Lexikon: Allgemeine deutsche Real-Encyklopaedie. 11. Band, Leo-Murray/F. A. Brockhaus. —13. Aufl.. —Leipzig: F. A. Brockhaus, 1885

956 S. ;25 cm.

H33-61/B864-13(13)

Brockhaus' Conversations-Lexikon: Allgemeine deutsche Real-Encyklopaedie. 13. Band, Phraates-Russkohle/F. A. Brockhaus. —13. Aufl.. —Leipzig: F. A. Brockhaus, 1886

948 S. ;25 cm.

H33-61/B864-13(14)

Brockhaus' Conversations-Lexikon: Allgemeine deutsche Real-Encyklopaedie. 14. Band, Russland-Spahis/F. A. Brockhaus. —13. Aufl.. —Leipzig: F. A. Brockhaus, 1886

954 S. ;25 cm.

H33-61/D845-5

Vollstaendiges Orthographisches Woerterbuch der deutschen Sprache: mit zahlreichen kurzen Wort- und Sacherklaerungen und Verdeutschungen der Fremdwoerter/Konrad Duden. —5. Aufl.. —Leipzig: Bibliographisches Institut, 1897

18,350 S. ;18 cm.

H33-61/D845-8

Orthographisches Woerterbuch der deutschen Sprache: Nach den fuer Deutschland, Oesterreich und die Schweiz gueltigen amtlichen Regeln/Konrad Duden. —8. Aufl.. —Leipzig: Bibliographisches Institut, 1908

24,415 S. ;18 cm.

H33-61/H541-3

Konversations-Lexikon/Herdersche Verlagshandlung. —3. Aufl.. —Freiburg im Breisgau: Herdersche Verlagshandlung, 1907

1838 S. ;25 cm.

H33-61/H541-3(1)

Herders Konversations-Lexikon: Reich illustriert durch Textabbildung, Tafeln und Karten. 1. Band, A bis Bonaparte/Herdersche Verlagshandlung. —3. Aufl.. —Freiburg im Breisgau: Herdersche Verlagshandlung, 1902

1740 S. ;25 cm.

H33-61/H541-3(4)

Herders Konversations-Lexikon: Reich illustriert durch Textabbildung, Tafeln unf Karten. 4. Band, H bis Kombattanten/Herdersche Verlagshandlung. —3. Aufl.. —Freiburg im Breisgau: Herdersche Verlagshandlung, 1905

1790 S. ;25 cm.

H33-61/H541-4(1)

Der grosse Herder: Nachschlagewerk fuer Wissen und Leben. 1. Band, A bis Battenberg/Herder & Co. G. m. b. H. Verlagsbuchhandlung. —4. Aufl.. —Freiburg im Breisgau: Herder & Co. G. m. b. H. Verlagsbuchhandlung, c1931

1696 S. ;25 cm.

H33-61/H541-4(3)

Der grosse Herder: Nachschlagewerk fuer Wissen und Leben. 3. Band, Caillaux bis Eisenhut/Herder & Co. G. m. b. H. Verlagsbuchhandlung. —4. Aufl.. —Freiburg im Breisgau: Herder & Co. G. m. b. H. Verlagsbuchhandlung, c1932

1632 S. ;25 cm.

H33-61/H541-4(4)

Der grosse Herder: Nachschlagewerk fuer Wissen und Leben. 4. Band, Eisenhuette bis Gant/Herder & Co. G. m. b. H. Verlagsbuchhandlung. —4. Aufl.. —Freiburg im Breisgau: Herder & Co. G. m. b. H. Verlagsbuchhandlung, c1932

1632 S. ;25 cm.

H33-61/H541-4(5)

Der grosse Herder: Nachschlagewerk fuer Wissen und Leben. 5. Band, Ganter bis Hochrelief/Herder & Co. G. m. b. H. Verlagsbuchhandlung. —4. Aufl.. —Freiburg im Breisgau: Herder & Co. G. m. b. H. Verlagsbuchhandlung, c1933

1680 S. ;25 cm.

H33-61/H541-4(7)

Der grosse Herder: Nachschlagewerk fuer Wissen und Leben. 7. Band, Konservativ bis Maschinist/Herder & Co. G. m. b. H. Verlagsbuchhandlung. —4. Aufl.. —Freiburg im Breisgau: Herder & Co. G. m. b. H. Verlagsbuchhandlung, c1933

1696 S. ;25 cm.

H33-61/H541-4(8)

Der grosse Herder: Nachschlagewerk fuer Wissen und Leben. 8. Band, Maschona bis Osman/Herder & Co. G. m. b. H. Verlagsbuchhandlung. —4. Aufl.. —Freiburg im Breisgau: Herder & Co. G. m. b. H. Verlagsbuchhandlung, c1934

1696 S. ;25 cm.

H33-61/H541-4(9)

Der grosse Herder: Nachschlagewerk fuer Wissen und Leben. 9. Band, Osman bis Reuchlin/Herder & Co. G. m. b. H. Verlagsbuchhandlung. —4. Aufl.. —Freiburg im Breisgau: Herder & Co. G. m. b. H. Verlagsbuchhandlung, c1934

1756 S. ;25 cm.

H33-61/H541-4(10)

Der grosse Herder: Nachschlagewerk fuer Wissen und Leben. 10. Band, Reue bis Sipo/Herder & Co. G. m. b. H. Verlagsbuchhandlung. —4. Aufl.. —Freiburg im Breisgau: Herder & Co. G. m. b. H. Verlagsbuchhandlung, c1935

1728 S. ;25 cm.

H33-61/H541-4(11)

Der grosse Herder: Nachschlagewerk fuer Wissen und Leben. 11. Band, Sippe bis Unterfranken/Herder & Co. G. m. b. H. Verlagsbuchhandlung. —4. Aufl.. —Freiburg im Breisgau: Herder & Co. G. m. b. H. Verlagsbuchhandlung, c1933

1775 S. ;25 cm.

H333. 2-61/T349

Woerterbuch sinnverwandter Ausdruecke/F. Tetzner. —Leipzig: Verlag von Philipp Reclam jun. , [?]

472,31 S. ;14 cm.

H333. 3/C978-3

Lebensweisheit: Ein Schatz von 2660 Zitaten, Sprichwoertern, Sinnspruechen und Sentenzen deutscher Dichter und Denker/Fidel Curti. —3. Aufl.. —Bonn: Emil Strauss, [?]

8,468,9 S. ;18 cm.

H333. 3/G312

Das Buch der Zitate: Ein Zitaten- und Sentenzenlexikon in deutscher und fremder Zunge/Stefan Geiger. —Berlin: Globus Verlag, [?]

312 S. ;19 cm.

H333. 3-61/L765

Spruchwoerterbuch/Franz Freiherrn von Lipperheide. —Berlin: Verlag von Franz Lipperheide, 1907

8, 1069 S. ; 25 cm.

H333. 3-61/S215-2

Zitatenlexikon: Sammlung von Zitaten, Sprichwoertern, Sprichwoertlichen Redensarten und Sentenzen/Daniel Sanders. —2. Aufl.. —Leipzig: Verlagsbuchhandlung von J. J. Weber, 1905

712 S. ; 17 cm.

H333. 3-62/L274

Handbuch englischer und deutscher Idiome zum Schulgebrauch und Selbstunterricht/Frank Lange. —Heidelburg: Julius Groos Verlag, [?]

149 S. ; 20 cm.

H333. 9-61/S349

Etymologisches Woerterbuch der Naturwissenschaften und Medizin/C. W. Schmidt. —Berlin: Vereinigung wissenschaftlicher Verleger, c1922

138 S. ; 19 cm.

H334/L522-2(2)

Unterrichtsstoff fuer die Deutsche Grammatik und Orthographie: Zum Gebrauch in Vorschulen und in den unteren Klassen hoeherer Buergerschulen und Toechterschulen. 2. Teil/Lehrer der Koeniglichen Vorschule zu Berlin. —2. Aufl.. —Berlin: Verlag von Carl Habel, 1898

308 S. ; 19 cm.

H334/S388-5

Deutsche Sprachlehre fuer Auslaender: Grammatik und Uebungsbuch/Hans Schulz, Wilhelm Sundermeyer. —5. Aufl.. —Shanghai: Van Chong Book Co., 1936

10, 228 S. ; 21 cm.

H334-61/V878

Ausfuehrliches grammatisch-orthographisches Nachschlagebuch der deutschen Sprache: mit Einschluss der gebraeulicheren Fremdwoerter und Angabe der schwierigeren Silbentrennungen/August Vogel. —Berlin: Langenscheidtische Verlagsbuchhandlung, 1902

8, 478 S. ; 20 cm.

H334-61/V878-8

Ausfuehrliches grammatisch-orthographisches Nachschlagebuch der deutschen Sprache unter steter Beruecksichtigung der neuesten orthographischen Spezial-Woerterverzeichnisse der einzelnen deutschen Bundesstaaten, Oesterreich und der Schweiz/August Vogel. —8. Aufl.. —Berlin: Langenscheidtische Verlagsbuchhandlung, 1912

50, 568, 24 S. ; 20 cm.

H335/M363-4(1)

Deutsches Stilbuch. Erster Kurs, Fuer die unteren Klassen hoeherer Lehranstalten, sodann fuer die Oberklassen gehobener Volks- und fuer Fortbildungsschulen/G. N. Marschall. —4. Aufl.. —Nuernberg: Verlag der Friedr. Kornschen Buchhandlung, 1882

284 S. ; 20 cm.

H335-62/F654-4

Der Kaufmaennische Korrespondent: Praktisches Handbuch der gesamten Handelskorrespondenz in deutscher, englischer, franzoesischer, italienischer und spanischer Sprache. Deutsch-Spanisch/Carl Foerster, Honore Maucher. —4. Aufl.. —Berlin: Neufeld & Henius Verlag, [?]

8, 680 S. ; 24 cm.

H335-62/G111-13

Allgemeiner deutscher Muster-Briefsteller und Universal-Haussekretaer fuer alle in den verschiedenen gesellschaftlichen Verhaeltnissen sowie im Geschaefts-, Gewerbs- und Privatleben

vorkommenden Faelle：Unentbehrliches Handbuch fuer Jedermann/Georg von Gaal.—13. Aufl..—Wien：A. Hartleben's Verlag,[?]
32,816 S.；22 cm.

H336/A239-5
Venns Deutsches Woerterbuch nach der neuen Rechtschreibung fuer Schule und Haus：Mit besonderer Beruecksichtigung der gebraeuchlichsten Fremdwoerter und Eigennamen/Verlag von Adolf Gestewitz.—5. Aufl..—Berlin：Verlag von Adolf Gestewitz,1891
320 S.；23 cm.

H336/H515
Deutsches Woerterbuch：Kleine Ausgabe/Moriz Henne.—Leipzig：Verlag von S. Hirzel,1896
1288 S.；27 cm.

H336/H699-3
Woerterbuch der deutschen Sprache nach dem Standpunkt ihrer heutigen Ausbildung/P. F. L. Hoffmann.—3. Aufl..—Leipzig：Friedrich Brandstetter,1884
705 S.；19 cm.

H336/H699-5
P. F. L. Hoffmanns Woerterbuch der deutschen Sprache nach dem Standpunkt ihrer heutigen Ausbildung/P. F. L. Hoffmann.—5. Aufl..—Leipzig：Friedrich Brandstetter,1905
620 S.；20 cm.

H336/L228-2
Woerterbuch der Antike：Mit Beruecksichtigung ihres Fortwirkens/Hans Lamer.—2. Aufl..—Leipzig：Alfred Kroener Verlag,c1933
16,892,42 S.；18 cm.

H336/M443-5
Das neue deutsche Woerterbuch：Unter besonderer Beruecksichtigung der Rechtschreibung sowie der Herkunft，Bedeutung und Fuegung der Woerter，auch der Lehn- und Fremdwoerter/Theodor Matthias.—5. Aufl..—Leipzig：Hesse & Becker Verlag,1931
24,432 S.；19 cm.

H336/S632
Deutsch-Kirchenlateinisches Woerterbuch/Albert Sleumer.—Berlin u. Bonn：Ferd. Duemmlers Verlag,c1937
275 S.；19 cm.

H336/W515-4
Grammatisch-stilistisches Woerterbuch der deutschen Sprache/Ignaz Emanuel Wessely.—4. Aufl..—Leipzig：O. R. Reisland,1911
10,198 S.；20 cm.

H336/W678
Deutsch-Chinesisches Woerterbuch：N-Z/Helmut Wilhelm.—[?]:[?],[?]
707-1256 S.；26 cm.

H336/W959-9
Duden，Rechtschreibung der deutschen Sprache und der Fremdwoerter：nach den fuer Deutschland，Oesterreich und die Schweiz gueltigen amtlichen Regeln/Ernst Wuelfing,Alfred S. Schmidt.—9. Aufl..—Leipzig：Bibliographisches Institut,c1919
48,565 S.；18 cm.

H339.4/B456(6)
Deutsch-englische Lesebuecher fuer katholische Schulen：Sechstes Lesebuch. 6. Band/Benziger Brothers.—New York：Benziger Brothers,c1912
272 S.；19 cm.

H339.4/B665-24(2)
Deutsches Lesebuch fuer die Beduerfnisse des Volksschulunterrichts：Kleinere Ausgabe（A.）fuer einfache Schulverhaeltnisse in zwei Teilen.

2. Teil, Deutsches Lesebuch fuer die mittlere und obere Stufe der ein- und zweiklassigen Volksschule/Eduard Bock. —24. Aufl.. —Breslau: Ferdinand Hirt, koenigliche Universitaets- und Verlags- Buchhandlung, 1885

16, 449 S. ; 20 cm.

H339. 4/D537

Nachlese: Easy short stories from contemporary German literature/William Diamond, Frank H. Reinsch. —New York: Henry Holt And Company, c1927

313 S. ; 19 cm.

H339. 4/E93(5)

Deutsches Lesebuch fuer hoehere Lehranstalten. 5. Teil, Obertertia/M. Evers, H. Walz. —Leipzig: Verlag von B. G. Teubner, 1903

8, 332 S. ; 22 cm.

H339. 4/H476-3(2)

Deutsches Lesebuch fuer hoehere Schulen. 2. Teil, Deutsches Lesebuch fuer Quinta/P. Hellwig, P. Hirt. —3. Aufl.. —Leipzig: Verlag von L. Ehlermann, 1903

12, 340 S. ; 21 cm.

H339. 4/K89

Deutsch-Chinesisches Lesebuch fuer Chinesen/P. Kranz. —Shanghai: The Commercial Press, [?]

203 S. ; 19 cm.

H339. 4/M862-4(2)

Deutsches Lesebuch fuer Volksschulen. 2. Band/Verlag Moritz Diesterweg. —4. Aufl.. —Frankfurt am Main: Verlag Moritz Diesterweg, [?]

288 S. ; 22 cm.

H339. 4/M862-10(2)

Lebensgut. 2. Teil/Verlag Moritz Diesterweg. —10. Aufl.. —Frankfurt a. M.: Verlag Moritz Diesterweg, 1935

271 S. ; 23 cm.

H339. 4/P153-5(2)

Deutsches Lesebuch: Ausgabe B fuer hoehere Maedchenschulen. 2. Teil, Drittes Schuljahr/F. C. Paldamus, Karl Rehorn. —5. Aufl.. —Frankfurt am Main: Moritz Diesterweg, 1901

20, 213 S. ; 21 cm.

H339. 4/P988-2(2)

Deutsches Lesebuch fuer gegliederte Volksschulen: Ausgabe C. 2. Teil, 3. und 4. Schuljahr/F. W. Putzger[usw.]. —2. Aufl.. —Leipzig: Verlag der Duerr'schen Buchhandlung, 1909

292 S. ; 22 cm.

H339. 4/S214-10(1)

Deutsches Lesebuch mit Erlaeuterungen fuer chinesische Schulen. 1. Band/H. Sander. —10. Aufl.. —Schanghai: A. B. C. Press, 1934

100, 25 S. ; 23 cm.

H339. 4/S388-3(5)

Berlinisches Lesebuch. 5. Teil, Oberstufe II. Abteilung/Otto Schulz. —3. Aufl.. —Berlin: Nicolaische Verlagsbuchhandlung, 1901

8, 592, 26 S. ; 22 cm.

H339. 4/U58(1)

Lesebuch fuer die evangelischen Volksschulen Wuerttembergs. 1. Teil, Zweites und drittes Schuljahr/Union Deutsche Verlagsgesellschaft. —Stuttgart: Union Deutsche Verlagsgesellschaft, 1910

256 S. ; 22 cm.

H339. 6/H792(1)

Meine Muttersprache: Ein Arbeitsbuch fuer die Spracherziehung in Haupt- und Mittelschulen. 1. Teil, Klasse 1-3/Willi Hopff. —Altenburg: Pierersche Hofbuchdruckerei Stephan Geibel & Co., 1941

182 S. ;21 cm.

H34/S875-6(4)

Gesammelte Werke. 4. Band, Spanisches fuer die gebildete Welt/Alban Stolz. —6. Aufl.. —Freiburg im Breisgau: Herder & Co. G. m. b. H Verlagsbuchhandlung, 1927

16,357 S. ;16 cm.

H35/M267-2(4)

Die Kunst der Polyglottie: Eine auf Erfahrung begruendete Anleitung jede Sprache in kuerzester Zeit und in Bezug auf Verstaendnis, Konversation und Schriftsprache. 4. Teil, Die Kunst der russischen Sprache durch Selbstunterricht schnell und leicht zu erlernen/B. Manassewitsch. —2. Aufl.. —Leipzig: A. Hartleben's Verlag, [?]

192 S. ;17 cm.

H771-61/B644-8

Lateinisch-Deutsches Schulwoerterbuch/Heinrich Blase, Wilhelm Reeb. —8. Aufl.. —Leipzig: Verlag von B. G. Teubner, 1909

66,921 S. ;25 cm.

H771-61/B644-9

Lateinisch-Deutsches Schulwoerterbuch: Neubearbeitung/Heinrich Blase, Wilhelm Reeb, Otto Hoffmann. —9. Aufl.. —Leipzig: Verlag von B. G. Teubner, 1927

76,940 S. ;25 cm.

H771-61/G351-13

Lateinisch-Deutsches und Deutsch-Lateinisches Schulwoerterbuch: Lateinisch-Deutsches Teil/K. E. Georges. —13. Aufl.. —Hannover: Hahnsche Buchhadlung, 1918

993 S. ;22 cm.

H771-61/M544

Taschenwoerterbuch der lateinischen und deutschen Sprache/Hermann Menge. —Berlin: Langenscheidtische Verlagsbuchhandlung, [?]

8,548,24 S. ;15 cm.

H771-61/M544(2)

Taschenwoerterbuch der lateinischen und deutschen Sprache. 2. Teil, Deutsch-Lateinisch/Hermann Menge. —Berlin: Langenscheidtische Verlagsbuchhandlung, c1910

548,16 S. ;15 cm.

H771-61/M544-2(1)

Langenscheidts Taschenwoerterbuch der lateinischen und deutschen Sprache. 1. Teil, Lateinisch-Deutsch/Hermann Menge. —2. Aufl.. —Berlin: Langscheidtsche Verlagsbuchhandlung, c1937

407,8 S. ;15 cm.

H771. 4/M946-9

Lateinische Schulgrammatik, vornehmlich zu Ostermanns lateinischen Uebungsbuechern. Ausgabe A. /H. J. Mueller. —9. Aufl.. —Leipzig: Verlag von B. G. Teubner, 1909

15,337 S. ;22 cm.

H772-43/H467-5

Kleines Lehrbuch der italienischen Sprache/Sophie Heim. —5. Aufl.. —Zuerich: Verlag von Schulthess & Co. , 1908

8,186 S. ;21 cm.

H773-43/H877

Praktisches Lehrbuch des Portugiesischen: mit Beruecksichtigung des brasilianischen Sprachgebrauches/Joseph Huber. —Hamburg: Deutscher Auslandverlag Walter Bangert, 1929

184 S. ;18 cm.

I 文学

I2/E65
Chinesische Literatur/Eduard Erkes. —Breslau: Ferdinand Hirt, c1922
104 S. ;19 cm.

I222.2/S912
Schi-king: Das kanonische Liederbuch der Chinesen/Victor von Strauss. —Heidelberg: Carl Winter's Universitaetsbuchhandlung, 1880
528 S. ;21 cm.

I222.7/B562
Die chinesische Floete/Hans Bethge. —Leipzig: Im Insel Verlag MCMXXVI, [?]
118 S. ;19 cm.

I222.7/H933
Chinesische Dichter in deutscher Sprache/Vincenz Hundhausen. —Peking: Pekinger Verlag, 1926
149 S. ;23 cm.

I242/H933-5
Der Oelhaendler und das Freudenmaedchen: Eine chinesische Geschichte in fuenf Gesaengen/Vincenz Hundhausen. —5. Aufl.. —Peking: Verlag der Pekinger Pappelinsel, c1926
165 S. ;15 cm.

I242.4/K96
Das Juwelenkaestchen/Menglong Feng, Franz Kuhn. —Dresden: Wilhelm Heyne Verlag, c1937
60 S. ;19 cm.

I242.7/F331
Das Perlenhemd: Eine chinesische Liebesgeschichte/Menglong Feng. —Leipzig: Insel Verlag, [?]
61 S. ;18 cm.

I247.7/S444
Zwischen zwei Goettern: Geschichten aus China/Fritz Secker. —Peking: Hartung's Verlag, c1942
151 S. ;19 cm.

I266.1/L735
Mein Land und mein Volk/Yutang Lin. —Stuttgart: Deutsche Verlags-Anstalt, [?]
439 S. ;22 cm.

I371.73/F962(4)
Tausend und eine Nacht: Arabische Erzaehlungen. 4. Band/Ludwig Fulda. —Berlin: Verlag Neufeld & Henius, c1914
327 S. ;26 cm.

I512.45/M558
Leonardo Da Vinci: Historischer Roman/Dmitri Mereschkowski. —Berlin: Verlag von Th. Knaur Nachf., [?]
728 S. ;19 cm.

I512.64/T654(2)
Fuer alle Tage: Ein Lebensbuch. II. Teil/Leo Tolstoi. —Dresden: Verlag von Carl Reitzner, 1907
712 S. ;21 cm.

I515.45/H324
Ungarische Rhapsodie: Der Lebensroman von Franz Liszt/Zsoll von Harsznyi. —Leipzig: Esche Verlag GmbH., [?]
1228 S. ;20 cm.

I516. 06/E88-82

Schattenbilder：Eine Fibel fuer Kulturbeduerftige in Deutschland/Herbert Eulenberg. —73. bis 82. Aufl.. —Berlin：Verlag von Bruno Cassirer，1923

28，345 S.；18 cm.

I516. 07/T559-16

Trost bei Goethe：Ein Buch des Trostes，der Freude，der Liebe，der Lebenskunst und des guten Gluecks/Heinrich Tieck. —11. bis 16. Aufl.. —Wien：F. G. Speidel'sche Verlagsbuchhandlung，1936

89 S.；19 cm.

I516. 09/W515

Zur Geschichte der deutschen Literatur/Rudolf Wessely. —Leipzig：Verlag von B. G. Teubner，1905

169 S.；20 cm.

I516. 11/H713

Ueber den Umgang mit Buechern/Josef Hofmiller. —Muenchen： Albert Langen/Georg Mueller，[?]

206 S.；20 cm.

I516. 11/S334

Schillers saemtliche Werke：in zwoelf Baenden/Friedrich Schiller. —Leipzig：Verlag von Philipp Reclam jun.，[?]

264，262，217 S.；16 cm.

I516. 11/S334(1)

Schillers saemtliche Werke：in vier Hauptbaenden und zwei Ergaenzungsbaenden. 1. Band，1. und 2. Teil/Friedrich Schiller. —Leipzig：Verlag von Philipp Reclam jun.，[?]

72，235，14，313 S.；16 cm.

I516. 11/S334(2)

Schillers saemtliche Werke：in vier Hauptbaenden und zwei Ergaenzungsbaenden. 2. Band，Dramen/Friedrich Schiller. —Leipzig：Verlag von Philipp Reclam jun.，[?]

192，485 S.；16 cm.

I516. 11/S334(3)

Schillers saemtliche Werke：in vier Hauptbaenden und zwei Ergaenzungsbaenden. 3. Band，Dramen-Erzaehlungen I-Philosophische und kritische Schriften/Friedrich Schiller. —Leipzig：Verlag von Philipp Reclam jun.，[?]

340，12，140，15，377 S.；16 cm.

I516. 14/E34

Von Wald und Welt/Josef Freiherrn von Eichendorff. —Muenchen：Wilhelm Langewiesche-Brandt，[?]

446 S.；19 cm.

I516. 14/E65(1)

Goethes Kunstschriften. Band I/Wilhelm Ernst. —Leipzig：MDCCCCXX im Inselverlag，[?]

878 S.；17 cm.

I516. 14/E87

Sieben Schwaben：Ein neues Dichterbuch/Eugen Salzer. —Heilbronn：Eugen Salzer，1910

276 S.；19 cm.

I516. 14/G599

Johann Wolfgang Goethe gesammelte Werke/Johann Wolfgang von Goethe. —Berlin：Hans Heinrich Tillgner Verlag，c1924

55，394，346 S.；19 cm.

I516. 14/G599(1)

Goethes Werke：Auswahl in sechzehn Baenden. 1. Band，Gedichte. Erster Teil/Johann Wolfgang von Goethe. —Leipzig：Max Hesse's Verlag，[?]

15，244 S.；16 cm.

I516. 14/G599(5)

Johann Wolfgang Goethe gesammelte Werke. 5. Band/Johann Wolfgang von Goethe. —Berlin: Hans Heinrich Tillgner Verlag, c1924

302,343 S. ;19 cm.

I516. 14/G599(9)

Goethes Werke: Auswahl in sechzehn Baenden. 9. Band, Wilhelm Meisters Lehrjahre. Erstes bis drittes Buch/Johann Wolfgang von Goethe. —Leipzig: Max Hesse's Verlag, [?]

216 S. ;16 cm.

I516. 14/H443(9-10)

Hebbels Werke in zehn Teilen. 9. Teil, Tagebuecher I. 10. Teil, Tagebuecher II/Friedrich Hebbel. —Berlin: Deutsches Verlagshaus Bong & Co. , [?]

497,465 S. ;18 cm.

I516. 14/L639(1)

Lessings Werke: Auswahl in sechs Teilen. 1. Teil, Gedichte und Fabeln - Miss Sara Sampson Philotas/Gotthold Ephraim Lessing. Leipzig: Deutsches Verlagshaus Bong & Co. , [?]

48,314 S. ;18 cm.

I516. 14/L639(3-4)

Lessings Werke: Auswahl in sechs Teilen. 3. und 4. Teil/Gotthold Ephraim Lessing. —Leipzig: Deutsches Verlagshaus Bong & Co. , [?]

344,511 S. ;18 cm.

I516. 14/M694

Moerikes Werke/Eduard Moerike. —Berlin: Deutsches Verlagshaus Bong & Co. , [?]

45,302,315 S. ;18 cm.

I516. 14/M694(3)

Moerikes Werke in vier Teilen. 3. Teil, Maler Nolten I/Eduard Moerike. —Berlin: Deutsches Verlagshaus Bong & Co. , [?]

281 S. ;18 cm.

I516. 14/S884(3)

Theodor Storm Ausgewaehlte Werke. Band III/Theodor Storm. —Hamburg: Hansa Verlag, [?]

480 S. ;17 cm.

I516. 15/K63

Kaempfer und Traeumer: und andere ausgewaehlte Werke/Walther Gottfried Klucke. —Dortmund: Westfalen Verlag GmbH. , [?]

255 S. ;23 cm.

I516. 15/W671

Erzaehlungen und Maerchen/Oscar Wilde. —Berlin: J. Gnadenfeld & Co. , [?]

280 S. ;19 cm.

I516. 2/A951

Das froehliche Buch: Aus deutscher Dichter und Maler Kunst gesammelt/Ferdinand Avenarius. —Muenchen: Georg D. W. Callwey im Kunstwart Verlage, 1910

10,426 S. ;20 cm.

I516. 2/A951-2

Das froehliche Buch/Ferdinand Avenarius. —2. Aufl. . —Muenchen: Georg D. W. Callwey, 1929

312 S. ;20 cm.

I516. 2/B338

Gedichte in Prosa/Charles Baudelaire. —Leipzig: Im Insel Verlag, [?]

59 S. ;18 cm.

I516. 2/F829

Joseph Victor von Scheffels saemtliche Werke/Johannes Franke. —Leipzig: Hesse & Vecker Verlag, [?]

192,144 S. ;17 cm.

I516. 2/G881

Quickborn/Klaus Groth. —Leipzig: Insel Verlag,[?]

96 S. ;18 cm.

I516. 2/V521

Gedichte: Eine Auswahl der besten Uebertragungen/Paul Verlaine. —Leipzig: Insel Verlag,[?]

72 S. ;18 cm.

I516. 2-09/R713-8

Geschichte der deutschen Dichtung/Hans Roe-Hl. —8. Aufl.. —Leipzig: Verlag von B. G. Teubner,1931

382 S. ;21 cm.

I516. 23/N299

Die Minnesinger in Bildern der manessischen Handschrift/Hans Naumann. —Leipzig: Insel Verlag,[?]

48 S. ;19 cm.

I516. 23/S451

Graf Albrecht von Mansfeld: Erzaehlende Dichtung aus dem Zeitalter der Reformation/R. Seehaussen. —Guetersloh: Verlag von C. Bertelsmann,1892

204 S. ;18 cm.

I516. 24/B347

Nordische Melodien: Gedichte/Nicolai Baumbach. —St. Petersburg: W. Erickson & Co.,1883

268 S. ;17 cm.

I516. 24/C615

Der Wandsbecker Bote: Eine Auswahl aus den Werken von Matthias Claudius/Matthias Claudius. —Leipzig: Insel Verlag,[?]

79 S. ;18 cm.

I516. 24/E65(2)

Goethes dramatische Dichtungen. Band II/Wilhelm Ernst. —Leipzig: MDCCCCXX im Inselverlag,[?]

904 S. ;18 cm.

I516. 24/H333(2)

Paelzer Ausles: Eine Sammlung bester Pfaelzer Mundartdichtungen. Band II/Ludwig Hartmann. —Ludwigshafen a. Rh.: Verlag Jul. Waldkirch & Cie. m. b. H.,[?]

200 S. ;18 cm.

I516. 24/H694

Hymnen an die Ideale der Menschheit/Friedrich Hoelderlin. —Leipzig: Insel Verlag,[?]

95 S. ;18 cm.

I516. 24/U31

Uhlands Gedichte: Auswahl/Ludwig Uhland. —Bielefeld: Verlag von Velhagen & Klasing,1893

14,150 S. ;17 cm.

I516. 24/W373-147

Dreizehnlinden/F. W. Weber. —147. Aufl.. —Paderborn: Verlag von Ferdinand Schoeningh,[?]

381 S. ;16 cm.

I516. 25/B981

Neuere Deutsche Lyrik/Carl Busse. —Halle a. d. S.:Verlag von Otto Hendel,[?]

16,471 S. ;18 cm.

I516. 25/E65(3)

Das Kaiserbuch. Die Schwabenkaiser/Paul Ernst. —Muenchen: Albert Langen / Georg Mueller,c1936

871 S. ;21 cm.

I516. 25/K63

Li-Tai-Pe/Klabund. —Leipzig: Insel Verlag, [?]

48 S. ;18 cm.

I516. 25/M851

Palmstroem/Christian Morgenstern. —Berlin: Verlag von Bruno Cassirer, 1926

82 S. ;18 cm.

I516. 25/W423

Kammermusik/Josef Weinheber. —Muenchen: Albert Langen / Georg Mueller Verlag, c1939

83 S. ;20 cm.

I516. 3/B928

Wonzeck: Eine Tragoedie/Georg Buechner. —Leipzig: Insel Verlag, [?]

48 S. ;19 cm.

I516. 34/G599

Torquato Tasso/Johann Wolfgang von Goethe. —Berlin: S. Fischer Verlag, [?]

28, 157 S. ;13 cm.

I516. 34/G599G368

Faust/Johann Wolfgang von Goethe. —Berlin: Verlag Gerhard Merian, [?]

445 S. ;17 cm.

I516. 34/G599L525

Goethes Faust/Johann Wolfgang von Goethe. —Leipzig: Insel Verlag, [?]

577 S. ;17 cm.

I516. 34/G599W126

Iphigenie auf Tauris/Johann Wolfgang von Goethe. —Bielefeld: Velhagen & Klasing, 1918

8, 116 S. ;17 cm.

I516. 34/S334(1)

Schillers ausgewaehlte Werke: Mit einer Einleitung von Heinrich Stiehler. 1. Band, Schillers Leben und Wirken/Friedrich Schiller. —Berlin: A. Weichert Verlag, [?]

318 S. ;18 cm.

I516. 35/B928

Dantons Tod/Georg Buechner. —Leipzig: Insel Verlag, [?]

79 S. ;19 cm.

I516. 35/M522

Fuehrer durch das Schauspiel der Gegenwart: Die dramatischen Werke der Gegenwart/Leo Melitz. —Berlin: Globus Verlag G. m. b. H. , [?]

363 S. ;16 cm.

I516. 4/D722(2)

Der Idiot. 2. Band/F. M. Dostojewski. —Leipzig: Insel Verlag, [?]

375 S. ;19 cm.

I516. 4/D722(3)

Der Idiot. 3. Band/F. M. Dostojewski. —Leipzig: Insel Verlag, [?]

432 S. ;19 cm.

I516. 4/E88

Till Eulenspiegels lustige Streiche/Till Eulenspiegel. —Stuttgart: Loewes Verlag Ferdinand Carl, [?]

94 S. ;20 cm.

I516. 4/L755-8

Vergib und Vergiss: Preisgekroente Novelle/Ernst Lingen. —8. Aufl. . —Koeln am Rhein: Verlag von J. P. Bachem, [?]

330 S. ;17 cm.

I516. 4/L941

Meine erste Liebe und andere: Skizzen aus der Grossstadt/Max Luckow. —Berlin: Rich. Eckstein Nachf. , [?]

160 S. ;18 cm.

I516. 4/N269

Spaetes Glueck/Clara Nast. —Berlin: Verlag von A. Weichert,[?]

96 S. ;18 cm.

I516. 4/S348

Genovefa: Eine der schoensten und ruehrendsten Geschichten des Altertums/Christoph Schmid. —Stuttgart: Verlag von D. Gundert, [?]

108 S. ;16 cm.

I516. 43/G197-73

Das Gotteslehen: Roman aus dem 13. Jahrhundert/Ludwig Ganghofer. —73. Aufl.. —Stuttgart: Verlag von Adolf Bonz & Comp., c1919

413 S. ;18 cm.

I516. 44/D485(1)

Novellenbuch. 1. Band, Conrad Ferd. Meyer, Friedr. Spielhagen, Ernst v. Wildenbruch, Detlev v. Liliencron/Verlag der Deutschen Dichter Gedaechtnis Stiftung. —Hamburg: Verlag der Deutschen Dichter Gedaechtnis Stiftung, 1910

194 S. ;18 cm.

I516. 44/D722

Die Sanfte: Eine phantastische Erzaehlung/Fyodor Dostoyevsky. —Leipzig: Insel Verlag, [?]

71 S. ;18 cm.

I516. 44/F652-4

Seefahrt ist not! /Gorth Fock. —4. Aufl.. —Hamburg: Verlag von M. Glogau jr., 1915

282 S. ;19 cm.

I516. 44/F815

Clio: Historische Miniaturen/Anatole France. —Muenchen: K. Piper & Co. Verlag, 1912

145 S. ;18 cm.

I516. 44/F982

Im Banne des deutschen Adlers/Alfred Funke. —Berlin: Verlag von W. Vobach & Co., c1915

349 S. ;20 cm.

I516. 44/G599

Die Leiden des jungen Werthers/Johann Wolfgang Goethe. —Berlin: Fritz Heyder,[?]

170 S. ;17 cm.

I516. 44/G599D485

Die Leiden des jungen Werthers/Johann Wolfgang v. Goethe. —Berlin: Buchverlag fuers Deutsche Haus, 1908

284 S. ;17 cm.

I516. 44/H537

Die Roemerin: Novelle aus dem vierten Jahrhundert nach Christi/M. Herbert. —Koeln: Verlag und Druck von J. P. Bachem, c1914

154 S. ;18 cm.

I516. 44/K29(1-2)

Der gruene Heinrich. 1. und 2. Band/Gottfried Keller. —Berlin: Deutsches Verlagshaus Bong &Co.,[?]

387 S. ;19 cm.

I516. 44/K29-38(4. 1)

Gottfried Keller's gesammelte Werke. 4. Band, Leute von Seldwyla/Gottfried Keller. —38. Auflge. —Stuttgart und Berlin: J. G. Cotta'sche Buchhandlung Nachfolger, 1904

310 S. ;19 cm.

I516. 44/K29F347

In deiner Kammer/Paul Keller. —Paderborn: Verlag von Ferdinand Schoeningh, 1922

254 S. ;18 cm.

I516. 44/K29P349

Der gruene Heinrich/Gottfried Keller. —Pe-

king: Verlag der Pekinger Pappelinsel,[?]
241 S.;19 cm.

I516.44/K29S378
Martin Salander/Gottfried Keller.—Berlin: Schreitersche Verlagsbuchhandlung,[?]
304 S.;19 cm.

I516.44/M281-77
Koenigliche Hoheit/Thomas Mann.—71. bis 77. Aufl..—Berlin: S. Fischer Verlag,c1909
453 S.;19 cm.

I516.44/M615
Des deutschen Spiessers Wunderhorn: Gesammelte Novellen/Gustav Meyrink.—Muenchen: Albert Langen,c1913
143,140,143 S.;19 cm.

I516.44/P324
Blumen-, Frucht- und Dornenstuecke aus Jean Paul's Werk/Jean Paul.—Muenchen: R. Piper & Co. Verlag,1924
20,252 S.;18 cm.

I516.44/P324B456
Blumen-, Frucht- und Dornenstuecke aus Jean Paul's Werk/Jean Paul.—Muenchen: R. Piper & Co. Verlag,1924
29,221 S.;18 cm.

I516.44/P324B456P613
Blumen-, Frucht- und Dornenstuecke aus Jean Paul's Werk/Jean Paul.—Muenchen: R. Piper & Co. Verlag,1924
22,278 S.;18 cm.

I516.44/P762
Bewegung ist alles: Novellen und Skizzen/Alfred Polgar.—Frankfurt a. M.:Literarische Anstalt Ruetten & Loening,1909
148 S.;19 cm.

I516.44/R111-18
Der Hungerpastor/Wilhelm Raabe.—18. Aufl..—Berlin: Verlag von Otto Janke,1903
384 S.;19 cm.

I516.44/R363-2
Aus den Tiroler Bergen: Lustige und leidige Geschichten/ReimmicHl..—2. Aufl..—Brixen: Verlag der Pressvereins-Buchhandlung,[?]
448 S.;16 cm.

I516.44/R447(1)
Ut mine Stromtid. 1. Band/Fritz Reuter.—Berlin: Deutsche Bibliothek,[?]
9,306 S.;17 cm.

I516.44/S854(4)
Adalbert Stifters ausgewaehlte Werke in sechs Baenden: mit Stifters Bildnis, einem Gedicht in Faksimile, einer Abbildung des Stifters Denkmals und Stifters Biographie. 4. Band/Adalbert Stifter.—Leipzig: Max Hesse's Verlag,[?]
334 S.;17 cm.

I516.44/T452
Das Kaelbchen: Der umgewendete Dichter, Onkel Peppi-Heimkehr/Ludwig Thoma.—Muenchen: Albert Langen,c1916
207 S.;18 cm.

I516.44/Z83
Die Erben/Hanns von Zobeltitz.—Jena: Hermann Costenoble Verlagsbuchhandlung,[?]
224,197 S.;19 cm.

I516.45/B517
Die Sonne Satans/Georg Bernanos.—Hellerau: MCMXXVII bei Jakob Hegner,[?]
357 S.;19 cm.

I516.45/B566
Die Gruppe Bosemueller/Werner Beumelburg.—Oldenburg I. O.:Gerhard Stalling,c1930

332 S. ;21 cm.

I516. 45/B612

Die Vogelscheuche/Rudolf G. Bingding. —Hamburg: Deutsche Dichter Gedaechtnis Stiftung, c1927

61 S. ;18 cm.

I516. 45/B673

Krach im Hinterhaus/Maximilian Boettcher. —Berlin: Buchwarte Verlag Lothar Blanvalet, 1936

281 S. ;19 cm.

I516. 45/B928

Der "Stern von Afrika": Eine Reise ins Weltall/Bruno H. Buergel. —Berlin: Verlag Ullstein, c1920

301 S. ;19 cm.

I516. 45/C181

Mein Dorf am See: Erzaehlungen aus der Innerschweiz/Josef Maria Camenzind. —Freiburg im Breisgau: Herder&Co. G. m. b. H. Verlagsbuchhandlung, 1937

199 S. ;19 cm.

I516. 45/C942

Kaleidoskop/Anna Croissant-Rust. —Muenchen: Thespis Verlag G. m. b. H. , c1920

289 S. ;15 cm.

I516. 45/D129-151(2)

Ein Kampf um Rom: historischer Roman. 2. Band/Felix Dahn. —136. bis 151. Aufl. . —Leipzig: Verlag von Breitkopf & Haertel, 1922

412 S. ;17 cm.

I516. 45/D129-151(3)

Ein Kampf um Rom: historischer Roman. 3. Band/Felix Dahn. —136. bis 151. Aufl. . —Leipzig: Verlag von Breitkopf & Haertel, 1922

438 S. ;17 cm.

I516. 45/D583-16

Die Suende wider Das Blut/Artur Dinter. —16. Aufl. . —Leipzig: Verlag Matthes und Trost, c1921

352 S. ;18 cm.

I516. 45/D722(1)

Die Daemonen: Roman in zwei Baenden. 1. Band/F. M. Dostojewski. —Muenchen: R. Piper & Co. Verlag, c1921

32,520 S. ;18 cm.

I516. 45/D772(2)

Die Daemonen: Roman in zwei Baenden. 2. Band/F. M. Dostojewski. —Muenchen: R. Piper & Co. Verlag, c1921

521-1138 S. ;18 cm.

I516. 45/E37

Geliebter Sohn: Elternbriefe an beruehmte Deutsche/Paul Elbogen. —Berlin: Ernst Rowohlt Verlag, c1930

514 S. ;21 cm.

I516. 45/E74

Felix Hopf, der verhinderte Braeutigam/Karl Escher. —Berlin: Dr. Eysler & Co. A. —G. , c1923

208 S. ;20 cm.

I516. 45/F596

Der Haupttreffer = Michl: Ein heiterer Roman/Victor Fleischer. —Leipzig: Verlag von Fr. Wilh. Grunow, c1921

258 S. ;19 cm.

I516. 45/F736

Die Opferflamme/Gertrud von le Fort. —Leipzig: Insel Verlag, 1938

54 S. ;18 cm.

I516. 45/F828

Erzaehlungen/Bruno Frank. —Berlin: Ernst

Rowohlt Verlag, c1926
311 S. ; 19 cm.

I516.45/G735
Roblanks Kinder: Roman einer Berliner Familie/Erdmann Graeser. —Berlin: Paul Franke Verlag, [?]
300 S. ; 19 cm.

I516.45/G775-32
Heimweh des Herzens/Traud Gravenhorst. —23. bis 32. Aufl.. —Berlin: S. Fischer Verlag, c1935
171 S. ; 19 cm.

I516.45/Gj48
Der Pilger Kamanita: Ein Legendenroman/Karl Gjellerup. —Frankfurt a. M. : Literarische Anstalt Ruetten & Loening, 1921
322 S. ; 18 cm.

I516.45/H135
Der Bankherr und die Genien der Liebe/Carl Haensel. —Berlin: S. Fischer Verlag, c1938
415 S. ; 18 cm.

I516.45/H374
Der Ketzer von Soana/Gerhart Hauptmann. —Berlin: S. Fischer Verlag, c1918
165 S. ; 22 cm.

I516.45/H459
Der Wetterwart/Jakob Christoph Heer. —Stuttgart: J. G. Cotta'sche Buchhandlung Nachfolger, 1927
416 S. ; 19 cm.

I516.45/H459C846
Felix Notvest/Jakob Christoph Heer. —Stuttgart: J. G. Cotta'sche Buchhandlung Nachfolger, 1922
385 S. ; 19 cm.

I516.45/H537
Prinz Spiro Maria/M. Herbert. —Koeln: Verlag von J. P. Bachem, c1919
223 S. ; 18 cm.

I516.45/H581
Der grosse Bischof/Franz Herwig. —Muenchen: Verlag Josef Roefel, c1930
340 S. ; 19 cm.

I516.45/H582
Die Wiskottens/Rudolf Herzog. —Stuttgart: J. G. Gotta'sche Buchhandlung Nachfolger, 1928
460 S. ; 19 cm.

I516.45/H592
Der falsche Claus Hartmann/Hans Heuer. —Berlin: Otto Uhlmann Verlag, c1934
279 S. ; 19 cm.

I516.45/H615
Unterwegs: Die Lebensfahrt eines romantischen Strolches/Artur Heye. —Berlin: Safari Verlag G. m. b. H. , c1925
288 S. ; 20 cm.

I516.45/H693
Koenigskinder/Sophie Hoechstetter. —Leipzig: Verlag von K. F. Koehler, c1928
297 S. ; 18 cm.

I516.45/H895
Der Kampf am Dober/Victor Hugo. —Berlin: Franz Schneider Verlag, c1922
207 S. ; 20 cm.

I516.45/K29
Waldwinter: Roman aus den schlesischen Bergen/Paul Keller. —Breslau: Bergstadtverlag, c1922
264 S. ; 18 cm.

I516.45/K63

Borgia：Roman einer Familie/Klabund.—Wien：Phaidon Verlag，c1928

283 S.；19 cm.

I516.45/K96-2

Fische im Fjord！/Artur Kuhnert.—2. Aufl..—Leipzig：Verlag vo Philipp Reclam jun.，c1930

278 S.；19 cm.

I516.45/L163

Fanale am Himmel：Technisch-politischer Roman/Karl-August von Laffert.—Leipzig：Ernst Keils Nachfolger（August Scherl）G. m. b. H.，c1925

205 S.；18 cm.

I516.45/L174

Die sieben Todfuenden：Ausgewaehlte Legenden und Erzaehlungen/Selma Lagerloef.—Muenchen：Albert Langen，1920

112 S.；17 cm.

I516.45/L346(1)

Auf zwei Planeten：Roman in zwei Buechern. 1. Band/Kurd Lasswitz.—Leipzig：Verlag von B. Elischer Nachfolger，[?]

421 S.；18 cm.

I516.45/L346(2)

Auf zwei Planeten：Roman in zwei Buechern. 2. Band/Kurd Lasswitz.—Leipzig：Verlag von B. Elischer Nachfolger，[?]

547 S.；18 cm.

I516.45/L433

Das Schweisstuch der Veronika/Gertrub von Le Fort.—Muenchen：Josef Koesel & Friedrich Pustet，c1928

356 S.；19 cm.

I516.45/L676

Die Hauptstrasse：Carola Kennicotts Geschichte/Sinclair Lewis.—Berlin：Verlag von Th. Knaur Nachf.，[?]

384 S.；19 cm.

I516.45/L676D485

Sam Dodesworth/Sinclair Lewis.—Berlin：Deutsche Buch-Gemeinschaft G. m. b. H.，c1930

515 S.；20 cm.

I516.45/M261-8

Der Gottesschatz：Roman aus der Gegenwart/E. von Maltzahn.—8. Aufl..—Schwerin：Verlag von Friedrich Bahn，1922

260 S.；19 cm.

I516.45/M281(2)

Buddenbrooks：Verfall einer Familie. 2. Band/Thomas Mann.—Berlin：S. Fischer Verlag，1922

477 S.；19 cm.

I516.45/M281-16

Herr und Hund/Thomas Mann.—16. Aufl..—Berlin：S. Fischer Verlag，1929

140 S.；18 cm.

I516.45/M281-138(1)

Buddenbrooks：Verfall einer Familie. 1. Band/Thomas Mann.—129. bis 138. Aufl..—Berlin：S. Fischer Verlag，c1922

499 S.；19 cm.

I516.45/M281-985

Buddenbrooks：Verfall einer Familie/Thomas Mann.—936. bis 985. Aufl..—Berlin：S. Fischer Verlag，[?]

729 S.；19 cm.

I516.45/M466

Der Waldschwarze und andere Erzaehlungen/Karl May.—Radebeul bei Dresden：Karl May Verlag，[?]

506 S. ;18 cm.

I516. 45/M687

Die Kaiserinnen/Jos. Mockenhaupt. —Waldsassen: Verlagsanstalt Albert Angerer,[?]

501 S. ;19 cm.

I516. 45/M699-2

Allhier verkauft man Weisheit: Treuherzige deutsche Geschichten/Heinrich Mohr. —2. Aufl.. —Freiburg im Breisgau: Herder & Co. G. m. b. H. Verlagsbuchhandlung,1936

a8,173 S. ;23 cm.

I516. 45/M899

Die verborgene Symphonie: Der Roman eines deutschen Musikers/Hans Joachim Moser. —Leipzig: L. Staackmann Verlag,c1936

281 S. ;19 cm.

I516. 45/M946-5

Das Schneiderchen von Mackebach: Ein Dorfidyll in Pfaelzer Mundart/Richard Mueller. —5. Aufl.. —Kaiserslautern: E. Lincks-Crusius, 1924

91 S. ;17 cm.

I516. 45/N684

Schwarze Schwaenke: Froehliche Geschichten aus unserem schoenen Alten Deutsch-Ostafrika/Ernst Nigmann. —Berlin: Safari Verlag G. m. b. H. ,c1922

166 S. ;22 cm.

I516. 45/Q1

Die Robbenfaenger/Hellmuth Quast-Peregrin. —Berlin: Peter J. Oestergaard Verlag, c1931

288 S. ;19 cm.

I516. 45/R813

Der Koenig der Vagabunden/Erwin Rosen. —Hamburg: Ernst Schwabe Verlag,[?]

238 S. ;18 cm.

I516. 45/S214

Ola, die Schwedin/Ulrich Sander. —Karlsbad: Adam Kraft Verlag,c1940

315 S. ;19 cm.

I516. 45/S313

Die schwarze Valtin und die weisse Osanna/Ruth Schaumann. —Berlin: G. Grote'sche Verlagsbuchhandlung,c1938

235 S. ;20 cm.

I516. 45/S349

Rosenfelix/Walter Schmidthaessler. —Berlin: Dr. Eysler & Co. G. m. b. H. ,c1919

269 S. ;20 cm.

I516. 45/S731

Kaeufer der Ehre/Otto Soyka. —Leipzig: Ernst Keil's Nachfolger,c1922

346 S. ;18 cm.

I516. 45/S864

Eine Stunde vor Tag/Juliana von Stockhausen. —Leipzig: L. Staackmann Verlag,c1933

352 S. ;19 cm.

I516. 45/T452

Heilige Nacht/Ludwig Thoma. —Muenchen: Albert Langen,1930

63 S. ;21 cm.

I516. 45/T584

Pallieter/Felix Timmermans. —Leipzig: Insel Verlag,[?]

290 S. ;20 cm.

I516. 45/T584M575

Bauernpsalm/Felix Timmermans. —Leipzig: Im Insel Verlag,[?]

218 S. ;21 cm.

I516. 45/T587-2

Barbaras froehlicher Hausstand/Carl Tinhofer. —2. Aufl.. —Freiburg im Breisgau: Herder & Co. G. m. b. H. Verlagsbuchhandlung, 1938

398 S. ; 19 cm.

I516. 45/U54

Viga-Ljot und Vigdis/Sigrid Undset. —Berlin: Bruno Cassirer, c1931

232 S. ; 19 cm.

I516. 45/V292

Der Schneider himmlischer Hosen/Daniele Vare. —Berlin: Paul Zsolnay Verlag, 1940

328 S. ; 18 cm.

I516. 45/W322(2)

Christian Wahnschaffe. 2. Band, Ruth/Jakob Wassermann. —Berlin: S. Fischer Verlag, c1919

453 S. ; 21 cm.

I516. 45/W426-2

Die Letzten von Sankt Klaren/Leo Weismantel. —Freiburg im Breisgau: Herder & Co. G. m. b. H. Verlagsbuchhandlung, 1940

342 S. ; 19 cm.

I516. 45/W642

Das einfache Leben/Ernst Wiechert. —Muenchen: Albert Langen/Georg Mueller, c1939

390 S. ; 19 cm.

I516. 45/Z19

Helden des Alltags: Ein Novellenbuch/Ernst Zahn. —Stuttgart: Deutsche Verlags-Anstalt, 1920

400 S. ; 18 cm.

I516. 54/R813-10(1)

Der Deutsche Lausbub in Amerika: Erinnerungen und Eindruecke. 1. Teil/Erwin Rosen. —10. Aufage. —Stuttgart: Verlag Robert Lutz, c1911

10, 302 S. ; 18 cm.

I516. 55/B242

Lule: Vaetersatzung und Vaeterbrauch in den albanischen Bergen/Fabian Barcata. —Muenchen: Dr. Franz A. Pfeiffer & Co. Verlagsgesellschaft m. b. H. , 1924

280 S. ; 18 cm.

I516. 55/E74

Erdachte Briefe/Ernst Wilhelm Eschmann. —Jena: Eugen Diederichs Verlag, c1938

153 S. ; 18 cm.

I516. 55/F528

Das Alte und das neue System: Die politischen Koepfe Deutschlands/Johammes Fischart. —Berlin: Oesterheld & Co. Verlag, c1919

210 S. ; 18 cm.

I516. 55/F528(3)

Koepfe der Gegenwart. 3. Folge, Das Alte und das neue System/Johammes Fischart. —Berlin: Oesterheld & Co. Verlag, c1920

280 S. ; 18 cm.

I516. 55/K87

Suedsee-Erinnerungen/Stefan von Kotze. —Berlin: Dom Verlag, c1925

178 S. ; 20 cm.

I516. 6/H882

Der letzte Sommer: Eine Erzaehlung in Briefen/Ricarda Huch. —Leipzig: Insel Verlag, [?]

79 S. ; 18 cm.

I516. 64/H468(1)

Heinrich Heine's saemtliche Werke. 1. Band, Franzoesische Zustaende/Heinrich Heine. —Hamburg: Hoffmann und Campe, 1872

8, 436, 264 S. ; 16 cm.

I516.64/K91

Deutsche Trostbriefe/Rudolf Krauss. —Stuttgart: Verlag von Julius Hoffmann, c1919

220 S. ;19 cm.

I516.64/M729(3)

Generalfeldmarschall Graf von Moltke Ausgewaehlte Werke: Vier Baende. 3. band, Feldherr und Staatsmann/Graf von Moltke. —Berlin: Verlag von Reimar Hobbing, c1901

14,414 S. ;29 cm.

I516.64/R573

Briefe an einen jungen Dichter/Rainer Maria Rilke. —Leipzig: Insel Verlag, [?]

54 S. ;18 cm.

I516.65/B721

Indienfahrt/Waldemar Bonsels. —Frankfurt a. M. :Verlag der Literarischen Anstalt Ruetten & Loening, c1916

259 S. ;21 cm.

I516.65/E33

Tubutsch/Albert Ehrenstein. —Leipzig: Insel Verlag, 1919

54 S. ;18 cm.

I516.65/E37

Lieber Vater: Briefe beruehmter Deutscher an ihre Vaeter/Paul Elbogen. —Berlin: Ernst Rowohlt Verlag, c1931

230 S. ;21 cm.

I516.65/E97

Hinter Pflug und Schraubstock: Skizzen aus dem Taschenbuch eines Ingenieurs/Max Eyth. —Stuttgart: Deutsche Verlags-Anstalt, 1922

558 S. ;20 cm.

I516.65/H249

Maerchenstadt und Sonnenvoegel/Hela Hansen. —Shanghai: Max Noessler & Co. , c1940

131 S. ;20 cm.

I516.65/H374

Griechischer Fruehling/Gerhart Hauptmann. —Berlin: S. Fischer Verlag, 1921

266 S. ;21 cm.

I516.65/H469

Maria im Volk/Borromaeus Heinrich. —M. Gladbach: Volksvereinsverlag GmbH. , c1927

141 S. ;27 cm.

I516.65/K44-6(1)

Das Reisetagebuch eines Philosophen. 1. Band/Hermann Keyserling. —6. Aufl. . —Darmstadt: Otto Reichl Verlag, c1922

32,412 S. ;19 cm.

I516.65/K44-6(2)

Das Reisetagebuch eines Philosophen. 2. Band/Hermann Keyserling. —6. Aufl. . —Darmstadt: Otto Reichl Verlag, c1922

413-886,44 S. ;19 cm.

I516.65/M894

Die Inseln der Weisheit: Geschichte einer abenteuerlichen Entdeckungsfahrt/Alexander Moszkowski. —Berlin: F. Fontane & Co. , c1922

283 S. ;22 cm.

I516.65/S558

Leberecht Huehnchen/Heinrich Seidel. —Stuttgart: J. G. Cotta'sche Buchhandlung Nachfolger, 1922

342 S. ;19 cm.

I516.65/T439

Das Gesicht des Jahrhunderts: Briefe an Zeitgenossen/Frank Thiess. —Stuttgart: J. Engelhorns Nachf. , c1923

272 S. ;22 cm.

I516.65/T587

Siebensorg：Ein Idyll von Liebe，Kindern und grossen Leuten/Carl Tinhofer.—Muenchen：Verlag Koesel & Pustet，c1932

263 S.；20 cm.

I516.65/T887

Rheinsberg：Ein Bilderbuch fuer Beliebte/Kurt Tucholsky.—Berlin：Josef Singer Verlag A.—G.，1930

110 S.；17 cm.

I516.72/E69(2)

Die Volkslieder der Deutschen：Eine vollstaendige Sammlung der vorzueglichen deutschen Volkslieder von der Mitte des fuenfzehten bis erste Haelfte des neunzehnten Jahrhunderts. 2. Band/Friedrich Karl Freiherrn von Erlach.—Mannheim：Heinrich Hoff Verlag，1834

631 S.；21 cm.

I516.72/E69(3)

Die Volkslieder der Deutschen：Eine vollstaendige Sammlung der vorzueglichen deutschen Volkslieder von der Mitte des fuenfzehten bis erste Haelfte des neunzehnten Jahrhunderts. 3. Band/Friedrich Karl Freiherrn von Erlach.—Mannheim：Heinrich Hoff Verlag，1835

632 S.；21 cm.

I516.72/S588

Die deutschen Volkslieder/Karl Simrock.—Basel：Venno Schwarbe Verlagsbuchhandlung，[?]

627 S.；18 cm.

I516.73/G864(2)

Deutsche Sagen：Gesammelt durch die Brueder Grimm. 2. Band/Brueder Grimm.—Muenchen：Georg Mueller，[?]

20，339 S.；

I516.73/R348

Thule：Ausgewaehlte Sagas von altgermanischen Bauern und Herden/Konstantin Reichardt.—Jena：Eugen Diederichs Verlag，c1934

236 S.；20 cm.

I516.73/S294

Wendekreis：neuer Anekdoten/Wilhelm Schaefer.—Muenchen：Albert Langen/Georg Mueller，1937

266 S.；18 cm.

I516.73/T123

Rumpelstilzchen Berliner Allerlei/Verlag der Taeglichen Rundschau.—Berlin：Verlag der Taeglichen Rundschau，c1922

306 S.；20 cm.

I516.82/D566

Mein Kinderhimmel：Gesammelte Kinderlieder und -Reime/Georg Dietrich.—Muenchen：Georg W. Dietrich Hofverleger，[?]

147 S.；22 cm.

I516.84/H185

Doris/M. Haller.—Berlin：Franz Schneider Verlag，c1936

79 S.；19 cm.

I516.85/Sp998

Kurze Geschichten：fuer Kinder und solche，die Kinder lieb haben/Johanna Spyri.—Reutlingen：Enszlin & Laibling Verlagsbuchhandlung，[?]

348 S.；21 cm.

I516.85/Sp998-3

Gritlis Kinder：Eine Geschichte fuer Kinder und solche，die Kinder lieb haben/Johanna Spyri.—3. Aufl..—Stuttgart：Loewes Verlag Ferdinand Carl，1935

128，124 S.；21 cm.

I516. 99/K66(1. 1)

Klopstocks gesammelte Werke: in vier Baenden. 1. Band, Der Messias. 1. Teil/Klopstock. —Stuttgart: J. G. Cotta'sche/Gebrueder Kroener,[?]

272 S. ;18 cm.

I516. 99/S741

Herzensheilige/Diedrich Speckmann. —Berlin: Martin Warneck,c1918

313 S. ;18 cm.

I516. 99/S875-9

Edelsteine aus reicher Schatzkammer: Eine Sammlung schoener Stellen aus den Schriften/Alban Stolz. —8. und 9. Aufl.. —Freiburg im Breisgau: Herder & Co. G. m. b. H. Verlagsbuchhandlung,1920

11. 334 S. ;16 cm.

I521. 34/H685(5-8)

Grillparzers Werke. 5. bis 8. Teil/Stefan Hock. —Leipzig: Deutsches Verlagshaus Bong & Co. ,[?]

212,258,308,187 S. ;18 cm.

I521. 34/H685(9-12)

Grillparzers Werke. 9. bis 12. Teil/Stefan Hock. —Leipzig: Deutsches Verlagshaus Bong & Co. ,[?]

436,152,11 S. ;18 cm.

I521. 65/A466-15

Wie ich es sehe/Peter Altenberg. —12. bis 15. Aufl.. —Berlin: S. Fischer Verlag,1919

14,332 S. ;19 cm.

I522. 34/B151

Grotesken: Der Klub der Erloeser-Der Faun-Die tiefe Natur/Hermann Bahr. —Wien: Verlagsbuchhandlung Carl Konegen,1907

264 S. ;18 cm.

I522. 44/K29

Das Faehnlein der sieben Aufrechten/Gottfried Keller. —Leipzig: Insel Verlag,[?]

79 S. ;18 cm.

I522. 54/S768

Heimat zu: Erlebnisse eines Schweizers in den Augusttagen 1914/Eugen F. Sprengler. —Bern: Verlag A. Francke,1916

192 S. ;16 cm.

I524. 45/J48-66

Caesar/Mirko Jelusich. —61. bis 66. Aufl.. —Wien: F. Speidel'sche Verlagsbuchhandlung, c1929

352 S. ;19 cm.

I533. 45/G971

Und ewig singen die Waelder/Trygve Gulbranssen. —Muenchen: Albert Langen Georg Mueller Verlag,c1935

257 S. ;19 cm.

I546. 23/A411

Die goettliche Komoedie/Dante Allighieri. —Berlin: Verlag von Th. Knaur Nachf. ,[?]

540 S. ;19 cm.

I546. 23/A411V597

Die goettliche Komoedie/Dante Alighieri. —Muenchen: Josef Koesel & Friedrich Pustet K. —G. ,1926

1123 S. ;19 cm.

I552. 24/B273

Sonette aus dem Portugiesischen/Elizabeth Barret-Browning. —Leipzig: Insel Verlag,[?]

46 S. ;18 cm.

I561. 33/S339(1)

William Shakespeare's saemtliche Dramatische Werke in drei Baenden. 1. Band/Schlegel [usw.]. —Leipzig: Verlag von Philipp Reclam

jun. ,[unbekannnt]
857 S. ;17 cm.

I561. 33/S339(2)
William Shakespeare's saemtliche Dramatische Werke in drei Baenden. 2. Band/Schlegel [usw.]. —Leipzig: Verlag von Philipp Reclam jun. ,unbekannnt
945 S. ;17 cm.

I561. 44/W671
Das Bildnis des Dorian Gray/Oscar Wilde. —Berlin: Th. Knaur Nachf. ,[?]
295 S. ;17 cm.

I561. 6/L351
Verborgene Helden/G. Latente. —Kaldenkirchen: Missionsdruckerei in Steyl,[?]
176 S. ;19 cm.

I561. 65/B648
Afrika: Dunkel lockende Welt/Tania Blixen. —Stuttgart: Deutsche Verlags-Anstalt,[?]
336 S. ;20 m.

I564. 44/C837
Uilenspiegel und Lamme Goedzak: Ein froehliches Buch trotz Tod und Traenen/Charles De Coster. —Leipzig: Im Insel Verlag,[?]
640 S. ;18 cm.

I712. 45/A518
Die Frauen der Coornvelts/Jo Van Ammers-Kueller. —Bremen: Carl Schuenemann Verlag,[?]
452 S. ;19 cm.

J 艺术

J110. 9/H198
Geschichte der Kunst: Von der altchristlichen Zeit bis zur Gegenwart/Richard Hamann. —Berlin: Verlag von Th. Knaur Nachf. ,c1932
959 S. ;24 cm.

J110. 9/W843(3)
Geschichte der Kunst aller Zeiten und Voelker. 3. Band, Die Kunst der christlichen Fruehzeit und des Mittelalters/Karl Woermann. —Leipzig: Bibliographisches Institut,c1918
18,574 S. ;25 cm.

J120. 9/M948(2)
Chinesische Kunstgeschichte. Band II, Die Baukunst Das Kunstgewerke/Oskar Muensterberg. —Esslingen a. N. :Paul Neff Verlag (Max Schreiber),1912
21,500 S. ;26 cm.

J131/G548
Die Kunst Ostasiens: Der Umkreis ihres Denkens und Gestaltens/Curt Glaser. —Leipzig: Insel Verlag,1922
8,207 S. ;22 cm.

J150. 9/P648
Das Problem der Generation: In der Kunstgeschichte Europas/Wilhelm Pinder. —Berlin: Frankfurter Verlags-Anstalt,c1926
32,160 S. ;21 cm.

J151. 61/M941-19
Deutsche Kunst: im Wandel der Zeiten/Wilhelm Mueseler. —19. Aufl. . —Berlin: Safari Verlag,[?]

206 S. ;25 cm.

J217/B888

Original-Graphik：Radierungen，Lithographien，Holzschnitte/F. Bruckmann A. —G.. —Muenchen：F. Bruckmann A. —G.，1925

160 S. ;20 cm.

J231/H811-2

Fuenfhundert Selbstportraets：Von der Antike bis zur Gegenwart <Plastik，Malerei，Graphik >/Horovitz. —2. Aufl.. —Wien：Phaidon Verlag，c1936

528 S. ;27 cm.

J293/W427-3

Schrift- und Buchwesen in alter und neuer Zeit/O. Weise. —3. Aufl.. —Leipzig：Verlag von B. G. Teubner，c1910

155，32 S. ;18 cm.

J331(516)/L729

Deutsche Plastik/Georg Lill. —Berlin：Volksverband der Buecherfreunde Wegweiser Verlag G. m. b. H.，1925

248 S. ;21 cm.

J339(516)/I59

Die Muttergottes：Deutsche Bildwerke/Insel Verlag. —Leipzig：Im Insel Verlag，[?]

63 S. ;18 cm.

J608/D485

Deutsches evangelisches Gesangsbuch/Der Deutsche Evangelische Kirchenausschuss. —Berlin：E. S. Mittler & Sohn，1926

8，488 S. ;18 cm.

J621. 1/P945

Schule fuer die Boehm-Floete/Emil Prill. —Leipzig：Musikverlag Wilhelm Zimmermann，[?]

123 S. ;28 cm.

J652/K11-12(3)

Liederbuch：Fuer hoehere Maedchenschulen，Lyzeen，Oberlyzeen und Studienanstalten. III. Teil，Oberstufe/Ludwig Kageler. —12. Aufl.. —Hannover：Norddeutsche Verlagsanstalt O. Goedel，1916

368 S. ;21 cm.

J652(516)/M463

Neues Deutsches Liederbuch/Max Noessler & Co.. —Shanghai：Max Noessler & Co.，1942

8，102 S. ;14 cm.

J652(516)/N489

Der Spielmann：Liederbuch fuer Jugend und Volk. Schulausgabe/Klemens Neumann. —Mainz：Matthias Gruenewald Verlag，1930

320 S. ;16 cm.

J652(516)/P725

Der Liederschrein：Hundertzehn deutsche，likauische und masurische Volkslieder aus Ostpreussen/Karl Plenzat. —Leipzig：Friedrich Hofmeister，1922

160 S. ;19 cm.

J652. 2/E69(1)

Volkslieder der Deutschen：Eine vollstaendige Sammlung der vorzueglichen deutschen Volkslieder der Mitte des fuenfzehnten bis in die erste Haelfte des neunzehnten Jahrhunderts. 1. Band/Friedrich Karl Freiherrn von Erlach. —Mannheim：Heinrich Hoff，1834

536 S. ;21 cm.

J652. 8/R739

Heididei：Ein Singebuechlein/P. Damian Rohrbach. —Werl i. Westf.：Franziskus Druckerei，1930

255，13 S. ;17 cm.

J838/B289

Preis-Verzeichnis von Bartl's Akademie fuer

moderne magische Kunst: Beste Bezugsquelle fuer Zauberapparate Illusionen, Schaustuecke u. Buehnen-Einrichtung sowie Vexier- und Geduldspiele/Janos Bartl. —Hamburg:[s. n.],[?]
316 S. ;22 cm.

历史、地理

K1/C443(1)
Die Grundlagen des neunzenten Jahrhunderts. 1. Haelfte/Houston Stewart Chamberlain. —Muenchen: F. Bruckmann A. —G. ,[?]
632 S. ;19 cm.

K1/C443(2)
Die Grundlagen des neunzenten Jahrhunderts. 2. Haelfte/Houston Stewart Chamberlain. —Muenchen: F. Bruckmann A. —G. ,[?]
633-1246 S. ;19 cm.

K1/G926-3
Das Zeitalter der Entdeckungen/S. Guenther. —3. Aufl. . —Leipzig: Verlag von B. G. Teubner,c1912
104,14 S. ;18 cm.

K1/O28-4(2-3)
Bilder aus der Weltgeschichte: Ein Lehr- und Lesebuch fuer Gymnasten, Lehrerseminarien und andere hoehere Schulen, sowie zum Selbstunterrichte. 2. und 3. Teil, Mittlere und neuere Geschichte/Wilhelm Oechsli. —4. Aufl. . —Winterthur: Verlag von Alb. Hoster,1903
8,314 S. ;19 cm.

K1/P729-11
Auszug aus der alten, mittleren und neueren Geschichte/Karl Ploetz. —11. Aufl. . —Berlin: Verlag von A. G. Ploetz,1895
8,434 S. ;18 cm.

K1/S918
Historische Miniaturen/August Strindberg. —Muenchen: Georg Mueller,c1926
407 S. ;20 cm.

K1/W641-3(2)
Illustrierte Weltgeschichte in vier Baenden. Band II, Geschichte des Mittelalters/S. Widmann. —3. Aufl. . —Wien: Allgemeine Verlags-Gesellschaft m. b. H. ,[?]
8,528 S. ;27 cm.

K1/W641-3(3)
Illustrierte Weltgeschichte in vier Baenden. Band III, Geschichte der neueren Zeit/S. Widmann. —3. Aufl. . —Wien: Allgemeine Verlags-Gesellschaft m. b. H. ,[?]
8,472 S. ;27 cm.

K1-43/H447-49
Auszug aus Welters Lehrbuch der Weltgeschichte fuer Schulen/A. Hechelmann. —49. Aufl. . —Muenster: Verlag der Coppenrath'schen Buchhandlung,1907
13,459 S. ;20 cm.

K107/H335-10
Der Treppenwitz der Weltgeschichte: Geschichte Irrtuemer, Entstellungen und Erfindungen/W. L. Hertslet. —10. Aufl. . —Berlin: Verlag der Haude & Spenerschen Buchhandlung Mar Paschke,1927
8,376 S. ;21 cm.

K107/S744-42(2)

Der Untergang des Abendlandes: Umrisse einer Morphologie der Weltgeschichte. 2. Band, Welthistorische Perspektiven/Oswald Spengler. —31. bis 42. Aufl..—Muenchen: C. H. Beck'sche Verlagsbuchhandlung Oskar Beck,1922

635,12 S. ;23 cm.

K107/S744-52(1)

Der Untergang des Abendlandes: Umrisse einer Morphologie der Weltgeschichte. 1. Band, Gestalt und Wirklichkeit/Oswald Spengler. —48. bis 52. Aufl..—Muenchen: C. H. Beck'sche Verlagsbuchhandlung Oskar Beck,c1923

10,557 S. ;23 cm.

K126/M733

Das Weltreich der Caesaren/Theodor Mommsen. —Wien: Phaidon Verlag,c1933

821 S. ;21 cm.

K25/W323

Die Erschliessung Chinas: Kulturhistorische und wirtschaftspolitische Aufsaetze zur Geschichte Ostasiens/W. P. Wassiljew. —Leipzig: Dieterich'sche Verlagsbuchhandlung,1909

11,236 S. ;23 cm.

K295.1/S444

Sehen: Studien aus einer chinesischen Weltstadt/Fritz Secker. —Schanghai: Max Noessler & Co. G. m. b. H. ,c1913

130 S. ;24 cm.

K382/K62-2(3)

Geschichte des Volks Israel. 3. Band,Die Zeit der Wegfuehrung nach Babel und die Aufrichtung der neuen Gemeinde/Rudolf Kittel. —1. und 2. Aufl..—Stuttgart: Verlag von W. Kohlhammer,1929

16,762 S. ;24 cm.

K382.8/K62-2

Gestalten und Gedanken in Israel: Geschichte eines Volkes in Charakterbildern/Rudolf Kittel. —2. Aufl..—Leipzig: Quelle & Meyer,[?]

9,535 S. ;21 cm.

K500/F928-5

Leitfaden der Geschichte: fuer die unteren und mittleren Klassen hoeherer Lehranstalten/J. Frohnmeyer. —5. Aufl..—Stuttgart: Verlag von Adolf Bonz & Comp,1909

290 S. ;21 cm.

K504/Z83-2(2)

Chronik der Gesellschaft unter dem letzten Kaiserreich. 2. Band,1902-1914/Fedor von Zobeltitz. —2. Aufl..—Hamburg: Alster Verlag, c1922

379 S. ;23 cm.

K516/G876

Geschichte und Sage/Anna T. Gronow. —Bosten: Ginn And Company,c1916

8,330 S. ;19 cm.

K516/R535-3

Grundriss der neueren Geschichte/Gustav Richter. —3. Aufl..—Leipzig: Verlag von B. G. Teubner,1901

14,164 S. ;21 cm.

K516/S294-9(2)

Deutsche Geschichte. 2. Band, Neuzeit/Dietrich Schaefer. —9. Aufl..—Jena: Verlag von Gustav Fischer,1922

10,574 S. ;23 cm.

K516/S744(1)

Jahre der Entscheidung. 1. Teil, Deutschland und die weltgeschichtliche Entwicklung/Oswald Spengler. —Muenchen: C. H. Beck'sche Verlagsbuchhandlung,1934

14,165 S. ;24 cm.

K516/S842-7

Geschichts-Erzaehlungen fuer die Unterstufe/Theodor Steudel. —7. Aufl..—Leipzig: Verlag und Druck von B. G. Teubner,1931

100 S. ;23 cm.

K516-43/B721-2

Lehrbuch der Geschichte fuer Lyzeen/Fr. zur Bonsen. —2. Aufl..—Duesseldorf: Verlag von L. Schwann,1924

8,382 S. ;22 cm.

K516-43/S324

Lehrbuch der Geschichte fuer hoehere Lehranstalten: in Uebereinstimmung mit den neuen Lehrplaenen/K. Schenk. —Leipzig: Verlag von B. G. Teubner,1899

70 S. ;21 cm.

K516. 31/F499

Vorreformationsgeschichtliche Forschungen. Geschichte des Armutsstreites im Franziskanerorden bis zum Konzil von Vienne/Heinrich Finke, Karl Balthasar. —Muenster i. W.: Aschendorffsche Verlagsbuchhandlung,1911

284 S. ;24 cm.

K516. 33/R198

Deutsche Geschichte im Zeitalter der Reformation/Leopold von Ranke. —Wien: Phaidon Verlag,[?]

1287 S. ;21 cm.

K516. 9/R918

Geschichtliche Heimatkunde des Kreises Brilon/Josef Ruether. —Bigge i. W.: Verlag der Josefs-Druckerei,1920

286 S. ;20 cm.

K827/B642-2

China unter der Kaiserin Witwe: Die Lebens- und Zeit-Geschichte der Kaiserin Tzu Hsi/J. O. P. Bland, E. Backhouse. —2. Aufl..—Berlin: Verlag con Karl Siegismund,1913

16,503 S. ;24 cm.

K827/P895

Das Erbe Tschingis-Chans/Michael Prawdin. —Stuttgart: Deutsche Verlags-Anstalt,c1935

294 S. ;20 cm.

K835. 16/C978(1)

Denkwuerdigkeiten des Fuersten Chlodwig zu Hohenlohe-Schillingsfuerst: Im Auftrage des Prinzen Alexander zu Hohenlohe-Schillingsfuerst. 1. Band/Friedrich Curtius. —Stuttgart: Deutsche Verlags-Anstalt,1907

8,440S. ;24 cm.

K835. 16/G926

Hausbuch schwaebischer Erzaehler/Otto Guentter. —Stuttgart: Verlag des Schwaebischen Schillervereins,1911

8,504 S. ;21 cm.

K835. 16/H674(2)

Mein Kampf. 2. Band, Die nationalsozialistische Bewegung/Adolf Hitler. —Muenchen: Verlag Franz Eher Nachfolger G. m. b. H. ,1933

16,409-782 S. ;19 cm.

K835. 16/L274

Goethe: Leben Gedanken Bildnisse/Karl Robert Langewiesche. —Koenigstein im Taunus: Verlag der Eiserne Hammer,[?]

64 S. ;20 cm.

K835. 16/W132

Beethoven/Richard Wagner. —Leipzig: Insel Verlag,[?]

87 S. ;18 cm.

K835. 165. 2/G846-10

Hermann Goering Werk und Mensch/Erich Gritzbach. —9. und 10. Aufl..—Muenchen:

Zentralverlag der NSDAP. , Franz Eher Nachf. , c1937
345 S. ;21 cm.

K835. 165. 2/K89
Das Kriegstagebuch des Johannes Krafft/Johannes Krafft. —Minden: Wilhelm Koehler, Vaterlaendische Verlagsanstalt, [?]
184 S. ;22 cm.

K835. 165. 2/M729(4)
Gesammelte Schriften und Denkwuerdigkeiten des General-Feldmarschalls Grafen Helmuth von Moltke. 4. Band, Briefe des General-Feldmarschalls Grafen Helmuth von Moltke an seine Mutter und an seine Brueder Adolf und Ludwig/Grafen Helmuth von Moltke. —Berlin: Ernst Siegfried Mittler und Sohn, 1891
15, 315 S. ;22 cm.

K835. 165. 38/K15
1834/1934 Vier Generationen Seidenweberei/Kampf & Spindler. —Hilden/Rhein: Kampf & Spindler, 1934
1 Heft;26 cm.

K835. 165. 6/B553
Friedrich Hoelderlin/Beate Berwin. —Stuttgart: Union Deutsche Verlagsgesellschaft, [?]
188 S. ;18 cm.

K835. 165. 6/G599(1)
Goethes autobiographische Schriften. Band I/Johann Wolfgang von Goethe. —Leipzig: MDCCCCXX im Inselverlag, [?]
829 S. ;17 cm.

K835. 165. 6/G599-5
Dichtung und Wahrheit/W. v. Goethe. —5. Aufl. . —Leipzig: Verlg von B. G. Teubner, [?]
204 S. ;17 cm.

K835. 165. 6/N726
Der Rembrandtdeutsche Julius Langbehn/Benedikt Momme Nissen. —Freiburg im Breisgau: Herder & Co. G. m. b. H. Verlagsbuchhandlung, 1926
358 S. ;24 cm.

K835. 165. 6/W136
Goethe und seine Welt/Hans Wahl, Anton Kippenberg. —Leipzig: Im Insel Verlag, 1932
306 S. ;25 cm.

K835. 167/B566
Der Koenig und die Kaiserin: Friedrich der Grosse und Maria Theresia/Werner Beumelburg. —Oldenburg i. O. : Gerhard Stalling Verlagsbuchhandlung, c1938
459 S. ;21 cm.

K835. 167/B624
Friedrich der Grosse/Theodor Bitterauf. —Leipzig: Verlag von B. G. Teubner, 1909
116 S. ;18 cm.

K835. 167/M621-2
Fuer Staat und Volk: Eine Lebensgeschichte/Georg Michaelis. —2. Aufl. . —Berlin: Furche Verlag, c1922
13, 440 S. ;21 cm.

K835. 167/P715
Das Leben Kaiser Ottos des Grossen/J. O. Plassmann. —Jena: Eugen Diederichs, 1928
80 S. ;20 cm.

K835. 167/R744
Die Buergermeister: Fuenf Fuehrer Hamburgs zu Einheit und Reich/Gertrud Rolm. —Hamburg: Verlagsbuchhandlung Broschek & Co. , 1931
207 S. ;19 cm.

K835. 167/S294(2)

Bismarck: Ein Bild seines Lebens und Wirkens. II. Band/Dietrich Schaefer. —Berlin: Verlag von Reimar Hobbing, 1917

240 S. ; 29 cm.

K835. 167. 2/W126

Duerer und seine Zeit/Wilhelm Waetzoldt. —Wien: Phaidon Verlag, c1935

592 S. ; 27 cm.

K835. 168/S326-7

Menschliche Tragikomoedie/Johannes Scherr. —7. Aufl.. —Leipzig: Hesse & Becker Verlag, [?]

137, 154, 176 S. ; 18 cm.

K835. 168. 5/B666-6

Charlotte von Stein/Wilhelm Bode. —6. Aufl.. —Berlin: E. S. Mittler & Sohn, c1926

22, 699 S. ; 20 cm.

K835. 168. 5/K22

Grosse Frauen/Elisabeth Kawa. —Paderborn: Verlag der Bonifacius-Druckerei, [?]

106 S. ; 19 cm.

K835. 168. 5/M614-8

Die kleine Chronik der Anna Magdalena Bach/Esther Meynell. —8. Aufl.. —Leipzig: Koehler & Amelang, 1934

300 S. ; 19 cm.

K835. 168. 9/L941

Seeteufel: Abenteuer aus meinem Leben/Felix v. Luckner. —Leipzig: Verlag von K. F. Koehler, c1921

318 S. ; 22 cm.

K835. 168. 9/N473

Joachim Nettelbeck: wundersame Lebensgeschichte von ihm selbst erzaehlt/Joachim Nettelbeck. —Ebenhausen bei Muenchen: Wilhelm Langewiesche-Brandt, 1925

409 S. ; 18 cm.

K835. 46/M992

Professor Contardo Ferrini: Ein moderner Gelehrter und Heiliger/D. W. Mut. —Kirnach: Verlag der Schulbrueder, 1925

8, 308 S. ; 19 cm.

K835. 465. 7/R749

Michelangelo/Romain Rolland. —Zuerich: Max Rascher Verlag, 1919

206 S. ; 18 cm.

K835. 65/B624-2

Napoleon I. /Theodor Bitterauf. —2. Aufl.. —Leipzig: B. G. Teubner, 1911

8, 112, 32 S. ;

K835. 655. 6/B573

Das Leben eines Sonderlings/Henri Beyle. —Leipzig: Insel Verlag, [?]

804 S. ; 17 cm.

K835. 657/C776

Talleyrand/Duff Cooper. —Leipzig: Insel Verlag, [?]

495 S. ; 21 cm.

K851. 662/S341

Besonnte Vergangenheit: Lebenserinnerungen (1859-1919)/Carl Ludwig Schleich. —Berlin: Ernst Rowohlt Verlag, c1924

348 S. ; 22 cm.

K885/S383

Alteuropa: in seiner Kultur- und Stilentwicklung/Carl Schuchhardt. —Strassburg: Verlag von Karl I. Truebner, 1919

12, 350 S. ; 22 cm.

K892/R933

Aus dem Lande der Mitte: Schilderungen der

Sitten und Gebraeuche der Chinesen/Ernst Ruhstrat. —Berlin: Alfred Schall,[?]
331 S. ;18 cm.

K892. 22/K14
Der Totenkult in Suedschantung: Ein Beitrag zur Volkskunde des Landes/P. L. Kalff. —Yenchoufu: Verlag der Katholischen Mission Yenchoufu,1932
8,109 S. ;22 cm.

K893. 811. 8/D148(1. 1)
Arbeit und Sitte in Palaestina. Band I, Jahreslauf und Tageslauf/Gustaf Dalman. —Guetersloh: Verlag von Bertelsmann,1928
14,279 S. ;24 cm.

K90/B983-2(21)
Monographien zur Erdkunde. 21. Band,Palaestina/Hermann Buthe. —2. Aufl.. —Bielefeld: Verlag von Velhagen & Klasing,1927
172 S. ;26 cm.

K91/H733-10
Erdbeschreibung: in zwei Lehrstufen/C. Holl. —10. Aufl.. —Stuttgart: Verlag der J. B. Metzlerschen Buchhandlung,1887
10,190,23 S. ;21 cm.

K928. 7/T877
Der T'ai-Schan und seine Kultstaetten/P. A. Tschepe. —Jentschoufu: Verlag der Katholischen Mission,1906
124 S. ;22 cm.

K928. 9/P426
Von Chinas Goettern: Reisen in China/Friedrich Perzynski. —Muenchen: Kurt Wolff Verlag,c1920
261 S. ;25 cm.

K928. 9/S819
Mit der Nord-China-Expedition: Reiseerlebnisse, Sitten und Gebraeuche der Chinesen und Mongolen/M. Steinle. —Hamburg: Weltbund Verlag,c1921
158 S. ;21 cm.

K938. 1/K77
Palaestina: Die Landschaft in Karten und Bildern/Robert Koeppel. —Tuebingen: Verlag von J. C. B. Mohr <Paul Siebeck>,1930
174 S. ;27 cm.

K939/W828
Sommer-Sonnentage in Japan und China: Reise-Erlebnisse in Ostasien im Jahre 1924/J. Witte. —Goettingen: Vandenhoeck & Ruprecht, 1925
218 S. ;20 cm.

K951. 6/O96
Ein Buch von der Stadt Soest/Julius Overhoff. —Leipzig: Verlag Jakob Hegner,1935
110 S. ;19 cm.

K951. 65/H887
Berlin: Berichte und Bilder/Martin Huerlimann. —Berlin: Atlantis Verlag,c1934
512 S. ;21 cm.

K952. 27/C183
Die Buendner Glocken: Eine kulturhistorische Studie aus Buenden/Christian Caminada. —Zuerich: Verlag Art. Institut Drell Fuessli,1915
112 S. ;22 cm.

K971. 29/H376-46
Kleine Liebe zu Amerika: Ein junger Mann schlendert durch die Staaten/Manfred Hausmann. —43. bis 46. Aufl.. —Berlin: S. Fischer Verlag,c1930
346 S. ;19 cm.

K991/H541
Herders Welt- und Wirtschaftsatlas/Herder &

Co. G. m. b. H. Verlagsbuchhandlung. —Freiburg im Breisgau: Herder & Co. G. m. b. H. Verlagsbuchhandlung, c1932
8,181,143 S.; 26 cm.

K991/S766-7
Dr. K. von Spruner's historisch-geographischer Schul-Atlas/K. von Spruner. —7. Aufl.. —Gotha: Justus Perthes, 1874
1 Heft; 25 cm.

N 自然科学总论

N/E65
Goethes naturwissenschaftliche Schriften in Auswahl/Wilhelm Ernst. —Leipzig: MDCCCCXX im Inselverlag, [?]
706 S.; 17 cm.

N09/W361-12(1)
Die Anfaenge der Naturbeherrschung. Fruehformen der Mechanik/Karl Weule. —12. Aufl.. —Stuttgart: Kosmos, Gesellschaft der Naturfreunde Geschaeftsstelle: Franckh'sche Verlagshandlung, c1921
76 S.; 20 cm.

N49/J43
Durch Raum und Zeit/James Jeans. —Stuttgart: Deutsche Verlags-Anstalt, [?]
260,54 S.; 21 cm.

O 数理科学和化学

O121-44/B245-6
Dr. E. Bardens Aufgabensammlung: methodisch geordnet, mehr als 8000 Aufgaben enthaltend ueber alle Teile der Elementar-Arithmetik, vorzugsweise fuer Seminare und Praeparanden-Anstalten/E. Bardens. —6. Aufl.. —Leipzig: B. G. Teubner Verlag, 1908
13,395 S.; 21 cm.

O121-44/B245-30
Dr. E. Bardens Aufgabensammlung: methodisch geordnet, mehr als 8000 Aufgaben enthaltend ueber alle Teile der Elementar-Arithmetik, vorzugsweise fuer Gymnasien, Realgymnasien und Oberrealschulen/E. Bardens. —30. Aufl.. —Leipzig: B. G. Teubner Verlag, 1911
14,329 S.; 21 cm.

O122/L716-14(2)
Leitfaden der Elementar-Mathematik: Nach den Bestimmungen der presslichen Lehrplaene vom Jahre 1901. 2. Teil, Arithmetik/H. Lieber, F. von Luehmann. —14. Aufl.. —Berlin: Verlag von Leohard Simion Nf., [?]
186 S.; 21 cm.

O123. 1/L716-30(1)
Leitfaden der Elementar-Mathematik. 1. Teil, Planimetrie/H. Lieber, F. von Luehmann. —30. Aufl.. —Berlin: Verlag von Leonhard Simion

Nf. ,1913
159 S. ;21 cm.

O14/B726-6(2. 1)
Mathematische Hauptsaetze: Ausgabe fuer Realgymnasien und Oberrealschulen. 2. Teil, Pensum der Oberstufe (bis zur Reisepruefung). 1. Abteilung/Heinrich Bork. —6. Aufl.. —Leipzig: O. R. Reisland,1919
14,399 S. ;21 cm.

O174/B586
Einfuehrung in die konforme Abbildung/Ludwig Bieberbach. —Berlin: G. J. Goeschen'sche Verlagshandlung G. m. b. H. ,1915
142 S. ;16 cm.

O39/K24-2(3)
Vortraege ueber Mechanik als Grundlage fuer das Bau- und Maschinenwesen. 3. Teil, Allgemeine Mechanik/Wilh. Keck. —2. Aufl.. —Hannover: Helwingsche Verlagsbuchhandlung,1915
12,350 S. ;23 cm.

O4/M396(1)
Die Physik: In zwei Baende. 1. Band/Hermann Maser[usw.]. —Neudamm: Verlag von J. Neumann,[?]
8,972 S. ;23 cm.

O4-61/A917
Woerterbuch der Physik/Felix Auerbach. —Berlin: Vereinigung Wissenschaftlicher Verleger,1920
10,466 S. ;20 cm.

O441-43/K21-10(4)
Mueller-Pouillets Lehrbuch der Physik und Meteorologie. 4. Band, Magnetismus und Elektrizitaet/Walter Kaufmann, Alfred Coehn. —10. Aufl.. —Braunschweig: Verlag von Friedrich Vieweg und Sohn,1909
12,622 S. ;24 cm.

O562/P499
Kuenstliche Verwendung der Elemente (Zertruemmerung der Atome)/Hans Pettersson. —Berlin: Walter De Gruyter & Co. ,1929
8,159 S. ;22 cm.

O6/C678-3
Einfuehrung in die Chemie in leichtfasslicher Form/Lassar Cohn. —3. Aufl.. —Hamburg: Verlag von Leopold Voss. ,1907
12,301 S. ;21 cm.

O6/H672-8
Katechismus der Chemie/Heinrich Hirzel. —8. Aufl.. —Leipzig: Verlagsbuchhandlung von J. J. Weber,1901
10,453,16 S. ;17 cm.

O6/M946(1)
Die chemische Technik. Band I/Arthur Mueller. —Leipzig: Verlag von B. G. Teubner,c1915
146,16 S. ;18 cm.

O6-43/O16
Einfuehrung in die Chemie: Ein Lehr- und Experimentierbuch/Rudolf Ochs. —Berlin: Verlag von Julius Springer,1911
8,502 S. ;24 cm.

O6-61/U41-2(1)
Enzyklopaedie der technischen Chemie. 1. Band, Abasin-Ausdehnung/Fritz Ullmann. —2. Aufl.. —[S. l. :s. n.],1928
10. 808 S. ;26 cm.

O6-61/U41-2(3)
Enzyklopaedie der technischen Chemie. 3. Band, Calciumcyanamid-Druckerei/Fritz Ullmann. —2. Aufl.. —[S. l. :s. n.],1929
828 S. ;26 cm.

O6-61/U41-2(5)

Enzyklopaedie der technischen Chemie. 5. Band, Faerben-Glyoxylsaeure/Fritz Ullmann. —2. Aufl.. —[S. l. : s. n.], 1930

836 S. ; 26 cm.

O6-61/U41-2(9)

Enzyklopaedie der technischen Chemie. 9. Band, Salpeter-Tinonfarbstoffe/Fritz Ullmann. —2. Aufl.. —[S. l. : s. n.], 1932

535 S. ; 26 cm.

O62/D561-2

Einfuehrung in die organische Chemie/Otto Diels. —2. Aufl.. —Leipzig: Verlagsbuchhandlung von J. J. Weber, 1919

12, 326 S. ; 22 cm.

O62/H887-3(2)

Theoretische Grundlagen der organischen Chemie. 2. Band/Walter Hueckel. —3. Aufl.. —Leipzig: Akademische Verlagsgesellschaft Becker & Erler Kom. —Ges. , c1941

15, 614 S. ; 20 cm.

O62/H944

Querschnitt durch die organische Chemie/Wilhelm Huntenburg. —Leipzig: Verlag von Leopold Voss, c1935

8, 180 S. ; 21 cm.

O62-43/B517-13

Kurzes Lehrbuch der organischen Chemie/A. Bernthsen. —13. Aufl.. —Braunschweig: Verlag von Friedr. Vieweg & Sohn, c1918

20, 672 S. ; 21 cm.

O62-43/K18-2

Lehrbuch der organischen Chemie/Paul Karrer. —2. Aufl.. —Leipzig: Georg Thieme Verlag, c1930

21, 889 S. ; 25 cm.

O621. 1/H518-5

Theorien der Organischen Chemie/Ferdinand Henrich. —5. Aufl.. —Braunschweig: Verlag von Friedr. Vieweg & Sohn Akt. —Ges, 1924

8, 515 S. ; 23 cm.

O64/E86-2

Grundriss der physikalischen Chemie: fuer Studierende der Chemie und verwandter Faecher/Arnold Eucken. —2. Aufl.. —Leipzig: Akademische Verlagsgesellschaft m. b. H. , c1922

12, 506 S. ; 23 cm.

O642. 1/S385-3(2)

Technische Thermodynamik. 2. Band, Hoehere Thermodynamik/W. Schuele. —3. Aufl.. —Berlin: Verlag von Julius Springer, c1920

16, 409 S. ; 23 cm.

O648/L716-2(6)

Naturwissenschaftliche Reihe. Band VI, Kolloidchemie/Raphael Ed. Liesegang. —2. Aufl.. —Dresden: Verlag von Theodor Steinkopff, c1926

12, 176 S. ; 22 cm.

O648/L884-3

Kurze Einfuehrung in die Kolloidchemie unter besonderer Beruecksichtigung der anorganischen Kolloide/Alfred Lottermoser. —3. Aufl.. —Dreseden: Verlag von Theodor Steinkopff, c1943

8, 260 S. ; 23 cm.

O65/O85-7

Die wissenschaftlichen Grundlagen der analytischen Chemie/Wilhelm Ostwald. —7. Aufl.. —Dresden: Verlag von Theodor Steinkopff, 1920

12, 238 S. ; 20 cm.

O65/P364-13

Volhard's Anleitung zur Qualitativen chemischen Analyse/H. v. Pechmann. —13. Aufl.. —Muenchen: Chemisches Laboratorium des Sta-

ates,1912
120 S. ;18 cm.

O661. 1/O42
Chemische Technologie des Wassers/W. Olszewski. —Berlin: Walter de Gruyter & Co. , 1925
138 S. ;16 cm.

P 天文学、地球科学

P1/W373
Eine Astronomie, die jeder verstehen kann: Nach den neuesten Errungenschaften der Wissenschaft/Edmund Weber. —Berlin: Wiedmannsche Buchhandlung,1926
8,187 S. ;18 cm.

P114/S934-3
Der Himmel im Bild: Ein astronomischer Bilderatlas/P. Stuker. —3. Aufl.. —Stuttgart: Franckh'sche Verlagshandlung,1927
8,72 S. ;25 cm.

P195. 516/Z11
Deutscher Faerberkalender fuer das Jahr 1939/W. Zaenker. —Muenchen: Verlag Deutscher Faerberkalender Franz Eder,1939
32,256,59,32,36 S. ;16 cm.

P3-62/Z73-4(1. 1)
Der Erdball und seine Naturwunder. 1. Band, Populaeres Handbuch der physischen Geographie. 1. Band/W. F. A. Zimmermann. —4. Aufl.. —Berlin: Verlag von Gustav Hempel,1855
8,378 S. ;22 cm.

P5/W237-4
Vorschule der Geologie: Eine gemeinverstaendliche Einfuehrung und Anleitung zu Beobachtungen in der Heimat/Johannes Walther. —4. Aufl.. —Jena: Verlag von Gustav Fischer,1910
10,293 S. ;19 cm.

P75/G926
Die Eroberung der Tiefe/Hanns Guenther. —Stuttgart: Kosmos, Gesellschaft der Naturfreunnde,c1928
79 S. ;20 cm.

Q 生物科学

Q5/C517
Fortschritte der physiologischen Chemie 1929-1934/Verlag Chemie. —Berlin: Verlag Chemie, G. m. b. H. ,[?]

311 S. ;23 cm.

Q5-43/H224-8

Lehrbuch der physiologischen Chemie/Olof Hammarsten. —8. Aufl.. —Wiesbaden: Verlag von J. F. Bergmann, 1914

8,961 S. ;26 cm.

Q53/B527

Grundzuege der Chemie und Biochemie der Zuckerarten/Konrad Bernhauer. —Berlin: Verlag von Julius Springer, c1933

11,365 S. ;25 cm.

Q94/K63

Grundriss der Pflanzenkunde fuer Schulen Ostasiens/P. Klautke. —Hannover: Hahnsche Buchhandlung, 1923

183 S. ;23 cm.

Q948.552.2/F529-8

Flora von Bern: Systematische Uebersicht der in der Gegend von Bern wildwachsenden und allgemein kultivierten Phanerogamen und Pteridophyten/L. Fischer. —8. Aufl.. —Bern: Verlag von Raillard & Schiller, 1911

40,342 S. ;19 cm.

Q949/M946-9

Das grosse illustrierte Kraeuterbuch: Ausfuerliche Beschreibung aller Pflanzen, ihres Gebrauchs, Nutzens, ihrer Anwendung und Wirkung in der Arzneikunde/Ferdinand Mueller. —9. Aufl.. —Ulm: Verlag der J. Ebner'schen Buchhandlung, [?]

8,912 S. ;22 cm.

Q95/K63

Grundriss der Tierkunde fuer Schulen Ostasiens/P. Klautke. —Hannover: Hahnsche Buchhandlung, 1923

223 S. ;23 cm.

Q958.1/M111

Lebensbedingungen und Verbreitung der Tiere/Otto Maas. —Leipzig: Verlag von B. G. Teubner, 1907

138 S. ;18 cm.

Q959/B834(6)

Brehms Tierleben: Jubilaeums-Ausgabe in acht Baenden: nach dem neuesten Stande der Wissenschaft. 6. Band, Kriechtiere, Lurche, Fische/A. E. Brehm. —Leipzig: Verlag von Philipp Reclam jun., c1928

551 S. ;19 cm.

Q959.7/B834(4)

Brehms Tierleben: Jubilaeums-Ausgabe in acht Baenden: nach dem neuesten Stande der Wissenschaft. 4. Band, Die Voegel. 1. Band, Leben der Gesamtheit Sperlingsvoegel, Rakenvoegel Raubvoegel/A. E. Brehm. —Leipzig: Verlag von Philipp Reclam jun., c1928

530 S. ;19 cm.

Q959.7/I59

Das kleine Buch der Voegel und Nester/[?]. —Leipzig: Insel Verlag, [?]

50 S. ;18 cm.

Q959.7/V891

Deutsches Vogelleben/Alwin Voigt. —Leipzig: Verlag von B. G. Teubner, 1908

156 S. ;18 cm.

Q959.8/B834(1)

Brehms Tierleben: Jubilaeums-Ausgabe in acht Baenden: nach dem neuesten Stande der Wissenschaft. 1. Band, Die Saeugetiere/A. E. Brehm. —Leipzig: Verlag von Philipp Reclam jun., c1928

493 S. ;19 cm.

R 医药、卫生

R-05/C238-19

Pastoral-Medizin/C. Capellmann, W. Bergmann. —19. Aufl.. —Paderborn: Verlag der Bonifacius Druckerei, c1923

13,472 S.; 22 cm.

R-55/S738(76. 2)

Muenchener Medizinische Wochenschrift. 76. Jahrgang II. Haelfte, (Juni-Dezember) 1929/ Bernhard Spatz. —Muenchen: J. F. Lehmanns Verlag, 1929

1117-2176,111 S.; 32 cm.

R1/R928-3

Krankheiten und Hygiene der warmen Laender: Ein Lehrbuch fuer die Praxis/Reinhold Ruge[usw.]. —3. Aufl.. —Leipzig: Georg Thieme Verlag, c1930

10,496 S.; 26 cm.

R179/D249

Koerperliche Verbildungen im Kindesalter und ihre Verhuetung: Ein Mahnwort an Eltern, Lehrer und Erzieher/Max David. —Leipzig: Verlag von B. G. Teubner, c1910

110,32 S.; 18 cm.

R3/M544

Das aerztliche Volksbuch: Gemeinverstaendliche Gesundheitspflege und Heilkunde/Heinrich Meng. —Stuttgart: Hippokrates Verlag G. m. b. H., c1930

24,1201 S.; 26 cm.

R322-43/K83-10(4)

Rauber's Lehrbuch der Anatomie des Menschen. Abteilung 4, Eingeweide/Fr. Kopsch. —10. Aufl.. —Leipzig: Verlag von Georg Thieme, 1914

424 S.; 27 cm.

R322-43/K83-11(1)

Rauber's Lehrbuch der Anatomie des Menschen. Abteilung 1, Allgemeiner Teil/Fr. Kopsch. —11. Aufl.. —Leipzig: Verlag von Georg Thieme, c1920

191 S.; 27 cm.

R322-43/K83-11(3)

Rauber's Lehrbuch der Anatomie des Menschen. Abteilung 3, Muskeln, Gefaesse/Fr. Kopsch. —11. Aufl.. —Leipzig: Verlag von Georg Thieme, c1919

513 S.; 27 cm.

R322-43/K83-11(5)

Rauber's Lehrbuch der Anatomie des Menschen. Abteilung 5, Nervensystem/Fr. Kopsch. —11. Aufl.. —Leipzig: Verlag von Georg Thieme, c1920

480 S.; 27 cm.

R322-43/K83-11(6)

Rauber's Lehrbuch der Anatomie des Menschen. Abteilung 6, Sinnesorgane/Fr. Kopsch. —11. Aufl.. —Leipzig: Verlag von Georg Thieme, c1920

370 S.; 27 cm.

R33-43/H693-3

Lehrbuch der Physiologie des Menschen/Rudolf Hoeber. —3. Aufl.. —Berlin: Verlag von Julius Springer, 1922

828 S.; 25 cm.

R361-43/A812-5(2)

Pathologische Anatomie: Ein Lehrbuch fuer Studierende und Aerzte. 2. Band, Spezielle pathologische Anatomie/L. Aschoff. —5. Aufl.. —Jena: Verlag von Gustav Fischer, c1911

9,1088 S. ;25 cm.

R363/K92-12

Pathologische Physiologie/Ludolf KreHl. —12. Aufl.. —Leipzig: Verlag von F. C. W. Vogel, c1923

15,719 S. ;22 cm.

R4/E71

Hausaerztliches Taschenbuch: Auch fuer die Reise/Wilhelm Ermer. —Nuernberg: Buecher Verlag Anzeiger fuer Aerzte und Apotheker, 1924

377 S. ;16 cm.

R4/R845-7

Klinische Terminologie: Zusammenstellung der in der klinischen Medizin gebraeulichen technischen Ausdruecke mit Erklaerung ihrer Bedeutung und Ableitung/Otto Roth. —7. Aufl.. —Leipzig: Verlag von Georg Thieme, 1908

32,673 S. ;19 cm.

R44-43/B891-5

Lehrbuch klinischer Diagnostik und Untersuchungsmethodik fuer Studierende, Medizinalpraktikanten und Aerzte/Theodor Brugsch, Alfred Schnittenhelm. —5. Aufl.. —Berlin: Urban & Schwarzenberg, c1921

20,968 S. ;24 cm.

R45/A252

Die praktische Therapie mit Hormonen und Vitaminen: unter besonderer Beruecksichtigung aktueller Ernaehrungsfragen/Verlag der Aerztlichen Rundschau Otto Gmaelin. —Muenchen: Verlag der Aerztlichen Rundschau Otto Gmaelin, 1930

138 S. ;23 cm.

R454. 6/B595

Das neue Naturheilverfahren: Unentbehrliches Ergaenzungswerk zu Bilz, Naturheilverfahren und jedem anderen naturheilkundlichen Buche/Verlag von F. E. Bilz. —Leipzig: Verlag von F. E. Bilz, [?]

1060 S. ;24 cm.

R5/D666-12

Grundriss der inneren Medizin/A. von Domarus. —12. Aufl.. —[S. l. :s. n.], 1938

15,697 S. ;23 cm.

R5-43/A844-4(2)

Lehrbuch der inneren Medizin. 2. Band/H. Assmann. —4. Aufl.. —[S. l. :s. n.], 1939

14,886 S. ;24 cm.

R5-43/S927-13(1)

Lehrbuch der speziellen Pathologie und Therapie der inneren Krankheiten fuer Studierende und Aerzte. 1. Band/Adolf Struempell. —13. Aufl.. —Leipzig: Verlag von F. C. W. Vogel, 1900

8,624 S. ;22 cm.

R52/L827

Vorlesungen ueber Bakteriologie, Immunitaet, spezifische Diagnostik und Therapie der Tuberkulose fuer Aerzte und Tieraerzte/Ernst Loewenstein. —Jena: Verlag von Gustav Fischer, c1920

8,476,11 S. ;25 cm.

R521/M184

Die Kollapstherapie der Lungentuberkulose: Mit besonderer Beruecksichtigung des kuenstlichen Pneumothorax/Hanns Maendl. —Wien: Verlag von Julius Springer, 1927

9,206 S. ;24 cm.

R6-43/L679-13(1)

Lehrbuch der allgemeinen Chirurgie zum Gebrauche fuer Aerzte und Studierende. I. Band/Erich Lexer. —12. und 13. Aufl.. —Stuttgart: Verlag von Ferdinand Enke, 1921

12,488 S.;24 cm.

R6-43/L679-13(2)

Lehrbuch der allgemeinen Chirurgie zum Gebrauche fuer Aerzte und Studierende. II. Band/Erich Lexer. —12. und 13. Aufl.. —Stuttgart: Verlag von Ferdinand Enke, 1921

8,499 S.;24 cm.

R61/S699-4

Grundriss der gesamten Chirurgie: Ein Taschenbuch fuer Studierende und Aerzte/Erich Sonntag. —4. Aufl.. —[S. l.:s. n.], 1937

12,1128 S.;21 cm.

R72-43/F295-8

Lehrbuch der Kinderheilkunde/E. Feer. —8. Aufl.. —Jena: Verlag von Gustav Fischer, c1912

8,762 S.;25 cm.

R749.92/E47

Die Krankhaften Geschlechts-Empfindungen auf dissoziativer Grundlage/Havelock Ellis. —Wuerzburg: A. Stuber's Verlag, 1907

13,317 S.;19 cm.

R759.1/M954-2

Praktische Anleitung zur Syphilisdiagnose auf biologischem Wege: Spirochaeten-Nachweis, Wassermannsche Reaktion/P. Mulzer. —2. Aufl.. —Berlin: Verlag von Julius Springer, 1912

8,129 S.;20 cm.

R9/A681-8

Spezialitaeten und Geheimmittel aus den Gebieten der Medizin, Technik, Kosmetik und Nahrungsmittelindustrie: Ihre Herkunft und Zusammensetzung/G. Arends. —8. Aufl.. —Berlin: Verlag von Julius Springer, 1924

564 S.;19 cm.

R96/S348-4

Grundriss der Pharmakologie in Bezug auf Arzneimittellehre und Toxikologie/Oswald Schmiedeberg. —4. Aufl.. —Leipzig: Verlag von F. C. W. Vogel, 1902

12,496 S.;22cm.

R97/G454-8

Von Kahlden's Technik der histologischen Untersuchung pathologisch-anatomischer Praeparate/Edgar Gierke. —8. Aufl.. —Jena: Verlag von Gustav Fischer, 1909

11,220 S.;25 cm.

S 农业科学

S184-62/K64(3.2.1)

Handbuch der Pflanzenanalyse. 3. Band, Spezielle Analyse. 2. Teil, Organische Stoffe. 1. Abteilung /G. Klein. —Berlin: J. Springer, 1932

806 S.;25 cm.

S184-62/K64(3.2.2)

Handbuch der Pflanzenanalyse. 3. Band, Spezielle Analyse. 2. Teil, Organische Stoffe. 2. Abteilung/G. Klein. —Berlin: J. Springer, 1932

1613 S.;25 cm.

S184-62/K64(4.3)

Handbuch der Pflanzenanalyse. 4. Band, Spezielle Analyse. 3. Teil, Organische Stoffe III/G. Klein. —Berlin: J. Springer, 1933

839-1868 S.; 25 cm.

S4/L275

Kurze Anleitung zur Ausuebung des Pflanzenschutzes: Zum Selbstunterricht und fuer landwirtschftliche Schulen bearbeitet/E. Langenbeck. —Berlin: Verlagsbuchhandlung Paul Parey, 1906

77 S.; 19 cm.

S436.3/S334

Die Schaedlinge des Gemuesebaues und deren Bekaempfung: Ein Volksbuch fuer Gartenfreunde, Gaertner, Samenzuechter, Wuerzkraeute- und Apothekerpflanzen Anbauende/Heinrich Freiherr von Schilling. —Frankfurt a. Oder.: Verlag der Koeniglichen Hofbuchdruckerei Crowitzsch & Sohn, [?]

64 S.; 22 cm.

S6/M612-4

Meyer's immerwaehrender Gartenkalender/J. G. Meyer. —4. Aufl.. —Berlin: Verlagsbuchhandlung Paul Parey, 1908

199 S.; 18 cm.

S6/T351

Der Jugend Gartenbuch: Zu deren Freude und Belehrung/Marie Teuscher. —Frankfurt a. M.: Verlag der Koeniglichen Hofbuchdruckerei Trowitzsch & Sohn, 1902

8, 184 S.; 23 cm.

S605/B673-8

Gartenbuch fuer Anfaenger: Unterweisung im Anlegen, Bepflanzen und Pflegen des Hausgartens im Obstbau, Gemuesebau und in der Blumenzucht/Johannes Boettner. —8. Aufl.. —Frankfurt a. Oder: Verlag der koeniglichen Hofbuchdruckerei Trowitzsch & Sohn, 1908

557 S.; 22 cm.

S68/B565-5

Praktische Blumenzucht und Blumenpflege im Zimmer/Robert Betten. —5. Aufl.. —Frankfurt a. Ober: Verlag der Koeniglichen Hofbuchdruckerei Troeitzsch & Sohn, 1907

292, 23 S.; 23 cm.

S68/H583-2

Anleitung zur Blumenpflege im Hause/Max Hesdoerffer. —2. Aufl.. —Berlin: Verlagsbuchhandlung Paul Parey, 1905

185 S.; 22 cm.

S68/S357-2(2)

Der praktische Schnittblumenzuechter der Neuzeit: Eine Zusammenstellung und Kulturbeschreibung der fuer den Schnittblumenzuechter wertvollsten Straeucher, Stauden, Knollen, Zwiebeln und einjaehrigen Pflanzen fuer Fruehjahr, Sommer und Herbst. II. Teil/Otto Schnurbusch. —2. Aufl.. —Leipzig: Verlag von Hugo Voigt, 1906

10, 133 S.; 23 cm.

S685.12/J91

Rosenbuch fuer Jedermann: Die Kultur, Behandlung und Pflege der Rose in monatlicher Arbeitseinteilung/Paul Juratz. —Berlin: Verlagsbuchhandlung Paul Parey, 1901

8, 128 S.; 19 cm.

S76-44/F654-4

Repetitorium zum Neudammer Foersterlehrbuch/Verfasser des Foersterlehrbuchs. —4. Aufl.. —Neudamm: Verlag von J. Neumann, 1912

229, 24 S.; 21 cm.

S829.2/O89

Der deutsche Schaeferhund in Liebhaberhand/

E. von Otto. —Berlin: Verlagsbuchhandlung Paul Parey, c1925
11, 167 S. ; 22 cm.

S852/J58
Kompendium der Bakteriologie und Blutserumtherapie fuer Tieraerzte und Studierende/Paul Jess. —Berlin: Verlag von Richard Schoetz, 1901
10, 102 S. ; 19 cm.

T 工业技术

T-62/H888-2
"Huette": Taschenbuch fuer Betriebsingenieure/Der Akademische Verein "Huette" E. V.. —2. Aufl.. —Berlin: Verlag von Wilhelm Ernst & Sohn, c1924
20, 1325 S. ; 18 cm.

T-62/H888-18(2)
"Huette" Des Ingenieurs Taschenbuch. Abteilung II. /Der Akademische Verein "Huette". —18. Aufl.. —Berlin: Verlag von Wilhelm Ernst & Sohn, 1902
867 S. ; 18 cm.

T-62/H888-23(2)
"Huette" Des Ingenieurs Taschenbuch. II. Band/Der Akademische Verein "Huette". —23. Aufl.. —Berlin: Verlag von Wilhelm Ernst & Sohn, 1920
8, 1077 S. ; 18 cm.

TG177/B918-5
Die Metallfaerbung und deren Ausfuehrung/Georg Buchner. —5. Aufl.. —Berlin: M. Krayn, c1914
20, 426, 10 S. ; 25 cm.

TH-62/K81-2
Praktische Herstellung und Loesungen: Ein Handbuch zum raschen und sicheren Aussinden der Loesungsmittel aller technisch und industriell wichtigen Koerper, sowie zur Herstellung von Loesungen solcher Stoffe fuer Techniker und Industrielle/Theodor Koller. —2. Aufl.. —Wien: A. Hartleben's Verlag, 1920
8, 308 S. ; 19 cm.

TH11/F654-6(1)
Vorlesung ueber technische Mechanik. 1. Band, Einfuehrung in die Mechanik/Aug. Foeppl. —6. Aufl.. —Leipzig: Verlag von B. G. Teubner, c1920
16, 414 S. ; 22 cm.

TH11/F654-7(3)
Vorlesungen ueber technische Mechanik. 3. Band, Festigkeitslehre/Aug. Foeppl. —7. Aufl.. —Leipzig: Verlag von B. G. Teubner, 1919
18, 446 S. ; 22 cm.

TH11/F654-7(4)
Vorlesungen ueber technische Mechanik. 4. Band, Dynamik/Aug. Foeppl. —7. Aufl.. —Leipzig: Verlag von B. G. Teubner, c1923
10, 417 S. ; 22 cm.

TH111-43/L366-9
Die Mechanik: Elementares Lehrbuch fuer den Schul- und Selbstunterricht sowie Gebrauch in

der Praxis/R. Lauenstein. —9. Aufl.. —Leipzig: Alfred Kroener Verlag, 1912
8, 245 S. ; 23 cm.

TH12/B118-11(1)
Maschinen-Elemente: Ihre Berechnung und Konstruktion mit Ruecksicht auf die neueren Versuche. 1. Band/C. Bach. —11. Aufl.. —Leipzig: Alfred Kroener Verlag, 1913
24, 525 S. ; 27 cm.

TH126/V916
Das Maschinenzeichnen des Konstrukteurs/C. Volk. —Berlin: Verlag von Julius Springer, c1921
73 S. ; 23 cm.

TH13/D875-5
Lehrheft fuer Maschinenteile/Verlagsanstalt zu Duisburg und Moers G. m. b. H.. —5. Aufl.. —Duisburg: Verlagsanstalt zu Duisburg und Moers G. m. b. H., 1912
56 S. ; 29 cm.

TM92/B467-5
Die wissenschaftlichen Grundlagen der Elektrotechnik/Gustav Benischke. —5. Aufl.. —Berlin: Verlag von Julius Springer, c1920
16, 640 S. ; 23 cm.

TQ/B658-11(1)
Auskunftsbuch fuer die Chemische Industrie. 1. Halbband/H. Bluecher. —11. Aufl.. —Berlin: Vereinigung Wissenschaftlicher Verleger, c1921
16, 800 S. ; 23 cm.

TQ/P256-4
Die maschinellen Hilfsmittel der chemischen Technik/A. Parnicke. —4. Aufl.. —Berlin: Verlagsbuchhandlung Paul Parey, 1922
8, 487 S. ; 24 cm.

TQ619/Z11
Die Kalkulation und Organisation in Faerbereien und verwandten Betrieben: Ein kurzer Ratgeber fuer Chemiker, Koloristen, Techniker, Meister und Kaufleute in Faerbereien, Druckereien, Bleichereien, Chemisch-Waeschereien, Appreturanstalten, Textilfabriken usw. /W. Zaenker. —Berlin: Verlag von Julius Springer, 1911
10, 72 S. ; 21 cm.

TQ62/B919
Die Mineral-, Pflanzen- und Teerfarben: Ihre Darstellung, Verwendung, Erkennung und Echtheitspruefung/Hans Th. Bucherer. —Leipzig: Verlag von Veit & Comp., 1911
8, 142 S. ; 22 cm.

TS1/H459
Technologie der Textilveredelung/Paul Heermann. —Berlin: Verlag von Julius Springer, c1921
10, 564 S. ; 24 cm.

TS102/H582(4.3)
Technologie der Textilfasern. IV. Band, 3. Teil, Chemische Technologie der Baumwolle, Mechanische Hilfsmittel zur Veredelung der Baumwolltextilien/R. O. Herzog[usw.]. —Berlin: Verlag von Julius Springer, c1928
14, 771 S. ; 25 cm.

TS102/S861
Chemische Technologie der Gespinstfasern/ Karl Stirm. —Berlin: Verlag von Gebrueder Borntraeger, c1913
16, 410 S. ; 25 cm.

TS112/E37
Die Bedienung der Arbeitsmaschinen zur Herstellung bedruckter Baumwollstoffe unter Beruecksichtigung der wichtigsten Arbeitsmaschinen der Spinnerei und Weberei/Wilh. Elbers. —

Braunschweig：Verlag von Friedrich Vieweg und Sohn，c1905
14，226 S.；29 cm.

TS193-43/B645
Der praktische Kleiderfaerber：Ein Lehr- und Nachschlagebuch ueber das gesamte Gebiet der Kleiderfaerberei fuer alle praktischen Kleiderfaerber，Meister，Gehilfen und Lehrlinge/Karl Blau. —Wittenberg：A. Ziemsen Verlag，1922
8，345 S.；23 cm.

TS193. 5/S819
Batik：Eine Einfuehrung in die Technik fuer Kunstgewerbler und Laien/Th. Steinoel. —Ravensburg：Verlag von Otto Maier，[?]
79 S.；20 cm.

TS2/F873-2
Ernaehrung und Volksnahrungsmittel/Johannes Frentzel. —2. Aufl.. —Leipzig：Verlag von B. G. Teubner，1909
120 S.；18 cm.

TS255/H148
Das Einmachen der Fruechte und Gemuese im Haushalt mit und ohne Apparat sowie Bereitung der Fruchtsaefte，Gelees，Konfitueren，Marmeladen und Likoere/Mary Hahn. —Wernigerode im Harz：Verlag M. Hahn，1917
139 S.；21 cm.

TS262. 6-44/H465
Praktische Uebungen in der Weinchemie und Kellerwirtschaft/C. von der Heide，F. Jakob. —Stuttgart：Verlagsbuchhandlung Eugen Ulmer，1911
121 S.；21 cm.

TS27/F829
Kakao，Tee und Gewuerze/Erwin Franke. —Wien：A. Hartleben's Verlag，1914
8，312 S.；18 cm.

TS275. 5/M498
Suessmost：Fachbuch der gewerbsmaessigen Suessmosterzeugung/Alfred Mehlitz. —Braunschweig：Dr. Serger & Hempel，1931
208 S.；21 cm.

TS38/F953
Salzbergbau- und Salinenkunde/F. A. Fuerer. —Braunschweig：Verlag von Friedrich Vieweg und Sohn，1900
22，1124 S.；22 cm.

TS761/H134
Die Herstellung von Buntpapier：Eine Anleitung zur Selbstherstellung von Kleisterpapieren，Stempel-，Tusch-，Tunk-，Del- und Schabionenpapieren/Marianne Finckhhaelssig. —Ravensburg：Verlag von Otto Maier，[?]
53 S.；20 cm.

TS972. 1/G479
Das "Weisse Haus" Kochbuch：Eine reichhaltige Enzyklopaedie nuetzlicher Belehrung fuer das Hauswesen/F. L. Gillette. —New York：The Saalfield Publishing Co.，1912
8，651 S.；24 cm.

TS972. 1/W642-36
Neues Illustriertes Kochbuch oder die Kunst ohne jede Vorkenntnis，Schmackhafte und wohlfeile Speisen fuer den einfachen wie auch reicheren Tisch bereiten zu koennen：Enthaltend gegen 900 erprobte und bewaehrte Rezepte/Gertrude Wiemann. —36. Aufl.. —Berlin：Verlagsdruckerei Merkur G. m. b. H.，1902
347 S.；20 cm.

TS972. 1-62/B171
Gastrosophie：Ein Brevier fuer Gaumen und Geist/Hans Balzli. —Stuttgart：Walter Haedecke Verlag，c1931
124 S.；21 cm.

TS972. 161/D249-41

Praktisches Kochbuch fuer die gewoehnliche und feinere Kueche: Unter besonderer Beruecksichtigung der Anfaengerinnen und angehenden Hausfrauen/Henriette Davidis-Holle. —41. Aufl.. —Bielefeld: Verlag von Belhagen & Klasing, 1904

52,826 S. ;19 cm.

TS972. 161/G382-4

Meine Diaet: Ein Ratgeber fuer Kranke und Gesunde/Max Gerson. —4. Aufl.. —Berlin: Verlag Ullstein, c1930

188 S. ;22 cm.

TS972. 18/R744-3

Bremer Kochbuch: Die jahrelang erprobten Rezepte der Wirtschaftsschule des Frauenerwerbs- und Ausbildungsvereins/Rolandverlag. —3. Aufl.. —Bremen: Rolandverlag H. Boesking & Co. , [?]

256 S. ;21 cm.

TU-49/O85-4(1)

Sechs Buecher vom Bauen: enthaltend eine Theorie des architektonischen Entwerfens. 1. Band, Einfuehrung/Friedrich Ostendorf. —4. Aufl.. —Berlin: Verlag von Wilhelm Ernst & Sohn, 1922

28,299 S. ;23 cm.

TU-885/P648

Die Bildwerke des Naumburger Doms/Wilhelm Pinder. —Leipzig: Insel Verlag, [?]

59 S. ;18 cm.

TU111. 43/K27-2

Die Feuchtigkeit der Wohngebaeude der Mauerfrass und Holzschwamm: fuer Baumeister, Bautechniker, Gutsverwalter, Tuencher, Maler und Hausbesitzer/Adolf Wilh. Keim. —2. Aufl.. —Wien: A. Hartleben's Verlag, 1901

8,141 S. ;18 cm.

TU241/D525

Das Wohnhaus von heute/Grete Dexel, W. Dexel. —Leipzig: Hesse & Becker Verlag, 1928

189 S. ;19 cm.

TU3/F899

Leitfaden fuer den Unterricht in der Bau-Constructionslehre/Johann Friedel. —Wien: Wilhelm Braumueller, 1900

975 S. ;22 cm.

TU311. 1-43/L366-15

Die graphische Statik: Elementares Lehrbuch fuer den Schul- und Selbstunterricht sowie zum Gebrauch in der Praxis/R. Lauenstein. —15. Aufl.. —Leipzig: Alfred Kroener Verlag, 1922

307 S. ;23 cm.

TU37-62/E55(2)

Handbuch fuer Eisenbetonbau in vier Baenden. 2. Band, Der Baustoff und seine Bearbeitung/F. von Emperger. —Berlin: Verlag von Wilhelm Ernst & Sohn, 1907

243 S. ;27 cm.

TU8/W415

Taschenbuch der handwerklichen Selbsthilfe fuer alle Arbeiten in Haus und Wohnung: Praktische Unterweisungen in Hauswerkstechnik fuer jedermann/Bernhard Weickmann. —Esslingen: Verlag von J. F. Schreiber, c1928

8,198,41 S. ;17 cm.

U 交通运输

U46-61/E65-4(1)

Autotechnisches Woerterbuch in vier Sprachen. Band I,Deutsch Franzoesisch-Englisch-Italienisch/Heinz Erblich. —4. Aufl.. —Berlin: Richard Carl Schmidt & Co. ,1929

233 S. ;17 cm.

U469-62/P478-8

Das moderne Automobil: Sein Bau und Betrieb seine Pflege und Reparaturen/M. Peter. —8. Aufl.. —Berlin: Richard Carl Schmidt & Co. , c1927

8,694 S. ;23 cm.

U472. 4/H713

Kraftfahrzeug-Reparaturwerkstaetten/Rich. Hofmann. —Berlin: Richard Carl Schmidt & Co. ,1926

8,236 S. ;17 cm.

U472. 42/S398-3

Stoerungen am Kraftwagen und seinen Teilen: Angaben ueber Merkmale, Ursachen und Abhilfe/Jac. Schwaiger. —3. Aufl.. —Berlin: Richard Carl Schmidt & Co. ,1927

230 S. ;17 cm.

U483/S394-6

Das Motorrad und seine Behandlung/Walter Schuricht. —6. Aufl.. —Berlin: Richard Carl Schmidt & Co. ,1928

273 S. ;17 cm.

U659. 516/W469-2

Der Hafen von Hamburg/L. Wendemuth,W. Boettcher. —2. Aufl.. —Hamburg: Meissner & Christiansen,1931

254 S. ;21 cm.

U675. 81/H113-8

See-Atlas: Eine Ergaenzung zu Justus Perthes' Taschen-Atlas/Hermann Habenicht. —8. Aufl.. —Gotha: Verlag von Justus Perthes,1911

46 S. ;17 cm.

V 航空、航天

V262/P529(1)

Der Bau des Flugzeug. Teil 1, Allgemeiner Aufbau und die Tragflaechen/E. Pfister. —Berlin: Verlag C. J. E. Volckmann Nachf. G. m. b. H. ,c1926

48 S. ;21 cm.

Z 综合性图书

Z2/F953

Das Buch der 1000 Wunder/Artur Fuerst, Alexander Moszkowski. —Muenchen: Albert Langen, c1916

12, 400 S. ; 22 cm.

Z22/M551

China/Gerhard Menz. —Berlin: Zentral Verlag G. m. b. H., 1930

88 S. ; 19 cm.

Z22/V834

China: 12 Vortraege ueber Geschichte, Kultur und Kunst/Carl Emmo Vissering. —Tientsin: Eigenverlag des Verfassers, 1943

191 S. ; 26 cm.

Z251. 6/H541(1)

Der kleine Herder: Nachschlagebuch ueber alles fuer alle. 1. Halbband, A bis K/Herder & Co. G. m. b. H. Verlagsbuchhandlung. —Freiburg im Breisgau: Herder & Co. G. m. b. H. Verlagsbuchhandlung, 1925

752 S. ; 20 cm.

Z251. 6/H541(2)

Der kleine Herder: Nachschlagebuch ueber alles fuer alle. 2. Halbband, L bis Z/Herder & Co. G. m. b. H. Verlagsbuchhandlung. —Freiburg im Breisgau: Herder & Co. G. m. b. H. Verlagsbuchhandlung, 1925

753-1531 S. ; 20 cm.

Z251. 6/W784(3)

Ewiges Deutschland: Ein deutsches Hausbuch. 3. Folge/Winterhilfswerk des Deutschen Volkes. —Braunschweig: Verlag Georg Westermann, c1940

352 S. ; 20 cm.

Z351. 6/B582-5(2)

Meyers Konversations-Lexikon: Ein Nachschalgewerk des allgemeinen Wissens. 2. Band, Asmanit bis Biostatik/Bibliographisches Institut. —5. Aufl.. —Leipzig: Bibliographisches Institut, 1895

1056 S. ; 24 cm.

Z351. 6/B582-5(8)

Meyers Konversations-Lexikon: Ein Nachschalgewerk des allgemeinen Wissens. 8. Band, Grosskreuz bis Huebbe/Bibliographisches Institut. —5. Aufl.. —Leipzig: Bibliographisches Institut, 1896

1056 S. ; 24 cm.

Z351. 6/B582-5(9)

Meyers Konversations-Lexikon: Ein Nachschalgewerk des allgemeinen Wissens. 9. Band, Huebbe-Schleiden bis Kausler/Bibliographisches Institut. —5. Aufl.. —Leipzig: Bibliographisches Institut, 1896

1060 S. ; 24 cm.

Z551. 6/W373-2

1848: Sechs Vortraege/Ottocar Weber. —2. Aufl.. —Leipzig: Verlag von B. G. Teubner, 1909

8, 136, 48 S. ; 18 cm.

Z651. 6/A474(1937. 9)

Das Innere Reich: Zeitschrift fuer Dichtung, Kunst und deutsches Leben. September 1937/Paul Alverdes, Karl Benno von Mechow. —

Muenchen: Verlag Albert Langen/Georg Mueller,1937
641-752 S. ;23 cm.

Z651. 6/A474(1937. 11)
Das Innere Reich: Zeitschrift fuer Dichtung, Kunst und deutsches Leben. November 1937/Paul Alverdes, Karl Benno von Mechow. —Muenchen: Verlag Albert Langen/Georg Mueller,1937
869-996 S. ;23 cm.

Z651. 6/A474(1937. 12)
Das Innere Reich: Zeitschrift fuer Dichtung, Kunst und deutsches Leben. Dezember 1937/Paul Alverdes,Karl Benno von Mechow. —Muenchen: Verlag Albert Langen/Georg Mueller,1937
997-1120 S. ;23 cm.

Z651. 6/A474(1938. 1)
Das Innere Reich: Zeitschrift fuer Dichtung, Kunst und deutsches Leben. Januar 1938/Paul Alverdes,Karl Benno von Mechow. —Muenchen: Verlag Albert Langen/Georg Mueller,1938
1121-1252 S. ;23 cm.

Z651. 6/A474(1938. 2)
Das Innere Reich: Zeitschrift fuer Dichtung, Kunst und deutsches Leben. Februar 1938/Paul Alverdes,Karl Benno von Mechow. —Muenchen: Verlag Albert Langen/Georg Mueller,1938
1253-1376 S. ;23 cm.

Z651. 6/A474(1938. 3)
Das Innere Reich: Zeitschrift fuer Dichtung, Kunst und deutsches Leben. Maerz 1938/Paul Alverdes. —Muenchen: Verlag Albert Langen/Georg Mueller,1938
1377-1484 S. ;23 cm.

Z651. 6/A474(1938. 4)
Das Innere Reich: Zeitschrift fuer Dichtung, Kunst und deutsches Leben. April 1938/Paul Alverdes. —Muenchen: Verlag Albert Langen/Georg Mueller,1938
1-112 S. ;23 cm.

Z651. 6/A474(1938. 5)
Das Innere Reich: Zeitschrift fuer Dichtung, Kunst und deutsches Leben. Mai 1938/Paul Alverdes. —Muenchen: Verlag Albert Langen/Georg Mueller,1938
113-240 S. ;23 cm.

Z651. 6/A474(1938. 6)
Das Innere Reich: Zeitschrift fuer Dichtung, Kunst und deutsches Leben. Juni 1938/Paul Alverdes. —Muenchen: Verlag Albert Langen/Georg Mueller,1938
241-360 S. ;23 cm.

Z651. 6/A474(1938. 11)
Das Innere Reich: Zeitschrift fuer Dichtung, Kunst und deutsches Leben. November 1938/Paul Alverdes. —Muenchen: Verlag Albert Langen/Georg Mueller,1938
845-964 S. ;23 cm.

Z651. 6/A474(1939. 1)
Das Innere Reich: Zeitschrift fuer Dichtung, Kunst und deutsches Leben. Januar 1939/Paul Alverdes. —Muenchen: Verlag Albert Langen/Georg Mueller,1939
1129-1254 S. ;23 cm.

Z651. 6/A474(1939. 3)
Das Innere Reich: Zeitschrift fuer Dichtung, Kunst und deutsches Leben. Maerz 1939/Paul Alverdes. —Muenchen: Verlag Albert Langen/Georg Mueller,1939
1391-1506 S. ;23 cm.

Z651. 6/A474(1939. 5)
Das Innere Reich: Zeitschrift fuer Dichtung, Kunst und deutsches Leben. Mai 1939/Paul Alverdes. —Muenchen: Verlag Albert Langen/

Georg Mueller, 1939
121-266 S. ; 23 cm.

Z651.6/A474(1939.6)
Das Innere Reich: Zeitschrift fuer Dichtung, Kunst und deutsches Leben. Juni 1939/Paul Alverdes. —Muenchen: Verlag Albert Langen/Georg Mueller, 1939
267-386 S. ; 23 cm.

Z651.6/A474(1939.8)
Das Innere Reich: Zeitschrift fuer Dichtung, Kunst und deutsches Leben. August 1939/Paul Alverdes. —Muenchen: Verlag Albert Langen/Georg Mueller, 1939
507-622 S. ; 23 cm.

Z651.6/A474(1939.9)
Das Innere Reich: Zeitschrift fuer Dichtung, Kunst und deutsches Leben. September 1939/Paul Alverdes. —Muenchen: Verlag Albert Langen/Georg Mueller, 1939
623-734 S. ; 23 cm.

Z651.6/A474(1939.10)
Das Innere Reich: Zeitschrift fuer Dichtung, Kunst und deutsches Leben. Oktober 1939/Paul Alverdes. —Muenchen: Verlag Albert Langen/Georg Mueller, 1939
735-798 S. ; 23 cm.

Z651.6/A474(1940.3)
Das Innere Reich: Zeitschrift fuer Dichtung, Kunst und deutsches Leben. Maerz 1940/Paul Alverdes. —Muenchen: Verlag Albert Langen/Georg Mueller, 1940
1035-1090 S. ; 23 cm.

Z651.6/A474(1940.4)
Das Innere Reich: Zeitschrift fuer Dichtung, Kunst und deutsches Leben. April 1940/Paul Alverdes. —Muenchen: Verlag Albert Langen/Georg Mueller, 1940
1-56 S. ; 23 cm.

Z651.6/A474(1940.6)
Das Innere Reich: Zeitschrift fuer Dichtung, Kunst und deutsches Leben. Juni 1940/Paul Alverdes. —Muenchen: Verlag Albert Langen/Georg Mueller, 1940
113-168 S. ; 23 cm.

Z651.6/A474(1940.7)
Das Innere Reich: Zeitschrift fuer Dichtung, Kunst und deutsches Leben. Juli 1940/Paul Alverdes. —Muenchen: Verlag Albert Langen/Georg Mueller, 1940
169-224 S. ; 23 cm.

Z651.6/A474(1940.9)
Das Innere Reich: Zeitschrift fuer Dichtung, Kunst und deutsches Leben. September 1940/Paul Alverdes. —Muenchen: Verlag Albert Langen/Georg Mueller, 1940
285-340 S. ; 23 cm.

Z651.6/D588(1930)
Regensburger Sonntagsblatt: Wochenschrift fuer das Bistum Regensburg/Dioezesan-Caritas-Verband Regensburg. —Regensburg: [s. n.], 1930
1 Heft; 33 cm.

Z651.6/W859(1937)
Regensburger Sonntagsblatt: Kirchenbaltt der Dioezese Regensburg/St. Wolfgangs Verlag. —Regensburg: St. Wolfgangs Verlag, 1937
1 Heft; 33 cm.

题名索引

—1—

—A—

—B—

—C—

—D—

—E—

—F—

—G—

—H—

—I—

—L—

—M—

—N—

—O—

—P—

—Q—

—R—

—S—

—T—

—U—

—V—

—W—

—Y—

—Z—

《中国图书馆分类法》类目

法语专辑

A 马列主义……

A742/1

La vie de Staline/Imam Raguza. —Paris: Librairie Arthème Fayard, 1938

416 p. ;18 cm.

B 哲学、宗教

B351/1

Les grands penseurs de l'Inde/Albert Schweitzer. —Paris: Payot, 1936

10,228 p. ;20 cm.

B565.26/1

La vie privée de J. J. Rousseau/René Trintzius. —Paris: Hachette, 1938

11,252 p. ;18 cm.

B565.4/1-14

Les idées et les âges/Alain. —4 ed.. —Paris: Gallimard, 1927

11,26 p. ;18 cm.

B565.5/1

La théologie de Saint Paul/F. Prat, S. J.. —Paris: Gabriel Beauchesne, 1908

591 p. ;22 cm.

B565.5/1-14

La théologie de Saint Paul/F. Prat, S. J.. —4 ed.. —Paris: Gabriel Beauchesne, 1913

607 p. ;22 cm.

B821/1

La vie et la mort/A. Dastre. —Paris: Ernest Flammarion, 1918

349 p. ;17 cm.

B83-0/1-6

Mes idées esthétiques/Léon Daudet. —Paris: Librairie Arthème Fayard, 1939

8,295 p. ;18 cm.

B843.3/1

Un art de vivre/André Maurois. —Paris: Librairie Plon, 1939

239 p. ;18 cm.

B848.6/1

L'art de connaître le caractère par la physionomie/Dr Jean Lefas. —Paris: Editions Médicales Norbert Maloine, 1928

326 p. ;22 cm.

B91/1

Brahma & Bouddha/H. V. Glasenapp. —Paris: Payot, 1937

18,286 p. ;21 cm.

B91/2

La grande porte/Maurice Maeterlinck. —Paris: Fasquelle, 1939

252 p. ;18 cm.

B911/1

Les grands cimetières sous la lune/Georges Bernanos. —Paris: Librairie Plon, 1938

361 p. ; 18 cm.

B920/1

Les pères du désert/Jean Bremond. —Paris: Librairie Victor Lecoffre, 1927

60, 263 p. ; 17 cm.

B94/1

L'église Jaune/Robert Bleichsteiner. —Paris: Payot, 1937

8, 292 p. ; 22 cm.

B97/1

L'évangile de Jésus-Christ/Le p. ; M. —J. Lagrange. —Paris: Librairie Lecoffre, 1932

12, 656 p. ; 22 cm.

B971/1(1)

Atlas historique de l'Ancien Testament/L. Tellier. —Rhône: Trait d'union, 1937

237 p. ; 22 cm.

B972/1(1)

Le corps mustique du christ 1/Emile Mersch. —Paris: Museum Lessianum, 1933

38, 477 p. ; 23 cm.

B972/1(2)

Le corps mustique du christ 2/Emile Mersch. —Paris: Museum Lessianum, 1933

10, 435 p. ; 22 cm.

B972/2

Origène/L'abbé Gustave Bardy. —Paris: Librairie Lecoffre, 1931

310 p. ; 18 cm.

B972/3

Tertullien et Saint Cyprien/Le Chanoine L. Bayard. —Paris: Librairie Lecoffre, 1930

285 p. ; 18 cm.

B972/4

Le catholicisme de Saint Augustin/Pierre Batiffol. —Paris: Librairie Lecoffre, 1929

555 p. ; 18 cm.

B972/5-7(1)

Histoire du dogme de ma Trinité/Jules Lebreton. —7 ed.. —Paris: Gabriel Beauchesne, 1927

24, 694 p. ; 22 cm.

B972. 1/1-10(2)

L'Enseignement de Saint Paul tome 2/François Amiot. —10 ed.. —Paris: Librairie Lecoffre, 1938

264 p. ; 17 cm.

B972. 1/1-12

L'enseignement de Saint Paul/François Amiot. —2 ed.. —Paris: Librairie Lecoffre, 1938

337 p. ; 18 cm.

B975/1

La Donation Totale(collection Nos Retraites)/T. R. Père Noël Gubbels. —[S. l.]: [s. n.], [?]

457 p. ; 21 cm.

B976. 1/1

L'Eglise naissante et le Catholicisme/Pierre Batiffol. —Paris: Librairie Victor Lecoffre, 1927

25, 520 p. ; 18 cm.

B976. 1/2-15(2)

La spiritualité chrétienne/P. Pourrat. —5 ed.. —Paris: Librairie Victor Lecoffre, 1924

535 p. ; 18 cm.

B976. 1/3(3)

La spiritualité chrétienne/P. Pourrat. —Paris: Librairie Lecoffre, 1927

607 p. ; 17 cm.

B976. 1/3(4)

La spiritualité chrétienne/P. Pourrat. —Paris: Librairie Lecoffre, 1930

12,672 p. ;17 cm.

B976. 1/4(3)

Histoire des dogmes dans l'Antiquité chrétienne/J. Tixeront. —Paris: Librairie Lecoffre, 1928

21,578 p. ;18 cm.

B976. 1/4-8(2)

Histoire des dogmes dans l'antiquité chrétienne II/J. Tixeront. —8 ed.. —Paris: Librairie Lecoffre, 1924

534 p. ;18 cm.

B976. 1/6(1)

La spiritualité chrétienne I Des origines de l'Eglise au Moyen Age/P. Pourrat. —Paris: Librairie Victor Lecoffre, 1926

502 p. ;17 cm.

B976. 1/7

Pascal /Jacques Chevalier. —[S. l.]: Librairie Lecoffre, 1927

295-560 p. ;18 cm.

B979. 198. 5/1-4

Lea paix constantinienne et le catholicisme/Pierre Batiffol. —4 ed.. —Paris: Librairie Lecoffre, 1929

530 p. ;18 cm.

B979. 9/1

La vie merveilleuse de Jésus/Gaston Varenne. —Paris: Fasquelle Editeurs, 1938

10,180 p. ;17 cm.

B979. 9/2

Vie de Jésus/François Mauriac. —Paris: Ernest Flammarion, 1936

284 p. ;18 cm.

B979. 9/3

Jésus [s. n.]/Dmitry Merejkovsky. —Paris: Editions Bernard Grasset, 1935

364 p. ;20 cm.

B979. 956. 5/1

Journal d'un curé de campagne/Georges Bernanos. —Paris: Librairie Plon, 1936

366 p. ;17 cm.

B979. 956. 5/2-6

La vie du Maréchal de Richelieu/Robert Honnert, Marcel Augagneur. —6 ed.. —Paris: Gallimard, 1929

8,226 p. ;18 cm.

B985/1

Quand Israël rentre chez soi/Pierre Goemare. —Paris: Denoël et Steele, [?]

184 p. ;17 cm.

C 社会科学总论

C525. 65/1

La théologie de Saint Paule/F. Prat, S. J. —Rennes: Gabriel Beauchesne et Cie, 1912

576 p. ;23 cm.

D 政治、法律

D091. 2/1
Athènes, une démocratie de sa naissance à sa mort/Robert Cohen. —Pa-ris: Arthème Fayard et Cie,1936
10,310 p. ;17 cm.

D1/1
L'idéologie du communisme/Colonel Résanov. —Paris: Editions Bossard,1923
10,11 p. ;18 cm.

D5/1
La politique et le partage de la terre/Georges Hardy. —Paris: Albin Michel,1937
18,494 p. ;21 cm.

D59/1
L'aventure de l'amiral koltchak/Général J. Rouquerol. —Paris: Payot,1929
9,187 p. ;22 cm.

D6/1
La Chine capitaliste/Maurice Lachin. —Paris: Librairie Gallimard,1938
22,303 p. ;21 cm.

D6/2
L'énigme Chinoise/Comte Sforza. —Paris: Payot,1928
7,204 p. ;23 cm.

D731. 3/1-4
L'honorable paix Japonaise/Jean Escarra. —4 ed.. —Paris: Bernard Grasset,1938
20,227 p. ;18 cm.

D731. 32/1
Le Monroïsme japonais/Georges Klévanski. —Paris: Librairie Arthur Rousseau,1935
10,157 p. ;24 cm.

D735. 65/1
Discours/M. André Maurois. —Paris: Bernard Grasset,1939
131 p. ;18 cm.

D742. 1/1
L'avion noir/Henry de Monfreid. —Paris: Bernard Grasset,1936
16,191 p. ;18 cm.

D75/1
Les débris de la guerre/Maurice Maeterlinck. —Paris: Eugène Fasquelle,1922
274 p. ;17 cm.

D75/2
La crise de l'Europe/André Siegfried. —Paris: Calmann Lévy,1935
125 p. ;17 cm.

D75/3-7
Dictateurs et dictures de l'après-guerre/Le comte Sforza. —7 ed.. —Paris: Gallimard,1931
15,264 p. ;18 cm.

D750. 9/1
La désagrégation de l'Europe/Francesco Nitti. —Paris: Editions Spes,[?]
17,564 p. ;18 cm.

D751. 2/1
Cavalerie rouge/I. Babel. —Paris: Les Editions

Rieder, 1928
26, 236 p. ; 17 cm.

D751. 2/2
La tyrannie soviétique et le malheur russe/Michel d'Herbigny. —Paris: Editions Spes, 1923
257 p. ; 18 cm.

D751. 2/3
La Russie sous les soviets/N. de Basily. —Paris: Librairie Plon, 1938
480 p. ; 22 cm.

D754/1
Les Etats Balkaniques et le principe confédératif/Société de Bienfaisance Slave de Sophia-Comité littéraire. —Sophia: Imprimerie de la Cour Royale, 1915
24 p. ; 20 cm.

D754/2
La Confédération balkanique et la question macédonienne/Société de Bienfaisance Slave de Sophia-Comité littéraire. —Sophia: Imprimerie de la Cour Royale, 1915
21 p. ; 20 cm.

D754. 1/1
La conférence nationale des études sociales/Naim Frashëri. —Tirana: Naim Frashëri, 1971
234 p. ; 16 cm.

D754. 109/1(1967-1968)
Discours 1967-1968/Enver Hoxha. —Tirana: Naim Frasheri, 1969
385 p. ; 16 cm.

D754. 6/1-9
La quatrième Italie/Maurice Lachin. —9 ed. . —Paris: Gallimard, 1935
12, 247 p. ; 19 cm.

D756. 4/1
Le roi des belges a-t-il trahi? /Robert Goffin. —[S. l.]: [s. n.], [?]
291 p. ; 18 cm.

D756. 5/1
Hommes et Doctrines/Arthur Huc. —Paris: Editions Bernard Grasset, [?]
9, 337 p. ; 18 cm.

D756. 5/2-11
Mes idées politiques/Charles Maurras. —Paris: Arthème fayard et Cie, 1937
295 p. ; 18 cm.

D756. 5/3
Mémoires clair de lune et taxi-auto/Elisabeth de Granmont. —Paris: Bernard Grasset, 1932
269 p. ; 18 cm.

D756. 5/4
L'hécatombe/Léon Daudet. —Paris: Nouvelle Librairie Nationale, 1923
7, 308 p. ; 18 cm.

D756. 5/5
La misère et nous/Daniel-Rops. —Paris: Bernard Grasset, 1935
140 p. ; 16 cm.

D756. 5/6
Dans la Ronde des Faunes/Isabelle Sandy. —Paris: Librairie Delalain, 1921
224 p. ; 16 cm.

D756. 5/7
Savoir réagir/Léon Daudet. —Paris: Albin Michel, 1935
187 p. ; 15 cm.

D756. 5/8-16
Paris qui disparait/G. Lenotre. —6 ed. . —Paris: Editions Bernard Grasset, 1937

290 p. ;18 cm.

D756. 5/9

Sur la pente/André Tardieu. —Paris: Ernest Flammarion,1935

120,25 p. ;18 cm.

D756. 5/10

France été 1940/Andre Morize. —Paris: [s. n.],1941

11,23 p. ;18 cm.

D756. 5/11

Sur la démocratie/Maurice Ségard. —Paris: Librairie Larousse,1930

14,192 p. ;18 cm.

D756. 5/12

Doit-on le dire? /Jacques Bainville. —Paris: Arthème Fayard,1939

14,396 p. ;19 cm.

D756. 5-532/1

Avec foch /André Tardieu. —Paris: Ernest Flammarion,1939

11,283 p. ;18 cm.

D756. 509/1

Discours/Henri-Robert. —Paris: Librairie Plon,1939

132 p. ;18 cm.

D756. 55/1

Toute la vérité sur un mois dramatique de notre histoire/Jean Montigny. —Paris: Editions Mont-Louis Clermont-Ferrand,[?]

5,157 p. ;18 cm.

D756. 56/1

La République des ducs/Daniel Halévy. —Paris: Bernard Grasset,1937

7,411 p. ;18 cm.

D756. 56/2

La légende des démocraties pacifiques/Georges Demartial. —Paris: Presses Univeritaires de France,1939

10,121 p. ;18 cm.

D756. 59/1

Carnets/Ludovic Halévy. —Paris: Calmann-Lévy,1935

224 p. ;18 cm.

D756. 59/2

La fortune publique de la France/Edmond Théry. —Paris: Librairie CH. Delagrave,1911

256 p. ;18 cm.

D756. 59/3

Notre pays et les autres pays/Neville Chamberlain. —Paris: Flammarion,1939

192 p. ;18 cm.

D80/1

Le diplomate/Jules Cambon. —Paris: Hachette,1926

122 p. ;15 cm.

D819/1

Le traité de paix/L. Barthou. —Paris: Bibliothèque-Charpentier,1919

249 p. ;18 cm.

D822/1

La vérité sur le différent sino-japonais/L'Association générale des étudiants chinois en France. —Paris: L'Association générale des étudiants chinois en France,1915

52 p. ;22 cm.

D822/2

Extrême-Orient et Pacifique/Roger Lévy. —Paris: Librairie Armand Colin,1935

232 p. ;18 cm.

D822.331.3/1

Le Japon en Chine/K. K. Kawakami. —Paris: Editions Bernard Grasset,1938

26,270 p.;18 cm.

D822.331.3/2

Chine et Japon 1938/R. D'Auxion de Ruffé. —Paris: Editions Berger-Levrault,1939

18,403 p.;22 cm.

D83/1

Unité de l'Asie/André Duboscq. —Paris: Editions Unitas,1936

96 p.;19 cm.

D831.32/1

L'Effort japonais/A. Gérard. —Paris: Bloud et Gay,1916

30 p.;19 cm.

D856.5/1

Quand Hitler espionne la France/Paul Allard. —Paris: Les Editions de France,1939

197 p.;17 cm.

D923/1

Règlement de Procédure Pénale de la république de Chine/La commission de l'exterritorialité. —Pékin: Merie du pei-T'ang, 1923

142 p.;26 cm.

D923.99/1

Législation commerciale de la République de Chine/La Commission de l'exterritorialité. —Pékin: Edition Bernard Grasset,1924

213 p.;25 cm.

E 军事

E115/1

Les marines étrangères/Marc Benoist. —Paris: J. De Gigord,1938

179 p.;21 cm.

E195/1

Vérité sur les combattants/Jean Labusquière. —Shanghai: Editions Typhon,1940

109 p.;20 cm.

E5/1

Combats et batailles sur mer/Claude Farrère et Paul Chack. —Paris: Ernest Flammarion,1925

283 p.;17 cm.

E509/1

Deux batailles navales/Paul Chack. —Paris: Les éditions de France,1935

349 p.;18 cm.

E512.5/1

L'armée russe telle qu'elle est/William Barnes Steveni. —Paris: Librairie Payot et Cie,[?]

5,127 p.;18 cm.

E565/1

Le péril sous-marin/Amiral Comte Jellicoe. —Paris: Editiond de la nouvelle revue critique, 1936

14,197 p.;23 cm.

E565/2

Missions Spéciales/Jacques Mortane. —Paris: Editions Baudinière,1929

10,308 p. ;18 cm.

E565/3

La France devant la guerre/André Labarthe. —Paris: Editions Bernard Grasset,1939

244 p. ;19 cm.

E565. 2/1

Démocratie beurre et canons/Robert de Saint Jean. —Paris: Gallimard,[?]

13,367 p. ;18 cm.

E565. 53/1

Nos marins a la guerre/Commandant Emile Vedel. —Paris: Librairie Payoy,1916

15,32 p. ;18 cm.

E565. 53/2-12

Dixmude/Charles le Goffic. —2 ed.. —Paris: Librairie Plon,1915

255 p. ;18 cm.

E83/1

Le diable noir/CH. Lucieto. —Paris: Berger Levrault,1928

258 p. ;18 cm.

E831/1

La guerre souterraine/Commandant Verdun. —Paris: Les éditions Denoël,1939

12,172 p. ;17 cm.

E92/1

Des anticipations de Jules Verne aux Réalisations d'aujourd'hui/A. Jacobson et A. Antoni. —Paris: J. de Gigord,[?]

14,197 p. ;18 cm.

F 经济

F039/1

Le sort du capitalisme/Louis Marlio. —Paris: Ernest Flammarion,1938

7,3 p. ;18 cm.

F156. 5/1

Produire d'une organisation économique du pays/Jean-Desthieux. —Paris: Editions Bossard, 1919

333 p. ;16 cm.

F832. 59/1

La crise bancaire en 1921-1923/André Buraeu. —Paris: Société Anonyme de Publications Périodiques,1923

144 p. ;24 cm.

G 文化、科学、教育、体育

G210/1-4

Bréviaire du journalisme/Léon Daudet. —4 ed.. —Paris: Gallimard,1936

250 p. ;17 cm.

G254. 37/1

Les beaux livres de notre temps/Jean de Pierrefeu. —Paris: Librairie Plon,1938

6,245 p. ;18 cm.

G40-095. 65/1

Emile ou de l'éducation/Rousseau. —Paris: Librairie de Paris,[?]

643 p. ;18 cm.

G811. 219/1

Le Paradis/Henry de Montherlant. —Paris: Bernard Grasset,1924

190 p. ;18 cm.

G861. 6/1

En plongée par 900 mètres de fond/william Beebe. —Paris: Bernard Grasset,[?]

9,320 p. ;18 cm.

H 语言、文字

H019/1-10

Variété IV/Paul Valéry. —10 ed.. —Paris: Qallimard,1938

265 p. ;18 cm.

H316/1

Dictionnaire Français-Anglais/Louis Chaffurin. —Paris: Librairie Larousse,1928

768 p. ;14 cm.

H323. 1-45/1-6

Apprenons L'Orthographe/E. Tribouillois. —6 ed.. —Paris: Librairie Delagrave,1938

10,214 p. ;17 cm.

H323. 2/1

Dictionnaire analogique/M. Charles Maquet. —Paris: Librairie Larousse,1936

591 p. ;19 cm.

H323. 3/1

Caractères et confidences/Maurice Martin du Gard. —Paris: Flammarion,1936

245 p. ;18 cm.

H324/1

Deuxième livre/M. D. Berlitz. —Paris: Nouvelle Edition,1923

8,142 p. ;19 cm.

H324-44/1

Grammaire cours supérieur/Claude Augé. —Paris: Librairie Larousse,[?]

472 p. ;18 cm.

H326/1

Manuel de conversations avec prononciation/S. Hirsch. —Paris: Librairie Garnier Frères,1933

129 p. ;13x12 cm.

H326/2

Dictionnaire Français-Italien et Italien-Français/A. Lacombe et p. ;Rouède. —Paris: Librairie Garnier Frères,[?]

768 p. ;18 cm.

I 文学

I313.45/1

Le roman de la Voie lactée/Lafcadio Hearn. —Paris: Mercvre de France,1922

254 p. ;17 cm.

I313.73/1

Légendes japonaises/Fukujirô Wakatsuki. —Paris: Georg et Duplat,1923

67 p. ;18 cm.

I421.073/1

Le drame éthiopien/Henry de Monfreid. —Paris: Bernard Grasset,1935

7,243 p. ;18 cm.

I512.44/1(2)

La Guerre et la Paix/Comte Léon Tolstoï. —Paris: Hachette,[?]

387 p. ;18 cm.

I512.45/1

Bêtes, Hommes et Dieux/Ferdinand Ossendowski. —Paris: Librairie Plon,1924

275 p. ;18 cm.

I512.45/2

Sulamite/Alexandre Kouprine. —Paris: Editions du monde nouveau,1922

27,165 p. ;16 cm.

I512.45/3-8

L'Antéchrist Pierre et Alexis/Dmitry Merejkovsky. —8 ed.. —Paris: Gallimard,1938

445 p. ;18 cm.

I516.45/1

L'Enfant perdu/Rahel Sanzara. —Paris: Arthème Fayard et Cie,1935

368 p. ;21 cm.

I516.45/2

La fabrique des hommes nouveaux/Alla Rachmanova. —Paris: Librairie Plon,1936

255 p. ;17 cm.

I516.45/3

Le dernier jour/Vicki Baum. —Paris: Emile-Paul Frères,1938

211 p. ;17 cm.

I516.45/4

La femme sans ombre/Hugo de Hofmannsthal. —[S. l.]:Librairie Stock,1930

3,213 p. ;16 cm.

I516.45/5

Retour à l'Aube/Vicki Baum. —[S. l.]:Émile-Paul Frères,1938

7,149 p. ;17 cm.

I545.73/1

Uranie/Camille Flammarion. —Paris: Ernest Flammarion,[?]

371 p. ;17 cm.

I546.45/1

Le prisonnier des Abyssins/Guglielmo Ferrero. —Paris: Les Editions Rieder,[?]

311 p. ;17 cm.

I546.45/2

Le feu/Gabriele d'annunzio. —Paris: Calmann-Lévy,1929

416 p. ;18 cm.

I561.45/1-10

Lord Jim/Joseph Conrad. —10 ed.. —Paris: Editions de la nouvelle revue française, 1922

10,346 p. ;18 cm.

I561.45/2

Intentions/Oscar Wilde. —Paris: Librairie, 1921

28,266 p. ;16 cm.

I561.45/3

Porgy/Du Bose Heyward. —Paris: Calmann-Lévy, 1929

198 p. ;17 cm.

I561.45/4

La Citadelle /A. J. Cronin. —Paris: Albin Michel, 1938

415 p. ;19 cm.

I561.45/5-8

Enfants des étoiles/H. G. Wells. —8 ed.. —Paris: Gallimard, 1939

204 p. ;18 cm.

I561.45/6

L'exilée/Pearl Buck. —Paris: Librairie stock, 1937

10,251 p. ;18 cm.

I561.45/7

La père de Christine-Alberte/H. —G. Wells. —Paris: Albin Michel, 1939

9,439 p. ;19 cm.

I561.45/8-4

Oscar Wilde et quelques autres/Lord Alfred Douglas. —4 ed.. —Paris: Gallimard, 1930

7,246 p. ;18 cm.

I561.45/9

Nevada/Zane Grey. —Paris: Editions Jules Tallandier, 1939

249 p. ;18 cm.

I561.45/10-9

La verge d'aaron/D. H. Lawrence. —9 ed.. —Paris: Gallimard, [?]

7,367 p. ;18 cm.

I561.45/11

Un crépuscule américain/Samuel Rogers. —Paris: Editions de la nouvelle revue critique, 1936

7,249 p. ;18 cm.

I561.45/12

Europe/Robert Briffault. —Paris: Albin Michel, 1936

495 p. ;19 cm.

I561.45/13

La Course du Thé/John Masefield. —[S. l.]: Plon, 1939

1,236 p. ;16 cm.

I561.45/14

Le Défenseur d'Herat/Maud Diver. —[S. l.]: Payot, 1936

7,325 p. ;19 cm.

I561.45/91

L'ange combattant/Pearl Buck. —Paris: Librairie stock, 1937

276 p. ;18 cm.

I561.5/1

Mes chasses en Chine/Harold Frank Wallace. —Paris: Payot, 1939

10,217 p. ;22 cm.

I561.5/2

Avoine sauvage/Eric Muspratt. —Paris: Bernard Grasset, [?]

7,287 p. ;18 cm.

I561. 6/1

L'ange et la bête/Aldous Huxley. —Paris: Editions Stock,1940

268 p. ;18 cm.

I564. 45/1

Le Guet-Apens/Henri Conscience. —Paris: Calmann Lévy,1897

240 p. ;17 cm.

I564. 6/1

La mort/Maurice Maeterlinck. —Paris: Bibliothèque-Charpentier,1928

272 p. ;18 cm.

I565. 09/1

Histoire de la littérature française/Albert Thibaudet. —Paris: Stock,1936

587 p. ;17 cm.

I565. 15/1(6)

Les oeuvres libres recueil littéraire mensuel/A. Fayard et cie. —Paris: A. Fayard et cie,1934

382 p. ;18 cm.

I565. 15/1(118)

Les oeuvres libres recueil littéraire mensuel/A. Fayard et cie. —Paris: A. Fayard et cie,[?]

377 p. ;18 cm.

I565. 15/1(156)

Les oeuvres libres recueil littéraire mensuel/A. Fayard et cie. —Paris: A. Fayard et cie,1934

373 p. ;18 cm.

I565. 15/1(161)

Les oeuvres libres recueil littéraire mensuel/A. Fayard et cie. —Paris: A. Fayard et cie,[?]

383 p. ;18 cm.

I565. 15/1(180)

Les oeuvres libres recueil littéraire mensuel/A. Fayard et cie. —Paris: A. Fayard et cie,1936

375 p. ;18 cm.

I565. 15/1(185)

Les oeuvres libres recueil littéraire mensuel/A. Fayard et cie. —Paris: A. Fayard et cie,1936

349 p. ;18 cm.

I565. 15/2

Bucoliques-Elégies prose/André Chénier. —Paris: Editions du Monde Moderne,[?]

10,275 p. ;18 cm.

I565. 2/1

Les Petites Ames/Paul Géraldy. —Paris: Albert Messein,1923

10,145 p. ;18 cm.

I565. 2/2

Histoire de mellila princesse de portugal/Louis Thomas. —Paris: Editions Baudiniere,1929

15,24 p. ;18 cm.

I565. 2/3

Les fleurs du mal/Charles Baudelaire. —Paris: Librairie des Bibliophiles,[?]

300 p. ;18 cm.

I565. 2/4-73

Aux flancs du vase/Albert Samain. —73 ed. . —Paris: Mercvre de France,1922

7,199 p. ;18 cm.

I565. 2/5

Traversées Epiques/Paul Chack. —Paris: Les éditions de France,1938

239 p. ;18 cm.

I565. 2/6-14

Le miroir des heures/Henri de Régnier. —4 ed. . —Paris: Mercvre de France,1919

9,239 p. ;16 cm.

I565.2/7-123

Le chariot d'or/Albert Samain.—23 ed..—Paris: Bloud et Gay,1925

7,236 p.;18 cm.

I565.2/8

Poésie Morceaux Choisis de Victor Hugo /Victor Hugo.—[S.l.]:Librairie Delgrave,1930

14,504 p.;15 cm.

I565.3/1

Aimer/Paul Geraldy.—Paris: Librairie Stock, 1921

129 p.;18 cm.

I565.3/2

Romanesques: Les deux pierrots/Edmond Rostand.—Paris: Fasquelle Editeurs,[?]

215 p.;19 cm.

I565.3/3

Chez Palmyre/Maurice Donnay.—Paris: Ernest Flammarion,[?]

61 p.;15 cm.

I565.3/4

Oeuvres de P. Corneille tome septième Agésilas/P. Corneille.—Paris: Libairie de L. Hachette et Cie,1862

8,526 p.;21 cm.

I565.3/5-25

La famille benoiton/Victorien Sardou.—25 ed..—Paris: Michel Lévy Frères,1867

1 p.;18 cm.

I565.3/6

Mademoiselle de la seiglière/Jules Sandeau.—Londre: Macmillan,1920

150 p.;15 cm.

I565.3/7(6)

Molière/Molière.—Paris: Nelson,1930

474 p.;16 cm.

I565.3/8

Guignol/Gaston Baty.—Paris: Editions coutan-Lambert,1934

202 p.;20 cm.

I565.3/9

L'Aiglon/Edmond Rostand.—Paris: Librairie Charpentier et Fasquelle,1919

262 p.;20 cm.

I565.3/10

Le Cid de Corneille/Henry Lyonnet.—Paris: Edgar Malfère,1928

171 p.;17 cm.

I565.3/11(2)

Théâtre choisi de Corneille/Corneille.—Paris: Editions Lutetia,[?]

571 p.;15 cm.

I565.3/12

L'étincelle/Edouard Pailleron.—Paris: Calmann-Lévy,1929

57 p.;16 cm.

I565.3/13

Merlusse Cigalon/Marcel Pagnol.—Paris: Fasquelle Editeurs,1936

9,211 p.;18 cm.

I565.3/14

Robert et Marianne/Paul Géraldy.—Paris: Librairie Stock,[?]

155 p.;18 cm.

I565.3/15

César/Marcel Pagnol.—Paris: Fasquelle,1937

247 p.;18 cm.

I565.44/1

Confessions Tome1/Jean-Jaques Rousseau.—

Paris: Librairie Plon,1930
14,345 p. ;19 cm.

I565. 45/1
Le passage des ombres /Maurice Clavière. —Paris: Editions Bernard Grasset,1935
260 p. ;18 cm.

I565. 45/2
L'oblat/J. K. Huysmans. —Paris: Librairie Plon,[?]
448 p. ;18 cm.

I565. 45/3
Les Soeurs Rondoli/Guy de Maupassant. —Paris: Librairie Paul Ollendorff,[?]
279 p. ;17 cm.

I565. 45/4
Un Sidi ou la Vie est belle/Marcelle Marty. —Paris: Albin Michel,1938
317 p. ;18 cm.

I565. 45/5-5
Conquête/C. J Odic. —5 ed.. —Paris: Editions R. —A. Corrêa,1938
250 p. ;18 cm.

I565. 45/6
Le journal d'un philosophe/Gyp. —Paris: Ernest Flammarion,[?]
283 p. ;18 cm.

I565. 45/7-23
Le temps du mépris/André Malraux. —23 ed.. —Paris: Librairie Gallimard,1935
16,169 p. ;18 cm.

I565. 45/8
Intempéries/Rosamond Lehmann. —Paris: Librairie Plon,1936
483 p. ;18 cm.

I565. 45/9
Nouvelle histoire de Mouchette/Georges Bernanos. —Paris: Librairie Plon,1937
223 p. ;17 cm.

I565. 45/10
Que ma joie demeure/Jean Giono. —Paris: Editions Bernard Grasset,1935
493 p. ;18 cm.

I565. 45/11-36
Les Pitards/Simenon. —36 ed.. —Paris: Librairie Gallimard,[?]
252 p. ;18 cm.

I565. 45/12
Jean Villemeur/Goger Vercel. —Paris: Albin Michel,1939
318 p. ;18 cm.

I565. 45/13
Xénia/Joseph Peyré. —Paris: Editions Bernard Grasset,1936
8,239 p. ;18 cm.

I565. 45/14
Frère et Soeur/Paul d'Aigremont. —Paris: Editions Jules Tallandier,1930
221 p. ;18 cm.

I565. 45/15-10
Baudouin des mines/O. —P. Gilbert. —10 ed.. —Paris: Librairie Gallimard,1939
6,262 p. ;17 cm.

I565. 45/16
Les deux soeurs/Paul Bourget. —Paris: Librairie Plon,[?]
366 p. ;18 cm.

I565. 45/17
Cagayous/[s. n.]. —Paris: Librairie Gallimard,1931

40,225 p. ;18 cm.

I565.45/18

La Bâtonnière/José Théry. —Paris: Albin Michel,1938

252 p. ;18 cm.

I565.45/19

La jeune fille secrète/Robert Francis. —Paris: Librairie Gallimard,1938

8,210 p. ;18 cm.

I565.45/20

Boule de Suif/Guy de Maupassant. —Paris: Albin Michel,[?]

285 p. ;17 cm.

I565.45/21

Le nouveau sphinx/Robert Goffin. —[S. l.]: [s. n.],[?]

235 p. ;18 cm.

I565.45/22

Varouna/Julien Green. —[S. l.]:[s. n.],[?]

4,275 p. ;18 cm.

I565.45/23

L'Américain/Marcel Prévost. —Paris: Les Editions de France,[?]

244 p. ;18 cm.

I565.45/24

Le Révolté/Maurice Larrouy. —Paris: Les Editions de France,1929

308 p. ;18 cm.

I565.45/25

Les abeilles d'or/Albéric Cahuet. —Paris: Fasquelle Editeurs,1939

283 p. ;18 cm.

I565.45/26

L'Affaire plantin/André Lang. —Paris: Librairie Plon,1936

2,242 p. ;18 cm.

I565.45/27

Claudine à Paris/Willy et Colette Willy. —Paris: Librairie ollendorff,[?]

276 p. ;17 cm.

I565.45/28

La Pologne de Pilsudski/Raymond Recouly. —Paris: Les Editions de France,1935

3,324 p. ;18 cm.

I565.45/29-2

Train de vies/Eugène Dabit. —2 ed.. —Paris: Librairie Gallimard,1936

10,239 p. ;18 cm.

I565.45/30-6

Le jour de Gloire/René Béhaine. —6 ed.. —Paris: Mercvre de France,1939

10,293 p. ;18 cm.

I565.45/31-10

Les Violents/Ramon Fernandez. —10 ed.. —Paris: Librairie Gallimard,1935

10,244 p. ;18 cm.

I565.45/32

Grand Hôtel/Vicki Baum. —Paris: Librairie Stock,1931

355 p. ;18 cm.

I565.45/33

Un gentilhomme maudit/Lucien Maulvault. —Paris: Librairie Artheme Fayard,1939

10,254 p. ;18 cm.

I565.45/34

Campagne en Chine/Charles Paul. —Paris: Editions Stock,1939

8,548 p. ;19 cm.

I565. 45/35

Le Château des Brouillards/Roland Dorgelès. —Paris: Albin Michel, 1932

8,305 p. ;18 cm.

I565. 45/36

El Requête/Lucien Maulvault. —Paris: Arthème Fayard et Cie, 1937

8,241 p. ;17 cm.

I565. 45/37

La Flamme Sauvage/Ludovic Massé. —Paris: Editions Bernard Grasset, 1936

10,240 p. ;17 cm.

I565. 45/38

La Bête du vaccarès/Joseph d'Arbaud. —Paris: Editions Bernard Grasset, 1926

28,378 p. ;17 cm.

I565. 45/39(1)

Les trois mousquetaires tome 1/Alexandre Dumas. —Paris: Calmann Lévy, [?]

384 p. ;17 cm.

I565. 45/40

Port-Arthur/Pierre Frondaie. —Paris: Librairie Plon, 1936

270 p. ;17 cm.

I565. 45/41

Cris dans le ciel/Andr Corthis. —Paris: Arthème Fayard, 1939

250 p. ;17 cm.

I565. 45/42

Le Garçon savoyard/C. —F. Ramuz. —Paris: Editions Bernard Grasset, 1937

214 p. ;17 cm.

I565. 45/43

Amour promis/Emile Clermont. —Paris: Editions Bernard Grasset, 1938

28,260 p. ;17 cm.

I565. 45/44-5

Les musiciens du ciel/René Lefèvre. —5 ed.. —Paris: Gallimard, 1938

10,174 p. ;17 cm.

I565. 45/45-3

La fenêtre refermée/Ami Chantre. —3 ed.. —Paris: Mercvre de France, 1938

231 p. ;17 cm.

I565. 45/46

L'eau trouble/Jean Davray. —Paris: Albin Michel, 1939

8,309 p. ;17 cm.

I565. 45/47

La guerre n'existe pas/Luc Durtain. —Paris: Flammation, 1939

219 p. ;17 cm.

I565. 45/48

L'oubli sur la gloire/L. Barot-Forlière. —Paris: Arthème Fayard et Cie, 1926

318 p. ;17 cm.

I565. 45/49

La reine Evanouie/Jean-Louis Vaudoyer. —Paris: Librairie Plon, 1923

291 p. ;17 cm.

I565. 45/50

La Colombe/Alexandre Dumas. —Paris: Librairie Larousse, [?]

252 p. ;17 cm.

I565. 45/51

Les Thibault septième partie: L'Eté 1914/Roger Martin du Gard. —Paris: Gallimard, 1936

285 p. ;17 cm.

I565.45/52
L'amour de Cécile Fougère/Edmond Jaloux. —Paris: J. Fernczi&Fils,[?]
164 p. ;19 cm.

I565.45/53
Un divorce/Paul Bourget. —Paris: Librairie Plon,1930
252 p. ;15 cm.

I565.45/54
L'Assommoir tome premier/Emile Zola. —Paris: Fasquelle Editeurs,1930
297 p. ;17 cm.

I565.45/55
Le Traquenard/André Cayatte. —Paris: Albin Michel,1939
382 p. ;21 cm.

I565.45/56
Sous le pied de l'archange/Roger Vercel. —Paris: Albin Michel,1937
286 p. ;17 cm.

I565.45/57
Colin ou Les voluptés tropicales/Paul Reboux. —Paris: Ernest Flammarion,1923
287 p. ;17 cm.

I565.45/58
Les enfants gâtés/Philippe Hériat. —Paris: Gallimard,1939
10,279 p. ;21 cm.

I565.45/59
Autres Montparnos/Michel Georges-Michel. —Paris: Albin Michel,1935
253 p. ;17 cm.

I565.45/60
Le chiffre/Alexandre Arnoux. —Paris: Editions Bernard Grasset,1926
243 p. ;17 cm.

I565.45/60
Le chiffre/Alexandre Arnoux. —Paris: Bernard Grasset,1926
7,243 p. ;18 cm.

I565.45/61
Bel-ami/Guy de Maupassant. —Paris: Ernest Flammarion,[?]
348 p. ;17 cm.

I565.45/62
Césette/Emile Pouvillon. —Paris: Librairie Plon,1912
12,240 p. ;15 cm.

I565.45/63
Quarantième étage/Luc Durtain. —Paris: Gallimard,1927
247 p. ;17 cm.

I565.45/64
La curée/Emile Zola. —Paris: Eugène Fasquelle,1929
387 p. ;17 cm.

I565.45/65
Les marchands d'ombres/André Cayatte. —Paris: Albin Michel,1938
443 p. ;19 cm.

I565.45/66-14
Aux sources de la liberté/Edouard herriot. —4 ed.. —Paris: Gallimard,1939
9,209 p. ;18 cm.

I565.45/67
Au mal assis/Marcel E Grancher. —Lyon: Les éditions Lugdunum,1934
17,255 p. ;18 cm.

I565. 45/68

Le retour du fils/Charles Plisnier. —Paris: Edition Corrêa et Cie,1939

12,371 p. ;18 cm.

I565. 45/69

Trois Récits/François Mauriac. —Paris: Bernard Grasset,1929

32,215 p. ;18 cm.

I565. 45/70

Arches de discorde/Maurice Larrouy. —Paris: Arthème fayard et Cie,1936

14,345 p. ;18 cm.

I565. 45/71

Un soir a cordoue... /Georges Grappe. —Paris: Albin Michel,1926

13,255 p. ;18 cm.

I565. 45/72(1)

Vingt ans après(tome 1)/Alexandre Dumas. —Paris: Nelson,[?]

9,572 p. ;15 cm.

I565. 45/72(2)

Vingt ans après(tome 2)/Alexandre Dumas. —Paris: Nelson,1930

10,569 p. ;16 cm.

I565. 45/73-6

La haute neige/Noel Vindry. —6 ed.. —Paris: Gallimard,1939

7,243 p. ;19 cm.

I565. 45/74-5

La felouque bleue/Léon Lafage. —5 ed.. —Paris: Editions spes,[?]

7,234 p. ;18 cm.

I565. 45/75

L'astre d'épouvante/Gustave le Rouge. —Paris: Librairie Larousse,1928

8,254 p. ;18 cm.

I565. 45/76

La vie douloureuse de Charles Baudelaire/François Porché. —Paris: Librairie Plon,1926

304 p. ;18 cm.

I565. 45/77-9

Mon premier voyage (tour de monde en 80 jours)/Jean Cocteau. —9 ed.. —Paris: Gallimard,1936

11,231 p. ;18 cm.

I565. 45/78

Les filles du rhône/Jean des vallières. —Paris: Albin Michel,1938

19,315 p. ;18 cm.

I565. 45/79

Les trois mousquetaires (tome 1)/Alexandre Dumas. —Paris: Nelson,1930

7,480 p. ;16 cm.

I565. 45/80-2

René Leys/Victor Segalen. —2 ed.. —Paris: G;Grès et Cie,1922

10,257 p. ;17 cm.

I565. 45/81

Correspondance de Sophie-Dorothée/G. du Boscq de Beaumont et M. Bernos. —Paris: Librairie Ambert,[?]

5,327 p. ;19 cm.

I565. 45/82

La prochaine dernière/Georges de la Fouchardière. —Paris: Editions Montaigne,1932

255 p. ;18 cm.

I565. 45/83

La double affaire du 20 avril/Georges Imann. —Paris: Edition Bernard Grasset,[?]

10,238 p. ;18 cm.

I565. 45/84

Mon petit trott/André Lichtenberger. —Paris: Librairie Plon,1931

11,252 p. ;16 cm.

I565. 45/85-117(1. 2)

Du coté de chez Swann/Marcel Proust. —117 ed.. —Paris: Gallimard,1919

301 p. ;18 cm.

I565. 45/85-124(2. 1)

A l'ombre des jeunes filles en fleurs/Marcel Proust. —124 ed.. —Paris: Gallimard,1919

7,242 p. ;18 cm.

I565. 45/85-124(2. 2)

A l'ombre des jeunes filles en fleurs/Marcel Proust. —124 ed.. —Paris: Gallimard,1919

230 p. ;17 cm.

I565. 45/85-124(2. 3)

A l'ombre des jeunes filles en fleurs/Marcel Proust. —124 ed.. —Paris: Gallimard,1919

260 p. ;18 cm.

I565. 45/85-21(3. 2)

Le temps retrouvé(A la recherche du temps perdu tome 3)/Marcel Proust. —21 ed.. —Paris: Gallimard,1927

7,261 p. ;18 cm.

I565. 45/85-23(8. 1)

Le temps retrouvé/Marcel Proust. —23 ed.. —Paris: Gallimard,1927

237 p. ;18 cm.

I565. 45/85-52(6)

La prisonnière(à la recherche du temps perdu tome 6)/Marcel Proust. —52 ed.. —Paris: Gallimard,1923

8,272 p. ;17 cm.

I565. 45/85-52(6. 2)

La Prisonnière/Marcel Proust. —52 ed.. —Paris: Gallimard,1923

287 p. ;19 cm.

I565. 45/85-74(5. 1)

A la recherche du temps perdu tome 5: Sodome et Gomorrhe II/Marcel Proust. —74 ed.. —Paris: Gallimard,1922

7,23 p. ;18 cm.

I565. 45/85-74(5. 2)

A la recherche du temps perdu tome 5: Sodome et Gomorrhe II/Marcel Proust. —74 ed.. —Paris: Gallimard,1922

7,236 p. ;18 cm.

I565. 45/86-3

Mélanges/Louis Pergaud. —3 ed.. —Paris: Mercvre de Rrance,1938

15,284 p. ;18 cm.

I565. 45/87-79

La rose de la mer/Paul Vialar. —79 ed.. —Paris: Robert Denoel,1939

7,214 p. ;18 cm.

I565. 45/88

Mon ami robespierre/Henri Béraud. —Paris: Librairie Plon,1927

5,283 p. ;18 cm.

I565. 45/89

Le magicien/Somerset Maugham. —Paris: Les édition de France,1938

218 p. ;18 cm.

I565. 45/90(1)

Vérité(tome 1)/Emile Zola. —Paris: Eugène Fasquelle,1924

381 p. ;18 cm.

I565. 45/92

Sylvie Velsey/Cilette Ofaire. —Paris: Edition stock,1938

254 p. ;18 cm.

I565. 45/93-3

L'homme élastique/Jacques Spitz. —3 ed.. —Paris: Gallimard,1938

10,206 p. ;18 cm.

I565. 45/94

Le coeur et les chiffres/Georges Imann. —Paris: Bernard Grasset,1927

7,261 p. ;18 cm.

I565. 45/95-22

Terre des hommes/Antoine de Saint Exupéry. —22 ed.. —Paris: Gallimard,1939

10,218 p. ;18 cm.

I565. 45/96

Andromède et le monstre/Henry Bordeaux. —Paris: Librairie Plon,1928

255 p. ;18 cm.

I565. 45/97

L'indochine en zigzags/Pierre Billotey. —Paris: Albin Michel,1929

7,251 p. ;17 cm.

I565. 45/98

Le jardin d'épicure/Anatole France. —Paris: Calmann-Lévy,1921

238 p. ;18 cm.

I565. 45/99

Le Procueur de la lanterne/Jean Martet. —Paris: Albin Michel,1935

11,315 p. ;18 cm.

I565. 45/100

La guerre des espions/Paul Allard. —Paris: Ernest Flammarion,1936

6,246 p. ;18 cm.

I565. 45/101

Un drame dans le monde /Paul Bourget. —Paris: Librairie Plon,1921

9,306 p. ;18 cm.

I565. 45/102

L'an mille... /Léo Larguier. —Paris: Albin Michel,1937

10,253 p. ;18 cm.

I565. 45/103

Ceux de la mer/A. T'serstevens. —Paris: Bernard Grasset,1937

11,290 p. ;18 cm.

I565. 45/104

Le secrèt de Babylone/Maurice Verne. —Paris: Albin Michel,1927

14,315 p. ;18 cm.

I565. 45/105

La guerre en dentelles/Georges d'Esparbès. —Paris: Albin Michel,[?]

11,285 p. ;18 cm.

I565. 45/106

Face au destin/Charles Robert-Dumas. —Paris: Librairie Arthème Fayard,[?]

8,252 p. ;18 cm.

I565. 45/107

Maternité/Alexis Danan. —Paris: Albin Michel,1936

10,252 p. ;18 cm.

I565. 45/108

Komlah visions d'Asie/Roland Meyer. —Paris: Edition Pierre Roger,[?]

247 p. ;18 cm.

I565. 45/109

Roméo et Juliette Amants de Vérone/Paul Reboux. —Paris: Librairie Arthème Fayard,1939

7,254 p. ;18 cm.

I565. 45/110

sang et lumière/Joseph Peyré. —Paris: Editions Bernard Grasset,1935

6,316 p. ;18 cm.

I565. 45/111

Les filles à marier/Léon Frapié. —Paris: Ernest Flammarion,1925

284 p. ;17 cm.

I565. 45/112-60

Le coté de Guermantes 2 Sodome et Gomorrhe 1 (A la recherche du temps perdu tome 4)/Marcel Proust. —60 ed.. —Paris: Librairie Gallimard,1929

6,282 p. ;18 cm.

I565. 45/113

Le Labyrinthe/Edouard Estaunié. —Paris: Librairies-Editeurs,1924

6,298 p. ;18 cm.

I565. 45/114

Les cavaliers de la déroute/Robert Goffin. —[S. l.]:[s. n.],[?]

10,355 p. ;19 cm.

I565. 45/115

Mariquita (Le Bossu: livre deuxième)/Paul Féval Fils. —Paris: Librairie Ollendoref,1922

185 p. ;19 cm.

I565. 45/116

La Famille Dispersée/Pearl S. Buck. —Paris: Payot,1935

442 p. ;18 cm.

I565. 45/117

Ténébreuse Affaire/H. De Balzac. —Paris: Librairie Plon,1928

6,245 p. ;15 cm.

I565. 45/118

Mitsou/Colette Ziily. —Paris: Arthème Fayard et Cie,[?]

94 p. ;23 cm.

I565. 45/119

Le Rêve/Emile Zola. —Paris: Ernest Flammarion,1926

78 p. ;23 cm.

I565. 45/120

Une corde sur l'abîme/Fean Lébédeff. —Paris: Arthème Fayard et Cie,1935

123 p. ;23 cm.

I565. 45/121(1)

Le Bossu 1: Le Petit Parisien/Paul Féval. —Paris: Librairie Ollendorff,[?]

202 p. ;19 cm.

I565. 45/121(2)

Le Bossu 2 Lagardère /Paul Féval. —[S. l.]: Librairie Ollendorff,[?]

5,234 p. ;19 cm.

I565. 45/122-25(7)

Albertine disparue/Marcel Proust. —25 ed.. —Paris: Gallimard,1925

213 p. ;18 cm.

I565. 45/123

Les Chevauchées de Lagardère/Paul Féval. —Paris: Librairie Ollendorff,[?]

202 p. ;19 cm.

I565. 45/124

Les trois crimes d'Arsène Lupin/Maurice Leblang. —Paris: Editions Pierre Lafitte,1910

96 p. ;23 cm.

I565. 45/125

Thérèse Raquin/Emile Zola. —Paris: Ernest Flammarion,[?]

91 p. ;24 cm.

I565. 45/126

La maitresse du Prince Jean/Willy. —Paris: Albin Michel,[?]

128 p. ;24 cm.

I565. 45/127(1)

Rouletabille chez le Tsar/Gaston Leroux. —Paris: Editions Pierre Lafitte,1921

80 p. ;24 cm.

I565. 45/127(2)

Rouletabille chez le Tsar/Gaston Leroux. —Paris: Editions Pierre Lafitte,1921

80 p. ;24 cm.

I565. 45/128

Tartarin sur les Alpes/Alphones Daudct. Paris: Ernest Flammarion,[?]

103 p. ;24 cm.

I565. 45/129

Les demi-vierges/Marcel Prévost. —Paris: Ernest Flammarion,[?]

78 p. ;24 cm.

I565. 45/130(2)

L'Ile aux trente cercueils/Maurice Leblang. —Paris: Editions Pierre Lafitte,1922

78 p. ;24 cm.

I565. 45/131

La maison thüringer/Panaït Istrati. —Paris: Arthème Fayard et Cie,1935

123 p. ;24 cm.

I565. 45/132

Arsène Lupin/Maurice Leblang. —Paris: Editions Pierre Lafitte,1921

80 p. ;24 cm.

I565. 45/133

Le bonheur immobile/Pierre Billotey. —Paris: Albin Michel,1930

13,254 p. ;18 cm.

I565. 45/134

La terre/Emile Zola. —Paris: Eugène Fasquelle,1925

281 p. ;18 cm.

I565. 45/135

La princesse des halles/Edouard Adenis. —Paris: Editions Jules Tallandier,1925

224 p. ;18 cm.

I565. 45/136

Le grand départ/Yves Gandon. —Paris: Albin Michel,1939

7,251 p. ;18 cm.

I565. 45/137

Le père Goriot/Honoré de Balzac. —Paris: Librairie Plon,1931

7,252 p. ;17 cm.

I565. 45/138-2

Les évadés de l'an 4000/Jacques Spitz. —2 ed. . —Paris: Gallimard,1936

7,217 p. ;18 cm.

I565. 45/139

La voie sans disque/Andre Armandy. —Paris: Librairie Alphonse Lemerre,1931

241 p. ;18 cm.

I565. 45/140

Provenge/Vieilles Moeurs, Vieilles Coutumes. —Paris: A. Lions,1905

286 p. ;18 cm.

I565.45/141

La carte Marine/Edouard Peisson. —Paris: Edition Bernard Grasset,1939

10,26 p. ;18 cm.

I565.45/142

Au soleil/Guy de Maupassant. —Paris: Ernest Flammarionmma,1925

248 p. ;18 cm.

I565.45/143

Les sept couleurs/Robert Brasiliach. —Paris: Librairie Plon,1939

244 p. ;18 cm.

I565.45/144

La meute/Alphonse de Chateaubriant. —Paris: Edition Bernard Grasset,1935

12,373 p. ;18 cm.

I565.45/145

Après l'orage/Jacques Brienne. —Paris: Editions Jules Tallandier,1925

7,222 p. ;18 cm.

I565.45/146

Mea culpa/Louis-Ferdinand céline. —Paris: Denoel et Steele,1937

7,124 p. ;18 cm.

I565.45/147

Climats/André Maurois. —Paris: Edition Bernard Grasset,1928

13,286 p. ;18 cm.

I565.45/148

Servante/Henri Duvernois. —Paris: Ernest Flammarionmma,1926

246 p. ;18 cm.

I565.45/149-30

L'évadé/Simenon. —30 ed.. —Paris: Gallimard,1936

7,25 p. ;18 cm.

I565.45/150

Les deux visages de l'amour/Henri Ardel. —Paris: Librairie Plon,1938

273 p. ;18 cm.

I565.45/151

Aux cent mille sourires/Maurice Dekobra. —Paris: Editions Baudiniere,1932

7,283 p. ;18 cm.

I565.45/152-6

Le brave soldat chvéik/Jaroslav Hasek. —6 ed.. —Paris: Gallimard,1932

317 p. ;18 cm.

I565.45/153

Ras el gua (Poste du sud)/René Guillot. —Paris: Les éditons de moghreb,1936

255 p. ;18 cm.

I565.45/154

Le fiancé excessif/André Dinar. —Paris: Albin Michel,[?]

216 p. ;18 cm.

I565.45/155

Le feu aux poudres/René Jouglet. —Paris: Edition Bernard Grasset,1937

7,213 p. ;18 cm.

I565.45/156

Les pieds du diable/François Dallet. —Paris: Les editions denoel,1937

7,235 p. ;18 cm.

I565.45/157

L'entrevue/Nature. —Paris: Librairie Nilsson,[?]

159 p. ;16 cm.

I565. 45/158

A salonique sous l'oeil des dieux/Jean-Jose Frappa. —Paris: Ernest Flammarionmma,1917

264 p. ;18 cm.

I565. 45/159-4

La vie commence/Marie Anne Comnene. —4 ed.. —Paris: Gallimard,1935

7,303 p. ;18 cm.

I565. 45/160-8

Pilotes de Ligne/O. —P Gilbert. —8 ed.. —Paris: Gallimard,1938

220 p. ;18 cm.

I565. 45/161-19

Les extravagants/Paul Morand. —19 ed.. —Paris: Gallimard,1936

10,256 p. ;18 cm.

I565. 45/162-23

Le repos de l'équipage/J. Kessel. 23 ed.. —Paris: Gallimard,1935

7,17 p. ;18 cm.

I565. 45/163

Claudine s'en va /Willy et Colette Willy. —Paris: Librairie Ollendorff,[?]

311 p. ;17 cm.

I565. 45/164-2

Belle France /Charles Silvestre. —2 ed.. —Paris: Librairie stock,1938

8,223 p. ;18 cm.

I565. 45/165

Les plus jolis contes de la Fontaine/Jean Fontaine. —Paris: Editions Nilsson,[?]

254 p. ;18 cm.

I565. 45/166

Le lépreux/Henry de monfreid. —Paris: Edition Bernard Grasset,1935

10,301 p. ;18 cm.

I565. 45/167-14

Gustalin/Marcel Aymé. —14 ed.. —Paris: Gallimard,1937

6,233 p. ;18 cm.

I565. 45/168

L'été 1914/Roger Martin du Gard. —Paris: Gallimard,1936

7,352 p. ;18 cm.

I565. 45/169

La Taiga de l'oussouri/Vladimier Arséniev. —Paris: Payot,1939

11,313 p. ;22 cm.

I565. 45/170

Nach Paris/Louis Dumur. —Paris: Payot et cie,1920

9,352 p. ;18 cm.

I565. 45/171

Passage de la ligne/Edouard Peisson. —Paris: Edition Bernard Grasset,1935

7,254 p. ;17 cm.

I565. 45/172-14

Le laurier d'Apollon/Maurice Bedel. —14 ed.. —Paris: Gallimard,1936

7,192 p. ;18 cm.

I565. 45/173

Les pirateries du capitaine singleton/Daniel De Foe. —Paris: Edition Française illustrée,1920

11,268 p. ;19 cm.

I565. 45/174

Deux/Irène Némirovsky. —Paris: Albin Michel,1939

9,254 p. ;18 cm.

I565. 45/175

Rue de la marine/André Tabet. —Paris: Albin Michel,1938

317 p. ;18 cm.

I565. 45/176

Suzanne/Léon Daudet. —Paris: Ernest Flammarion,[?]

70 p. ;24 cm.

I565. 45/177

Victime explatoire/André Corthis. —Paris: Arthème Fayard et Cie,1929

110 p. ;24 cm.

I565. 45/178

J'ai quatorze ans/A. Roubé-Jansky. —Paris: Arthème Fayard et Cie,1933

126 p. ;24 cm.

I565. 45/179

Bien et mal aimer/Jean Bertrand. —Paris: Editions Denoël et Steele,1935

250 p. ;18 cm.

I565. 45/180

La marche à l'étoile/E. Fernqnd Xau. —Paris: Fasquelle Editeurs,1937

215 p. ;17 cm.

I565. 45/181

Les compagnons d'Ulysse/Pierre Benoît. —Paris: Albin Michel,1937

314 p. ;17 cm.

I565. 45/181

Les compagnons d'Ulysse/Pierre Benoît. —Paris: Albin Michel,1937

314 p. ;18 cm.

I565. 45/182

Romanesques/Jacques Chardonne. —Paris: Librairie Stock,1937

10,224 p. ;17 cm.

I565. 45/183

Malombra/A. Fogazzaro. —Paris: Albin Michel,1926

12,365 p. ;17 cm.

I565. 45/184

Les disgrâces amoureuses/Lefebvre Saint-Ogan. —Paris: Ernest Flammarion,1927

248 p. ;16 cm.

I565. 45/185

L'homme de choc/Joserh Peyré. —Paris: Editions Bernard Grasset,1936

271 p. ;18 cm.

I565. 45/186

Les mohicans de babel/Gaston Leroux. —Paris: Editions Baudiniere,1926

320 p. ;18 cm.

I565. 45/187

Maison basse/Marcel Aymé. —Paris: Gallimard,1935

275 p. ;17 cm.

I565. 45/188

L'enfant sauvage/Henry de Monfreid. —Paris: Editions Bernard Grasset,1938

281 p. ;18 cm.

I565. 45/189

Boissière/Pierre Benoît. —Paris: Albin Michel,1935

315 p. ;17 cm.

I565. 45/190

J'avais un camarade/Paul Vialar. —Paris: Emile-Paul Frères,[?]

254 p. ;17 cm.

I565. 45/191

L'enfant des ruines/Max du Veuzit. —Paris: Editions Jules Tallandier, 1938

254 p. ;17 cm.

I565. 45/192

La vagabonde/Colette Willy. —Paris: Albin Michel, [?]

320 p. ;18 cm.

I565. 45/193-4(1)

Les enfants du Limon/Raymond Queneau. —4 ed.. —Paris: Gallimard, 1938

316 p. ;18 cm.

I565. 45/194

La piste du Sud/O. —P. Gilbert. —Paris: Gallimard, 1937

26, 155 p. ;17 cm.

I565. 45/195-16(2)

L'avènement de Bonaparte/Albert Vandal. —16 ed.. —Paris: Librairie Plon, 1907

540 p. ;22 cm.

I565. 45/196

La dame de Malacca/Francis de Croisset. —Paris: Edition Bernard Grasset, 1935

11, 355 p. ;18 cm.

I565. 45/197(2)

L'Argent/Emile Zola. —Paris: Eugène Fasquelle, 1922

223 p. ;18 cm.

I565. 45/198

Monsieur des lourdines/A. de Chateaubriant. —Paris: Le livre moderne illustré, [?]

156 p. ;20 cm.

I565. 45/199

Némésis/Paul Bourget. —Paris: Le livre moderne illustré, [?]

174 p. ;20 cm.

I565. 45/200

Mon cher Tommy/Marcel Prvéost. —Paris: Arthème Fayard et Cie, 1920

298 p. ;20 cm.

I565. 45/201

Katia/Lucile Decaux. —Paris: Gallimard, 1938

246 p. ;18 cm.

I565. 45/202

Le mémorial de la rue Saint-Hélène/Henri Béraud. —Lyon: Les éditions de Guignol, 1919

91 p. ;17 cm.

I565. 45/203

La prison de velours/Louis Roubaud. —Paris: Gallimard, [?]

254 p. ;18 cm.

I565. 45/204-7(1)

Le Suborneur/Abel Hermant. —7 ed.. —Paris: Editions de la nouvelle revue française, 1923

206 p. ;18 cm.

I565. 45/205

Au pays des mannequins/Louis Roubaud. —Paris: Les éditions de France, 1928

224 p. ;18 cm.

I565. 45/206

Wang/Louis Patelle. —Paris: Gallimard, 1937

245 p. ;18 cm.

I565. 45/207-6

Brune/François de Roux. —6 ed.. —Paris: Gallimard, 1938

255 p. ;18 cm.

I565.45/208

Fièvres/Jean d'Esme. —Paris: Flammarion, 1935

248 p. ;18 cm.

I565.45/209

Le voyage de Shakespeare/Bibliothèque Plon. —Paris: Librairie Plon,[?]

256 p. ;18 cm.

I565.45/210

Félicie/Florise Albert-Londres. —Paris: Albin Michel,1939

249 p. ;18 cm.

I565.45/211

Sonnica la courtisane/V. Blasco-Ibanez. —Paris: Ernest Flammarion,1926

10,318 p. ;18 cm.

I565.45/212

Quand le coeur nous mène... /Paul Darcy. —Paris: Editions du livre national,1927

126 p. ;22 cm.

I565.45/213

L'épouse traquée/Marcel Priollet. —Paris: Editions du livre national,1927

126 p. ;22 cm.

I565.45/214

Le secret de la Flibustière/Edouard Adenis. —Paris: Editions du livre national,1926

126 p. ;22 cm.

I565.45/215

Le berceau sous l'orage/Marcel Priollet. —Paris: Editions du livre national,1927

126 p. ;22 cm.

I565.45/216

La vengeance du Caïd/Edouard Adenis. —Paris: Editions du livre national,1927

126 p. ;22 cm.

I565.45/217

Occupation /André Savignon. —Paris: Les éditions de France,1938

249 p. ;18 cm.

I565.45/218

Platon cherche l'amour/Nicolas Ségur. —Paris: Ernest Flammarion,1926

10,234 p. ;18 cm.

I565.45/219

Pacifique/Jean Martet. —Paris: Albin Michel, 1938

320 p. ;18 cm.

I565.45/220

Zigoël ou l'Aventurier de l'idéal/Pierre Frondaie. —Paris: Librairie Plon,1932

15,316 p. ;18 cm.

I565.45/221(1)

Vingt ans après/Alexandre Dumas. —Paris: Nelson et Calmann-Lévy,1931

572 p. ;16 cm.

I565.45/221(2)

Vingt ans après/Alexandre Dumas. —Paris: Nelson, Calmann-Lévy,[?]

569 p. ;15 cm.

I565.45/222

Mirentchu/Pierre Lhande. —Paris: Librairie Plon,1914

253 p. ;15 cm.

I565.45/223

Monsieur, Madame et Bébé/Gustave Droz. —Paris: Albin Michel,[?]

318 p. ;18 cm.

I565. 45/225

Le centaure de Dieu/La Verende. —Paris: Bernard Grasset, 1938

328 p. ; 18 cm.

I565. 45/226

Port de l'air/Hedwige de Chabannes. —Paris: Librairie Arthème Fayard, 1938

242 p. ; 18 cm.

I565. 45/227(1)

Nana/Emile Zola. —Paris: Fasquelle éditeur, 1930

259 p. ; 18 cm.

I565. 45/228

L'affaire Sauvenir/Charles-Henry Hirsch. —Paris: Ernest Flammarion, 1928

285 p. ; 18 cm.

I565. 45/229

La dernière harde/Maurice Genevoix. —Paris: Flammarion, 1938

235 p. ; 18 cm.

I565. 45/230

Quand les loups ont faim/Isabelle Sandy. —Paris: Editions Jules Tallandier, 1937

256 p. ; 18 cm.

I565. 45/231-26

Le testament donadieu/Simenon. —26 ed.. —Paris: Gallimard, 1937

9, 318 p. ; 18 cm.

I565. 45/232

Meurtres/Charles Plisnier. —Paris: Editions Corrêa, 1939

344 p. ; 19 cm.

I565. 45/233

Napoléon Noir/Paul Haurigot. —Paris: Albin Michel, 1935

256 p. ; 19 cm.

I565. 45/234

Les hallucinations du lieutnant Darnoux/Jean Cossart. —Paris: Editions Berger-Levrault, 1936

291 p. ; 18 cm.

I565. 45/235

La Seconde/Colette. —Paris: J. Ferenczi et Fils, 1929

270 p. ; 18 cm.

I565. 45/236

L'Empreinte du Dieu/Maxence van der Meerrsch. —Paris: Albin Michel, 1936

254 p. ; 18 cm.

I565. 45/237

Codine/Panait Istrati. —Paris: F. Rieder et Cie, 1926

9, 235 p. ; 18 cm.

I565. 45/238

Le violier d'amour/Pierre Devoluy. —Paris: Eugènr Fasquelle, 1927

256 p. ; 18 cm.

I565. 45/239

Marylène ou à qui le dire/Vassily Photiadès. —Paris: Bernard Grasset, 1936

11, 222 p. ; 18 cm.

I565. 45/240

Pilotage sans visibilité/Jean-Pierre Duret. —Paris: Librairie Plon, 1938

186 p. ; 18 cm.

I565. 45/241

Les Javanais/Jean Malaquai. —Paris: Robert Denoël, 1939

322 p. ; 18 cm.

I565.45/242
Présages/Henri Louis-Mill. —Paris: Edition Bernard Grasset,1935
264 p. ;18 cm.

I565.45/243
Sur l'écran/Robert Hichens. —Pris: Les éditions de France,1938
214 p. ;18 cm.

I565.45/244
La cavalière Elsa/Pierre Mac Orlan. —Paris: Edition de la nouvelle revue française,1921
10,219 p. ;18 cm.

I565.45/245
Monsieur Parent/Guy de Maupassant. —Paris: Albin Michel,1925
7,318 p. ;17 cm.

I565.45/246
Colomba/Prosper Mérimée. —Paris: Nelson, 1930
7,286 p. ;16 cm.

I565.45/247
Bethsabée/Pierre Benoit. —Paris: Albin Michel,1938
7,311 p. ;18 cm.

I565.45/248
Pêcheur de Goémon/Yvonne Pagniez. —Paris: Librairie Plon,1939
263 p. ;18 cm.

I565.45/249-45
La passante du sans-souci/J. Kessel. —45 ed.. —Paris: Gallimard,1936
12,251 p. ;18 cm.

I565.45/250
La partie de boules/Jean Martet. —Paris: Albin Michel,1935
73,174 p. ;18 cm.

I565.45/251
Si le soleil ne revenait pas /C. —F. Ramuz. —Paris: Bernard Grasset,1939
7,238 p. ;18 cm.

I565.45/252
Les dessous des prisons de femmes/Robert Boucard. —Paris: Les Editions Documentaires, 1930
24,255 p. ;18 cm.

I565.45/253
Le bois du templier pendu/Henri Béraud. —Paris: Les éditions de France,1926
300 p. ;18 cm.

I565.45/254
Les silences du Colonel Bramble/André Maurois. —Paris: Bernard Grasset,1921
10,253 p. ;18 cm.

I565.45/255
Les damnés de la terre 1906-1910/Henry Poulaille. —Paris: Bernard Grasset,1935
10,487 p. ;18 cm.

I565.45/256-15
La maison thuringer/Panait Istrati. —15 ed.. —Paris: Editions Rieder,1933
25,271 p. ;18 cm.

I565.45/257
Faux Passeports/Charles Plisnier. —Paris: Editions R. A. Corrêt,1937
16,382 p. ;18 cm.

I565.45/258
Le songe du voyageur/Jean Fontenoy. —Paris: Bernard Grasset,1939
10,281 p. ;18 cm.

I565. 45/259

L'enchantement de la nuit/Jean Guirec. —Paris: Albin Michel, 1938

7, 253 p. ; 18 cm.

I565. 45/260-10

La croisière du jour sans fin/Maurice Constantin-weyer. —10 ed.. —Paris: Editions Rieder, 1935

11, 234 p. ; 18 cm.

I565. 45/261

La vieillesse d'Hélène/Jules Lemaitre. —Paris: Calmann-Lévy, 1914

283 p. ; 18 cm.

I565. 45/262

Maria Chapdelaine/Louis Hémon. —Paris: A. Fayard et cie, [?]

126 p. ; 23 cm.

I565. 45/263

Le bonheur de Barbezieur/Jacques Chardonne. —Paris: Librairie stock, 1938

9, 197 p. ; 18 cm.

I565. 45/264

Le rire de la naiade/Princesse Bibesco. —Paris: Bernard Grasset, 1935

10, 256 p. ; 18 cm.

I565. 45/265-2

L'expérience du docteur mops/Jacques Spitz. —2 ed.. —Paris: Gallimard, 1939

200 p. ; 18 cm.

I565. 45/266-20

Hollywood Dépassé/Luc Durtain. —20 ed.. —Paris: Gallimard, 1928

249 p. ; 18 cm.

I565. 45/267

La grande peur des Bien-pensants/Georges Bernanos. —Paris: Bernard Grasset, 1931

29, 458 p. ; 18 cm.

I565. 45/268

La montagne paienne/Paul Mousset. —Paris: Bernard Grasset, 1937

8, 254 p. ; 18 cm.

I565. 45/269

Autour de la terre/Magdeleine Cluzel. —Paris: Etidions Baudiniere1937, 1937

8, 287 p. ; 18 cm.

I565. 45/270

Rue de la roquette/Laurence Algan. —Paris: Librairie Plon, 1938

246 p. ; 18 cm.

I565. 45/271

Hirondelles de plages/Tristan Bernard. —Paris: Albin Michel, 1929

7, 253 p. ; 18 cm.

I565. 45/272

Un homme libre chez les soviets/Jean-Gérard Fleury. —Paris: Les éditions de France, 1936

257 p. ; 18 cm.

I565. 45/273

L'approbaniste/André Billy. —Paris: Ernest Flammarion, 1937

7, 212 p. ; 18 cm.

I565. 45/274

La vie amoureuse de Louis XIV/Louis Bertrand. —Paris: Ernest Flammarion, 1924

7, 203 p. ; 17 cm.

I565. 45/275

Par delà suez/Paul A. Fouletier. —Paris: Union Commerciale, 1935

254 p. ; 18 cm.

I565. 45/276

Macao enfer du jeu/Maurice Dekobra. —Paris: Editions Baudiniere, 1939

7, 299 p. ; 18 cm.

I565. 45/277

Le quart d'heure d'Anibal Bumbo/Jean Martet. —Paris: Albin Michel, 1938

7, 315 p. ; 18 cm.

I565. 45/278

Anna, premier visage /Luce Amy. —Paris: Bernard Grasset, 1938

10, 199 p. ; 18 cm.

I565. 45/279

Jeanne d'Arc/Joseph Delteil. —Paris: Edition Bernard Grasset, 1925

262 p. ; 18 cm.

I565. 45/280

Le jugement des ténèbres/André Demaison. —Paris: Bernard Grasset, 1935

11, 243 p. ; 18 cm.

I565. 45/281

Jamais plus... /Armand Praviel. —Paris: Bloud et Gay, 1922

259 p. ; 18 cm.

I565. 45/282

Eugénie Grandet/Honoré de Balzac. —Paris: Librairie Plon, 1932

11, 252 p. ; 18 cm.

I565. 45/283

Ceux de la cave/Claude Jan. —Paris: Librairie Arthème Fayard, 1939

9, 247 p. ; 18 cm.

I565. 45/284

Bella-vista/Colette. —Paris: Ferenczi, 1937

9, 248 p. ; 18 cm.

I565. 45/285

Mademoiselle Fifi/Guy de Maupassant. —Paris: Ernest Flammarion, 1926

250 p. ; 18 cm.

I565. 45/286

L'inconstante/Gérard d'Houville. —Paris: A. Fayard et cie, 1925

9, 125 p. ; 23 cm.

I565. 45/287

Aurora ou le rancho de l'ombu/Lise de Maureilhac. —Paris: Editions de la vraie France, 1929

13, 296 p. ; 18 cm.

I565. 45/288

Le mauvais génie/La Comtesse de Ségur. —Paris: Libraiire Hachette et Cie, 1914

330 p. ; 18 cm.

I565. 45/289

Les vacances/[incunnu]. —Paris: Libraiire Hachette et Cie, [?]

315 p. ; 18 cm.

I565. 45/290

Don Juan les pins/Constantin. —Paris: Librairie Plon, 1930

271 p. ; 18 cm.

I565. 45/291

Le scandale du gazon bleu/Maurice Leblanc. —Paris: Ernest Flammarion, 1935

242 p. ; 18 cm.

I565. 45/292

La femme et le pantin/Pierre Louys. —Paris: Eugènr Fasquelle, 1925

254 p. ; 18 cm.

I565. 45/293

La belle inutile/Yves Gandon. —Paris: Albin

Michel,1935
11,317 p. ;18 cm.

I565. 45/294
Constantinople sous les barbares/Jacques Fontelroye. —Paris: Calmann-Lévy,1924
293 p. ;18 cm.

I565. 45/295
Le passant d'éthiopie/Jérôme et Jean Tharaud. —Paris: Librairie Plon,1936
257 p. ;18 cm.

I565. 45/296
la Peau de l'ours/Marcel Griaule. —Paris: Gallimard,1936
15,219 p. ;18 cm.

I565. 45/297
Justice suprême/Paul D'aigremont. —Paris: Editions Jules Tallandier,[?]
192 p. ;18 cm.

I565. 45/298
Rap et vaga/Henry Bordeaux. —Paris: Librairie Plon,1927
274 p. ;18 cm.

I565. 45/299
Axelle/Pierre Benoit. —Paris: Albin Michel, 1928
7,351 p. ;17 cm.

I565. 45/300
Le rossignol napolitain/Alexandre Arnoux. —Paris: Bernard Grasset,1937
253 p. ;18 cm.

I565. 45/301
Le démon impur/Maurice Betz. —Paris: Edition Emile-Paul Freres,1926
234 p. ;18 cm.

I565. 45/302
Les termagies/Jeanne Nabert. —Paris: Librairie Plon,1936
320 p. ;18 cm.

I565. 45/303
La comtesse Sarah/Georges Ohnet. —Paris: Albin Michel,[?]
254 p. ;18 cm.

I565. 45/304
Plongées/François Mauriac. —Paris: Bernard Grasset,1938
13,248 p. ;18 cm.

I565. 45/305
Manon l'escroc/Geo London. —Paris: Les Editions de France,1938
248 p. ;18 cm.

I565. 45/306
Didi, Niquette et cie/G. de la Fouchardière. —Paris: Albin Michel,1926
7,314 p. ;18 cm.

I565. 45/307-3
La grande peur de Kong Sinn Fat/Puisné Landais. —3 ed.. —Paris: Bernard Grasset,1936
243 p. ;18 cm.

I565. 45/308-34
Quartier nègre/Georges Simenon. —34 ed.. —Paris: Gallimard,1935
7,252 p. ;18 cm.

I565. 45/309
Man'd'arc/Jean de la varende. —Paris: Bernard Grasset,1939
11,387 p. ;18 cm.

I565. 45/310
Le haut-du-seuil/Claire sainte-Soline. —Paris: Les Editions Rieder,1939

7,249 p. ;22 cm.

I565. 45/311

La grande fraude/Maurice Larrouy. —Paris: A. Fayard et cie,1937

10,331 p. ;18 cm.

I565. 45/312

Lyon ville secrète/Maurice Privat. —Paris: Les Documents secrets,1931

10,62 p. ;18 cm.

I565. 45/313

Brumes/Francis Carco. —Paris: Albin Michel, 1935

10,319 p. ;18 cm.

I565. 45/314

Les Hommes de bonne volonte XIII: Mission à Rome/Jules Romains. —Paris: Ernest Flammarion,1937

310 p. ;18 cm.

I565. 45/315

Adrienne Mesurat/Julien Green. —Paris: Librairie Plon,1927

355 p. ;18 cm.

I565. 45/316

La barette rouge/André de Richaud. —Paris: Bernard Grasset,1938

11,256 p. ;18 cm.

I565. 45/317

Vamireh/J. H Rosny. —Paris: Librairie Plon, 1902

260 p. ;18 cm.

I565. 45/318

Denise la fille du sorcier/Maurice Mario. —Paris: Editions Jules Tallandier,1926

224 p. ;18 cm.

I565. 45/319

La reine évanouie/Jean-Louis Vaudoyer. —Paris: Librairie Plon,1923

291 p. ;18 cm.

I565. 45/320

Nulle part dans le monde Le dernier bateau/ Michel Georges-Michel. —Paris:[s. n.],[?]

250 p. ;18 cm.

I565. 45/321

L'homme vierge/Marcel Prévost. —Paris: J. Ferenczi et Fils,1929

221 p. ;19 cm.

I565. 45/322

L'homme de minuit/Francis Carco. —Paris: Albin Michel,1938

252 p. ;18 cm.

I565. 45/323

Terres permises/Noël Félici. —Paris: Albin Michel,1940

253 p. ;18 cm.

I565. 45/324

L'éther consolateur/Willy. —Paris: Albin Michel,[?]

313 p. ;18 cm.

I565. 45/325

Le coup de grace/J. Kessel. —Paris: Les éditions de France,1931

251 p. ;18 cm.

I565. 45/326

Le vin de solitude/Irène némirovsky. —Paris: Albin Michel,1935

311 p. ;18 cm.

I565. 45/327(3)

Le vicomte de Bragelonne/Alexandre Dumas. —Paris: Calmann-Lévy,[?]

400 p. ;18 cm.

I565. 45/327(5)

Le vicomte de bragelonne/Alexandre Dumas. —Paris: Calmann-Lévy,[?]

394 p. ;18 cm.

I565. 45/328

Le panier flottant/Guy Mazeline. —Paris: Gallimard,1938

220 p. ;18 cm.

I565. 45/329

Les révélées/Michel Corday. —Paris: Ernest Flammarion,1925

246 p. ;18 cm.

I565. 45/330

Précoce Avril/Yvonne Schultz. —Paris: Bernard Grasset,1924

286 p. ;17 cm.

I565. 45/331

Père/André Lichtenberger. —Paris: J. Ferenczi,1921

250 p. ;17 cm.

I565. 45/332

La haute nuit/Pierre Audiat. —Paris: Les éditions de France,1939

232 p. ;17 cm.

I565. 45/333

Les plumes d'oie/Marguerite d'Escola. —Paris: Editions Spes,1928

271 p. ;15 cm.

I565. 45/334

Thérèse Raquin/Emile Zola. —Paris: Fasquelle Editeurs,[?]

509 p. ;16 cm.

I565. 45/335

Mère et fils/Charles Silvestre. —Paris: Librairie Plon,1938

286 p. ;16 cm.

I565. 45/336-7

Série de Sept/Pierre Véry. —7 ed.. —Paris: Gallimard,1938

220 p. ;17 cm.

I565. 45/337

Les grands cimtières sous la lune/Georges Bernanos. —Paris: Librairie Plon,1938

361 p. ;17 cm.

I565. 45/338

Abel et Caïn/Emile Baudann. —Paris: Bernard Grasset,1930

263 p. ;17 cm.

I565. 45/339

Les sacrifiés/Olivier Carignan. —Paris: Les éditions du Mercure,1927

228 p. ;17 cm.

I565. 45/340

Jean d'Agrève/E. —M. de Vogüe. —Paris: Librairie Plon,1929

253 p. ;16 cm.

I565. 45/341

Le Lama aux cinq sagesses/Lama Yongden et Alexandra David-Neel. —Paris: Librairie Plon, 1935

389 p. ;17 cm.

I565. 45/342

La maison Tellier/Guy de Maupassant. —Paris: Albin Michel,

10,276 p. ;17 cm.

I565. 45/343

L'âme des hommes/André Billy. —Paris: Er-

nest Flammarion,1935
283 p. ;16 cm.

I565. 45/344
Le Padrao/André Armandy. —Paris: Librairie Plon,1939
244 p. ;18 cm.

I565. 45/345
L'ombre des ailes/Maurice Maeterlinck. —Paris: Bibliothèque-Charpentier,1936
253 p. ;18 cm.

I565. 45/346
Ces dames aux chapeaux verts/Germaine Acremant. —Pris: Librairie Plon,1922
196 p. ;18 cm.

I565. 45/347(2)
Journal/François Mauriac. —Paris: Bernard Grasset,1937
230 p. ;18 cm.

I565. 45/348
Promenades en Indochine/H. Célarié. —Paris: Editions Baudiniere,1937
10,282 p. ;18 cm.

I565. 45/349
O toi que j'eusse aimée/Edmond Jaloux. —Paris: Librairie Plon,1936
254 p. ;18 cm.

I565. 45/350
J'aurai un bel enterrement... /Pierre la Mazière. —Paris: Editions Baudiniere,1924
9,22 p. ;18 cm.

I565. 45/351
Anatole France/Michel Corday. —Paris: Ernest Flammarion,1927
7,247 p. ;18 cm.

I565. 45/352
Louise de Prusse/Albert-Emile Sorel. —Paris: Bernard Grasset,1937
9,273 p. ;19 cm.

I565. 45/353
Les trois glorieuses/Recits d'Autrefois. —Paris: Hachette,1927
7,127 p. ;18 cm.

I565. 45/354
Moeurs du jour/Marcel Boulenger. —Paris: Librairie Plon,1926
250 p. ;18 cm.

I565. 45/355
Mon oncle et mon curé/Jean de la Brète. —Paris: Librairie Plon,1929
8,251 p. ;15 cm.

I565. 45/356
Pêcheurs d'hommes/Maxence Van Der Meersch. —Paris: Albin Michel,1940
11,318 p. ;18 cm.

I565. 45/357-10
Loulou prince impérial/Lucile Decaux. —10 ed.. —Paris: Gallimard,1938
8,211 p. ;18 cm.

I565. 45/358
Le matelot moravine/Jean Feuga. —Paris: Librairie Arthème Fayard,1937
7,256 p. ;18 cm.

I565. 45/359
Les sentiers dans la montagne/Maurice Maeterlinck. —Paris: Bibliothèque-Charpentier,1923
304 p. ;18 cm.

I565. 45/360
Le cercle de famille/André Maurois. —Paris: Bernard Grasset,1932

12,339 p. ;18 cm.

I565. 45/361

Ni ange ni bête/André Maurois. —Paris: Bernard Grasset,1919

15,187 p. ;19 cm.

I565. 45/362

Escales Jaunes/André Bernis. —Paris: Les éditions de France,1935

236 p. ;18 cm.

I565. 45/363

Le crime de Sylvestre Bonnard/Anatole France. —Paris: Calmann-Lévy,1469

323 p. ;18 cm.

I565. 45/364

On disait en France/Paul Péladeau. —Paris: [s. n.],1941

17,238 p. ;18 cm.

I565. 45/365

Nous avons fait un beau voyage/Francis de Croisset. —Paris: Bernard Grasset,1930

11,286 p. ;18 cm.

I565. 45/366

Ce qui était perdu/François Mauriac. —Paris: Bernard Grasset,1930

7,267 p. ;18 cm.

I565. 45/367

Un rude hiver/Raymond Queneau. —Paris: Gallimard,1939

7,221 p. ;18 cm.

I565. 45/368

L'amour camarade/Maurice Bedel. —Paris: Bernard Grasset,1931

7,248 p. ;18 cm.

I565. 45/369-50

Sainte-Colline/Gabriel Chevallier. —50 ed.. —Paris: Les Editions Rieder,1937

7,315 p. ;18 cm.

I565. 45/370

Le toutounier/Colette. —Paris: Ferenczi,1939

12,17 p. ;18 cm.

I565. 45/371

Le compagnon/Victor Margueritte. —Paris: Ernest Flammarion,1923

11,311 p. ;18 cm.

I565. 45/372

Le vicomte de Bragelonne/Alexandre Dumas. —Paris: Calmann-Lévy,[?]

386 p. ;18 cm.

I565. 45/373

L'amour et le feu/Albert Bailly. —Paris: Fasquelle,1938

218 p. ;19 cm.

I565. 45/373

L'amour et le feu/Albert Bailly. —Paris: Fasquelle Editeurs,1938

7,218 p. ;18 cm.

I565. 45/374

La onzième heure/Claude Farrère. —Paris: Ernest Flammarion,1940

339 p. ;18 cm.

I565. 45/375

Saint Jean d'Acre/Pierre Benoit. —Paris: Albin Michel,1936

7,25 p. ;18 cm.

I565. 45/376

Quand l'amour a passé/Edouard de Keyser. —Paris: Albin Michel,1924

7,317 p. ;18 cm.

I565. 45/377
Beloukia/Drieu la Rochelle. —Paris: Gallimard, 1936
9,219 p. ;18 cm.

I565. 45/378
L'héroine de Thermidor/Mademoiselle de Lagardère. —Paris: Editions Baudiniere, 1929
7,251 p. ;18 cm.

I565. 45/379
Les tendres ménages/P. —J. Toulet. —Paris: Le divan, 1923
7,196 p. ;18 cm.

I565. 45/380-16
Le trésor du pèlerin/Henry de Monfreid. —16 ed.. —Paris: Gallimard, 1938
9,255 p. ;18 cm.

I565. 45/381
Le fuseau d'or/Jean Rameau. —Paris: Librairie Plon, 1914
7,23 p. ;18 cm.

I565. 45/382
L'ile des Misanthropes/Xavier de Courville. —Paris: Société des Editions Fast, 1927
15,278 p. ;18 cm.

I565. 45/383
Sous le règne de Raspoutine/Carlos d'Eschevannes. —Paris: Albert Méricant, 1924
13,255 p. ;17 cm.

I565. 45/384
Pontcarral/Albéric Cahuet. —Paris: Bibliothèque-Charpentier, 1937
13,283 p. ;18 cm.

I565. 45/385
Une créature de dieu/Edouard Schneider. —Paris: Plon, 1939
245 p. ;18 cm.

I565. 45/386
Antée/Gaston Chérau. —Paris: Ferenczi, 1938
7,238 p. ;18 cm.

I565. 45/387-86
L'ordre/Marcel Arland. —86 ed.. —Paris: Gallimard, 1929
9,542 p. ;18 cm.

I565. 45/388
Le serpent de Cheik hussen/Henry de Monfreid. —Paris: Editions Pierre Tisné, 1937
10,192 p. ;19 cm.

I565. 45/389
Sept mystères du destin de l'Europe/Jules Romains. —Paris: Ernest Flammarion, [?]
17,33 p. ;18 cm.

I565. 45/390-2
Germinal/Emile zola. —2 ed.. —Paris: Bibliothèque-Charpentier, 1924
263 p. ;18 cm.

I565. 45/391
L'épée de feu/Daniel-Rops. —Paris: Librairie Plon, 1939
530 p. ;18 cm.

I565. 45/392
Monsieur Paquebot/Georges le Fevre. —Paris: Editions Baudiniere, 1929
7,256 p. ;18 cm.

I565. 45/393
Jeunes filles d'autrefois/Ernest Daudet. —Paris: Edition Moderne, [?]
126 p. ;18 cm.

I565. 45/394
Toum/Louis Faivre. —Paris: Bernard Grasset, 1926
7,308 p. ;17 cm.

I565. 45/395
La Chine en folie/Albert Londres. —Paris: Albin Michel, 1925
11,254 p. ;18 cm.

I565. 45/396
Ma charmante/Claire et line Droze. —Paris: Librairie Plon, 1938
249 p. ;18 cm.

I565. 45/397
Les lys sanglants/Léon Daudet. —Paris: Ernest Flammarion, 1938
7,29 p. ;18 cm.

I565. 45/398-2
La guerres mouches/Jacques Spitz. —2 ed.. —Paris: Gallimard, 1938
7,226 p. ;18 cm.

I565. 45/399
Le Rosier de Mme Husson/Guy de Maupassant. —Paris: Albin Michel, [?]
9,281 p. ;17 cm.

I565. 45/400
S'il est minuit dans le siècle/Victor Serge. —Paris: Bernard Grasset, 1939
9,294 p. ;18 cm.

I565. 45/401
Le pilote/Edouard Peisson. —Paris: Bernard Grasset, 1937
9,244 p. ;18 cm.

I565. 45/402
Magistrats et Policiers/Léon Daudet. —Paris: Bernard Grasset, 1935
7,24 p. ;18 cm.

I565. 45/403
Dossoers de police/G. Lenotre. —Paris: Bernard Grasset, 1935
7,246 p. ;18 cm.

I565. 45/404
Marguerite de la nuit/Pierre Mac Orlan. —Paris: Bernard Grasset, 1926
11,211 p. ;18 cm.

I565. 45/405
Le tigre/Jean Martet. —Paris: Albin Michel, 1930
15,313 p. ;18 cm.

I565. 45/406-3
Jean de fodoas/Maurice Magre. —3 ed.. —Paris: Gallimard, 1939
7,27 p. ;18 cm.

I565. 45/407
Patrice ou de l'éducation des parente/Jean Dufourt. —Paris: Librairie Plon, 1939
14,229 p. ;18 cm.

I565. 45/408
Toine/Guy de Maupassant. —Paris: Albin Michel, [?]
9,311 p. ;17 cm.

I565. 45/409
Le bal des ardents/René Jouglet. —Paris: Librairie Plon, 1926
244 p. ;18 cm.

I565. 45/410
Léna/Roger Vercel. —Paris: Albin Michel, 1936
253 p. ;18 cm.

I565.45/411
La route mouvante/Germaine Acremant. — Paris: Librairie Plon, 1939
243 p.;18 cm.

I565.45/412
Contes de la bécasse/Guy de Maupassant. — Paris: Ernest Flammarion, [?]
252 p.;18 cm.

I565.45/413-17
Le boeuf clandestin/Marcel Aymé. —17 ed.. —Paris: Gallimard, 1939
221 p.;18 cm.

I565.45/414
A Paris, sous l'oeil des métèques/Jean-José Frappa. —Paris: Ernest Flammarion, 1926
248 p.;18 cm.

I565.45/415
Morceaux Choisis/Jacques de Lecretelle. — Paris: Gallimard, 1938
11,332 p.;17 cm.

I565.45/416(2.4)
Cocardasse et Passepoil/Paul Féval Fils. — Paris: Librairie Ollendorff, 1923
219 p.;20 cm.

I565.45/417
Les Navires Truqués/Jacques Baïf. —[S. l.]: Éditions Denoël, 1939
12,382 p.;17 cm.

I565.45/418
Les moyens du bord/Tristan Bernard. —Paris: Fernczi et fils, 1927
159 p.;19 cm.

I565.45/419
Marthe et Marie/Pierre Sales. —Paris: Ernest Flammarion, [?]
428 p.;18 cm.

I565.45/420
Le voleur de femmes/Pierre Frondaie. —Paris: Editions Emile-Paul Frères, 1931
300 p.;18 cm.

I565.45/421
Les Léreeuses/H. de Montherlant. —Paris: Editions Bernard Grasset, 1939
332 p.;18 cm.

I565.45/422
Les Chemins De La Mer/François Murac. — [S. l.]: Bernard Grasset, 1939
9,322 p.;16 cm.

I565.45/423
Les contes de la Dierge/Jérôme Tharaud et Jean Tharaud. —[S. l.]: Librairie Plon, 1940
1,245 p.;16 cm.

I565.45/424
La pharmacie des prés/J. h. Rosny Jeune. — [S. l.]: Albin Michel, 1939
13,251 p.;16 cm.

I565.45/425
Ne dites pas Mais dites.../Étienne le Gal. — [S. l.]: Librairie Delgrave, 1924
1,111 p.;16 cm.

I565.45/426
Le courrier de la Mer Blanche /Édouard Peisson. —[S. l.]: Des Portiques, 1929
7,231 p.;16 cm.

I565.45/427
Travail/Emile Zola. —[S. l.]: Bibliothèque Charpentier, 1925
1,329 p.;16 cm.

I565.45/428
retour de l. U. R. S. S. /André Gide. —[S. l.]: Gallimard,1936
9,123 p. ;16 cm.

I565.45/429
Prométhée Délivré /Georges Blond. —[S. l.]: Arthème Fayard,1938
7,301 p. ;17 cm.

I565.45/430
La Rue/Francis Carco. —[S. l.]: Albin Michel,1930
11,254 p. ;17 cm.

I565.45/431
Le Génie et les Vices de Rémi Canari/René Collard. —[S. l.]:Denoël,1939
1,205 p. ;16 cm.

I565.45/432
Les Œuvres libres/Plusieurs. —[S. l.]: Arthème Fayard,1926
5,311 p. ;16 cm.

I565.45/433
Maripepa/Raymond Escholier. —[S. l.]: Albin Michel,1935
11,249 p. ;16 cm.

I565.45/434
L'injustice est en moi/Gabriel D'Aubarède. —[S. l.]:Librairie Plon,1927
1,258 p. ;15 cm.

I565.45/435
Le Mannequin D'Osier/Anatole France. —[S. l.]:Calman Lévy,
1,351 p. ;17 cm.

I565.45/436
Iris Perdue et Retrouvée /Pierre Frondaie. —[S. l.]:Émile-Paul Frères,1931
3,307 p. ;17 cm.

I565.45/437
Notre Cher Péguy/Jérôme et Jean Tharaud. —[S. l.]:Librairie Plon,1926
1,255 p. ;18 cm.

I565.45/438
Le Jardin Qui Chante/Charles de Vitis. —[S. l.]:Maison Alfred Mame et Fils,
7,123 p. ;17 cm.

I565.45/439
Le Cabaret de la Belle Femme/Roland Dorgelès. —[S. l.]:Albin Michel,1928
9,287 p. ;17 cm.

I565.45/440
Bourguignottes et Pompons Rouges/Charles le Goffic. —[S. l.]:Georges Crés & Cie,1916
1,287 p. ;18 cm.

I565.45/441
Clemenceau Dans la Retraite /René Benjamin. —[S. l.]:Librairie Plon,1930
1,254 p. ;17 cm.

I565.45/442
Cécile de la Foile /Marc Chadourne. —[S. l.]: Librairie Plon,1930
1,175 p. ;19 cm.

I565.45/443
Les Femmes Aux Ménages /Albéric Cahuet. —[S. l.]: Bibliothèque Charpentier Fasquelle Éditeurs,1938
11,190 p. ;18 cm.

I565.5/1-3
Au coeur de la tartarie/Peter Fleming. —3 ed. . —Paris: Librairie Gallimard,1938
12,278 p. ;19 cm.

I565.5/2

Caraja... Kou/Rayliane de la Falaise. —Paris: Librairie Plon, 1939

3,292 p. ;17 cm.

I565.5/3

Les Manants du roi/Jean de la Varende. —Paris: Librairie Plon, 1938

271 p. ;18 cm.

I565.5/4

Escales et paysages/Général Pierre Weiss. —Paris: Bernard Grasset, 1939

228 p. ;19 cm.

I565.5/5

Au coeur sauvage des philippines/René Jouglet. —Paris: Bernard Grasset, 1934

7,235 p. ;19 cm.

I565.5/6

L'Appel de la Route/Edouard Estaunié. —Paris: Librairie Académique, 1922

355 p. ;18 cm.

I565.5/7

La machine à lire les pensées/André Maurois. —Paris: Gallimard, 1937

6,211 p. ;18 cm.

I565.5/8

Journal intime/Pierre Loti. —Paris: Calmann'Lévy, 1929

197 p. ;18 cm.

I565.5/9

Au pays où les femmes sont reines/Ardien de Meeüs. —Paris: Les Editions de France, 1940

210 p. ;17 cm.

I565.5/10

Nous autres Français/Georges Bernanos. —Paris: Gallimard, 1939

290 p. ;20 cm.

I565.5/11

Les Etats-Désunis/Vladimir Pozner. —Paris: Les éditions Denoël, 1937

308 p. ;20 cm.

I565.5/12

Quédar/Bernard Vernier. —Paris: Librairie Plon, 1938

244 p. ;18 cm.

I565.5/13

Chez les brigands de la vielle Chine/Jean Perrigault. —Paris: L. Fournier, 1935

251 p. ;19 cm.

I565.5/14

Les derniers jours de la marine à voiles/Marcel Rondeleux. —Paris: Librairie Plon, 1929

10,300 p. ;19 cm.

I565.5/15

Morvan/M. Constantin-Weyer. —Paris: Les éditions Rieder, 1929

218 p. ;18 cm.

I565.5/16

Les bestiaires/Henry de Montherlant. —Paris: Bernard Grasset, 1926

10,288 p. ;17 cm.

I565.5/17

Okoumé bêtes et gens de l'afrique noire/Georges Trial. —Paris: Editions Je sers, 1939

9,298 p. ;18 cm.

I565.5/18(1914-1918)

Les crapouillots 1914-1918/Général J. Rouquerol. —Paris: Payot, 1935

11,188 p. ;21 cm.

I565. 6/1

Le rire/Henri Bergson. —Paris: Librqirie Félix Algan,1936

8,208 p. ;18 cm.

I565. 6/2

Histoires de très loin ou d'assez près/Claude Farrère. —Paris: Ernest Flammarion,1923

284 p. ;17 cm.

I565. 6/3

Crainquebille/Anatole France. —Paris: Calmann-Lévy,[?]

314 p. ;18 cm.

I565. 6/4

Gargantua/Francoys Rabelais. —Paris: Editions de la Sirène,1919

294 p. ;18 cm.

I565. 6/5

L'école des femmes: Robert/André Gide. —Paris: Gallimard,1934

254 p. ;16 cm.

I565. 6/6

Le sauvagine/Joseph d'Arbaud. —Paris: Bernard Grasset,1929

304 p. ;18 cm.

I565. 6/7(1)

Au soir de la pensée 1/Georges Clemenceau. —Paris: Librairie Plon,1927

477 p. ;22 cm.

I565. 6/8

Défense des lettres/Georges Duhamel. —Paris: Mercvre de France,1937

17,312 p. ;18 cm.

I565. 6/9-73

Le peseur d'âmes/André Maurois. —73 ed.. —Paris: Gallimard,1931

174 p. ;16 cm.

I565. 6/10

Domnitza de Snagov/Panaït Istrati. —Paris: J. Fernczi et fils,1926

156 p. ;20 cm.

I565. 6/11

Le séducteur/Gérard d'Houville. —Paris: Arthème Fayard et Cie,1926

126 p. ;22 cm.

I565. 6/12

La petite fille de Jérusalem/Myriam Harry. —Paris: Arthème Fayard et Cie,1927

126 p. ;22 cm.

I565. 6/13

L'île de volupté/Myriam Harry. —Paris: Arthème Fayard et Cie,1927

125 p. ;22 cm.

I565. 6/14

Morte la bête.../Henri Duvernois. —Paris: Arthème Fayard et Cie,1924

125 p. ;22 cm.

I565. 6/15

Une femme dans chaque port/André Savignon. —Paris: J. Fernczi et fils,1918

188 p. ;19 cm.

I565. 6/16

Manitoba/M. Constantin-Weyer. —Paris: Fernczi et fils,1924

157 p. ;19 cm.

I565. 072/1

Rainer Maria Rilke/Robert Pitrou. —Paris: Editions Albin Michel,1938

14,238 p. ;18 cm.

I565.73/1

Croisière Blanche/Roger Vercel. —Paris: Albin Michel,1938

255 p. ;17 cm.

I565.73/2

Les Gilberts/Robert-Louis Stevenson. —Pris: Edition de la Sirène,1920

9,231 p. ;18 cm.

I565.73/3

Huit gouttes d'opium/Ernest Pérochon. —Paris: Librairie Plon,1925

256 p. ;18 cm.

I565.73/4

Dames et cavaliers/Edmond Pilon. —Paris: Edition Bernard Grasset,1936

11,286 p. ;18 cm.

I565.73/5

Le pain blanc/Jean Buhot. —Paris: J. ferenczi et Fils,[?]

158 p. ;19 cm.

I565.73/6

Contes réels et fantaisistes/Pierre Frondaie. —Paris: Emile-Paul Frères,1930

12,244 p. ;18 cm.

I565.73/7

La clef des choses cachées/Maurice Magre. —Paris: Fasquelle éditeur,1935

10,196 p. ;19 cm.

I565.73/8

Béhanzigue/P. J. Toulet. —Paris: Librairie Edgar Malfère,1921

7,174 p. ;18 cm.

I565.73/9

L'étrangère /Jacques Bompard. —[S. l.]: Perrin et clé,1921

1,228 p. ;16 cm.

I565.74/1

Fables de la Fontaine/L'Aimabel Mentor. —Paris: Librairie Générale Catholique,1899

10,182 p. ;15 cm.

I565.99/1

Les contes du rabbin/D. Acques. —Paris: A. Quignon,1927

313 p. ;18 cm.

I712.45/1

La mère/Pearl Buck. —Paris: Librairie Stock, 1934

15,238 p. ;17 cm.

I712.45/2

Radieuse Aurore/Jack London. —[S. l.]: Librairie Plon,1932

7,252 p. ;16 cm.

J 艺术

J234(565)/1

De la marne au Rhin/Forain. —Paris: Librairie Hachette,1920

1 v. ;19 cm.

J234(565)/2(1)

De la maine au Rhin Tome 1/Forain. —Paris: Editions Pierre Lafitte, 1920

1 v. ; 19 cm.

J617.6/1

Phonographes et Musique Mécanique/Eugène H-Weiss. —Paris: Librairie Hachette, 1930

6,184 p. ; 18 cm.

J895.65/1

La vie parisienne au théatre/Francis de Croisset. —Paris: Bernard Grasset, 1929

11,231 p. ; 18 cm.

K 历史、地理

K1/1

L'invasion de la Chine par l'occident/E. R. Hughes. —Paris: Payot, 1938

11,288 p. ; 22 cm.

K1/2(1)

Histoire universelle/Pierre de Coubertin. —Paris: Société de l'histoire universelle, [?]

18,92 p. ; 24 cm.

K143/1

L'armisrice du 11 novembre 1918/Général H. Mordacq. —Paris: Librairie Plon, 1937

247 p. ; 17 cm.

K143/2

La Guerre et les Hommes/Général Debeney. —[S. l.]: Librairie Plon, 1937

3,378 p. ; 19 cm.

K2/1

La Naissance de la Chine/H. G. Creel. —Paris: Payot, 1937

11,357 p. ; 22 cm.

K2/2

Le chemin de Changhaï/Henry Champly. —Paris: Jules Tallandier, 1933

8,246 p. ; 19 cm.

K2/3

Histoire du la Chine/René Grousset. —Paris: Arthème Fayard et Cie, 1942

426 p. ; 17 cm.

K203/1

Sur la route de la soie/Louis Audouin-Dubreuil. —Paris: Librairie Plon, 1935

291 p. ; 19 cm.

K25/1

Les Peuples d'Extrême-Orient La Chine/Emile Hovelaque. —Paris: Ernest Flammarion, 1920

17,269 p. ; 18 cm.

K25/2

La civilisation chinoise/Henri Berr. —Paris: La Renaissance du livre, 1929

21,523 p. ; 19 cm.

K3/1

Forces spirituelles de l'Orient/Claude Farrère. —Paris: Flammarion, 1937

244 p. ; 18 cm.

K313.4/1

Le Japon mort et vif/François de Tessan. —Paris: Editions Baudinière, 1928

12,241 p. ;18 cm.

K351/1

L'Inde aux cent couleurs/Jacques le Bourgeois. —Paris: Librairie Hachette,1935

248 p. ;17 cm.

K371/1

Le pays sans ombre/Hans Helfritz. —Paris: Bernard Grasset,1936

11,306 p. ;19 cm.

K421/1

Le masque d'or/Henry de Monfreid. —Paris: Bernard Grasset,1936

10,244 p. ;18 cm.

K5/1-18

Les batisseurs de l'europe moderne/Le comte Sforza. —18 ed. . —Paris: Gallimard,1931

17,408 p. ;18 cm.

K5/2

Vive la liberté/Roland Dorgelès. —Paris: Albin Michel,1937

311 p. ;17 cm.

K5/3

La vérité sur l'armistice/le Général Mordacq. —Paris: Editions Jules Tallandier,1929

15,124 p. ;18 cm.

K503/1

La Renaissance/Frantz Funck-Brentano. —Paris: Arthème Fayard et Cie,1935

442 p. ;17 cm.

K512.5/1

Les précurseurs de lénine/Maurice Paléologue. —Paris: Librairie Plon,1938

7,247 p. ;18 cm.

K516/1

Histoire d'Allemagne/Charles Bonnefon. —Paris: A. Fayard et cie,1925

13,542 p. ;18 cm.

K516.44/1

La gerbe des forces/A. de Chateaubriant. —Paris: Editions Bernard Grasset,1937

356 p. ;18 cm.

K516.44/2

Idoles Allemades/Max Hermant. —Paris: Editions Bernard Grasset,1935

10,348 p. ;17 cm.

K516.9/1

Histoire secrète de la concilitation de Munich/Alfred Fabre-Luce. —Paris: Editions Bernard Grasset,1938

118 p. ;18 cm.

K551.4/1

La Corrida/Marcel Sauvage. —Paris: Les éditions Denoël,1938

226 p. ;18 cm.

K551.5/1

Les leçons de la guerre d'Espagne/Général Duval. —Paris: Librairie Plon,1938

247 p. ;18 cm.

K565.0/1

En France jadis/G. Lenotre. —Paris: Editions Bernard Grasset,1938

348 p. ;17 cm.

K565/1

L'homme qui était trop grand/Pierre Benoît et Claude Farrère. —Paris: Les Editions de France, 1936

337 p. ;17 cm.

K565/2-9

Histoire sommaire de la France jusqu'a 1610/G. Pagès. —9 ed.. —Paris: Librairie Hachette, [?]

5,280 p. ;17 cm.

K565/3-2

Les grandes Légendes de France/Edouard Schuré. —2 ed.. —Paris: Librairie Académique Didier, 1895

299 p. ;18 cm.

K565/4

Anatole France Anecdotique/Nicolas Segur. —Paris: Albin Michel, 1929

10,241 p. ;18 cm.

K565/5

Histoire de France/Jacques Bainville. —Paris: A. Fayard et cie, 1924

11,572 p. ;18 cm.

K565/6

Histoire des romanov 1613-1918/V. V. Funk et B. Nazarevski. —Paris: Payot, 1930

11,4 p. ;21 cm.

K565.3/1(1)

Les grands procès de l'histoire/Henri-Robert. —Paris: Payot, 1922

15,302 p. ;19 cm.

K565.3/1(2)

Les grands procès de l'histoire (deuxième série)/Henri-Robert. —Paris: Payot, 1923

257 p. ;19 cm.

K565.3/2

Les Bourbons (1518-1830)/Baron Andre de Maricourt. —Paris: Edition Emile-Paul Freres, 1936

15,315 p. ;18 cm.

K565.4/1

La vie parisienne à l'époque romantique/Henry Bidou. —Paris: Payot, 1931

190 p. ;19 cm.

K565.4/2

Le seconde empire/Octave Aubry. —Paris: Librairie Arthème Fayard, 1938

7,697 p. ;18 cm.

K565.4/3-14

Les guerriers de l'ogaden/Henry de Monfreid. —14 ed.. —Paris: Gallimard, 1936

10,344 p. ;19 cm.

K565.4/4(12)

Histoire du Consulat et de l'Empire/M. A. Thiers. —Paris: Paulin, 1855

40,709 p. ;21 cm.

K565.4/5(3)

Histoire du Consulat et de L'Empire/M. A. Thiers. —Paris: Paulin, 1845

570 p. ;20 cm.

K565.4/5(9)

Histoire du Consulat et de L'Empire/M. A. Thiers. —Paris: Paulin, 1849

596 p. ;20 cm.

K565.4/5(10)

Histoire du Consulat et de L'Empire/M. A. Thiers. —Paris: Paulin, 1851

511 p. ;20 cm.

K565.4/5(11)

Histoire du Consulat et de L'Empire/M. A. Thiers. —Paris: Paulin, 1851

476 p. ;20 cm.

K565.4/6(2)

Dans les Coulisses de l'histoire 2/Docteur Cabanès. —Paris: Albin Michel, 1937

7,381 p. ;17 cm.

K565. 4/7(2)

Mon temps/Gabriel Hanotaux. —Paris: Société de l'histoire nationale et librairie Plon, 1938

531 p. ;19 cm.

K565. 4/8

L'orme du mail/Anatole France. —Paris: Calmann-Lévy,[?]

340 p. ;18 cm.

K565. 4/9(1)

Mon Temps/Gabriel Hanotaux. —[S. l.]: Librairie Plon,1933

1,342 p. ;19 cm.

K565. 41/1(1)

Histoire de la Révolution française/M. A. Thiers. —Paris: Furne et Cie,1845

591 p. ;20 cm.

K565. 41/1-13(2)

Histoire de la révolution française /M. A. Thiers. —13 ed. . —Paris: Furne et Cie,1845

466 p. ;21 cm.

K565. 41/1-13(9)

Histoire de la Révolution française/M. A. Thiers. —13 ed. . —Paris: Furne et Cie,1847

427 p. ;21 cm.

K565. 41/1(6)

Histoire de la Révolution Française 6/Thiers. —Paris:[s. n.],[?]

595 p. ;22 cm.

K565. 41/1(8)

Histoire de la Révolution française tome 8/M. A. Thiers. —Paris: Furne et Cie, Librairie-Editeurs,1846

437 p. ;21 cm.

K565. 41/2

La troisième République/Jacques Bainville. —Paris: Arthème Fayard et Cie,1935

12,305 p. ;17 cm.

K565. 41/3

La vie à Paris pendant la Révolution/G. Lenotre. —Paris: Calmann-Lévy,1936

6,266 p. ;20 cm.

K565. 41/4

Le tribunal révolutionnaire/G. lenotre. —Paris: Librairie Académique,1924

364 p. ;19 cm.

K565. 41/5

L'histoire de France sous le règne de Napoléon/Sainte-Hélène. —Paris: Michel Lévy Frères,[?]

14,557 p. ;18 cm.

K565. 41/6(1)

Histoire du consulat et de l'empire(Tome 1)/M. A. Thiers. —Paris: Paulin,1845

494 p. ;21 cm.

K565. 41/6(4)

Histoire du consulat et de l'empire(Tome 14)/M. A. Thiers. —Paris: Paulin,1847

684 p. ;21 cm.

K565. 41/6(5)

Histoire du consulat et de l'empire(Tome V)/M. A. Thiers. —Paris: Lheureux et Cie,1845

473 p. ;21 cm.

K565. 41/6(6)

Histoire du Consulat et de l'Empire/M. A. Thiers. —Paris: Paulin,1857

693 p. ;20 cm.

K565. 41/6(7)

Histoire du consulat et de l'empire(Tome 7)/M. A. Thiers. —Paris: Paulin, 1847

684 p. ;21 cm.

K565. 41/6(8)

Histoire du consulat et de l'empire/M. A. Thiers. —Paris: Paulin, 1849

679 p. ;21 cm.

K565. 41/6(13)

Histoire du Consulat et de l'Empire/M. A. Thiers. —Paris: Paulin, 1856

583 p. ;23 cm.

K565. 41/6(14)

Histoire du consulat et de l'empire(Tome 14)/M. A. Thiers. —Paris: Paulin, 1856

686 p. ;22 cm.

K565. 41/6(20)

Histoire du consulat et de l'empire (Tome XX)/M. A. Thiers. —Paris: Lheureux et Cie, 1862

814 p. ;21 cm.

K565. 41/7

L'ascension de Bonaparte/Louis Madelin. —Paris: Libraiire Hachette, 1937

6,39 p. ;22 cm.

K565. 41/8

Napoléon et Alexandre ler 2/Albert Vandal. —Paris: Librairie Plon, 1918

570 p. ;18 cm.

K565. 41/9

Barnave/Jean-Jacques Chevallier. —Paris: Payot, 1936

360 p. ;20 cm.

K565. 41/10

Paris révolutionnaire/G. Lenotre. —Paris: Librairie académique, 1912

12,388 p. ;20 cm.

K565. 45/1

Magie noir/Paul Morand. —Paris: Bernard Grasset, 1928

15,303 p. ;18 cm.

K565. 45/2

Le mois (synthèse de l'activité mondiale)/. —Paris: Maulde et Renou, 1936

9,319 p. ;21 cm.

K565. 46/1

1940: Année de Grandeur Française/Maurice Privat. —Paris: Editions Médicis, 1939

228 p. ;19 cm.

K565. 9/1

Cela dépend de vous /Joules Romains. —Paris: Flammarion, 1939

134 p. ;17 cm.

K812/1

Grandeur des élites/Maurice Muret. —Paris: Albin Michel, 1939

314 p. ;18 cm.

K812. 4/1(1)

Napoléon et Alexandre I/Albert Vandal. —Paris: Librairie Plon, [?]

24,527 p. ;21 cm.

K815. 7/1

La musique/Henri de Curzon. —Paris: Librairie Plon, 1914

341 p. ;18 cm.

K831. 984. 7/1

Alcibiade/Jean Babelon. —Paris: Payot, 1935

14,242 p. ;22 cm.

K835/1

Les dictateurs/Jacques Bainville. —Paris: Denoel et Steele, 1935

17,300 p. ;18 cm.

K835. 125. 6/1

Mes co-détendus au Guépéou/Boris Wartanoff. —Genève: Librairie et Edition J. H. Jeheber S. A. ,[?]

10,214 p. ;19 cm.

K835. 125. 6/2

Dostoïevsky/Henri Troyat. —Paris: Librairie Arthème Fayard, 1940

632 p. ;18 cm.

K835. 125. 7/1

Ballets Russes/Tamar Karsavina. —Paris: Librairie Plon, 1931

19,304 p. ;18 cm.

K835. 125. 7/2

Tourguéniev/André Maurois. —Paris: Edition Bernard Grasset, 1931

15,248 p. ;18 cm.

K835. 125. 19/1

Scènes du monde criminel russe/Général A. de Kochko. —Paris: Payot, 1929

12,361 p. ;18 cm.

K835. 125. 76/1

Pages de ma vie/Fiodor Chaliapine. —Paris: Librairie Plon, 1927

256 p. ;17 cm.

K835. 165. 7/1-2

La vie de Robert Schumann/Alfred Colling. —2 ed. . —Paris: Librairie Gallimard, 1931

15,223 p. ;18 cm.

K835. 165. 7/2

La vie d'amour de Beethoven(Collection "leurs amours")/René Flament. —Paris: Ernest Flammarion, 1928

6,178 p. ;18 cm.

K835. 217/1

Zita, princesse de la paix/Antoine Redier. —Paris: Alexis Redier, 1930

276 p. ;17 cm.

K835. 225. 6/1

Des monts célestres aux sables rouges/Ella Maillart. —Paris: Editions Bernard Grasset, 1934

300 p. ;18 cm.

K835. 418/1

Georges Kastriote-Skanderbeg et la guerre albano-turque au quinzième siècle/Université d'Etat de Tirana, Institut d'histoire et de linguistique. —Tirana: Université d'Etat de Tirana, Institut d'histoire et de linguistique, 1967

147 p. ;20 cm.

K835. 465. 72/1

Raphael ou la puissance de l'esprit /Fred Bérence. —Paris: Payot, 1936

11,33 p. ;22 cm.

K835. 466. 1/1-5

Vie et Aventures de Marco Polo/Antonio Aniante. —5 ed. . —Paris: Mercvre de Fance, 1936

12,294 p. ;18 cm.

K835. 618/1

Avoine Sauvage/Eric Muspratt. —Paris: Editions Bernard Grasset, [?]

287 p. ;18 cm.

K835. 647/1(1)

Deux années à Berlin/Baron Beyens. —Paris: Librairie Plon, 1931

300 p. ;22 cm.

K835.647/1(2)

Deux Années à Berlin/Baron Beyens. —[S. l.]:Librairie Plon,1931

1,326 p. ;18 cm.

K835.65/1

lettres choisies de Madame de Sévigné/Collection des classiques français. —Paris: Firmin-Didot et Cie,1928

100,651 p. ;19 cm.

K835.65/2

Jeanne d'Arc Louis X IV Napoléon/Charles Maurras. —Paris: Ernest Flammarion,1937

20,240 p. ;18 cm.

K835.655.2/1

Lke général Daumesnil/Groger Baschet. —Paris: Librairie Hachette,1938

10,243 p. ;19 cm.

K835.655.2/2

Valbelle "le tigre"/Charles de la Roncière. —Paris: Editions Bernard Grasset,1935

252 p. ;19 cm.

K835.655.2/3

Mes souvenirs de la légion étrangère/S. A. le prince Aage de Danemark. —Paris: Payot,1936

10,206 p. ;22 cm.

K835.655.3/1

Le désert de bièvres/Georges Duhamel. —Paris: Mercvre de France,1937

324 p. ;17 cm.

K835.655.6/1-6

Cinq éclats de Silex/M. Constantin Zeyer. —6 ed.. —Paris: Les Editions Rieder,1927

8,151 p. ;17 cm.

K835.655.6/2

Visions/Henri Fauconnier. —Paris: Editions Stock,1938

8,279 p. ;17 cm.

K835.655.6/3

Racine/Saint-René Taillandier. —Paris: Librairie Plon,1927

124 p. ;18 cm.

K835.655.6/4-29

Géographie cordiale de l'Europe/Georges Duhamel. —29 ed.. —Paris: Mercvre de France, 1931

279 p. ;18 cm.

K835.655.6/5

Mes origines-Mémoires et récits/Frédéric Mistral. —Paris: Librairie Plon,1929

253 p. ;15 cm.

K835.655.6/6

De l'affaire dreyfus au dimanche rouge à saintptersbourg/J. Tchernoff. —Paris: Editions Rieder,[?]

233 p. ;22 cm.

K835.655.6/7(8)

Les grands écrivains de la France: oeuvres de p. ;Corneille /M. AD. Regnier. —Paris: Librairie de L. Hachette et Cie,1862

23,695 p. ;21 cm.

K835.655.6/7(10)

Les grands écrivains de la France: oeuvres de p. ;Corneille /M. AD. Regnier. —Paris: Librairie de L. Hachette et Cie,1862

24,551 p. ;22 cm.

K835.655.6/8

Les caprices du poète/Francis Jammes. —Paris: Librairie Plon,1923

212 p. ;17 cm.

K835. 655. 6/9

Hommes et oeuvres du 20e siècle/Henri Peyre. —Paris: Edition R. A Corrêa,1938

343 p. ;22 cm.

K835. 655. 6/10

L'aventure de Paul-Jean Toulet/Jacques Dyssord. —Paris: Bernard Grasset,1928

230 p. ;18 cm.

K835. 655. 6/11

Voltaire/John Charpentier. —Paris: Editions Jules Tallandier,1938

8,310 p. ;18 cm.

K835. 655. 6/12

Mes Apprentissages/Colette. —Paris: Ferenczi,1936

10,209 p. ;18 cm.

K835. 655. 6/13

Le Bateau Pervers/Pierre Lestringuez. —Paris: Les Editions de France,1929

247 p. ;17 cm.

K835. 655. 6/14-5

La jeunesse d'un clerc/Julien Benda. —5 ed. . —Paris: Gallimard,1936

221 p. ;17 cm.

K835. 655. 6/15

L'amie de la Rochefoucauld/André Beaunier. —Paris: Ernest Flammarionmma,1927

7,281 p. ;18 cm.

K835. 655. 6/16

Poètes angevins d'aujourd'hui/Société des Artistes Angevins. —Paris: Librairie Paul Lefebvre, 1922

131 p. ;18 cm.

K835. 655. 6/17

Journal intime 1878-1884/Pierre Loti. —Paris: Calmann-Lévy,1925

282 p. ;18 cm.

K835. 655. 6/18

Les Pécieux et les Précieuses/Collection des plus belles pages. —Paris: Mercvre de France, 1939

250 p. ;17 cm.

K835. 655. 6/19(3)

Oeuvres de p. ; Corneille/Librairie de L. Hachette et Cie. —Paris: Librairie de L. Hachette et Cie,1862

104,468 p. ;22 cm.

K835. 655. 6/19(4)

Oeuvres de p. ; Corneille/Librairie de L. Hachette et Cie. —Paris: Librairie de L. Hachette et Cie,1862

514 p. ;20 cm.

K835. 655. 6/19(6)

Oeuvres de p. ; Corneille/Librairie de L. Hachette et Cie. —Paris: Librairie de L. Hachette et Cie,1862

660 p. ;22 cm.

K835. 655. 6/19(10)

Oeuvres de p. ; Corneille/M. CH. Marty-Laveaux. —Paris: Librairie de L. Hachette et Cie, 1862

488 p. ;21 cm.

K835. 655. 6/19(12)

Oeuvres de p. ; Corneille/Librairie de L. Hachette et Cie. —Paris: Librairie de L. Hachette et Cie,1862

572 p. ;22 cm.

K835. 655. 6/20

Tournant dangereux/Vlaminck. —Paris: Librairie Stock,1929

275 p. ;18 cm.

K835. 655. 6/21

Les amours d'un poète/Louis Barthou. —Paris: Arthème Fayard et Cie,[?]

12,114 p. ;23 cm.

K835. 655. 6/22

Mes évasions/Georges Rème. —Paris: Les editions de France,1928

258 p. ;19 cm.

K835. 655. 6/23

Sixième numéro de Chronique/Le Roseau d'or. —Paris: Librairie Plon,1928

310 p. ;19 cm.

K835. 655. 6/24

La vie amoureuse de Charles Baudelaire/Camille Mauclair. —Paris: Ernest Flammarion,1927

16,169 p. ;17 cm.

K835. 655. 6/25

La vie et les opinions d'Anatole France/Jacques roujon. —Paris: Librairie Plon,1925

275 p. ;18 cm.

K835. 655. 6/26

Anecdotes/Frenand Herbert. —Paris: Edition Franco-allemand,1900

240 p. ;18 cm.

K835. 655. 6/27(1)

Carnets/Ludovic Halévy. —Paris: Calmann-Lévy,1935

230 p. ;18 cm.

K835. 655. 6/28

Mes années d'appentissage/Louis Bertband. —Paris:[s. n.],1938

270 p. ;18 cm.

K835. 655. 6/29-3

Un réculier dans le siècle/Julien Benda. —3 ed.. —Paris: Gallimard,1937

253 p. ;18 cm.

K835. 655. 6/30

Cruelle Espagne/Jérôme et Jean Tharaud. —Paris: Librairie Plon,1937

254 p. ;18 cm.

K835. 655. 6/31

Dingley l'illustre écrivain/Jérôme et Jean Tharaud. —Paris: Emile-Paul,[?]

272 p. ;18 cm.

K835. 655. 6/32

Stendhal/Alain. —Paris: Les éditions Rieder, 1935

106 p. ;18 cm.

K835. 655. 6/33

Le paradis perdu/André Rousseaux. —Paris: Bernard Grasset,1936

18,277 p. ;17 cm.

K835. 655. 6/34

Johanna Beaumont/Pierre Gourdon. —Paris: Bloud et Gay,1922

226 p. ;17 cm.

K835. 655. 6/35

Oeuvres de p. ; Corneille/Librairie de L. Hachette et Cie. —Paris: Librairie de L. Hachette et Cie,1862

644 p. ;20 cm.

K835. 655. 6/36

Graziella/A. de Lamartine. —Paris: Librairie Plon,1925

252 p. ;15 cm.

K835. 655. 6/37

Souvenirs d'un temps disparu/Marie Scheikevitch. —Paris: Librairie Plon,1935

260 p. ;18 cm.

K835. 655. 6/38

Mémorandum D'un Éditeur /P-V. Stock. —[S. l.]:Libraire Stock,1935

4,323 p. ;16 cm.

K835. 655. 6/39

À la recherche de Marcel Proust/Lucien Aressy. —[S. l.]:Triptyque,1930

3,190 p. ;18 cm.

K835. 655. 7/1

Nicolas Pousin/Pierre Courthion. —Paris: Librairie Plon,1929

10,122 p. ;18 cm.

K835. 655. 7/2

Claude Monet/Georges Clémenceau. —Paris: Librairie Plon,1928

124 p. ;17 cm.

K835. 655. 7/3

Le roman d'un chansonnier populaire/Maurice Hamel. —Paris:[s. n.],[?]

12,146 p. ;19 cm.

K835. 656. 2/1

Devant la douleur/Léon Daudet. —Paris: Editions Bernard Grasset,1931

262 p. ;17 cm.

K835. 656. 2/2

La Guillotine/G. Lenotre. —Paris: Perrin et Cie,1912

375 p. ;18 cm.

K835. 656. 13/1

Lavoisier/Lucien et Désiré Leroux. —Paris: Librairie Plon,1928

123 p. ;17 cm.

K835. 657/1

Laurent le Magnifique/Marcel Brion. —Paris: Albin Michel,1937

14,353 p. ;18 cm.

K835. 657/2

Le secret de Napoléon/Médecin général R. Brice. —Paris: Payot,1936

12,292 p. ;22 cm.

K835. 657/3

Richard Wagner: révolutionnaire/Henry Malherbe. —Paris: Albin Michel,1938

10,338 p. ;21 cm.

K835. 657/4

La vie amoureuse de la Grande Mademoiselle/Duc de la Force. —Paris: Ernest Flammarion, 1927

162 p. ;17 cm.

K835. 657/5

Soliveau/Georges-Armand Masson. —Paris: Editions du siècle,1923

121 p. ;17 cm.

K835. 657/6

Auguste/Léon Homo. —Paris: Payot,1935

10,330 p. ;22 cm.

K835. 657/7

Neville Chamberlain/Pierre Belperron. —Paris: Librairie Plon,1938

7,91 p. ;19 cm.

K835. 657/8

Louis XVI/J. —B. Ebeling. —Paris: Librairie Plon,1939

246 p. ;19 cm.

K835. 657/9

Napoléon/E. Guillon. —Paris: Librairie Plon, 1912

316 p. ;18 cm.

K835.657/10(3)

Mémoires de Napoléon/Bibilothèque des Mémoires historiques et militaires. —Paris: Garnier Frères,[?]

467 p. ;18 cm.

K835.657/11

La reine Marie-Antoinette/Pierre de Nolhac. —Paris: Calmann-Lévy,[?]

332 p. ;20 cm.

K835.657/12

Napoléon Ⅲ secret/Jules Bertaut. —Paris: Bernard Grasset,1939

301 p. ;18 cm.

K835.657/13

La guerre vue d'en bas et d'en haut/Abel Ferry. —Paris: Bernard Grasset,1920

14,314 p. ;18 cm.

K835.657/14

Louis XV et Marie Leczinska/Pierre de Nolhac. —Paris: Calmann-Lévy,[?]

345 p. ;18 cm.

K835.657/15

Les amours de Napoléon Ⅲ/Adrien Dansette. —Paris: Librairie Arthème Fayard,1938

286 p. ;18 cm.

K835.657/16

Sous la menace des idoles/Révérend père A. Flachère. —Paris: Librairie Plon,1938

305 p. ;19 cm.

K835.657/17

Talleyrand/Comte de Saint Aulaire. —Paris: Dunod,1936

435 p. ;18 cm.

K835.657/18

La vie et les prophéties du comte de Gobineau/Robert Dreyfus. —Paris: Calmann-Lévy,1875

344 p. ;17 cm.

K835.657/19

La jeunesse de Bonaparte/Louis Madelin. —Paris: Hachette,1937

13,357 p. ;22 cm.

K835.657/20

François/Auguste Valensin. —Paris: Librairie Plon,1938

29,278 p. ;19 cm.

K835.657/21

Vie de Louis XⅢ/Louis Vaunois. —Paris: Editions Bernard Grasset,1936

10,533 p. ;19 cm.

K835.657/22

Napoléon/J. —G. Prod'homme. —Paris: Mercvre de France,[?]

651 p. ;19 cm.

K835.657/23

La vie privée de Louis XIV/Georges Mongredien. —[S. l.]: Hachette,1938

13,225 p. ;16 cm.

K835.658/1

La Castiglione/Abel Hermant. —Paris: Hachette,[?]

20,230 p. ;18 cm.

K835.658/2

Confession amoureuse de la femme qui devint homme/Marcel Allain. —Paris: Les Editions de France,1939

22,162 p. ;17 cm.

K835.658/3

La vie amoureuse de la Belle Hélène/Gérard d'Houville. —Paris: Ernest Flammarion,1928

8,191 p. ;16 cm.

K835.658/4

Le livre de mon père/Emile Henriot. —Paris: Librairie Plon, 1938

278 p. ;18 cm.

K835.658/5

Un aide de camp de Napoéon/Comte Philippe de Ségur. —Paris: Edition R. Simon, [?]

15, 286 p. ;18 cm.

K835.658/6-16

Le duc de lauzun et la cour de marie-Antoinette/Gaston Maugras. —16 ed.. —Paris: Librairie Plon, 1893

8, 470 p. ;20 cm.

K835.658/7-27

Les Maîtres/Georges Duhamel. —27 ed.. —Paris: Mercvre de Fance, 1937

314 p. ;18 cm.

K835.658/8

L'initiatrice aux mains vides/Jeanne Galzy. —Paris: Les Editions Rieder, 1929

10, 251 p. ;18 cm.

K835.658/9

La gracieuse histoire de la petite Anne de Guigné/Etienne-Marie Lajeunie. —Paris: Editions de la vie spirituelle, 1924

81 p. ;18 cm.

K835.658/10

Bayard 1476-1524/Paul Ballaguy. —Paris: Payot, 1935

14, 360 p. ;22 cm.

K835.658/11

En Armagnac aux temps romantiques/Fernand Laudet. —Paris: Editions de la vraie France, 1930

230 p. ;18 cm.

K835.658/12

Le stupide XIX siècle/Léon Daudet. —Paris: Npivelle Librairie Nationale, 1922

7, 31 p. ;18 cm.

K835.658/13(2)

Frédéric II/Pierre Gaxotte. —Paris: Librairie Arthème Fayard, 1938

9, 547 p. ;18 cm.

K835.658/14

soeurs de grands hommes /Victor Giraud. —Paris: Les éditions G. Crès et Cie, 1926

216 p. ;18 cm.

K835.658/15

La belle Gabrielle qu'aima Henri Ⅳ/Paul Reboux. —Paris: Arthème Fayard, 1938

285 p. ;17 cm.

K835.658/16

Lucile de chateaubriand/Albéric Cahuet. —Paris: Fasquelle, 1935

286 p. ;19 cm.

K835.658/17

Le Film de Ma Vie/René Lefèvre. —[S. l.]: Gallimard, 1937

7, 220 p. ;18 cm.

K835.7/1

Les pilotes de l'europe/John Gunther. —Paris: Bernard Grasset, [?]

7, 381 p. ;18 cm.

K892/1

En Chine/Abel Bonnard. —Paris: A. Fayard et cie, 1924

7, 362 p. ;18 cm.

K895.652.6/1

La politesse/Duc de Lévis Mirepoix, comte Félix de Vogüé. —Paris: Les éditions de France,

1937
304 p. ;18 cm.

K897. 21/1
Mexique terre indienne/Jacques Soustelle. —Paris: Editions Bernard Grasset, 1936
270 p. ;18 cm.

K91/1
Le beau voyage autour du monde/Dr Fred. Blanchod. —Paris: Payot, 1939
214 p. ;22 cm.

K919/1-8
La croisière d'anahita/Louis Bernicot. —8 ed.. —Paris: Gallimard, 1939
176 p. ;18 cm.

K919. 2/1
Kaimiloa/Eric de Bisschop. —Paris: Librairie Plon, 1939
358 p. ;18 cm.

K919. 2/2
Journal de bord du Snark/Madame Jack London. —Paris: Hachette, 1938
10,245 p. ;18 cm.

K919. 2/3
Tour du Monde/Henri de Rothschild. —Paris: Hachette, 1936
284 p. ;17 cm.

K919. 2/4
Rien que la terre/Paul Morand. —Paris: Bernard Grasset, 1926
9,258 p. ;18 cm.

K93/1
Tour d'asie/Maurice Percheron. —Paris: Denoel et Steele, 1936
9,258 p. ;21 cm.

K93/2
Lueur d'Asie/Waddy. —Paris: Librairie Picart, 1935
191 p. ;18 cm.

K935/1
Dans le sillage des jonques/René Jouglet. —Paris: Bernard Grasset, 1935
13,252 p. ;18 cm.

K935. 19/1
Les tigres parfumés/Maurice Dekobra. —Paris: Les éditions de France, 1929
318 p. ;18 cm.

K935. 655/1
Feuilles de calendrier/Princesse Bibesco. —Paris: Librairie Plon, 1939
278 p. ;18 cm.

K939/1-10
Connaissance de l'Est/Paul Claudel. —10 ed.. —Paris: Mercvre de France, [?]
258 p. ;17 cm.

K939/2
Mes Voyages/Claude Farrère. —[S. l.]: Ernest Flammarion, 1923
5,246 p. ;17 cm.

K94/1
Au Moghreb parmi les fleurs/Alice-Louis Barthou. —Paris: Bernard Grasset, 1925
176 p. ;18 cm.

K941. 19/1
La caravane sans chameaux/Roland Dorgelès. —Paris: Albin Michel, 1928
301 p. ;17 cm.

K949/1
Les bâtisseurs de royaumes/Jean Martet. —Paris: Albin Michel, 1934

7,314 p. ;18 cm.

K95/1-151
Ouvert la nuit/Paul Morand. —151 ed. . —Paris: Editions de la nouvelle revue française, 1922
200 p. ;16 cm.

K951. 22/1
La sibérie et l'extrême-nord soviétique/Charles Steber. —Paris: Payot,1936
9,245 p. ;21 cm.

K954. 25/1
Bucarest/Paul Morand. —Paris: Librairie Plon,1935
10,203 p. ;18 cm.

K954. 69/1
La fête à Amalfi/A. T'Serstevens. —Paris: Albin Michel,1933
314 p. ;17 cm.

K954. 69/2
L'Ardente Sicile/Camille Mauclair. —Paris: Bernard Grasset,1937
6,259 p. ;18 cm.

K954. 69/3
Promenades Italiennes/Emile Henriot. —Paris: Edition d'Art H. Piazza,1930
13,181 p. ;18 cm.

K956. 4/1-8
Croisières en eaux troubles/Jacques de Lacretelle. —8 ed. . —Paris: Librairie Gallimard,1939
8,181 p. ;18 cm.

K956. 5/1
Terre de France/Comte Serge Fleury. —Paris: Editiond Fernand Sorlot,1939
17,78 p. ;18 cm.

K956. 54/1
Le Mont-Saint-Michel/Ch. —H. Besnard. —Paris: Henri Laurens,1945
144 p. ;19 cm.

K956. 55/1-20
La bête du vaccacarès/Joseph d'Arbaud. —20 ed. . —Paris: Bernard Grasset,1926
43,364 p. ;18 cm.

K956. 59/1-10
La cote de Jade/Francis de Croisset. —10 ed. . —Paris: Editions Bernard Grasset,1938
9,271 p. ;18 cm.

K956. 59/2-2
Femmes tahitiennes /Louis-Charles Royer. —2 ed. . —Paris: Les éditions de France,1939
229 p. ;18 cm.

K956. 59/3
En campant du cap nord au cap de Bonne-Espérance/Jo Roger-Tourte. —Paris: Les Oevres Françaises,1937
313,362 p. ;18 cm.

K971. 29/1
L'Amérique toute nue/Louis-Charles Royer. —Paris: Les éditions de France,1938
233 p. ;18 cm.

K971. 3/1
Sur les hauts plateaux groenlandais/D ED. Wyss-Dunant. —Paris: Payot,1939
17,207 p. ;22 cm.

K973/1-2
Amérique latine/André Siegfried. —2 ed. . —Paris: Librairie Armand Colin,1934
14,160 p. ;17 cm.

K975/1
Villes et paysages d'ametique/Jean Canu. —

Paris：J. De Gigord，1937
363 p. ；22 cm.

K979. 951. 2/1-2
Saint Basile/L'Abbé Jean Rivière. —2 ed. . —Paris：Librairie Victor Lecoffre，1925
24，296 p. ；18 cm.

O 数理科学和化学

O181/1
Théorie des groupes finis et continues et la géométrie differenielle/Elie Cartan. —Paris：[s. n.]，[?]
269 p. ；21 cm.

O6-3/1
Dictionnaire-Manuel du Maître de Chai/Edouard Feret. —Paris：Librairie Associés，1896
650 p. ；19 cm.

P 天文学、地球科学

P1/1
De mercure à pluton/Pierre Humbert. —Paris：Albin Michel，1937
11，181 p. ；18 cm.

P468. 252/1
La température de Tsingtao/P. J. Tsiang. —[S. l.]：[s. n.]，1929
79 p. ；25 cm.

P725/1
L'Atlantique：histoire et vie d'un océan/André George. —Paris：Albin Michel，1938
42，248 p. ；18 cm.

P941. 6/1
A l'assaut des pôles/Roger Vercel. —Paris：Albin Michel，1938
10，253 p. ；18 cm.

Q 生物科学

Q434/1
Physiologie du gout/Brillat-Savarin. —Paris：Eugène Fasquelle，1918
525 p. ；17 cm.

Q95/1

La Harde/Joseph de Pesquidoux. —Paris: Librairie Plon, 1936

5, 282 p. ; 18 cm.

Q969. 554. 2/1

La vie des fourmis/Maurice Maeterlinck. —Paris: Bibliothèque-Charpentier, 1930

11, 254 p. ; 18 cm.

T 工业技术

TQ658. 1/1

Manuel de parfumerie/L. Lazennec. —Paris: Librairie J. —B, 1922

10, 326 p. ; 15 cm.

TS19/1

La teinture et l'impression/Albert Letellier. —Paris: Librairie scientifique J. Hermann, 1924

17, 608 p. ; 22 cm.

TU-095. 65/1

Les dessous de Scotland yard/Georges Lafumée. —Paris: Les éditions de France, 1934

237 p. ; 18 cm.

Z 综合性图书

Z/1

La Baule/[s. n.]. —[S. l.]: [s. n.], [?]

142 p. ; 24 cm.

Z235. 65/1

Les oeuvres libres/Arthème Fayard et Cie. —Paris: Arthème Fayard et Cie, [?]

349 p. ; 20 cm.

Z256. 5/1

Les oeuvres libres/Librairie A. Fayard. —Paris: Librairie A. Fayard, [?]

347 p. ; 17 cm.

Z256. 5/2

Les oeuvres libres/Marcel • Boulenger[etc]. —Paris: Arthème Fayard et Cie, [?]

383 p. ; 17 cm.

Z256. 5/3(4)

La nouvelle Revue Française/[pas en détail]. —Paris: [s. n.], 1935

497-976 p. ; 21 cm.

Z256. 5/4

Première étape/OTTO F. Bond. —Paris: The university of chicago, 1936

1 v. ; 18 cm.

Z256. 5/5(56)

Les oeuvres libres/Arthème Fayard et Cie. —Paris: Arthème Fayard et Cie, [?]

377 p. ; 17 cm.

Z256. 5/5(123)
Les oeuvres libres/Arthème Fayard et Cie. —Paris: Arthème Fayard et Cie,[?]
383 p. ;18 cm.

Z256. 5/5(193)
Les oeuvres libres/Arthème Fayard et Cie. —Paris: Arthème Fayard et Cie,[?]
351 p. ;18 cm.

Z256. 5/5(195)
Les oeuvres libres/Arthème Fayard et Cie. —Paris: Arthème Fayard et Cie,[?]
315 p. ;18 cm.

Z256. 5/6(198)
Les oeuvres libres/Librairie A. Fayard. —Paris: Librairie A. Fayard,[?]
349 p. ;19 cm.

Z256. 5/7
Le Larousse pour tous/Claude Augé. —Paris: Librairie Larousse,[?]
986 p. ;30 cm.

Z656. 5/1(38)
Europe/Editons Rieder. —Paris: Editions Rieder,1935
152 p. ;21 cm.

Z656. 5/2(34)
Les oeuvres libres/Arthème Fayard et Cie. —Paris: Arthème Fayard et Cie,[?]
380 p. ;16 cm.

Z656. 5/2(61)
Les oeuvres libres/Arthème Fayard et Cie. —Paris: Arthème Fayard et Cie,1926
379 p. ;18 cm.

Z656. 5/2(62)
Les oeuvres libres/Arthème Fayard et Cie. —Paris: Arthème Fayard et Cie,[?]
375 p. ;18 cm.

Z656. 5/3(7)
Le mois/Maulde et Renou. —Paris: Maulde et Renou,1936
320 p. ;22 cm.

Z656. 5/3(10)
La nouvelle revue Française/Paul Claudel. —Paris: Gallimard,1935
481-968 p. ;22 cm.

Z656. 5/3(12)
Le mois/Maulde et Renou. —Paris: Maulde et Renou,1936
160 p. ;22 cm.

Z656. 5/4
La nouvelle revue française/[pas en détail]. —Paris:[s. n.],1936
1016 p. ;20 cm.

Z656. 5/5
Lecteurs pour tous/[pas en détail]. —Paris: [s. n.],1927
154 p. ;22 cm.

题名索引

—1—

—A—

—B—

—C—

—D—

—E—

—F—

—M—

—N—

—O—

—P—

—Q—

—R—

—S—

—T—

—U—

—V—

—W—

—X—

—Z—